Date Due

LaRue T. Hosmer

University of Michigan

Arnold C. Cooper

Purdue University

Karl H. Vesper

University of Washington

THE ENTREPRENEURIAL FUNCTION

Text and Cases on Smaller Firms

Prentice-Hall, Inc., Englewood Cliffs, New Jersey   07632

Library of Congress Cataloging in Publication Data

HOSMER, LARUE T
    The entrepreneurial function.

    1. Small business—United States—Management.
I. Cooper, Arnold C., joint author. II. Vesper,
Karl H., joint author. III. Title.
HD69.S6H62   658′.022′0973   76–50928
ISBN 0–13–283093–0

The following cases in this book were authored by Professor LaRue Tone Hosmer, © 1976, The University of Michigan, which retains the copyright and reserves all rights in connection therewith: The TEF-CHROME Process; Michigan Canning Lids, Inc.; WFF 'N' PROOF Learning Games Associates; Treasure Systems, Inc.; Housing Components, Inc.; Racketball Corporation of New England; Alarm Systems, Inc.; Electronic Accounting Associates, Inc.; Natural Foods Warehouse Corporation; Robinson Upholstery Company; Sawmill Machinery Corporation; Michigan Demolition and Salvage Company; Maryland Electronic Instrument Corporation; Hampfel-McFarland Company; Coldwater Container Corporation; and Ann Arbor Brewery, Inc.

Prentice-Hall International, Inc., London
Prentice-Hall of Australia Pty. Limited, Sydney
Prentice-Hall of Canada, Ltd., Toronto
Prentice-Hall of India Private Limited, New Delhi
Prentice-Hall of Japan, Inc., Tokyo
Prentice-Hall of Southeast Asia Pte. Ltd., Singapore
Whitehall Books Limited, Wellington, New Zealand

To Our Wives

> *Jane*
> *Jean*
> *Joan*

Contents

The essential function of the entrepreneur is to recognize the commercial potential of a product or service; to design consistent operating policies in marketing, market research, production, finance, product development, and the organizational structure and systems for that product or service; and then to supervise the changes required in the strategy through the various stages of company growth. The ability to conceptualize, to design, and to supervise are all needed by the successful small business manager. Smaller business firms lack, almost by definition, the financial resources and the market size that provide competitive advantages to the larger corporations; the small business manager must design operating policies—in all of these functional areas and through all of the stages of growth—that adjust to these inherent deficiencies. Small business management requires imagination, perception, and innovation to survive and to grow; it is very different from the management of larger companies that can utilize capital and market size to maximize a return on investment. This book uses short sections of text and related cases to explain and illustrate the functions of the entrepreneur and the particular characteristics of small business management.

Small companies are much more important in the American economy than is commonly recognized. The image of these small businesses is often based on the marginal companies—ill-conceived, ill-financed, and ill-managed—that are readily apparent in almost every geographic and industrial area. However, there are many local "family" businesses, stable "high-payoff" companies, and energetic "rapid-growth" firms that have been exceedingly successful. The short cases which

follow, designed for the early class sessions of a course, describe companies with
the potential for high payoff or rapid growth, but with problems in the design of
operating policies and strategy.

2 Marketing Management   *17*

Marketing management refers to the development of a plan for the pricing,
distribution, promotion, and eventual sale of a good or service. It is difficult for
smaller companies to compete with larger firms in marketing since they lack the
established products and mass markets that make the pricing, distribution, promotion, and eventual sale of goods and services much easier. In order to be
successful, the smaller company must develop a complete marketing plan, coordinating the elements of product characteristics, customer requirements, and market
segments with the pricing policies, distribution channels, and promotional methods. The smaller company must substitute perception and understanding of
customer needs and motives for large scale expenditures on distribution and
promotion.

3 Market Research   *78*

Market research refers to the systematic and comprehensive collection and analysis
of information to improve the marketing plan for a good or service. Smaller
companies have difficulty competing with larger firms in market research since
they lack both the financial resources to pay for the comprehensive collection and
analysis of information and the mass markets to repay the investment. The smaller
company must develop an inexpensive research plan, coordinating the use of
published information, the results of market tests, and the opinions of customer
interviews, all at minimal cost. The small company must substitute perception
and imagination in finding personally-reliable market information for large-scale
expenditures on statistically-reliable surveys.

4 Operations Management *125*

Operations management includes the design of a system to produce a given good or service and the planning, scheduling, and control of that system for optimal performance. Smaller companies are at a disadvantage with larger firms in production since they lack both the financial resources to design and build the physical facilities to exactly match the productive requirements of a given good or service, and the managerial resources in staff training and computer capability to schedule and control those facilities for optimal utilization. The smaller company must substitute imagination for money in the design of its productive facilities—often remodeling used equipment and reconstructing older buildings, and it must use innovative scheduling and control methods to take the place of the quantitative and computer-based systems developed for the larger firms.

5 Financial Management *152*

Financial management is the effective utilization of the assets—both current (short-term) and capital (long-term) —and the provision of funds to support those assets through the use of current liabilities, intermediate loans, and capital debt or equity. It is difficult for smaller companies to compete with larger firms in finance since, very simply, they lack money. To make the new investments in product development, market expansion, and process improvement needed for growth, the management of a smaller company must conserve its available funds by preparing such detailed financial plans as cash budgets, pro-forma statements, and capital investment analyses; it must find additional funds from such diverse financial sources as current liabilities, bank loans, equity investments, and retained earnings; and it must obtain external funds through financial presentations such as loan requests and venture capital proposals. In short, smaller companies must practice careful financial management for growth, combining the uses, plans, sources, and presentations for funds in a consistent financial program.

6 Product Development   *204*

Product development refers to improvements in the design of existing products and to inventions of entirely new products, both of which are needed to maintain the competitive position of a business firm. Smaller companies often lack either the financial resources or the technical capabilities available to larger firms. The smaller company must use its limited resources and capabilities efficiently, and this requires a specific sequence of decisions on technical feasibility, market feasibility, development time and cost, manufacturing compatibility, and strategic fit.

7 Organizational Management and Control   *241*

Smaller companies go through identifiable stages of growth. This growth affects more than just sales and profits; it brings a need for increased specialization in the tasks of the employees, increased delegation on the part of the founder or general manager, and increased systemization of the information and accounting procedures. Although these changes are often neglected during growth, they definitely affect the potential and final outcome of the firm, so there is a need for specific consideration of detailed plans to structure and control the activities of the members of the smaller company.

8 Formation   *267*

The formal or legal procedures for starting a small company are numerous, but they are neither difficult to learn nor nearly as important as the informal requirements, which include a knowledge of the market or technology which will be involved, an acquaintance with people whose cooperation and assistance will be needed, a definition of the product or service which will be offered, a listing of the resources—both physical and financial—which will be available, and a set of customer orders that can be accepted. Anticipation of and planning for the problems that will follow the acceptance of customer orders is also needed. But small company formation is not solely a process of meeting legal requirements and contemplating possible problems; it is also a continuous course of search, personal encounter, investigation, negotiation, commitment, and action.

9   Purchase of a Smaller Company   *358*

It is, of course, possible to purchase an existing company rather than start a new venture, and there are definite advantages, as well as disadvantages, to this form of entry into small business management. The purchase of a small company involves a series of decisions in identifying the opportunities for acquisition, screening the candidates, evaluating each firm, negotiating the purchase, and, finally, structuring the payment.

10   Consolidation of a New Company   *394*

The period of time between starting a business and reaching a constant and reliable break-even level of operations is of critical importance. This is a period that can be measured in weeks for some small companies that are almost immediately successful, and in years for others that seem to drift along, reporting alternate profits and losses, with final success always delayed. It is a period that requires intense conservation of the company's cash, firm limitations on the company's expenses, and continual examination of the company's strategy.

11   Expansion of a Smaller Company   *423*

Rapid growth is not inevitable in most small companies. Rather, the rate of growth should be the result of deliberate management decisions that take into account both the advantages and the disadvantages that come with changes in sales revenues, product lines, market areas, and market share. Rapid growth requires explicit consideration of the firm's strategy, that is, the type of business the company presently conducts and the type of company it seeks to become. The formulation of the corporate strategy is an iterative process involving evaluation of current performance trends, present environmental threats and opportunities, existing company strengths and weaknesses, and future performance targets. Stra-

tegic planning and revision is the last of the requirements for success of the
expanding small business firm.

12   Final Outcomes   *474*

The final disposition of a small company is usually neglected during the formation, consolidation, and expansion stages; there are inevitably more important
or more pressing concerns for the attention of the entrepreneur. However, it is
essential that early consideration be given to the alternatives of a public stock
sale, merger with a larger firm, continuation with management succession, sell-out
with business continuation, close-down with liquidation of the assets and full
repayment of creditors, or bankruptcy without full repayment. Planning is necessary to achieve the optimal return to the entrepreneur and the other participants
in the small business venture.

13   Careers in Small Firms   *480*

Acknowledgments

The authors are grateful to many individuals for helping to make this book possible. Dean Floyd A. Bond and Associate Dean Alfred W. Swinyard of the University of Michigan, Dean John S. Day and Associate Dean Frank M. Sterner of Purdue University, and Dean Kermit O. Hanson and Department Chairmen Jim Rosenzweig and Borje O. Saxberg of the University of Washington provided helpful support and encouragement. Many former students contributed both in case materials and evaluation of the work. These included Thomas Forestek, Charles Houy, Ronald Hwang, Steven Kasiske, In-Kuin Kim, Andrew Lawlor, and Joseph Shipley of the University of Michigan; William Leber, Raymond Lindstrom, Cameron McLeod, David Putnam, and Arthur Rizer of the University of Washington; and William Sandberg of Purdue University.

Others who contributed were Professor Robert T. Lund of M.I.T., who wrote the Smalltren Engineering, Inc. case, and Mr. John Uhles, who wrote the Crain's English Pig & Whistle case. The President and Fellows of Harvard College have granted permission for the Technifax case, which was written earlier by one of the authors and revised for use in this casebook, and for Smalltren Engineering, Inc.

Valuable assistance in preparing the manuscript was received from Mrs. Judith Armstrong and Mrs. Linda Graf at the University of Michigan, Mrs. Maureen Bart of Purdue University, and Mrs. Margaret Melzer and Mrs. Sandra Goodman of the University of Washington.

1

Introduction

Small business has always played an important role in the American economy. This is still true in the last quarter of the twentieth century. Furthermore, although it is not generally recognized, this segment of our economy includes some of the most dynamic, profitable, and, in our opinion, interesting firms to be found.

There are a number of reasons why smaller firms are of importance to our economy and are worthy of study, for example:

1. They are important sources of competition and challenge the economic power of larger firms.

2. They offer a wider range of choice to the consumer. Larger firms must be oriented toward the mass market, but smaller firms can serve specialized needs.

3. They broaden the distribution of economic and political power. In many areas, small business provides local leaders with strong local roots.

4. They are sources of innovation and creativity. Many innovations in services and technology have originated in small firms.

5. They offer career opportunities to those who are happiest and most productive in the unstructured environment of a small company.

The study of small firms is of value not only to those who are attracted to careers in small organizations. Many students will move into career positions in which they will deal with and must understand the special characteristics of small companies. Bankers, purchasing agents, salesmen, investment analysts, venture capitalists, and consultants are examples. Managers in large firms that compete with small companies can also benefit from a better understanding of their adversaries. Finally, particularly in the study of management through cases, there is much to be said for analyzing problems within the context of a small company,

1

regardless of the career objectives of the students. It is easier "to get your arms around the situation" and to understand the interrelationships in a small company than in a large one.

SMALL BUSINESS IN THE AMERICAN ECONOMY

In this book we shall deal mainly with companies that have fewer than 100 employees and that are characterized by small, cohesive management groups in direct contact with customers, with workers, and with day-to-day problems.

The high visibility of giant corporations means that many people do not realize that most American firms are small. Consider the following:

1. Of the 12 million businesses in this country, only 13.9% are corporations; the rest are organized as proprietorships or partnerships and tend to be small.

2. Of the active corporations, 57.7% have less than $100,000 in assets and 93.7% have less than $1 million in assets.

3. Approximately 95% of all businesses have fewer than 20 employees. These account for approximately 23% of all employment by industry.

By all measures, small business constitutes an important part of the American economy.

The population of small firms is highly dynamic, and the overall figures conceal a great deal of churning, as companies start and discontinue. The importance of small business varies widely across industries. Furthermore, in some industries, small firms are enlarging their market share, but in others the tides of competition are favoring the large companies.

1. In 1972, 317,000 new corporations were established. In a typical 40-hour week, approximately 158 new corporations were established per hour and almost as many were discontinued.

2. Approximately two out of three new businesses discontinue in the first four years after founding. As a business gets older, the probability that it will survive each additional year increases.

3. Some industries, for example, primary aluminum, automobiles, and cigarettes, are highly concentrated, with small firms playing a minor role except as suppliers and distributors. Other industries, for example, furniture, apparel, and printing and publishing, are highly fragmented, with many small companies.

4. Brewing, bread, and photographic equipment and supplies are examples of industries in which large companies have been expanding their market shares. In meat packing, plastics materials and resins, and knit fabrics the contrary is true, for these industries are becoming less concentrated.

Available profitability data suggest that, when averaging all manufacturing firms within a given size class, profitability increases with size of firm, as indicated below.

Within each of these size categories, however, there are wide differences in profitability. The smaller size categories, in particular, include well-established profit-

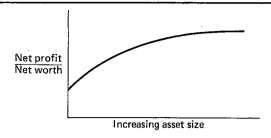

Net profit / Net worth

Increasing asset size

able firms, new companies showing what is often an expected loss in their first year, and, unfortunately, thousands of companies that should never have been started. In the large firm categories, there is also dispersion, but much less so. The performance of these large companies reflects the averaging of many products, many facilities, and many people. Some of these resources are outstanding, but some are not, and the result is that the performance of the larger firms as a group is stabilized and brought toward the middle.

The image of small business in the United States is highly influenced by the many marginal small companies. Many of these firms—ill-conceived, ill-financed, and ill-managed—are doomed to failure before they ever start. In every town there are retail locations that need revolving doors, not for the few customers, but for the stream of entrepreneurs who come and go.

Nevertheless, the dismal performance of these marginal companies should not obscure the presence of another class of small firms. These well-planned and excellently managed businesses are, as a group, showing some of the highest returns to be found in American industry. They are demonstrating what can be done in small business.

In selecting the cases for this book, we have included very few "mom 'n pop" businesses of limited potential. The selection is biased toward businesses that have a record of success or, at least, that have some potential. We feel that more can be learned from studying these companies, and, furthermore, we feel that these firms should be of greatest interest to students who may have a variety of career alternatives.

TYPES OF SMALLER FIRMS

As indicated previously, small business includes a variety of companies and encompasses a wide range of performance. One way of classifying these firms is as follows: (1) Mom 'n pop companies, (2) stable, high-payoff companies, and (3) rapid growth companies. The strategies, available resources, and potential rewards vary widely among these types of firms. They also differ greatly in the kinds of careers they make possible.

Mom 'n Pop Company. The Yellow Pages of any phone book contain a large number of companies, mostly retail or service firms, which are very small and which will always remain small. Many have no hired employees and rely only on the proprietor or members of the family. It is difficult to operate a chain of beauty shops or newsstands because the profit margins are generally not great enough to slip in the additional layer of overhead that would pay the person who owns but does not personally operate more than one outlet. The shops have to be geographically scattered because customers prefer to use those nearest to them. Because the shops are scattered, one owner finds it difficult to control more than one or two.

Because relatively little capital must be invested to start and own such a business, those who are qualified to manage them often prefer to start or buy their own instead of managing a second outlet for someone else. This ease of entry also keeps the pace of competition up and the profit margins down, so that owning such firms often results in only modest returns at best.

Many of the owner–managers of these businesses have only modest education and no previous managerial experience. For them, the alternative to self-employment is working as a factory worker or salesclerk. Often, the business supports a family in a satisfactory but not lavish way.

By far the largest number of small companies is found in this group. To an even greater extent, the start-ups and discontinuances are also found in this group. Franchising has been applied to many of these businesses, sometimes with excellent results that move the franchisee into the category described below, that of stable, high-payoff companies. In other instances, however, the effect has been to increase competition in particular market segments, such as "fast food" outlets. Successful franchisors, for example, Colonel Sanders, have been able to build rapid growth companies, with high-profit multiples, but they represent an extremely small fraction of the total.

Stable High-Payoff Company. A small percentage of retail and service firms and a high percentage of manufacturing companies, particularly those that have proprietary products, provide their owners with high incomes, substantial freedom, and many fringe benefits. Some owners of such companies put in long hours, but many do not. This can be verified experimentally by phoning some companies listed with proprietary products, for instance, in the manufacturers' directory, and seeing how many of them are present late Friday afternoon or early in the morning. In many of these firms, the owner who chooses to do so can employ or train others to handle most of the day-to-day operations, freeing the owner to concentrate on broad policy issues and to participate in such outside activities as community affairs, recreation, and, of course, ownership of additional high-payoff companies. Fringe benefits include travel, entertainment expense accounts, leased cars, and the opportunity to buy items through the company at discounts.

These companies usually use strategies that to a degree insulate them from the competitive pressures that can keep profit margins low. Sometimes they have a virtual monopoly in a particular local market. Competitors may be unable to enter the market because they are unable to get a local franchise, because of high capital requirements, or because of specialized know-how or patents. Often the market is not large enough to attract vigorous competitors.

Rapid Growth Company. Rapidly growing companies offer the possibility of high payoff through selling out or through floating public issues of stock. The owners can also prosper by keeping control of a growing profitable business. Many family fortunes had their origin with such companies. Although the ultimate rewards can be greatest with this kind of company, the interim experience can be different. High-growth companies more often have multiple owners who collaborate and therefore do not enjoy as much independence as owners of stable high-payoff companies. Moreover, the growth phase is often more personally demanding than running a stable firm in which much of the work can be routinized and turned over to others. Growth usually requires a succession of commitments that involve risking what has been achieved. Also, as will be developed in the section on managing the growing firm, growth calls for adaptation, constant change, new systems, and development of new skills by the managers.

Clearly, rapid growth companies are much less numerous than the other classes of firms discussed. A combination of a strategy with high potential, capable management willing to take risks, and satisfactory financing is required.

These companies usually are positioned in growing markets. It is much easier to grow by participating in overall industry growth than by taking market share away from competitors. These companies have functional policies that lead to strong competitive positions that are possibly based upon unique products or lower prices. They can "live with" some inefficiencies or poor decisions because they are carried along by the inherent strength of their strategies. One executive in the computer peripheral equipment field commented, "An industry growth rate of 30% per year can overcome a lot of mistakes."

Rapid growth firms usually have strong management. Unlike the managers in mom 'n pop businesses, their managers usually have previous managerial experience. In fact, the early competitive strength of the firm is often based upon the founders' unique skills in engineering, or sales, or cost control. The managers of the firms also must be willing to take risks—to broaden their product lines, to add facilities, to build their organizations. Management must also be willing to work hard and to meet the succession of challenges associated with growth.

Rapidly growing companies usually need external sources of funds. Management must be skilled in setting terms of sale, in negotiating with suppliers for trade credit, in working with bankers, and, sometimes, in raising additional equity capital. If the firm is fortunate enough to be located in an area where there are supportive and creative financial institutions, it is more likely to be able to realize its growth possibilities.

It should be recognized that these categories of firms are fluid and that not all firms can be neatly pigeonholed. For instance, some high-potential firms never grow because of poor decisions or inadequate resources. Furthermore, vigorous leadership and sound policies can sometimes move a firm from one category to another.

The TEF-CHROME Process

John Schaffner was graduated in the spring of 1975 from the M.B.A. program at the University of Michigan. He was older than many of the other students, having worked a number of years in industry, and he wanted to found his own company immediately after graduation rather than return to work for a large corporation. He thought that he had the product or service that would permit him to achieve this personal goal: the application of the TEF-CHROME process to small home appliances.

TEF-CHROME is a patented chemical process that locks polytetrafluoroethylene, popularly known as Teflon but referred to phonetically as TEF, into a hard electrodeposited surface such as hard anodize or chromium. The result is a new surface with all the sliding, low-friction and anti-stick properties of Teflon plus the hardness and durability qualities of the anodize or chrome. An independent inventor in Cincinnati developed the process for industrial use on steel dies and shear plates to prolong life and reduce wear. Mr. Schaffner had worked for the inventor over the summers while he was in college and graduate school. Then he was offered the rights to the process for consumer products.

> He (the inventor) felt that the consumer industry was just a bag of worms, and he did not want to get involved. When I said that I would be interested, he told me that I could have the rights to his invention; the next day he came in with a contract that his attorney had drawn up that gave me the rights in return for a royalty based upon sales. It was a very fair document. (Statement of Mr. Schaffner.)

Mr. Schaffner decided to start his company by applying the TEF-CHROME process to the aluminum surface of electric frying pans and electric irons, two consumer products that caused customer dissatisfactions because of continual sticking and difficult cleaning. He explained the technical details of the TEF-CHROME process applied to aluminum as follows:

> You start with a hard anodize surface; hard anodize is an electrochemically produced surface that is formed on aluminum by oxidizing the aluminum surface in a concentrated sulphuric acid bath. You apply a large positive potential to the aluminum piece and a negative potential to a titanium cathode at the side of the tank; this causes the SO_3 ions to migrate to the aluminum surface, and the result is that the aluminum oxidizes forming Al_2O_3, the chemical compound of saphire.
>
> The normal thickness of this saphire surface is 0.002 in. to 0.003 in. and, because one of the side reactions involved is the breakdown of water into hydrogen and oxygen gases which bubble through this thin surface during the

electrochemical process, the anodized surface is minutely porous, with 186,000 very small cracks and fissures per square inch.

To TEF-CHROME the anodized surface, the aluminum is heated to 375°F to thermally expand these cracks and fissures. The tetrafluoroethylene particles are cooled to −100°F to cryogenically contract their size; the cooled particles are then pressed into the heated porous surface. As the aluminum cools, the expanding particles lock into the contracting fissures; since fluorocarbons have a very high coefficient of expansion, the lock fit is permanent.

Mr. Schaffner explained that Teflon was commonly used as a nonstick surfacing agent on consumer products, but that it was applied by spraying TEF particles with a resin binder onto the metallic surface, which was then sintered at 780°F to form a uniform coating. The problem is that this sintered coating is very readily scratched or scraped, and it gradually wears off; it has very limited durability. For example, only nylon or wooden spoons can be used to stir the food cooking in a Teflon-coated frying pan or broiler; metal spoons would damage the very soft surface. Some very preliminary market research indicated that both retailers and consumers were disillusioned with the usual Teflon coatings because of their softness and resultant short life; however, both groups indicated that a much harder nonstick surface and a 5-year guarantee would be the answer to this negative response, and that this new approach would have a very considerable appeal in the market.

> It would not bother me at all to put a 5-year guarantee on our process; you can't damage an anodized or chromed surface with anything found in the home, and the anodize or chrome protects the Teflon. (Statement of Mr. Schaffner.)

Mr. Schaffner investigated the production process and found that the smallest practical equipment to anodize and then TEF-CHROME the finished surface of either electric irons or frying pans would cost $60,000 and would produce 600 units per 8-hour shift, or approximately 150,000 per year. The variable costs of operating this equipment were as follows:

Anodize process for labor, power, sulphuric acid, and maintenance	$0.69/unit
TEF-CHROME process for labor, power, Teflon particles, and maintenance	0.32/unit
Packing and preparation for shipment	0.03/unit
Royalty, at 5% of the industrial sales price (estimated at $1.60/ea.)	0.08/unit
	$1.12/unit

Mr. Schaffner also found that because of the inherent labor in handling the individual pieces in the anodizing and TEF-CHROME processes, there were few economics of scale in this industry. That is, to increase the production rate by a factor of 10 would require nearly 10 times as much capital ($600,000) and would not substantially reduce the cost below the existing estimate ($1.12/ unit).

Mr. Schaffner then estimated the fixed costs at a production rate of 600 units per shift. He expected most of these costs to be only semifixed and to vary as a step function with production; he thought that only the executive salary figures would be completely fixed:

Building rental, for 2,000 sq ft at $0.30 per sq ft per month	$ 7,200/yr
Equipment depreciation, at 12 years on $60,000 investment	5,000/yr
Interest costs, at 8½% on $50,000 bank loan	4,250/yr
Administrative overhead for secretary, telephone, insurance, etc.	10,000/yr
Executive salary at $10,000/year plus employment costs	12,000/yr
	$38,450/yr

The marketing expenses for promotion and personal selling were not included in the fixed cost forecast given above since Mr. Schaffner had not decided upon a marketing plan. He knew that a very substantial and competitive market existed [9.5 million electric irons and 3.6 electric frying pans are sold in the United States each year by two major manufacturers (General Electric and Sunbeam) and a few smaller firms], but he was not certain how to reach that market.

ASSIGNMENT

Propose three or four alternatives to market the TEF-CHROME process, which will provide a durable nonstick and low-friction surface for small home appliances. Evaluate each alternative.

Trailhouse Enterprises

In the fall of 1975 Frank Zarth, a graduate student in architecture at Western Idaho University was considering how best to arrange a compensation scheme for his new venture to produce foldout camping trailers.

The trailer idea was one that he had been contemplating for over 5 years during service in the Army prior to returning to graduate study in architecture. He liked to camp with his family but was dissatisfied with available alternatives for obtaining shelter in public camp grounds. Using a tent required a substantial amount of packing, unpacking, and setting up, while the other alternative of buying a travel trailer constituted, in his view, too great an expense. He thought it should be possible to design a plywood trailer that would fold open, cost less than existing trailers, and at the same time by utilizing an attached tent enclosure would provide more room space than other trailers on the market.

Undertaking the development of the design as a student project, he became further convinced of its feasibility and began to develop the idea of forming a company to produce the vehicle. He immediately recognized that he could not do so alone. His personal finances were limited to savings of around $3,000, his time at present was restricted by the need to complete other course work, and he also had to hold down some sort of income-producing job. By drawing on his G.I. bill, his wife's income as a secretary, and a half-time research assistantship, he was able to make ends meet adequately for his wife and small child, but upon graduating he could see most of this income disappearing.

Working out the design of the trailer and its novel features was where he felt strongest. He was also skilled as a carpenter so that he could fabricate any parts of the prototypes himself except the welded steel frame, off-the-shelf components such as the stove, sink and toilet, and the fabric needed for the tent extension. From his school training, moreover, he had the ability to produce graphic renderings for brochures, advertising, and display copy. Because his Army experience had thrust him into command of substantial construction projects, he felt competent to handle tasks of cost estimation, planning, supervision of fabrication, and control of manufacturing quality. He had been in touch with real estate firms to explore possible sites and was convinced that he could obtain suitable plant space at an attractive price by handling negotiations himself and that he would have no difficulty

in selecting appropriate used machinery and laying out the plant arrangement himself.

He could also see areas in which he would need substantial help. From the graduate school of business he intended to recruit someone majoring in marketing to help manage sales, an area with which he was himself completely unacquainted, and also a finance major to help both in dealing with banks and in preparing an accounting and financial forecasting system. He also thought he should recruit an operations major to oversee the day-to-day problems of fabrication and working with suppliers. He had talked to several students in these specialties who had expressed enthusiasm for the idea of participating in the new venture on some basis, and he had found a law student who said she would like to help the firm work with whatever counsel was engaged. Frank's expectation was that by having someone in the company who understood legal matters it should be possible to minimize the costs of legal services obtained on the outside.

Several meetings were held among these interested participants as Frank began fabricating a prototype in the shop of the Architecture School. Workdays for Frank grew progressively longer as he called on suppliers, worked out designs, sawed and assembled wood, enlisted collaborators, chaired meetings, and worked out plans. His short-run target was to complete the prototype in time for presentation at a recreational vehicle show 2 months hence, and beyond that he wanted to start turning out salable units. So far he was meeting both the time and cost schedules, and he expected to meet the short-run goal.

His savings, however, were rapidly dwindling as he bought materials, paid for legal assistance in a patent application and formation of a corporation, and traveled to make arrangements with suppliers and the trade show. He also began to feel the limits of what he could do in the waking hours of a day, and to keep the prototype on schedule he felt that he would need more hands to help with the work. Consequently, he inquired through friends and family about who might be willing to invest in the project to provide capital and he also contemplated recruiting more students to help do the manual labor in production.

"The question now," he said, "is what should I offer these people in return for their contributions? Suppose, for instance, one of the potential investors thinks he can put in $5,000 for stock. How should I decide how much of the company to give him in return for that? Should the people who contribute time to the project be paid in stock or notes, or should they be allowed to make that choice themselves? Also, how should the rates be set? Should they be paid by the task or by the hour, and how should the rules be arranged for deciding what tasks should be performed and how many hours should be spent? Should each participant make his own decisions about what to work on and how much time to spend, or should I do it for every person and every task and negotiate it individually each time? And what should I do about the fact that I simply can't map it all out in advance because we have to find out what needs doing as we work along.

"I figure I have invested about $2,500 cash and well over 400 man-hours in this personally so far. Should I use that as some sort of base for establishing who gets what? If I figure, for example, that this company should have a million dollar potential and that creating it in the first place was my doing, how much does that make my contribution worth? Can I say that the business at this stage is worth, considering the potential and the probability of success, maybe $150,000, and then distribute shares as pay on that basis? And what if one of the participants doesn't work out and I decide he should be out of the picture? Is there some arrangement I should make in advance to preclude an awkward legal hassle with the individual?

"It seems to me, and I gather to the potential participants I have been talking to, that this venture shows real promise and therefore has a value. But what is the way to utilize that value to bring in the help needed to bring the venture to fruition?"

ASSIGNMENT

Formulate a set of procedures to answer Mr. Zarth's questions and invent a hypothetical case with specific events and figures to illustrate application of your procedures.

Man-Tal, Inc.

In November 1974 Bill Morter, Jim Zuber, Rich Dirlam, and Paul Richardson met to discuss an interesting career opportunity. All were students in the Masters Program in Industrial Administration at Purdue University, with the first three expecting to grad-

uate in the next month and Paul Richardson expecting to graduate in May 1975.

A prominent Indianapolis businessman had expressed the belief that good men, supported for a year, ought to be able to develop business ventures that would not only support them, but would also, in time, provide a good return for financial backers. He had first met the younger men while taking some courses at Purdue. He had proposed the venture that they were now considering.

A new corporation, Man-Tal, Inc., was to be organized with initial capital of $100,000, with the stock to be subscribed by ten corporations in the Indianapolis area. The officers of these companies all knew the sponsoring businessman. The four young entrepreneurs would each own 10% of the stock in return for services. They were to give the corporation their personal notes for $2,000 each as indications of their commitment. The notes were to come due within 2 years of their leaving the corporation. The sponsoring businessman would provide guidance and have the title of chairman; he would receive 10% of the stock, but would receive no salary. The ten corporate investors would each supply $10,000 and receive $9,000 notes, due in ten years and paying 10% annual interest; they would also receive 5% of the equity. Each investor would appoint one member to an advisory board.

The young men were to develop ventures that could support them and hopefully be highly profitable to investors. They were to devote particular attention to finding attractive local businesses that might be purchased and that needed additional management, particularly businesses that were suffering from management succession problems. As a secondary activity, they might also be involved in starting new ventures. In fact, the proposed chairman suggested that they might design and produce a component that his own company needed.

If a particular acquisition or start-up venture required additional capital, the entrepreneurs would go back to the original investors to seek financing. Man-Tal would also hold equity positions in the new ventures.

No investor would be obligated to invest in additional ventures, but presumably most would do so. The terms would be negotiated separately for each venture.

The entrepreneurs were to be paid salaries for the first year of $15,000 each. Considering expenses, they thought the initial $100,000 would support them for 12 to 15 months. They might do some consulting to help cover expenses.

Bill Morter was 27, had B.S. and M.S. degrees in biology, and had 2 years of experience as a research assistant at Purdue in a group studying plant physiology. Jim Zuber was 27, had B.S. and M.S. degrees in psychology, and had worked throughout his student career. Rich Dirlam was 28, had been a captain in the army, and had worked in large-scale farming; his B.S. degree was in civil engineering. Paul Richardson was 26, had an interdisciplinary engineering degree, and had served $3\frac{1}{2}$ years in the army, achieving the rank of captain. All had attractive job offers from larger companies, with annual salaries (not including fringe benefits) of $14,000 to $18,000. All were married and their wives were willing to see them start the venture if this was what they wanted.

Some of the men were concerned because it was difficult to analyze such an open-ended opportunity. In contrast, their other opportunities involved specific industries, duties, and compensation. Nevertheless, the flexibility of the situation was also attractive.

ASSIGNMENT

Appraise this opportunity from the point of view of these four men.

Michigan Canning Lids, Inc.

During the summer of 1974 there was a growing shortage of canning lids. Both experienced and novice home canners were buying the lids as rapidly as they could be stocked on the shelves of suburban and rural stores, and the manufacturers were explaining that they were producing additional lids as quickly as possible. The shortage had come as a surprise to retailers and manufacturers alike, and it was caused by a dramatic increase in the number of persons who wished, either for economic or ecological reasons, to produce and then preserve home-grown fruits and vegetables.

From 1940 to 1970 the number of home gardeners had remained at a relatively constant 14 million, but in the early 1970s a national interest in gardening began to develop, and the number of gardeners began to grow, reaching 20 million in 1974. Many of the companies that supplied seeds, tools, fertilizers, and other necessities for this market appeared to have been unprepared for the growth in demand. These companies, most of which had been in operation for decades and had apparently been satisfied with the moderate level of industry activity, attempted to adjust to the change, but, of course, there were substantial lead times involved in increasing production. The first shortages were apparent in seeds during the spring of 1974, but the major shortage developed in canning lids during the late summer and early fall.

Canning lids are necessary for food preservation. Although some gardeners grow only enough produce to fill their daily needs, most, and especially the newcomers who always underestimate the power of a seed packet, manage to grow far more than can

be freshly consumed, necessitating either wastage or some form of preservation. Drying and freezing have been used to some extent, but they are limited in the home market because of a lack of the knowledge and equipment required. The primary method of preservation for home-grown fruits and vegetables is canning. A glass jar is used, rather than a metal can, with a flat replaceable tin lid equipped with a rubber or neoprene seal, and a screw top that holds the flat lid onto the jar. The filled jars, with the lids very lightly screwed in place, are placed upright in a bath of boiling water. The heat kills the microorganisms in the contents and also generates steam which drives much of the air from the jars. When the jars are removed from the boiling water to cool, the air pressure inside drops, forming a partial vacuum, and the canning lid with the rubber or neoprene ring is "vacuum sealed" onto the mouth of the jar. The screw top is then tightened to prevent any accidental breaking of the seal, and the produce is preserved for use during the remainder of the year.

Charles Houy, who was an avid gardener as well as an M.B.A. student at the University of Michigan, felt that the shortage of canning lids provided an opportunity to start a small company that would be of definite benefit to its customers, as well as highly profitable to its owner. Mr. Houy had helped to organize and direct a community gardening effort in Ann Arbor which provided plots of public land for several thousand "landless" gardeners, primarily university students and apartment dwellers, and he had watched with concern as the supply of canning lids dwindled and finally all but disappeared at local stores. In some stores the price for a dozen lids, which had been at the 39¢ level for years, went as high as 99¢, and harried gardeners paid the higher price almost without hesitation. The community gardeners, whom Mr. Houy had encouraged to start by explaining the savings and other benefits of home canning, kept his telephone ringing with complaints that their efforts would be wasted if they could not find additional lids. Mr. Houy called the major manufacturers, Ball Manufacturing Company and Kerr Glass Company, but they explained that they were unable to make additional shipments to the Ann Arbor area, although they did state that they planned to increase production 30% for the coming year.

> We got through the 1974 season, primarily because there had been a large inventory build-up in the distribution channels over the prior years: almost every family that did any canning at all had an extra box or two of the lids, and every store that handled canning supplies had an extra carton or two at the start of the summer. But it was obvious that the real crunch would come in 1975. The lids aren't reusable; once you break the seal, you have to throw away that lid and buy a new one. That meant that every existing home canner would have to get a new supply in 1975, and there were going to be a lot of new gardeners wanting lids that year too.
>
> By April of 1975 I was convinced that the number of gardeners had increased far more than 30%. For one thing, the number of people who applied to get plots through our community gardening group more than doubled over the 1974 level; for another, the economy was in terrible shape, especially here in Michigan because of the auto industry slump, and prices of food had skyrocketed with inflation. I just knew that more people would *need* to garden during 1975. The final clincher came when the conservative U.S. Department of Agriculture announced that they expected 50% of all American families to garden during 1975, an increase of about 80% over 1974. (Statement of Mr. Houy.)

Mr. Houy was convinced that the lids would be easy to make. A roll of coated 4-in. wide, 32-gauge tinplate is fed into a stamping press which cuts out a circle and shapes

the edge into a trough to mate with the lip of the canning jar. A two-stage progressive die is necessary for the stamping machine to accomplish the two steps of cutting and forming. A sealing compound is then applied to the lid's circumference trough; it can be done by either spraying a liquid sealing compound such as is used for the lids by baby food jars, or a pre-formed rubberized ring can be applied with heat and minimal pressure to the through. Then the lids can dry and cool, be inspected, and packaged.

Because of the auto slump, used stamping machines were readily available in the area for about $2,500 apiece, and the tool and die shops were eager to construct the two-stage dies for $3,500 each. A new seal sprayer would cost $4,000. Three presses would balance production with one seal sprayer, and this combination could easily produce 2,000 finished lids per hour. The costs for the tinplate and sealing compound would run about 1¢ per lid. Packaging each dozen would add another 1¢ since Mr. Houy intended to use clear plastic bags so that the consumer could inspect the new brand of lids before purchase. Because of the few steps necessary to complete the manufacturing process, he felt that he would only have to hire four people per shift, and he planned to operate the machines three shifts per day, and seven days per week, which would result in approximately 336,000 lids each week.

In May of 1975 Mr. Houy realized that he would have to move forward quickly with his idea if he wanted to start the new company. Gardeners around the country were already complaining about the expected shortage of canning lids, and newspapers and magazines were running stories on the "panic buying" of the few available lids. A Congressional investigation was scheduled by the House Subcommittee on Commodities and Services to look into reasons for the lid shortage. Mr. Houy had firm commitments on the delivery of the stamping machines and dies, the availability of workers, and the rental of a suitable building, but he hesitated to start the business.

I had to convince myself that the market existed, so I called a buyer for the Meijer's Thrifty Acres chain (a regional group of discount stores in the midwest); he told me that Meijer's had ordered more than 7 million lids from Ball and Kerr, but they expected to receive only 25% of that order and would be willing to pay 50¢ per dozen to *anyone* who had canning lids for sale.

At 50¢ per dozen, I stand to make $6,000 per week contribution to overhead and profits, and that's after paying for all the material and for the workers at $5.00 an hour. At that rate, I could wind up the year with about $300,000 before taxes, which is not a bad return on a $22,500 investment. The machinery is available; if I could get the money, I could double or triple the production and the profits. I could retire before I got the M.B.A.

But one thing continues to bother me: if this is as good as it looks, why hasn't someone else thought of it before me and plunged in just as I want to do. What can go wrong? (Statement of Mr. Houy.)

ASSIGNMENT

What would you recommend to Mr. Houy, and why?

The Taco Works

When one of the workers in the Taco Works Collective complained to another worker that she could not live adequately on the standard $1.60 per hour member wage, he replied, "I'd like to make more from this operation too, but how can I change it?" He went on to say that 3 others of the 13 members had voiced similar complaints, but the rest of the 13 total members, all of whom had equal votes, had either shown no concern or had expressed satisfaction with current policies.

Located a few blocks from the University of California, Berkeley, campus, the Works served a variety of taco combinations, sandwiches, salads, and non-alcoholic drinks to a mostly young, "hip" local clientele. In a 372 sq ft area there were five tables that gave seating to a maximum of 30 customers. Homemade partitions waist high left the 204-sq ft kitchen area open to view and allowed easy conversation between customers and operators. The decor was characterized as "twentieth-century scrounge," but customers, some of whom hung around for hours drinking coffee refills at 10¢ each, said they found the atmosphere relaxing and congenial.

The building lease still had $2\frac{1}{2}$ years to run, but a house next door in which the collective rented commissary storage space was scheduled to be torn down in 6 months to make room for an apartment building. There was no other rentable space on other sides of the Works, and no search or plans had been undertaken to find additional space. One member who thought something should be done about this pointed out that the kitchen space was crowded already. When the refrigerator doors were open they blocked traffic, and insufficient sandwich making space sometimes caused 30 to 45 minute backlogs on orders or parts of orders.

Operations required three people in each of three shifts per day. The cook prepared hot dishes, while the person on counter duty was to take orders for, prepare, and serve sandwiches, salads, and drinks. A backup person had the job of bussing, cleaning tables, washing dishes, and helping with counter work as needed. Each Friday a signup sheet allowed selection of jobs on a first-come first-served basis. There was no "rank" associated with any position, and no individual was designated to be "in charge" of any shift.

The average tenure of employees was 8 months. Replacements, who came from among friends of the members, had to work 20 hours for each of 3 weeks running at $1 per hour to join the partnership. A unanimous vote by the existing partners was also required. Currently, there were five on the waiting list to begin this initiation. "Most people who are competent enough to get another job leave before long," commented one former member. "The ones who are left, and the ones who apply are generally either fanatics who worship poverty or misfits nobody else will hire." Substitutes were supposed to be arranged for by any members who missed shifts for which they had signed. This obligation occasionally went unfulfilled, however, causing overloading in the kitchen with slower output and lowered quality. Customers sometimes had to wait 45 minutes for orders. Errant members usually said they had been unable to find substitutes who would work for the standard wage of members.

No attempts were made to "cut corners" on food quality. For example, meat in the tacos was not diluted with soybean additives, and opportunities to buy such things as overripe tomatoes at discounts were not taken. Prices charged were generally 10% to 30% below competitors, of which there were four in the general area. The exact markups tended to vary, however, because there were no standards for the amounts of ingredients used in preparing dishes and sandwiches. The possibility of introducing tighter control over portions had been considered but voted down by the group as too regimented; consequently, each cook was free to "personalize" servings.

Money was handled on an "honor system." The cash register was to be opened with $60 each day, but rarely was the amount counted. During rush periods the register was operated by as many as 12 people per day without recording of the changes. Workers who took money from the register for personal or business needs were supposed to leave a signed explanatory note. It was found that some of these notes bore only the amount and date, others only date or amount. Someone on the last shift each day was supposed to count the balance and put it into a bank envelope for deposit the next morning. One member noted that at least 30 people must know that the envelope, which might contain as much as $1,000 Sunday night, was left in the register overnight.

The Taco Works sometimes provided food in barter exchange for such things as cover charge admission to a nearby bar, merchandise from a health food store and two second-hand stores, and admission to a local movie. Records were kept, but according to one member "not fastidiously." He observed that the movie operators, for instance, ate an estimated $7 in food per week while the same show played for 3 straight months. Yet members had voted against eliminating the barter.

Other "leaks" observed in the system were beer drinking and "clubhouse privileges." No record was kept of who consumed the average of six cases of beer per week brought in for members and friends. (The consumption record was five cases in 8 hours one Saturday.) On a few occasions the beer had been blamed for cutting into performance by producing swearing and sloppy food preparation in the kitchen and rudeness to customers. Clubhouse privileges included allowing members and friends to fix food for themselves without charge. "One such leech," a member observed, "had been living in his converted van in the parking lot for 11 months with free run of the premises."

Occasionally, bookkeepers had attempted to curb members in ways that would facilitate record keeping and reduce leaks, but such efforts had been rebuffed. Four different members, selected on the basis of interest in the job and trust by the other members rather than training or experience, had taken on the bookkeeper role in the preceding 3 years. The current bookkeeper had never worked as such before and claimed his college major had been "anarchy." Discrepancies between the books and bank records were great as $1,000 when the books changed hands.

A recent overstatement in the books had prompted members to declare a $100 Christmas bonus to all members in December 1974. This "profit" was shortly discovered to be an accounting error, however, and only thanks to unusually high New Year's sales was the checking account overdraft covered. The company had tried using professional public accounting services. But members had been unable to understand the resulting statements and had become impatient with what seemed to them high charges by the bookkeeping firms. At present no financial reports were given by the bookkeeper to members, although the records were accessible to anyone. "The members don't want to mess with the technicalities," he observed. "They simply feel they should be entitled to better pay for the work they do."

ASSIGNMENT

Formulate advice in response to dissatisfactions expressed by members of the Taco Works, explain how you would attempt to get your suggestions implemented, and describe the sequence and timing of events you would expect to follow.

Land Reclamation, Inc.

In the spring of 1975, Mr. Robert Speake,[1] president of Dakota Fertilizer Equipment, was considering an opportunity to buy a company called Land Reclamation, Inc. (LRI).

LRI was located in southern Illinois in an area that had been heavily strip-mined. After it had been strip-mined, the soil was acidic and of such poor quality that it was difficult to get anything to grow upon it. It was also very uneven, even after having been leveled to a degree by bulldozers. LRI reclaimed this land; all of its work had been done under contract for a large local coal company. LRI disked the land and then applied lime, fertilizer, and seed. Its charges were proportionate to the number of acres treated or to the tons of lime applied. LRI also made a profit from

Reprinted by permission. Copyright © Purdue Research Foundation, 1975.

[1] *See Dakota Fertilizer Equipment case, pp. 258–67.*

selling the fertilizer and seed which were applied.

Because of the uneven ground, LRI's heavy equipment tilted and jolted as the land was being treated. There was the constant danger that equipment might tip over, although this had happened only once. Nearby farmers did not seek contracts to do this work because ordinary farm equipment was not large enough and rugged enough. LRI had 6 trucks, 3 tractors, 5 disks, blending equipment, and a leased front-end loader. The original cost of this equipment had been $110,000. The company also owned a building (7,000 sq ft), which sat on 1½ acres of land.

LRI had treated about 3,000 acres of land in each of the 2 years it had been in operation. There was no contract, but a "continuing assurance of future work" from the company for which all of the work had been done. The company had asked LRI to expand its capacity. More than 30 other coal companies did strip mining in the general area.

There were 8 local employees and the manager, Mr. Robert Hart. Mr. Hart, about 45, had previously worked for the owners in their fertilizer business. He repaired the equipment and supervised the relatively uneducated workers, but he did not appear to have the managerial ability to do more than supervise day-to-day operations. His salary was $12,000 and he seemed to like the work.

LRI was owned by 2 businessmen who were successful as fertilizer dealers. Their fertilizer business operated 24 plants that mixed fertilizer; these were centered about 135 miles away. They found LRI difficult to manage because of the geographical distance and the demands of their other business.

Summarized versions of the financial statements are given in Table 1-1.

The owners offered to sell the common stock of LRI for $300,000.

Mr. Speake and his friend had the cash to make the initial payment if they chose to buy LRI. However, both devoted long hours to their own businesses, and they realized they would have little time to supervise LRI, which was over 250 miles from their homes. Nevertheless, they were impressed by the profitability of LRI and felt that they should consider the opportunity carefully.

ASSIGNMENT

Appraise the opportunity from the point of view of Mr. Speake.

TABLE 1-1

BALANCE SHEET
DECEMBER 31, 1974

Assets		Liabilities and equity	
Current assets	$ 21,400	Current liabilities	$ 18,200
Investments	27,600	Note payable	8,600
Net fixed assets	99,500	Capital stock	1,800
Other assets	1,300	Retained earnings	121,200
Total	$149,800	Total	$149,800

OPERATING STATEMENT
YEAR ENDING 12/31/74

Sale of product		$232,000
Cost of sales		182,000
Gross margin		50,000
Service income		241,500
Total income		$291,500
Operating expenses:		
Payroll	$86,500	
Rent	27,900	
Other expenses	47,300	
Depreciation	20,900	
Interest	3,700	
		$186,300
Income before taxes		$105,200
Taxes		44,200
Net income after taxes		$ 61,000

2

Marketing Management

Small companies face the same array of variables in managing marketing functions as do big companies. These variables are shown in Table 2–1. In making decisions regarding them, however, most small companies find their choices automatically narrowed because both the markets they serve and the resources they individually can apply to them are more limited. The successful small firms are those that use these limitations to their advantage.

Not all these components of marketing management are subject, no matter what the size of the firm, to company control. Demand variables, such as the demographic, economic, social, political, and competitive factors in the market environment and the psychological, social, and economic patterns in customer motivations, are autonomous. Semidemand variables, which include market segmentation and customer behavior, are only partially under the control of the company, while decision variables, which are product characteristics and pricing, distribution, and advertising policies, are totally under company control. The essential function of marketing management is the design of an integrated marketing plan that relates the demand and semidemand variables of the market and the consumer to the product and decision variables of the firm to generate an optimal sales response. This integrated marketing plan in smaller firms should be different from the integrated marketing plan in larger corporations.

TABLE 2–1

Product variables	*Demand variables*	*Decision variables*
Product policy	Customer motivation	Pricing
Product characteristics	Customer behavior	Distribution
Product development	Market segment	Personal selling
	Market environment	Advertising
	Company sales	

The plan also depends on which of the following three businesses the company is in:

1. Retailing. Marketing here is virtually the whole purpose of the firm. There is no R&D, no manufacturing, and probably no servicing of products sold. The only control over what is sold is in terms of what is selected for purchase from other firms. Location of the business and pricing are extremely important in attracting customers. Advertising and personal selling may also play important roles.

2. Service. Quality, promptness, and price are very important. Advertising and personal selling may also play key roles, but location may or may not, depending on whether customers come to the firm or the firm takes its service to the customers.

3. Manufacturing. The full range of marketing variables may apply, including R&D. Exceptions may also occur. For example, one producer of eye drops does no selling. She simply collects orders in the mail from druggists and physicians, has them filled by a contract packaging firm, sends out the bills, and collects the money. More typically, however, several of the variables discussed below come heavily into play.

PRODUCT OR SERVICE CHARACTERISTICS

Product and service areas that exclude small firms are those requiring large capital investment and those permitting significant economies of scale. Nuclear submarines, which are expensive and technically complex, are made only by large companies, although small suppliers of those companies may be employed to make some of the parts. Electric toasters, although neither complex nor expensive, are made by large rather than small companies because toasters can be produced more cheaply in large volume. Airlines that maintain schedules to many destinations are large. Even though theoretically several small companies could accomplish the same things, it is more efficient to operate centralized management and common facilities.

Small companies compete better for smaller markets that have specialized needs. Custom manufacturers of few-of-a-kind products are small because large companies have difficulty administratively coping with many small orders from individual customers. Work involving individual expression, as opposed to mass production, is normally performed in small firms that make such things as artifacts, highest quality cuisine, and highest quality musical instruments. When personal service is important, for example, in beauty shops, portrait studios, ballet schools, and interior decorating, small firms are the only kind to survive. Finally, when entry is relatively easy, for example, in such lines of work as heat treating, electroplating, gardening, house painting, and auto repair, small firms predominate.

PRODUCT DEVELOPMENT

Most products and services tend to change over time, whether made by either small or large companies, and this is symptomatic of the need in most firms for product development. There are exceptions (products that remain virtually unchanged over time, such as some types of musical instruments), and there are many small companies that do not operate formal research and development programs as such. Some of these firms pass from the scene as competitors surpass them with innovations; others adapt innovations from elsewhere. Generally, it is advisable for any firm, large or small, to devote conscious attention to the need to develop new products and new features in existing products and to weed out obsolete products. Management of the R&D process in small firms is discussed in Chapter 6.

PRODUCT POLICY

A small firm must develop a conscious product policy that recognizes the competitive situation and adjusts to the alternative products or services that are available. It is not difficult to think up one or more classification schemes that describe the company's offerings in terms of *product types* which have similar features, *product lines* which separate different features, and an overall *product mix* which represents the composite offering of the company. Because of their limited resources, smaller firms typically concentrate on a single product line or product. Viewing the products or services as part of the broader array in which they fit, however, can help in anticipating both competitive threats and new opportunities.

MARKET ENVIRONMENT

The market environment includes (1) *demographic* factors such as population characteristics and how they change, (2) *economic demand factors* such as changes in personal and disposable income and costs of goods and services, (3) *social demand factors* such as education levels, leisure time, mobility, and patterns of taste, (4) *political demand factors* such as welfare programs, government services, and military expenditures, and (5) *competitive demand factors* introduced by other firms. Large companies sometimes spend substantial amounts to collect data on these factors and to hire professionals to analyze the data. In smaller firms this is impossible and the task is usually left to the intuitive judgment of the chief executive. Experience indicates that the large companies, in spite of their great intelligence resources, often miss the target (as their critics continually delight in pointing out), and that individual entrepreneurs, in spite of the informality of their methods in assessing these factors, often succeed.

MARKET SEGMENTATION

Part of the process of analyzing markets involves subdividing the markets according to demand factors such as those mentioned above or according to others which may be important, such as the geographical distribution or behavioral characteristics of different potential customer groups. Often a small company will concentrate on one particular market segment. For instance, most independent retail and service firms are restricted to serving only customers within a small distance radius. Others may deal only with very wealthy clients or with those who have particular problems, for example, with blind people or with the physically disabled. Being aware of the segments that a company serves and does not serve, however, may trigger ideas for new opportunities. Consideration of the market segment that was buying its musical instruments, for instance, led one company to start selling mugs, T-shirts, and other mementos emblazoned with the company's trademark. This policy helped the company to expand its profitable product lines and to obtain further advertising.

CUSTOMER BEHAVIOR

For consumer products, participants in the buying decision include family members and friends who may influence the purchase or use of the product. For industrial products, participants in the buying decision include technical, production, or financial personnel who may influence the purchase or use of the product. The process of buying includes the normal time, place and frequency of purchase, the method of delivery, and the terms of payment. Stages in the buying decision include felt need, pre-purchase comparisons, purchase choice, product or service use, and post-use reactions. All these factors must be considered important regardless whether the firm is small or large. In a small company, however, it is more often possible for top management to know many of the customers personally and to be attuned to individual customer behavior. Here, customers are people, not just statistics.

CUSTOMER MOTIVATION

In interpreting, understanding, and predicting customer behavior, it is possible to complement the intuition on which most small business operators exclusively rely with several theories that may increase their insights. The small business firm that is able to use these theories effectively will be exceptional (most firms are not sufficiently aware of them) and hence may derive substantial competitive advantages. A marketing plan should attempt to specifically identify the reasons that a specific product line is purchased; some of the theories explaining these reasons are as follows:

1. Economic theory explains that the purchasing decision is the result of rational and conscious economic calculations; the buyer seeks to maximize his or her utility function by setting marginal utility proportionate to price. The purchase is rational.

2. Psychological theory explains that the purchasing decision is a learned response to marketing stimuli, for example, product features or promotion. The purchase is habitual instead of rational.

3. Psychoanalytical theory explains that the purchasing decision is a response to symbolic as well as to economic and functional product features. The purchase is controlled by unconscious constraints, hopes, fears, duties, etc., instead of by conscious thought processes.

4. Social–psychological theory explains that the purchasing decision is the result of the individual's conforming to the norms, beliefs, and values of the various groups, organizations, and subcultures to which he or she belongs. The purchase is for social approval.

PRICE DECISIONS

The selection of the price level is the first of the decision variables that relate the marketing plan to the product characteristics, market segment, and customer behavior. Pricing is important, for both large and small firms, because it limits or expands the potential market. The two major methods used to determine price are as follows:

1. Theoretical pricing models have been developed for firms that know their demand and cost functions; these models use mathematical programming to maximize profits within market and financial parameters.

2. Pragmatic pricing methods are used by firms that do not know their demand and cost functions; these methods include markups over cost at a standard percentage, target returns on investment at a standard volume, variable pricing for variable demands, standard pricing at competitive levels, exceptional pricing of "loss leaders" and sales, etc.

Smaller firms generally use pragmatic methods and are constrained to follow the competition's price. Seldom do they set the price themselves. They occasionally may be able, however, to influence the prices of larger competitors. For instance, discount stores and gas stations have at times had substantial effects on retail prices and have forced larger firms to follow them. Small companies more often must compete on the basis of price in bidding situations. Job machine shops, of which there are many in every metropolitan area, are virtually always small and compete on the basis of bid prices, as do many small construction firms. A major part of the art in bid pricing is the ability to forecast the costs of performing the work. In a small company, this art is usually based on the chief executive's prior experience rather than on the formal procedures and statistical data that might be used in the more impersonalized organizational machinery of larger companies.

Terms for payment are sometimes treated differently in small firms than in large ones. A small company cannot use the enormous legal forces accessible to large companies to force recalcitrant customers to pay. Some customers take advantage of this fact and are slower to pay small suppliers; consequently, small suppliers must be on guard against them. At the same time, smaller companies are less able to "play the numbers" in accepting losses on bad debts. A few slow-paying customers or a few bad checks may wipe them out. Therefore, small companies are sometimes more cautious in extending credit to new accounts. It is not uncommon to see "no credit sales" or "no checks accepted, cash only" signs posted on their walls. At the same time, because top management in a small firm knows customers personally and does not have to deal with the customers through bureaucratic organizational structures, credit policies may be more flexible and tailored to the individual customer. This can be a selling advantage that big companies lack.

DISTRIBUTION DECISIONS

Most small firms deal directly with their customers. These firms include retail stores, restaurants and other food outlets, and service operations from barber shops to law firms. Many of the advertisements for direct-mail items seen in newspapers and popular magazines are placed by small firms, as are advertisements received through the mail. Some small firms sell directly from the factory through their own sales forces. Examples of these firms are small storage battery companies that serve a few large customers in a limited geographical area.

Small manufacturing firms that serve broader geographical markets may sell through the same combinations of wholesalers, jobbers, and retailers that are used by larger companies. These firms face the same kinds of distribution needs for such things as representation, credit screening, transportation, storage, delivery installation, and repair as do larger companies, and they face the same problems, for example, cost of direct customer contacts, lack of control over indirect contacts, and possibilities of conflicts with multiple channels.

PERSONAL SELLING DECISIONS

The role played by personal selling ranges in a small business as it does in a large business from virtually zero, as in the case of mail order sales, to very great, as in the life insurance industry. It is more often in smaller companies, however, that strong relationships develop between members of top management and particular customers. Sometimes small companies maintain some of their larger customers as "house accounts," but they sell to other customers through various combinations of representatives, wholesalers, jobbers, etc. Some small companies have only one customer. An example would be a small furniture factory that produces a special line for a chain of retail stores; here there is no sales force and no channels whatever except the contact between the owners of the manufacturing company and the buyers of the chain.

It is a common practice for small manufacturers to handle personal selling through manufacturers' representatives at first. Since these representatives carry several lines from different manufacturers, the costs of the representatives' selling efforts are shared and are not too high for any particular product. By this means a new company can quickly secure coverage for widespread geographic areas, and may be able to obtain entrée to needed customers through the relationships of established representatives. The disadvantage is that the company then has no control over its representative, who may push the new product or not at his or her discretion and who may or may not choose to approach new customers. This lack of control typically prompts companies to shift away from these representatives as soon as their sales grow large enough to support their own sales forces on the payroll. This method, although common in practice and simple in concept, actually involves many difficult decisions, not only in finding and selecting representatives, but also in changing from them to recruit "house" representatives for whom choices must be made regarding recruitment, hiring terms, compensation, and management.

ADVERTISING DECISIONS

The decision area in which smaller companies are more at a disadvantage than larger companies is advertising. Because of its high-volume national sales, a large company can justify the maintenance of its own advertising department and very high-cost and elaborate advertising campaigns, but a small company cannot. In dealing with an advertising agency, the small company is at a disadvantage because the prospect of its account ever becoming large and lucrative for the agency is usually small, and therefore the agency will be more loathe to put substantial effort into developing ideas for the small client and at times will even be hesitant to extend credit.

Nevertheless, it is sometimes necessary for small firms to engage in advertising campaigns to let their potential customers know about them. In this regard, the following are the four important areas in which decisions must be made:

1. Expenditure levels may be limited by the firm's financial capabilities, but, nonetheless, they must be made realistically. Since the amounts are often set as percentages of sales, the question becomes one of what can be bought with that amount that will be most effective. For some very small companies, the limit may only allow erection of a sign, listing in the Yellow Pages, and perhaps limited distribution of circulars or flyers.

2. Media include those mentioned above plus direct mail, newspapers, magazines, radio, television, and displays at trade shows. The decision process must strike a balance between not only which of these are chosen and how funds are allocated between them but also the amount spent on preparing the display for any of them.

3. Advertising agencies can be chosen to help with these decisions and to prepare the art work and campaign, although there may be limitations if the company's resources are small. The small company may have to cast its lot with new and untried agencies that are struggling themselves in order to obtain accounts and show what they can do.

4. The message projected is limited only by the imagination of the agency and the preference of management. For smaller firms, simple messages are often most effective. Assessment of results, particularly in small campaigns, can be very difficult. For this reason, some small companies make it a policy always to include a coupon or other feedback device as part of the message so that they can learn who receives the message and how it is received.

STRATEGY

By definition, large companies have established products and big markets; they sell their output by first positioning each product in a specific market segment and then by adjusting the price margin to the distribution and promotional expenses, and the consequent sales volume, to optimize the expected return on their product and process investments. Although these marketing plans are subject to the uncertainties of the national economic system, they do have the advantages of an existing product reputation, which provides continued sales through brand recognition and loyalty, a large market area that maintains existing sales through the diversified wants of many individual consumers, and the substantial financial and managerial resources that together can develop additional sales through increased advertising or expanded distribution. The management of a larger company seldom has to consider the full range of the product, market, consumer, and decision variables in the design of a marketing plan; the large company has established products, positions, and procedures, and it can use these resources to adapt to changing market conditions. Even in expansion it can use known products in a new market area, or familiar market segments for a new product line, or available financial assets and managerial contacts to overcome problems with either the new products or the new markets; thus the company seldom has to design a full marketing plan from the beginning. It operates, in large measure, with the comforting certainty of an established product market position and with adequate resources.

The smaller company, and particularly the beginning company, does not have these advantages, its product market position is not as secure, and its resources are not as extensive. Despite these problems, it has to compete in an economy dominated by larger firms. The management of the smaller company can do this provided they design a distinctive marketing plan so that they do not have to compete on a product-to-product basis with larger firms that offer the same goods to the same customers through the same channels of distribution. This plan, of course, must be different, but it must be rational as well—not merely eccentric; it has to be based upon a complete understanding of the customers' needs, motives, and purchasing methods within a specific industry. Management of the smaller company should design a complete marketing plan based upon these customer needs, motives, and purchasing methods, and it should carefully consider the following questions:

1. Who are the customers? What are the characteristics of the market segment selected for the product or service?

2. What do these customers want in the way of product characteristics, purchasing convenience, and continuing service?

3. How can the company offer these products and services to these specific customers? What price level, distribution method, and advertising means are needed to sell the products and services to these customers?

Because of the rigidity of their established marketing plans, larger companies tend to neglect these questions and to make only minor changes as the market environment (and the consequent customer needs and motives) changes over time. Smaller companies are, or should be, more flexible, and they should be better able to devise—through perception, imagination, and innovation—a different product market position, based upon an accurate understanding of their customers' needs and motives and upon continual redesign of the company products and services and supported by consistent pricing, distribution, and promotional policies. For the smaller firm, perception, imagination, and innovation are the keys to marketing success, for they result in a distinctive marketing plan. The following cases illustrate the need for this distinctive marketing approach.

Tecnifax Corporation

The Tecnifax Corporation was founded in 1949 to manufacture a new type of coated paper, called diazotype, for the reproduction of engineering and architectural drawings. The company was immediately successful, helped by the rapidly expanding market for the new product and by the general industrial prosperity of the early 1950s, and sales increased from $170,000 in the first year of operations to $2,600,000 in the fourth year. This rapid growth strained the financial resources and productive facilities of the firm, so that in 1952 Joe Coffman, the president and founder, was forced to borrow a substantial sum of money to purchase a new building, to construct additional equipment, and to finance expanded sales. It is often difficult, of course, for a small or beginning company to borrow money; this loan was only granted because of the superior growth history of the Tecnifax Corporation and because of the rapid repayment that seemed possible if this growth continued as expected. The bank insisted upon closing out the loan for both working capital and fixed assets within four years, so a loan schedule with large monthly payments was established, and a loan provision was included that permitted the bank to take control if the payments were not made by a specified date, or if the working capital dropped below a specified level. These conditions were considered to be strict but not onerous by Mr. Coffman, since the company had been profitable during each year of operations and since the profits were expected to continue to increase with sales. In early 1953, however, the largest competitor in the diazotype industry, with

68% of the industry sales (88% prior to the formation of Tecnifax), announced price reductions on their products that averaged 14%. Hurried computations on the recently received 1952 income statement (Exhibit 1) revealed that if Tecnifax met these price reductions, the decreased margin would result in a substantial loss, and that if Tecnifax did not meet the new prices, the decreased volume, estimated at 30%, would result in a profit level insufficient to make the required bank payments.

At first glance, it seemed obvious that the only possible course of action for the Tecnifax Corporation was to maintain its list prices, despite the resultant reduction in sales volume, and to hope that the price cuts initiated by its largest competitor would prove to be only temporary. However, it was not certain that the reduction in sales volume would be limited to 30%; that was only the optimistic forecast of the sales manager. The salesmen, individually called by Mr. Coffman, estimated that they could hold no more than 50% of their customers, and that their larger volume customers would be the first to change suppliers, so that the total company sales decline might be in the range of 50% to 60%. Also, Mr. Coffman was worried about the effect of the reduced sales volume upon the morale and effectiveness of the sales force; the salesmen were paid by commission, and a 30% or 50% reduction in sales volume for the company would result in a 30% or 50% reduction in personal income for the salesmen. Mr. Coffman felt that the company would have to cover at least a portion of this income loss, or the best salesmen

This case was based upon the Tecnifax Corporation (A) case copyrighted in 1960 by the President and Fellows of Harvard College, written by Arnold Cooper and W. A. Hosmer.

EXHIBIT 1 Income statement for the Tecnifax Corporation for 1952, as reported, and as changed to reflect the effects of the announced price reduction or the estimated volume reduction.

	1952 as reported	1952 with 14% price reduction	1952 with 30% volume reduction
Net sales	$2,600,000	$2,236,000	$1,820,000
Cost of goods sold (68% of list)	1,768,000	1,768,000	1,237,000
Gross margin	832,000	468,000	583,000
Administrative expenses	159,000	159,000	159,000
Engineering and research	96,000	96,000	96,000
Selling expenses (14% of sales)	359,000	314,000	255,000
Operating profit	$ 218,000	$ (101,000)	$ 73,000
Taxes (52% of operating profits)	113,000	—	37,000
Net profit after taxes	$ 105,000	$ (101,000)	$ 36,000

might move over to one of the competitors, with a further reduction in sales volume. In short, Mr. Coffman was not at all certain that the profit of $36,000 forecasted as a consequence of maintaining the existing list prices was an accurate figure. Despite this lack of information, Mr. Coffman had to decide within a matter of days on the proper course for his company to follow; salesmen, distributors, and customers were calling to request an immediate decision. The balance of the case provides background information on the diazotype industry and on the Tecnifax company to permit students to recommend to Mr. Coffman the best alternative open to the company.

The diazotype process was developed in Germany during the 1920s, but it was not introduced into the United States until shortly before World War II (1939–1945). The process was used, as described previously, primarily for the reproduction of engineering and architectural drawings, but also for the copying of technical documents such as manufacturing bills of required materials, or construction sets of bidding specifications, and for the printing of catalog pages and advertising pages. The diazotype process produced black lines on white paper, rather than the more familiar white lines on a blue background. This black and white contrast made drawing details, dimensions, tolerances, and specifications much clearer, and

much less likely to be misinterpreted, than on blueprints. The diazotype process was also quicker and more easily automated than the earlier blueprint method.

Diazotype prints were prepared by first making an original drawing or document on translucent drafting paper; then, the original was placed on top of a sheet of diazotype copying paper. The two sheets were fed together through a machine which exposed them to ultraviolet light from a mercury vapor lamp. The ultraviolet light passed through the translucent drafting paper, except where the opaque lines and characters covered the original, and formed an impression on the diazotype copy. The copy was then developed by passing it through a moist ammonia atmosphere, generally in the same machine, which turned the unexposed portions of the paper black and left the exposed background pure white.

Since the diazotype, or whiteprint, process was simple, fast, and accurate, it rapidly supplanted the earlier blueprint process in popularity (See Exhibit 2).

The diazotype process had been introduced into the United States by the Ozalid Division of the General Analine and Film Corporation, a German-owned firm that had been expropriated by the U.S. government during World War II. It was managed by the Alien Property Commission of the government following the war, while the eventual

EXHIBIT 2 Industry production of blueprint and white-print paper, 1948 to 1952. (Source: company records.)

Year	Blueprint paper (tons)	Whiteprint paper (tons)
1948	11,400	2,600
1949	10,000	4,200
1950	11,500	6,500
1951	11,900	11,100
1952	13,200	13,600

disposition and sale of the assets of the company were being arranged. Ozalid dominated the diazotype market; the division not only had introduced the process in the United States, it also was the only manufacturer of the equipment needed to expose and develop the whiteprints, and it sold, in 1948 at the time of the formation of the Tecnifax Company, 88% of the diazotype paper used within the country. Other competitors in the industry were manufacturers of engineering equipment, such as Dietzgen, Keuffel & Esser, or Frederick Post, that sold diazotype paper as part of their full line of precision drafting tools and supplies, and small paper converting firms, termed "garage coaters," that produced diazotype paper at reduced prices for a local or regional market.

The Ozalid Division of the General Analine and Film Corporation had dominated the diazotype industry from the introduction of the process in 1937, but by 1952 the Tecnifax Corporation had taken nearly a third of the market, and the trends indicated that the new company would continue to increase its market share (see Exhibit 3).

The sales of the Tecnifax Corporation had nearly doubled each year; this success was due, in the opinion of management, to its attention to quality in both its product line and marketing methods. The diazotype paper manufactured by Tecnifax was produced with continual tests and inspections of the purchase materials, the coating process, and the finished product. Every roll produced had to meet company standards on printing speed, color contrast, detail clarity, texture evenness, and background whiteness. It was felt that the Tecnifax product standards were the highest in the industry.

It was also felt that the Tecnifax product line was the largest in the industry. Drafting standards are variable, with basic drawing sizes of 8½ in. x 11 in., 9 in. x 12 in., 9½ in. x 13 in., and 10 in. x 14 in., and with all the multiples of these sizes, in black, blue, and green colors in use by different companies. In addition to the reproduction of

EXHIBIT 3 Industry sales (in tons) of whiteprint paper, by producer, 1948 to 1952. (Source: company estimates.)

Year	Ozalid Division	Tecnifax Corporation	Engineering supply firms	Local paper firms
1948	2,300	—	200	100
1949	3,400	200	400	200
1950	4,700	1,000	500	300
1951	7,200	2,400	800	700
1952	7,800	4,200	800	800

engineering and architectural drawings, the diazotype process was used as an inexpensive printing method for short runs of advertising brochures and catalog pages, which required cellulose acetate and plastic coated papers in various sizes and colors. The process was also used for the simple copying of office documents, which required lower grade paper in various sizes and forms. Tecnifax manufactured and stocked for immediate shipment over 2,000 different types, sizes, colors, and grades of diazotype paper.

Tecnifax distributed the diazotype paper directly to the consumer through the use of company salesmen. Twenty-two men were employed, working through 11 sales offices in major cities throughout the country. Management felt, since the diazotype process was relatively new, that personal assistance was needed to help customers with any technical problems that might arise, particularly since many firms attempted to use the new white-print paper on exposing and developing equipment designed for the earlier blueprint process. Company salesmen were trained in the operation and repair of the various types of equipment available for the reproduction of engineering and architectural drawings and documents, and it was felt that the Tecnifax sales force was the most technically competent in the industry. The salesmen were even instructed to help customers using competitive diazotype paper, for management believed that this technical assistance would expand the use of diazotype paper and eventually expand the sales of this paper by Tecnifax.

In addition to the 11 sales offices, a number of distributorships were established in areas where the volume was not sufficient to support a branch. Both branches and distributors carried in stock a full line of the diazotype paper in the various types, sizes, colors, and grades, so that it was generally possible to provide "sameday" shipment of a customer's requirements. In addition, the salesmen carried stocks of the more standard types and sizes in their cars, in order to make "rush" shipments and prevent a customer from running out of needed paper. In

short, the function of the sales force was to provide excellent customer service and to support the company motto, "It's easy to do business with Tecnifax."

Until January 1953 Tecnifax sold the diazotype paper at the list prices established by Ozalid. Historically, most companies in the industry had followed the volume leader in price changes, though the engineering supply firms normally priced their diazotype paper approximately 5% below list since they carried a large number of drafting tools and materials and were unable to provide the emphasis upon this one item in their personal sales calls that Ozalid and Tecnifax naturally gave. The local paper converting firms, or "garage coaters," sold at prices that were 10% to 20% below Ozalid, but they provided neither personal selling nor technical assistance, and it was said that their quality standards were considerably lower. All companies gave volume discounts based upon annual usage.

Tecnifax engaged in only limited advertising in engineering or architectural journals. None of the other firms in the industry advertised heavily either; instead, they tended to compete on either personal service (Ozalid and Tecnifax) or price (the engineering supply firms and the local paper converters).

Production of diazotype paper required continual attention to quality. Purchased paper (in rolls) was processed by a machine 120 ft in length on which the paper was first immersed in a sensitizing solution and then, after passing over an "air knife" that controlled the amount of solution remaining on the paper, it was pressed by large heated rolls that dried the paper and formed the texture. The rolls were then cut into large sheets, which were individually checked for defects, counted, stacked in 500-sheet lots, sheared to required size, and then wrapped in light-proof polyethylene-coated kraft paper for shipment and eventual sale. The equipment at the Tecnifax factory was of modern design and, except for the inspection step, all of these functions were performed by automated machinery.

The growth of the company was financed

by retained earnings and bank loans, while the amounts required were kept to a minimum by very stringent controls on the size of the accounts receivable and inventory. Despite these controls, total debt in 1952 was 140% of equity, a condition which Mr. Coffman felt was unbalanced, but also unavoidable given the recent rapid growth of the firm. Mr. Coffman was hesitant to release detailed information of the financial position of the company; however, he did approve the summary balance sheet shown in Exhibit 4.

Mr. Coffman owned a majority of the stock of the Tecnifax Corporation, and the remainder was held by a wealthy businessman in Holyoke, Massachusetts, who was the president of a small paper mill in the area and who had thus been able to supply both the capital needed to start the company and the facilities required to manufacture the diazotype paper during the early years of operations. Mr. Coffman had been able to arrange this advantageous combination of financing and production since he was exceedingly well-known and respected in the technical printing industry. He had been the first director of visual education for the Atlanta school system (1925–1930), an early producer of scientific and educational films (1930–1935), marketing vice president of Scientific Films (1935–1937), a division of General Analine and Film, and eventually general manager of the Ozalid Division of

G.A.F. (1938–1947). His assignment at Ozalid had been to introduce the diazotype process to the United States, and he had succeeded so well that in 1947 Ozalid was, as described previously, the dominant company in the diazotype market, with 88% of the total market sales. However, Mr. Coffman objected to certain developments in the top management group, and he subsequently resigned on May 1, 1948. After considering a number of other job offers, he decided to start a new company to manufacture and sell diazotype paper.

Originally, Mr. Coffman was the only employee of Tecnifax. The diazotype paper was produced and packaged by the paper mill in Holyoke to Mr. Coffman's specifications, and then it was shipped to customers sold by Mr. Coffman. As the company grew, and as more people were needed, Mr. Coffman was able to recruit salesmen and departmental managers from Ozalid, many of whom were either eager to leave New York City for the pleasant and rural atmosphere in western Massachusetts or eager to work for Mr. Coffman in a new and expanding company. Eventually, 20 people came from Ozalid to Tecnifax, including the best 12 salesmen, the production manager, the maintenance superintendent, and the research director.

As sales expanded, Tecnifax rented office and warehouse space in various buildings near the parent paper mill in Holyoke. In 1952, however, company sales exceeded the

EXHIBIT 4 Balance sheet for the Tecnifax Corporation as of December 31, 1952 (disguised figures).

Cash	$18,700	Accounts payable	$ 39,200
Accounts receivable	141,200	Bank loan—due within 1 year	78,300
Inventory	158,800		$117,500
	$318,700		
		Bank loan—due past 1 year	229,400
Building and equipment	$295,700		
Less reserve for depreciation	21,100	Common stock	63,000
	$274,600	Retained earnings	183,400
			$246,400
Total assets	$593,300		
		Total liabilities and equity	$593,300

capacity of that mill, so that Mr. Coffman was forced to look for larger facilities. In the spring of 1952 the company purchased a group of buildings that had been constructed in 1888 by the American Thread Company and abandoned in 1950 when that company moved to the South. Although the buildings were 64 years old, Mr. Coffman felt that the property was nearly ideal, since it was clean and well maintained, although larger than needed, with 250,000 square feet. It was estimated that Tecnifax sales of $25 million per year could be produced in the compound. Mr. Coffman offered $100,000 for the real estate and water-power rights, 15% of the amount asked. The offer was accepted.

After acquiring the plant, Tecnifax made a number of changes: new floor covering, improved lighting, air conditioning, the conversion of the former engine room into modern offices, landscaping, and the leveling of two unneeded warehouses to make parking spaces. The company also designed and built a new, very high-speed process machine to accurately coat paper rolls with the diazotype solution and installed improved equipment to automatically shear, wrap, and label the finished diazotype paper in standard packages. The total cost of the new property, with the equipment installed, running, and capable of producing approximately $8 million in sales per year, was nearly $300,000; this was more than Mr. Coffman wanted to spend, given the beginning nature and limited finances of his company, but it was also less than one-third of the cost of constructing new buildings and installing purchased machinery for the same capacity, and this capacity could be tripled within the existing buildings:

> We knew that we were taking a chance, since we had more plant than we needed. But, I couldn't find anything else that was suitable in the area, and we wanted the high-speed processing equipment to keep our costs low, and we wanted the big buildings for our future expansion. The problem was the financing; we could not get a 10-year or 15-year mortgage. The note meant that we were vulnerable to a business downturn, since I knew

that we could not obtain additional financing if things went wrong, but we expected to easily be able to pay off the note through retained earnings. Our pro forma statements showed a profit of $160,000 for 1953, more than twice the required annual payments. We did not worry about meeting these payments. But, we did not expect Ozalid to cut their prices. (Statement of Mr. Coffman.)

During the first week of January 1953 Tecnifax learned that telegrams had been sent by Ozalid to all the principal users of diazotype paper with the following message:

PRODUCTION ECONOMIES DUE TO GREATLY INCREASED VOLUME PERMIT SUBSTANTIAL IMMEDIATE REDUCTION IN LIST PRICE FOR OZALID SENSITIZED PAPERS. YOUR USUAL VOLUME DISCOUNT STILL APPLIES. THIS UNUSUAL AGAINST-TREND REDUCTION OFFERS YOU THE OPPORTUNITY TO OBTAIN QUALITY AT REDUCED COSTS, DOING BUSINESS WITH THE INDUSTRY LEADER AND ORIGINATOR OF THE DIAZOTYPE PROCESS. OZALID DIVISION, GENERAL ANALINE AND FILM CORPORATION. (Source: Company Records.)

Within a week the new price list was available, indicating price cuts of from 9% to 16% on various items, but averaging 14%. A 14% price reduction would, as shown in Exhibit 1, have resulted in a substantial loss on 1952 sales. The lost sales volume that would come from attempting to maintain the original list prices in the face of serious price competition would have resulted in a profit figure far too low to meet the required bank payments for the recently completed plant expansion.

> It certainly seemed as if Ozalid picked the 14% figure since they knew that it would hurt us badly, and it certainly seemed as if they picked the time for the same reason. It also seemed as if everyone in this company had a different idea as to what we should do. (Statement of Mr. Coffman.)

The Tecnifax executives agreed that the annual sales increase, which was estimated by company officials to be in the range of 25%

to 40% for 1953, and which could be expected as a result of the continued growth of
the diazotype market nationwide, would help
to mitigate the effects of the price cut, provided Tecnifax met the new prices. However,
company officials were not at all certain that
they could expect higher sales in 1953 if they
did not meet the lower prices, since they felt
that they might not be able to maintain their
existing market share of the new customers;
that is, many of the new customers might go
directly to Ozalid because of the lower prices,
and only the established customers, because
of supplier loyalty, would remain with Tecnifax. Company officials also felt that there
was a chance that the new prices might
greatly expand the market, with a 50% to
75% increase in 1953, since the lower costs
might now appeal to the large number of
industrial and architectural concerns still using the older blueprint process.

The size and character of the future national market were not definite as a result of
the change in price level initiated by Ozalid,
and the proper competitive reaction by Tecnifax was not at all clear either. Some executives argued for an immediate price reduction, while others wanted to maintain the
established list prices:

> Look, all industries mature, and when they
> mature you get price cuts and price compe-
> tition. We spent 4 years building up our
> market position, and we just acquired this
> plant in order to support a higher sales vol-
> ume. We have to keep our sales volume; we
> have to keep our market position; we have to
> lower our prices. (Statement of Tecnifax
> executive.)

> Our relationships with our customers are
> our most important asset, and we should not
> jeopardize that asset. If we do not lower our
> prices, every company in the industry can
> undersell us, and eventually our relationships
> with our customers will deteriorate. (State-
> ment of Tecnifax executive.)

> Our profits in 1952 before taxes were only
> 8.1% of sales. If we meet the new prices, we'll
> be selling our products at a loss. Why stay in

business if you have to sell at a loss? It is sui-
cidal to follow the lower prices now offered by
others in the industry. (Statement of Tecnifax
executive.)

Despite these disagreements on policies,
the Tecnifax executives were in firm agreement that the reason given by Ozalid for the
lower prices, economies in production, was
not at all valid. They were certain that the
Tecnifax manufacturing costs, because of
their recently constructed processing machinery and new facilities generally, were at
least as low as any in the industry. They also
considered their expenditures for administration and research to be reasonable, given
their size and position in the industry. They
admitted that their selling costs might be
considered somewhat high, but they also
pointed out that the results of this selling
effort, with annual volume increases averaging over 100%, were impressive:

> We may spend a little more in selling, but
> we get a lot more in return. We have nearly
> doubled our sales each year, and there are not
> many companies in any industry that have
> done that. (Statement of Tecnifax executive.)

In late January 1953 Mr. Coffman had to
decide upon the proper pricing level for the
Tecnifax Corporation. All the other competitors in the diazotype industry had met
the new Ozalid prices. Now Tecnifax salesmen, distributors, and customers were pressuring him to follow the lead of the other
firms.

ASSIGNMENT

Prepare a marketing plan for the Tecnifax
Corporation, relating price, distribution,
and promotion to the needs and wants of
the customers and the characteristics of
the product. Specifically, what price level
would you recommend?

WFF 'N PROOF
Learning Games Associates

WFF 'N PROOF Learning Games Associates was formed by Professor Layman E. Allen in 1962 to produce and market the WFF 'N PROOF series of educational games, of which he is the principal author or designer. The production function has caused no difficulties; the company is easily able to purchase the components and to assemble, box, and ship the games in quantities of 30,000 to 50,000 units per year, and could readily multiply that production rate by a factor of 10 or even 15 within the existing facilities. Marketing, however, has been a continual problem, and the annual sales of the games have never approached the potential envisaged by the company founder and president. Professor Allen describes the past marketing efforts as "an amateur night operation," and he feels that the lack of a successful marketing plan is partially because he has no training or experience in business administration, but primarily because his principal interests are in continuing research in the educational and motivational values of the games, not in maximizing profits, and his principal activities are in teaching law and conducting legal research, not in operating a small business. In 1975 he was still managing WFF 'N PROOF Learning Games Associates because, after numerous unsuccessful attempts to distribute his games through a variety of publishers and other manufacturers, this was the only way he was able to continue to manufacture and distribute his products. At this time, he decided that he would much prefer to supervise only the manufacturing and financial operations and leave the marketing to a younger person, trained in the area, who could devise and implement a new

marketing plan. The purpose of this case is to describe the problems and requirements of marketing the WFF 'N PROOF series of educational games so that potential candidates for the position can design a workable marketing plan.

EVOLUTION OF THE WFF 'N PROOF SERIES OF EDUCATIONAL GAMES

The evolution of the WFF 'N PROOF series of games can probably be best characterized as a sequence of happy accidents. A decade ago, if anyone had suggested to me as a young lawyer just beginning a teaching career at Yale Law School, that I would be seduced into devoting so much time and attention to the use of games as instructional and therapeutic devices, I believe that my reaction would have been a dandy guffaw. (Statement by Professor Allen, quoted in Layman E. Allen, "Some Examples of Programmed Non-Simulation Games" in P. J. Tansey (ed.), *Educational-Aspects of Simulation*, p. 63. Copyright © 1971 McGraw-Hill Book Co. (UK) Limited. Reproduced by permission.

Layman E. Allen had earned a bachelor's degree in Public and International Affairs at Princeton, a master's degree in Public Administration at Harvard, and a law degree at Yale before joining the faculty at Yale Law School. It was during his early years at Yale that he first became intrigued by the potentials of educational games.

As is so often the case, there were a variety of fortuitous circumstances that kindled my interests in the potentials of games as teaching devices. Among the recollections that stand out are discussions during the 1956–1957 academic year with Richard Helgeson, then a law student at Yale. He, also, had become interested in symbolic logic and its usefulness for lawyers in dealing with certain kinds of communication problems. At the time, Helgeson and his family lived in one of the Yale Bowl Quonset huts just across the way from ours. Frequently in the wee hours of two and three in the morning I would tap on his still-lit kitchen window, and we would wind up chatting about logic problems. Invariably, that is what he would be working on at that time in the morning. I well understood the feeling of exhilaration that accompanied such efforts, being then deeply involved in the study of, and being stimulated by, logic myself. Frequently expressed at those sessions was our surprise that other law students and lawyers had not discovered the joy and usefulness of modern logic. We were even more surprised that so many of the extraordinarily bright students we happened to know, then enrolled at Yale Law School, seemed apprehensive about learning something that "looked like" mathematics. We were certainly aware that many persons in America do not understand very much about mathematics, are not interested in it, do not like to deal with it, and given free option will avoid studying it whenever possible. I guess, however, we expected that the exceptionally intelligent Yale Law School group would be different. We attributed our impressions to attitude more than aptitude, and, as I recall, it was in this context that we talked about games involving mathematical logic as a possible way of developing more favorable attitudes toward such kinds of symbol-handling activities. We tinkered with a notion of using a big, stuffed white rabbit with movable ears for signaling messages to nursery-school and kindergarten children about binary logic, and somehow arranging the activity in the form of a game that would be enjoyable and, hopefully, cultivate a favorable attitude toward the subject matter involved. We also considered a card game involving mathematical logic. We went as far as making a preliminary mock-up of such a game, but it really did not seem to be a very interesting one and was never finished. (Statement by Professor Allen, quoted in *Educational Aspects of Simulation*, pp. 64–65.)

In 1958, while teaching a seminar on symbolic logic and law at Yale Law School, Pro-

fessor Allen was discouraged to find that many of the bright students seemed to have difficulty with the course material. That same year he was teaching a sixth-grade class in the Sunday School of the New Haven Unitarian Society; convinced that reasonably bright 12-year-olds could handle introductory work in modern logic, Professor Allen spent 10 minutes each Sunday morning for a term introducing logic concepts to his young students. Not only did they demonstrate their ability to handle these concepts, they were genuinely enthusiastic about working logic problems. Professor Allen was very much encouraged by the attitude displayed by members of his Sunday School class, and he wondered if other young children could be motivated to learn and enjoy modern logic. He prepared a proposal for a research project to develop methods of teaching logic to elementary school children. In 1959 the Carnegie Foundation provided a 3-year grant to fund Professor Allen's project, which was termed Accelerated Learning of Logic (ALL). The objectives of the ALL project were twofold: (1) to develop a program of self-instructional materials for teaching logic to elementary school children and (2) to develop a series of games to complement the programmed self-instructional materials and generate enthusiasm for learning logic among elementary school children.

Professor Allen and his three graduate student research assistants considered the goal of the games to be to teach, through active participation, the symbol-handling skills of logic in a competitive and entertaining atmosphere to students of widely varying skills and abilities. There were seven characteristics that were incorporated into the original games and, in fact, into most of the games that were to be developed in later years, that Professor Allen felt would make the games especially useful for facilitating learning:

1. Practice in logic should come as a byproduct of an activity that is enjoyable in itself.

2. Although young children enjoy these

games, the more intricate ones should pose a genuine challenge for adults.

3. In the play of the games there should be no waiting time. Each player should proceed at his own pace throughout the entire time of play. The more adept player should not be delayed by those who play more slowly.

4. Everyone else in these games should learn from the best player. His strategies should be displayed openly so that all others may learn to adopt them. In effect, the best players should act as teachers, although they are not formally assigned this role by the rules of the game.

5. The games should be so ordered that each new game is slightly more intricate than the previous one, and each later game will use the skills learned in earlier games.

6. The games should emphasize individual rather than collective decision making. Each player should plan and execute his own strategy independently in order to achieve specified goals.

7. The games should be flexible both in the number of persons who may play (two or more) and in the length of time for a game to be played (5 minutes or more). (Statement by Professor Allen.)

Through 1960 Professor Allen and his three assistants worked on the development of the self-instructional materials and the games, and both were ready for testing in the spring of 1961. During a 17-week testing period in a sixth-grade classroom at the Mary L. Tracy School in Orange, Connecticut, half an hour per day was devoted to the Accelerated Learning of Logic project. Four of the daily sessions each week were spent working through the self-instructional materials and the fifth session was devoted to playing one of the versions of the game then developed. In less than four weeks the students were requesting that more of the sessions be spent playing the games and fewer spent working through the programs. Then, the students began building their own game equipment so that they could play outside the classroom. Overall, the tests were considered an outstanding success, and the results of the initial testing period were confirmed by further experimentation with elementary students at the Yale–North Haven Summer School during the summer of 1961.

Encouraged by the results of the tests, Professor Allen and his brother, Robert, who was a junior high school teacher, together prepared the first commercial version of *WFF 'N PROOF: The Game of Modern Logic,* which was privately published in the fall of 1961. (The self-instructional materials from this early version of the games were ultimately published as *Symbolic Logic and Language: A Programmed Text* by McGraw-Hill in 1965.)

The first version of WFF 'N PROOF was a 24-game kit, with a programmed text of self-instructional material for each game. However, it was quickly noted in all of the testing that the games were much more popular than the self-instructional programs, so an effort was made to incorporate much of the programmed material into the games and to make the learning programs much more game-like. Professor Allen worked on this change during the 1961–1962 academic year while he was a Fellow at the Center for Advanced Study in the Behavioral Sciences at Stanford University in Palo Alto, California. The result of this effort was a new version of WFF 'N PROOF with an instruction manual that incorporated the required set of programmed materials in game-like fashion, requiring participation by the learner. Professor Allen felt that this new version would provide a means to reach the unmotivated student and to instill positive learning attitudes.

> It is in giving practice and building confidence in an enjoyable and stimulating setting that I believe that games have a useful role in mathematics and logic education. This results in developing positive attitudes toward the subject matter, and if used appropriately, it seems likely that games can also contribute significantly to a learner's self-esteem. The most clear-cut impressionistic result of the use of such games in the classroom is the building of self-confidence, the emergence of an "I can

do it" attitude. This is also true of the subsequent games that have been developed along the lines of the WFF 'N PROOF game. (Statement by Layman Allen, quoted in *Educational Aspects of Simulation,* p. 69.)

During the two years of refinement of the WFF 'N PROOF game, Professor Allen also created his second game, *EQUATIONS: The Game of Creative Mathematics.* The EQUATIONS game, like WFF 'N PROOF, was found to be both educational and fun in tests conducted in 1963 in the California school system.

> An experimental group of 43 students, in junior and senior high schools, after 3 weeks of intensive exposure to WFF 'N PROOF materials, scored an average increase in non-verbal IQ of 20.9 points, or 14.3 points better than a similar control group not using the materials. At the same time, the EQUATIONS game was used in instructing 84 basic mathematics students for 4 months, after which tests showed that their average increase in arithmetic reasoning was 1.3 years, or 7 months more than their control group. (John Edgerton, "Academic Games: Play as You Learn," *Southern Education Report,* March–April 1966, p. 27.)

Professor Allen was very much encouraged by the test results and published reports. He established an informal information exchange with other researchers interested in the interrelationship between education and motivation, and he continued to develop and refine the games. To satisfy his interests he sought a position at a university that would allow him the opportunity to both continue his research in the field of educational games and to teach in a distinguished law school. In 1966 he accepted an offer to join the faculty at the University of Michigan, with a dual appointment at the Law School and at the Mental Health Research Institute. As a Professor of Law, he continued to teach courses in contracts, symbolic logic, and communication sciences. At the same time, as a Research Social Scientist, he was able to formalize his work in game design and motivation as related to instructional and therapeutic performance.

Professor Allen feels that many other persons have contributed to the WFF 'N PROOF series of educational games, and he wishes very specifically to credit them for their efforts as authors and for other assistance:

Mr. Robert W. Allen, Director
National Academic Games Program

Professor Robin Brooks
Bowdoin College

Professor William Dickoff
Kent State University

Professor Harold L. Dorwart
Trinity College

Professor Frederick L. Goodman
The University of Michigan

Mr. Lorne Greene
NBC—Paramount Studios

Professor Bruce L. Hicks
University of Illinois

Professor Hervey C. Hicks
Carnegie-Mellon University

Ms. Doris J. Humphrey
The University of Michigan

Professor Patricia James
Kent State University

Professor Peter Kugel
M.I.T.

Professor George H. Moulds
Kent State University

Mr. James R. O'Neil
U.S. Treasury Department

Dr. Martin F. Owens
Mitre Corporation

Mrs. Joan K. Ross
The University of Michigan

Professor Harry D. Ruderman
Hunter College

DESCRIPTION OF
THE WFF 'N PROOF SERIES
OF EDUCATIONAL GAMES

The name of the first game developed by Professor Allen, WFF 'N PROOF, has been carried over to the 11 other games that he and other professors and research specialists have developed so that currently the WFF 'N PROOF series consists of 12 distinct games:

1. WFF 'N PROOF: The Game of Modern Logic, which teaches abstract thinking and symbolic logic.
2. WFF: The Beginner's Game of Logic, which also teaches abstract thinking and symbolic logic, but designed for younger children through the use of the simpler problems from the WFF 'N PROOF game.
3. EQUATIONS: The Game of Creative Mathematics, which teaches arithmetic operations (addition, subtraction, multiplication, division, exponents, and radicals) in a variety of numerical systems (decimal, octal, binary, etc.).
4. ON-SETS: The Game of Set Theory, which teaches the basics of set theory (union, intersection, complement, identity, inclusion, null, and universal sets) and provides an introduction to "new math."
5. REAL NUMBERS: The Beginner's Game of Mathematics, which prepares younger children for playing EQUATIONS and deals with real, rational, irrational, integer, and natural numbers.
6. CONFIGURATIONS: Number Puzzles and Patterns for All Ages, which teaches logical reasoning through a series of geometric and mathematical problems.
7. QUERIES 'N THEORIES: The Game of Science and Language, which teaches inductive reasoning and the scientific method of inquiry.
8. ON-WORDS: The Game of Word Structure, which teaches spelling, grammar, phonetics, word roots, inflectional endings, prefixes, and suffixes.

9. PROPAGANDA GAME, which teaches the techniques such as faulty analogy, out-of-context quotes, rationalization, technical jargon, emotional appeals, etc., used by both individuals and groups to influence public opinion.
10. TRI-NIM: The Game for Complete Strategists, which teaches sequential decision making leading toward a specific objective or strategy in mathematical terms. The name is derived from the triangular board that is used and from a very ancient game called *nim*, which is based upon counters, laid out in piles of agreed numbers, from which the players draw according to set rules.
11. TAC-TICKLE: A Game of Pure Strategy, which also teaches decision making leading toward an optimal objective.
12. QWIK-SANE: A Topological Puzzle, which teaches both patience and concentrated effort to resolve a series of problems that involves specific spatial relationships.

The name of the WFF 'N PROOF series of educational games is, of course, very similar to that of the Whiffenpoof singing group at Yale, and many former or present college beer-drinkers may have inferred that the game was conceived at the "tables down at Mory's" for the amusement of the "poor little lambs who have gone astray." The name actually is a semi-acronym and is descriptive for the first game in the series; a WFF (pronounced "woof") is a "well-formed formula," or logic sentence, and is the basic concept upon which the game builds. By applying rules of inference, players utilize WFFs to construct a PROOF, which is the aim of the WFF 'N PROOF game.

WFF 'N PROOF is actually a series of 21 games, rather than a single game, designed to provide practice and favorable attitudes for mathematical logic and abstract thinking. The 21 games systematically introduce a total of 13 ideas, which comprise one formulation of the system of logic called "propositional calculus," the most elementary branch of logic. The beginning games teach the idea of a well-formed formula, and the subsequent games introduce, one at a time, the 11 rules of inference necessary for the proofs. As the 11 rules of inference are added, the proof games become more and more difficult, and the final games certainly rival chess in complexity. Whenever a player is not already familiar with the ideas to be used in the play of the game, he can achieve at least a minimum level of understanding and competence by working through the appropriate learning program provided in the WFF 'N PROOF instruction manual. This 224-page book contains learning programs for each of the 13 ideas, rules for playing the games, and several sample games.

The play of WFF 'N PROOF is essentially the same as the play of EQUATIONS and ON-SETS. Since the subject matter of these latter two games, mathematics and set theory, is much more familiar to most people than the subject matter of WFF 'N PROOF, propositional calculus and rules of logical inference, the rules and play of the two quantitative games will be described.

EQUATIONS: The Game of Creative Mathematics was developed by Professor Allen in 1962 and 1963 to enable students to practice the basic operations of mathematics (addition, subtraction, multiplication, division, exponentiation, and roots) as a competitive group activity, and thus encourage both intellectual mastery and favorable attitudes toward the subject matter. EQUATIONS can be played by two or more players and may be played at many levels of difficulty. The level of difficulty is determined by the number and color of the dice-like cubes that are used, and by the sophistication of the rules that are applied, during the play.

The EQUATIONS game kit includes 1 playing mat (illustrated in Exhibit 1), 12 red cubes (imprinted with $+$, $-$, 0, 1, 2, 3 on the 6 sides), 8 blue cubes (imprinted with $\times$, $\div$, 0, 1, 2, 3), 6 green cubes (imprinted with $-$, $\times$, * [exponentiation], 4, 5, 6), 6 black cubes (imprinted with $+$, $\div$, $\sqrt{}$ (radical), 7, 8, 9), a one-minute timer, and a 55-page instruction manual, all boxed in a 6 in. $\times$ 4¾ in. $\times$ 1 in. plastic case.

Prior to the start of each game, the players must decide which cubes and how many to use. (The instruction manual mentions that

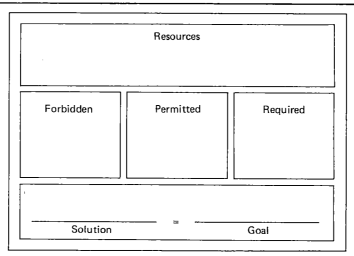

EXHIBIT 1 Playing mat for EQUATIONS: The Game of Creative Mathematics, ½ scale.

a good beginning game for 6-year-olds uses just the 12 red cubes and that 11-year-olds can learn to play with all 4 colors of cubes.) The player chosen to go first rolls the selected cubes out onto the table. The symbols that appear on the upward faces of the cubes are the "Resources." From these Resources, the first player sets a "Goal" (the right side of the equation) for which a "Solution" (the left side of the equation) can be built from the remaining Resources. The player then constructs the Goal in the Goal section of the playing mat; this must be a string of not more than 5 cubes that expresses a number. However, if it is not possible to set a Goal for which a Solution can be built from the remaining Resources, the first player must declare "no Goal," and his declaration is then evaluated by the other players. After a Goal has been set, the players proceed to take turns moving Resource cubes, one at a time, from the Resource area to the "Forbidden," "Permitted," or "Required" sections of the playing mat. By their moves, the players shape the eventual Solution that will be reached. To complete his turn, a player must either move one of the Resource cubes as described above, or claim that a Solution can be built with just one more cube from Resources, or claim that a Solution can no longer be achieved because of the earlier moves of other players. The Solution, of course, must be equal to the Goal, and each player must conceive of a Solution, yet continually change that conception as the cubes are moved into the Forbidden, Permitted, or Required sections of the mat. Cubes in the Forbidden section must not be used in building a Solution; cubes in the Permitted section may be used if desired; all of the cubes in the Required section must be used; and one cube (and sometimes all cubes) from Resources may be used.

Whether or not it is his turn, a player may at any time Challenge the player who has just completed a move. The Challenger must specify what kind of "Flub" he thinks the player has made. Each of the following constitutes a Flub: (1) a player makes a move that destroys all possibilities of building a Solution from the remaining Resource cubes; (2) a player makes a move that permits a Solution to be built with just one more cube from Resources when he could have avoided doing so; or (3) a player makes a move when he could have correctly challenged the previous move because it was a Flub.

When there has been a Challenge, all other players must side with either the Challenger or the Mover, and all the players who have sided with the player who has the burden of proving the existence of a Solution must sustain the same burden of proof by independently writing a Solution. The Challenger scores 2 points if he is correct; the Mover scores 2 points if he is correct; and each of the other players scores 1 point if he has correctly sided with the Challenger or 2 points if he has correctly sided with the Mover. Any player who is incorrect scores 0. If there has not been a Challenge but a player claims that a Solution can be built with just one more cube from Resources, then each player who writes a Solution within the specified time limit scores 1 point; if the player who claimed that a Solution could be built cannot in fact build one, then he loses 1 point and all other players score 0. The "specified time limit" is measured by the timer provided with the game. Any player who cannot complete his move, does not decide with whom to side after a Challenge, or does not build a Solution when required, within the specified time period, loses 1 point. Thus, a player wins by correctly Challenging when another player has Flubbed, or by being Challenged incorrectly when he has not Flubbed, or by correctly claiming that a Solution can be built, or by siding correctly with other players who have done any of the above, all within a specified time limit.

The EQUATIONS game, although basically simple, can become complex. For example, a Goal of 9 could be reached by a Solution as simple as "8 + 1" or "(3 × 4) − 3," or it could be reached by "(7 − 4) * (5 − 3)" where "*" denotes exponentiation, or by "(1 ÷ 2) √3," with roots. Further, the

Basic EQUATIONS game can be elevated into Adventurous EQUATIONS by requiring that each player introduce one additional rule to be in force before the cubes are rolled at the beginning of a game. Additional rules might be as simple as a "wild card" that would make one of the numbers on the cubes represent a vector of all possible numbers; or they might be as complex as permitting the ÷ symbol on the cubes to represent either the division operation or the log operation, or permitting both sides of the equation to be interpreted as base-8 expressions rather than base-10. These advanced rules require a more thorough understanding of mathematical concepts, and they encourage creativity in the formulation of complex Solutions to seemingly simple Goals. Professor Allen believes that the EQUATIONS game can be played by either fourth graders or advanced students of mathematics, each at his own level of complexity.

ON-SETS: The Game of Set Theory is patterned after EQUATIONS, though it builds upon the basic ideas of set theory rather than the elementary operations of mathematics. ON-SETS is a competitive game for two or more players and may be played at various levels of difficulty. The level of difficulty is determined by the number of symbol cubes and set cards used and by the level of understanding of set theory among the players. To develop the set-theoretic ideas used in the game, and to introduce the game rules, the instruction manual contains a programmed series of 28 games of increasing complexity. Some of the introductory games are simple enough to be played by kindergarten children, but the advanced examples are challenging for intelligent adults.

The ON-SETS game kit contains a playing mat, similar in general outline to that shown in Exhibit 1; 16 color cards, each with a blue, red, green, or orange dot, or any combination of these dots; 8 color cubes, each imprinted with blue, red, green, and orange dots; 4 red-symbol cubes, each imprinted with the symbols u (union), n (intersection), − (difference), and ' (complement); 3 blue-symbol cubes, each imprinted with ∨ (universal set), ∧ (null set), ⊆ (set-inclusion), and = (set-identity); 3 numeral cubes, each imprinted with 1, 2, 3, 4, and 5; a timer; and a 114-page instruction manual.

Play begins with the building of a Universe, which is accomplished by turning at least 6 of the color cards face up. The first player then shakes and rolls out a set of cubes consisting of the 3 numeral cubes, at least 3 of the red-symbol cubes, and at least 4 of the color cubes. The symbols and colors that appear on the upward faces of the cubes are the Resources. The first player then sets a Goal, which must consist only of numbers, for which a Solution can be built from the remaining Resources. After setting the Goal, all unused numeral cubes are placed in the Forbidden section of the playing mat. As each player proceeds to take a turn, he must either Challenge another player, claim (without Challenging) that a Solution can be built with just one more cube from Resources, or move a Resource cube to the Forbidden, Permitted, or Required sections of the playing mat. The rules for Challenging, Flubbing, and Scoring are all the same as those used in Equations. However, in ON-SETS, the Solution is the name of a set that contains exactly the number of cards from the Universe that is stated in the Goal. For example, consider a Universe consisting of the following cards, with the colored dots as shown:

| B R G | | G | B R | B O | O | R G |

If the Goal in this example were four, then sets with four cards should be selected for the Solution. Some of the Set-Names which would be possible Solutions are: BuR, BuO, GuR, Gu (O $\wedge$ B), Gu (R $\wedge$ B), O', (BuG) — O, BuG', etc. The acceptable Solution at the end of this game will be determined by the movement of the Resources to the Forbidden, Permitted, and Required sections of the playing mat during the game, which, of course, gradually shapes the final Solution.

The more advanced form of ON-SETS utilizes all of the color cubes and all of the symbol cubes, including the blue-symbol cubes. The Solution can then be either the name of a set with the proper number of cards from the Universe, or the combination of both the name of a set and a group of one or more statements/restrictions about the sets, which would utilize the set-inclusion and/or set-identify symbols. Using all of the symbol, color, and numeral cubes as resources, and all of the color cards as the Universe, Professor Allen believes that an advanced game of ON-SETS will test the insights of graduate students into set-theoretic concepts.

TESTING
THE WFF 'N PROOF SERIES
OF EDUCATIONAL GAMES

The primary objective of the WFF 'N PROOF series of instructional games is to change the students' traditional attitudes toward learning by making learning fun. The games have been designed to help develop more favorable attitudes toward mathematics and other rigorous symbol-handling activities. The game rules encourage the players to create and solve problems at the outer limits of their knowledge, thus instilling in each player a feeling of competence; but, because of the very gradually increasing complexity of the games, no player is likely to be overwhelmed by a problem, thus increasing self-confidence. Feelings of technical competence and personal confidence encourage students to try more difficult problems and to pursue further learning, both of which result in more positive attitudes by the student toward himself or herself. It also should be apparent from the descriptions of EQUATIONS and ON-SETS that the games help to teach the subject matter involved— be it mathematics, set theory, logic, critical analysis, science, or language—as well as problem-solving methodologies generally.

The games in the WFF 'N PROOF series have a number of other characteristics, in addition to the seven design requirements listed earlier in the case; together these make the games especially useful for facilitating learning:

1. The game rules promote the teaching of students by students since, in order to win, a player must reveal his solution and thoroughly explain its derivation.

2. The group nature of the games permits a teacher to work with one group, while other members of the class are actively engaged in play and learning.

3. The feedback from the games is fast and unequivocal, for a player who makes a mistake is immediately challenged and corrected, and effective performance is rewarded by winning.

4. The variability of the games permits play at a level adapted to the age and prior instruction of the students.

5. Flexibility is encouraged since there is no single solution, and alternative solutions must be identified and adapted to fit the constraints.

6. Continuous attention is required since each move affects the alternative solution possibilities of each of the players.

7. Creative, rather than repetitive, thinking is essential because of the continuously evolving nature of the games.

8. Enjoyment, rather than routine activity, results from the nonsimulation nature of the games; a simulation game deals with a model of a system and usually can be played only once or twice without repetition, whereas a nonsimulation game deals with the system itself and can normally be played over and over.

The incorporation of these characteristics into the games in the WFF 'N PROOF series has produced instructional methods which several studies have shown to have had significant impacts on student attitudes and achievements.

> Our general conclusion is that combining the nonsimulation game EQUATIONS with team competition significantly increased students' mathematics achievement over that of a traditionally taught class. The effect was observed for skills specific to the game as well as more general arithmetic skills. . . . The classroom teacher noted several key aspects of the experimental classes. First, the game succeeded in "turning on" students who had not been putting forth any effort. Second, the team competition feedback to the students via a newsletter was important to them. On two occasions when the experimenters failed to return the newsletters to the teacher on time, she reported that the classes became upset because they wanted to see how their teams had done. Third, during the periods of game play, the teacher found it much easier to give help to individual students while the rest of the class kept busy with the game. Fourth, students had a reason to help fellow team members to improve their team's performance. Fifth, the game competition gave the students a reason to learn mathematics (to win the game). It is likely that the other classroom instruction benefited from this motivation. Sixth, playing the game was involving and fun. (This excerpt from "Games and Teams: A Winning Combination," by Keith J. Edwards, et al, is reprinted from *Simulation and Games*, Vol. 3, No. 3 (Sept. 1972) pp. 260–1 by permission of the publisher, Sage Publications, Inc.)

Other researchers investigated the effect of playing WFF 'N PROOF on the nonlanguage IQ scores of junior high school students in Burbank, California. Members of the experimental group played WFF 'N PROOF for 45 minutes to an hour each day, 5 days a week, for 6 weeks during the summer. In each 2-hour class the remaining time was spent discussing the rules of the game and the concepts underlying them and taking tests to determine the players' progress in learning. The control group consisted of students enrolled in the regular fall classes, and this group spent its 6-week period on regular classwork. Pretests and post-tests were administered to both groups.

> The overall comparison of mean change scores in the junior high experimental and control groups were found to be highly significant. The mean change in nonlanguage IQ score for the experimental group was +17.3, while the mean change for the control group was +9.2. By a t-test this difference between the two groups could have occurred by chance about twice out of a hundred times ($P = 0.02$). (Allen, Allen, and Miller, Programmed Games and the Learning of Problem-Solving Skills," *The Journal of Educational Research,* September 1966, p. 23.)

In a further study conducted in Bethel Park, Pennsylvania, students in the fourth, fifth, and sixth grades played EQUATIONS in place of their "regular textbook" work for 50 minutes per week for a total of 9 weeks. The results showed that on the average the students almost doubled their usual increase in arithmetic concepts understanding and arithmetic problem-solving skills during the 9-week period.

One of the most successful, and most personally rewarding, programs built upon Professor Allen's games was conducted at the Pelham Middle School in innercity Detroit. A chronic problem at many innercity schools has been student absenteeism, reflecting student indifference toward learning. In an effort to improve the students' attitudes toward the learning environment, Professor Allen and Dr. Dana Main, also a member of the Mental Health Research Institute at The University of Michigan, introduced EQUATIONS and tournament play to an experimental group of seventh and eighth grade mathematics classes. The experimental group devoted two mathematics sessions a week to an EQUATIONS classroom tournament and had "ordinary" math classes and worked problems during the other three sessions per week. The control groups had "ordinary" math classes and worked problems during all five class sessions during the week. The groups participated in the program for two terms of the school year. The impact of the games upon the students' attitudes toward the learning environment was measured in terms of student absentee rates, since it was felt that this measure would reflect student attitudes more accurately than would the more usual self-opinionnaire tests of motivation.

> The absentee study was undertaken during the third year of the program at Pelham School. This study confirmed that absenteeism averaged three times as high in the nongame classes as in the EQUATIONS classes.
>
> We arranged for the students at Pelham Middle School to play against students in suburban schools by telephone; we had six games going at once, with six teams in each classroom. I think that this sort of thing may turn out to be important as an easier first step toward achieving the educational and social benefits of racial integration, rather than the currently more controversial alternative of busing.
>
> Lastly, the educational results are the most important of all the possible benefits; we found that after two years of the EQUATIONS game program the students in the games classes were significantly better than students in nongame classes in both computing with and applying mathematical concepts. (Statement by Professor Allen.)

In addition to the numerous studies that have reported the success of the games, both WFF 'N PROOF and EQUATIONS, in stimulating student achievement and learning, the WFF 'N PROOF series of educational games has received enthusiastic recommendations from the editors of professional journals and from consultants to educational systems.

> Introduction of the first WFF 'N PROOF game . . . was, in our estimation, a significant event in the teaching of logic—as significant in its field as the launching of the first satellite in the space race field. If this seems a bit extravagant, let us point out that challenging, competitive games capable of teaching with unadulterated enjoyment still are a rarity. . . . Therefore, we enthusiastically recommend the new WFF 'N PROOF game. . . . WFF 'N PROOF can be the first exhilarating challenge

> to children of six and, as the games progress, stimulate the intellect of people of any age or capability. (Statement in professional journal.)
>
> . . . Junior high school students will find the games fun, challenging, and stimulating, and will play them during their free time at lunch and after school. . . . (Statement in professional journal.)
>
> . . . We congratulate this "Layman" on his excellent contribution to mathematical education. (Statement in professional journal.)
>
> Layman E. Allen's contribution to modern educational technology is a set of game-like rules the effects of which are quite analogous to the processes determined by the program of a sophisticated teaching machine. These rules not only allocate active participation, immediate reinforcement, and individual pacing but also control the adaptation of learning materials to the increasing competence of the learners during a game without requiring a complex and expensive piece of hardware. . . . The possibilities of combining principles of sophisticated teaching machines with motivations inherent in game situations have been demonstrated here impressively. (Statement in professional journal.)
>
> . . . nothing has excited nor stimulated the students more than WFF 'N PROOF. This is evidenced by the outside time spent by the students in playing the games, their purchasing of their personal sets, students volunteering to take a course during their free time, and the general conversation concerning the game which has resulted. . . . This excitement has brought about easily observable learning of a higher order. (Statement in letter from North Carolina teacher.)
>
> I was fortunate enough to borrow games for one day to introduce EQUATIONS to my seventh graders on Friday. After one period of introduction and a second period of actually playing the game, their reaction was sheer enthusiasm. Early Monday morning two of my boys rushed in to inform me that they had spent Saturday at the Franklin Institute in Philadelphia and had seen EQUATIONS in the gift store there. They pooled their allowance money and bought a game together. This particular game is getting hard usage as these boys play at home and at school. Every available activity period they invite their friends into my room to "shake the math cubes."

(Statement in unsolicited letter from Pennsylvania teacher.)

Since organizing the EQUATIONS Math Club at our school, the game of EQUATIONS has continued to be a most popular and enjoyable way of stimulating mathematics beyond the confines of the classroom . . . there is a tremendous personal desire to be able to compete at a higher level. In this alone one can recognize a true educational value. . . . Having taught mathematics for several years, it is gratifying to see children enjoy the application of the skills they have learned without being compelled to under a classroom situation. (Statement in unsolicited letter from Connecticut teacher.)

PRODUCTION OF
THE WFF 'N PROOF SERIES
OF EDUCATIONAL GAMES

It is impossible to quote from more than a very small fraction of the enthusiastic editorials in the educational media and the whole-hearted letters from educational personnel; the WFF 'N PROOF series of instructional games were very well received during the period of experimentation and introduction, from 1962 to 1964. Professor Allen was convinced that the games should be distributed commercially, not to maximize his personal profit or income, but to achieve the widest possible usage and educational benefits. He contacted a large number of publishing firms, but quickly found that they were not interested in producing and distributing this type of educational material.

The book publishers didn't want our games because they were not books; it was just that simple. (Statement of Professor Allen.)

After he became discouraged with his attempts to convince a publishing firm to produce and distribute WFF 'N PROOF or EQUATIONS as a book, Professor Allen started contacting game manufacturing companies. He was amazed by the number of individual inventors who were trying to have their games adopted, and he was disheartened by the rapid rejections that he received.

The game manufacturers didn't want our games because they did not think they would sell well enough. I understand that Parker Brothers receives new game proposals from 7,000 to 8,000 inventors each year, and somebody has told me that they will not even consider one of those proposals unless they can see sales of at least 100,000 units the first year. (Statement of Professor Allen.)

After receiving rejections from book publishers and game manufacturers, Professor Allen decided that it would be necessary to produce and market himself the games that he and his colleagues had designed. He started by conducting an extensive search for manufacturers who could supply the components that he needed, and he found this search to be well worth the effort since the quotations he received to produce the parts for the games varied by a factor of 10 to 1. A company in West Germany was selected to make the playing cubes and timers, and one in New Haven, Connecticut was chosen to make the playing mats. These two companies still supply these parts. The instruction manuals have been printed both in the United States and the Far East, but presently are prepared by a local firm in Ann Arbor, while the plastic game boxes have been molded by different companies throughout the United States.

The rapid initial growth in sales of the games during 1965 and 1966, together with the extremely favorable publicity that they received during the earlier period of experimentation and testing, led Professor Allen to estimate a much higher level of annual sales than is now realized. Consequently, the facility that was acquired has the capacity to handle 10 to 15 times the number of games than are now assembled and stored there. Presently, the games are produced in lots of 5,000 to 10,000 and are stocked with a minimum 6-month inventory for each of the games in the series. The assembly point and warehouse are located in Professor Allen's hometown of Turtle Creek, Pennsylvania. Seven persons are employed there, including Professor Allen's father, who is the manager. The inventory, purchasing, assembly, order-filling, and mailing (of both advertising materials and games) responsibilities are centered in Turtle Creek. The bookkeeping, order-receiving, sales liaison, advertising, and promotion functions are the responsibilities of the Ann Arbor office. Three housewives work part-time here in a very informal atmosphere.

Out-the-door purchasing, assembly, and shipment costs have usually totalled about 30% to 35% of the retail price, but have recently, in 1975, risen because of inflation, necessitating an anticipated price increase. WFF 'N PROOF Learning Games Associates is an especially small producer of games, with no economies of scale or leverage in purchasing, so that their cost-of-goods-sold expense as a percentage of the retail price is considerably higher than that of the typical game manufacturer. The production and assembly costs of the larger game companies have traditionally averaged 25% of the retail cost, but recently the national marketers in this industry, in order to allow greater expenditures for advertising and promotion, have deliberately reduced the production and assembly costs to only 15% or 20% of the retail price.

The overhead and administrative expenses for WFF 'N PROOF Learning Games Associates currently run about $45,000 per year, while the advertising and promotional costs have ranged from $20,000 to $60,000. Professor Allen considered the advertising and promotional costs to be fully variable, and he usually set these expenditures at the highest level that he believed the contribution from anticipated sales could support.

MARKETING THE WFF 'N PROOF SERIES OF EDUCATIONAL GAMES

The retail prices of the WFF 'N PROOF games have increased gradually over the past 10 years as production and shipment costs have risen because of inflation. The price history of the instructional games is shown in Exhibit 2.

WFF 'N PROOF Learning Games Associates offers standard discounts off the customer selling price to retail outlets, schools, and sales representatives; these discounts are standard throughout the industry and are similar to those offered by other game manufacturers or textbook publishers on their products (see Exhibit 3).

Exhibit 4 indicates the effects of the discount and commission structure on the contribution margin of a single game when a dozen or more are sold to a retail outlet through a sales representative. The 1974 cost, commission, and sales price figures have been used.

The net dollar sales of WFF 'N PROOF Learning Games Associates, after applicable discounts to retailers and schools and after

---

EXHIBIT 2 Retail prices of the WFF 'N PROOF series of educational games, 1962 to 1974. (Source: company records.)

	1962	1966	1970	1974
WFF 'N PROOF	$6.50	$6.50	8.75	$9.75
EQUATIONS	—	3.50	5.50	6.50
ON-SETS	—	4.50	5.50	6.50
PROPAGANDA	—	5.50	6.50	7.50
REAL NUMBERS	—	1.75	2.25	2.25
WFF	—	1.50	1.50	2.25
CONFIGURATIONS	—	—	5.50	6.50
TAC-TICKLE	—	—	1.25	1.25
TRI-NIM	—	—	4.50	5.50
QUERIES 'N THEORIES	—	—	8.75	9.75
QWIK-SANE	—	—	1.75	2.25
ON-WORDS	—	—	—	6.50

EXHIBIT 3 Retail price discounts of the WFF 'N PROOF series of educational games, 1974. (Source: company records.)

Retail book, toy, game, or gift store	40% when the order is less than 12 50% when the order is more than 12
School or educational institution	Net when the order is less than 12 10% when the order is more than 12
Sales representative or wholesaler	10% commission on net sales (retail price less applicable store or school discounts)

EXHIBIT 4 Retail prices, retail discounts, sales commissions, manufacturing costs, and total contributions of sample games produced and sold by WFF 'N PROOF Learning Games Associates, 1974. (Source: company records.)

Game	Retail price	Retail at 50%	Representative's Commission at 10% net	Manufacturing cost	Contribution
WFF 'N PROOF	$9.75	$4.87	$0.49	$3.90	$0.46
EQUATIONS	6.50	3.25	0.33	2.60	0.32
TAC-TICKLE	1.25	0.62	0.06	0.50	0.07

EXHIBIT 5 Net sales, less discounts and commissions, of WFF 'N PROOF Learning Games Associates, 1962 to 1974. (Source: company records.)

	1962	1966	1970	1974
Net sales in dollars	$10,000	$235,000	$270,000	$225,000

net commissions to the sales representatives, are shown in Exhibit 5.

The sales of the company have traditionally been derived 75% from retail outlets, 15% from schools, and 10% from individual mail orders. Records are not available to determine the division of sales between games, but Professor Allen believes that WFF 'N PROOF has always been the best seller and still accounts for nearly half of the dollar sales volume. EQUATIONS normally takes the second place in sales volume each year.

The games are actually more widely played than the sales figures might indicate. Professor Allen frequently receives inquiries, especially from teachers, requesting his permission as author to allow them to make their own WFF 'N PROOF series games by electrostatically copying the instruction manuals and by reproducing the playing cubes and mats. He readily approves such requests since he wants to encourage widespread use of the concepts of the games to foster better attitudes toward learning and since he believes that wider use of the games will eventually result in increased retail sales.

The major marketing problem has always centered on the distribution of the WFF 'N PROOF series of instructional games. The potential channels that are open for distribution of books or games are shown in Exhibit 6.

Wholesalers, who are the first link in many distribution networks, and who normally stock the items they purchase from manufacturers and then resell to retailers and large institutional users, are not an important factor in book and game distribution. There are very few wholesalers who operate in this area, and the ones who do usually sell only repetitive supply items, such as paper, pencils, notebooks, typewriter ribbons, etc. Most contacts between game manufacturers or textbook publishers and retail stores are either direct, through company salesmen, or semidirect, through manufacturer's representatives.

Manufacturer's representatives in the game and textbook market can be either single individuals selling to retail outlets within a fairly limited geographic area, such as southeastern Michigan and northwestern Ohio, or reasonably large firms, with a number of employees and geographically dispersed offices, selling in a large section of the country, such as the Northeast or the South Central states. Both individuals and firms generally represent 20 to 100 manufacturers and publishers, and the common complaint against both is that they carry so many items that they find it impossible to devote adequate time to any single product line or any new product. Professor Allen has never been able to persuade the larger firms to distribute the WFF 'N PROOF series of educational games since demand had never been demonstrated to be very large, and the

larger representatives stated that they were not going to act as missionaries for any manufacturer or publisher. Only the smaller representatives have been willing to take on the WFF 'N PROOF products.

Currently only four representatives carry the WFF 'N PROOF series of games, and their sales account for less than 20% of the total company sales; the balance of the company's orders come by mail, from retail stores, schools, and individual customers, in response to direct-mail ads and magazine promotions. Even the best representative (in New York City, covering New England and the Middle Atlantic states) accounts for less than $15,000 annually in sales of the games.

Over the years, about 30 different manufacturer's representatives, all of the smaller size, have carried the WFF 'N PROOF games, but none has been successful, and most have now dropped the line completely. Many of the earlier representatives complained about the competitive overlap that came from WFF 'N PROOF Learning Games Associates' accepting direct-mail orders from retail stores within their areas. To avoid this resentment, Professor Allen for a few years agreed to pay the representatives their usual 10% net commission on all sales to commercial outlets within their territories, no matter how the orders were received by the company. This practice proved to be unsatisfactory, however, and had to be discontinued since many of the representatives performed no service whatever and just collected the commissions on direct sales.

Professor Allen has thought that one of

EXHIBIT 6   Potential distribution channels for retail sale of games and books.

		Book stores
	Wholesalers	Toy or hobby stores
Game manufacturer		Gift stores
or	Manufacturer's representatives	Department stores
Textbook publisher		Discount stores
	Company salesmen	Chain stores
		Mail-order firms

the reasons for the disappointing sales through manufacturer's representatives was the fact that WFF 'N PROOF Learning Games Associates never had a sales manager to work directly with them, to improve their sales methods, and to encourage their sales activities. Twice he has tried to remedy this situation by employing management consultants from New York and Chicago as the sales manager for these representatives. Each time a consultant was interviewed, selected, and given $10,000 to start, and each time the plan was to make an initial big push on the WFF 'N PROOF games for the Christmas season. Both efforts turned out to be complete failures, with inadequate sales to recoup the $10,000 investment, and both efforts were terminated after 6 months.

WFF 'N PROOF Learning Games Associates once hired a direct company salesman; he was located in California and was paid a very moderate salary plus commissions. This field employee, who was the younger brother of one of the workers in the Ann Arbor office, was a shoe salesman with a chemistry degree and was employed during 1968–1969. Although he followed a non-aggressive approach to selling, he was soon sending in annual orders much greater than any of the sales representatives, but he quit his job because he could not make enough money to cover his expenses and provide an acceptable standard of living.

The WFF 'N PROOF games currently are largely sold by independent retail stores who mail their orders directly to the Ann Arbor office, either in response to direct-mail ads or when their existing stock of the educational games is depleted. Company records have never been analyzed to determine the type of geographic location of the retail stores that sell the majority of the games.

> The company records were never analyzed, primarily because they are not well-organized. But, I don't think that this analysis, even if it were possible, would tell us anything. I don't think that there is any pattern to the retail distribution. The stores that handle the games seem to do so because the owner likes them or because one of the schools in the area used

them so that there is a generated demand. Probably the best example of the unusual nature of the retail distribution is a small store that is located on the ground floor of a large apartment complex here in Ann Arbor. The store sells newspapers, magazines, food staples, beer, wine, ice cream, and WFF 'N PROOFs.

> The owner plays both WFF 'N PROOF and ON-SETS, and since he likes the games, he sells them in his store. He has a wire rack right next to the cash register, and he sells about 75 to 100 games each year. People in that apartment house, who are mostly young professionals and some graduate students, play the games as if they were Monopoly or chess, but the same people, in an equivalent apartment complex about a mile away, don't play because the games aren't available. If you could talk owners of similar apartment house stores into selling and promoting the games, you could sell millions of dollars worth each year, but I don't know how you can get that distribution. (Statement of M.B.A. employed part-time to supervise distribution for WFF 'N PROOF Learning Games Associates in 1974.)

WFF 'N PROOF Learning Games Associates has, of course, made continual efforts, but it has never been successful in having the games adopted by national chain stores such as Sears Roebuck or discount chain stores such as K-Mart.

> Small game manufacturers and book publishers have a large disadvantage since they don't know the buyers for the big retail chains and discount stores and since they don't even know how to reach these buyers. You might think that it would be easy. You might think that all you would have to do is to pick up a telephone, call the national headquarters, and ask to talk to the buyer in charge of games. But you will be shunted back and forth, since each chain assigns responsibilities for educational games differently, between toy buyers, book buyers, gift buyers, etc. In one chain, I found the right person in "home improvements." Finally, you will get the right office, and you will talk to a secretary, who says that she will take your message and ask the buyer to call you back. You never hear from the buyer.
>
> The buyer at a national chain is an important executive; he or she—and this is an area

111355

in which you will find a good many women—is the head of a staff organization that includes product testing, product costing, and market research. Approval by the buyer will put your product on either an "approved to buy" listing, which means that the assistant buyers in all the districts can recommend it to the store buyers, or on a "required to buy" listing which means that each store must take a specified quantity, depending on demographic statistics in its market area. The volume you can get is immense, so everybody wants to see the buyer to get their products into this product evaluation, costing—they'll tell you what price they will pay for your product if you get it approved—and market research sequence. The result is that it is very hard to contact the buyers, and it is particularly hard if you don't know them.

We have the headquarter offices of two large chains here in Michigan: K-Mart in Southfield and Meijers (a regional discount firm) in Grand Rapids. I've been to both. At Meijers I waited all day to see the buyer, but he told me, "Look, we tried 'em; they didn't sell; we don't want 'em. Thanks for coming to see us." At K-Mart I waited a couple of days, because I kept getting the wrong person recommended to me. Finally, I got to the right office, but the buyer wouldn't see me. She sent out her assistant, who told me that we had to get some sex appeal into the games. If you think about it, her suggestion is ludicrous.

The buyers at large chains are professionals; they are well paid not to make mistakes. This is a competitive industry; if the buyers make too many mistakes, they lose their jobs in a hurry to one of their assistants. The result is that they will not take a chance. They evaluate each new product on a simple basis: "will it sell?" If their intuitive judgment is that it won't sell, you can't get your product into the evaluation process. This may be shortsighted, but it is the way the large retail chains operate. (Statement by M.B.A. employed part-time to supervise distribution for WFF 'N PROOF Learning Games Associates in 1974.)

The potential distribution channels for institutional sale of games and books to schools and other educational agencies are shown in Exhibit 7. Again, the wholesalers, who stock the materials they provide, generally concentrate upon repetitive supply items such as paper, pencils, and notebooks; while the sales representatives, both companies and individuals, offer textbooks and other instructional materials. Some of the educational sales firms are large and have national coverage; the problem, again, is that they represent so many publishers and manufacturers that any one product line receives very little emphasis.

The sales people for the larger manufacturers' representative firms selling to school systems pick their most popular product or products to push and leave the balance unmentioned in their sales calls. The catalogs those people carry are in the shape of a briefcase, 12 in. to 15 in. thick, and filled with descriptive folders, price lists, and shipping information. The sales people don't even look at many of their folders. The result is that they won't push a product on their sales calls; they just provide information if the customer asks, and they accept orders. You can't get a new product started that way. (Statement of M.B.A. employed part-time to supervise distribution for WFF 'N PROOF Learning Games Associates in 1974.)

WFF 'N PROOF Learning Games Associates has also tried individual manufacturer's representatives, who tend to carry a much smaller product line than the larger firms, and has experimented with direct sales to school systems, obtained through mail advertising and trade magazine promotion, but neither approach has been successful. Institu-

---

EXHIBIT 7   Potential distribution channels for institutional sales of games and books.

| Game manufacturer or Textbook publisher | Wholesalers Manufacturer's representatives Company salesmen | School systems or Educational agencies |

tional sales have never risen above 15% of the company's revenues, despite the very large apparent potential.

School sales have always come very hard, and even in Ann Arbor where the games are quite popular, the local schools purchased less than $125 worth of the WFF 'N PROOF products last year. A big problem is the amount of time it takes to sell to institutions. A salesman can contact about 12 commercial outlets per day, but only 1 or 2 schools; the reason is that the arrangements for selling to schools vary considerably among, and even within, school districts. School administrations are usually highly decentralized and, depending on the individual system involved, you may have to make the sales presentation and secure the order approval from individual teachers, department chairpersons, vice principals, school principals, curriculum coordinators, district administrators, and purchasing agents. Then, problems concerning funding and other administrative-type matters can cause delays. All in all, it is difficult to sell to school systems. (Statement of M.B.A. employed part-time to supervise distribution for WFF 'N PROOF Learning Games Associates in 1974.)

Approximately 15% of the annual revenues of WFF 'N PROOF Learning Games Associates is derived from sales to school systems throughout the country. Schools currently order the WFF 'N PROOF games by responding to direct-mail advertisements or by calling their local bookstores, which usually also extend a 10% discount to educational institutions on orders of 12 or more books or games.

Over the past 10 years the WFF 'N PROOF series of educational games has been advertised in more than 200 magazines and newspapers, including *Scientific American, Saturday Review, The New Republic, Atlantic Monthly, Harpers, Data Processing Digest, The Arithmetic Teacher,* and *The Mathematics Teacher.* In addition to describing and promoting the games, the advertisements included information on how to order directly from WFF 'N PROOF Learning Games Associates. Most advertisements today are concentrated in *Scientific American* (in

four or five issues per year), toy and hobby trade journals, and in educational magazines for the mathematics teachers in elementary, junior high, and senior high schools. In 1974 over half of the advertising and promotional expenditures were for magazine and journal advertising.

The balance of the advertising and promotional expenditures has normally been for direct mailings to previous customers, teachers, attendees of toy and hobby fairs, and numerous retail outlets. Although it would seem that teachers would be very interested in the educational and motivational values of the games, Professor Allen doubts that their orders in response to the mailings even cover the cost of the postage.

When sales were more profitable, the WFF 'N PROOF games were also exhibited at many teachers' conventions and toy and hobby fairs. Although the WFF 'N PROOF booth was often the most popular location at these affairs, very few sales were made. Consequently, with an estimated cost of $1,500 to $2,500 per convention, Professor Allen feels that WFF 'N PROOF Learning Games Associates can no longer afford to send a representative to these functions.

Perhaps the greatest promotion that the WFF 'N PROOF series of educational games will ever receive occurred on one Thanksgiving Eve. Lorne Greene, the star of the TV series *Bonanza,* and the co-author of the PROPAGANDA game, was a guest on Johnny Carson's *Tonight Show.* He brought with him some of the games, and for 10 minutes he and Johnny discussed PROPAGANDA, WFF 'N PROOF, and EQUATIONS. No one could ask for any better 10-minute exposure, but Professor Allen estimates that no more than 10 game sales can be traced to that extraordinary publicity; he feels that WFF 'N PROOF Learning Games Associates simply does not have an adequate distribution network to take advantage of such promotions.

Popularity of the games, although not game sales, has benefited from the WFF 'N PROOF tournaments that have started recently. Schools have organized intraschool and interschool competition and have conducted Saturday morning tournaments which encourage the general public to attend. The enthusiasm generated at the tournaments has prompted some schools to print newsletters to summarize records of individual and team performances and to provide puzzles and problems that help to teach the strategies that are often used in the game.

Recently Professor Allen has introduced some of the WFF 'N PROOF games on a local cable television channel. The TV channel conducts a weekly "TV Thinkers' Tournament" and invites the viewers to participate. Players are matched up according to their demonstrated skills; then they play a game, which can be accomplished over the telephone, during the week. The players record the results on a postage-paid card supplied by a local bank and mail it to the Tournament in care of the bank that serves as the collection point. The results are noted, and the standings are then tabulated and displayed on the TV screen the following week. During the initial debugging phase the Tournament had about 100 players, and Professor Allen is optimistic about the future of this program; he hopes to involve other institutions such as the telephone company, radio stations, and local newspapers in helping to sponsor community tournaments.

On a national level, schools in Alabama, California, Florida, Louisiana, Maine, Michigan, Mississippi, North Carolina, Pennsylvania, Tennessee, West Virginia, Wisconsin, and other states are playing WFF 'N PROOF games. These states have all been represented by students from their elementary, junior high, and senior high schools at the National Academic Olympic Games. Every year for the past 10 years these Olympics have provided the occasion for intellectual competition through the play of instructional games that have been designed by university professors and other subject-matter specialists. Four of the eight games played at the Olympics are from the WFF 'N PROOF series: WFF 'N PROOF, EQUATIONS, ON-SETS, and PROPAGANDA. The National Academic Olympics was designed to encourage students' learning by recognizing and reward-

ing academic achievement in a way that had previously been reserved for athletic accomplishments.

FINANCING
THE WFF 'N PROOF SERIES
OF EDUCATIONAL GAMES

Professor Allen was reluctant to disclose the financial position of WFF 'N PROOF Learning Games Associates since a profit has been realized in only 4 of the 14 years of operations, so that it has been necessary for Professor Allen to subsidize the operations with his personal income. He did, however, explain that losses have never been overwhelming because whenever a loss was foreseen, expenditures on direct-mail advertising, especially the advertising sent to schools, were cut back. Profits from commercial sales to retail outlets and individuals have traditionally supported, or nearly supported, the school sales effort. Losses have never been incurred in the commercial sales side of the business, but overall losses have continued as a result of the unprofitable efforts to reach the school market. Professor Allen felt, however, that it would be possible to make a small additional investment, perhaps on the order of $10,000, to support a new marketing plan.

> Up until now, the losses have been controllable, and the company has not been as much of a cash drain as one might expect. I should think that a new marketing proposal could be financed, perhaps up to $10,000, but I also think that this marketing plan should be self-supporting and should generate the cash flow out of increased sales that will pay for the proposed selling and advertising expenses. This is central to the problem of smaller businesses; they never have enough money to market their products the way the larger firms do, and they have to "boot strap" their way to success. (Statement of Professor Allen.)

PRESENT POSITION OF
THE WFF 'N PROOF SERIES
OF EDUCATIONAL GAMES

Professor Allen has been concerned by the declining sales and rising production costs of the WFF 'N PROOF games. Nevertheless, he wishes to continue promotional efforts. He has witnessed the motivational and educational benefits derived when the traditional teaching methods in the classroom are supplemented by instructional games, and he has set a specific objective for WFF 'N PROOF Learning Games Associates to "encourage others to do it"; i.e., he wants to prompt companies with much greater resources to invent, produce, and market games that will improve classroom learning and stimulate student interactions. He feels that he can accomplish this by increasing the sales of the WFF 'N PROOF series of games to well over 250,000 units annually, thus demonstrating to the large textbook publishers and game manufacturing companies that the educational game business can be profitable as well as beneficial. He feels strongly that this can be done.

> People in the book industry and the game industry think that we're crazy. I was hired to help Professor Allen with the distribution of the WFF 'N PROOF series last year, and the people I've met in book publishing and game manufacturing keep telling me that there is no market for educational games, but I think that they're wrong, and I'll give you just three examples of why I think that they're wrong:
> 1. If we can get one of our games started in a classroom, I will guarantee you that 15% to 20% of the children in the class will borrow the game sets so that they can play at home after school. If they can't borrow the games, they'll make the pieces necessary to play. The games enable children to learn, and many children like to learn.
> 2. If we can get one of our games started in a young adult group, such as a social club or apartment house, I will guarantee you that 15% to 20% of the members will play. These games force people to think, and many young adults like to think, and they like to compete on an intellectual rather than on an athletic basis.
> 3. There have been a great many research studies that have demonstrated the educational benefits of the WFF 'N PROOF games, but I think they can all be summed up in one example. I was talking to a student here at the Business School who heard that I was doing some work for Professor Allen; he told me that he took an elective course in logic in the Philosophy Department, and got an A+ since many of the logic concepts were familiar to him from playing WFF 'N PROOF with his father years ago. These games enable parents to help their children, and many parents like to do this.
> Fifteen percent of the children, 15% of the young adults, and 15% of the parents in this country add up to about 30,000,000 people. There is a large market out there. The problem is that we don't know how to promote and distribute the WFF 'N PROOF games so that we can reach that market. (Statement of M.B.A. employed part-time to supervise distribution for WFF 'N PROOF Learning Games Associates in 1974.)

ASSIGNMENT

Develop a marketing plan for the WFF 'N PROOF series of educational games, with specific recommendations for pricing, distribution, and promotion, all within the financial limitations described by Professor Allen.

Treasure Systems, Inc.

Treasure Systems, Inc. was founded in 1968 as the Saginaw Scientific Corporation, in Saginaw, Michigan, to provide electronic circuit design and development capability, on a subcontract basis, for large manufacturing firms in the midwestern area. This subcontracting service was not successful, partially because of the economic recession which, though mild, decreased the amount of subcontract work available generally, but more particularly because of the termination of the government-sponsored research in aerospace and military technology which, though spread out over a number of years, decreased the amount of experimental design and development work available specifically for companies similar to Saginaw Scientific. The company had been formed with the concept of doing short-run, high-precision fabrication, working out the problems of making and assembling the components of advanced electronic and electromechanical instruments. Companies formed to provide similar subcontracting services in the area of electronic instrumentation from 1958 to 1967 were generally successful, because of the large-scale effort in aerospace; companies formed after 1967 were often not successful, because of the changes in the economy. It was a matter of timing, and Saginaw Scientific was just a year or two too late.

Lawrence Van Eulen, the owner of the company and a man whom many considered a genius in electronic design ("if he is not a genius, then he is certainly exceedingly proficient") recognized the problem of timing and, as contracts became more and more difficult to obtain, and then more and more difficult to complete at a profit, he began looking for proprietary products that the company could build and sell itself:

> When electronic R&D began to slow down, the big firms, like Burroughs, Honeywell, Sycor, and Reliance, gave their jobs to subcontractors they had worked with in the past. That's only natural, and you can't blame the purchasing agents; they wanted to give the work to people they knew, with competences they knew. The only jobs we got were the offbeat ones, where they wanted to try something new but they did not think that it would work, and they thought that they might as well let some poor soul out in the hills lose a little sleep and a little money trying to make it work.
>
> I knew that we needed our own products to put a floor under our sales and soak up some of our overhead; but, it is easier to say that—and our banker in Midland said it continually—than it is to think of the products. That is not quite true; it is easy to think of new products that you can make, but it is hard to think of new products that you can make and sell at a profit. We did not do too well. (Statement of Mr. Van Eulen.)

The company made a slot-car tester for hobby shops, a spinner magnetometer for paleomagnetic analysis, an interuterine device validation unit for medical diagnosis, a nictitated (sequential blinking) lamp for paramedical motor response evaluation, a precision coil winder for manufacturing speciality transformers, a portable optical scanner with data accumulation and cross-tabulation features for onsite investigation of market research and political survey results, and a submersible gradient-field magnetometer for locating magnetic anomalies underwater. None of these products was successful; two were eclipsed in the market when they were released first by a competitor, one never worked consistently, one was too expensive to manufacture, and two were too difficult to sell.

In 1969 and 1970 every electronic instrument company in the country was trying to develop proprietary products, thinking that if they had them, the existing market channels would handle them, and everyone would make money. This just was not true. We made two instruments for the medical electronics market, and in each case I found that somebody else had made one just a few months before and the distributors were already handling the competitive unit. We made two magnetometers, nice, precise instruments, and we sold a few, but the market was not big enough for the distributors to push them. Then, we made a coil winder for speciality transformers; this may sound simple, but it was inordinately complex, and we never got it to work consistently, though it was better than anything else on the market. We tried all of the glamour fields—medical electronics, oceanographic research, geological surveys, electronic data processing—but we didn't do much. We spent a lot of money, but we didn't come up with a single profitable product. Warn your class that the area of product development is the one that makes or breaks most small companies; you have to invest your limited funds in R&D before you know what the manufacturing cost, the sales price, the market size, or the product performance will be. I enjoy the technological challenge of R&D work, but I don't like the uncertainties of manufacturing and marketing that go with it. I don't know how other companies handle this, but we did not do it very well. (Statement of Mr. Van Eulen.)

The company lost money in 1969 and 1970. In early 1971, however, the submersible magnetometer, which had been built for professional oceanographic research, was adopted by amateur divers in Florida and the Caribbean Islands for treasure hunting. The instrument had been designed for underwater exploration, to locate large magnetic objects, such as ore bodies, shipwrecks, buoy anchors, etc., while being towed behind a oceanographic survey ship; the unit was small enough and precise enough, however,

so that it could be held by a skin diver to locate the small iron objects—spikes, blocks, strapping, and cannon—that were part of the wreck of a wooden ship. The company sold over 80 of the submersible magnetometers in 1971, which brought the profit and loss statement to a break-even point for the year, and Mr. Van Eulen decided to start a crash program to design other instruments for electronic treasure detection:

It's fairly simple to design instruments for treasure detection since you're using an established technology. The magnetometer is not the right instrument, except for marine work, since a magnetometer operates only on the distortion of a magnetic field caused by the presence of ferrous material within that field; that is, a magnetometer can find only iron or steel. Fortunately, there was a good deal of iron in earlier ships, and fortunately the iron is still there; iron rust, salt water, and sand form an extremely hard calcified mixture that coats iron objects and preserves them in a crust 2 in. to 6 in. thick. You can crack this crust off a cannonball, for example, and the shot will roll out in a perfect state of preservation, like a nut from its shell. The iron is there, generally sunk into the sand or mud on the sea bottom, and it is usually well-preserved, so that you can use the magnetometer to find wrecks offshore. But, for most treasure hunting, you want a beat frequency oscillator.

A beat frequency oscillator generates microwaves at a given frequency, and material within the range of the generator reflects those microwaves. Each material has a characteristic resonance, which is nonlinear, in reflecting the microwaves. So, you can filter out most of the frequency range and tune in on the resonance of gold and silver. There are some problems involved; one is the fact that since the frequency associated with any material is nonlinear, that you get a spectrum of response, and since you can't filter it all out, you always have a background level of noise that can override a weak signal from a small find. Also, since you have the problem that the aluminum alloy used in beer-can lids and the pull-top tabs and in tinfoil gum wrappers happens to have a frequency range close to that of the more valuable materials, you can get erroneous signals. Unfortunately, the most common debris of our civilization seems to be pull-top tabs from beer cans and tinfoil wrappers from chewing gum; but, overall, the beat frequency oscillator works reasonably well.

You can vary the power of the generator, the sensitivity of the receiver, the sophistication of the filter, and the appearance and convenience of the controls, but that is about all that you can do in design. And, of course, there are some pretty well established cost trade-offs associated with each change in design, since the generator, the receiver, the filter, and the controls are off-the-shelf items, available from numerous manufacturers at consistent Original Equipment Manufacturer (O.E.M.) prices. As a result, you can build models of the basic unit to sell in different price ranges, and you can compare the cost of your model to the cost of your competitor's model pretty accurately. But one thing you can't do is convince a non-engineer of any difference in quality. Quality and cost are an exponential function, but you can't talk about cost in your ads, and you can't describe quality in nontechnical terms. It may seem obvious to me that the filter we use in our Starline series is much better, and nearly twice as expensive, as the one used by Garrett (one of the dominant competitors in the industry), but I couldn't convince you of the difference. It's a lot like selling hi-fi equipment; some people know the technical specifications and buy on that basis, but most people just want something that works at a price that they think is reasonable. We have the best units available, by far, in our price range, but it hasn't done us much good.

Last year I worked on the idea of comparing the different makes and models of oscillators on the basis of locating objects of a given size, say half-dollars, buried in the ground at various depths. The best machine would be the one that could find the deepest coin. The problem I encountered is that detecting ability varies with the soil conditions (sand, loam, clay, or rocks) and with soil moisture content (dry, moist, damp, or wet) so that it is hard to set up standards; and then it is hard to define "finding" the coin. You can get an indication, so slight that you would never notice it in actual use, but still an indication, from the cheapest machine and the deepest coin. Probably all manufacturers of treasure hunting equipment have worked on this concept of objective comparisons, and evidently

all of them have decided that it can't be done because their ads are filled with subjective assertions, such as "30% greater depth penetration," or "50% larger sweep area," or "greatly improved handling ease," or "more convenient controls." If you have to talk about where you put the on–off switch, it means that you don't have much else to talk about in comparing machines. We couldn't prove that our detectors were any better than the others, either, so we just designed a wide range of models and hoped that people would discover the quality for themselves. (Statement of Mr. Van Eulen.)

The company designed seven models of beat frequency oscillators, in two distinct series, and redesigned the magnetometers in a single series of four instruments for use in treasure hunting. The professional series of oscillators was intended for the serious treasure hunter, who wanted a high-quality instrument and was willing to pay to purchase it; Mr. Van Eulen felt that the quality in this series was higher than that of any competitive line. The economy series was intended for the amateur, or occasional, treasure hunter; Mr. Van Eulen termed these instruments "toys that work."

Mr. Van Eulen felt that the domestic market for these treasure hunting instruments could be divided into three major geographical areas, with a number of different kinds of treasure hunters in each area, and with each treasure hunter having different requirements for equipment. The areas, in their order of potential importance to the company, were Florida and the Caribbean Islands, where gold and silver coins and jewelry could be found as a legacy from the wrecks of the Spanish Plate Fleets during the sixteenth, seventeenth, and eighteenth centuries; the western states of Arizona, California, Colorado, Nevada, New Mexico, and Utah, where gold and silver nuggets and ore bodies could be found as a remnant of the mining that had taken place during the nineteenth century, and the rest of the country, where finds were generally either lost artifacts or buried coinage, not gold and silver. Mr. Van Eulen also felt that the amount of treasure available for both the

EXHIBIT 1 Product line of Treasure Systems, Inc., with 11 instruments in 3 series. (Source: company records.)

Professional Series:

Starline I	12-in. search head, for locating objectives up to 20 in. in the ground. Land use only.	$249.00
Starline II	12-in. search head for general sweeping and 5-in. search head for precision location. Land use only.	279.00
Starline III	12-in. search head and 5-in. search head. Designed for marine use; submersible to 300 ft.	495.00

Economy Series:

Money Mouse	4-in. search head, for locating objects up to 3 in. in the ground. Land use only.	$ 29.00
Wildcat	6-in. search head, for locating objects up to 5 in. in the ground. Land use only, but waterproof extension permits use in shallow stream, lakes, beaches, etc.	37.50
Coin Clam	6-in. search head. Designed for marine use, but submersible only to 50 ft.	49.50
Surf-N-Turf	6-in. search head. Designed for either land or marine use; submersible to 100 ft.	79.50

Magnetometer Series:

Discoverer I	For locating magnetic (iron or steel) objects only. Hand-held unit for land use.	$795.00
Discoverer II	For locating magnetic (iron or steel) objects only. Hand-held unit for marine use; submersible to 200 ft.	$895.00
Discoverer III	For locating magnetic (iron or steel) objects only. Boat-mounted unit, for trolling at reduced speed.	$695.00
Discoverer IV	For locating magnetic (iron or steel) objects only. Boat-mounted unit, for trolling at normal speed.	$1,495.00

professional and amateur treasure hunters was greater than might be expected, particularly in Florida and the Far West:

Florida is the center of treasure hunting in the United States for the simple reason that there is a lot of treasure there. From the discovery of the New World in 1492 until the series of successful revolts of the Spanish colonies in the late 1800s, the Spanish government systematically looted gold, silver, platinum, pearls, and emeralds from Central and South America. This material, in the form of coinage, jewelry, and plate, was gathered together in Havana, the center for the administration of the New World, and was shipped back to Castile once each year by the Plate Fleet, which crossed the Florida Straits, between Cuba and the Keys, and then hugged the Eastern coast of Florida up to the vicinity of St. Augustine, where they turned and rode the prevailing westerly winds home. Each year from 10 to 20 ships sailed from Havana to Cadiz, and each year one or two were driven ashore by storms or sunk on the uncharted reefs off Florida.

The amount of treasure off Florida is uncertain, but it has to be immense. The Spanish gathered between $10,000,000 and $20,000,000 each year from Royal mints that had been established by 1540 at Mexico City, Panama City, Sante Fe de Bogota, Lima, and Concepcion. Each mint was responsible for gathering treasure within a given district and then forwarding at least $2,000,000 annually to Havana. At first, this was easy since the gold and silver bracelets, necklaces, rings, brooches, plates, bowls, and religious objects of the Indians could be taken, melted down, and cast into ingots or hammered into coins for shipment. Then, as the stored wealth of the Aztec, Mayan, and Inca empires was gradually exhausted, it became more difficult for each mint to meet the annual quotas, and so the natives were forced to open and work the mines that had originally produced the gold and silver for the Indian rulers, priests, and aristocracy. Hundreds of Indians were tortured and beaten to death to force them to divulge the location of the mines; thousands more died from impressment and slavery in the mining camps; tens of thousands of others died from hunger and sickness as mining replaced food gathering and farming as the principal occupation for the people. It was a miserly, rapacious performance; most people in North America never think about what happened in Central and South America where three large, wealthy, and culturally advanced empires were systematically looted, enslaved, and destroyed.

No one knows how many people died, and no one knows how much treasure was shipped. The official amounts were between $10,000,000 and $20,000,000 per year, but unofficial amounts for bribes, commissions, and private fortunes were at least equal, and probably greater. Since the looting and robbery and theft went on for nearly three centuries, the total amount shipped was probably between $8,000,000,000 and $12,000,000,000; this may seem to be only a nominal amount now that it takes a few billion dollars to run the Pentagon for a week, but at the time this was simply incomprehensible wealth. This flood of gold and silver converted Spain from a barren, impoverished peninsula, held partially by the Moors from North Africa, to the major military and diplomatic power in Western Europe. Much of this wealth was wasted by an incredibly corrupt administrative structure, but you can still see the results of it in the palaces and churches and cities of Spain.

Not all of this wealth got to Spain. The Caribbean was infested with pirates, buccaneers, and privateers, who differed only in the degree of legitimacy claimed for their operations; the buccaneers and privateers were commissioned by Holland and England to use their own ships as warships and to seize and plunder Spanish shipping during the constant European wars of that period. Spain countered the threat to their shipments of treasure by arranging an annual convoy, termed the Plate Fleet, which was escorted by heavily armed galleons. This convoy sailed from Havana during the late summer months since it took the rest of the year to gather the treasure from the colonies that stretched over 6,000 miles along the Pacific coast from California to Chile, then to transport it by mule caravans over the Isthmus of Panama, and finally to ship it, in small convoys, to Havana. It had to be continually moved from one form of transport to another, continually guarded, continually supervised; all this took time and resulted in the late summer sailing. The problem with the late summer sailing was that this was the season for tropical storms and hurricanes.

The Spanish galleons were heavy, cumbersome, and unwieldy vessels; they were large enough for the 2- or 3-month voyage across the Atlantic, and they were strong enough to resist attack by the Dutch or the English, but they were not maneuverable enough to be able to set out to sea in the face of a tropical storm; instead, they would be driven onto the coast. The east coast of Florida is lined with reefs and sandbars and has no protected harbors. It is estimated that 10% of the ships of the Spanish Plate Fleets were wrecked off Florida. That means that gold and silver with a monetary value of at least $1,000,000,000, and with a numismatic value perhaps 5 times greater, is strewn along the Florida coast.

Mr. Van Eulen felt that there were three distinct kinds of treasure hunters in Florida, all attempting to find portions of this treasure.

First are the large-scale marine salvage operators, oceanographic research firms, and marine archaeologists; these people generally have an ocean-going ship, a permanent organization, high fixed costs, and excellent equipment. You need good equipment if you are going to base the success of a 2-week expedition, at $4,000 per week for the ship and crew, on the ability of a trolling magnetometer to pick up the indications of a specific wreck site. These people spend a very small percentage of their time hunting for treasure since their primary objective is commercial salvage or scientific research, but the lure of treasure hunting gets to them eventually, and then they often do quite well since they can keep their ship over the wreck site for a considerable period of time and recover much of the wreck material by either diving or dredging. Jacques Cousteau operates that way in the Mediterranean, and Florida Salvage, the company that has found three complete wrecks of the Spanish Plate Fleet of 1715, does the same thing in the Caribbean. Both use our trolling magnetometers, which they bought directly from us.

Next in line are the skindivers, in Florida and the Caribbean, who are usually private individuals, without a ship or an organization, and who search for wrecks close offshore that can be reached by swimming from the beach or from a small boat. These people don't have the equipment for the salvage of a full wreck; instead, they look for the cargo that was scattered over the sea bed when the wreck broke up. You realize that you could never hope to find an intact hull, with a treasure chest bolted to the deck in the center of the captain's cabin, covered with long strands of seaweed gently waving in the current and guarded by a huge octopus, as in an Errol Flynn movie. Instead, a wreck breaks up quickly, generally as a result of the storm that drove the ship ashore in the first place, and the ballast stones and cannon sink about where the ship hit the reef, but everything lighter is torn apart and spread over 10 to 20 acres of sea bottom, covered with sand by the ocean currents, and then discolored by the sea water and coated with growths by the sea organisms. The gold and silver will be in patches, and skin divers either look for these patches with marine oscillators or they look for the iron of the shipwreck with marine magnetometers.

You need the instruments. The sand may be washed away by storms, but the coins will be dark gray or black in color, cemented together by corrosion, and covered with mollusks or algae. They don't look at all like treasure; certainly, they don't glitter. There are lots of stories in Florida of divers who found a trench or hollow in the ocean floor filled with "funny flat stones" and never realized that they were swimming over a couple of million dollars worth of silver coinage. I don't blame them; you have to know what you're looking for, and particularly you have to know that the Spanish pieces of eight, so-called because they were worth eight reals, which made up probably 80% of the treasure shipped on the Plate Fleets, were formed by chiseling each coin off a rough bar of hammered silver, and then marking the coin with a simple die indicating the mint of origin. These coins were rough, crude, and irregularly shaped; they were not the neat, round discs with milled edges that you might expect. They were made this way, by unskilled native labor, because they were temporary coins, for counting, handling, and shipping only, not for circulation. The silver was remelted, alloyed, and made into official currency, each valued at one real, in the royal mints at Barcelona, Madrid, and Seville.

There are probably 2,000 skindivers in Florida who spend some time each year looking for this treasure, but that number includes both the professional, full-time divers and the amateur, or weekend, hobbyists. Both groups would get their equipment from the diving shops that abound in Florida, although they might buy direct from the manufacturer to save a little money. Skindiving is an expensive hobby.

Last on the list of Florida treasure hunters are the beach searchers, who use oscillators to find single coins that have washed up to the shore. You might think that the coastal areas would have been pretty well worked over by now, but each storm brings in new coins, and more searchers. I don't know how many people do this, but it's a big thing in Florida, and you find retired couples, children, housewives, and working people on their day off all walking along the beach with a treasure detector, searching for coins. Many of them wade in shallow water, using waterproof search heads on their instruments. These beach searchers use a wide range of equipment from war-surplus mine detectors to very expensive oscillators, depending on their interest in the hobby and their income. They buy the equipment from treasure shops, hobby shops, and, occasionally, sporting-good stores. (Statement of Mr. Van Eulen.)

Mr. Van Eulen was not as knowledgeable about treasure hunting in the western states as he was about Florida; he had spent much less time in the area, and his products were not as well-received there. However, he felt that this was the second largest market for treasure hunting equipment in the United States:

> Western United States is a big market for treasure hunting equipment, primarily because people out there combine treasure hunting and prospecting. Mining was the major industry in the west during the last half of the nineteenth century; and the amounts of gold and silver that were recovered were simply incredible. $9,000,000,000 in gold and $4,000,000,000 in silver from all the mining states during the period from 1850 to 1900 is the usual estimate. Just one mine, the Comstock at Virginia City, Nevada, shipped $10,000,000 worth of silver each year for 30 years. This gold and silver paid for the railroads and the industrial development of the west, for the mansions and public buildings of San Francisco and Denver, and for many private fortunes in New York, London, and Paris. It must have been an exciting time in which to have lived.
>
> Now, people search for the gold and silver that was lost or buried in earlier days; they look over the dumps and tailings at old mining camps for material that was discarded as being too low in value at the time, and they hunt for new nuggets and new bodies of ore. People in the western states combine treasure hunting and prospecting; this is very different from the activities of treasure hunters in other sections of the country, and the instruments reflect this. The treasure detectors that are sold in the western states have to be able to be tuned for both magnetic and nonmagnetic metals, since most of the silver and gold ore is found in either sand or rock that is heavily magnetic, with a strong concentration of iron particles. In the old days, the prospectors looked for black sand as an indication of gold and silver. The sand was black because it had a high concentration of iron oxide. It is a sad tale, but the original Henry

Comstock, who found the Comstock lode in Nevada, decided that the material had little value since there was no iron mixed in with it, and he sold the claim for a pittance. There was no iron since it was a vein of almost pure silver; the only impurity was a little gold. But, most ore in the west is found with iron, and the oscillators used there have to have this additional feature. It is an easy change to make; you just change the rectifier, but we haven't had much success selling our instruments in that area. I think that a magnetometer would be better, but you can't get people to carry both instruments, although there might be some market for our Discoverer II (land magnetometer) there.

> There may be some professional prospectors left in the west, and certainly there must be some mining companies still searching for new ore, but the primary market for metal detectors in the area is among individuals and families that combine treasure hunting, prospecting, and camping. There is a lot of open space in the six states (Arizona, California, Colorado, Nevada, New Mexico, and Utah), and there are a lot of people in the urban centers who like to get out camping, hiking, and exploring, and treasure hunting and prospecting provide both an excuse and an activity. People drive out to the old ghost towns and hike back in the mountains. They use jeeps to get off the road in the deserts, and they seem to have a good time. They are looking for gold and silver, and certainly there are enough legends of lost mines and undiscovered lodes (did you know that the Lost Dutchman Mine probably exists and that there doubtless are other lodes fully as rich as the Comstock waiting to be found?) to keep them looking and enough nuggets and grains of gold (did you also know that you can still pan for gold in many streams in the area?) to show that they are on the right track. Also, they are looking for relics of the old days, for anyone who goes prospecting in the west now can't help but become intrigued with the stories of discoveries and disappointments in the mining period of western history.
>
> I don't know how many treasure hunters there are in the area, but there are a lot of them. The two magazines for this hobby—*Treasure Guide* and *Treasure World*—each have a circulation of about 20,000 and 80% to 90% of their subscriptions are in the western states, so I would guess that there are

25,000 to 50,000 potential customers out there. But many of these people already have treasure hunting instruments, and I think that they tend to buy additional equipment from western manufacturers. There is no reason for a treasure hunter in Southern California to buy an oscillator from a manufacturer in Saginaw, Michigan, particularly since the electronics industry is so strong on the coast and since the three largest manufacturers of electronic treasure detectors are located in that area.

Mr. Van Eulen felt that the last market area, which consisted of the eastern and midwestern states, was probably the smallest in sales potential for electronic treasure detectors, but that this potential was still reasonably large, and that it was still reasonably free of competition since the other manufacturers of detection equipment tended to concentrate in the other areas. Mr. Van Eulen also explained that treasure hunters in this area looked for lost artifacts and buried money, not for silver and gold:

When you talk about treasure, most people generally think of gold and silver coins in an old oaken chest, or of an old map on parchment that is tattered and torn at the edges, stained with salt water and, hopefully, blood, smelling of rum and tobacco smoke, and marked with an X on an uninhabited inlet along a mysterious coast. Unfortunately, there aren't many treasure maps around, outside of nineteenth-century English fiction, and there never was much buried pirate treasure anyway. Pirates tended to be consumers, not investors, and the bars and grog shops of Kingston and Port Royal provided ample opportunities for immediate consumption. If they did want to save some of their booty, it was not necessary to bury it in a chest; they could invest their ill-gotten gains in the respectable private banks and merchant houses of Boston, New York, or Philadelphia. You may not believe it, but the founding capital for the Bank of Boston, which became the First National Bank of Boston and is now listed on the New York Stock Exchange, was subscribed in Spanish octo reals, or pieces of eight, by three old traders and sea captains, and no one ever inquired how they got them. Many of the old fortunes on the East Coast were based on rum, slavery, and piracy.

The real treasure in the East and the Midwest is not pirate's gold; instead, it is the old household artifacts and farm implements, which were lost 50 to 100 years ago and have now achieved considerable value as antiques, and the caches of coins or household silver, which were buried 50 to 100 years ago for protection and then forgotten. You might think that there would be a limited amount of buried money in this country, but you have to remember that in olden times banks were often either unavailable or untrustworthy and that farmers and merchants would often bury their funds for safekeeping and then forget where they put them or die before they were able to recover the money. Also, women would often bury table silver and other valuable household items and jewelry during the wars or depressions that occurred during the nineteenth century.

I think that a good example of the sort of treasure that can be found in this area is the experience of a friend of mine, George Bowersox. George did not believe in treasure hunting and tried to talk me out of building this line of treasure hunting instruments. He said that there just wasn't any material left to find in most of the country. When his 12-year-old daughter became interested during a visit here last summer, George borrowed one of our Starline models and searched around his home. Now, they live in an old farmhouse outside Toledo, and they found the usual horseshoes, barn hardware, and farm tools that you might expect. George got a lot more interested when his daughter dug up a big strap hinge that had been hand forged. For years George and his wife had been trying to buy a pair for their front door at antique shops. George began looking seriously for the other hinge. He got a very strong indication on the instrument, so they dug down near the roots of an old lilac bush and found 22 silver spoons wrapped in a piece of heavy velvet. When they cleaned the spoons with silver polish, they found the initials of the family from whom they had bought the farm. Now, there was only one member of that family left, a very old woman living in a nursing home near South Bend, Indiana. When they called her up, she was so surprised that she could hardly speak. Her mother had buried that silver in 1885, when there had been a series of robberies of rural farmhouses along the Ohio–Michigan border, and then her mother had never been able to find the cache again. She said that the spoons had been brought to America by her great-grandfather before the Revolution, and she was right. The spoons were Georgian silver; you could tell by the hallmarks.

The find was reported in the Toledo paper, and then it was reprinted in other papers, even *The New York Times*. Antique shop owners and collectors began calling them, and they found that the spoons were worth $200 a piece. They did not sell them; they gave them back to the old woman in South Bend. That woman told them that her mother had buried 40 silver dollars and one $10 gold piece, payment for that year's wheat crop, at the same time, so now George is looking for the money, which would be worth a lot more than $50 if he could find it.

People buried money, table silver, and jewelry in the old days, and they lost iron, copper, and brass tools, utensils, and hardware. It's all there waiting to be found. We have a big copper pot that I found buried near the foundations of an old farmhouse near Midland. Last year alone here in Michigan someone in Saline found a wooden box with over 100 silver dollars near the back porch of an old farmhouse. In Grand Rapids a jar of coins valued at more than $15,000 was found in the backyard of a 70-year-old house right in the city.

Old coins and antique hardware items are not the only valuable finds in this section of the country; the other objective for many treasure hunters in the urban areas of the eastern and midwestern states is, of course, lost money. People lose quite a few pennies, nickles, dimes, and quarters and there is no question but that you can find $10 to $20 worth per day if you look in the right places, such as parking lots, school yards, fair grounds, shopping centers, bathing beaches, etc. It seems a little ghoulish to me, but you can also find a lot of wedding rings and watches at beaches, as well as money. I sold our littlest detector to a 13-year-old boy here in Saginaw, and he found enough money and jewelry in one month to buy our most expensive Starline model. People who look for modern coins instead of historical finds are called "coinshooters."

There are a good many treasure hunters and coinshooters in the East and the Midwest, but I don't know how many. My best estimate would be 5,000. But, there must be 5 to 10 times as many people who would like to try the hobby, but they have either never thought about it seriously or they don't know where to go to buy the equipment. There are only a few treasure stores in this area, and they are usually very small, poorly located, and do very little business. There's one in a small town in the central part of Michigan, for example, that sells motorcycles, used television sets, and treasure detectors; I don't think that the people who ride motorcycles are usually interested in antiques or historical finds, or that the people who look at used television sets normally have the money or inclination to buy a frequency beat oscillator. It is one of the three treasure stores in the state, however. One of the others is even smaller; it is called Herb's Relic and Bottle Shop and is located in the side porch of the owner's home in the western part of the state. The third is the largest; it is about the size of a barber shop, and it is Mt. Clemens, Michigan, just north of Detroit. It is not easy to sell treasure detectors through dealers in this section of the country. (Statement of Mr. Van Eulen.)

In 1971, when Mr. Van Eulen first designed the line of instruments for treasure detection, most sales were made through dealers. The company advertised both the professional and the economy series of the oscillators and the marine models of the magnetometer in *Treasure Guide Magazine*, which at that time had a very limited circulation (about 4,000 professional and part-time treasure hunters), but which was read by nearly all dealers. These dealers, concentrated in the areas of greatest interest in treasure hunting, Florida and the Far West, would often write requesting further information; Mr. Van Eulen would reply, with pamphlets giving technical data about the various models of instruments and with an offer to supply one model on consignment. The dealers would usually accept this offer, since it required no cash investment on their part, and would eventually sell this instrument to a customer. They would then send an order for two or three more treasure detectors with their payment for the first instrument. Mr. Van Eulen gave a 30% discount to the dealers but did not offer exclusive territorial rights or encourage volume purchases since he did not feel that the dealers were essential in the distribution system; he felt that the users would specify his instruments because of their inherent quality. Also, he did not visit the dealers, both because of the distance and the expenses of travel and because of his predominant interest in original research and product development work. In retrospect, he felt that this lack of personal contact with the dealers was a mistake:

In 1971, when we designed our first treasure detector, there were only two or three other electronic companies that were at all active in this industry, and since we had instruments that were either better than any others in the market (professional series), or cheaper than any others in the market (economy series), we did fairly well; the dealers would contact us, take one of our instruments on consignment, make the retail sale to the consumer, and then order a few more. We did not have to do anything beyond running monthly advertisements, at about $400 per month for a full page, in the trade magazine. It was lucky that it worked that way since dealers at that time were small shops, generally selling skin-diving equipment in Florida or prospecting and camping equipment in the Far West, and we never could have found them. Instead, they found us.

But then other companies began to get into the treasure detection market, and they spent more time on marketing concepts than they did on technological improvement. Treasure-hunting instruments are simple to design, which gave these other companies a low cost of entry to the market, and there were a lot of other electronic firms, particularly on the West Coast, that were looking for new products due to the financial crunch that came with the slowdown of aerospace and military spending. They had less sophisticated instruments, but they signed up the dealers with an exclusive territory, stocked them with a full line of inventory, and gave them a 50% discount off list. This change to exclusive distributors was a gradual process that took place during 1971 and 1972, but our orders from dealers kept declining, and by 1973 they had almost completely terminated. I would call up a person in Anaheim, California who had sold 10 or 12 of our instruments each year, and he would say "Sorry, I'm handling the White line now." Or I'd call the owner of the diving shop in Fort Pierce, Florida that sold our marine oscillators

and magnetometers, and he would say, "Garrett gave me 50% off to sell only their instruments, and I'm sorry but I had to do it; expenses have been too high this year to continue with your detectors at a 30% discount." They were always "sorry," but they were always selling somebody else's treasure detectors. Had we been calling on them, we would have known about this before it happened, and we probably could have made a competitive offer. But, we didn't call on them, and now we're in the soup.

The problem is that the dealers are now bigger, more prosperous, better located, and much more important in the distribution network for treasure detectors. Treasure hunting as a leisure time activity grew rapidly during 1971 and 1972 in Florida and the mining states of the Far West as more accurate and less expensive equipment became available. The increase in the number of customers enabled the treasure shops to move out of the downtown sidestreets and out of people's homes and into the shopping centers. These stores now carry detectors, books on treasure hunting, camping or diving equipment, prospecting supplies, and materials for rock collectors or coin hobbyists. These stores now are much more accessible and much more respectable. People go to them in Florida and the Far West for advice on the best makes of treasure detectors. The dealer, of course, recommends the one that he is handling on an exclusive basis; we don't get many orders from dealers any more. (Statement of Mr. Van Eulen.)

The advertising agency for Treasure Systems planned to counter this decline of orders from dealers with a new emphasis on direct-mail order sales from consumers, but this change in the marketing plan did not seem to be working in the winter of 1973:

Our agency changed the message in the *Treasure Guide* ads from a hidden appeal to dealers to a blatant appeal to consumers, but our direct-mail orders from individual treasure hunters or coinshooters have not been numerous enough to pay for the advertising and agency costs. You never really know why anything happens in marketing a consumer product, but I think that the reason for our lack of success was the increase in the number of manufacturers of treasure hunting equipment and the consequent increase in the number of ads in the treasure hunting magazines.

Before, there were just two or three full-page ads in each issue; now there are 20 or 30 because the agency for each manufacturer convinces the manufacturer to spend more for advertising. But this advertising is not productive since there is so much of it. No potential customer is going to study 20 or 30 ads, then write 20 or 30 letters to the manufacturers, and finally sift through all the technical data and promotional claims for 20 or 30 instruments before ordering the best one. Instead, he writes to a few of the better known manufacturers. They send him an expensive color brochure and a list of dealers where he can see the detectors and try them out. We can't send expensive brochures since it costs so much to print them in small volume, and we can't send a list of dealers since we don't have any.

Our current advertising policies are simply not effective. (Statement of Mr. Van Eulen.)

In the winter of 1973 there were over 30 manufacturers of electronic treasure detecting equipment that advertised in *Treasure Guide* and *Treasure World*. These magazines are published for professional and part-time treasure hunters. Since Mr. Van Eulen had written for brochures from most of these manufacturers, he knew the prices of the various models they offered. He also requested Dun and Bradstreet credit reports on each firm. These reports gave the approximate sales level and the primary means of distribution for each form. This information is contained in Exhibit 2.

EXHIBIT 2 Competitive manufacturers of electronic treasure detection equipment, in order of size by annual sales. (Source: company records.) Except for the industry leaders, the names of all companies have been disguised.

Company name	Product line	Annual sales	Distribution method
White Electronics Sweet Home, Oregon	24 models; from $79.50 to $975.00	Approx. $2,500,000	Exclusive dealers in treasure shops
Garrett Electronics Garland, Texas	6 models; from $149.00 to $449.50	Approx. $1,000,000	Exclusive dealers in treasure shops
Carson Electronics Forest Grove, Calif.	12 models; from $89.95 to $249.50	Under $1,000,000	Non-exclusive treasure shops, diving shops, etc.
Pacific Detectors Salem, Oregon	8 models; from $49.95 to $395.00	Under $1,000,000	Exclusive dealers in western treasure shops
Jair Electronics Riverside, Calif.	4 models; from $69.50 to $189.50	Under $750,000	Sporting good stores only
Tolman Corporation Ft. Meyers, Florida	2 models at $129.50 and $219.50	Under $500,000	Non-exclusive treasure shops, diving shops, etc.
New Mexico Electronics Tala, New Mexico	2 models at $89.50 and $169.50	Under $250,000	Non-exclusive treasure shops
Surefind Electronics Tampa, Florida	3 models at $129.50, $149.50, and $169.50	Under $250,000	Non-exclusive treasure shops, diving shops
Treasure Finders Glendale, Calif.	4 models; from $84.50 to $269.50	Under $250,000	Non-exclusive treasure shops in the west only
A.B.C. Electronics San Diego, Calif.	2 models at $149.00 and $199.00	Under $100,000	Direct mail and occasional dealers
Electronic Systems Haddenfield, Calif.	2 models at $89.50 and $139.50	Under $100,000	Direct mail and occasional dealers

Company name	Product line	Annual sales	Distribution method
Folts Electronics Odessa, Texas	1 model at $179.50	Under $100,000	Direct mail and occasional dealers
Garden City Corp. Phoenix, Arizona	2 models at $74.50 and $124.50	Under $100,000	Direct mail and occasional dealers
Goldman Corporation Glendale, Calif.	1 model in kit form at $79.50	Under $100,000	Radio supply stores only
Homer–Davis Supply Renfrew, Calif.	6 models from $49.50 to $249.50	Under $100,000	Direct mail and occasional dealers
Katz Engineering Hollywood, Calif.	3 models at $79.50, $90.50, and $149.50	Under $100,000	Direct mail and occasional dealers
Manion Electronics Los Angeles, Calif.	2 models in kit form at $39.50 and $59.50	Under $100,000	Direct mail only
Nussbaum Corporation Palo Alto, Calif.	1 model at $239.95	Under $100,000	Direct mail and occasional dealers
Pafko Electronics Ocala, Florida	2 marine models at $199.00 and $269.00	Under $100,000	Diving shops only
Riter Systems San Diego, Calif.	3 models at $119.50, $149.50, and $199.50	Under $100,000	Direct mail and occasional dealers
Sporting Electronics South Bend, Indiana	1 model at $69.50	Under $100,000	Sporting good stores only
Treasure Systems Saginaw, Michigan	7 models from $29.95 to $495.00	Under $100,000	Direct mail and occasional dealers
Treasure Trove Corp. Tyler, Texas	2 models at $99.50 and $169.50	Under $100,000	Direct mail and occasional dealers
Waffler Electronics Davis, Calif.	3 models at $69.50, $99.50, and $149.50	Under $100,000	Direct mail and occasional dealers

Mr. Van Eulen felt that the market for electronic treasure detection equipment was saturated, with too many manufacturers attempting to sell to too few customers, and that there would be a rapid shakeout of the smaller firms over the coming year. He wanted his company to be one of the survivors, but he was uncertain of the marketing plan that he should adopt:

Look, since we're a small company with limited overhead, we don't have to sell many treasure detectors to survive. And we have the best instruments, and the cheapest instruments, so we ought to be able to sell them. My problem is that I don't know how to let people know that we have them.

I do know, however, that advertising in the treasure hunting magazines is not the answer; we spent over $17,000 there last year, but there are too many other manufacturers of treasure detection equipment advertising in those two trade journals for us to have an impact, and many of the readers must already have instruments. I want to find either an entirely new means of advertising or greater impact from our existing ads.

The agency has not been much help. They just ask me where and when I want the ads to appear, and then they do some uninspired artwork and write some typical copy. We need a new approach, but they don't have the imagination to provide it. And, of course, they say that we are too small an account for them to spend the time needed for them to develop this new approach.

I thought that I had a new approach, but it did not work out. We made up a large, full-color poster, with a picture of an extremely attractive and buxom neighborhood girl wearing an open work shirt and shorts and using our treasure detector near an old mine shaft. At the top of the poster was the slogan that treasure hunting could be both fun and profitable, and at the bottom we had our name and address and brief descriptions and prices of the various models of our detectors. We sent that poster to all the barber shops in Michigan. We got 11 orders for our least expensive instrument and the threat of a law suit from the National Organization for Women claiming that we were exploiting sex.

We have to change our advertising to get more exposure or more impact, and we have to do this quickly, since our sales have been declining and we are back in a loss situation. I don't know how to do this; perhaps you can help. (Statement of Mr. Van Eulen.)

ASSIGNMENT

Develop an advertising program for Treasure Systems, Inc., with specific plans for the magazines to be used and the messages to be printed in each ad. To help with this assignment, Exhibit 3 gives advertising rates, page sizes, and subscription/newsstand sales of consumer magazines that might be considered suitable for Treasure Systems advertising. The page rate is for a full page in black and white;

color, if required, adds about 20% to the cost for the ad, and fractional pages (one-half page, one-quarter page, and one-eighth page, etc.) may be used at roughly proportional costs. For further guidance, Mr. Van Eulen stated that he felt that he could invest $25,000 in the advertising program, although he hoped that the sales generated by the advertising would generate a margin adequate to repay this investment during the first year. He also stated that at existing list prices the margin above direct labor, materials, and overhead on all models of the treasure detectors was approximately 50%. That is, for instruments sold directly from the factory, without dealer discounts, one-half of the sales price was for direct costs of manufacture and one-half for administrative and selling expenses.

Mr. Van Eulen also explained that if this advertising program was not successful, the company would have to close. He felt that he needed the contribution from sales of at least $80,000 of treasure detection instruments to cover selling and administrative costs of the company and to provide time for him to develop a new line of oceanographic instrumentation for which he had been promised an immediate market. He stated that he did not wish to close the company and to go back to working for a large corporation, but he felt that there was no alternative if the program was not successful. Given these circumstances, what specific advertising program do you recommend?

EXHIBIT 3 Advertising rates, page sizes, and subscription/newsstand sales of consumer magazines suitable for Treasure Systems Advertising. (Source: company records. Report prepared for Mr. Van Eulen by local advertising agency.)

Magazine name	Page rate	Page size	Subscription sales	Newsstand sales
Antique Collecting				
1. *Antiques*	$1,058	8″ × 10½″	60,223	298

Antiques is for the serious collectors of antiques and works of art and for students of early American social history and culture. Feature articles deal with furniture, painting, prints, architecture, ceramics, glass, metals, etc.

Magazine name	Page rate	Page size	Subscription sales	Newsstand sales
2. *Antiques Journal*	$120	8″ × 11″	24,663	2,200

Antiques Journal is for the beginner as well as for the advanced antique collector. Writers cover a wide range of interest which varies from chinaware, clocks, bottles, and dolls to cut and colored glass, metal objects, etc.

Camping

3. *Better Camping*	$650	7″ × 10″	27,371	18,688

Better Camping is for families and individual campers who enjoy all types of camping; from backpacking, canoe camping, tent camping through the range of vehicles which include camping trailers, pickup campers, and motor homes.

4. *Camper Coachman*	$440	5″ × 7½″	30,697	10,185

Camper Coachman is devoted to the self-propelled recreational vehicle and its maintenance, upkeep, and uses (hunting, fishing, and touring, etc.) .

5. *Camping Guide*	$750	7″ × 10″	61,578	19,231

Camping Guide Magazine covers the spectrum of recreational vehicle travel and family camping. Other subjects covered are trail bikes, all-terrain vehicles, small boats, snowmobiles, etc.

6. *Camping Journal*	$2,190	7″ × 10″	243,264	17,843

Camping Journal is for the outdoor enthusiast—fishermen, hunters, boatmen, hikers, and others who vacation in the out-of-doors. Where to go and how to do it topics and test reports and roundups on camping equipment are included.

7. *Wheels Afield*	$975	7″ × 10″	32,349	24,669

Wheels Afield is for those who are interested in recreational vehicles, especially in pickup campers, motor homes, travel trailers, and tent trailers. The magazine stresses practical solutions to trailering and camping problems.

8. *Woodall's Trailering*	$2,350	7″ × 10″	9,548	212,374

Woodall's Trailering Parks and Campground describes and rates private, federal, state, county, and municipal parks and campgrounds in the U.S., Canada, and Mexico.

Crafts and Hobbies

9. *Coinage*	$400	7″ × 10″	41,200	84,675

Coinage is directed toward the interest levels of both old and new coin collectors. Feature articles emphasize the human stories and history behind the coins rather than the straight reporting of coin values.

10. *Coin Mart*	$225	Not given	Not given	84,200

Coin Mart is for the coin collector who, by choice or necessity, adds to his collection through mail order purchase; it also publishes a price guide and interprets the trends of the coin investment market.

11. *Coins*	$302	Not given	95,790	Not given

Coins is for the coin hobbyist. It deals with the how-to of coin collecting: cataloging, selecting, grading, storing, and displaying. It publishes a price guide, reports on activities of coin clubs, and prints articles on the history of coinage.

EXHIBIT 3 (*Continued*)

Magazine name	Page rate	Page size	Subscription sales	Newsstand sales
12. *Coin World*	$668	10″ × 16″	104,018	23,765

Coin World uses the newspaper concept for national and international news coverage and in-depth illustrated features on U.S. and world coins, tokens, medals, and paper money for beginning, intermediate, and advanced coin collectors.

13. *Lapidary Journal*	$564	7½″ × 10″	40,011	10,595

Lapidary Journal is for the amateur outdoor gem hobbyist (rockhound), for the collectors of gemstones and objects of gold and silver, and for the makers of jewelry and users of lapidary equipment.

14. *Numismatic News*	$387	9¼″ × 15″	56,803	Not given

Numismatic News is for the coin hobbyist who, in addition to collecting, occasionally buys, sells, and trades coins. Current pricing, as reflected in coin marketing exchanges, is featured.

15. *World Coins*	$105	4⅝″ × 7″	6,935	1,309

World Coins' editorial objectives are to serve collectors and dealers of modern and ancient coins of foreign nations by providing news and pictures of new issues, new discoveries, and new market value trends. In-depth research in numismatics is also reported.

Men's Magazines

16. *American Legion*	$6,930	7″ × 10″	2,615,638	Not given

American Legion Magazine is primarily a general-interest consumer magazine. Major articles deal with the background of events and trends in the world today, with subjects of broad consumer interest and with milestones of history.

17. *Argosy*	$7,455	7″ × 10⅛″	1,130,969	266,044

Argosy is for the young adult men. Articles explore the responsibilities of men as present or prospective heads of households, discuss the role of men in political and social events, and report on male-oriented leisure activities.

18. *Esquire*	$9,990	9⅜″ × 12″	1,004,603	173,611

Esquire is for a wide range of masculine interests. Monthly features include articles on travel and fashion, literary fiction, and reviews of books, records, and films. The major portion of the content of each issue is devoted to articles and special features on sports, personalities, recreation, the performing arts, alcoholic beverages, automotive topics, current social and political affairs, and a variety of other contemporary subjects.

19. *Modern Man*	$550	7″ × 10″	2,783	112,703

Modern Man offers a combination of beautiful women, masculine adventures, and sports features for men who have a wide range of interests. Article features deal with current events, such as the American involvement in Viet Nam and the Detroit auto industry controversy. Photo features range from wild parties and nude movies to MM's "Doll of the Month" and "The Uncovered Cover Girl."

20. *Penthouse*	$3,000	7″ × 10″	6,130	361,130

Penthouse is for the sophisticated male reader. Its editorial scope ranges from outspoken contemporary comment to photographic essays on beautiful women. Penthouse

Magazine name	Page rate	Page size	Subscription sales	Newsstand sales

features interviews with personalities, sociological studies, cartoons, travel, humor, food and wines, and fashion and grooming for men. Its editorial attitude is to reflect the new liberalism in social and intellectual morality and the spread of affluence in the Euro-American community.

| 21. *Playboy* | $25,200 | 7″ × 10″ | 1,315,630 | 3,974,397 |

Playboy is an entertainment magazine that offers fiction, serious and satirical articles, cartoons, and picture stories of pretty girls. It includes service features such as monthly articles on male fashion, food and drink, gifts and other merchandise, travel, etc., and, less regularly, apartment and office furnishings, automobiles, sports, and other leisure and avocational interests. The editors also review books, records, movies, legitimate plays, restaurants, night life, etc.

| 22. *True* | $4,400 | 7″ × 10¼″ | 2,111,574 | 298,419 |

True is for today's men. It is concerned with the major issues and questions of American society, the Washington scene, jobs and careers, adventure, travel, health, hunting and fishing, money management, marriage and the family, leisure, and recreation. It is editorially directed toward the American males who are on the way up in life and want information as well as entertainment.

Outdoor Activities

| 23. *Arizona Wildlife* | $325 | 7½″ × 10″ | 11,596 | 2,349 |

Arizona Wildlife is for all sportsmen, covering aspects of fishing, hunting, skin diving, boating, jeeping, and camping. The emphasis is on family participation.

| 24. *Colorado* | $2,000 | 7⅛″ × 10″ | 27,049 | 2,082 |

Colorado Magazine is for readers interested in Colorado and the Rocky Mountain West. Special editorial attention is focused on the outdoor sports and recreational opportunities in the Rocky Mountains.

| 25. *Field and Stream* | $7,800 | 7″ × 10½″ | 1,407,144 | 278,211 |

Field and Stream is for outdoor sportsmen and their families, with emphasis on both the experienced person and the beginner. Features and monthly departments cover a range of outdoor activities, especially hunting, fishing, camping, boating, archery, hiking, conservation, legislation, and reviews of new products.

| 26. *Florida Sportsman* | $440 | 7¼″ × 10″ | 8,000 | 16,000 |

Florida Sportsman is for those who have outdoor interests in Florida, the Bahamas, The Virgin Islands, and Puerto Rico. Feature articles deal with boating, fishing, camping, hunting, archery, skin diving, underwater photography, etc.

| 27. *Michigan Out-of-Doors* | $770 | 10″ × 13¾″ | 125,000 | 500 |

Michigan Out-of-Doors is for outdoorsmen, nature lovers, and those who have a high interest in the conservation of natural resources. Feature articles deal with wildlife, hunting, fishing, camping, and general conservation.

| 28. *Outdoor Life* | $8,040 | 7″ × 10″ | 1,409,084 | 341,400 |

Outdoor Life is for sportsmen. The major editorial stress is on the possibilities for active participation in field sports. Feature articles are on fishing, hunting, boating, camping, hiking, and archery. Where to go and travel information for the ardent sportsman are also included.

EXHIBIT 3   *(Continued)*

Magazine name	Page rate	Page size	Subscription sales	Newsstand sales
29. *Outdoor Sports*	$500	7″ × 10″	2,856	99,275

Outdoor Sports Life is for sportsmen. The major emphasis is on field sports. Articles and regular columns appear each month on salt-water and fresh-water fishing, hunting, boating, camping, and hiking. Travel information, articles about dogs, and advice on arms and ammunition are also given.

30. *Sports Afield*	$6,300	7″ × 10¼″	1,130,407	263,093

Sports Afield is for the outdoors sports enthusiast. Illustrated articles cover all outdoor activity, and advice on camping, hunting, arms and ammunition, fishing, boating, sporting dogs, and trap and skeet is given by experienced departmental editors, who also inform about new products in their fields.

31. *Western Outdoor News*	$618	9⅜″ × 14″	64,298	5,574

Western Outdoor News is for California sportsmen. It features reports on fishing, hunting, boating, and camping conditions in the state. Editorial format stresses timely, on the spot news reports.

32. *Western Outdoors*	$645	7¼″ × 10″	65,531	16,696

Western Outdoors is for active sportsmen who live in the 13 Western states. The magazine provides information on where to go in the West for recreational activities. Emphasis is on new places for fishing, hunting, camping, hiking, and pleasure boating.

Science and Mechanics

33. *Mechanix Illustrated*	$5,915	5½″ × 8″	1,270,270	285,337

Mechanix Illustrated is for men who are interested in scientific and mechanical subjects in general, for home workshop enthusiasts, and for car owners and fans. Subjects covered include cars, boating, aviation, popular medicine, inventions, vacation activities, business opportunities, and scientific developments; all articles are as nontechnical as possible.

34. *Popular Mechanics*	$4,425	5½″ × 8″	1,277,304	443,030

Popular Mechanics is primarily a service magazine for men, with regular features on automobiles and driving, science and inventions, new products for the home, boating and outdoor recreation, jobs and careers, photography, and aerospace.

35. *Popular Science*	$7,370	7″ × 10″	1,318,600	335,519

Popular Science concentrates on new products that may be of special usefulness to its readers: men who have strong interest in their homes, their transportation needs, and their recreational activities. Major articles cover such product areas as automobiles, boats and engines, home workshop tools, garden and lawn equipment, electronic, TV, and photographic products, etc.

36. *Science Digest*	$750	4⅜″ × 7″	108,618	50,475

Science Digest reports and explains the news of the month in science and technology for the general public. Feature articles cut across all disciplines and are designed to provide readable understanding of topics in the news for an audience of college and upper-level high school students and teachers, science-oriented laymen, and scientists interested in a quick review of important developments in the many fields of science.

Magazine name	Page rate	Page size	Subscription sales	Newsstand sales
37. *Science and Mechanics*	$995	$5\frac{1}{2}'' \times 8''$	207,588	112,667

Science and Mechanics is for young men who are interested in new developments and current research in physical and behavioral sciences, including space exploration, medicine and health, psychology, transportation, electronics, etc. Special emphasis is given to new cars, boats, planes, engines, and inventions.

38. *Scientific American*	$5,200	$7'' \times 10''$	369,831	84,060

Scientific American chronicles the developments in science and technology. The magazine is addressed to the scientists, engineers, and technically oriented executives of industry, government, and universities.

Sports and Sporting Equipment

39. *Dive Magazine*	$875	$7'' \times 10\frac{1}{2}''$	9,143	35,563

Dive Magazine is a consumer magazine in the skin and scuba diving fields. Feature articles include spearfishing, adventure underwater, photographic equipment, treasure seeking, new equipment, travel (where to dive), and fiction.

40. *Skin Diver*	$1,655	$7'' \times 10''$	55,063	26,737

Skin Diver Magazine is devoted to the underseas world of recreational diving, and it is designed to satisfy the novice, intermediate, and expert diver. Underwater activities covered include snorkling, skin diving, and scuba diving, with regular monthly features on boating, photography, shipwreck exploration, new equipment, and underseas science.

41. *Sports Illustrated*	$14,660	$7'' \times 10''$	1,962,895	80,516

Sports Illustrated reports and interprets each week the world of sport, recreation, and active leisure. It previews, analyzes, and comments on major games and events, as well as those noteworthy for character and spirit alone.

42. *Oceans Magazine*	$750	$7'' \times 10''$	Not given	Not given

Oceans Magazine is for readers who have ocean-related interests. Feature articles report contemporary developments in oceanography, hydrography, and ocean engineering. Regular topical departments discuss geopolitics, legislation, fisheries, naval science, merchant commerce, aquatic recreation, ocean-borne adventure, and exploration.

43. *Treasure Guide*	$850	$7\frac{1}{2}'' \times 10''$	21,238	2,333

Treasure Guide is for those who are interested in the location and recovery of lost or buried treasure, both on land and underwater. Regular monthly articles report on treasure sites, legend, and lore; regular monthly departments include reviews of treasure-seeking equipment, questions and answers for readers, how-to-do-it advice for beginners, etc.

44. *Treasure World*	$695	$7\frac{1}{2}'' \times 10''$	17,010	Not given

Treasure World offers news and articles of interest to the amateur treasure seeker. Articles on treasures recently found and on the legends of treasures still unfound predominate, together with news of new equipment and advice on new methods.

Women's Magazines

45. *Cosmopolitan*	$6,250	$7'' \times 10\frac{3}{4}''$	83,293	1,147,801

Cosmopolitan is for young women, married or single, interested in self-improvement, careers, clothes, beauty, travel, entertainment, and the arts, with special interest on the world outside the home.

EXHIBIT 3 *(Continued)*

Magazine name	Page rate	Page size	Subscription sales	Newsstand sales
46. *Family Circle*	$23,450	7″ × 10¼″	Not given	7,051,254

Family Circle is edited for homemakers. Approximately 90% of the editorial content is devoted to service features dealing with home management, family care, and self-improvement.

47. *Good Housekeeping*	$22,765	7″ × 10¼″	4,401,634	1,272,241

Good Housekeeping is for housewives. Readers' interests include purchase of a house, interior decoration, household appliances, food preparation and entertaining, and information on child care, family relations, fashion, and beauty.

48. *Ladies Home Journal*	$28,600	9⅜″ × 12″	6,141,244	865,833

Ladies Home Journal is a personal magazine for women. It is edited to supply information and inspiration to the younger woman on her world of fashion, home-making, personal appearance, and current interests. The subject matter ranges, literally, from pickles to politics, to provide a balance of interests in women's lives.

49. *Woman's Day*	$24,200	6¾″ × 10″	Not given	Not given

Woman's Day aims to satisfy the home-oriented interests of younger women. Fashion, beauty, food, decorating, gardening, and travel pages deal strictly with workable ideas and with merchandise, services, and projects that are within the reader's reach.

Housing Components, Inc.

Housing Components, Inc. was founded in Albany, New York, in 1872 as the Northern Sash and Door Corporation to manufacture windows, doors, and wooden moldings. The company was successful from the start, probably because of the population increase brought about by the railroad expansion in the area; the completion of the Hoosac Tunnel in 1874 provided for the first time direct rail service from Boston, through the Berkshire Mountains, to northern New York and the major routes farther west. Mechanicsville, 6 miles north of Albany, became the junction of the Boston and Albany, the Delaware and Hudson, the New York Central, the Ontario and Western, and the Central of Vermont. The location of the state government at Albany also provided an impetus for the development of the area.

In 1887 the company built a large steam-powered sawmill at Troy, New York, directly across the Hudson River from Albany, to manufacture lumber for the molding plant. Pine and spruce logs were driven down the Bennington Creek from the western slopes of the Green Mountains; since this was an area that had not previously been cut-over, the logs were of excellent quality and the sawmill was also financially successful.

The company easily survived the various

depressions and financial panics of the late nineteenth and early twentieth centuries. It was even able to operate profitably through much of the Great Depression of the 1930s. By 1950, however, the death of the founder and the subsequent management of the firm through the trust department of a New York City bank brought a series of losses, and in 1952 the company was sold to Henry Trotter, a graduate of the Yale School of Forestry.

> The old gentleman had the rough and crusty reputation of many of the early lumbermen and, while I never met him, I guess it was deserved.
> There were pictures of him around the office when I moved in; he was a tall, strong man, with a big hawk nose; one of the photographs showed him after he had wrestled a bear at a traveling circus or carnival and won.
> He lived until he was 96. The winter before his death he was still able to cruise timber (walk through a track of timber to estimate the volume of merchantable logs and prepare a bid for their purchase from the landowner). He was an institution in the area, and the farmers liked to deal with him. He treated the mill hands harshly; I know that he paid well below the minimum wage, but he provided company housing, and there was always a turkey at Thanksgiving and extra money to meet any medical or emergency expense. It sounds pretty awful now, but the men stayed with him, and he never had a strike.
> The bank, of course, did not know how to run a sawmill, and in their defense it must be admitted that he was a tough act to follow. They sent up that year's graduate of the Harvard Business School in a grey flannel suit and polished, pointed toe shoes. The shift foremen wanted more money and the farmers began bringing in every log the old man had ever refused (because of poor quality), and the profits quickly disappeared.
> The estate was also confused. Since he outlived all his children, his property was split among 25 to 30 grandchildren, great-grandchildren, and cousins twice removed, none of whom lived in the area or wanted to manage the company. They could not agree on what they did want, beyond more income, so the cash reserves disappeared rapidly in losses, estate taxes, and dividends. The bank was looking for a buyer, but it is difficult to sell

an 1872 molding plant and an 1887 sawmill to anyone except the Smithsonian. Eventually the price got down to the level where I could make an offer, and it was accepted. (Statement of Mr. Trotter.)

Mr. Trotter had purchased the company with the intention of producing precut and prefabricated housing components. He closed the sawmill, which had been unprofitable for years, brought the molding plant across the river from Albany to consolidate all operations at Troy, upgraded the machinery, revamped the product line, and changed the company name. The business, now termed Housing Components, Inc., became profitable again almost immediately.

> The sawmill was so ancient it was a curiosity. It had been built in the days of the large original-growth timber, when logs 4 ft in diameter and 20 ft long were common, but it was cutting second-growth scrub pine and hardwood when I bought it, with logs 6 in. or 8 in. or 10 in. in diameter and 10 ft long: Everything was handled at least a dozen times, including the sawdust and wooden scrap which was shoveled by hand into the boilers for fuel.
> I felt badly about closing the mill, since I didn't think that the employees could get other jobs. But many had been there so long that they were eligible for retirement under social security, and the others all seemed to come up smiling. The sawyer, who was 64 and apparently had never spent a nickel of his salary, moved to Florida and made a fortune in real estate speculations. The boilermaker, who was a large and burly citizen, opened a bar in an old stone engine house in Mechanicsville and has been deluged with customers from the local colleges ever since.
> With the sawmill shut down, the cash drain disappeared. Then we were able to use the funds we got from selling the real estate in Albany and the housing in Troy to buy some new machinery and put it in a new building right next to the existing dry kilns, storage sheds, and lumber yard. This gave us the basis for the economical production of millwork (finished wooden pieces).
> I wanted to manufacture pre-cut and prefabricated housing components. This sounded pretty advanced in 1952, but you have to remember that doors and windows and ·the

installation frames for each are, after all, prefabricated housing components, so we did not
change that much. We continued to make
window sash and doorways, both in standard
and special-order sizes, and we kept the machinery to make strip and plank hardwood
flooring. Then we added the equipment to
laminate (glue short pieces into a continuous
structural member) and finish beams and
trusses and to assemble plywood siding and
roofing panels. (Statement of Mr. Trotter.)

The company sold its full line of wooden
doors, windows, flooring, structural members, and panels to lumber yards, building
supply firms, and the larger construction
contractors in the Troy–Albany–Schenectady
area of central New York, though the market
for the laminated beams and roofing panels
extended over much of the northeastern
portion of the United States. Sales during the
period 1952–1965 remained fairly constant
at approximately $1,500,000 per year, and
profits after taxes were in the range of 4%
to 8%.

Two salesmen were employed; both had
been with the company for a number of
years before Mr. Trotter purchased control,
but there seemed to be no reason to make
a change, for they both were well-acquainted
with their customers and conscientious in
their sales calls. The company did a limited
amount of advertising primarily in the form
of support for high school yearbooks and
charitable programs.

> There was no question but that we were
> the dominant factor in our market area; if you
> wanted a window in northeastern New York
> State you came to us. Or, more properly, you
> went to a lumber yard and they came to us.
> We also got quite a bit of business from
> outside our area. This was at a time when the
> large West Coast mills were advertising lami-
> nated beams heavily, with full color ads in
> architectural and housing journals showing
> glowing wooden arches in churches, gymnasi-
> ums, and assembly halls. The architect would
> design the roofing system around the beams
> and then the contractor would get them from
> us to save money. Our prices and margins were
> good since we always knew that we could beat
> the freight from Oregon on a 12-ton beam.

> This was a pleasant time for us. I did not
> have to work too hard and was able to spend
> a lot of time with my family, which I enjoyed.
> (Statement of Mr. Trotter.)

Sales began to decline in 1965, and in
1970 the company recorded the first loss in
18 years. This was disturbing to Mr. Trotter,
who felt that the declining sales reflected a
basic trend in the construction industry away
from quality wooden components, and toward the use of substitute materials.

> Part of the trouble, of course, was the hous-
> ing market in our area. Residential and com-
> mercial construction was down; every index
> showed this, and every person gave this as the
> reason for our loss. Yet, I knew this could
> happen when I bought the company, and it
> was one of the reasons for the low price; this
> is a mature area, and you can't expect the
> growth here that is common in the suburbs
> of Boston, New York, or Philadelphia, or the
> resort areas of Florida.
> Still, there was enough construction to sup-
> port us; there was even enough activities in
> single-family dwellings, which is our primary
> market. I thought that the real trouble was in
> the substitution of materials and methods that
> had come about slowly over the last 20 years.
> Nothing very big ever happens in housing
> technology, but the cumulative effect of these
> minor changes was substantial. First, were the
> doors. We make a rail and mullion type of
> door that is attractive, sturdy, and used to be
> standard; now the West Coast veneer mills
> make a plywood door with flush sides and a
> honeycomb core that is lighter weight, more
> easily damaged, but less expensive. Then, our
> hardwood flooring market disappeared because
> people went to wall-to-wall carpeting laid di-
> rectly on the subfloor or to linoleum and tile.
> When we bought the business, you could not
> even talk to an architect about steel windows
> because of the closure and insulation prob-
> lems. Now, windows come in steel, aluminum,
> vinyl-coated wood, or double-plated glass, and
> they are all acceptable quality. Lastly, many
> companies have gotten into the laminated
> beam and roofing panel business in the north-
> east, all as part of the industrialized housing
> trend of the last few years, so that source of
> sales is closed to us except on a price com-
> petitive basis. The housing components busi-

ness has changed, but we did not change with it. (Statement of Mr. Trotter.)

Mr. Trotter felt that it would not be worthwhile to simply copy some of the newer products among the competitive components since his company seemed to lack the large potential market that was required to repay the necessary investment. Instead, he planned to combine the existing components into a package of prefabricated vacation housing. An architect friend of Mr. Trotter had designed six models of A-frame vacation houses using the company components exclusively. The A-frame is a dwelling unit whose cross section looks like the letter "A"; the steep roof structure forms both the sides and the roof, and the only windows are on the ends. Sleeping accommodations are normally on the balcony, at the crossbar of the "A," while the living room, kitchen, dining room, and bath are on the base. It is a form of construction that is used mainly for vacation but not year-round homes, probably because of its chalet-like appearance and space limitations. It is also a form of construction that is considered to be among the least expensive to build, because of the double function of the roof, and one that is particularly suitable for the do-it-yourself builder because there are no side walls and because the design is simple.

Mr. Trotter was pleased with the design of the prefabricated vacation homes, and he was certain that the company could manufacture and sell the package of components at a competitive price:

> We never sold a package of components before because we thought that any effort we made would conflict with our own customers, who are the lumber yards, the large contractors, and the custom builders. But those people stay pretty close to their own area, and they don't really care what we do over in Vermont or up in the Adirondacks, which is where we intend to sell our vacation homes. Also, I have never been convinced of the value of the modular approach in most single-family residential housing; you always get somebody who wants an extra room for the grandmother or a picture window overlooking the rose

garden, and there is no way to add features in a production-line factory on Long Island. But you can standardize a vacation home because people don't want the extras and that is what we have tried to do. Also, the prefabricated components package does offer some flexibility, anyway.
>
> We feel that we have a good, standard design. We know that we can compete on a price basis since we know our costs on all the components. The other companies that offer A-frame vacation homes on a prefabricated basis just purchase and assemble the parts for shipment; since we make all our parts, we have a savings right at the start. (Statement of Mr. Trotter.)

The vacation home to be offered by Housing Components, Inc. was technically termed a prefabricated shell. It comprised a set of laminated structural members and the two-dimensional panels required for the roof, flooring, and interior partitions; these components were transported to the site by truck and assembled on a concrete foundation by a builder or the customer. A single purchase order would ensure delivery to the site of all necessary components to complete a home of a specific model and size.

The prefabricated shell differed from the prefinished modular house, which was comprised of three-dimensional rooms that were completely finished at the factory and then shipped to the site by truck to be bolted together on the foundation. Because of the prefinishing, the modular house required less labor at the site, but it also demanded much greater standardization since each unit left the assembly line with flooring, carpeting, plumbing, electric, and heating installed and operating. Because of trucking limitations, the prefinished modular house tended to be a blocky, rectangular structure made up of units 12 ft wide and 40 ft long. The prefabricated shell could be of variable size and appearance because it was easy to load and transport the unassembled components.

Prefinished modular housing achieved an unfavorable public image in the summer of 1972 because of the industry problems that resulted in the financial collapse of the Sterling–Homex Corporation. Sterling–Homex had been considered one of the industry leaders, but after reporting a $26.3 million loss for the 10-month period ending May 31, 1972, the company petitioned for a Chapter XI Bankruptcy Act proceeding. This action shocked the housing industry and much of the financial community:

> Sterling-Homex . . . collapsed in July with a bang that is still echoing throughout the industry. . . . The concern is stuck with thousands of modular units—boxlike rooms that are combined to make houses—that it can't deliver, and shareholders are stuck with a stock that sells for less than $1.00 a share in over the counter trading. The stock once traded as high as $51.
>
> Modular, or factory-built housing, to be sure, remains an intriguing idea—producing modules on a factory assembly line, then transporting them to a building site, and swiftly putting them together into a house or an apartment building. Thanks to the factory, builders can avoid the delays of weather and the cost of local labor on the eventual home-sites. Thanks to the assembly line, wage costs should be relatively low. Thanks to both, quality control should be easy. It sounds like an efficiency expert's dream. . . .
>
> Yet, as is now starkly clear to a number of bloodied builders, anguished analysts, and ill investors, it isn't at all what it sounds like. A large factory means high fixed costs and requires high volume. Moving modules can cost $1.00 or more per mile, and laws prohibiting night-time transportation of modules can limit the effective marketing area sharply. Erection can be delayed interminably by local zoning red tape and a welter of conflicting building codes clutched in the hands of skeptical building inspectors. (Making Modular Units Is Easy; Making Money at It Isn't, *The Wall Street Journal*, September 7, 1972, p. 1. Reprinted with permission of *The Wall Street Journal*, © 1972 Dow Jones & Company, Inc. All rights reserved.)

Mr. Trotter planned to avoid the investment, transportation, and zoning problems that he foresaw might be associated with prefinishing modular housing by concentrating exclusively on the prefabricated shell form of construction. As a start toward investigating the feasibility of this new product pack-

age, he commissioned a study of the costs to the customer of three alternative means of constructing a standard three-bedroom A-frame on a 24 ft x 32 ft base. The three alternatives that were considered in these cost comparisons were (1) a custom A-frame, which was considered to be a vacation home of this style and size designed by an architect and built by union labor using commercial lumber and othes materials; (2) a competitive A-frame, which represented an average of the purchase price and construction costs for an equivalent vacation home ordered from the four other companies that offered standard prefabricated A-frames in the northeast; and (3) the Housing Components A-frame, which was designed as described, by a friend of Mr. Trotter. Mr. Trotter was pleased that these comparisons showed an overall cost savings for the Housing Components design (see Exhibit 1).

The additional expenses for land acquisition and road access and for sewage, water, and electrical connections were considered to be equivalent for the three alternatives and were not included in the comparison. The variations in the cost factors that were included in the comparisons can be explained as follows:

1. Material Costs. Housing Components expected the material cost of the completed structure to be considerably greater for their design than for others since their prefabricated methods would carry the components much closer to the finished form, and thus reduce construction labor at the site.

> Our laminated roof beams are surface finished, sanded, and stained, completely ready for use, and they will be shipped with the holes drilled to bolt to the tie plates on the foundation. This raises our sales price—though not as much as you might expect since we can do much of the work by machine—but it definitely reduces the overall cost of construction since it saves onsite labor. Our roofing will be roof length double plywood panels, filled with styrofoam insulation; these go up much more quickly than the usual roofing boards or deck-

EXHIBIT 1 Comparison of consumer costs for custom, competitive, and company designs of three-bedroom A-frame vacation homes, size 24 ft × 32 ft base. (Source: company records.)

	Custom A-frame	*Competitive A-frame*	*Company A-frame*
Material, including structural members, decking, and panels	$ 3,800	$ 4,400	$ 6,000
Freight, from the West Coast	900	900	—
Foundations, prepared by the builder or owner	1,200	1,200	1,200
Assembly labor, performed by the builder or owner	8,000	4,700	3,900
Plumbing, heating and electrical material, and installation	4,700	4,700	3,700
Architectural fee	1,100	—	—
	$19,700	$15,900	$14,800

ing which has to be individually nailed in place. (Statement of Mr. Trotter.)

2. Freight Costs. Housing Components expected to use Eastern spruce and fir lumber, purchased from local sawmills, to laminate their roof beams and to frame their roof and floor panels. Their competitors used white spruce and Douglas fir from the West Coast; three of these companies were located in Washington and Oregon, while the fourth was located in Massachusetts but used western lumber and components exclusively. The use of western lumber generated a savings in fabrication since the roof beams could be sawn timbers and not laminated because of the large size of the logs, but it also resulted in a considerable freight charge on the transportation of the housing package.

We can easily pick up a $900 savings on freight, since all of our present competitors use western lumber. There is actually a greater savings than that since none of them does much manufacturing; they all purchase structural timbers and roofing and floor decking, cut the material to length, combine it with commercially available windows and doors, and ship it as an architectural package. They

have extra costs that we don't have. (Statement of Mr. Trotter.)

3. Assembly Costs. Housing Components expected the construction labor at the site to be an inverse function of the material cost because of the varying degree of prefabrication of the material in each of the three designs. Two contractors who were both customers and friends of Mr. Trotter had furnished estimates of the labor costs for the three designs.

Our design can be built quickly, particularly if the contractor uses a mobile crane to put the A-frame beams and roofing panels in place. The "do-it-yourself" builder may have some trouble here, but he could use deadfalls (a tripod frame built of timbers or structural steel with a manual block and tackle system for hoisting) that we would rent to him. (Statement of Mr. Trotter.)

4. Plumbing, Heating, and Electric. The installation and connection of electrical appliances and plumbing fixtures has always been considered a problem in prefabricated home design.

A prefab isn't always a case of pure pleasure and value for your money. . . . Conventional electrical, plumbing, and heating equipment can be costly. Remember that everything must be transported to the vacation site. The equipment must be correctly installed, often by local workers. You may save on the house shell and lose money on the bath and kitchen. (Prefabs: Summer Homes for the Cost Conscious," *Business Week*, June 27, 1970, p. 105.)

To reduce the plumbing, heating, and electrical expenses, the architect for Housing Components had designed pre-wired and pre-piped kitchen, bath, and utility room (heating, storage, and fireplace) modules that could be assembled at the Troy plant on a timber floor and sidewalls and then shipped to the site by a company truck equipped with a short crane for unloading and placement. These modules were each 6 ft × 12 ft and could be combined in various patterns, provided the foundations were properly prepared. The modules met the rather limited housing codes of northern New York and Vermont and required only connection to water and sewer or septic tank pipes for operation.

I think that the modules are one of the features of our design, although I am not certain how we should sell them. If we talk about modules, people think about something that looks like a house trailer, but all we mean is something that provides a real cost savings. (Statement of Mr. Trotter.)

5. Location. One definite advantage that Housing Components had, which did not appear in the customer cost analysis, was the company location. Troy is just northeast of Albany and just off the New York Thruway and Northway highway systems. It is probably the center of a vacation area that serves the entire metropolitan East Coast.

Our real advantage is our location. The Vermont border is 18 miles to the northeast; Lake George and Lake Champlain are 50 miles to the north, and the Adirondacks are off to the northwest, and these are all vacation areas. Then, the Catskills are to the southwest and the Berkshires to the southeast. The northern areas have not developed much until now,

primarily because of their distance from New York City, but that is changing with the new highway system. Before only the professional skier would drive up to Stowe (in the northern portion of Vermont), but now it is only 2 hours past Troy, and family skiers are going there and building A-frames and condominiums. The State Development Agency in Vermont is talking about 5,000 vacation homes to be built in their state each year for the next 10 years; we ought to be able to get our share of that business. (Statement of Mr. Trotter.)

Mr. Trotter was confident that a potential market existed for the proposed product line of A-frame vacation homes within his natural trading area, and he was certain that the components for these prefabricated homes could be produced and packaged competitively by his millwork plant at Troy; yet he was hesitant to commit the resources necessary to start the new program mainly because he was concerned about the proper marketing of the product.

Everyone tells me that I am ridiculous in not going ahead and that I may miss this opportunity by waiting. My banker says that I ought to just jump in and get my feet wet, but it is not his money that he wants me to invest, it's mine; and I don't like these simple analogies. A lot of people have lost a lot of money in modular housing, prefabricated housing, developmental housing; and I don't like to lose money.

I am concerned mainly about marketing. We have a sales department here, but it consists of two older men, both conscientious and hardworking, but they have been calling on the same lumber yards and contractors for the past 30 years; they don't know how to sell a house. I don't either. I've always looked upon my job as making certain that after receiving an order we produced it as economically and delivered it as quickly as possible. We provided service, and we made money. But, in selling homes, you have to offer something more than service, and I'm not certain what that something is. I'm not even certain who our customers would be: the housewife, the husband, the builder, or the developer.

I don't suppose it is a good term, but there seems to be a bit of P. T. Barnum in every successful real estate man, since they have to sell something that isn't there yet. That is something that we don't have. (Statement of Mr. Trotter.)

In order to limit the financial liability of his company, and to provide a situation that would be attractive to a younger and more aggressive marketing oriented person, Mr. Trotter decided to found a new corporation, Vacation Homes, Inc., with an initial capital in the range of $30,000 to $50,000 and hire a recent M.B.A. as Executive Vice President and General Manager of the firm.

The assignment for the new executive would be to develop a marketing plan for the Housing Components product line of pre-fabricated vacation housing and to supervise sales. Payments to the new company would be on a commission basis, with an 8½% discount, which was standard in the industry for dealers, allowed on the list price of all Housing Components products, including both the A-frame material package and the kitchen, bathroom, and utility room modules. Payments to the new executive would include a salary and a personal commission, both to be charged as expenses against the Vacation Homes 8½% discount income, and the right to purchase equity in the new company on a sliding scale leading toward eventual control and full ownership.

> My idea is to get a good man and let him market the homes his way, and I think that we have to make the package financially attractive to get him. My idea is that he could buy the Vacation Homes division out of his income, using retained profits to build up the company. If he is successful, then we can talk about selling Housing Components to him out of the profits of the combined companies. I would like to get out of the business over the next 10 years, and this seems to offer a way to do it.
> I thought that I could talk to 10 or 15 students who are graduating from business schools this year and who have an interest in either real estate sales or small business management, pick 7 or 8 whom I like and ask them to draw up a marketing plan summarizing

their recommendations for the sale of the A-frames, and then pick one person based upon this competition. The plan would have to be ethical, complete, and understandable to me. (Statement of Mr. Trotter.)

Mr. Trotter was hesitant to release financial information; he did, however, state that Housing Components, in which he owned 100% of the equity, was clear of debt and had a net worth of slightly over $2,000,000. He also stated that the material package for the A-frame homes and the kitchen, bath, and utility room modules was priced to yield a 20% contribution to the overhead and profits of Housing Components, Inc., before subtracting the 8½% sales discount to Vacation Homes.

> 12½% contribution is about as low as I want to go. This is less than we make on our individual components, but I wanted to keep the final price of our A-frame below that of our competition.
> Also, I don't want to be in the position of guaranteeing loans for the new company. I look upon this firm (Housing Components) as my retirement insurance. It was saddled with heavy debt charges when I bought it, and I never want to get into that situation again. The person who comes here is going to have to make do with $30,000 or $50,000 and build the company himself. I had to make sacrifices 20 years ago to get this company going; I want him to make sacrifices now to show his commitment. (Statement of Mr. Trotter.)

ASSIGNMENT

Assume that you are one of the seven or eight students selected to prepare a marketing plan for the A-frame vacation homes and that the salary, personnel commissions, responsibility assignments, ownership possibilities, and the living accommodations in the area are such that you wish strongly to obtain the job offer. What would you recommend?

3

Market Research

In Chapter 2 marketing management was described as the process of adapting the characteristics of a product to fit the needs and wants of customers in a specific market segment and then combining the pricing level, distribution method, personal sales effort, and advertising program into a consistent marketing plan that is adjusted to the characteristics of the product or service and the needs of the customers and their motives for purchase. To repeat the simplified outline of Table 2–1, marketing management can be considered as a sequence of decisions relating product, demand, and decision variables, as shown in Table 3–1.

Marketing success for smaller companies was defined as the design of a distinctive marketing plan that relates the product characteristics, market segment, customer needs, and the pricing, distribution, personal sales, and promotional decisions in an innovative or imaginative manner. Innovation or imagination is needed because it is important that smaller companies not attempt to compete on a product-to-product basis with larger firms, offering the same goods or services to the same customer through the same channels of distribution at approximately the same prices. Instead, they must do something different. This "something different," however, has to be rational and not merely eccentric; the marketing plan has to be based upon a specific identification of the market segment and a

TABLE 3–1

Product variables	Demand variables	Decision variables
Product policy	Customer motivation	Pricing
Product characteristics	Customer behavior	Distribution
Product development	Market segment	Personal selling
	Market environment	Advertising
	Company sales	

definite understanding of the customers' needs and purchasing methods. The identification of the market segment and the understanding of the customer motives and purchasing methods are the functions of market research.

Market research refers to the systematic and comprehensive collection and analysis of information to improve the marketing plan; this research should reduce the uncertainty inherent in the design of the plan, and it should provide some estimate of the resultant market size so that the company can judge the potential of its current products and the opportunity for future ones. The market size, which is dependent on the demand variables, will, of course, vary with the product characteristics and decision variables. This definition of market research can also be expressed graphically:

Customer motivation ⎤		Product characteristics ⎤
	Market size potential	Pricing level
Customer behavior ⎟	↓	
	Market research techniques	Distribution methods ⎬
Market segment ⎬	↓	
	Market size estimate	Advertising program ⎦
Market environment ⎦		

Larger companies employ a wide range of market research techniques, for example, consumer panels, trial markets, test sampling, controlled experiments, and national surveys, that are not directly transferrable to smaller companies. Since the smaller firm, and particularly the beginning company, has to obtain meaningful market information quickly and inexpensively, it must use the simpler and more direct methods of market research, such as publication surveys and customer interviews.

PUBLICATION SURVEYS

There is an enormous amount of published information available. A printing company interested in providing office supplies to business firms within a specific geographic region can easily find the names and addresses of its potential customers in area directories. A software firm that plans to offer production scheduling and inventory control services to a specific industry, rather than to a geographic area, can also identify its potential customers in industry lists. Consumer product companies can obtain data on the income levels, educational achievements, employment types, residential locations, etc., of their potential customers. Although so much published information is available, the problem is to find it and then to evaluate it.

It is not easy to locate directly relevant market information during a publication survey, but some of the sources to be considered by a small business firm are government publications, industry associations, area organizations, trade journals, and business magazines:

1. Government Publications. The U.S. census is not only the best known, it is also the most complete of the government publications; it is summarized in the *Statistical Abstract of the United States,* which is probably the most useful, for it provides basic background information on income levels, employment figures, industry outputs, etc. The *Statistical Abstract* is available in nearly every library. In addition to the census, there is a wide range of material available from such agencies as the Department of Commerce or the Department of Labor; all of this material that was prepared specifically for smaller business firms is listed in *A Survey of Federal Government Publications of Interest to Small Business,* available from the Small Business Administration. Materials prepared for other purposes, such as studies by regulatory agencies or reports by congressional committees, are much more difficult to find and are generally available only at the large libraries of major universities, but they are often worth the search. Much of the needed background data for small business market research is available through government publications.

2. Industry Associations. Almost all industries, such as the Woodworking Machinery Manufacturers or the Welding Supply Distributors, have an association of members; very often these associations will supply to their members information on legislative problems, market trends, or comparative costs. Some of these associations will supply copies of their reports to anyone who contacts their headquarters office. Another method is to contact one of the local members of the association and ask permission to read his reports. There is seldom any strictly confidential material in the association reports, but much of the market and cost information may not be available elsewhere.

3. Area Organizations. Within each state there is a Department of Commerce, or the equivalent, which will provide a list of companies—generally broken down into industry, size, and geographic location—that operate within the state. In addition, the Department of Commerce may also publish reports on the more important industries operating in the region; although these reports are prepared to further industrial development, they do contain data on wage rates, material supplies, etc. The reports may be obtained from the state capitol. The Chamber of Commerce within each major city usually publishes a list of companies located within the area; this list is very useful for industrial sales information.

4. Trade Journals. Many industries have a weekly or monthly trade journal, for example, *Electronic News* or *Railway Age.* The material published in trade journals normally deals with product improvements or process descriptions; little direct information on markets or marketing is included, but the indirect statements and summaries can be very useful.

5. Business Magazines and Newspapers. The last sources of published information are the articles in business magazines, such as *Fortune* or *Business Week,* and in business newspapers, such as *The Wall Street Journal* or *The New York Times.* These articles usually describe existing companies or proposed products or processes; again, they include relatively little direct information on customers or markets, but they do offer general industry information that can be useful for market research by small business firms.

The data found in the publication survey should be evaluated carefully before reliance is put upon it for small business decisions. The problem is not that the information is deliberately misleading or inaccurate; it is that since the reports, whether from government publications, industry associations, area organizations, trade journals, or business magazines, were prepared for a different use, the data may be incomplete, inapplicable, or, occasionally, poorly prepared and wrong.

The smaller business firm generally does not have the time and is too far away from a large research library to verify the published data for currentness, completeness, and accuracy. The smaller company has to rely on personal interviews and informed opinions to verify and interpret the published sources.

PERSONAL INTERVIEWS

Although there is a tremendous amount of market information available through published sources, there is also a lot of market information available through talking with people, both potential customers and others who are active in the industry or in an associated industry. Smaller business firms, or people who are planning to start a small company, probably cannot ask competitors for market information, but they can and should ask distributors, suppliers, and customers. The opinions of wholesalers or retailers in the channels of distribution for a new product can be very helpful; there is a small but very successful construction equipment manufacturer in Iowa that performs market research on new products by asking competitive dealers, not customers or company representatives, for their opinions on alternative product features. Suppliers also often have both opinions and market data that can be useful to the smaller company. A small restaurant chain in western Michigan relies on location studies provided by one of the large breweries as an aid in starting new franchises. The final customer, obviously, also has opinions on market needs and product characteristics that must be understood by the smaller business firm.

Not only is contacting distributors, suppliers, and customers time-consuming and costly, it may also provide misleading information if the interview process is not carefully planned. It is necessary to plan, in detail, the interview type and method, product or service definition, question content and wording, answer format, market segment, sample selection, interview process, response recording, and data analysis before calling or meeting the first informant.

1. Interview Type. The interview may be either structured, in which the interviewer asks the same questions in the same order from each person, or unstructured, in which any questions are asked in any order. The structured interview is usually used for customer interviews, for personal opinions, not definite information, are expected. The unstructured interview is for suppliers or distributors, who can supply informed opinions and industry information. Nevertheless, the unstructured interview should still be carefully planned. General questions should be prepared in advance in order to obtain the needed market information quickly and accurately.

2. Interview Method. The method of an interview refers to the form of communication; this form may use personal conversations, telephone calls, or direct mail. Personal interviews permit longer questionnaires and a much less structured format, but they are very time-consuming and expensive; telephone calls are less costly, but they are also less satisfactory, for many people dislike giving opinions or information over the telephone; direct mail contacts are the lowest-cost form of primary data collection, but they tend to be biased, for the returns come only from persons who have an interest in the subject.

3. Product or Service Definition. One of the major problems in market research for the smaller business firm is the definition of the product or service that is to be offered. Smaller companies tend to provide specialized products or personalized services in order to avoid competition with the larger firms. It is difficult to describe the important characteristics of these special products or personal services in concise terms that are meaningful to the respondent, who may well be an uninformed potential customer. The smaller business firm or the person planning to start a small company should spend a very considerable amount of time defining the features, both tangible and intangible, of the product or the advantages, both personal and financial, of the service. The person who can concisely and accurately explain what the sale of his product or service will do for the benefit of his customer, rather than for the benefit of himself, will probably be successful in operating a smaller business.

4. Question Content. The question content refers to the information sought by each question during the interview. Obviously, this information should relate to the features and advantages that have been defined for the product or service. In order to avoid bias and misunderstanding, it is also useful to consider the probable answer to each question, and the range of possible answers, in the design of question content.

5. Question Wording. Because there are assumptions and ambiguities inherent in almost all communication, it is necessary to consider both the wording and the content of the questions carefully so that bias and misunderstandings can be reduced, if not eliminated. It is also useful to test the questionnaire in experimental interviews in order to recognize and remove these biases and misunderstandings.

6. Answer Format. The answer format refers to the measurement structure designed to record the information sought by each question during the interview process. The questions range from open-ended (accept any response that can be written down verbally), to multiple-choice (accept any of a specified number of responses that can be recorded on a chart or list), to dichotomous (accept only one of two definite responses). Dichotomous questions are very easy to record, code, and analyze, but they severely limit customer replies. Open-ended questions are difficult to record, code, and analyze, but they do permit complete and in-depth replies. Multiple choice questions occupy a middle ground, with some of the benefits and some of the problems of the other two types.

7. Market Segment. Another of the major problems in market research for the smaller business firm is the definition of the market segment that has been selected for the product or service. Smaller companies tend to sell to small but very specific market segments in order to avoid competition with larger firms; it is difficult, however, to describe the important characteristics of these segments in concise and measurable terms. In conducting market research, it is not enough to have a general and intuitive feeling for the members of the market segment. Instead, it is necessary to define the members of the target market by describing their socioeconomic characteristics (age, sex, income level, etc.), their geographic characteristics (section of the country, residential area, etc.), and the behavioral characteristics (usage rate, buyer motives, etc.) so that the individuals can be located and identified for interviews. Since smaller companies usually sell distinctive products or services to definite groups of people, it is necessary to be able to identify these groups accurately in order to be able to gather their opinions and evaluate their responses through the interview process. The person who can concisely and accurately explain the salient characteristics of his customers will probably be successful in operating a smaller business.

8. Sample Selection. After the members of the market segment have been clearly identified, it is necessary to select a sample of the total membership for the interviews. This selection process can either be based upon a probability sample, in which each person or organization within the market segment has a known and equal chance of being chosen, or upon a nonprobability sample, in which some members are deliberately chosen, without an equal chance at being selected, because of their particular knowledge or position. Nonprobability sampling ranges from asking a few friends and neighbors to a systematic selection of participants based upon known characteristics. For example, a company planning to start a sailboat distribution center, with discounted prices and immediate delivery, similar to the much more familiar discount appliance or furniture stores, could research the concept by using a probability sample drawn from all the residents of the area or by using a nonprobability sample drawn only from those residents who are also members of a yacht or boat club in the region. These two methods of sampling would provide very different responses to items on the questionnaire, but hopefully the data analysis would eventually provide the same forecast of the market size potential. Overall, it is necessary to decide which of the two methods of sample selection is most likely to give the most reliable information about a specific product or service.

9. Interview Process. After the market segment has been defined and after the means of sampling from the total population has been selected, it is necessary to conduct the field interviews. Interviewing with a prepared questionnaire and a defined sample is not technically difficult, but it is time-consuming and can be very tiresome. Many small business owners, or potential owners, have found that their informants have a very limited interest in the subject matter of the questionnaire, and an even lesser tolerance for being interrupted in their normal activities. Most people, however, are willing to help a smaller firm, but this, too, can be a problem: people give answers that they believe the interviewer wants to hear, not their true opinions, if they feel sympathetic toward the interviewer or supportive of the topic of the market research. The questions must be carefully designed in order to avoid this kind-hearted but disruptive bias.

10. Response Recording. Answers obtained from the interview process must be edited, coded, and tabulated. Editing eliminates errors or interprets incomplete or unclear responses. Coding establishes the categories for the classification of the edited responses, following the requirements of the answer format, that is, open-ended, multiple-choice, or dichotomous. Tabulation records the number of responses in each category and summarizes the results.

11. Data Analysis. After the review responses are edited, coded, and tabulated, they must be analyzed in order to develop meaningful conclusions from the research and practical recommendations for the design or improvement of the marketing plan. For larger companies, this is the task of statistical inference and estimation, which can provide either a confidence interval, or a nonparametric test of significance for measurements of large-scale probability samples. The relationships within the statistical data can also be examined by multiple correlation and regression analysis. Since the smaller company, however, does not normally have a large enough sample to enjoy statistical validity, it must attempt to analyze the data and understand the results by simpler means, for example, by cross tabulation or simple regression.

Both published sources and personal interviews provide information for smaller firms interested in investigating the market size potential for new or improved products or services. However, the process of collecting this information differs markedly between large and small companies, and the entrepreneur must be able to recognize these differences.

Executives in large companies are concerned with selling established products to substantial markets in which there are hundreds of thousands or even millions of customers in large regional or national market segments; the executives, however, are generally separated from their customers by a complicated distribution network of division headquarters, branch offices, area wholesalers, and local retailers so that casual observation of the market is neither sufficient nor possible. Instead, they have a need for a systematic and comprehensive collection and analysis of market and customer data to improve the marketing plan for their products. Large-scale market research performs this function.

Large-scale market research, however, is expensive; it is very easy to spend $250,000 in package research to determine the "right" size, shape, color, and material for the packaging of a consumer product or to spend $1,000,000 in a motivational study to investigate the reasons for the purchase of the product. The larger firm can spend these substantial sums since success in the market guarantees recovery of the investment. The smaller firm has neither the money, the potential market size, nor the established products; it must gather market and customer information, but it must do it by innovative, nonconventional, inexpensive means and not by systematic and comprehensive research studies. The smaller firm must recognize that it will probably never have statistically reliable data upon which to base marketing decisions.

Yet, the smaller company needs an estimate of the potential market size for its products, and it needs an understanding of the influence of the various decision variables (product characteristics, pricing level, distribution channels, and promotional methods) on this market size. For the beginning company, this market evaluation and customer understanding are essential. The executives of these smaller or beginning firms have an advantage in that they are closer to the market and to their customers, and they are better able to design a market research method that will provide the needed information at minimal expense. They also have disadvantages, for the product or service they are offering is usually specialized or personalized (thus, the product characteristics may not be known to their potential customers and may be difficult to describe briefly), the market segment they are supplying is usually narrow, and the members may be difficult to locate and identify precisely. The smaller company or beginning company also has the disadvantage that both time and money are limited. Nevertheless, these disadvantages can be overcome. Market research for the smaller company does not have to be complex and costly; it does, however, have to be planned. The executives of a smaller company engaged in a market research study to improve their marketing plan or to estimate their market potential should plan their approach carefully and pay particular attention to the following questions:

1. What are the features, both tangible and intangible, of the product or service that is being offered for sale?

2. What questions should be asked about this product or service in order to obtain needed information without incurring bias or misunderstanding?

3. What are the characteristics, in specific and measurable terms, of the customers in the market segment selected for the product or service?

4. How should people be selected from the market segment in order to get responses that are representative of all the members of the segment?

5. How should the responses to the questions asked during interviews be evaluated and analyzed?

The managers of small companies have to understand what questions they should ask, who they should ask, and how they should analyze the responses, but they don't have to ask large numbers of potential customers, and they don't have to limit their market research activities to formal interviews. Government publications, industry associations, and area organizations have market and customer information, much of which is available in printed form, and suppliers and distributors of equivalent products or substitute products are often willing to provide some help and assistance. Experimental market testing can also provide information at minimal cost. Planned customer interviews, though statistically unreliable because they are on a small scale, can offer definite evidence of customer wants and needs. Useful facts about the market and the customer for a new or existing product are available, but the executive of the smaller firm has to use imagination, innovation, and perception to find them. The three following cases illustrate the need for this nonsystematic approach to market research for the smaller firm.

Racketball Corporation of New England

Racketball is a game that is played with a short strung racket and a lively ball in an enclosed handball court; the object of the game is to hit the ball against the front wall of the court in such a way that it cannot be returned before it has bounced twice on the floor. Since the ball is kept in play by the side walls, the back wall, and the ceiling, each point tends to be closely contested, with numerous shots by each player; the result is that the game is both exciting and strenuous:

> You keep hearing that 20 minutes of racketball is equivalent to 1 hour of tennis or 4 hours of golf, and I guess that's true for well-conditioned athletes. But, for the rest of us, it's possible to slow down the pace and rest between points. The real advantage of racketball is that it's a lot of fun. The ball stays in

play because it's kept within the court, and two players who aren't very good can keep an exchange going because the ball has to bounce off the walls and come someplace where they can hit it. In tennis, the duffer always hits the ball out of the court; in racketball, that's impossible, so that you get these long exchanges. The long exchanges provide the excitement, the exercise, and variety since you can angle your shots off any of the walls. You win in racketball by using the angle shot and by out-thinking your opponent; you pretend that you're going to hit a soft tap off the front wall, so that you get him running forward, and then you hit a hard smash that will go all the way to the back wall. He has to reverse directions, hurry back, and try to return it on the first bounce. The game is a lot of fun; I don't know why it has never caught on in the East. (Statement of George Stapleton.)

Racketball is played primarily in the midwest since it was developed in that area. There are a number of traditions that ascribe the development of racketball to various colleges or universities, but all are in general agreement that the game started during the 1930s as a means of using the handball courts that had been built during the previous decade by most of the members of the Big-Ten athletic conference. Handball requires very precise hand–eye coordination and continual practice to sling the ball rather than slap at it; it is a difficult, demanding game that, since it helps to develop speed, coordination, and endurance, was used during the 1920s as a conditioning program for other sports. The longer seasons and extended practice for football, basketball, and baseball meant that the handball courts were no longer needed for conditioning and training varsity athletes. Many remained vacant until the development of an easier game:

> Handball is played on public outdoor courts in New York City and California and on private indoor courts in some of the athletic clubs in the larger cities, but it is not a popular sport because of the skill and stamina required. There is a small band of very devoted handball enthusiasts, whom you could not get to play any other game, but

there just aren't enough of them to use the available courts at the larger colleges and universities. There were 14 courts at the University of Michigan, for example, 30 at the University of Chicago—before they converted most of them there to the first atomic laboratory, and 24 at Ohio State. These athletic facilities were built when the schools were much smaller than they are now, and most of the members of the faculty and the students had no use for them. Some athletic director somewhere had the idea of making the game easier by hitting the ball with a big Ping-Pong paddle (for paddleball) or with a short tennis racket (for racketball). These new sports caught on, but only in the midwest where the courts were available. Racketball could be popular everywhere if the courts were available and if the sport were promoted. I want to build the courts and promote the sport. (Statement of George Stapleton.)

George Stapleton, a 1968 graduate of the University of Wisconsin with a B.S. in electrical engineering and a 1970 graduate of the University of Pittsburgh with an M.B.A. in quantitative methods, wanted to build six racketball courts and promote racketball in Dedham, Massachusetts, a southwestern suburb of Boston. He had selected Dedham because he worked for a software consulting firm in that area which permitted its employees to work part-time for local, noncompetitive businesses in that area:

> The company I work for encourages us to participate in local politics and to invest in local firms. This attitude is not entirely gratuitous on its part, of course; it wants to keep its employees happy and content and fully occupied since it is so easy for a competent systems analyst, who is not happy and content or fully occupied, to start a new software firm, particularly in our field which combines the behavioral implications of information with the technical design of the system. The owners of the company will even put up half of the equity for these ventures, provided there is a good market potential. I'm certain that there's a good market potential for racketball in this area. (Statement of George Stapleton.)

Mr. Stapleton recognized that indoor tennis would affect the market potential for racketball, because of the similarity between the two sports, and he knew that 3 clubs with a total of 20 indoor courts were already in existence in the southwest suburban area and that 2 more clubs, each with 6 indoor courts, were in the tentative planning stage, but he was not overly concerned about this competition. He believed that the popularity of tennis would continue to increase, with more players each year looking for indoor accommodations either for tennis or for an equivalent racket sport during the winter months. He also felt that the existing and planned indoor tennis courts in the area could not satisfy this potential demand for racket sports during the winter. He was certain that racketball had enough competitive advantages over indoor tennis to capture this demand.

Tennis has increased rapidly in popularity over the past 10 years; it is now estimated that there are approximately 13,000,000 tennis players in the United States, or 6.3% of the total population (see Exhibit 1).

The reasons usually given for this increased growth in the popularity of tennis, which became particularly noticeable after 1965, include the increased television coverage of the major tournaments, which started in about that year, and the emergence, also at about the same time, of attractive new stars such as Stan Smith, Chris Evert, Arthur Ashe, Billie Jean King, Rod Laver, and John Newcombe. It has been claimed, though this is probably an overstatement, that the Billie Jean King vs. Bobby Riggs match on television induced nearly one million people to try the sport. It is known that large numbers of new people do try the sport each year because the sales of tennis equipment, rackets, balls, and clothing are now growing at 12% compounded annually.

Other reasons for the growth in tennis, in addition to the televised promotions and attractive players, would certainly include the much more widespread interest in exercise and physical conditioning, as a preventive against heart attacks, and the increased affluence and family income that have generated much more leisure time. The definite increase in family income, if corrected for inflation, almost exactly matches the estimated increase in the number of tennis players (see Exhibit 2).

Mr. Stapleton felt that the close correlation between the increase in family income and the increase in tennis popularity indicated that tennis remained a game of the more wealthy segments of society:

> There used to be a considerable element of snobbishness in the game of tennis. It was originally a royal game in medieval Europe, played by kings and nobles in a castle courtyard (that is why the present area where one plays tennis is called a court). Do you remember in the play by Shakespeare on Henry V that King Louis of France sends him a gift of tennis balls to indicate that he was a player and wastrel? And did you know that the scoring system still in use today comes from court expressions, for example, "love" for zero is derived from the French "l'oeuf" for goose egg and "deuce" for an even score between two players comes from "deux" for two? Even the name of the game is derived from the French "Tenez," or "take it," which the players called as they gave up a point.
>
> Tennis was reinvented as a lawn game in England during the late nineteenth century,

---

EXHIBIT 1 Total population and tennis players (estimated) within the United States, 1950 to 1972. (Source: U.S. Bureau of the Census, *Statistical Abstract of the U.S.,* 1973.)

	1950	*1960*	*1965*	*1970*	*1972*
Total population (millions)	151.3	180.7	199.3	204.9	208.8
Tennis players (millions)	1.5	2.0	4.0	11.0	13.0
Tennis players as percentage of the total population	1.0%	1.1%	2.0%	5.3%	6.3%

EXHIBIT 2 Number of households earning over $15,000 per year and number of tennis players (estimated) within the United States, 1950 to 1972. (Source: U.S. Bureau of the Census, *Statistical Abstract of the U.S.,* 1973, p. 39 for number of households and p. 328 for distribution of income of households. Industry estimate for the number of tennis players.)

	1950	1960	1965	1970	1972
Number of households over $15,000 income (millions)	1.49	2.17	4.96	15.0	17.5
Index of households over $15,000 (1960 = 100)	70	100	228	691	892
Number of tennis players in U.S. (millions)	1.5	2.0	4.0	11.0	13.0
Index of tennis players in U.S. (1960 = 100)	75	100	200	550	650

and for a short time this game was called lawn tennis, while the earlier version was called court tennis. But since lawn tennis came to be played on a hard-surfaced court, the distinction became very confusing, and you seldom run across it today except in very old-fashioned texts and in the Wimbledon championships. You do have to remember, however, that lawn tennis is a very recent innovation in the U.S.; the first trophy for a match between Great Britain and the U.S. was provided by a Harvard undergraduate named Dwight Davis in 1905. This is now the well-known Davis Cup for international competition.

The tradition of royal antecedents, the invention among the English country gentry, and the introduction in private colleges and clubs in the U.S. all served to provide tennis with a certain element of snobbishness and social superiority. But, thankfully, that has largely disappeared today, since public courts were built throughout the country during the 1950s and the game was energetically promoted on television during the 1960s. Tennis, however, still remains a game that you are more likely to play if you come from the upper 25% of the income distribution rather than the lower 25%; this is very much in our favor since this southwestern area is an upper-income suburb. (Statement of Mr. George Stapleton.)

Mr. Stapleton defined his market area in the southeastern suburbs by drawing a circle on a map of Boston with a radius of 7 miles and the center on the proposed location of the indoor courts, on High Street in Dedham, just off Route 128, which is the major arterial highway into Boston. He selected the radius of 7 miles because he considered this to be the equivalent of 20 minutes driving time at an average city speed of 25 miles per hour, and he felt that this was the maximum time that people would travel to play either indoor tennis or racketball. This circle included portions of the suburban towns of Dedham, Westwood, Norwood, Canton, Randolph, Milton, Mattapan, Roslindale, Brookline, Newton, and Needham. Working from the census data and market statistics compiled by the chambers of commerce for each of these towns, he developed a profile of the area, which indicated that it was young, affluent, and growing (see Exhibit 3).

Mr. Stapleton had reliable information only up to 1970, but he extrapolated that in 1972 there were 229,000 persons and 63,000 households in the market area. Exhibits 4 and 5 break the 1970 households down according to age and income.

Mr. Stapleton estimated (also by extrapolation) that in 1972 there were 33,500 households in the market area with an income greater than $15,000 per year. If he assumed that 20% of the members of these households with an income over $15,000 played tennis, and this seemed to be a safe

EXHIBIT 3 Actual and projected growth of the market area of the Racketball Corporation of New England (circle with a 7-mile radius centered on Dedham, Massachusetts), 1960 to 1980 (estimated). (Source: company records.)

	1960	1965	1970	1975 (est.)	1980 (est.)
Population within area	137,300	170,100	209,700	261,000	295,000
Households within area	36,400	44,700	56,200	73,000	86,000
Persons per household	3.76	3.80	3.73	3.57	3.43

EXHIBIT 4 Age distribution of heads of households within the market area of the Racketball Corporation of New England, 1970. (Source: company records.)

	Under 25	25–34	35–44	45–54	55–64	Over 65
Percentage	4.8%	20.9%	26.5%	23.5%	13.3%	11.1%
Number (1970)	2,500	11,700	14,900	13,200	7,500	6,400

EXHIBIT 5 Income distribution of households within the market area of the New England Racketball Corporation, 1970. (Source: company records.)

	Under $5000	$5–10,000	$10–15,000	$15–20,000	$20–25,000	Over $25,000
Percentage	7.2%	20.4%	19.4%	25.6%	22.6%	4.8%
Number (1970)	4,000	11,400	10,900	14,500	12,700	2,700
Number over $15,000 income:				29,900		

assumption since 6.3% of the total population nationally played tennis (see Exhibit 1), then there were 24,120 tennis players in the market area (33,500 households with an income greater than $15,000 × 20% for the ratio of tennis players × 3.6 for the number of persons per household).

In addition to the residents within the southwestern suburban area, Mr. Stapleton recognized that there were a number of executives, engineers, and scientists who worked for the electronic, data processing, and high technology firms that were located along Route 128, the peripheral highway around Boston. These firms had been attracted to the Boston area by the availability of scientific talent from the Cambridge universities and venture capital from the Boston banks, and they had become established in the suburbs because the cost of land was low and because commuting was easy. Again, using census data and market statistics from the chambers of commerce in each of the 11 cities and towns within his market area, Mr. Stapleton estimated that there were 68 manufacturing and research firms inside the 7-mile circle, with 11,500 employees divided by function and position as shown in Exhibit 6.

Mr. Stapleton believed that, in addition to the 4,400 executives and scientists employed in the local manufacturing and research firms, he could count upon an equal amount of managers in the area in the wholesale and retail trades, service and utility firms, and finance, insurance, and real estate offices. Again, assuming that 20% of these managerial and professional people played tennis, there were probably another

EXHIBIT 6 Employment distribution of manufacturing and research firms within the market area of the Racketball Corporation of New England, 1970. (Source: company records.)

	Executives and managerial personnel	Scientists and professional personnel	Hourly paid employees
Employment	2,100	2,300	7,100

2,000 potential customers for the existing indoor tennis courts and the planned racketball facility.

The 24,000 estimated residential tennis players and the 2,000 estimated employed tennis players in the area seemed to indicate to Mr. Stapleton an unsaturated market for the 20 existing indoor tennis courts. He felt that each indoor court would be open 16 hours per day (8:00 in the morning to 12:00 at night) for 7 days each week during the winter season, and that an average of 3 persons (half of the games would be singles and half doubles) would use each court each hour; this meant that each indoor court could accommodate 336 persons playing once per week. Since there were 20 indoor courts in the area, only about 6,700 persons could play indoor tennis during the winter; this was less than 25% of the potential market.

Mr. Stapleton felt that not only did he have an unsaturated market, but that he also had a superior product. Racketball, he was certain, was inherently less expensive than indoor tennis, easier to learn, more fun to play, and a welcome wintertime change from the outdoor tennis that is popular during the summer. He felt that racketball would be less expensive (in court rental charges for the players) because the courts are much smaller, and, therefore, less costly to enclose (see Exhibit 7).

The reduced court rental charges for racketball reflected the nearly 3:1 construction cost advantage of the sport; this 3:1 ratio could be increased to 4:1 if the concrete walls of the racketball courts were also used as the exterior walls of the building and as the support columns for the roof. Indoor tennis courts require a 100-ft wide

EXHIBIT 7 Comparison of indoor tennis and racketball court dimensions, construction costs, and typical rental charges. (Source: company records.)

	Indoor tennis	Racketball
Court size	27' × 78' (singles) 36' × 78' (doubles)	20' × 40'
Court size, with margin for play	45' × 120'	20' × 40'
Court area	5,400 sq ft	800 sq ft
Building cost to enclose each court at $14/sq ft for steel building	$75,600	$11,200
Court cost, to construct each court:	$6,500	$17,600
At $1.20/sq ft for tennis court for court surface and net		
At $22.00/sq ft for racketball for court surface and walls		
Total cost per court	$82,100	$28,800
Typical rental charges per court	$12 to $16 per hour	$4 to $6 per hour

clear expanse without columns or posts to support the roof; consequently, strong and expensive steel trusses must be used. Racketball courts can be covered crosswise so that lighter and less expensive bar joists only 20 ft long are required. Combining the structure of the courts with the components of the building in this fashion could, Mr. Stapleton was told, reduce the total cost of each racketball court to $24,000.

Mr. Stapleton believed that the reduced court rental charges for racketball made available through the decreased court construction costs for the sport would be important to potential customers even though they were in the higher-income market segment. He thought that most people like to play a competitive sport, such as tennis or racketball, at least twice a week, and that the confirmed amateur athlete likes to play three or four times a week, but that very few persons can afford the luxury of repetitive play on indoor tennis courts. For indoor tennis, the usual arrangement is that a person pays an annual membership charge and then signs up for a seasonal court reservation at a specific time each week; additional time is available, on an optional basis, if the courts are not reserved. Both the seasonal and the optional charges vary, depending on the time selected; weekday evenings and weekend mornings and afternoons are the most popular, while week-

days before 5:00 p.m. and weekends after 6:00 p.m. are less in demand, and consequently about 25% less in price. Despite subtracting the discounts available for the less popular times, and despite dividing the court rental charges by the number of persons playing, the cost per hour for each individual remains high for indoor tennis (see Exhibit 8).

Most indoor tennis courts stress the $3.50 per hour individual charge for doubles, but they don't mention the need to have four people who can meet at the same hour each week throughout the season; often one member of the group is ill or out of town on a business trip, and it is necessary either for two of the others to play singles and pay the increased cost per person or for the three to find a substitute at very short notice. Also, the individual cost per person is not really applicable to married couples, who might like to play tennis in the evenings. The charge is $16.00 per hour, nearly equivalent to the cost of a restaurant dinner, and certainly a substantial portion of the entertainment or recreational budget of any family on a repetitive basis.

Racketball has a definite price advantage because the courts are so much smaller, but the courts don't look much smaller. A racketball court looks very big when you are inside playing, much bigger than the typical squash

---

EXHIBIT 8 Comparison of indoor tennis and racketball membership fees and court rental costs. (Source: company records.)

	Indoor tennis	*Racketball*
Annual membership charges:		
Single person	$100/season	$100/season
Family membership	$150/season	$100/season
Annual court rental charges:		
Evenings and weekend prime time	$416/season	$156/season
Mornings and afternoons	$312/season	$104/season
Optional court rental charges:		
Evenings and weekend prime time	$16.00/hour	$6.00/hour
Mornings and afternoons	$12.00/hour	$4.00/season
Average court rental per person:		
For singles (2 persons)	$7.00/hour	$2.50/hour
For doubles (4 persons)	$3.50/hour	$1.25/season

court, so that people will think that we offer more value for their money, and that is a good position for us to be in relative to indoor tennis. (Statement of George Stapleton.)

In addition to the lower price, Mr. Stapleton felt that racketball had a number of other competitive advantages over indoor tennis. He believed that racketball was much simpler to learn and much easier for the beginning player to enjoy, since the ball stayed within the court and thus stayed in play for the lengthy exchanges which made the game both energetic and exciting:

> Very simply, racketball is more fun than tennis. The ball has to stay inside the court, so that it has to come someplace where you can hit it, and you can hit it as hard as you like. Coordination and skill are useful, but they're not essential in racketball. I think that we can even get people who don't play tennis to start with this sport.
>
> I don't think that anyone sympathizes enough with beginning tennis players. When they go out on a tennis court for the first time, they hit the ball onto the next court and have to go to get it. Then they hit the ball over the fence, and all the good players glare at them. It isn't much fun. This doesn't happen in racketball since they are inside a closed court, without anyone watching them or anyone criticizing them. They can practice as much as they want and hit the ball as hard as they like without annoying anyone else, and they have a good time. The four walls and ceiling of a racketball court can hide a thousand errors and can make a beginning player or inexperienced athlete feel like a world champion. You know, last week I was dictating a letter to a banker in which I was trying to describe the benefits of the game for beginners, and the girl in the stenographic pool said that she had never played tennis because she was too embarrassed to start, but that she would like to try this game.
>
> Nevertheless, I don't want your students to think that this game is just for timid stenographers or beginning tennis players. Racketball is easy to learn, which is good since there aren't many experienced players in this area, but it is also cheaper than indoor tennis and more fun to play, so that most of our customers will be good tennis players who want

a change during the winter or confirmed athletes who want to play any sport more often than once a week.

Lastly, the game can be more energetic than tennis. Since it has been described as "enjoyable jogging," we ought to get the people who are concerned about physical health and weight control. We have a good game that happens to be new to this area, but it has so many advantages that I'm not concerned about the competition with indoor tennis. (Statement of George Stapleton.)

Mr. Stapleton planned to construct a building with six racketball courts, showers and dressing room facilities, office, lounge, and bar. He thought that it was essential that the building be clean, colorful, well-lighted, and attractive, in order to avoid the stereotyped college or Y.M.C.A. locker room atmosphere, and he expected to spend more money than was basically required at the start in order to achieve this. He intended to cover the entrance hall, lounge, office, and dressing rooms with a bright red carpet that would contrast with the white walls of the courts but would match the paint of the bar and office trim. He also intended to install individual tiled showers for each dressing room and to provide extra-large lockers. Each player would use a private locker, with a key to protect his or her belongings, but these would not be permanently assigned since it is difficult to prevent stale odors if the players leave sweaty gym clothing in the dressing room. The courts were to be built with floors and walls of poured concrete covered with interlocking hardwood panels, since this construction method was considered to combine the finest playing surface with the simplest maintenance characteristics. In short, Mr. Stapleton was determined that the entire racketball facility was to be well-built, clean, colorful, and attractive:

> Many of the early indoor tennis courts were too spartan; they were put in a bare steel building, without insulation, that was often cold and drafty; many of them had good courts, but the showers were cheap, the lockers were smelly, and the dressing rooms were

cramped. I think that this cut-rate approach is the wrong atmosphere for recreation. It's hard to have a good time if you're cold, cramped, and uncomfortable.

We don't expect our building to be opulent, but we do expect it to be comfortable. We're going to spend the extra money to have a clean, well-lighted, pleasant building; we're going to keep it warm during the winter, and we're going to provide oversize towels that will be crisp from a heated storage bin, and we're going to have individual soap bars and plenty of hot water. Then, we'll serve free coffee or iced tea to the players after they've finished their game, and we'll also, of course, have a small bar and sell homemade sandwiches, snacks, beer, and mixed drinks, so that people can sit in the lounge after they play, watch some of the other games through the plate-glass window at the back of each court, relax, and have a good time. Some people have told me that our customers will drive to Boston to play racketball or handball at the Y.M.C.A. Well, they can't have a good, cold martini on the rocks with a twist of lemon at the "Y." We'll have the right atmosphere for recreation. (Statement of George Stapleton.)

An architect had estimated the cost of the racketball facility proposed by Mr. Stapleton at $253,000, with the construction details as described in Exhibit 9.

Mr. Stapleton recognized that the proposed building with its 6 racketball courts would provide 672 court hours per week, which he divided into the time periods shown in Exhibit 10 for pricing and promotion.

Mr. Stapleton then estimated that the total revenues from these courts (over a 26-week season) and including membership fees, rental charges, and contributions from the sale of auxiliary services, would be $125,220. This estimate was based upon a 75% occupancy rate, which he felt could easily be achieved over the first season (see Exhibit 11).

Mr. Stapleton also estimated the costs of operation, including interest on the mortgage and depreciation on the building, at $49,110 (shown in Exhibit 12).

Lastly, Mr. Stapleton estimated that the occupancy would increase from 75% in the first year of operations to 90% in the second year and then to 100% in the third year, and he computed the profits after taxes (at a corporate tax rate of 20% on the first $25,000 of profits and 52% on all subsequent profits annually) and the cash flow (profits after taxes plus depreciation) for these three years. The total cash flow for the period was $193,200 (see Exhibit 13).

The total cash flow for the period of $193,200 was almost enough to pay off the mortgage on the building 17 years early; the average annual cash flow of $64,400 constituted a return on equity of 128%. Mr.

EXHIBIT 9 Construction costs of the proposed building for the Racketball Corporation of New England. (Source: company records.)

Six racketball courts, with poured concrete floors and walls, covered with interlocking hardwood panels, and designed to utilize the court structure for the exterior walls of the building and the interior supports of the roof	$144,000
Two large dressing rooms with individual showers and lockers	22,000
Office, lounge, and bar area, with finished trim and wiring	14,000
Office, lounge, and bar furniture, lighting fixtures, and carpeting	10,000
Furnace and forced hot-air heating system	13,000
Asphalt parking lot for 14 cars	5,000
Total building cost	$208,000
Real estate, with 1 acre of land located on High Street in Dedham	45,000
	$253,000

EXHIBIT 10 Time periods and court hours of the Racketball Corporation of New England. (Source: company records.)

Weekday mornings and afternoons		
10 hours/day × 5 days/week × 6 courts	8:00 a.m. to 6:00 p.m.	300 court hours
Weekday evenings		
6 hours/day × 5 days/week × 6 courts	6:00 p.m. to 12:00 a.m.	180 court hours
Weekend mornings and afternoons		
10 hours/day × 2 days/week × 6 courts	8:00 a.m. to 6:00 p.m.	120 court hours
Weekend evenings	6:00 p.m. to 12:00 a.m.	72 court hours
Total		672 court hours

Stapleton was particularly impressed by the financial performance indicated in the pro forma statements since he felt that the cash flow from the first racketball facility could be used to build other facilities in other sections of the country.

Mr. Stapleton proposed to the company for which he worked, which was willing, as stated previously, to participate in the financing of new ventures for their employees, that he and the company should each advance $25,000 for the equity of the Racketball Corporation. The senior executives of the company were interested in the proposal and were impressed by the amount of work done by Mr. Stapleton in preparing plans and estimating revenues and costs, but they were concerned by the assumption of 75% occupancy for the first year, which was, of course, central to the pro forma cash flow; they asked

EXHIBIT 11 Estimated revenues of the Racketball Corporation of New England over the first year of operations. (Source: company records.)

Membership fees. 672 court hours × 75% occupancy × 1 membership for each hour of court usage × $100 per membership		$ 50,400.00
Weekday morning and afternoon rental charges. 300 court hours × 75% occupancy × $4.00/hour × 26-week season		23,400.00
Weekday evening rental charges. 180 court hours × 75% occupancy × $6.00/hour × 26-week season		21,060.00
Weekend morning and afternoon rental charges. 120 court hours × 75% occupancy × $6.00/hour × 26-week season		14,040.00
Weekend evening rental charges. 72 court hours × 75% occupancy × $4.00/hour × 26-week season		5,620.00
Sandwich, beer, and mixed drink sales at average of $0.50 per player. 672 court hours × 75% occupancy × 2 players per court hours × $0.50 per player × 26 weeks.	$ 13,120	
Less cost at 33% of revenues:	−4,370	8,750.00
Racketball and athletic supply (rackets, balls, club shirts, shorts, etc.) sales, at average of $200 per week × 75% occupancy × 26-week season.	$ 3,900	
Less cost at 50% of revenues	−1,950	1,950.00
Total revenues for the first year of operations:		$125,220.00

EXHIBIT 12 Estimated costs of the Racketball Corporation of New England over the first year of operations. (Source: company records.)

Court attendants, to take reservations, assign courts, allocate lockers, and serve sandwiches, beer, and mixed drinks. The courts will be open 112 hours per week so that 3 people will be required, each working 40 hours per week, with some overlap at shift changes for simple maintenance and cleaning. 3 people × 40 hours/week × 26-week season × $3.00 per hour plus 12% for FICA, etc.	$10,480.00
Building janitor to clean courts, dressing rooms, lounge, office, and bar for approximately 20 hours per week. 1 person × 20 hours/week × 26-week season × $2.50 per hour plus 12% for FICA, etc.	1,460.00
Court supplies, including laundry of towels, bar soap, and general cleaning materials	1,500.00
Heat, light, and water, estimated at $0.80 per square foot of building area (6,000 sq ft)	4,800.00
Insurance, for both property and liability, estimated at $0.22 per square foot of building area (6,000 sq ft)	1,320.00
Maintenance of property, estimated at $0.28 per square foot of building area (6,000 sq ft)	1,680.00
Telephone, with one installation at the desk for the use of the court attendant and one installation in the lounge for the use of members, both restricted to local area service only, at $25.00 per month for each line	600.00
Real estate taxes, estimated at $70 per $1,000 assessed value (assessed value in Dedham is computed at 50% of the actual value, or building and land cost of $253,000)	8,860.00
Interest, estimated for a mortgage on 80% of the building and land cost of $253,000, at annual rate of 9% over 20 years	9,110.00
Depreciation, divided into three separate schedules:	

Racketball courts, dressing rooms, office, lounge and bar area, on a 30-year schedule	$6,000	
Office, lounge, and bar furniture and fixtures, on a 5-year schedule	2,000	
Furnace and heating system, on a 10-year schedule	1,300	$ 9,300.00
Total costs over the first year of operations		$49,110.00

EXHIBIT 13 Profit after taxes and cash flow for the first three years of operations of the Racketball Corporation of New England. (Source: company records.)

	First year, at 75% occupancy	Second year, at 90% occupancy	Third year, at 100% occupancy
Revenues	$125,200	$150,200	$166,900
Costs	49,100	49,100	49,100
Gross profits	76,100	101,100	117,800
Income taxes	31,600	44,600	53,500
Net profits	44,500	56,400	64,300
Depreciation	9,300	9,300	9,300
Cash flow	53,800	65,800	73,600

that he perform market research to support this assumption.

> The executives in the company want me to do market research. But I'm a systems analyst, not a marketing man, and I don't know how to design a market research plan or how to carry it out. Perhaps your students can help; what should we do to support our occupancy projections? (Statement of George Stapleton.)

ASSIGNMENT

Prepare a market research program to provide reliable information on the potential market size for a racketball facility in the southwest suburban market area of Boston. In the program include specific information sources, interview questions, respondent samples, and process methods.

Alarm Systems, Incorporated

Alarm Systems, Incorporated was formed by two friends, Greg Ehrman and Brian Wesolowski, who had become acquainted while they both attended the M.B.A. program at The University of Michigan and who had continued their friendship after graduation since they both worked for the same department of a large automobile firm and they both lived in the same suburb north of Detroit. They often drove to work together, and during the commuting time they talked about starting a small business that could be run under their direction while they continued to work for the automobile firm and that they would take over on a full-time basis only when it was ready to be franchised outside the Detroit area. Both men were interested in substantial capital gains in order to be able to eventually finance real estate developments in northern Michigan, and they thought that the establishment of a successful local business and the subsequent sale of the rights to this business in other areas through franchised contracts would be the best means to obtain these capital gains quickly. They considered different concepts in fast-food restaurants and in discount-store operations, but the markets in both fields seemed crowded with competitors, and the

start-up capital for both businesses seemed greater than they could raise. It was not until the Ehrman's home was burglarized, while Greg and his wife were on a short skiing vacation in Aspen during the early spring of 1973, that the two friends decided that they had the right idea for a successful local business: rented burglar alarms to temporarily protect the homes of families going on vacation.

Numerous types of burglar alarms are available for sale, from approximately 100 different manufacturers within the United States; but for effective operation, they all require extensive wiring at installation, and this wiring, if done on the surface of the walls, is unsightly, and if done inside the walls, is exceedingly expensive. The various types of intruder alarms are described in Exhibit 4, but one of the more effective types is the perimeter system, with pressure-sensitive or movement-sensitive switches at each possible point of entrance into the home, such as doors, windows, skylights, etc., and with double wiring from each switch to the central control panel. Since wiring is normally done in series, the wires extend around the house, going from opening to opening, but for a permanent installation these wires have to be either stapled to the inner surface of the walls or threaded between the inner and outer surfaces. Neither alternative is satisfactory, and the partners felt that their ability to avoid the appearance and expense problems connected with a permanent installation would be their major sales point:

> Everybody else in this industry offers permanent installations, and while the salesman tells you that the wires are thin and that you will hardly notice them, you do notice them and they are a nuisance. The wires run along the baseboard and up to each window and over each door, and there have to be holes drilled in the ceiling to get the wires up to the second floor or down to the basement. We would avoid all of that hassle since we would put in our equipment on a temporary basis, for a week or two weeks or a month while the family is away; since no one would be living in the house, we would just string the wires across the floor. We would put in the system on the day the family leaves for vacation, and we would take it up on the day they come back, and we would charge them only for the time that they need the protection. If we had had this service when we went on vacation, we would have saved about $500 in stolen property and a lot of grief in dealing with the insurance company and the police. There must be many people who feel the same way, not only here in Detroit, but also throughout the country. I think that we have the product that we were looking for to start our business. (Statement of Mr. Ehrman.)

There appeared to be grounds for the two friends' optimism as they considered the size of the potential market for their rental burglary alarm service. Residential burglaries, defined as the unlawful entry by a person or persons into a private dwelling unit to commit a felony or theft, had increased nationwide by 70% in the 5-year period 1967 to 1971; and the burglary rate, or number of reported unlawful entries per 100,000 population, had risen from 710 to 1,148. That meant that in 1971 each 100 persons had an equal 1.148% chance of being victimized by a burglar, and, since the average dwelling unit contained 4.1 persons, the typical house or apartment had an equal 4.592% chance of being entered by a burglar. These percentages, of course, were based on the 1971 figures; if the rate of increase were projected to 1975, each house or apartment would have nearly an equal 10% chance of being burglarized. At that time, each home within the United States would be ransacked by a burglar, on the average, once every 10 years. These statistics, and particularly the figures of the rate of increase for burglaries within metropolitan areas, were not reassuring to suburban homeowners.

Crimes of illegal entry within the metropolitan area were not limited to the central city; burglaries within the suburbs were increasing even more rapidly (see Exhibit 2).

Along with the increase in the reported burglary rate nationwide and the increase in the reported burglary offenses in both Detroit and the suburbs came an increase in the concern felt by homeowners about burglaries. People were worried about the possibility of losing personal property, household items and, particularly, inherited silver and table settings, and they were frightened at the possibility of personal injury. This concern, worry, and fear increased much more rapidly than did the rate of actual crimes (see Exhibit 3).

EXHIBIT 1 Reported burglary rate (crimes of unlawful entry into private dwellings) per 100,000 population for the total U.S. and for cities over 250,000 population. (Source: Federal Bureau of Investigation, *Uniform Crime Reports for the United States,* annual editions.)

	1960	*1967*	*1968*	*1969*	*1970*	*1971*
Total U.S. burglary rate	457.9	643.1	868.4	1031.1	1228.5	1282.7
Metropolitan burglary rate	742.1	982.6	1473.8	1759.1	2026.1	1949.3

EXHIBIT 2 Reported burglary offenses (crimes of unlawful entry into private dwellings) for selected Michigan cities and towns, 1960 and 1967–1971. (Source: U.S. Federal Bureau of Investigation, *Uniform Crime Reports for the United States,* annual editions.)

	1960	1967	1968	1969	1970	1971
Detroit	21,474	38,307	37,932	41,264	50,868	51,531
Dearborn	722	967	761	847	1,075	1,090
Dearborn Heights	297	625	581	739	832	919
Livonia	108	762	774	1,193	1,640	1,569 .
Southfield	—	477	509	556	909	880
Ann Arbor	236	524	877	1,488	2,734	3,154

EXHIBIT 3 Percentage of homeowners interviewed reporting personal concern about the possibility of burglary within their house or apartment, 1960 and 1967–1971. (Source: company records; original source not recorded.)

	1960	1967	1968	1969	1970	1971
Percentage of persons expressing concern	25.2%	68.7%	77.5%	85.6%	92.4%	95.3%

People were worried about the possibility of burglary within their homes; one form of response to this worry was the purchase of a burglar alarm that would either alert the resident to the entry of an outside person within their house or apartment or that would notify the police department or a protective agency about this entry. Burglar alarms are manufactured, as described previously, by over 100 different companies within the United States and are available in a wide variety of models. The major types, methods of operation, price ranges, applications, and problems associated with these models are described in Exhibit 4.

There are, as described below, 10 different intruder protection devices and more than 100 different models in the various types. In discussing the applications of this wide variety of equipment, the partners of Alarm Services, Incorporated felt that there were a number of distinctions and problems that should be made clear to persons interested in burglar alarm sales:

1. Burglar alarm sales are only part of the overall protection industry. The total sales of the protection industry are esti-

mated at $1.8 billion per year; these sales are concentrated among five large companies: Pinkerton Detective Agency; William J. Burns Detective Agency; Globe Security Company; ADT (American District Telegraph Company); and Mosler Safe Company. These companies provide cash delivery services, security patrol services, general alarm services, and proprietary protection devices. The alarm systems offered by these companies are often costly and complex, and they are normally connected to a central station that is continually manned by company employees, who evaluate and then respond to each alarm, either with their own personnel or by calling in the police or fire departments or by notifying the company maintenance crews. The alarm systems can report fires, holdups, burglaries, or equipment failures. One of the services offered by these companies, for example, is continual monitoring of the sprinkler system for fire protection within large buildings; the central control console can indicate when a water supply valve is turned off, either accidentally or maliciously or for unauthorized repairs, and can also detect leaks within

EXHIBIT 4 Major types of burglar alarms available within the United States. (Source: company records.)

Type	Description and costs	Application and problems
Point alarm	The point alarm is a self-contained unit, often battery powered, that can be attached to a door or window to operate a warning bell or buzzer. The cost is $2.50 to $10.00 per unit, with very simple installation (the unit is screwed or clamped to the door jamb or window sill) required.	Point alarms are sold by department stores, hardware stores, and drug stores, generally to elderly people who are unable to afford or install more complex systems. They are considered largely ineffectual because the batteries deteriorate over time, making the unit unreliable, and because the control mechanism can be broken or the alarm bell can be turned off at the site of the break-in.
Perimeter system	The perimeter system consists of a series of electronic switches, either pressure or movement sensitive, that can be mounted on all points of entry (doors and windows, etc.) and connected to a central control panel to operate a warning light or buzzer or to notify, via a recorded message, either the police department or a protective agency. For retail stores, metallic tape is placed on plate glass to activate the alarm if the display windows are broken. A closed circuit is used so that if the wires are cut or if a sensor switch is disconnected, the alarm is triggered. The cost is $10 to $25 per sensor and approximately $500 for the control panel, plus the installation wiring.	The perimeter system is the most common for retail stores; it can be defeated only by a burglar who either hides in the store after the closing hour or who breaks in through the roof or walls. It is not considered suitable for large department stores or warehouses due to the number of possible hiding places or possible points of entry. The system is not extensively used in private homes because the cost for the wiring for permanent installations is very high.
Barrier alarm (infrared)	The infrared barrier alarm consists of a photoelectric cell and an infrared (invisible) light source that is mounted in a hallway or room that must be crossed by a burglar to reach valuable items. The cost range is $200 to $750 per unit, plus the installation.	Infrared barrier alarms are generally effective, but they protect only one line within a building and they can be detected and bypassed (by shining a flashlight on the photoelectric cell) by sophisticated burglars. Barrier alarms are often used as a crisscross system within banks and brokerage houses and to protect paintings and works of art in museums and wealthy private homes.
Barrier alarm (laser)	A laser beam may also be used as a barrier alarm; the light is not necessarily visible if a nonruby crystal is used. The cost range is $500 to $1,100.	The advantage of the laser beam barrier is that the beam cannot be bypassed, except by another laser of precisely the same frequency. The visible light from a ruby crystal is often considered a deterrent; it is eerie in the darkness of a warehouse or department store. The laser can extend over a long distance, but, as with the infrared barrier, it protects only one line.

EXHIBIT 4   (*Continued*)

Type	Description and costs	Application and problems
Movement alarm (sound)	Movement alarms operate on the principle that any relative motion between a sound source and a receiver causes a frequency shift; this is known as the Doppler effect. An oscillator is used to energize a transducer, which floods an area with ultrasonic waves; any movement within this area changes the frequency at the receiver and triggers the alarm. The cost range is $650 to over $5,000.	Movement alarms are used in large department stores and warehouses; each unit can protect an enclosed space of about 200,000 cu ft. Since the transducer and receiver can be mounted in a single unit, motion alarms are often sold for residential protection because the installation is simple. However, moving air currents and household pets can cause false alarms inside the house, and external noises such as thunder, wind, and traffic can trigger the alarm from outside.
Movement alarm (radio)	Another type of movement alarm operates on the principle that any motion within a field of ultrahigh-frequency radio waves causes a distortion of those waves and a consequent change in the loading of the uhf oscillator, which triggers the alarm. The cost range for uhf radio alarms is also $650 to over $5,000. Note: This alarm is frequently mis-termed a "radar" unit; it is not radar because it does not operate with a receiver.	Movement alarms based on uhf radio waves are much less likely to externally cause false alarms, but, again, household pets, open windows, moving draperies, etc., can all trigger the alarm, particularly in the less expensive models.
Presence alarm (electromagnetic)	Every object whose temperature is above absolute zero radiates electromagnetic energy; the human body radiates energy at wavelengths between 3 and 8 microns. This human radiation can be detected by photoconductive cells at distances up to a 60-ft radius. The cost is approximately $700 per unit.	Presence detectors based upon electromagnetic energy are a new development. They were originally designed for military use in Southeast Asia. The number of civilian applications at present is limited because the electronic system required is very complex.
Presence alarm (visual)	Closed-circuit TV cameras have been used for some time to scan an area; the system, however, has always required a human viewer to monitor a bank of cameras. A new system uses a digital memory and a comparator; the comparator translates bits of the scan into a digital code stored on a magnetic loop that is synchronized with the scan. The stored data is compared with each subsequent scan; any major changes in the picture activates the alarm. The cost for the complete system (closed-circuit TV transmitter and	Many retail stores have closed-circuit TV cameras to supervise sales personnel and to control shoplifting during store hours. It is expected that presence alarms based upon optical comparisons will be added to these systems to provide burglary protection when the store is closed. Because of the cost and complexity, it is not expected that the system will be used in private homes.

Type	Description and costs	Application and problems
	receiver, optical comparator, and magnetic tape data storage) is $2,500. The comparator and digital memory can be added to existing TV systems for approximately $900.	
Presence alarm (noise)	Microphones can be used for listening and, as with the visual presence alarm, the normal background can be converted into digital code. A chromatic converter compares the frequency and intensity of sounds picked up by the microphones to the expected background noise; any major changes in the sound type or level activates the alarm. The cost for the complete system (microphones, central station, and chromatic converter) is approximately $2,500, but the system can monitor a large area that has numerous microphones.	It is expected that the automated presence alarms based upon sound will be used to protect factories, engineering offices, etc., because the cost for protecting a large area is low. It is not expected that the system will be used in private homes because the system is too complex and too costly for protecting a small area.
Presence alarm (odor)	Another type of presence alarm operates on the effusion of ammonia by the human body; the amount of ammonia is frequently increased under stress, as in breaking into a private home. A chromatograph, which is an electronic device for determining the percentage of a particular constituent gas in a complex vapor mixture, can be programmed to detect any increase in the ammonia present within a room. The cost is approximately $700 per unit.	Presence detectors based upon chromatography were also originally designed for military use in Southeast Asia. The number of civilian applications at present is limited because the electronic system required is very complex. Also, since the speed of gas dispersion is slow, a rapidly moving intruder might not be detected until after he had left the protected area.

the system and the waterflow indicating a fire or a broken pipe. Other controls detect smoke in air ducts, storage vaults, washrooms, etc., or unusually high temperatures in offices, elevator shafts, utility areas, etc. These protection industry companies provide a wide range of services to commercial, financial, and industrial clients. Alarm Services, Inc. did not expect to compete directly against these services:

We can't compete against ADT or the others for total protection sales since they offer such a wide range of services and since they have the central stations for the reception of the alarm and the trained personnel for the evaluation of the alarm. This evaluation is important because it limits the number of false alarms; if you were to turn a cat loose in the Detroit Museum of Fine Arts late at night, the central station would pick up the movement of the cat, but the station personnel would not call the police department since no barrier alarms would be triggered, and the station people would know that the movement was caused by a small animal, less than 12 in. tall, probably a cat or a very small dog. But, if you tried to walk across the room where the Rembrandt is hung, they would have you identified as an intruder within 5 seconds and could tell the police where you were and what you were doing. Since large clients like the service that is available from the established protective agencies, they simply won't deal with a small or local firm, such as ourselves. (Statement of Mr. Ehrman.)

2. Burglar alarm sales are concentrated in the commercial, financial, and industrial sectors of the economy, not in residential housing. The large protective agencies, such as ADT or Globe Security, etc., primarily provide alarm services to retail stores, commercial banks, brokerage offices, insurance firms, storage warehouses, and manufacturing plants since these companies normally purchase a full range of services at prices that are not constrained by excessive competition. Protective agencies do not emphasize private homes in their sales approach, except for exceedingly wealthy clients who want the same range and quality of fire, burglary, and intruder alarm services at the same prices as those offered to business firms, since they feel that most homeowners want limited service at lower prices. The partners at Alarm Services, Inc. felt that this concentration upon business firms was due at least partially to the terms of the insurance contracts that required commercial, financial, and industrial companies to have adequate systems:

Insurance companies require retail stores, particularly jewelry, clothing, appliance, liquor, and drug outlets, to have both burglary alarms and fire alarms for a rate reduction in the premiums, and the insurance companies will accept only the top-quality alarm units from established manufacturers and installed by protective agencies with good reputations. That is why you will see a retail store put in a complete barrier system, with the distinctive metallic tape on the windows, and with a vibration detector in the ceiling to prevent thieves from breaking in through the roof, which is much more common than you might expect because of the low-quality construction used in many shopping centers, and with some sort of a presence detector, often of the ultrahigh-frequency radio-wave type, to catch the burglar who hides in the store until it closes. This system costs from $8,000 to $12,000 installed and has a monthly central station charge of from $50 to $100, but the store can

generally save the cost in 5 or 6 years on insurance premiums. Many insurance companies will not even take a store now if they don't have this sort of equipment. The same thing is true of commercial banks, brokerage firms, office buildings, and manufacturing plants; they can pay for the cost of their alarm system in a few years through savings on the cost of their insurance. Private individuals can't do that; there is almost no savings on the cost of the typical homeowner's insurance policy for either a fire alarm or a burglary alarm system. Since there is no savings, there is not as much money available to pay for the system, and so the protective agencies simply don't pay much attention to residential housing. (Statement of Mr. Ehrman.)

3. Burglar alarms for the residential market are sold by local retail outlets at reduced prices. Since the large protection agencies generally have tended to concentrate upon the commercial, financial, and industrial markets, the residential housing market has been left to smaller firms, usually without central station facilities, that serve as licensed distributors and local installers for national manufacturers of burglar alarms and to large department stores, hardware stores, and discount store chains that sell burglar alarms as appliances and expect their customers to install the equipment themselves. The local installers may offer a perimeter system, but because of the high cost of wiring to each door and window at installation (estimated at $3,500 for concealed wiring in a three-bedroom ranch house), they normally recommend barrier alarms (photoelectric cell units with an infrared light source), point alarms (battery-powered units for attachment to a door or window), or movement alarms (electronic units operating on ultrasonic sound or ultrahigh-frequency radio waves), with much lower installation costs. Department stores, hardware stores, discount stores, drug stores, and radio supply stores usually offer only movement alarms since these are assembled units (transmitter, receiver, and alarm mounted in a single

box), and the purchaser need only place this box on a table in the living room or front hall, plug it into the house current (110 volts AC), and run two wires to the central box, usually in the master bedroom, and to a key-operated entrance box, usually near the front door. The control box and the entrance box both contain a switch to turn the unit on and off and a "panic" button that activates the alarm regardless of whether the unit is on or off. The alarm usually consists of a circuit that will turn on some of the lights within the house, to frighten away a burglar or intruder, and a loud electric bell or buzzer that will awaken the homeowners so that they will call the police. It is also possible to add an automatic dialer that will call the police automatically and give a recorded message. These units, without the automatic dialer, are not expensive in comparison to those sold for commercial, financial, or industrial protection; barrier alarms are sold for under $100 and movement alarms for less than $200:

I can bring a unit to your house and install it for $169.50. This unit will detect anyone entering the house, through any door or window; it is a radar set that operates on radio waves that hit a robber or thief and bounce back to the set to turn on the alarm, but these radio waves are so high frequency that they don't interfere with your television watching or radio listening. The reason for the low price is solid-state electronics, just like the new calculators and the new computers. Isn't the security of your home worth $169.50? (Statement of Detroit area dealer and installer.)

We have an electric eye that works with invisible light; we recommend this strongly for stairways since no one can come upstairs to the bedrooms without setting off the alarm before they take two steps. The electric eye alarm is only $89.50 and will protect you and your family from attack. (Statement of second Detroit area dealer and installer.)

There are over 4,000 installers who are members of the National Burglar and Fire Alarm Association, and these people are usually local shop owners who specialize in resi-

dential protection; they sell burglar alarms, fire alarms, fire extinguishers, heavy door locks, etc. They concentrate on alarm systems that sell for under $200 since this is where the big market is. Many of these shops are not overly profitable, and some of the shop owners are not overly reliable; it has been known for the person who installed the burglar alarm one day to come back the next night as the burglar. (Statement of Mr. Ehrman.)

With locked homes being broken into every 23 seconds in the U.S., it is small wonder that there is a boom in sales of burglar alarms systems. . . . But the homeowner who decides to buy such a system should move with care. Some fly-by-night opportunists in the security business are happy to make a few quick sales and then vanish even more quickly. ("Burglar Alarms for the Home: Choose with Care," *Business Week*, March 27, 1971, p. 87.)

Department stores and discount chains, as well as the local installers, offer primarily movement alarms since these are so easy to demonstrate and to install. They don't work very well, but that has never stopped the mass merchandising of a consumer product. (Statement of Mr. Ehrman.)

4. Burglar alarms for the residential market are often of poor quality. Many of the barrier alarms that sell for under $100 and the movement alarms for less than $200 are not reliable in operation; they can both be bypassed by cutting the control wires or disconnecting the power supply, and they both generate numerous false alarms. The movement alarm is particularly susceptible to false alarms since it is based upon relative motion within a field of ultrasonic sound waves causing a detectable frequency shift or upon movement within a field of ultrahigh-frequency radio waves causing a detectable loading distortion. Any internal movement, whether of household pets, air currents, or draperies, and many external events, such as loud sounds or electronic interference, can trigger the alarm, to the dismay of the householder:

Your typical householder buys an alarm from a discount store, after reading the advertising claims on the outside of the carton, or from a local installer who comes out and sets the black box in the living room and the controls in the hall. After talking about "space-age electronics" and "solid-state components," he shows how it works by walking into the living room from the hall and, of course, the lights all come on and the bell rings. The couple who bought it are as happy as hell. Then, he goes outside and opens a window into the living room and the same thing happens. The couple go to bed that night with the control console right next to the telephone and the flashlight on the night table. They feel secure and happy and certain that it is the best $169.50 that they ever spent. Then, three nights later they forget to lock the cat in the basement, and about 3:00 or 4:00 in the morning the lights come on and the bell rings. They call the police and sit huddling up in the bedroom until the patrol car comes, and then they rush downstairs and open the door. When the officers come in, they find the damn cat sitting on top of the box cleaning its fur. Well, they don't like that too much, but then a few nights later one of them gets up to go to the bathroom, upstairs, mind you, and out of the range of the machine, and the draft from an open window in the bedroom sets off the alarm. This time they don't call the police. Instead, they stand in the upstairs hall listening, and when they don't hear any movement they come downstairs very slowly, turn off the bell, and look around. Everything is secure, so they know that it is another false alarm. That happens a few more times. When there is a thunderstorm the alarm goes off every time there is a close flash of lightning. Well, now they don't feel so good about the alarm, so they call up the fellow who sold it to them and complain, but he says, "Don't worry, it's just set a little too tight; it's a little too sensitive. You just have to adjust it. I'll come out this afternoon and take care of it." Well, they don't ask him why he didn't adjust it when he was out the first time; but he does come out and fiddles with a couple of screws and a rheostat inside the box, and there are no more false alarms. The trouble is that they never notice that now you could hold a convention of burglars in the living room, and the alarm wouldn't go off until one of them kicked the box. The $169.50 alarm just doesn't work very well, and a good movement alarm costs about $1,300. The typical householder isn't going to spend that sort of money at a discount store or pay that sort of money to the local installer. (Statement of Mr. Ehrman.)

5. Burglar alarms for the residential market often do not have the approval of the police. Since false alarms are a continual problem with the less expensive barrier systems and movement systems sold for residential protection, the police in many areas have become hesitant in responding to home alarms. The police believe that over 95% of the home alarms they receive are caused by either malfunctions of the equipment or malperformance by the owners, and they are certain that these false alarms waste money and manpower. In some cities (New York City), the police now charge for responding to false alarms; in others (Philadelphia, Los Angeles, and San Francisco), the police now refuse to respond to all home alarms not reported personally by the homeowner or the neighbors:

Local police also have not been entirely happy with some new devices, particularly electronic alarms that automatically telephone the local station house with recorded messages indicating criminal entry. Too often police have rushed to the address to find that the family cat or the householder himself had bumbled into range of the sensor device. Having had enough of this, Los Angeles and Philadelphia police obtained local legislation banning devices linked to official switchboards. ("Security Men Thrive on Wages of Fear," *Business Week*, June 20, 1970, p. 112.)

We will always respond to a telephone call from a resident of this town requesting police assistance, and a call reporting possible breaking and entry into a private dwelling gets first priority with us; we try to send two patrol cars to handle it properly. But I would be less than honest with you if I didn't tell you that we don't like people calling in to say that an automatic alarm has gone off in their neighbor's house, and we certainly don't like automatic dialers calling in a recorded message. The advantage of the direct call from a homeowner is that he can meet the officers at his front door, take them through his house, and report what prompted his call in the first place. Our patrolmen are trained to evaluate these reports and either reassure the homeowner or take corrective action. In the event of an actual break-in, which occurs on less than 10% of all break-in calls, the officers ·in the first car can take evidence on the spot while the men in the second car drive along the streets in the neighborhood looking for someone who is carrying household items. We can often recover the property and make a positive identification within 5 or 10 minutes of the call, and that is the sort of police service we want to perform.

But the problem with an automatic alarm is that the homeowner is not there when we arrive; instead, he is on vacation or visiting on the other side of town or at a party, and we cannot deal effectively with the situation. The officers have to walk around the house, checking for evidence of illegal entry. You'd be surprised at how many people, even in this day and age of publicity about crime, who still leave a door or window open while they are away from home. Warn the students in your class not to do this, since this is how the real kooks break in; but what do the officers do when they find a window open? They have to find a neighbor who has a key, and then they have to go through a strange house, but they can't tell if anything is missing. Meanwhile the thief, if there is one, has carried the color television set over to the next block, put it in the trunk of his car, and is just waiting for our men to go into the house before he drives away. We can't deal effectively with an automatic call since we don't know what has happened. (Statement of Detroit area police chief.)

6. Burglar alarms for the residential - market have not become an important factor in the total protection industry. Despite the rapidly increasing burglary rate in metropolitan areas, and despite the rapidly rising level of civilian concern about these crimes of unlawful entry, the actual sales of alarm units for home protection have remained relatively constant at the 1967 sales level of $14,000,000. Each year industry spokesmen forecast rapidly increasing sales, but each year the actual sales remain at disappointing levels for industry members. This lack of growth is ascribed partially to the low quality of many of the barrier and movement alarms

sold for electronic home security and partially to the availability of many alternative means of protecting a house or apartment, such as heavy locks, improved lighting, firearms, and watch dogs:

Many of the nation's mass merchants are now strongly committing themselves to the growing home protection market—offering the consumer a variety of sophisticated devices to fight crime—and a growing number of electronic and appliance manufacturers are ready to supply these devices. In sharp contrast to several years ago, a consumer may visit the hardware department of most major retail chains and find a large assortment of alarm systems; but sales have not kept pace with expectations. (*Merchandising Magazine,* July 20, 1970, p. 4.)

The (residential burglar) alarm will be one of many on a market that has drawn competing hardware and service salesmen like flies. But though the boom in home protection continues, it has not been without misfortunes and setbacks. Two years ago May Department Stores Company had high hopes for its Citadel Alarm and Security Corporation in St. Louis, aimed at the home market. But a personal protection department it set up in the Famous-Barr Company store in downtown St. Louis is now closed, and May is trying to sell its security company. ("Security Men Thrive on Wages of Fear," *Business Week,* June 20, 1970, p. 112.)

Burglar alarms for the residential market have not sold very well since they don't have the approval of the police. If you ask the police about any of the alarm systems available from the discount stores or the local installers, they will not only refuse to recommend that specific model, but they will also attempt to dissuade you from installing any system. And they can be quite blunt about it: they will tell you that none of the alarms provides adequate protection, except for the very expensive perimeter systems connected to the central station of a protective agency, such as ADT or Globe Security. Insurance agents will give you the same story. The two groups of people to whom the homeowner turns for advice on burglar alarms, the police departments and the insurance companies, both recommend against the installation of inexpensive residential alarms. These alarms will never sell well without the enthusiastic support of those two groups. (Statement of Mr. Ehrman.)

You have to remember that burglar alarms are only part of the total package of products for home protection; there is a wide variety of anti-burglar devices, as opposed to burglar-detection devices, available. These anti-burglar devices include dead bolts, window locks, door chains, outside lights, peepholes, guns, and dogs. You'd be surprised at the number of people who keep a shotgun in the corner near their front door or a revolver on the night-stand in their bedroom. Gun sales are up 300% over 1967, and not all of those guns are used by the crooks; the honest household-ers have quite a few of them also. Then, peo-ple have big dogs now. I don't mean to be philosophical about it, but if you tell me the breed of dog that is most popular, I can tell you the stage of civilization that has been reached. In the Middle Ages the wolfhound and the greyhound were kept since it was a lawless time, but by the Victorian Age, the poodle was most popular since that was a se-cure period. Small dogs, poodles, and spaniels were the most common household pets until the 1960s when retrievers, larger but still friendly, took over. Now, the most popular breed is the Doberman pinscher, large and not friendly. Did you know that you can buy a tape recording of an angry snarling and growling Doberman pinscher? It is one of the more ingenious anti-burglar devices, for an angry Doberman pinscher or German shep-herd will discourage most burglars. As a mat-ter of fact, lights, locks, and an attentive householder will discourage most burglars. You don't really need a burglar alarm unless you're not there. (Statement of Mr. Wesolowski.)

The two partners were in agreement that inexpensive burglar alarms for the residen-tial market would never sell very well, de-spite the continually optimistic forecasts of industry spokesmen, since these alarms were generally of poor quality, unapproved by the police departments and insurance com-panies, and ineffectual in preventing intru-sions into the home. The partners were also in agreement that the expensive burglar alarm systems provided for commercial, fi-nancial, and industrial concerns by the large protective agencies, which were approved by

the police and effectual in operations, would also never sell very well in the residential market because of the high initial cost for installation and the continuing charge for the central station service. They felt, how-ever, that there was a gap in the market structure between these two alternatives in home protection; and they wanted to pro-vide a high-quality alarm system of the pe-rimeter type on a temporary basis, with only a minimal installation charge and no central station costs, to families going on vacation:

> The typical home in the suburbs away from the high-crime areas is reasonably safe from intrusion as long as the lights are on, the doors are locked, the dog is asleep on a rug in the rec room, and the family is at home. No burglar really wants to walk into that sort of situation. But let the family go away for vacation for a few weeks. The grass is not cut during the summer or the snow is not plowed during the winter. The newspapers and circulars pile up around the front door, despite the efforts of the homeowner to stop them before he went away. The house looks deserted and, to a burglar, open and inviting. You can have a timer to turn on one light at 7:30 each night and off at 11:00, but that just advertises your absence to the experienced burglar; he will call you on the telephone and, if there is no answer, he assumes that you won't be back for that night, at least, or you would not have set the automatic timer. No one would attempt to burglarize my house while I'm here [Mr. Wesolowski was correct in that assumption; he had been a defensive lineman and heavyweight wrestler as an under-graduate at Indiana University, and he re-mained in good physical condition by playing handball on a semi-professional basis and by walking the two large German shepherds owned by the family], but when we leave on vacation, then it's an open season on all of our property. I thought that we were smart in putting our silver in the dirty clothes hamper and our jewelry in the freezing com-partment of the refrigerator when we went on vacation but after Gary's house was broken into, I learned from the police that those are the first two places even the most amateur burglar will look. The trouble is that the burglar knows much more about his business than you do. Another thing, neither Gary nor

I thought that our families had much silver or jewelry, except for the wedding presents and a few inherited pieces, but you find out when you try to add things up after a burglary that you had a lot more valuable items than you thought. People need protection at home when they go on vacation, and we can provide that protection. (Statement of Mr. Wesolowski.)

The partners' plan was to purchase the components for a number of perimeter alarm systems, including movement-sensitive switches for each door and window, a central control panel for the electrical connections, and an automatic dialer to report intrusions to the police, and then to install these components on a temporary basis in the home of a family leaving for vacation. They felt that there would be few false alarms from this perimeter system since the movement-sensitive switches would require a deliberate movement of over $\frac{1}{2}$ in. of the window or door before operating. Winds, drafts, noises, or pets could not trigger the alarm; it would require the forcing of a lock or the breaking of a window to activate the system. The partners planned to hire a retired police captain or lieutenant to supervise the installation of the equipment since this would provide reassurance to the homeowner and approval by the police. The installation would be simple since it would be temporary. Each switch could be clamped to a window or door, and the wires to the central control panel could be laid on the floor. In actual practice, there would be a junction box for each room, with a number of wires and sensors permanently connected; the person installing the system would then have only to connect each junction box to the control panel and plug the automatic dialer into the telephone jack. The time for installation would be short, perhaps an hour for the typical home, and it could be done the day before the family left for vacation. When they left, they would activate the system with a key at the front door. The family would rent the system for the period that they would be gone; when they came back, they would turn off the system with the key and then call to have the components removed.

The rented burglar alarm system was to be the primary service of the new company, but the partners felt that they would also offer an electronic timer that could turn the lights on and off throughout the house in a realistic pattern and a telephone answering device that could provide a short recorded message that would be noncommittal about the length of time that the family would be away. It was expected that most prospective burglars would not attempt to hold a conversation with the voice that answered the telephone and that they would hang up without realizing that they were listening to a recording. The company could also provide adjustable window braces that would make it impossible to "jimmy" (use an iron bar to pry open a door or window by tearing the lock out of the wood) the windows without breaking the four panes of glass at each corner and special door wedges that would make it impossible to "shimmy" (use a flexible piece of steel or plastic to open a door or window by forcing back the spring latch on a simple lock) a door without breaking the hinges. It was again expected that most prospective burglars would not wish to break the window glass or the door hinges because of the noise involved and that they would leave without gaining entry. If they did gain entry, the alarm system was certain to go off.

The last service that the partners expected their new company to offer was supervision of the home maintenance. A representative of the company could visit each home each day to make certain that the mail, newspapers, and pamphlets were picked up and that the companies or individuals who had contracted to mow the lawn or shovel the snow were performing as promised. Each service, from the basic alarm system rental to the light timer, telephone answering device, door and window braces, and supervisory visits, would be provided at a reasonable daily charge.

The partners were certain that they had the basic concept for an extremely successful business, and they felt that they had an excellent means of distribution through franchised offices headed by retired police officers, but they were uncertain about the price that should be charged for the service, the method of promotion that should be used, and the area that should be selected for the first office:

> Our price per week for the alarm system rental should not be just the initial cost of the unit divided by 52 weeks in the year times 3 or 4 years plus a percentage for overhead and profit, since we aren't going to rent every system every week. Vacations tend to cluster in the summer, although they are much more spread out throughout the year now than they used to be. People go to Europe in the fall, to Florida during the winter, and skiing in the spring, but we've got to get some idea of the value of the property that needs protection so that we won't price ourselves out of the market.
>
> We originally thought that we would promote our business by advertising in the suburban newspapers, but people seem to have a general impression that goods and services advertised in the weekly town papers are poor in quality. Both of our wives say this, and I guess I tend to agree; certainly most of the other advertisers are discount department stores, chain drug stores, small jewelry stores, etc., but I wish that we had a better cross section of opinion.
>
> Again, originally we thought that we would set up our first office in Southfield, which is an affluent suburb to the northwest of Detroit, with 23,200 families and a median family income of $14,660. These people must take a lot of vacations, and they must have a lot of personal property to protect, but they also have a good police department there and a low crime rate. Maybe we would be better off to move in closer to Detroit, say to Dearborn, with 36,200 families and a median family income of $11,707, and a much higher burglary rate. We don't know the facts, but we don't want to make any mistakes in choosing our first location.
>
> Have you realized how big this business could be? If we could get just one out of five of the families in Southfield, all of whom must go on at least a two-week vacation each year, and if we charged $100 per week for the complete home protection, which is cheap compared to what they have to lose, then we

would have $1,000,000 in revenues. And Southfield is just one of probably 50 good suburbs around Detroit, and Detroit is just one of probably 100 metropolitan areas in the United States. We have to move quickly to forestall competition, but we have to do things right to be successful, and to do things right we have to know more about the market. That is our problem right now. (Statement of Mr. Ehrman.)

The partners wanted to engage in market research prior to establishing the pricing, promotion, and location policies, and they wanted positive results from this market research prior to making the necessary investment in equipment and operating capital:

> I think that we should have the equipment for 50 complete systems before starting so that we can handle the initial demand. If we don't have the equipment, somebody else could just come in and take over after we establish the service and prove that the market is there. Each system would cost $1,300 at retail, but we can get the components for about $780 from the wholesaler or manufacturer. Our problem is that we don't have the necessary $39,000 for equipment or the necessary funds for start-up expenses and working capital. I don't think that many M.B.A.'s have that sort of money after paying for their education and making the down payment on their home, despite working for a few years at a good salary; expenses just naturally seem to expand to the level of your salary, and you can't save much money. We can get the start-up funds from the bank, provided we each put in $5,000 of our own money, or of our families' money, and we can finance the equipment through a commercial finance company at 9% add-on interest (9% on the beginning balance of the loan, for a true interest rate of 18%), but we have to personally pledge all of our assets and agree that the finance company could attach a percentage of our salaries for repayment. We want some pretty firm assurances about the market before we go into a deal like that. (Statement of Mr. Wesolowski.)

The partners had tried three different methods of market research in order to provide the needed information about the size and the characteristics of the market; none of the three had been successful:

1. Direct Mail. The partners and their wives, working in the evenings, had selected the names of 980 residents at random from the telephone directories for Southfield, Dearborn, and St. Clair Shores, and had sent a mimeographed letter detailing the service they proposed to offer and asking for consumer reactions and consumer information on a prepaid 4 in. x 6 in. postcard they enclosed with the letter (see below).

Only 17 cards were returned, for a response rate of 1.7%. Fifteen of the cards indicated that the respondents already had a burglar alarm system installed; the other two cards were not signed and only partially filled out.

2. Telephone. To check on the reasons for the lack of response to their direct mail questionnaire, the partners began telephoning persons on the mailing list; the following quotations were recorded verbatim from calls made by Mr. Wesolowski while the case writer was at his home:

WESOLOWSKI

Hello, I'm from Alarm Systems, Incorporated; we rent burglar alarms to protect your home and your property while you're on vacation. I'd like to ask you a few questions about our service.

RESPONDENT

(Silence)

WESOLOWSKI

Hello . . . Hello. . . . I'm from Alarm Systems Incorporated; we rent burglar alarms. . . .

RESPONDENT

(Young child's voice) Hello.

WESOLOWSKI

Hello, is your mother there?

RESPONDENT

(Silence)

WESOLOWSKI

Hello, is your mommy there?

Do you believe that rented burglar alarms are needed to protect your home during vacation periods?   Yes_____ No_____

Property you would want to protect (estimate the value in dollars)

        Silverware _____   Hi-fi equipment _____

        Jewelry_____   Coin/stamp collections_____

        Television sets_____   Paintings/works of art_____

Vacation periods when you would be absent from your home and need protection from our rented burglar alarm service (estimate time in weeks, and give approximate dates)

        Fall_____   Spring _____

        Winter_____   Summer_____

Do you now have a burglar alarm system?   Yes_____   No_____

Name:_____

        (include your name and address only if you wish further information)

Address:_____

RESPONDENT

No.

WESOLOWSKI

Who is there?

RESPONDENT

Daddy.

WESOLOWSKI

Can I speak to him?

RESPONDENT

He's in the bathroom. (Long silence; the child did not hang up, but no adult came to the telephone.)

WESOLOWSKI

Hello, I'm from Alarm Systems, Incorporated; we rent burglar alarms to protect your home and your property while you're on vacation. I'd like to ask you a few questions about our service.

RESPONDENT

(Older child's voice) Mom, there's a guy on the phone who wants to rent burglar alarms. Cool, huh? (Mother's voice clearly audible) Tell him we don't want any. (Child's voice again) We don't want any. (Hangs up)

WESOLOWSKI

Hello, I'm from Alarm Systems, Incorporated; we rent burglar alarms to protect your . . .

RESPONDENT

(Interrupts impatiently) I'm sorry but I don't like telephone solicitations. (Hangs up)

The partners did not get enough valid interviews by telephone to form any estimate of the market size or any impression of customer attitudes. Over 50% of the calls were answered by children, and then it was difficult to get an adult to come to the telephone. Between 50% and 60% of the adults refused to be interviewed by telephone. The seriousness and validity of the statements made by adults who did

agree to be interviewed were questionable. Almost all of the respondents claimed to have burglar alarms, although many qualified their assertions with comments such as "My burglar alarm has a cold nose" or "I've got the biggest four-footed burglar alarm you'll ever see." Mr. Wesolowski felt that the telephone interviewing process was distinctly unsuccessful:

I'll never call 200 strangers again as long as I live. Toward the end, the only thing I wanted to do was to wring their scrawny, little, snotty necks. (Statement of Mr. Wesolowski.)

3. *Personal Interviews.* Since the direct-mail and telephone interviewing methods had not been successful, the partners tried personal interviews. They stood on the sidewalks at shopping centers on Friday and Saturday evenings asking questions of persons who stopped, and they tried calling on neighbors at their homes; neither method was successful:

At shopping centers you are always surrounded by children who think that interviewing is some sort of a circus. I don't know what they're doing there, but they are a damn nuisance. They'll sit right next to you on a bicycle, right in your way, and they'll give smart-alecky answers to your questions, confusing the person you're interviewing. You can't push them out of the way, and you can't get away from them.

Also, most people won't stop to be asked questions. But you can see some people who are so eager to be interviewed that they'll come past you three or four times; they must think you're giving away prizes. I know that we didn't get a representative sample out there.

Interviewing in your neighborhood is sort of fun, at first, since you're calling on people you know. Our neighbors all thought that we had a good idea and said to let them know when we started in business, but the further we got away from our own house, the less cordial and less informative the interviews became. My wife went along with me so that people would not worry that I was trying to break into their homes, but it got so that people were not even polite to her; they would just say, "We don't want any" and slam the door before I could explain what we were after. (Statement of Mr. Wesolowski.)

ASSIGNMENT

The partners were discouraged by the continual rebuffs they received while they tried to gather market information. Prepare a market research program, with specific information sources, interview questions, respondent samples, and process methods, to provide reliable information on the market size and on the pricing, promotional, and area policies.

Ann Arbor Brewery, Inc.

Over the past 20 to 25 years the economics of the brewing industry have emphasized the importance of the large, central brewery, producing a uniform beer in massive volume that could be marketed as a consumer product, with national advertising and national distribution. During this time period, which roughly followed the advent of commercial television in 1948, the number of independent brewers has declined from 611 to 129, and the larger of the national firms have taken an increasing share of the market. The outlook for the small local brewery was considered to be doleful.

The steady expansion of market shared by a handful of major brewing companies at the expense of smaller beer makers has continued right through the recession and appears to be inexorable. Last year the five largest beer companies wound up with 63.6% of total brewing industry barrelage, up from 40.9% in 1968, 55.5% in 1972, and 59.4% in 1973. ("Beer Drinkers Continue to Favor Big Brewers," *The Wall Street Journal,* July 18, 1975, p. 28. Reprinted with permission of *The Wall Street Journal,* © 1975 Dow Jones & Company, Inc. All rights reserved.)

In its frothiest days, the American brewing industry was a cheerful fraternity. There were hundreds of firms, family-owned in the main,

each with its own territory; and when the brewers met for conventions, beer flowed, big-name entertainers performed, and *Gemütlichkeit* prevailed. Today things aren't so *gemütlich* anymore. A handful of big brewers are flourishing, mainly by taking business away from weaker competitors, many of whom are headed for extinction. Charles G. Burck, "While the Big Brewers Quaff, the Little Ones Thirst," *Fortune,* November 1972, p. 103.)

There are some indications that this economic dominance of the large brewers may be ending. New techniques and equipment for the brewing process, primarily in the form of micro-filtration to eliminate the need for aging tanks and computerized instrumentation and feedback controls to eliminate the need for batch rather than line processing, have given the smaller brewery a production cost advantage. This advantage has been multiplied in the past few years by the continuing increases in packaging, freight, and distribution costs caused by inflation and the possibility of legislation against the disposable beer container, brought about by environmental concern:

The brewing industry today is based upon the one-way container. We brew 120 million barrels of beer, and we put that beer in 40 billion cans and bottles and ship them all over the country and then let someone else worry about picking up the empties. How much longer can that go on? We make the cans out of aluminum and the bottles out of glass, the two most resistant materials we can find; in a few years we will be up to our earlobes in beer cans. You know there will be legislation in a few years prohibiting the one-way container. What is the big brewery going to do then? It costs as much to ship back the empties (because of bulk) as it does to ship out the full ones. Maybe Gussie Busch can pick them up with his Clydesdales.

The container is only part of the problem. Do you realize that all the beer in a six-pack is worth only 7¢. You pay more than 7¢ since you pay for the advertising and the sporting events and the expense accounts and the most inefficient distribution system since Noah carried animals around in a raft. The large brewers are in trouble, but they don't know it yet. You can't ship beer from St. Louis, Missouri to Manistique, Michigan, handle it six times, pay three discounts, and expect to make money much longer. Beer is 96% water, 3.8% alcohol, and 0.2% flavor; you can't afford to ship water around in rail cars, so you have to brew it locally and sell it locally. The day of the giants is past; there will be a highly successful local brewery in every major trading area within the next 10 years. They are as logical as shopping centers or discount houses, and people will stand in line to get in. (Statement of industry executive.)

There is convincing evidence, as described in the balance of the case, to support the viewpoint that a small brewery, selling to a local trading area through a limited distribution system, is a viable economic concept, provided that the beer can be sold at a reasonable price. There is substantial disagreement here. The opponents of the local brewery say that lower-priced beers are available in most markets now, but they do not sell in competition to the national brands because consumers believe that price equals quality. The proponents reply that this consumer reaction is not a bias since the present lower-priced beers are poorer in quality and

that no one has yet offered a premium quality beer at a discount price through an improved distribution system.

PRODUCTS OF THE BREWING INDUSTRY

Beer, of course, is the primary product of the brewing industry, but beer is not perhaps as totally undifferentiated as is commonly assumed; there are a number of varieties of types:

1. *Premium beers.* (Budweiser, Schlitz, Pabst, or Millers, etc.) are normally brewed by a national company and supported by extensive national advertising, particularly on television. In Michigan during the summer of 1972 premium beers sold at $6.25 per case of twenty-four 12-oz bottles or cans.

2. *Regional beers.* (Carlings, Hamms, Strohs, Shaffers, Blatz, Falstaff, Coors, etc.) are often made from the same ingredients and by the same process as the premium beers, with equivalent aging and quality control, but since they are not equally advertised, they sell at a discount of from 3% to 5% from the price of the premium beers. In Michigan, again during the summer of 1972, regional beers sold at $5.95 per case. It is alleged that because of the reduced turnover some regional beers in low-volume stores may become overaged, and therefore "flat" or "bitter" in taste, and that this accounts for an erroneous reputation for poorer quality.

3. *Price beers.* (Buckeye, Right Time, Rolling Rock) are specifically designed to sell at a discounted price; materials are reduced in cost and the process in duration; the result may be a beer that tastes "thin" to persons accustomed to the premium and regional brands since the alcoholic content may be at 3.0%, not at the generally accepted 3.8%. Price beers are designed to sell at a discount of 20% to 25% from the premium beers; in Michigan during the summer of 1972 price beers

sold in the range between $4.50 and $5.50 per case.

4. *Malt liquors* are beverages similar in flavor and other characteristics to the premium and regional beers, but they have an alcoholic content ranging from 4% to 8% by weight.

5. *Beer* is brewed with a top raising yeast, that is, one that floats on the surface of the vat during fermentation. Ale is made with a bottom floating yeast, although this distinction is followed only in the United States. Beer and ale are synonymous in Europe. Additional hops may be added to ale in the United States to accentuate the slight distinction in flavor.

6. *Dark beer* is brewed with roasted malt; light beer is brewed with dried malt.

7. *Lager or pilsner beer* is light beer that has been aged for a period of from 30 to 60 days to permit the suspended protein matter and yeast to settle out; porter or stout is dark beer that has not been aged so that it still contains the protein and yeast, though fermentation has been stopped by pasteurization.

MANUFACTURING PROCESS OF THE BREWING INDUSTRY

Beer is manufactured, or brewed, from cereal grains, often with nearly equal amounts of corn, rice, and malted barley. Malted refers to a process of controlled germination; the barley is softened by soaking in water, which causes the grains to germinate; this growth is allowed to continue for 7 or 8 days and then stopped by either drying or roasting. Drying produces a light beer; roasting a darker beer. The germination develops an enzyme, diatose, that is capable of changing the starch of raw corn or rice into sugar, which in turn can be changed, through fermentation, into alcohol. Malt is therefore an essential ingredient of brewing and distillation and has been described as one of the major but least known benefits of the human condition.

The cereal grains are crushed by large rollers; then they are mixed and cooked, as a mash, in a pressure vessel; this dissolves all of the fermentable portions of the grains and allows the enzymes from the malted barley to convert the starches of the other cereals to dextrose. The mash is then drained, and the liquid portion is piped to a brewing kettle where hops, which provide the sharp and characteristically bitter flavor of beer, are added. The solid residue from the mash is pressed, dried, and sold as cattle or poultry feed.

The liquid in the brewing kettle is cooled to about 65°F, and yeast is added. Yeast is a unicellular vegetable organism that induces alcoholic fermentation. Cells absorb the fermentable sugars as food and throw off carbon dioxide gas and alcohol in approximately equal quantities. The formula, very simplified, is:

$$C_6H_{12}O_6 \longrightarrow 2C_2H_5OH + 2CO_2$$

$$\underset{\text{dextrose}}{} \qquad \underset{\substack{\text{ethyl} \\ \text{alcohol}}}{} + \underset{\substack{\text{carbon} \\ \text{dioxide}}}{}$$

When fermentation is complete, the liquid is drained and piped to lagering, or aging, tanks, while the yeast is pressed, dried, and again sold as cattle or poultry feed. During lagering, which extends over 30 to 60 days, a slow second fermentation takes place, carbon dioxide is dissolved within the beer, and suspended protein matter and yeast settle out; the beer becomes lighter in color and more mellow in taste. It is then piped to storage, or "government," tanks; all liquid taken from these tanks must be metered. Federal and state taxes are assessed against the withdrawals that are packaged in kegs, bottles, or cans for shipment and eventual retail sale. Production in the United States is measured as "tax-paid withdrawals" in barrels of 31 gallons, or 14 cases of twenty-four 12-oz bottles or cans.

Brewing, prior to the advent of chemical and biochemical analysis, was an indefinite and arcane art. The brewmaster knew, from years of experience, the appearance, taste, odor, and texture of the product in its many stages and could adjust the process for the infinite number of possible variations to achieve a reasonably tasty beer. Breweries at this time were small, usually about 10,000 barrels per year, since they had to be under the control of a single man, and they were local since the storage and traveling qualities of the product were unreliable. Extra yeast left in the bottles or kegs might continue fermentation with startling results.

Science, in the form of corporate laboratories and white-coated technicians, eliminated, as in so many other professions, the responsibilities, position, and status of the brewmaster. Samples could be taken of all input materials and of the resultant mixtures at every stage of the process; these samples could be analyzed and corrective action taken by the improved mechanical and electromechanical equipment for input and process controls. Breweries became larger, for the product was now uniform enough for sale and reliable enough for shipment over a large area. The small local brewer succumbed to competition, and large national firms such as Anheuser-Busch, Schlitz, or Pabst,

each with a marketing orientation and funds for television advertising, have dominated the industry since the 1950s.

ECONOMIC CHARACTERISTICS OF THE BREWING INDUSTRY

The first characteristic of the beer industry is that it is large, and it is now growing rapidly (see Exhibit 1).

After a stagnant period in the 1950s, when per capita consumption actually declined, production and consumption both began to grow rapidly in the middle of the 1960s. During this decade production increased from 88.9 million to 122.5 million barrels, a jump of 38.1%. This substantial increase was the result of an increasing population, up 12.8% over the same period, and an expanding consumption per person, up 21.5%. This increase also calmed the fears of the brewing industry, for it demonstrated that younger people would still drink beer in volume.

There is no doubt that the beer business is going to grow. Beer drinkers come from the ranks of the young—those in the 21–34-

EXHIBIT 1 Taxpaid withdrawals of malt beverages, population, and consumption per capita, 1870 to 1970. Withdrawal and population figures in thousands. (Source: United States Brewers Association, Inc., *Brewer's Almanac*, 1974, p. 13.)

Year	Taxpaid withdrawals (barrels)	National population (persons)	Per capita consumption (gallons)
1870	6,570	38,560	5.3
1880	13,350	50,160	8.2
1890	27,560	62,950	13.6
1900	39,330	75,990	16.0
1910	59,480	91,970	20.0
1920	27,590	104,340	8.2
1930	Prohibition	122,470	—
1940	53,020	131,670	12.5
1950	83,510	150,700	17.2
1960	88,930	179,320	15.4
1970	122,550	203,180	18.7
1973	133,960	209,850	19.8

year-old category. Thanks to the post-war baby boom, that happens to be the group that is growing the fastest. From 1965 to 1975, adults in the 21–34 age group are slated to increase by 13.4 million to 46.5 million. By contrast, this group grew only 385,000 in the prior decade. To quench the thirst of this exploding multitude will take an ocean of suds. ("Cold Drafts? Life Isn't All Beer and Skittles for the Brewers," *Barrons,* July 13, 1970, p. 116.)

The second characteristic of the beer industry is that, as mentioned in the introduction, the industry is economically concentrated. This concentration has developed over an extended period of time, but it ac-celerated during the 1950s (see Exhibit 2).

In 1973 there were 129 breweries operating in the United States; these were not equal in size, and the larger companies were getting bigger. There seemed to be a direct correlation between size and profitability (see Exhibits 3, 4, and 5).

There is no question but that the larger breweries were the most profitable during the 1960s; note particularly the profit/size correlation even among the three largest companies in the industry. There is also little doubt that the smaller breweries were finding the competition exceedingly difficult during this time.

EXHIBIT 2 Taxpaid withdrawals of malt beverages, number of breweries, and production per brewery, 1900 to 1970. Withdrawal and average production figures in thousands. (Source: United States Brewers Association, *Brewer's Almanac,* 1974, pp. 12–14.)

Year	Taxpaid withdrawals (barrels)	Number of breweries	Per brewery production (1,000 barrels)
1900	39,330	1,400	28
1910	59,480	1,270	48
1920	27,590	925	29
1930	Prohibition	—	—
1940	53,020	611	80
1950	83,510	507	203
1960	88,930	229	390
1970	122,550	154	780
1973	133,960	129	1,038

EXHIBIT 3 Numbers, sales, and profits after tax of all breweries in 1970, by asset size class. Dollar figures in thousands. (Source: United States Brewers Association, *Brewer's Almanac,* 1974, pp. 44, 50, 52.)

Asset size class (000 omitted)	Number of breweries	Average sales	Average profits	Profits % of sales
Under $100	0	—	—	—
$100 to $500	36	$ 619	$ 12	1.9
$500 to $1,000	14	769	0	0.0
$1,000 to $10,000	50	5,234	117	2.2
$10,000 to $50,000	25	44,805	1,105	2.5
$50,000 to $100,000	6	135,061	1,877	1.4
Over $100,000	8	361,409	17,024	4.7

EXHIBIT 4 Numbers, net worth, and profits after tax of all breweries in 1970, by asset size class. Dollar figures in thousands. (Source: United States Brewers Association, *Brewer's Almanac,* 1974, pp. 44, 49, 52.)

Asset size class (000 omitted)	Number of breweries	Average net worth	Average profits	Profits % net worth
Under $100	0	$ —	$ —	—
$100 to $500	36	245	12	4.9
$500 to $1,000	14	317	0	0.0
$1,000 to $10,000	50	1,495	117	7.8
$10,000 to $50,000	25	16,282	1,105	6.8
$50,000 to $100,000	6	42,255	1,877	4.4
Over $100,000	8	143,770	17,024	11.8

EXHIBIT 5 Sales, expenses, and profits for the three major breweries in 1971. Dollar figures in thousands. (Source: Moody's Investors Services, Inc., *Moody's Industrial Manual,* 1972, pp. 214, 2468, 2917.)

	Anheuser-Busch	Schlitz	Pabst
Net sales	$902,450	$522,090	$416,730
Cost of sales	658,890	360,820	330,950
Selling and administrative expenses	108,090	85,570	36,800
Operating profit	135,480	74,700	48,980
Other income, expenses, and taxes	63,840	39,450	23,630
Net profit after taxes	71,640	35,250	25,350
Net profit % of sales	7.9%	6.8%	6.1%

There are a few discordant notes in the U.S. beer barrel polka. One reason is that the big brewers are getting bigger. Last year the industry leaders—Pabst, Schlitz, and Anheuser-Busch—accounted for 38% of the country's beer sales. This year, using their abundant resources to build new plants and expand their reach, the king pins may grab off 43% of the total.

With lots of new capacity coming on stream, it's conceivable the nationals may resort to price cutting to move the product off the shelves. The immediate sufferers would be the small beer makers, the so-called "regionals," which are short of funds and locked into specific territories. (*Barrons,* July 13, 1970, p. 115.)

The brewery industry has a lot going for it: rising levels of disposable income; an accelerated growth rate in the key 22–40-year-old group; increased leisure time; and more lenient attitudes toward beer drinking. But not all brewers are benefiting. While the top 25 firms in the industry posted an average gain last year of 4.5%, the rest showed an average drop of 11.4%.

What happened is that the big brewers are getting bigger and either swallowing up their small rivals through mergers or squeezing them out of business altogether. Where there were some 700 independent brewers in the thirties, the number now is well under 200—and indications are their ranks will continue to dwindle. Many of the small brewers are finding it increasingly difficult to turn a respectable profit as price wars, seasonal fluctuations, high fixed expenses, and encroachment by the industry giants keep whittling away at margins. (*Financial World,* October 2, 1968, pp. 11–12.)

CHANGES IN
THE CHARACTERISTICS
OF THE BREWING INDUSTRY

The possibility of economic change that might deteriorate, if not destroy, the current pronounced dominance of the large breweries can be seen in an analysis of the estimated costs of beer manufacture and distribution.

Packaging, shipment, and distribution costs are 67% of the retail price, while brewing costs are only 4.5%; the large, national brewery does not have direct control over the major portion of its costs (see Exhibit 6).

Packaging, shipment, and distribution expenses are the major portion of the retail price of beer, and yet these costs are not

EXHIBIT 6 Estimated costs of beer manufacture and distribution, 1971, per barrel and per case. A barrel equals 31 gallons and contains 14 cases. A case contains twenty-four 12-oz bottles/or cans. (Source: company records.)

	Costs per barrel	*Costs per case*
Brewing costs		
Raw materials (grain, malt, water)	$ 1.50	
Direct labor	0.80	
Brewery overhead	0.60	
	$ 3.90	$0.28
Tax costs		
Federal excise tax	$ 9.00	
Michigan excise tax	6.30	
	$15.30	$1.09
Selling and administrative costs		
Advertising and public relations	$ 3.00	
Missionary sales effort	1.00	
Administrative overhead	1.00	
Operating profit before taxes	5.00	
	$10.00	$0.71
Packaging costs		
Raw materials (bottles, cans, etc.)	$ 0.90	$0.90
Direct labor		0.14
Packaging overhead		0.07
		$1.11
Shipment costs		
Warehouse labor and overhead		$0.07
Freight from brewery to wholesaler		0.70
		$0.77
Total price to the wholesaler		$3.90
Distribution costs		
Wholesale discount of 14% of retail sales price		0.87
Retail discount of 23% of retail sales price		1.42
		$2.29
Total price to the retail customer		$6.25

under the control of the brewery. These are also the areas in which change is occurring most rapidly.

1. Packaging trends and costs. Beer is packaged for shipment and eventual retail sale in metal cans, glass bottles, and draft kegs or barrels. The bottles may be either one-way nonreturnable or two-way returnable. The percentage of beer sold in disposable containers, either metal cans or one-way nonreturnable bottles, has increased substantially, from less than 20% of sales in 1950 to more than 72% in 1973 (see Exhibit 7).

Over this same time period, the cost of disposable bottles and cans has risen rapidly (see Exhibit 8).

The combined result of the increased use of nonreturnable bottles and cans and the increased price of these disposable containers is a substantial increase in the cost of packaging beer; the beer industry now pays $0.90/case for packaging materials, nearly triple the $0.35/case of 1960. Returnable containers are considered to be much less expensive. Once back at the brewery, they can be auto-

matically cleaned in a hot caustic solution that will remove all organic material, and they can be electronically inspected by a light refraction test that will reject all bottles that have inorganic matter. The problem is in the return freight; empty containers are bulky, and it is estimated that the cost of the return shipment and handling would be equal to the outgoing charge of $0.77/case. There is also felt to be a consumer and distributor prejudice against the returnable containers.

No one likes the idea of going back to the two-way bottle. The customers don't like to return them; the retailer does not like to pay the refunds and store them; the distributor does not like to handle them; but most of all the brewery does not like to ship them: A carload of empty bottles may weigh only a few tons, but the railroad will charge the minimum car loading of 80,000 lb, and it will cost as much to get the empties back as it did to ship out the full ones. Also there is breakage, and the attendant mess and claims for Workman's Compensation from the broken glass; empty bottles rattling about in a freight car and handled four or five times just naturally break. The only way to do it is the way the soft drink

EXHIBIT 7 Taxpaid withdrawals of malt beverages from 1950 to 1970, by type of container. (Source: United States Brewers Association, *Brewer's Almanac,* 1961, pp .17, 23; *Brewer's Almanac,* 1973, pp. 14, 16.)

Type of container	1950	1955	1960	1965	1970	1973
Metal cans	18.4%	26.5%	30.5%	33.1%	44.7%	53.4%
One-way bottles	2.2%	4.1%	6.6%	15.2%	20.6%	19.0%
Two-way bottles	51.9%	47.2%	43.5%	34.0%	20.4%	14.7%
Kegs and barrels	27.5%	22.2%	19.3%	17.7%	14.3%	12.9%

EXHIBIT 8 Index of disposable container prices from 1967 to 1970. 1967 = 100. (Source: U.S. Department of Commerce, *Containers and Packaging Publication,* January/April 1972, p. 12.)

	1967	1968	1969	1970
12-oz beer can index	100.0	102.9	107.1	121.1

companies do; they have local filling plants, and the same truck that makes deliveries pick up the returns, with minimal handling. The large breweries can't do that; they serve much too large a geographic area for direct truck delivery. Budweiser, for example, serves 22 states from their St. Louis brewery; they brew over 9,000,000 barrels there, and you can't send out a couple of trucks every morning to deliver that. (Statement of industry executive.)

2. Shipment trends and costs. The beer industry, as explained previously, is economically concentrated; beer production is centralized not only among a few companies, but also among only a few plants for each company (see Exhibit 9).

The average plant production for these five large national brewers is 2,600,000 barrels, or roughly 400,000 tons of beer annually. These brewers distribute their products over the entire country from an average of six brewery locations. Freight from the brewer to the wholesaler is an important expense (an estimated $.77 per case) for the large national firms.

3. Distribution trends and costs. Beer is distributed in the United States by wholesalers who typically handle the output of only one or two brewing companies and who sell to both on-premise outlets such as bars, restaurants, nightclubs, etc., and to off-premise retail stores. The wholesaler provides a warehouse for storage and trucks for delivery of the beer, and he either is paid a commission or he receives a discount from the retail price. This wholesale discount ranges from 12% to 17%; 14% is considered standard in the industry.

The wholesaler is often a small, local businessman who services an area of one to four counties; his responsibilities include, beyond storage and delivery, personal selling, billing, credit, and setting up point-of-sale promotional devices. Beer distributorships were once considered very profitable concessions, but now because of the increased costs of labor and delivery services, they are now reputed to be in a severe profit squeeze, as are the independent wholesalers in other consumer product industries, since the larger manufacturers are hesitant to increase their commissions and consequent distribution expenses.

The beer distributor is helped to some extent by missionary salesmen employed by the brewer, who call upon both the on-premise outlets and the off-premise stores to take orders, service complaints, encourage advertising, and generally promote the sale and consumption of their brand or brands of beer. Personal selling in the beer industry is notoriously expensive; the missionary sales-

EXHIBIT 9 Total taxpaid withdrawals, number of breweries, and production per brewery for five national companies, 1974. Withdrawal and production figures are in thousands. (Source: Moody's Investors Service, Inc., *Moody's Industrial Manual,* 1974, pp. 86, 1424, 2188, 3082, 3247.)

Company	Total taxpaid withdrawals (barrels)	Number of breweries	Production per brewery (1,000 barrels)
Anheuser-Busch	34,100	9	3,800
Schlitz	22,700	7	3,200
Pabst	14,300	5	2,900
Millers	9,100	3	3,000
Falstaff	5,800	7	800
Totals	86,000	31	2,800

men generally offer to provide customers in bars and nightclubs with free samples of their product, tip bartenders and waitresses generously, and chat with the owner or manager. The ideal combination for beer sales is felt to be a wholesaler's driver who is on a friendly basis with the employees at each stop on his route and a company salesman who is a personal friend of the owner. This double selling, however, is expensive.

Discounts for the retail outlets, whether on-premise or off-premise, are standardized at 23% of the final price. Widespread retail distribution is felt to be desirable; small stores, with total sales of perhaps 20 cases per week of all brands, are solicited by both the wholesaler's drive and the brewing company's salesman, since it is believed that the customer will not go a long distance to purchase beer.

CUSTOMERS OF THE BREWING INDUSTRY

The average per capita consumption of beer in the United States, as indicated earlier in the case, was 19.8 gallons in 1973; this is an impressive statistic since, if one exempts just children under 18 years of age and 30% of the remaining adult population, it means that all the rest of us consume 40 gallons, or more than four hundred 12-oz bottles or cans, per person per year.

Beer consumption is widespread. Surveys indicate that 75% of all men and 50% of all women are beer drinkers and that over 80% of younger persons of both sexes, below age 35, consume at least an occasional glass of beer. These averages tend to be misleading, however, since it is believed that 80% of all beer sold is consumed by only 20% of the population. This is the prime beer market, but it is difficult to identify because very few persons during an interview will admit that they are heavy beer drinkers. For years it was believed that members of this market, almost by stereotype, were blue-collar workers, often in difficult or demanding jobs such as loggers, miners, steel workers, etc. It is now accepted that professional people, including lawyers,

doctors, university faculty, etc., and students are members of the prime beer market.

PRODUCTION AND MARKETING PLANS OF THE ANN ARBOR BREWERY

There has been a proposal, which is still in the planning state, to start a small, local brewery with a capacity of 30,000 barrels per year in the Ann Arbor area, primarily because of the large student (35,000) and professional (perhaps 8,000) population, but also because of the massive urban markets in Dearborn, Flint, and Detroit, all less than 50 miles away.

The economic justification of the investment and the explanation of the proposed production and marketing plans can be described first by a comparison of the costs for the typical national brewery (from Exhibit 6) and for the new local company. The strategy of the new brewery, in brief, will be to sell premium beer, equal in taste, alcoholic content, and quality to Budweiser, Schlitz, Millers, etc., at $3.80 per case, or $0.95 per six-pack, to local residents and students, primarily those in the prime beer market, through selected retail outlets by means of extensive newspaper, radio, and television advertising. The price provides a considerable savings. It is expected that the heavier beer drinkers, the professionals, students, and working men, or those planning to entertain friends and needing a large quantity of beer to do so will drive either to the brewery for direct sales or to a limited number of retail stores. The advertising, which is all to be on local media and consequently relatively inexpensive, will be used to inform customers about the product and where it can be purchased. Additional details of the production, marketing, and financial plans follow:

1. Brewing Costs. Brewing costs are expected to be equal; the process for the Ann Arbor Brewery will probably be less expensive to operate (a result of automation and reduced labor charges), but the input grains and malt may be more expensive to purchase because the quantities required are smaller:

Since we are going to brew premium beer, we will have no savings on our raw materials; we can make some savings on the process costs, but we don't have to count on that. It will be nice if we get it; it will not hurt us if we don't. (Statement of potential investor.)

Water, which is important in brewing, is not expected to be a problem in Ann Arbor; the company can use either artesian wells or the city water system:

Years ago, the quality of the water decided the location of the brewery. Now we can use any water that is free of bacterial contamination, malodorous content, or iron. The Ann Arbor water qualifies very well on those tests. You will find now that most brewers use the community water system in their process if not in their advertising. (Statement of potential investor.)

2. *Tax Costs.* Tax costs are also expected to be equal; these are federal and state excise taxes, assessed at a specified rate on brewery withdrawals for shipment.

We can't save money on taxes; everyone pays the same rate. (Statement of potential investor.)

3. *Selling and Administrative Costs.* Selling and administrative costs for the national brewery include an allowance of $5.00/barrel ($0.35/case) for profit. No equivalent allowance has been included for the Ann Arbor Brewery, so a more valid comparison would be $0.36/case for the national brewery ($0.71/case listed less $0.35/case profit allowance) and $0.30/case for Ann Arbor. The difference is because of the limited nature of the promotional program proposed for the local brewery:

$0.30 per case for selling and administration expenses equals $4.20 per barrel, and we expect to spend most of that for local advertising. We won't use missionary salesmen and we will keep our administrative expenses lean, so we ought to have $3.00 (per barrel) available for advertising; at 30,000 barrels a year, we can spend $90,000. This is just a drop in the bucket compared to the advertising expenditures of the national brewers, but we won't be advertising nationally; we will be selling on the local level where expenses are lower and where we can have a definite impact. On the local radio station we can sponsor a 5-minute news/weather program for $80, and in the local newspaper we can have a quarter page for $375. We will have to go to Detroit for television, but we can pick up 30 seconds there for $400 during AA time (6:00 P.M. to 10:00 P.M.). We will have to spend more than this at the start, of course; we will have to make an investment in adver-

---

EXHIBIT 10 Estimated costs of beer manufacture and distribution for a national premium brewery and the proposed Ann Arbor brewery. (Source: company records.)

	National brewery	*Ann Arbor brewery*
Brewing costs	$0.28/case	$0.28/case
Tax costs	$1.09/case	$1.09/case
Selling and administrative costs	$0.71/case*	$0.30/case
Packaging costs	$1.11/case	$0.30/case
Shipment costs—brewery to wholesaler	$0.77/case	—
Wholesale distribution costs	$0.82/case	$0.20/case
Retail distribution costs	$1.42/case	$0.65/case
	$6.25/case*	$2.81/case

* National brewery costs include (in the selling and administrative category) an allowance of $5.00/barrel ($0.35/case) for operating profit before taxes; no equivalent allowance has been included for the Ann Arbor Brewery.

tising during the first 3 months so that people get to know us, but after that the ads can be on a sustaining basis for about $90,000 per year.

The ads will be simple; we'll just explain that we have premium beer available at a discount price direct from the brewery. Then we'll show the places where they can buy it.

We'll also do a lot of the "conducted tour of the brewery" advertising; breweries are interesting places. You have to keep them very, very clean to avoid contamination of the yeast, and, of course, all the pipes are stainless steel and all the valves are brass-plated. If you keep everything polished and painted, people like to look. If you then offer them a free sample, you often have a new customer. (Statement of potential investor.)

4. Packaging Costs.

Packaging costs for the local brewery are expected to be considerably lower because we plan to use two-way returnable bottles which, as described previously, can be cleaned, inspected, and reprocessed inexpensively. The problems for larger brewers are the handling and return freight. The Ann Arbor Brewery expects all sales points to be within the range of their delivery trucks, which can pick up and bring back the empty bottles in permanent racks rather than in cardboard cartons.

Our trucks will stop at each retail point daily; they will deliver our beer in permanent plastic rack-type cases that hold 24 bottles and pick up the empties in the same cases. Daily service will prevent the clutter and smell around the retail store that is usually associated with returnable bottles.

We will use two-way bottles because they represent a very considerable savings which we can use both to generate and to explain the low price. But, to be honest, I wish we had better information here. Many people don't like the returnable bottle; they don't like the inconvenience of bringing them back and they don't think that we can really clean them. Everyone has heard the stories about the dead mouse or the old cigarette butts in the bottle; I can guarantee you that that won't happen with hot caustic cleaning. But, will our customers believe us? There are people, of course,

who are concerned about the environment and prefer returnable bottles, but we don't know if they drink beer; they may prefer milk or coke or martinis. (Statement of potential investor.)

5. Shipment Costs.

Shipment costs, from the brewery to the wholesaler, will be nonexistent for the Ann Arbor Brewery; they do not expect to ship any greater distance than can be served by their wholesale delivery trucks.

One major savings is that we won't have to ship by rail or by long-haul trucks. Every major brewer has to do that, and it is expensive. (Statement of potential investor.)

6. Wholesale Distribution Costs.

The Ann Arbor Brewery expects to serve as its own wholesale distributor, which will eliminate most handling and storage costs; delivery costs will be reduced since the company expects to sell 20% to 30% of the production through the retail office at the brewery and the balance through a limited number of company branches and selected retail stores, all within 20 miles of the brewery.

Since it costs as much for the delivery truck to drive to and stop at a small outlet as at a large outlet, we expect to have large outlets only, and not too many of them, and not too far away. Thus, our delivery costs should be low.

We will have 2 trucks, each operating about 150 miles per day, and 2 drivers. Many beer trucks have to have a driver and an assistant to handle the beer, which is heavy; we will deliver much of our product to our own retail outlets, and our clerks there can help with the handling.

Our 2 trucks will operate a total of 300 miles per day, at a maximum of $0.50 per mile, for $150 per day. Then we can get good drivers who will be courteous in their contacts with the store personnel at $50 per day, which means that our total delivery expenses will be $250 per day; over 300 days this is $75,000. We have allocated $0.20 per case, which is $2.80 per barrel, or $84,000 per year; I know that we can keep our wholesale distribution costs within that. (Statement of potential investor.)

7. Retail Distribution Costs.

The Ann Arbor Brewery expects to sell 25% to 30% of their production through a retail store at the brewery, 40% to 50% through branch locations in shopping centers or on heavily traveled routes, and the balance through selected retail stores:

We expect to keep our retail costs down by using our own stores and by allowing a discount of only 20% instead of the standard 25%. We will have a volume item that will build traffic, so I know that the retail grocery and package stores will ask us to let them handle it, despite the discount, but I think that we can do it cheaper and better with our own stores. We could have one store at the brewery and three branch locations, each in a modern, attractive building, well-lighted, with plenty of parking. The branch stores would be in places that are easy to get to, such as out in the parking lot of a shopping center. People drive out to discount stores; they will certainly drive out to a shopping center to save money on beer.

We have allocated $0.65 per case for retail distribution costs; this is $9.10 per barrel, or $273,000 per year. Our expenses would be as follows:

Brewery retail store, open 12:00 noon to 10:00 P.M. 6 days a week and 1:00 to 5:00 on Sunday. Wages, with an average of 2 clerks on duty, would be $380 per week; maintenance, utilities, etc., would add another $120 per week. This would be $26,000 per year.

Branch locations, also open 12:00 noon to 10:00 P.M. 6 days a week and 1:00 to 5:00 on Sunday. Wages, with an average of 2 clerks on duty, would be $380 per week at each, rent would be $400 per week, and maintenance, etc. would be $120. This totals $900 per week for each location. We would have 3 locations, so that annual cost would be $135,000.

Retail stores will probably sell at most one-third of our production at a 20% discount, or $0.76 per case on the customer price of $3.80 per case. About 140,000 cases would cost $110,000 per year through the retail stores.

Eventually we will probably sell our beer only through our own locations, but at the start we do want some grocery and drug stores to get wider distribution and to introduce more people to our product. (Statement of potential investor.)

8. Expected Investment and Returns.

A small local brewery, with automated instrumentation and controls for line processing as described previously, can be built for a capital cost of $30.00 per barrel capacity, complete with bottle washing and filling equipment. The capital cost of the new brewery is expected, then, to be $900,000; an additional $250,000 has been allocated for start-up expenses and working capital. Working capital needs are believed to be minimal, since beer manufacture and marketing is a cash business, with very limited accounts receivable or inventory required. Start-up expenses will consist primarily of an intensive advertising campaign over the first 3 months of operation to acquaint customers with the beer.

Revenues and expenses for the Ann Arbor Brewery have been estimated as follows:

Net sales, 30,000 barrels, or 420,000 cases, sold at $3.80/case	$1,600,000
Total expenses, 30,000 barrels, or 420,000 cases, brewed and distributed at $2.81/case (from Exhibit 10)	$1,180,000
	$ 420,000

Financially, of course, this seems to be a most attractive business; pre-tax profits run about 40% of the total investment required, and after-tax profits will pay off the capital investment in just over 3 years. Since the capital investment is largely for bricks and mortar, which we can mortgage, we should be able to obtain quite a leverage.

I particularly like the thought that the cash flow from this one brewery could be used to start others in college towns throughout the country. There are a lot of universities, so this company could get very large very fast. Then, of course, we could expand to manufacturing and urban centers. There is only one problem in all of this: we don't know if anyone will buy our low-priced beer. (Statement of potential investor.)

9. Expected Problems.

The major problems facing the company are a bias

against the local or regional brewer and a definite prejudice against low-priced beer. The national firms, through their extensive advertising, have established brand consciousness among consumers and a general belief that price equals quality. Lower-priced beers are felt to be less desirable in taste, less reliable in quality, and less prestigious to drink or to serve to others. This attitude has been confirmed by a large number of market research studies, undertaken both by the American Brewers Association and by local and regional brewers themselves, in which persons randomly selected for interviews described imported German and Danish beers as "distinctive" and "satisfying," premium American beers as "smooth" or "full-bodied," and lower-priced local beers as "thin," "green," or "bitter"; none of these respondents, however, was able to distinguish between these beers when offered samples of each in unidentified glasses.

ASSIGNMENT

The problem for the Ann Arbor Brewery is the very definite existing bias against lower-priced, locally brewed beer, irrational though this attitude may be. The company wants to start production and marketing in a university town, since it is believed that students and faculty members are less likely to accept existing social attitudes and conventions and would be more likely to purchase the new product. The assignment for the market research groups (three to five students) of the class is to investigate student, faculty, professional, and working class attitudes within the community to form an estimate of the potential market size within the area and to recommend a course of action, with supporting evidence, for the potential investors in the local brewery. Remember that the branch stores, under the existing cost structure, may be situated up to 20 miles from the central brewery to serve an adequate market area.

4

Operations Management

Operations management is concerned with the design of a system to produce a given good or service and the scheduling and control of that system for optimal performance. As such, it is a more general form of production. Production has traditionally been associated with the factory, and with the design and control of large-scale manufacturing processes; operations management has expanded this field of study to apply the principles and techniques of systems design, scheduling, and control to such nonfactory settings as retail stores, financial offices, and whole-sale firms, and such nonbusiness establishments as educational institutions, health care organizations, and governmental units. It follows, then, that the principles and techniques of operations management are applicable to the smaller business firm engaged in either manufacturing, service, or distribution.

Operations management can be summarized as the process of designing and utilizing the physical resources of the firm to maximize the operational capabilities of the company. This view of operations management is shown below:

Product/service design
Process design
Job design
Job standards
Physical facilities
Planning models
Scheduling methods
Control techniques

Company operational capabilities

In short, operations management is a combination of the product, process, and job design with the establishment of job standards to define efficient physical facilities and the planning, scheduling, and control of those facilities for effective usage. It is the means of "getting shipments out the door on time" or of "getting things done" within a business organization. It is particularly important in smaller companies since the smaller firm generally has to provide specialized few-of-a-kind products and personalized services, without the benefits of mass production and mass distribution. Large firms have an inherent advantage in the economies of scale, for they have established products and large markets; smaller companies have to compete against the large corporations and have to produce a much more limited volume of goods and services at a quality and price that will still appeal to the market segment selected. Since the products of the smaller company are usually specialized, the price does not have to be equal, but it does have to seem comparable to the customer. The quality has to be at least equal, if not often higher. In order to be able to compete on this price and quality basis but with limited financial and professional resources, the management of a smaller firm has to develop a complete and efficient productive system, with innovative product designs, process designs, job designs, and job standards, and it has to manage this system effectively by using quantitative planning models, scheduling methods, and control techniques.

PRODUCT OR SERVICE DESIGNS

The first step in the development of an efficient operational system is the design of the product or service that is to be offered. This operational design is in addition to the engineering design that earlier has determined the performance and appearance of the product; the operational design is concerned with the efficient production of the item or service. It is necessary to review the product features to determine which can be standardized and which can be simplified in order to improve the productive process.

Standardization involves the reduction of product or service variations to gain uniformity and interchangeability. Since uniform and interchangeable parts are usually manufactured in volume by mass-production techniques, the concept of standardization is often believed to be applicable only to large manufacturing firms in the basic industries. Standardization, however, is equally useful for smaller companies and service organizations. The quick-service restaurant chains, most of which started as small local companies, are based on the time and cost savings of standardized food servings. A very successful repair service for automatic car washers in Pennsylvania and Ohio performs standardized preventive maintenance on a weekly basis so that its customers can avoid the much more expensive emergency repairs over the weekends, which are, of course, the periods of greatest use, and consequently the periods of greatest probability of breakdowns and greatest potential for lost revenues. The concept of standardization can even be of benefit to small retail stores, for example, "tall girl" shops which can offer a much wider range of styles, fabrics, and colors in a standardized range of sizes.

Simplification involves the reduction of product or service complexities to gain easier operational methods, and it includes substitution of materials, relaxation of tolerances, and combinations of operations. Again, since simplification is often illustrated in textbooks by examples from metal-working machine tools, it is sometimes believed that the concept is applicable only to large manufacturing firms. Simplification is equally useful for smaller service and retail companies. An extremely successful ice cream shop in Massachusetts has simplified its operations by making only one flavor of ice cream that is very similar in texture and consistency to that made in an old-fashioned freezer. Then whatever flavors or natural fruits or nuts the customer wants are stirred into the ice cream. Strawberries are added for strawberry ice cream; chocolate chips for chocolate chip ice cream, etc. The customers evidently enjoy being able to choose their own combinations, for during the spring and summer there is a continual line outside the shop. The owner is able to offer extremely high quality at reasonable prices through an efficient operational system that is based upon a simplified products design.

PROCESS DESIGNS

The second step in the development of an efficient operational system is the design of the process to meet the product or service specifications. Process planning includes the selection of operations, facilities, and sequences.

The selection of operations is, of course, based upon the design characteristics of the product or service. In a manufacturing company the engineering drawings provide the specifications for each part and the bills of material list the number of parts in each assembly. These are translated into routing slips that show the operations required to manufacture each part and each assembly. The same breakdown of design characteristics is required in a service firm; for example, the owners of the ice cream shop described previously had to list the individual operations required before they could design the new system. A complete and accurate breakdown of operations is essential for innovative process design.

The selection of facilities is then based upon the list of required operations. The actions necessary to manufacture each part and assembly or to provide each element of the service are translated into the equipment or process machinery capable of performing these operations at various levels of demand. Many times the equipment necessary to manufacture the specialized products of the smaller firm or to provide the individualized services, is not commercially available and has to be designed. The ice cream shop owners, for example, were unable to purchase a suitable freezer. They had to build a special unit, using commercial parts, to produce the high-quality ice cream mixture they offer to their customers. The success of many other small companies is based upon the design of special-process machinery that provides a distinctive competitive advantage in either quality or cost.

The selection of sequences is the last step in the design of the productive process. The operations required to manufacture each part and assembly of a product or to provide each element of a service can be sequenced in different ways, depending on the product or service characteristics and the expected volume. The sequence of operations governs the flow of material through the productive process. There are two basic material flows that are possible: continuous (line production) and intermittent (job–shop production), with combinations between these two extremes. The ice cream shop is a good example of a combined process. The preparation of the basic mixture is a continuous line operation; the addition of flavors, fruits, and nuts to the customer's order is equivalent to an intermittent job shop. The management of a smaller company should carefully consider the cost advantages associated with the different methods of sequencing—and not automatically accept the common or traditional method—in order to develop an efficient productive process.

JOB DESIGN

Despite recent advances in automation technology, manual work is still prevalent in most manufacturing and service industries. Therefore, job design remains an important consideration in operations management. Job design may be divided into determination of the work content, recommendations for the work methods, and design of the work environment.

Work content is not consciously designed; it is the direct result of prior decisions on product or service design and process planning. It is what the workers must do to accomplish a given task, and it can be schematically represented by an operator chart that shows the motions of a typical worker in performing an existing job.

Work methods are consciously designed; they are the direct results of efforts to improve the performance of the work content through changes in the work-place arrangement or process machine controls. They are what the workers should do to accomplish a given task in the most economical fashion, and they can be schematically represented by an operations chart that shows the motions of an efficient worker in performing an improved job.

Work environment is the setting in which the work methods are performed. It includes temperature, humidity, noise, lighting, etc., all of which can have a marked effect on productivity and quality levels.

Many small companies, of course, do not employ industrial engineers to help in the design of work methods and the improvement of the work environment, and the managers are often too busy to spend time on these details. In some industries this neglect may be costly. There is a small company in northern Indiana that manufactures formed wire parts for the automobile industry. This is a very competitive and labor intensive industry in which many small companies fail; yet the major problem of this firm is where to invest the surplus cash generated by the operations. The owner individually designs very efficient work methods for each new contract, before the contract is accepted, and personally supervises the conditions of the work environment. This entrepreneur, who started with one machine in the basement of his home and now employs more than 100 people in a modern factory building, has stated that efficient work methods and a pleasant work environment are much more central to the success of his company than either marketing or finance.

JOB STANDARDS

A job standard is the amount of time it should take an average worker to perform a specific job after the essential work content has been defined and after the optimal work methods and work environment have been established. Job standards are used for production planning, scheduling, and control and for product costing and wage incentives. They are normally set by time study in which either a stopwatch or synthetic times are used.

Small companies often neglect job standards, for they assume that the close personal rapport that often exists between the owner and the employees will ensure high productivity, and they feel that time study by a stopwatch under those conditions would be both awkward and unrewarding. Again, in some industries these assumptions may be wrong. The owner of the formed wire products company in northern Indiana sets the standard for each job simply and accurately by measuring the amount of time it takes him, after study of the work content and design of the work methods, to make the part. Production schedules, employee wages, and contract bids are all based upon that standard; the owner feels that accurate job standards are the second central element in the success of his company.

PHYSICAL FACILITIES

The physical facilities for most small firms, and for almost all beginning companies, do not have to be luxurious. It is undoubtedly true that more successful small companies have been started in basements, garages, and barns, with used and remodeled machinery, than in modern buildings with new equipment. As a matter of fact, many customers prefer to see the older facilities, since they feel that this indicates that they are not being charged for the high overhead associated with modern buildings and equipment, and many financial people, both bankers and credit analysts, share this attitude since they believe that the management of a growing firm should put their limited resources into current working capital rather than long-term fixed assets. There are exceptions to this rule, of course. A small store that specializes in the retail sales of expensive watches and personally designed jewelry probably cannot be located in a garage, and a high technology firm, requiring exceedingly close tolerances in its productive process, probably cannot employ used and remodeled equipment. Overall, however, small and growing firms should not invest excessive amounts in fixed assets but should use existing buildings and used machinery. Both are usually available at reasonable costs; it is one of the functions of the entrepreneur to find and refurnish the necessary physical facilities.

The physical facilities for most small firms do not have to be expensive, but they do have to be designed for efficient operations (the result of careful decisions on product or service design, process design, job designs, and job standards), and to utilize the available capacity, they have to be effectively managed through quantitative procedures for production planning, scheduling, and control. It is not the intention of the balance of this chapter to review these quantitative procedures, which normally form a central portion of the undergraduate and M.B.A. curricula at many schools of administration, but merely to indicate their applications and usefulness in small business situations.

PRODUCTION PLANNING MODELS

Production planning involves the adjustment of the designed capacity of the physical facilities to meet variations in aggregate product or service demand. These adjustments may be made by changes in the employment level, in overtime or undertime, in order backlogs or inventory build-up, or in make-buy decisions. The objective of production planning is to minimize the total costs of meeting expected but uncertain demand under the restrictions of a given productive system. Decisions on how to minimize these total costs can be made by expressing the relationships between variables and constraints within the system through such techniques as linear cost models, quadratic cost functions, queuing networks, or computer simulations.

Small service companies, retail stores, and wholesale firms particularly need to pay attention to production planning because the quality of their service, which is really what they are selling and central to the success of their business, often depends on the number of employees and the costs of providing available capacity to meet customer demands quickly. The relationships between known costs and anticipated revenues can be expressed by production planning models.

PRODUCTION SCHEDULING TECHNIQUES

Production scheduling involves the adjustment of the designed capacity of the physical facilities to meet variations in individual product or service demand. These adjustments may be made by changes in the product mix, the facilities assignment, or both. The objective of production scheduling is to minimize the total costs of meeting existing demand under the restrictions of a given productive system. Decisions on how to minimize these total costs can be made by expressing the relationships between variables and constraints through such methods as linear programming, integer programming, or dynamic programming.

Small job shop operations that provide machined parts and assembly services to larger companies should pay particular attention to production scheduling because it is necessary to balance the available jobs on the existing equipment. Most contract jobs like these can be done on different pieces of equipment in different sequences at different costs. The successful operation of a job shop often depends on finding the lowest-cost product mix, operational sequence, and facility assignment. This can be done by using production scheduling techniques.

PRODUCTION CONTROL METHODS

Production control involves the supervision of the output of the physical facilities to adjust for variations in individual worker or machine performance. Supervision is performed by recording the output (in product units, machine times, and quality tolerances) and comparing these measurements with accepted standards. The objective of production control is to maintain performance at the anticipated unit, cost, and quality standards. The methods that are employed use computerized or graphic data processing because the amount of information needed even in a small productive system is so enormous. Production control is important for almost all small companies. Management must supervise operational costs and quality because these are central to successful competition with larger firms.

The management of a smaller company has a difficult task in designing an efficient productive system for the firm and in arranging the planning, scheduling, and control of that system for effective operation. The problem is that the smaller firm, and particularly the beginning company, does not have adequate financial resources to design and build the physical facilities to exactly match the operational requirements of a given product or service; instead, existing facilities often have to be adapted, with compromises made in the engineering of the product, the planning of the process, and the translation of these decisions into the plant or shop layout. The larger company can invest substantial funds in physical plant and equipment, and it can build exactly what is needed since efficient production, given the larger market size, guarantees eventual recovery of the investment. The smaller company has neither the money nor the potential market size, and yet it must operate at least as economically to maintain control of its product or service. That is, if its production costs are excessive, the smaller firm can easily find itself in a position in which it is unable to market its product (because of price) or to finance additional development (because of costs) and, thus, it may be gradually squeezed out of its industry position. To avoid this, the management of the smaller company must substitute imagination and innovation for money in the design of their productive facilities; they must remodel used equipment and reconstruct older buildings to have a comparable productive system at substantially reduced cost. This is difficult but not impossible. More successful firms have undoubtedly started in old warehouses, garages, or mill buildings than in new structures, and probably one of the marks of the successful smaller company is the ability to make or remodel inexpensive production and test equipment.

The smaller firm also has to use imagination and innovation in planning, scheduling, and controlling its productive facilities for efficient utilization. The larger firm often has the managerial resources, particularly in staff personnel and computer capability, to apply the newer managerial techniques, such as linear programming, computer simulation, or heuristics, to optimize its plant or shop utilization. Again, the larger firm has the production base and market share to support these resources; the smaller firm does not, but it still must compete in performance. Again, this is difficult but not impossible. Operations management is not entirely quantitative and computer-based; many graphic and mechanical planning, scheduling, and control techniques are available and apply to the simpler productive systems of the smaller firms.

In both the design and management of the productive system of the firm, the executives of the smaller company must recognize the opportunities for compromise, adaptability, and innovation, but they must also understand the need for competitive performance. The objective in the management of the operations of the firm must be to produce a given good or service at a definite capacity and quality level and at a competitive cost. To accomplish this objective, management should think in terms of a complete productive system, relating the product and process designs to the job methods and the job standards, in order to develop efficient physical facilities. Then management should employ planning, scheduling, and control techniques to utilize those facilities effectively. The following cases illustrate the need for this complete approach to operations management.

Electronic Accounting Associates, Inc.

John Chesin, a 1972 graduate of the M.B.A. program at the University of Chicago, was interested in starting a consulting business that could offer operations research and management science services to smaller firms:

The management at most smaller companies doesn't have the expertise or the time to make use of the standard quantitative methodologies that are now just accepted procedures at most of the bigger firms. I'm not talking about advanced mathematical techniques such as branch and bound algorithms or transformation equations. I'm talking about just such basic methods as linear programming, computer simulation, and network models and just such basic functions as sales forecasting, production scheduling, inventory control, quality review, and financial planning. Most smaller firms don't perform these functions in an orderly, systematic managerial process that uses mathematics, statistics, or computation; instead, they tend to rely on intuition and hope. I want to change this. I want to apply quantitative techniques to the problems of small business management. (Statement of Mr. Chesin.)

Mr. Chesin was looking at the problems of smaller business firms because he was dissatisfied with his present position in the management services division of a major accounting firm; he felt that his assigned task, which was writing computer programs for use in the information and control systems that were being developed for large clients, was dull and unimaginative, and he complained that he was not improving his competence in mathematics and statistics:

As you well know, there is a lot of detail work in getting a complex program to run properly in a large corporate environment. Technically, I'm classified as one of the firm's Information Systems Analysts, and we do have programming assistance, but the programmers aren't really capable of tracing down system problems in the more economical languages, so that as long as we have to do most of this work, we all feel that we might as well closely supervise the original program preparation. The result is that I spend 70% to 80% of my time working at my desk on program development, about 20% on information system design in the field, and almost none on decision system research, which is what I'm really interested in. I think that I'm good at my job [Mr. Chesin has an undergraduate major in mathematics and a masters degree in computer science], and I'm certainly well paid for my age, but I want to get into more interesting and original work. Also, and your students may laugh at this but I could not be more serious, I feel that the large multinational corporations are taking over the world, and I don't want to be part of the supporting services that help them to do this. I feel that it is important that smaller companies remain a viable force in the economy, to give us all a choice in employment and in products and services, but I don't believe that smaller firms can continue to exist if they don't make use

of mathematics and statistics to optimize their use of limited capital and other resources. I want to help them here. (Statement of Mr. Chesin.)

In order to follow up on his interests and his ideals, Mr. Chesin began to devote much of his free time, on evenings and over weekends during the summer months of 1974, to market research on the need for quantitative assistance to the management of smaller business firms. He made appointments with the owners and managers of independent retail stores and local manufacturing firms, talked with them about their problems, and asked for their opinions. The results of these interviews were not encouraging:

There was one problem that was apparent right at the start, one that probably could be resolved over time through customer education. There was a second problem that was not as apparent at the start, and it seemed to grow worse the further I got into it.

The first problem is that small business people generally have very limited experience with quantitative methodologies, and they tend to view the computer as some sort of expensive marvel that has no possible application to their operations. Most of the owners and managers of small firms graduated from college 15 or 20 or more years ago, if they had a college education at all, and they never had an introductory course in computing, which is almost standard now, and they had very little work in the application of mathematics and statistics. The social sciences, particularly economics, did not have the quantitative base they have now, so there was very little reason for anyone except a physicist or an engineer to spend much time on quantitative analysis. I can explain the advantages of quantitative managerial methods, but it takes time. I met the owner of an alloy casting firm who described, as his major problem, classic blending decisions that were textbook examples of linear programming, but it took me all of one evening to explain the process, and even then he wasn't convinced. I wasn't worried here, however; good O.R. really is research into the operations of a firm for the purpose of improving those operations, and I knew that I could demonstrate those improvements. The small business people I talked with had a lot of problems, some of which I could help them with. I felt then, and I still feel, that there is a lot of opportunity here.

The major problem, the one that I did not anticipate at the start of my market research study, but that became clearer and more troublesome the further I got into it, was the lack of an accurate and organized data base. Bookkeeping and accounting are just not very well done at most smaller firms, and, therefore, you can't get detailed sales revenues or cost figures for analysis. In the case of the smallest companies, the bookkeeping is often done by the owner in the evening and in his spare time over weekends. You know that it is the last item on his agenda. Slightly larger firms have a high school girl who comes in every afternoon, but she doesn't know anything about systems; she just keeps the debits and the credits balanced. The larger companies have one or two permanent people who have considerable bookkeeping competence, but they generally follow a system that was set up years before, with just the basic records in the journal and a few subsidiary ledgers. The entries may be accurate, but they are hard to pick out quickly for analysis.

Most of the smaller companies have a C.P.A. firm come in once or twice a year to close out their books, take a trial balance, and prepare an income statement and balance sheet. But since this is done primarily for tax reasons, the information in the reports is too late for use in management decisions. Some of the companies have quarterly or monthly services from a local accounting firm, but most of the people with whom I spoke felt that this was too expensive, at $40.00 per hour, which is the standard charge from an auditing firm, and, again, the reports are usually late.

Almost all the owners and managers of the smaller companies I surveyed felt that bookkeeping and financial accounting were a major problem. But they did not know what to do about this problem. They said that it is difficult to hire competent people. For example, one of the men I spoke with picked up the local newspaper and showed me the classified ad section; in a city of only 100,000 population there were 14 ads under the "Help Wanted—Bookkeeper" classification. There are a number of companies that offer specialized bookkeeping services, such as computerized payroll or billing, and there are standard forms that simplify bookkeeping, such as carbon overlays that record the check stub and the journal entry at the same time, and there are a few accountants who keep the books totally as a favor to their clients, but it is very difficult for the typical small business to obtain competent bookkeeping and accurate and timely accounting statements. Most owners and managers have an intuitive feeling for the operations of their companies—one of them talked about the "droop in my right hip pocket"—but few of them have the sort of financial and managerial accounting services that large companies automatically provide.

It was obvious that there was a huge market for bookkeeping and accounting services to smaller businesses, but I talked to people on our audit staff, and they told me that no one can really afford to provide the level of service that these people want and need. Since the account classification system at most smaller firms is not good, you are faced with reviewing all the entries in order to offer meaningful sales or cost analysis. Since there are errors and omissions in many of the accounts, you have to balance and confirm the cash and receivables and inventory and payables before you really get down to work. After you've classified and verified the entries, you still can't use the computer for electronic data processing because you can't afford to enter each item on a terminal or key punch.

I was discouraged at the end of the summer. It appeared that I couldn't offer the service on decision systems that I wanted since the smaller companies lacked the necessary data base, and I couldn't offer the service on information and control systems that they wanted since it was too expensive to classify, verify, and record all the entries.

As a result of his market research survey, Mr. Chesin decided to forget his concept of offering operations research and management science services to smaller companies. He had resolved to work harder at his present job in order to be promoted to a more responsible and more intellectually challenging position. Then he suddenly had an idea for a means of low-cost data entry:

It was a Saturday afternoon. My wife and I had driven out in the country to look at a possible home site. On the way back we stopped at McDonalds for lunch, and Judith [Mrs. Chesin] asked me about the electronic cash registers (keyboard shown in Exhibit 1), and I explained that they were part of an E.D.P. system that provided cash records, inventory control, sales analysis, and even production scheduling. The four or five registers at the counter are connected to a very simple minicomputer in the office. The manager can see at a glance the trend of sales and compare this trend with standard forecasts, so that he knows when to start more hamburgers or cheeseburgers or french fries. He can enter the production orders on his terminal, which gives him a real-time inventory on all prepared food items, plus an accurate total on all the raw materials, so that he knows when to requisition additional meat patties or buns or even ketchup from the district warehouse. A physical inventory at the end of each day lets him know exactly where and when losses are occurring. It's a beautiful little system, and it's one of the major reasons McDonalds has been able to push out the small, local restaurants, which may offer better quality food but can't hope to equal this degree of accurate and current management information and control.

Then, we stopped at a convenience food store, one of those that stock only the most popular items, such as bread and milk and beer, and provide quick service—you go in, find what you want easily, pay for it quickly, without standing in line, and leave—at a fairly high price. Judith wanted some cigarettes. This store was one of a chain, and it too had electronic cash registers (keyboard shown in Exhibit 2). This system was even more advanced than the one at McDonalds; it obviously had an input tape with the prices of all the items, by code number, and an output tape for data transmission to the company headquarters. You could change the prices just by changing the input tape, and you could send the sales data to headquarters for processing just by mailing the output tape. Each item in the store was marked with an adhesive tag that gave the primary classification and the code number. For example, we bought one pack of Winstons, and the girl punched "Tobacco" for the primary classification and "304" for the code number for one pack of Winstons; one carton of Win-

stons would probably be "303" and one pack of Camels might be "313." Codes are usually set up with some inherent order, not just in simple numerical sequence. With the primary classification and the code, the machine recorded the deduction from inventory, searched for the price on the input tape, listed the item code and the item price on an electronic display board, recorded the sale, added the tax, showed the total, and printed a receipt. Since there was a telephone coupler, it was obvious that the tape would be run at night on the main computer, which would give the company headquarters daily cash receipts, sales analysis, tax liabilities, inventory control, and reorder information by store, by district, and by company. Since they would have standard costs for all merchandise and fixed costs for most of the overhead, they could have daily income statements by store. Again, it was a beautiful system—and another reason why the large corporation was able to drive out the independent retailer.

I was halfway out to our car before I realized that these were really very simple systems and that I could devise an equivalent system for a group of small businesses, such as gas stations, men's clothing stores, or local manufacturing plants. Each customer would need a system designed specifically for its industry, but the system could then be sold or leased to a large number of individual customers within that industry. That is, I would have to design a system specifically for gas stations, but once it was designed and operating, I could sell or lease it to 100 or more similar stations, and so amortize the cost of development on a pro-rata basis, just as the large chains did with their individual stores.

The only problem I could see was with the hardware. I would have to use an electronic cash register as the input terminal, or accounting machine, for expense items as well as sales revenues, and to do this I would have to design a special keyboard, with keys for the classification and coding of the various expenses. I didn't know if the manufacturers would be willing to make special keyboards in relatively small lots, so I was in a hurry to get home and call one of them. My wife didn't understand what I was thinking about; I was too excited to be able to explain it sensibly, and she thought that I was ill.

When we got home, I looked up the names of the electronic cash register manufacturers in a data processing journal and called the smallest one since I felt that it might be more flexible and more willing to make special models. I got the sales manager on the telephone, even though it was Saturday afternoon, and he said that his company manufactured cash register terminals to order, on a modular basis, so that if I could use standard modules, I could have as few as 10 units at list price. He also said that he would send me a copy of the specifications and prices for the various modules (Exhibit 3). Hardware, he explained, would be no problem; his company would supply the input terminals, and I could rent the equipment for data processing and output printing at any computer time-sharing facility. The only problem, he felt, would be in the design of the software system.

He suggested that I start with the format and content of the output statements and reports that I wished to provide each group of customers, then look at the original sources of this data within each company, divide these sources into various classes of standard transactions, provide each standard transaction with a code, and then design the keyboard of the terminal for the entry of this classification, code, and amount in a logical sequence. I explained that I was an information systems analyst, and that this was the way I normally worked. He said, "Good luck, I think that you've got the idea for a hundred million dollar business, and we'll help you get started by offering a special discount on our terminals, but you've got to design both the product that you're going to offer and the process by which you'll offer it, and that is going to take some time and effort." (Statement of Mr. Chesin.)

ASSIGNMENT

Design the weekly balance sheet and income statement, and any supplementary reports that you think necessary, that you would propose to offer to gas station owners who would lease your electronic cash registers as the data input device for both sales revenues and expense items. Your plan is to pick up the output tapes on Saturday evening, process the data, and mail back the computer printouts on Monday morning. Consider the original sources of this data, classify this data into standard transactions, code the possible entries within each transaction class, and then design the terminal keyboard for these entries. The terminal you select may have any of the options listed as available modules in Exhibit 3. I would suggest that you design the first system for a very simple gas station operation, with the accounting on a cash basis rather than accrual (payment is made in cash for all materials and services delivered at the time of delivery, and payment is received in cash for all materials and services sold, at the time of sale; there are no accounts payable or accounts receivable), and with the sales limited to two grades of gasoline, three grades of motor oil, a few tires, batteries, and other accessories, and no regular services beyond oil changes, car lubrications, and tire punctures.

After designing the electronic accounting system for a gas station, consider the additional problems involved for a men's clothing store that (1) maintains records on an accrual basis, (2) has some credit sales and therefore accounts receivable, (3) has extensive credit purchases and therefore accounts payable, and (4) has a much larger number of items in inventory than does the gas station.

Then consider the complex problems involved in designing an electronic accounting system for a local manufacturer of a consumer product, such as a snowmobile. There are 3 models and each model has 100 purchased parts and 50 manufactured parts that partially overlap.

Lastly, given the existence of a detailed and accessible data base, suggest some applications of management science and O.R. that might substantially improve the operations and profitability of these firms.

As an optional assignment, consider how you would market this electronic accounting and management science service to a given group of customers after it was designed.

EXHIBIT 1 Keyboard design of the electronic cash register used at a fast-food restaurant chain.

Quantity	Item sold			Price Per Item			Function
9	Hamburger	Small fries	Small drink	9	9	9	Enter item
8	Cheese-burger	Large fries	Large drink	8	8	8	
7	Super Burger	Misc #1 food	Misc #1 drink	7	7	7	Void item
6	Quarter pounder	Misc #2 food	Milkshake	6	6	6	
5	Quarter & cheese	Misc #3 food	Misc #2 drink	5	5	5	Sales tax
4	Q.L.T.	Apple pie	Coffee	4	4	4	
3	Fish fillet	Fruit pie	Tea	3	3	3	Sales total
2	Misc #1 sandwich	Cherry pie	Milk	2	2	2	
1	Misc #2 sandwich	Misc #1 dessert	Misc #3 drink	1	1	1	
0	Misc #3 sandwich	Misc #2 dessert	Misc #4 drink	0	0	0	Clear total

136

EXHIBIT 2 Keyboard design of electronic cash register at convenience store chain.

Department	Item code	Quantity	Miscell.	Function
Baked goods 9	9 9	9	Store coupon	Enter item
Dairy products 8	8 8	8	Store special	
Packaged foods 7	7 7	7	Vendor coupon	Void Item
Canned goods 6	6 6	6	Vendor special	
Frozen foods 5	5 5	5	Blank	Sales tax
Household product 4	4 4	4	Blank	
Personal product 3	3 3	3	Food stamps	Sales total
Tobacco 2	2 2	2	Credit slip	
Beer & drinks 1	1 1	1	Check	
Paid out 0	0 0	0	Cash	Clear total

EXHIBIT 3 Specifications and costs of standard modules available for electronic cash register terminals.

5	Classification keys (1/2 in. wide × 1 1/2 in. long) with alphabetic titles, in a single row, for primary classification of transactions.	$50
	Each additional classification key (up to 10) in single row.	$10
10	Coding keys (1/2 in. wide × 3/4 in. long) with alphanumeric titles, in a single row, for coding within each classification of transaction.	$80
	Each additional row of 10 coding keys.	$70
	Note: It is recommended that coding keys over four rows (four-digit code, expressed as 0000 to 9999) be broken into groups of three rows and separated by hyphens (six-digit code expressed as 000-000 to 999-999) for operator convenience.	
10	Quantity keys (1/2 in. wide × 3/4 in. long) with numeric titles, in a single row, for quantity within each transaction.	$80
	Each additional row of 10 quantity keys.	$70
	Note: It is recommended that quantity keys over three rows (three-digit number, expressed as 000 to 999) be broken into groups of three rows and separated by commas (six-digit number expressed as 000,000 to 999,999) for operator convenience.	
	Note: Decimal for quantity keys may be either permanent (three-digit number would be always 0.00 to 9.99) or temporary and located by striking a special decimal key (three-digit number could be 000 or 999 or 00.0 to 99.9 or 0.00 to 9.99 or .000 to .999). Special decimal key is located at the base of the quantity key rows and costs $10.00.	$10
10	Price keys (1/2 in. wide × 3/4 in. long) with numeric titles, in a single row, for dollar price of cost within each transaction.	$80
	Each additional row of 10 price keys.	$70
	Note: It is recommended that price keys over three rows (three-digit price, expressed as $000 to $999) be broken into groups of two rows for the decimals and three rows for integers (five-digit price, expressed as $000.00 to $999.99).	
10	Deduction keys (1/2 in. wide × 3/4 in. long) with alphanumeric titles in a single row, for standard discounts that affect the total of specific transactions, such as "store coupons," "vendor coupons," etc.	$80
5	Functional keys (1/2 in. wide × 1 1/2 in. long) with alphabetic titles, in a single row, for standard steps in the transaction, such as "make entry," "void entry," "sales tax," "sales total," or "clear keyboard."	$100
	Each additional functional key (up to 10) in single row.	$20
	Note: Calculations of addition, subtraction, multiplication, and division are performed on the functional keys.	

Input Options. Input data for large stores may be entered by digital readers from customer credit cards or merchandise tags by using machine-encoded data forms such as optical bar codes, color bar codes, magnetic strip codes, or optical number codes. Input data in small installations is expected to be entered solely through the electronic register keyboard.

Output Options. Output data for large stores may be transmitted by wire to a store controller (minicomputer) or by telephone coupler or tape cartridge to the company headquarters (main-frame computer) for processing. Output data in small installations is expected to be recorded solely on tape cassettes for daily or weekly pick-up by a courier. Each output tape cassette has a capacity of 60,000 lines, and each line has 15

EXHIBIT 3 *(Continued)*

---

spaces for the classification, code, quantity, price, and deduction digits. Only one output option is available:

60,000 line output cassette, with tape drive and recorder	$450

Storage Options. Stored data for input may be requested by the coding keys on the keyboard. The data is stored in random access files, with 500 items per file; each consists of the code number and either 15, 30, or 50 alphanumeric characters:

500-item file, with 15 alphanumeric characters per item	$1,200
500-item file, with 30 alphanumeric characters per item	$1,500
500-item file, with 40 alphanumeric characters per item	$1,750

Display Options. Input, stored, and output data may be shown in illuminated electronic digital displays or on alphanumeric cathode-ray tubes; three alternatives are available:

Illuminated digital display, with 15 numeric characters per display	$400
Illuminated digital display, with 30 numeric characters per display	$750
Cathode-ray tube, with 50 alphanumeric characters per display	$1,700

Printing Options. Input, stored, and output data may be printed on paper journal tape (locked in the register for verification, if needed of the electronic data) and on paper receipt tape or forms (tear off for the customer). Three printing options are available:

15 alphanumeric characters per line, printed on 1¼ in. receipt tape	$500
30 alphanumeric characters per line, printed on 2¼ in. receipt tape	$900
50 alphanumeric characters per line, printed on 5 in. receipt forms	$1,450

Natural Foods Warehouse Corporation

The Natural Foods Warehouse Corporation was formed by two young dropouts from the University of Indiana, Henry Lukaski and David Goldstein, during the fall of 1969 to distribute organically grown health foods throughout the tri-state area of southern Michigan and northern Indiana and Ohio. Health foods, or natural foods, are normally defined as cereal grains and dried vegetables, fruits, nuts, and seeds that are planted in composted soil enriched with organic materials such as leaves, straw, and manure, without chemical fertilizers. They are grown under natural conditions of wind, rain, and sunlight, without chemical insecticides, pesticides, or fungicides, and they are prepared and packaged for shipment by drying, without chemical additives or preservatives. Advocates of natural foods are concerned by the growing list of chemicals used in most food production and processing and by the lack of nutrition in many food products:

> There's polysorbate 60 in your pickles. There's ethylenediamine tetracetate in your mayonnaise. There's butylated hydroxytoluene in your breakfast cereal. These complex chemicals are hardly household words. But they and hundreds of others are being used more and more to flavor, color, fortify, preserve, and otherwise alter everyday foods. . . . The advocates of food additives, including food industry executives and many scientists in and out of government, insist that they are safe, nutritious, and essential for satisfying con-

sumers' tastes and convenience. . . . The critics, including consumer spokesmen, certain lawmakers, and some leading scientists, contend that some food chemicals are clearly hazardous to humans, others are suspect, and most are needless additions designed to deceive the food purchaser. ("Our Daily Bread; Use of More Chemicals in Food Products Stirs a Heated Controversy," *The Wall Street Journal*, January 13, 1971, p. 1. Reprinted with permission of *The Wall Street Journal*, © 1971 Dow Jones & Company, Inc. All rights reserved.)

The large companies do some ridiculous things in food processing. For example, did you know that they use talc to polish white rice and to remove the brown outer husks. The problem is that natural talc is usually contaminated with asbestos fibers, and asbestos is known to be a cancer-causing agent when absorbed in the body. (Statement of food industry executive.)

In a review of studies of vitamin and mineral nutrition from 1960 to 1968 among Americans above poverty status, doctors found that the "nutrition of a significant portion of the American public is inadequate, and has become worse during the past 10 years." . . . For the poor, of course, nutritional difficulties are usually caused by the lack of money to buy proper food. But that's clearly not the case with most Americans. In the middle-income groups there's a huge amount of food available, tremendous variety, and the money to buy it. . . . The problem is that through ignorance, apathy, or confusion, many people get led or pushed into eating the wrong things, medical experts say. ("Our Daily Bread; Nutritional Experts Say Americans Are Eating Themselves to Death," *The Wall Street Journal*, January 6, 1971, p. 1. Reprinted with permission of *The Wall Street Journal*, © 1971 Dow Jones & Company, Inc. All rights reserved.)

The large companies do some equally ridiculous things in food marketing. The prices are high in order to pay for the promotion. Food industry commercials show suburban kitchens, with modern appliances and a happy, healthy family—always four persons, with one daughter and one son—gathered around the dinner table and exclaiming with delight at the prospect of eating some packaged food product. The message, of course, is that it's the

intelligent, thrifty, caring woman who serves prepared products; that message is blatantly false. (Statement of food industry executive.)

The concern of many Americans over the lack of nutrition and the chemical content of many food products has led to the very rapid growth of the natural foods market. Statistics on national sales of natural foods are hard to obtain because of the fragmented and informal nature of the industry, but the sales of individual companies within the health foods industry have increased by approximately 50% each year since 1968.

Perhaps the most marked development lately has been the surge of public interest in so-called health foods, particularly those organically grown, using only natural fertilizers and no pesticides and free of artificial preservatives and additives. ("Our Daily Bread; Food Fadism Spurts as Young, Old People Shift to Organic Diets," *The Wall Street Journal*, January 21, 1971, p. 1. Reprinted with permission of *The Wall Street Journal*, © 1971 Dow Jones & Company, Inc. All rights reserved.)

I could name five companies, two on the East Coast and three on the West Coast, that are active in natural food distribution, and they have doubled their sales every year for the past 5 years. (Statement of food industry executive.)

Since we started from a very low base, it is not fair for us to say that our business has grown some stupendous figure such as 5,000% since the beginning, but our wholesale business does go up at least 50% each year. That makes it very hard for us to organize our warehouse and our distribution. (Statement of Mr. Lukaski.)

Natural Foods Warehouse, which was located in South Bend, Indiana, had originally been a retail store that sold, in addition to the usual cereal grains and dried vegetables, fruits, seeds and nuts, various herbs, teas, spices, fresh organic produce in season, yogurt, home-baked bread, kitchen utensils, books and magazines, and some natural soaps and cosmetics. It was termed a warehouse since it was located in an industrial section of the city far from the central shopping district. It was in an abandoned building that had been a storage warehouse on the team tracks of the New York Central. (The "team tracks" were the public unloading area provided by each railroad prior to the advent of motor transport; small merchants and farmers could back a wagon pulled by a team of horses up to a rail car to load or unload less-than-carload lots of merchandise.) The partners in the company soon found that there was only a limited retail demand for their products, perhaps because their store was nearly inaccessible, but they also found that there was a definite wholesale demand from the natural food shops and restaurants that were opening in other sections of the midwest, particularly in the college towns:

> We went into the business because it seemed to be a good idea. There was no place else to buy organic food in South Bend, so we rented the warehouse—no one else wanted the place; it had been vacant for 20 years—and set up a stone mill and opened a few sacks of grain and beans and put the bread on the counter. We soon found out that there was no place else to buy organic food in South Bend because no one else wanted any. People stayed away from here in droves. Neither David nor I are businessmen, and we certainly did not take marketing courses at Indiana, but we thought that it would be easy to run the store. We found out that it was not easy and

that we were probably going to lose the money we got from our families, which was not good, but then the wholesale business began to pick up.

> Just because of our name, everybody in the midwest thought that we were the central warehouse, and they began calling in orders. We would not see a retail customer all day, and then up would pull a panel truck from Ann Arbor or East Lansing or Columbus or Lafayette and in would come a good old boy with bib-overalls and a long beard and a purchase order for 500 lbs of grainola and 400 lbs of short-grain brown rice. We got in the wholesale business because there wasn't any retail business.

The Natural Foods Warehouse Company handled 370 separate items in 17 different product classifications, such as grains, cereals, flours, beans, seeds, nuts, oils, butters, dried fruits, natural cosmetics, kitchen utensils, cooking instructions, etc. The 370 separate items consisted of 137 different products, such as rice, wheat, rye, corn, millet, barley, popcorn, and buckwheat in the grains, and 213 different size packages of these products, such as 1-lb, 2-lb, and 4-lb boxes and 50-lb sacks of the various grains, cereals, and flours. The total list of products is too long to include in the case, but Exhibit 1 lists the grains and butters as examples of the full company product line.

EXHIBIT 1 Grain and butter products of the Natural Foods Warehouse Company, January 1973. Package sales are sales for the October–December quarter, 1972.

Product	Package size	Package cost	Package sales
Brown rice, short grain, California	1-lb box	$ 0.36	18
Brown rice, short grain, California	2-lb box	0.63	43
Brown rice, short grain, California	4-lb box	1.20	227
Brown rice, short grain, California	50-lb sack	14.00	326
Brown rice, medium grain, Louisiana	1-lb box	0.36	23
Brown rice, medium grain, Louisiana	2-lb box	0.63	37
Brown rice, medium grain, Louisiana	4-lb box	1.20	184
Brown rice, medium grain, Louisiana	50-lb sack	14.00	225
Brown rice, long grain, Texas	1-lb box	0.33	14
Brown rice, long grain, Texas	2-lb box	0.59	37
Brown rice, long grain, Texas	4-lb box	1.10	123
Brown rice, long grain, Texas	50-lb sack	12.50	172

EXHIBIT 1 *(Continued)*

Product	Package size	Package cost	Package sales
Wheat, hard red winter, Texas	1-lb box	0.22	47
Wheat, hard red winter, Texas	2-lb box	0.37	77
Wheat, hard red winter, Texas	4-lb box	0.70	380
Wheat, hard red winter, Texas	50-lb sack	5.75	593
Wheat, soft white winter, Michigan	1-lb box	0.20	29
Wheat, soft white winter, Michigan	2-lb box	0.35	38
Wheat, soft white winter, Michigan	4-lb box	0.65	201
Wheat, soft white winter, Michigan	50-lb sack	5.25	251
Wheat, hard red spring, Montana	1-lb box	0.22	18
Wheat, hard red spring, Montana	2-lb box	0.37	33
Wheat, hard red spring, Montana	4-lb box	0.70	193
Wheat, hard red spring, Montana	50-lb sack	5.75	214
Wheat, hard durum, Montana	1-lb box	0.22	6
Wheat, hard durum, Montana	2-lb box	0.37	19
Wheat, hard durum, Montana	4-lb box	0.70	43
Wheat, hard durum, Montana	50-lb sack	5.75	51
Rye, winter, Texas	1-lb box	0.20	11
Rye, winter, Texas	2-lb box	0.35	25
Rye, winter, Texas	4-lb box	0.65	45
Rye, winter, Texas	50-lb sack	5.25	130
Corn, open-pollinated, Iowa	1-lb box	0.20	14
Corn, open-pollinated, Iowa	2-lb box	0.35	29
Corn, open-pollinated, Iowa	4-lb box	0.65	68
Corn, open-pollinated, Iowa	50-lb sack	5.25	119
Millet, yellow, Colorado	1-lb box	0.30	7
Millet, yellow, Colorado	2-lb box	0.45	17
Millet, yellow, Colorado	4-lb box	0.85	38
Millet, yellow, Colorado	50-lb sack	8.50	71
Barley, pearled, Minnesota	1-lb box	0.24	5
Barley, pearled, Minnesota	2-lb box	0.40	13
Barley, pearled, Minnesota	4-lb box	0.75	28
Barley, pearled, Minnesota	50-lb sack	6.00	54
Popcorn, yellow, Iowa	1-lb box	0.55	183
Popcorn, yellow, Iowa	2-lb box	1.05	108
Popcorn, yellow, Iowa	4-lb box	1.85	43
Popcorn, yellow, Iowa	50-lb sack	15.50	45
Peanut butter, organic, Deaf Smith	1-lb jar	0.71	272
Peanut butter, organic, Deaf Smith	2-lb jar	1.36	243
Peanut butter, organic, Deaf Smith	40-lb tin	24.80	89
Safflower butter, organic, Deaf Smith	1-lb jar	0.65	49
Safflower butter, organic, Deaf Smith	2-lb jar	1.24	40
Safflower butter, organic, Deaf Smith	40-lb tin	21.40	23
Sesame butter, organic, Erewhon	1-lb jar	0.71	49
Sesame butter, organic, Erewhon	2-lb jar	1.36	31
Sesame butter, organic, Erewhon	40-lb tin	24.80	5

The partners agreed that the sales of many of the products, such as Yellow Colorado Millet or Pearled Minnesota Barley in 1-lb boxes, were too low for economical warehouse operations, yet they felt that it was necessary to continue to offer these products because of consumer demand:

> Our markets are communes, health food restaurants, and natural food stores, and each group wants a different product and a different package size. You just can't talk standards to these people; if we don't have what they want, they'll go someplace else. We seem to have what they want now, and I think that we ought to stay with it. (Statement of Mr. Goldstein.)

The product line offered by the warehouse, with 17 different product classifications and 370 separate product types and package sizes, apparently fitted the midwestern market, for the company grew rapidly and operated profitably, after the start of the wholesale service in early 1970. Exhibit 2 gives the profit and loss statement for each of the years the company has been in business.

The partners were concerned by the decreasing profit margins (9.9% in 1971 and 6.7% in 1972, despite nearly doubled sales volume) and by the increasing cost of labor (9.5% in 1970 and 12.9% in 1972, despite greatly increased mechanization) to unload, sort, and store the incoming goods and to assemble, pack, and load the outgoing shipments. They were particularly concerned by a prospective increase in rent ($275 per month under a 4-year lease due to expire in September, 1973), which they felt might double or triple their building expenses, and by a future need to borrow substantial funds to finance their food inventory, which they felt might double or triple their interest expenses. Despite the fact that both Mr. Lukaski and Mr. Goldstein were members of the counter-culture in dress and appearance, and despite the fact that they had founded the Natural Foods Warehouse as a form of protest against normal corporate practices in the food industry, both partners were very interested in the future financial success of the company:

> Your class is going to say we're hypocrites, so O.K., we're hypocrites. We're hypocrites who've got a good thing going. My father thinks that it is the funniest thing he has ever heard; he gave us a few bucks to get started, so now he tells everyone at the synagogue about the company. "Set them up in business," he says, "and they'll start making money just the way we did." Well, I'm not going to do it

EXHIBIT 2 Income statement for the Natural Foods Warehouse Corporation, 1969–1972.

	1969 (3 months only)	1970	1971	1972
Net sales	$31,640	$146,080	$262,740	$484,720
Cost of goods sold	23,610	106,010	187,270	338,550
	8,030	40,070	77,470	147,170
Payroll for warehouse labor	5,670	13,820	29,010	62,630
Rent for warehouse	1,320	3,300	3,300	3,300
Local taxes and license fees	1,130	920	2,720	4,970
Depreciation on equipment	740	1,840	2,390	7,410
Interest on bank and family loans	—	340	2,640	6,550
Selling and administrative expense	3,970	15,320	22,140	29,460
	12,830	35,540	62,200	115,320
Profit (loss) before taxes	(4,800)	4,530	25,070	31,850
Federal and state income taxes	—	—	6,340	9,820
	$ (4,800)	$4,530	$18,730	$22,030

the way he did, because that ruined his life. I'm going to do it my way, but I'm going to do it. (Statement of Mr. Goldstein.)

I guess that I feel the same way about it as David does. This is our thing, and we've got to keep it going. About every month we have to go down to the bank to pay back a loan or get some more money. There are 9:00 to 5:00 people there, with 9:00 to 5:00 souls, and I don't want to have to join them. Right now they envy us. At first they just laughed at us—they would have made us come in the back door if they could and sit up in the balcony if they had one—but now they envy us, and they're jealous of us, and they'd like to see us fail. If we went bankrupt, they'd be happy because that would prove to them that they were right and that they were better after all. We're not going to go bankrupt. We're going to make a lot of money, and then sell the warehouse and go and live in Spain, and I'll send those poor bastards at the bank a postcard every year. (Statement of Mr. Lukaski.)

Part of the reason that we've been successful up until now has been the low rent. Nobody wanted this building, so we got it for $275 a month. But, now we've fixed it up [Mr. Lukaski and Mr. Goldstein had replaced the broken windows, repaired the leaking room, cleaned the storage area, painted the wooden trim, swept the cobblestoned yard in front of the building, and planted window boxes filled with peonies, petunias, and begonias near the entrance]. And, the landlord now realizes that this building is almost ideal for a food warehouse (the heavy stone walls kept the storage area cool in the summer, which prevented both food spoilage and insect infestation, and warm in the winter, which reduced the heating bills, and the thick concrete floors made forklift operations simple, and almost eliminated the rodent problem), so I expect that we are going to pay at least $1.00 per square foot ($10,000 annually for the 50 ft × 200 ft structure) when our lease runs out, despite the location. If he charges too much, though, we'll just move over to the roundhouse. (An abandoned railroad roundhouse, built in the middle of the nineteenth century to house steam locomotives, and also well constructed with heavy stone walls and thick concrete floors, was located on the other side of the cobblestoned team track yard, about 100 ft from the present warehouse). (Statement of Mr. Lukaski.)

We've got some problems in finance, with the rent increase and the interest costs, and we're going to have more competition in marketing (an established food broker in Chicago had just announced that his company would distribute a popular line of health foods, and two of the larger grocery chains in the Midwest were starting to carry organic products), but our major problems are in operating the warehouse. We keep spending money on forklift trucks and on mechanized handling equipment, but our labor costs keep going up. We keep spending money on inventory, but the number of stockouts keeps going up. We don't understand what is happening. We just don't know what to do. (Statement of Mr. Goldstein.)

The major problems in the operation of the warehouse, although interrelated, could be separated into four specific areas for description: (1) planning the general inventory level for all the products handled by the company; (2) planning the staffing level for the warehouse employees to receive, sort, store, select, package, and ship these products; (3) scheduling the production amounts and times of the proprietary products such as stone-ground flour, roasted nuts and seeds, and mixed or ground cereals; and (4) controlling the stock level and issuing replenishment orders for the individual products.

1. Planning the General Inventory Level. The partners thought of the general inventory level as the overall dollar volume of goods to be stocked as a percentage of overall company sales. That is, if company sales per quarter were $100,000, as they were in 1972, then a primary operating decision was whether the inventory level should be at $80,000, $100,000, $120,000, $150,000, or $180,000. The greater the amount of inventory that was stocked, or the higher the inventory level, the greater would be the interest charge for the loan necessary to finance it, but the lower would be the labor and administrative costs since much of the existing work seemed to be concerned with "stockouts," when the inventory for a particular item was not available for the prompt shipment of an order. Stockouts delayed the packaging of an order while the worker came to the office for instructions. One of the partners then had to call the customer and ask for permission to substitute another product; this permission was generally refused, so the item then had to be back ordered. The clerks had to keep track of all of the back orders and prepare individual shipping documents when the required material was finally received from the supplier. It was not unknown for existing back orders to cover all the material received, so that it seemed as if no inventory could be built up for some very popular items.

Originally, the partners had set the inventory level for each of their products by using intuitive estimates of demand for a 3-month period, and then changing these estimates as customer orders were received and as inventory stocks were depleted. Reordering was on an informal basis: when one of the partners observed or was told that the stock of a particular item was low, he would have a new purchase order issued to bring the inventory level back to the original or adjusted estimate. This method, however, required constant observation of the inventory level and continual attention to the market demand for each product by the partners; as the number of products carried by the company expanded, and as the claims upon the time of the partners increased, it became necessary to substitute a more automatic system. Therefore, the company started to order, at the beginning of each 6-month period, a supply of each item equal to the sales for the prior 6 months plus a 25% allowance for sales expansion. This method, however, resulted in excessive inventory, which the company found difficult to finance, at the start of each period, and in depleted inventory, which the company found expensive in stockouts and emergency reorders, toward the close of the period. Also, products that had

seasonal swings in demand, such as dried fruits and vegetables, were always either overstocked or understocked by this system; and popular products that had greater growth than 25%, such as most of the grains, flours, and cereals, were never in adequate supply. To counter these problems, the company adopted a system that required continual rather than bi-annual review and reordering. The partners, following the advice of a friend who was the inventory clerk for a large local hardware wholesaler, set a minimum stocking level and a standard reorder quantity for each product, based upon past demand; then when the inventory fell below the minimum stocking level, the partners were to automatically reorder the standard amount. For example, they set the minimum stocking level for brown rice, long grained, in 1-lb boxes, at 12 boxes (one case), and the standard reorder quantity at 24 boxes (two cases). It was felt that this would result in an average inventory for this product of 18 boxes, since each time the inventory fell below 12 boxes the partners would order an additional 24, which would come in about 6 weeks, hopefully just before the safety stock of 12 was exhausted.

The new method, however, still resulted in stockouts and emergency reorders for the popular products because the demand increased more than the expected amount and in larger inventories for the slower-moving items. The partners now felt that the minimum stocking level and the standard reorder quantity should be adjusted each quarter to reflect the changing pattern and the volume of sales, and they also thought that the overall inventory level of the company (total inventory of all products/company sales for all products) should be adjusted quarterly to balance the costs of holding the inventory (interest on the investment and overhead on the storage space) and the costs of not holding enough inventory (extra labor and shipping costs caused by stockouts).

There are two interrelated things here: one is the cost of carrying the inventory, which includes interest on the loan used to buy the stuff and the operating costs of the building used to store it, and the other is the cost of not having the inventory when a customer wants it. Stockouts irritate the customer, of course, but they also cost us a lot of money. They slow down the warehouse crew, they slow down the office people, and they make a lot of extra paper work. We have to back order the stuff, keep track of the back orders in a special file, and then make up a special shipment to the customer when the product finally comes in.

This may seem like a minor matter to you, and it will probably seem miniscule to your students, but I am certain that all of us—the warehouse crew, our secretaries, David and I —spend at least 25% of our time dealing with stockouts and with the problems connected with stockouts, such as inquiry calls from customers, emergency reorders to suppliers, the back order file, and special shipments. This company would be a lot easier to run and would provide much better service to customers if we did not have stockouts.

We have two problems in trying to offer this better service. The first is that we don't really know what the demand will be in the next quarter; we can make an estimate based upon sales in the past few quarters, but we are never exactly right. [Company records indicated that the forecasts had been approximately correct nearly half the time, but that the balance had ranged between 40% too high and 100% too slow.] Also, we don't know exactly when the goods will be received after we order them; they generally come in in about 6 weeks, but they can get here in 2 weeks or in 3 months.

We have to arrange our inventory planning better than we have in the past, or we're not going to stay in this business very long; the problem is that we don't know how to do it. We do know that we have to forecast sales and receipts for each product, and then we have to relate the cost of having the inventory (interest and building expenses) to the costs of not having it (stockouts), but we don't know how to do this. (Statement of Mr. Lukaski.)

For assistance in designing a forecasting method for use by the Natural Foods Warehouse, Exhibit 3 gives the company sales by quarters, for rice and wheat in 50-lb sacks, as an example of a product group with only minimal seasonal influence. Exhibit 4 gives the company sales, again by quarters, for dried raisins in 20-lb crates and 1-lb boxes, as an example of another product group with considerable seasonal fluctuation.

As a final assistance in designing an inventory planning system for the Natural Foods Warehouse, estimate the interest costs of loans to this company at 8% and the current (1973) weighted average cost of capital for this company at about 29%.

2. Planning the General Staffing Level. The company products were purchased from a variety of sources, ranging from the established suppliers of natural foods, such as Erewhon Company in Boston and Deaf Smith in Texas, to small grain dealers and local farmers who specialized in organic products. The purchases were shipped to the Natural Foods Warehouse by truck, where they were unloaded, sorted, and stored. Smaller items, such as the 1-lb, 2-lb, and 4-lb boxes of grain, flours, and cereals, were taken from the shipping cartons and stacked on metal shelving which the partners had purchased inexpensively from a bankrupt automotive supply firm; larger items, such as the 50-lb sacks of grain, were placed on wooden pallets, with 4 sacks strapped to each pallet, and then carried to open storage by a forklift truck. In most commercial food warehouses, pallets with cartons or sacks of produce were piled on top of each other, up to a height of 12 ft or 15 ft; this was not required at the Natural Foods Warehouse due to the surplus space that was available in the building. In the latter part of 1972 the company received about 150,000 lb of health food products per month; this was delivered by approximately 50 trucks. Loads ranged between 1,000 lb and 30,000 lb and averaged 3,000 lb.

The company products were shipped to approximately 300 customers in the tristate area of southern Michigan and northern Indiana and Ohio. Customer

EXHIBIT 3   Company sales for rice and wheat in 50-lb sacks, by quarters, for 1971 and 1972.

	July–Sept 1971	*Oct–Dec 1971*	*Jan–Mar 1972*	*Apr–Jun 1972*	*July–Sept 1972*	*Oct–Dec 1972*
Brown rice, short grain	186	212	225	268	290	326
Brown rice, medium grain	22	47	74	136	162	225
Brown rice, long grain	36	51	76	101	141	172
Wheat, hard red winter	322	382	470	401	513	593
Wheat, soft white winter	28	46	66	108	148	251
Wheat, hard red spring	—	—	—	82	110	214
Wheat, hard durum	—	—	—	19	30	51

EXHIBIT 4   Company sales for raisins in 20-lb crates and 1-lb boxes, by quarters, for 1971 and 1972.

Raisins, Thompson, 20 lb	14	30	43	27	19	38
Raisins, Thompson, 1 lb	—	—	—	3	10	27
Raisins, Monukka, 20 lb	5	21	29	17	12	28
Raisins, Monukka, 1 lb	—	—	—	3	9	22

orders were received by mail and telephone; the information in each order was transcribed to a combined shipping document and invoice, one copy of which went to the warehouse for shipment. The products on each order were picked off the metal shelves (small boxes, jars, and cans) and pallets (50-lb sacks, 40-lb tins, and 20-lb crates) by hand and carried to a central shipping point where the smaller items were packed into a shipping carton. The carton, sacks, crates, etc., were addressed and then piled into a pallet ready to be carried to a truck by the forklift. Commercial trucks came daily. Waiting orders were sorted among the trucks going in the right direction and covering the right geographic area in their routes. Again, in the latter part of 1972 the company shipped about 150,000 lb per month; this was divided into approximately 1,000 orders, with a weight range of 10 lb to 2,000 lb, and an average of 150 lb. These numbers and weights of outgoing shipments disregarded the back orders, which were shipped individually as soon as the material required for each was received. About 200 back orders were shipped per month, with a weight average of only 50 lb.

The company had been given, by the friend of the partners who was the inventory clerk for a hardware wholesaler, a set of work standards for warehouse operations that were used by most food, hardware, and automotive parts supply distributors. These work standards were expressed in the form of the pounds per hour that could be expected for different materials that were handled in different ways. These standards are described in Exhibit 5, which gives the expected hours per month for the warehouse operations of the Natural Foods Warehouse.

The total standard hours for the company, estimated by means of the standards reportedly used by other wholesale food distributors, showed a requirement for 620 hours, or 4 men per month (620 standard hours ÷ 160 hours per month per man = 3.7). This concerned Mr. Lukaski, since the company employed 8 men in 1972 at an annual cost per man of $7,830:

What is wrong here? We have tried running the warehouse with just 4 men, but it

EXHIBIT 5 Pounds per month, work standards, and standard hours per month for the warehouse of the Natural Foods Company.

Type of freight and weight per month	Standards for work performed by type of freight and weight of material	Standard hours per month
Incoming freight 100,000 lb	2,000 lb/hr for heavy sacks, cartons, or drums, to be placed on pallet and carried to open storage by forklift	50
Incoming freight 50,000 lb	300 lb/hr for light boxes, cans, bottles, or tins, to be taken from shipping cartons and hand carried to shelf storage	170
Outgoing freight 100,000 lb	1,000 lb/hr for heavy sacks, cartons, or drums, to be taken from pallet storage, carried to central shipping by handtruck, and addressed	100
50,000 lb	200 lb/hr for heavy sacks, cartons, or tins, to be taken from shelf storage, carried to central shipping by hand, packed in shipping cartons, and addressed	250
Back orders 10,000 lb	200 lb/hr standard used, even though many of the items back ordered were actually of the heavy type	50
	Total standard hours:	620 hours

just doesn't work; they get behind and they can't catch up. And neither David nor I want to be a slave driver. But this is a small company, and we can't afford to keep 4 extra people around, particularly at a cost of $30,000 per year. How many people should we have working in the warehouse? (Statement of Mr. Lukaski.)

3. Scheduling Production of Proprietary Products. The Natural Foods Warehouse manufactured a number of prepared and semiprepared products for their customers. They ground flour on an old stone mill from the different types of organic wheat, rye, corn, rice, millet, and barley grains stocked by the company; they roasted the various seeds and nuts in a gas-fired oven; and they prepared a number of flavors of grainola cereal by mixing cracked, rolled, or ground grains, roasted seeds, shredded nuts, and dried

fruits with natural sweeteners such as honey or maple syrup. The roasting and mixing operations were simple and caused no problems in scheduling; the foreman in the warehouse merely waited until the stocks were low and then prepared a 2- or 3-week supply. Neither roasting nor mixing required much set-up time, and they were tasks that could be fitted in with the regular receiving and shipping activities in the warehouse. Grinding was more of a problem; the stone grinding mill was old and slow, with a daily production rate under 1,000 lb, but it would run unattended so that the costs of producing flour were not excessive. The warehouse crew, however, had gotten into the practice of grinding most of the flour to order, which meant that since the orders for flour varied among all the different types of grain stocked by the company and since the mill had to be cleaned and readjusted for each new order, the mill was shut down for cleaning and adjustment during a considerable portion of each day. The set-up procedure, including both the cleaning and adjustment took only 30 minutes, but it was being done five or six times each day since the flour orders averaged less than 100 lb per order and the set-up man was not available for regular warehouse work during this time. The partners were concerned about the cost of this lost time and about the resulting lack of capacity of the mill:

I don't think that we could find another used stone mill—they're in demand now by all the natural food stores—and new ones are available only from Sweden, for about $20,000. We've got to use the one we've got more productively.

Also, 30 minutes per changeover is not much and it probably only costs us about $5.00, but the cost mounts up if you think about 5 or 6 changes a day times the 220 working days in the year. We don't want to keep too large an inventory of flour on hand, which is the alternative to grinding to order, but we ought to be able to save some money here by better scheduling of the production runs. What should we do? (Statement of Mr. Lukaski.)

To assist in designing a production scheduling system to determine the length of runs on the stone mill, Exhibit 6 gives the annual sales in pounds of five varieties of stone-ground flour and the cost per pound of grinding.

The formula most commonly used for setting the economical order quantity (EOQ), when costs, delivery times, and market demands are known with certainty, is given in Assignment question 3 on p. 151.

4. Scheduling Truck Deliveries of Company Products. The Natural Foods Warehouse was considering the purchase of 2 trucks to make regular weekly runs to customers in the tri-state area. Since mileage costs were estimated at $0.18 per mile, and since the daily routes would average about 300 miles each, the partners were interested in methods of minimizing the total mileage required for these deliveries:

If you start drawing out routes on a map, there are hundreds of different ways you can go. It ought to be easy to save 50 miles a day on each truck, but we don't know how to do this. (Statement of Mr. Lukaski.)

5. Controlling the Inventory of Company Products. The last figure that concerned the owners of the Natural Foods Warehouse in the early winter of 1973 was the difficulty they experienced in controlling the inventory. They felt that they could establish optimal figures for the minimum stocking level and the standard reorder quantity for each product, but that these were valueless unless they knew immediately when the inventory dropped below the minimum stocking level so that a purchase order could be issued for replenishment.

The best inventory level planning system in the world won't work unless you know when to reorder. You would think that the

---

EXHIBIT 6 Annual sales in pounds and cost per pound of grinding five varieties of stone-ground flour at the Natural Foods Warehouse.

Variety of grain	Annual requirements (lb)	Cost per pound
Wheat, hard red winter	75,000	$0.15
Wheat, soft white winter	45,000	0.12
Wheat, hard durum	25,000	0.18
Corn, open-pollinated	120,000	0.05
Rye, winter	12,000	0.10

workers in the warehouse would tell us when the stock begins to get below a figure posted in the stockbook, but they won't; they'll wait until the stock is nearly all gone. Right now our secretary spends most of her time (3 days a week) just looking at the inventory out in the bins; she carries the book with her, and when she sees that something is low, she comes in and orders it. There must be a better way to do it. (Statement of Mr. Lukaski.)

In summary, there are five operating problems that affected the market success and the financial position of the Natural Foods Warehouse. These problems, and their potential costs per year, were:

1. Planning the general inventory level of the firm. The costs of this decision are a balance between inventory stocking (interest on the investment and overhead on the storage area) costs and stockout (extra labor and supervision and customer dissatisfaction) costs, and this balance is a significant amount. In 1972 interest costs were $6,550, and stockout costs were estimated at 25% of all warehouse labor and administrative effort, or $23,000; the potential savings is on the order of:

$16,500

2. Planning the general staffing level of the firm. The costs of this decision are those associated with the extra labor, above that actually needed for the standard operations of the warehouse. In 1972 the standard hours for the weights and types of material handled indicated a need for 4 men, at an annual cost of $31,300; the actual labor charge was for 8 men, at $62,630; the potential savings is on the order of:

$31,000

3. Scheduling the production of proprietary products. The costs of this decision are a balance between inventory stocking (interest on the investment and overhead on the storage space) and set-up (cleaning and adjustment of the stone mill) costs, but this balance again would be significant. In 1972 set-up costs were

estimated at $30 per day ($5.00 per set-up times 6 set-ups per day); the potential savings is on the order of:

$6,600

4. Scheduling the truck deliveries of company products. The costs of this decision are those associated with the extra mileage driven by 2 prospective delivery trucks; it was felt that 50 miles per day could be saved on the route design for each truck, at $0.18 per mile, so the potential savings are:

$4,000

5. Controlling the inventory of company products. The costs of this decision are again the costs of stockouts which might have been avoided with better control of the inventory for each product. No estimate of potential savings was given by the partners, but a reasonable estimate might be:

$4,000

6. Total potential savings with improved planning, scheduling, and control:

$62,400

We want to stay in business, but in order to do so we've got to start using modern business methods. We've got an increase in rent coming; we've got an increase in interest coming; and we've got an increase in competition on the way. But we ought to be able to operate our warehouse just as well as the large commercial food distributors. We just have to learn how to do it quicker. (Statement of Mr. Goldstein.)

ASSIGNMENT

Improve the operations of the Natural Foods Warehouse by using more careful planning, scheduling, and control systems and procedures, in order to realize as much as possible of the potential savings of $62,000 and to enable the company to survive in a more competitive, and more costly, environment:

1. Design a planning system for the general inventory level of the firm, relating the costs of inventory to the costs of stockout, given the uncertain demand and deliveries of the individual products. It is suggested that a computer-based system be designed, because of the volume of data to be processed. It is also suggested that the planning system not attempt to minimize directly the overall costs, because of the mathematical complexity involved; instead, the planning system might show the variations in total costs associated with stepped variations in the overall inventory level. No solution is required, although adequate information is included in the case for a solution to the optimal inventory level for rice, wheat, and raisins.

2. Design a planning system for the general staffing level of the firm, relating the variable work requirements associated with the actual shipments and deliveries to the standard hours computed for the firm. Again, it is suggested that a computer-based system be designed, because of the volume of data to be processed. The planning system could either minimize the total labor cost directly or show the expected delays in handling shipments and deliveries for stepped variations in the overall staffing level. No solution is required, although adequate information is included in the case for a solution to the optimal staffing level for warehouse employees.

3. Design a scheduling system for the size of runs of proprietary products, relating the costs of inventory to the costs of set-up, given the known demand and deliveries of the individual products. It is suggested that a manual system be designed by using the formula:

$$EOQ = \sqrt{(2 \times R \times S) / (C \times K)}$$

EOQ = economic order quantity (optimal production run in lb)
  R = annual requirements, in units (lb)
  S = set-up cost in dollars ($)
  C = cost per unit in dollars ($ per lb)
  K = annual carrying charge for inventory as percentage (%)

A solution should be obtained for the products listed in Exhibit 6.

4. Design a scheduling system for the routes of the prospective company trucks, relating the delivery points and the intermediate distances between them. It is suggested that a computer-based system be designed, because of the volume of data to be processed. The scheduling system should minimize directly the total distance or cost required to serve the delivery points. No solution is required, for adequate information is not included in the case.

5. Design a control system for the inventory of company products. The system may be either manual or computer-based.

5

Financial Management

Financial management in small companies typically is different from what it is in larger firms. The president of a smaller company is unlikely to employ staff schooled in high sophisticated theories of capital budgeting and economics, and even if there are such people on his staff, their energies will likely be harnessed to tasks more directly connected to immediate cash needs and profits. Probably less useful to the small company manager than to the manager in a big company will be knowledge of major considerations involved in selection of marketable securities or of traditional vs. modern practices regarding dividend payout rates.

While finance departments of big companies may be able to use quantitative methodology of financial management (which can be seen as a development from economics to maximize through differential calculus, mathematical programming, or probabalistic simulation the return on capital), smaller companies usually have no finance staffs at all. Instead, the small company may or may not have an accountant who keeps the books, possibly only a bookkeeper who makes entries under instruction from an outside accounting firm which in turn uses those entries periodically to prepare statements. Possibly there will be no accounting at all beyond the owner's checkbook and income tax records. The only other members of the small company's "financial staff" will probably be the company's banker and the company president, who will not likely bother with discounting expected cash flows to present value, even if the concepts are known to him or her. More often equipment purchase decisions, for instance, will be based on "Do we *have* to have it?" or "How badly does the owner want one?" "or "How long will it take to pay for itself?"

Capital rationing (typically assumed not to be present in theoretical cost of capital calculations) is an ever-present circumstance in most small companies. Although they have access to some forms of capital which large companies do not, such as loan guarantees from the Small Business Administration and money from venture capital firms and small business investment companies, there are other capital sources such as the public bond market and lending institutions such as pension trusts which make capital much easier to come by in large companies than in small ones. There are some small companies that yield profits in excess of what they need for growing. But most are not so comfortable and never seem to have money enough.

It will be convenient to consider financial management under four conditions in smaller companies. First is the *start-up* that requires seed capital which usually begins with the entrepreneur's personal savings and extends to savings of family and friends. This topic is discussed in the section on company formation. Second is a relatively *steady-state* operation in which the company "cruises" under fairly constant financial pressures. Third is the *financial setback* in which operating losses impose the need for additional capital to "bail out" the company and restore it to profitable status. Fourth is the *rapid growth* in which the company is profitable but its capability to expand generates the need for cash beyond what current operating surplus provides.

STEADY STATE

In steady-state or "normal" operation of a small business, financial management calls for not only keeping an eye on costs and profits, but also on items of the balance sheet in order to avoid running out of cash. It is possible for a company to earn a steady profit and still "go broke" by running out of cash through such things as understating depreciation, allowing inventory and accounts receivable to grow too large, and neglecting accounts payable to the point where creditors "crack down" and call for payment at a time when the company can't muster enough cash. Typically, each small company president will use certain favored reports to keep track of the company's status. Some will follow closely the company's cash account at the bank, especially as each payroll approaches. Others will monitor the accounts of particular customers who tend to be slow in paying. Many now obtain computer-produced monthly financial statements submitted by the company's accountant. A useful rule of thumb is that financial statements should be complete not later than 2 weeks after the close of each month. Many small company operators, however, use only annual financial statements and in the meantime monitor financial status through weekly and daily reports of selected key figures on their businesses.

The thoughts that might run through the mind of a manager in a small, as opposed to large, company in looking at a balance sheet could include the following:

Cash Account. There has to be enough ready to meet the payroll, which is one obligation that can't be delayed. At the same time, not too much money can be accumulated in this account for the Internal Revenue Service can levy severe penalties in the form of an "accumulated earnings tax." (A company can accumulate at least $100,000 in earnings before risking such a tax, but a small company may not be allowed to accumulate much more.)

Securities. Most small companies own no negotiable securities. Those which do must watch out for the accumulated earnings tax noted above.

Accounts Receivable. Because small companies are not in a position either to provide as much credit extension to customers or to marshall a legal department to crack down on "deadbeats," they sometimes have more difficulty collecting and may be pushed around by customers who are slow to pay. The small business manager may personally review each credit purchase by a customer and instruct his secretary not to ship to anyone except regular paying customers without checking with him first. At the same time, the small business manager may cherish credit purchases by very large companies or the government because those receivables can generally be used as collateral for borrowing at the bank.

Inventory. Since they are usually not publicly held and have no particular incentive for displaying high earnings, which draw corresponding taxes, small companies generally like to value inventory as low as they can. Borrowing from banks against small company inventory is generally very difficult or impossible. Banks will, however, sometimes lend against clearly salable raw materials, and other innovative lending arrangements are possible. One bank, for instance, itself bought the inventory from a small company's supplier, had it stored in a warehouse, and transferred it to the company as needed in lieu of lending against it.

Fixed Assets. The smaller company prefers to state fixed assets as low as possible in order to realize maximal depreciation and correspondingly lowered profits and taxes. Many small companies that have been in business for a number of years operate with fixed assets valued at next to nothing. Nevertheless, their owners are keenly aware of the higher potential market value of such assets, knowing they may be able to borrow on a chattel mortgage against them at the bank. Land and buildings may actually be increasing in value as collateral over time.

Intangibles. Organization expenses, patents, and goodwill are items that the owner and others generally recognize as having no cash value whatever.

Accounts Payable. Because they are typically a most important source of capital, the small business operator will watch accounts payable to make sure that they are not stretched too far. The risk of overextension is that suppliers may put shipments on a C.O.D. basis or possibly cut them off entirely. In addition, the small business that is too slow in paying will find itself hounded by supplier salesmen for payment, which will drain off time from the small company for more productive activities. Prompt payment can earn other rewards, such as purchase discounts, a good reputation for obtaining hard-to-get credit from other suppliers, fast and attentive delivery, and possibly access to hard-to-tap supplies in times of shortage.

Bank Debt. This source of capital too must be carefully tended by the small business operator. It will be discussed further below.

Longer-term Debt. Small companies generally cannot obtain longer-term debt unless it is secured by some sort of mortgage. There is no public market for small company bonds.

Equity. Many small companies manage to get by on amazingly little equity, though suppliers of credit naturally resist it. For example, one small manufacturer who sold retail and thereby managed to avoid having to carry accounts receivable boasted that his account payable to his advertising agency alone was larger than his total net worth. Understatement of inventory and rapid depreciation, which are common in small companies, both work to minimize this item.

Although careful financial planning is widely extolled among academicians and is widely used by large companies, the managers of small companies often relegate it to a minor role, particularly in steady-state operation. A survey of small manufacturing companies found that in general most of them believed that they performed sufficient cash planning. While the study revealed no minimum requirements for planning in the small manufacturing firms, it also showed that there was no relationship between financial health and the amount of formal cash planning done.[1] The study concluded that cash planning was important when the company was undercapitalized, when the company was having problems, when it needed to approach lending institutions for money, or when it was undergoing substantial growth.

FINANCIAL SETBACKS

In a company in which serious problems have consumed its cash, financial forecasting can be essential in formulating and implementing a cure. Presumably, the objective of a remedy will be to improve financial performance, and forecasting is a way to plan out in detail just how the mechanisms of improvement are supposed to work. If the company needs an injection of money to make the turnaround, it will be necessary to have forecasts, since an investor or lender will undoubtedly ask to see just how the additional money will be used and how the payoff will come about in terms of dollars before agreeing to put money into the company.

At the same time, although written financial plans may not be essential to effective operation in steady state for some companies, they may be very useful to others in steady state for anticipating changes, including either financial setbacks or rapid growth needs. A useful set of policies for financial planning in a small company might include the following:

1. Cash budgets should be prepared for planning up to 1 year. A cash budget should be prepared quarterly and should combine expected monthly sales revenues, cash receipts, material, labor and overhead expenses, and cost disbursements in order to anticipate fluctuations in the level of cash and to plan short-term borrowings and investments.

2. Pro forma statements should be prepared for planning up to 3 years. These should include both the income statements and balance sheets, and they should be revised quarterly to combine quarterly expected sales revenues, production, marketing, and administrative expenses, resultant profits, product, market or process investments, and supplier, bank, or investment company borrowings in order to anticipate the financial results of operations and to plan intermediate-term borrowings and investments.

---

[1] *Joseph C. Schabacker,* Cash Planning in Small Manufacturing Companies *(Washington, D.C., Small Business Administration, 1960)* .

3. Capital investment analyses and capital source studies should be prepared for planning up to 5 years. The investment analyses should compare rates of return for product, market, or process investments. Source alternatives should compare the cost and availability of debt and equity and the expected level of retained earnings, which together will support the selected investments. Capital investment analyses and source studies should be prepared quarterly in order to anticipate the financial consequences of changes in the strategy of the firm and to plan long-term borrowings, equity placements, and major investments.

Financial planning of this nature on three levels, and on a quarterly basis, can force the management of small companies to consider the results of their actions. Managerial estimates have to be explicit; managerial records have to be examined and evaluated; and managerial agreements have to be resolved, or at least discussed and understood.

RAPID GROWTH

When a company expands rapidly it typically needs money for increases in accounts receivable, inventory, tooling, other fixed assets, such as physical space, and sometimes research and development. There may be need to invest in recruitment and training of personnel at all levels, in expanded advertising, and in handling additional customer problems and servicing. If these needs are not anticipated, the company may find itself unable to service demand. As a result, the company may create customers who are unhappy because deliveries are late. At the same time competitors may spring in to take advantage of the unutilized market potential. Consequently, in times of rapid growth it is particularly desirable to perform financial planning, especially if the growth will require additional outside capital. Again, the use of cash budgets, pro forma statements, and capital investment analyses will be of great use on a regular basis as suggested above.

COMMERCIAL BANKS

Commercial banks are only one of many financial institutions in the country, but they are the major source of loan funds for smaller business. Many other lending institutions, such as insurance companies, commercial paper firms, brokerage houses, etc., simply refuse to deal with smaller companies because of the greater risk involved and the increased time and effort per dollar of loan required. The risk arises from the fact that small companies tend to go bankrupt more often than larger ones do. In addition, smaller companies generally have shorter operating histories that lenders can use to appraise the management and the competitive position, and smaller companies often have fewer assets for the lender to consider as his security for the loan. Despite these problems, banks and other financial institutions do grant loans to smaller companies, but they usually insist upon a rigorous examination of the loan requests before they advance funds.

Some other lending institutions, such as finance companies, state and local development agencies, and the Small Business Administration, do make loans to small companies, but they are often on a participatory basis with a local commercial bank: The bank is expected to be the administrator and contact point for these loans. Therefore, it is important for the smaller company manager to maintain communicative, if not cordial, relations with the bank.

It is not difficult for the manager of a smaller company to maintain friendly relations with most commercial banks. The manager should simply explain exactly what the company will do with the funds requested. Then the company should do exactly what it says it will do. The company should furnish realistic financial projections, including a monthly cash budget, a quarterly pro forma statement, and an annual investment analysis, in the loan request, and then it should meet the projections. Since few small companies do this, banks tend to value those that do.

It is, of course, important for the manager of a smaller business to select a bank that is at least partially sympathetic to the aims and objectives of his company and to meet an officer within that bank who is willing to make the necessary effort to understand the operations of his firm. In this respect, the manager of the smaller company should recognize that the loan officer will, to a considerable extent, be held responsible for the success of the loan; a failure will reflect upon his judgment and his record. To share this personal responsibility, bank officers will often present loan applications from small or beginning businesses to a committee for review. Bank policy may require this if the amount of the proposed loan is over a level established by the bank, for example, $25,000. In order to support the loan officer before the committee, the company should present a written loan request that presents a careful picture of the company, where it is headed, and what it needs to get there. This takes substantial thought and effort. Few small companies carry the task through, but those that do consequently appear in an exceptionally favorable light.

In examining loan requests from smaller companies, banks and other financial institutions traditionally have relied on the "three C's," character, capital, and collateral, but most bankers admit that character is difficult to judge in younger companies, that capital is often limited in growth situations, and that collateral may be of questionable value in conditions of rapid technological and economic change. What bankers consequently look for in evaluating loan requests are information on the company's current status and history, its future prospects, the purpose of the loan, and the repayment schedule.

Status and History. If the company is new to the bank, it will be a good idea to take along brochures that illustrate what the company does, samples, if possible, pictures of the plant and operations, and copies of any publicity the company may have received. A resumé of the owner and background information on other key people in the company, for example, financial backers and directors, will be of interest. Of particular interest will be a list of the customers to whom the company sells and copies of any major contracts it has. It would also be desirable to have a list of the major assets of the company and their values, plus a list of the main assets and liabilities of the owner or main shareholder.

Most banks would like to see financial statements for the past 3 years of operations. (Ideally, these should be audited, but in most small companies they are not.) The banker will be interested in the growth of sales and profits and in the liquidity and debt position of the company, but he will be even more interested in how well management is using the resources available, as may be indicated by the aging of accounts receivable, the turnover rate of inventory, and the return on assets and on equity. Since the bank will note any changes in these ratios over the history of the company, and since it will compare the ratios to published averages for industry, a well-prepared loan request contains summary statements, calculated ratios, industry comparisons, and an explanation of any meaningful differences between the company and the industry or any substantial changes in the company ratios over time. In discussing the past operations of the firm, it should be noted that most banks do not like start-up situations (beginning companies) in which there is no history of operations upon which to base their judgment of the product, market, and process and their evaluation of the management. For new companies, the bank will often look to the prior experience and financial worth of the managers and will generally ask for personal guarantees of the loan.

Company Future. Most banks advance funds to smaller companies not because of the profitability of the current loan, which often is minimal despite the higher interest rate charged to smaller companies because of the small size of the amounts involved and the increased expenses required for investigation and administration; instead, they make loans based on an expectation of growth and eventually greater profits from company deposits and normal bank services. Since the bank is interested in the future of the company, a well-prepared loan request will include a short description of the direction of the firm. The description should include the major investments anticipated in products, markets, and processes and the expected sources of funds from debt, equity, and retained earnings.

Loan Purpose. Most banks want very specific information on the full amount of the loan and the expected use of the funds, with details of both capital investment and current asset financing needs. They are particularly interested in knowing that the amount requested is adequate for the purpose envisaged so that supplementary loan appeals will not have to be made. When a banker asks whether or not the management of a small company is certain that the amount requested is enough, it does not mean that he is going to offer additional funds; instead, he is asking for reassurance that the management of the firm has considered the possible variations of all of the costs and the probable delays in all of the revenues connected with the loan project. Since the bank is interested in the use and amount of the loan, a well-prepared loan request will detail the amount, broken down into the major categories, and will explain the use, for either sales expansion or production improvement, and will then confirm the adequacy of the amount by a monthly cash budget showing fluctuations in the expected level of the cash reserves over the coming year. In discussing the use of the loan, it should be noted that most banks will advance funds for the physical facilities needed for either marketing area expansions, manufacturing process improvements, or for the working capital needed to support sales increases, all of which generate tangible assets in plant and equipment, inventory, or accounts receivable; but most banks will generally not finance product or market development activities that produce only the intangible assets of capitalized R&D expenses or goodwill. Banks expect the product and market development expenses of smaller companies to be financed by the owners and investors through equity.

Repayment Schedule. Most banks want very definite information on the period of time the loan will be outstanding and on the method of payment. They are particularly interested in making certain that repayment can be made from the normal cash flow of the loan project without straining the operation of the company. Even though most loans generate tangible assets, the bank does not want to rely on liquidation of these assets for repayment, for it would defeat the purpose of the loan. Since the bank is interested in the length of time and the method of repayment, a well-prepared loan request will contain quarterly pro forma operating statements, with both balance sheets and income statements, showing the expected revenues generated by the loan project and the effect of the repayments on the operations and financial condition of the firm. It should be noted that most banks will provide funds for equipment purchases or working capital needs for a period up to 3 years. General-purpose machinery that has immediate resale value might be financed for 5 years. Buildings and real estate projects are a special case and may be mortgaged for 12 to 15 years. Seasonal inventory or accounts receivable financing is also special, but it is on the other end of the scale; seasonal loans are generally expected to be paid off in full within 12 months.

VENTURE CAPITAL

For most small companies, personal savings, trade credit, and bank loans are the main sources of capital. Companies that grow rapidly, however, may need more capital than these sources plus earnings can provide. Such additional needed money is often referred to as *venture capital* and may be obtainable from a number of sources, including the following.

Wealthy Individual Backers. Every town has its wealthy people, and among these can be found a few who like to lay bets on small companies. These people may include big company executives, heirs, successful entrepreneurs, medical people, widows, airline pilots, etc. Often they prefer not to be widely known for this interest lest they be besieged with supplicants for capital. Sometimes they personally seek out the kinds of small company investments they want, and sometimes they work through intermediaries, for example, bankers, lawyers, and brokers whom they rely upon to tell them of opportunities. Consequently, a way to learn about these possible investors is to ask the intermediaries.

Tax breaks are important inducements to investors. Both the subchapter S provision of the Internal Revenue Code, which allows operating losses to be deducted from regular income, and the provision for Section 1244 stock, which allows capital losses as an ordinary income deduction can be important in making investment attractive and should therefore be considered when a new corporation is being formed.

Clearly, it is important to take care in joining forces with investors. If people are selected who can be considered as "unsophisticated," the sale of stock can be legally regarded as a public offering, which carries a host of complications, as will be discussed below. If false promises mislead people into investing, the investors may charge the company with fraud. If the investors are people who cannot place a bet and forget it for a while, they may pester the company management unduly over concern for their money and they may impede its operations. If they are people who expect too much from the company, they may become disgruntled and cause no end of problems. There are, however, many people who make a practice of making these investments and do so skillfully and in ways that are helpful in guiding their investments toward success. The best clue in seeking out such investors is usually their reputation in the banking and entrepreneurial communities. Therefore, one who seeks investment from such people would do well to "ask around" regarding their reputations in the local business community.

Venture Capital Companies. Generally, there are two types of companies formed for the purpose of providing venture capital. The first are private venture capital companies that invest in ventures according to their own rules. The second are the small business investment companies (SBIC's) that agree to operate according to investment rules set forth by the Small Business Administration of the U.S. Department of Commerce in return for being able to borrow investment money from that agency under favorable terms designed to encourage these investments. From the small company manager's point of view, however, these two types of investment companies are essentially the same.

Because the ventures they invest in tend to be risky (possibly only one investment out of ten turning out to be highly profitable, with a larger fraction failing entirely and the rest doing only moderately well), these venture capital firms have to seek high return, a rule of thumb for many being the aim of multiplying the investment from threefold to fivefold in 5 years. These firms will want to be able to have stock for their money at some point. Often they invest through convertible debentures, bonds that can be converted into stock according to some fixed formula over a stated period of time. Sometimes they base the formula upon the company's forecast. Thus, the better the company does, the smaller the fraction of stock they can take through conversion, and vice versa. Often they will require a seat on the board of directors, and they may impose other constraints, for example, interest charges, consulting retainer fees, maintenance of certain performance limits by the company, and so forth.

Before investing in a small company, a venture capital firm will usually undertake an extensive investigation of the company, its industry, and the prospects for the company's future. Because the investigation costs time and money and because many proposals are typically screened for each one accepted (roughly 30 out of 100 may receive serious attention and fewer than 5 will be accepted), the venture capital firm must confine its attention to companies in which the investment and potential payoff are large in absolute dollar amounts. Investments of less than $150,000 are usually regarded as too small to warrant serious attention and investigation. However, the investment may be staged in increments according to the new company's progress and needs, so that the initial investment by the venture capital firm may be small with larger amounts being added later. Typically, the venture capital firm will want to see a payback of approximately from $500,000 to $1 million within 5 years to be seriously interested in a proposition.

As in dealing with private investors, the small company should select venture capital firms carefully. Some firms have more experience than others and can be of more help to the company. Others have reputations for "bleeding" the companies they invest in by extracting high interest or consulting fees or for meddling unhelpfully in management. A particularly important point in the relationship with a venture capital firm can be the time at which the small company must return for a "second round" of financing. Experienced venture capitalists are better able to anticipate and be helpful when such needs arise, but less experienced investors have been known to panic or get tough in these circumstances.

Reputable venture capitalists usually realize that they will fare best by assisting the companies they invest in rather than by squeezing all they can get from them and thereby killing the incentive of the entrepreneurs they are backing.

Private Stock Offering. Instead of looking for one wealthy individual, the company may be able to interest several investors in providing smaller amounts to the company in return for stock or partnership interest. If the number of people *approached* is small (typically fewer than 25) and if they can all be considered sophisticated investors who know what they are buying, the offering can be made on a private basis, which means that the offering need not be registered with the Securities Exchange Commission. This way a great amount of red tape and legal expense can be avoided.

Advantages of this approach are that through teaming up people of smaller means can participate and through selecting investors judiciously it may be possible to recruit supporters who can help the company in other ways in addition to providing money. Investors can include suppliers, customers, professional experts of any type, and/or employees, all of whom may be able to render valuable service and advice because of their personal financial interest in the company. They may also later serve as sources of still further capital if needed.

At the same time, however, the manager of the company will be acquiring other owners to contend with, and if things do not go well this can become a severe problem. Also, the fact that a company is owned by a number of people instead of just one or two can make it more difficult to interest some other types of investors, for example, venture capital firms that do not like to become involved when ownership is complicated. Thus, by recruiting many investors at one stage in its progress the company may cut off access to some other sources of money later.

Registered Stock Offering. To be able to approach larger numbers of potential investors, the company must first register with appropriate governmental agencies. Three choices open in this direction are as follows:

1. *Full Registration.* If the company wants to raise a large amount of money, say $1 million or more, it may be worthwhile to go to the expense (typical cost is $100,000, plus any sales expenses for legal, accounting, and other red tape services) of filing a full registration statement with the Securities Exchange Commission. Typically, however, this method of raising capital is only used by large companies and only in times of favorable stock market conditions.

2. *Regulation A Offering.* If the amount to be raised is less than $500,000, the company may be able to sell stock publicly by a short-cut registration procedure with the SEC known as *Regulation A*. Total costs may be in the range of $20,000. Any number of potential investors may be solicited, and as with the full registration, they may be approached in any states where permission is obtained. This method of raising money is used exclusively by smaller companies. Successful clearing of the bureaucratic and legal hurdles does not guarantee that the issue will sell, however, and many small companies have gone to the trouble and expense of arranging such an offering only to find that people will not buy the stock.

3. *Intrastate Offering.* If the company operates mainly within one state and if the stock is to be sold only to residents of that state, then no federal registration is required, and the company can seek to raise any amount from any number of people in the state simply by clearing the sale with the appropriate state government authorities. Such a sale can become a sticky matter, however, if investors do not wish to be restricted on resale of their stock to people in other states or if the company wants to make other offerings at later dates.

Since all these offerings are much more complicated than described above, it is advisable to contact the Securities Exchange Commission to learn its rules regardless what type of offering planned and it is advisable to hire a lawyer who is experienced in stock registrations.

Other Companies and Approaches. There are many other potential sources of capital for small companies. Although they are usually only accessible to larger companies that offer more "prudent" investments, there are vast amounts of capital in pension funds, family trusts, insurance companies, foundations, and mutual funds that can sometimes be tapped by small enterprises. Accounts receivable can be sold to factoring companies which are in business for that purpose. Equipment can be leased instead of bought. Money can be borrowed from finance companies and savings and loans against some types of assets.

Other novel approaches are also possible. When the bankers tried to foreclose on Henry Ford, he managed to survive by requiring each of his many dealers to advance the company money, enough collectively to bail him out. The K-2 Ski Company, expanding faster than its internal sources would allow, decided to go public for more capital, but this became impossible when the stock market fell off sharply. As a result, the company sold its stock to the Cummins Diesel Company which essentially became a cash source for K-2 while allowing the company to continue operating as a highly independent (since diesels and skis have so little in common) subsidiary. Many companies have sold off fixed assets and leased them back to generate working capital for expansion. Still others have sold franchises or rights to products and processes both to generate cash for expansion and to expand at the same time.

PROSPECTUS FORMULATION

The central concept of the securities laws, which apply to all types of offerings whether private or public, is full disclosure. Full disclosure requires that no information important to the decision to invest in a company be held back from the buyer by the seller. Prospectuses for sale of stock to individuals in response to this injunction normally include a section on risk factors that points out the weaknesses and dangers that the company faces. Prospectuses designed to interest venture capital firms do not generally include a risk factor section, presumably because the capital firms will themselves decide which factors constitute risk and how much. Examples of prospectuses for public sale of stock are readily available from brokerage firms and illustrate the standard format used. Although not a public offering circular, the Wheels of the World prospectus in Chapter 8 of this book was cast in the standard pattern, just in case the company found it necessary to obtain SEC permission to solicit capital from a large rather than small number of individuals. There is no standard format for private venture capital proposals. The Camping Resorts of Puerto Rico case in Chapter 8 illustrates a prospectus prepared with this aim in mind.

EVALUATION

Although a small business operating in steady state may be able to get by, even possibly do well, with no written planning and with informal monitoring procedures only, the company aiming at rapid growth has much better odds of success in the eyes of professional evaluators, such as venture capitalists, if it operates from a well-prepared written plan. That is not to say the plan must be followed. In fact, it has been observed that companies that don't follow their plans often do better than those that do, but both do better on growth trajectories if they have formal plans. The advantages of plans are that they force management to think through in detail what must happen in order to achieve success, that they provide lead time for acquisition of resources that cannot be obtained on the spur of the moment, that they give members of the company a common understanding of what is to be done, that they make people in the company think harder about what is to be done and thereby raise the odds of getting better ideas on how to accomplish it, and that once plans are prepared they allow people to concentrate on doing the job instead of constantly having to worry about what the job should be. At the same time, willingness to depart from plans allows flexibility to take advantage of new ideas and unforeseen opportunities. Flexibility is often cited as a major advantage unique to small companies.

Other factors that venture capitalists consider are (1) how promising the product or service of the company appears to be, (2) whether there is a well-balanced management team or a "lone wolf" entrepreneur, (3) what sort of "track record" the entrepreneur(s) and the company can display, (4) what sort of reputation the principals in the company have built up, how dedicated they appear to be (for instance, have they fully committed their own resources to the company before seeking resource commitments from others?), how satisfactory the principals will be to work with ("No prima donnas, thank you," commented one venture capitalist), and (5) overall the expected payout to the venture capital firm, which is a function of expected growth, profitability, risk, and method of capital recovery.

Not the least important of these assessment factors will be the degree to which management of the company displays an appreciation for financial management, the need to control costs and utilize financial resources shrewdly. "A gut feel for profits" is what one expert characterized as a particularly important characteristic in entrepreneurs seeking backing. "There must be a realization of the importance of selling at a good margin and of controlling expenditures to maximize what is left to grow with," he continued. "That is the point of financial management in a small company that aims to become something greater."

Robinson Upholstery Company

During the summer of 1972 two students in the M.B.A. program at The University of Michigan were asked to volunteer financial consulting services to the owner of a small company in downtown Detroit that manufactured upholstered furniture for the local market. The owner of the company, Isaiah Robinson, wanted to obtain a bank loan to finance the expansion of his company into direct retail sales at a suburban shopping center; he felt that the growth and profitability of his firm had been constrained by the declining population, reduced consumer income, and general physical deterioration of the central city, and he thought that he could overcome these problems by selling his products in a more affluent suburb. The bank, however, had not approved his loan application; Mr. Robinson believed that he had been refused the loan because he was black and had attempted to open a retail store in a white community:

> I started this business back in 1954 when Detroit was a good place to live. Then, all these homes were painted, the yards were neat, and the streets were clean. Each house had a front porch where people sat in the evenings. You could drive up and down the streets, and you would see people who were proud of their homes. Those people didn't have much money, but they wanted good things for their homes, and they came to us because we were a local business and because we made good furniture. We had more business than we could handle in those days. Now you can see what is wrong. You drove down here this morning. You saw what the houses look like. Nobody has any pride in his home anymore; nobody wants good furniture in the city.
>
> I can't sell furniture in the city anymore, so I've got to sell outside the city. But, I can't

open up the store in Troy unless I get a bank loan, and the bank surely doesn't want to lend me any money. Maybe you can help. (Statement of Mr. Robinson.)

Mr. Robinson was a short, active man who had come to Detroit from rural Arkansas in 1933. He had found a job as a janitor at a reupholstery shop run by one of the larger department stores in the city. During the depression many of the department stores had offered reupholstering services to promote the sale of their fabrics. Mr. Robinson continued as a janitor until the war years when, because of the shortage of labor, he was asked to help in gluing the wooden frames, webbing the steel springs, and stuffing the burlap casings. These were hard and unpleasant jobs: the wooden parts for each frame had to be coated with animal glue, which was hot and sticky and often caused burns, before being fitted by hand into clamps for curing; then the steel springs, which had sharp edges and could easily cut, had to be interlaced tightly within the frame to form the base for the seat; and finally the stuffing, which at that time was horse hair or cattle hair and was dusty, dirty, and very likely to cause skin infections, had to be packed closely into the canvas and burlap cases that formed the body of the chair or sofa. Mr. Robinson, however, devised simple tools and fixtures to help in the performance of these jobs, so that by the end of the war he was easily the fastest and most productive worker in the shop. Since many of the prewar workers did not want to return to the upholstery business, he became the senior worker in 1947 and was promoted to shop foreman in 1950. His wife, who had been a seamstress at the upholstery shop since 1934, was put in charge of the sewing operations at the same time. This arrangement, which gave them a better-than-average income and enabled them to buy their own home, did not last very long, however. The department store decided to discontinue the reupholstery service in 1953, and, after unsuccessfully looking for equivalent employment for nearly 3 months, the Robinsons decided to start their own company in the basement of their home.

The new company was almost immediately successful. Customers heard of the company through friends or were referred by the downtown department store. They came directly to the shop, bringing their furniture to be repaired or reupholstered. Mr. and Mrs. Robinson were able to offer high-quality workmanship, based upon their own experience and competence, at a reduced cost because their overhead was low and they had no promotion or distribution expenses. The volume of business increased until the Robinsons had to hire additional people in 1956, and then they had to move the shop from their home to a storefront location in 1957 to accommodate the extra workers. The company was profitable for each of the first 5 years, except for 1957 when they had extra expenses connected with the change of location (see Exhibit 1).

The company continued to expand over the next 5 years, particularly after 1961 when Mr. Robinson designed a sofa, chair, and coffee table suite of furniture in a modern Danish style which the company manufactured for retail sale. Mr. Robinson frankly admitted that he had copied the design from a line of very popular imported furniture that was displayed and sold by the department store for which he had previously worked. As a result of this style plagiarism, the department store stopped referring customers for reupholstery and repair work, but Mr. Robinson felt that the new products more than canceled any possible loss of business and balanced out the seasonal swings in the reupholstery sales. Most reupholstery and repair work is done during the winter, when people are kept inside by the weather and are consequently concerned about the condition and appearance of the older furnishings of their homes; most upholstered furniture, however, is bought during the summer and early fall when people travel to look at new furniture displays. Also,

EXHIBIT 1 Income statements for the Robinson Upholstery Company, 1954–1958.

	1954	*1955*	*1956*	*1957*	*1958*
Retail sales	$28,730	$34,890	$47,420	$58,790	$72,470
Material costs	9,450	9,360	12,430	15,920	17,950
Labor costs	2,780*	4,170*	8,770*	14,860*	20,060*
Shop overhead cost	2,190	2,850	2,140	14,330†	9,830
Total manufacturing costs	14,420	16,380	23,340	45,110	47,840
Gross margin	14,310	18,510	24,080	13,680	24,630
Administrative expenses	13,890	13,710	14,560	15,970	17,110
Gross profit	420	4,800	9,520	(2,290)	7,520
Income tax	—	1,060	2,080	—	1,180
Net profit	$ 420	$ 3,740	$ 7,440	$ (2,290)	$ 6,340

Source: Company records. Some figures are disguised.
* *The salaries of Mr. and Mrs. Robinson during 1954 to 1958 were allocated to administrative expenses, although both worked in the shop for 50 to 60 hours each week. The combined salary of both partners during this period was $12,000 per year.*
† *The shop overhead in 1957 included approximately $6,000 in moving expenses connected with the relocation of the company.*

of course, the new line of proprietary products enabled the company to build for inventory during slow periods throughout the year:

> I don't know why we didn't start our own line of furniture much before 1961 since it has worked out so well for us. People would drive down to our shop to talk about repairing or reupholstering their old furniture, and then they would look at our new line which was modern and stylish, and they would generally buy the new rather than repair the old. We got a lot more business during the summer, which had been our slow period, and so we could work steadily right through the year. Before, when we did only reupholstery and repair, we had to let some of our good workers go during the summer, and sometimes they didn't come back in the fall. Now, we can offer employment right through the year, and we can keep the good workers. It was in 1961 that we began to think about having a furniture company and not just an upholstery shop. (Statement of Mr. Robinson.)

Sales and earnings for the second 5-year period of the company are given in Exhibit 2; both show continued growth after the mild recession of 1959. Because it needed increased work area and inventory storage, in 1963 the company moved from the storefront location on 12th Street to an abandoned laundry building on West Fort Boulevard, near the river. There were extra expenses connected with this move also, although they resulted in decreased profits and not an actual loss.

During the third 5-year period the company continued to grow in sales volume in 1964 and 1965, but the expenses increased proportionately more than sales, and the profits began to decline. Then, in 1966 racial unrest greatly accelerated the migration of middle-class families from the city and deterred many suburban customers from driving into Detroit to shop for clothing, jewelry, or home furnishings. All retail stores within the city lost business during this period, which culminated in the riots of 1967:

> Michigan Governor Romney today ordered 1,100 National Guardsmen and 370 state troopers into Detroit as Blacks looted, burned, and fired shots at police. The violence spread

EXHIBIT 2 Income statements for the Robinson Upholstery Company, 1959–1963.

	1959	1960	1961	1962	1963
Reupholstery service	$68,710	$79,040	$79,590	$ 86,720	$ 86,650
Upholstered furniture	—	—	10,070	21,820	34,760
Total retail sales	68,710	79,040	89,660	108,540	121,410
Material costs	17,540	19,610	21,840	25,040	28,900
Labor costs	18,760*	21,460*	27,090*	34,760*	39,460*
Shop overhead costs	9,030	10,320	10,700	13,040	19,650†
Total manufacturing costs	45,330	51,390	59,630	72,840	88,010
Gross margin	23,380	27,650	30,030	35,700	33,400
Administrative expenses	16,540	18,560	19,440	21,370	22,530
Gross profit	6,840	9,090	10,590	14,330	10,870
Income tax	1,450	1,990	2,350	3,160	2,350
Net profit	$ 5,390	$ 7,100	$ 8,240	$ 11,170	$ 8,520

Source: Company records. Some figures are disguised.
* *The salaries of Mr. and Mrs. Robinson during 1959 to 1963 were again allocated to administrative expenses, although both continued to work in the shop when they were not occupied with sales, deliveries, purchases, or general supervision.*
† *The shop overhead in 1963 included approximately $5,000 in moving expenses connected with the relocation of the company.*

throughout a mile-long section of the city, and Romney said that it was based on "a general disregard for law and order." (*The Wall Street Journal,* July 24, 1967, p. 1.)

About 4,700 paratroopers were prepared to move into the streets of Detroit today to help quell an epidemic of looting and arson that caused more than $150 million of fire damage in 2 days, and ground to a halt most of the normal activities of the nation's fifth largest city. (*The Wall Street Journal,* July 25, 1967, p. 2.)

Detroit's economy, battered by three days of looting, burning, and violence, struggled to get going again, but the first tasks of many businesses were merely trying to assess damages. Movement of Federal troops into the city late Monday night helped to restore some measure of order, but most office and factory workers stayed away from their jobs, fearful of encountering any of the sporadic incidents that continued during the day, or of getting cut off from their homes in the evening. (*The Wall Street Journal,* July 26, 1967, p. 3.)

Detroit rioting was apparently checked as troops took control of the streets. Foot patrols continued in most sections, but a Federal official said that "the worst is over," after 4 days of rioting that took 28 lives and caused over $500 million in damages. (*The Wall Street Journal,* July 28, 1967, p. 1.)

A major worry is that the little businessman has been hardest hit, and will have trouble snapping back when the tanks and the soldiers leave. (*The Wall Street Journal,* July 29, 1967, p. 5. All the above excerpts reprinted with permission of *The Wall Street Journal,* © 1967 Dow Jones & Company, Inc. All rights reserved.)

The Robinson Upholstery Company was hard hit by the riots of 1967, but not in the usual sense; their building was not damaged and their inventory was not destroyed, but their retail business nearly disappeared for a period of almost 4 months during the late summer and early fall, which was normally the season of greatest customer interest and sales activity, and afterward their sales never regained the former level or the former rate of growth:

Our business almost came to an end during the summer and fall of 1967. None of our property was damaged, and our people came to work almost every day during the riot, which was much more in the Northwest section of the city than around here. We would have been right in the middle of it in our 12th Street store, but here it worried us but did not bother us, right then. But our customers didn't come back. People didn't stop to think that there were sections of the city that were clear of trouble; they just didn't want to come into the city for any reason. That attitude has continued; people don't come into the city for shopping now. Instead, they go to the big shopping centers in the suburbs; they can get everything they need at those shopping centers, so there is no reason for them to come into the city anymore. Our sales went down and stayed down. (Statement of Mr. Robinson.)

In 1968 Mr. Robinson, discouraged by the continual lack of retail sales, decided to begin selling to credit furniture stores on a wholesale basis. These credit stores, which specialized in providing easy consumer credit at very high interest rates for the purchase of poorer quality furniture and appliances, normally obtained their merchandise from manufacturers in the South and Southwest. The owners of the credit stores had often asked Mr. Robinson to sell to them in the past because of the potential savings on freight, but he had refused, partially because of their reputation for poor quality and service, and partially because they had insisted upon a purchase price 25% lower than his normal retail price. He felt that there was only a limited profit to be made in selling to these stores on their terms, but he also felt that this wholesale business did increase sales volume and did provide some contribution to profit and overhead. The sales and profits or losses during this period are given in Exhibit 3.

Company sales to the credit furniture stores in the Detroit area expanded enough in 1969 to bring the company back to profitable operations, but the series of losses during 1966, 1967, and 1968 had seriously deteriorated the financial condition of the company, and Mr. Robinson had been forced to borrow funds from the local branch of the

EXHIBIT 3   Income statements for the Robinson Upholstery Company, 1964–1968.

	1964	1965	1966	1967	1968
Reupholstery service	$ 87,780	$ 85,180	$ 63,430	$ 45,960	$ 43,510
Upholstered furniture	50,050	53,940	49,810	32,570	36,800
Wholesale sales, 25% off	—	—	—	—	40,570
Total sales	137,830	139,120	113,240	78,530	120,880
Material costs	32,420	32,180	25,550	18,230	33,080
Labor costs	48,130	54,020	47,490	40,560	53,440
Shop overhead costs	15,460	18,530	17,430	15,410	15,860
Total manufacturing costs	96,010	104,730	90,470	74,200	102,380
Gross margin	41,820	34,390	22,770	4,330	18,500
Administrative expenses	27,450	29,560	29,840	28,170	29,490
Gross profit (or loss)	14,370	4,830	(7,070)	(23,840)	(10,990)
Income tax or refund +	−3,280	−1,090	—	+6,370	+2,530
Net profit (or loss)	$11,090	$ 3,740	$ (7,070)	$(17,470)	$ (8,460)

*Note: The salaries of Mr. and Mrs. Robinson during 1964 to 1968 were again allocated to administra-
tive expenses. This is correct since both had stopped working in the shop as extensively as before; they
were now almost fully occupied with sales, deliveries, purchases, supervision and, after 1967, financing.
Source: Company records. Some figures are disguised.*

Woodward National Bank for working capital. Previously, he had borrowed only to finance specific assets, such as a delivery truck that he used to provide home delivery and pick-up service in the suburbs or an automatic stapling machine that he used to reduce labor costs on the furniture manufactured in the shop; these had been installment loans, written over 2 or 3 years, secured by the asset to be financed, and repaid by a monthly payment schedule with small, equal payments. Now he had term notes, renewable every 90 days, secured by a general assignment of the accounts receivable and inventory of his firm, and subject to fairly continual pressure from the bank for repayment of the full amount, or at least reduction of the principal. Mr. Robinson found it difficult to pay off these notes since the wholesale business, which continued to expand during the next 4 years, did not generate adequate profits to finance this expansion. The income statements for this period, 1969 through the first 6 months of 1972, are given in Exhibit 4, and the balance sheets for the

close of each period are given in Exhibit 5.

Mr. and Mrs. Robinson were very discouraged during the summer of 1972 by the deteriorating financial condition of their company and by the lack of profits that resulted from their sales to the credit furniture and appliance stores. There seemed to be a substantial volume of wholesale business available, but the Robinsons had to meet the prices of the small Southern manufacturers who used poorer grade materials and lower paid help to produce much cheaper merchandise.

Most credit store owners admitted that the furniture manufactured by the Robinson Upholstery Company was better made and better designed, but they were not willing to pay a differential for this higher quality:

They (the credit store owners) want big, bulky pieces, so the customer will think that he is getting a lot of furniture for his money and also so that it will hide the junk that is inside. They don't care what you use. You can put split wood in the frame, sisal or cotton fibers in the stuffing, or reject fabrics in the

EXHIBIT 4   Income statements for the Robinson Upholstery Company, 1969–1972.

	Dec. 31 1969	*Dec. 31 1970*	*Dec. 31 1971*	*June 30 1972 (6 months)*
Reupholstery service sales	$ 50,510	$ 48,390	$ 46,150	$ 21,510
Retail furniture sales	47,620	46,860	47,760	19,250
Wholesale furniture sales	87,340	114,600	137,270	74,940
Total company sales	185,470	209,850	231,180	115,700
Material costs	50,270	57,950	65,310	37,590
Labor costs	84,540	97,560	110,070	52,870
Total direct shop costs	134,810	155,510	175,380	90,460
Shop supervision	9,600	9,900	10,200	5,100
Shop supplies and small tools	3,140	3,870	4,290	2,240
Shop repairs and maintenance	2,310	2,620	3,420	1,750
Heat, light, and power	2,760	3,710	4,260	2,070
Depreciation on equipment	1,140	1,270	1,430	1,160
Depreciation on leasehold improvements	950	960	980	490
Total indirect shop costs	19,900	22,330	24,580	12,810
Gross margin	30,760	32,010	31,220	12,430
Salaries of owners	12,000	12,000	12,000	6,000
Lease payments on building	2,600	2,600	2,600	1,300
Interest on loans	720	790	1,510	750
Legal and accounting	870	640	1,050	640
Bookkeeping service	340	380	470	260
Delivery van and auto costs	3,140	3,270	3,790	2,040
Insurance	1,810	1,870	2,220	1,840
Telephone	1,170	1,410	1,680	1,040
State and local taxes	460	1,670	1,460	1,430
	23,110	24,630	26,780	15,300
Gross profit	7,650	7,380	4,440	(2,870)
Income taxes (federal and state)	1,920	1,870	1,290	—
Net profit	$ 5,730	$ 5,510	$ 3,150	$ (2,870)

Source: Company records. Some figures are disguised.

cover, and they don't care as long as the customer can't see what you've done. It's an insult to work on that sort of stuff, and yet we have to. We need the work since we can't sell our good furniture here in the city. (Statement of Mr. Robinson.)

Mr. and Mrs. Robinson had not been able to arrange the financing necessary to offer credit to their retail customers, so they sold very little of their new furniture or reupholstery work to local people, who generally were on the edge of poverty and in need of credit for any major purchases. Most of their retail sales were made to people in the northern and western suburbs who knew of the company and called Mr. Robinson to ask him to build or repair their upholstered furniture, but this telephoned business now declined slightly each year as the older customers either died or moved away from the area. The younger customers generally went directly to the large furniture stores in the suburban shopping centers where they had a much wider choice of styles and fabrics than

EXHIBIT 5 Balance sheets for the Robinson Upholstery Company, 1969–1972.

	Dec. 31 1969	Dec. 31 1970	Dec. 31 1971	June 30 1972
Cash	$ 1,830	$ 2,410	$ 670	$(1,940)
Accounts receivable	6,200	9,730	17,590	25,610
Raw material inventory	15,630	17,090	19,670	22,300
In-process inventory	6,380	7,480	8,670	8,240
Finished goods inventory	4,680	3,320	1,410	910
Total inventory	26,690	27,890	29,750	31,450
Total current assets	34,720	40,030	48,010	55,120
Machinery and equipment	32,820	31,520	34,770	35,430
Less reserve for depreciation	18,010	16,890	18,320	19,480
Total machinery and equipment	14,810	14,630	16,450	15,590
Trucks and cars	7,040	7,040	9,770	9,770
Less reserve for depreciation	3,650	5,590	5,480	7,260
Total trucks and cars	3,390	1,450	4,290	2,510
Leasehold improvements	18,420	18,690	21,430	22,290
Less reserve for depreciation	9,480	10,440	11,420	11,850
Total leasehold improvements	8,940	8,250	10,010	10,440
Miscellaneous and prepaid expenses	1,870	2,470	1,890	1,410
Total assets	$63,730	$66,830	$80,650	$85,070
Accounts payable	$ 2,620	$ 3,400	$ 7,190	$15,540
Term loans	5,260	7,760	10,000	12,000
Equipment and automobile loans portion due within 1 year	2,640	2,430	5,370	4,070
Advance from owner	2,600	1,100	1,100	1,100
Income taxes due	1,920	1,870	1,290	650
Withholding taxes due	—	—	—	2,520
Miscellaneous and accrued expenses	870	540	1,090	1,840
Total current liabilities	15,910	17,100	26,040	37,720
Equipment and automobile loans portion due after 1 year	5,890	3,460	6,410	2,620
Preferred stock	2,400	2,400	2,400	2,400
Common stock	2,800	2,800	2,800	2,800
Retained earnings	36,730	41,070	43,000	39,530
Total equity	47,820	49,730	54,610	47,350
Total liabilities and equity	$63,730	$63,830	$80,650	$85,070

Mr. Robinson could possibly offer and where they had much more rapid delivery. Mr. Robinson had, of course, attempted to sell directly to these large suburban furniture stores, but he could not produce in the volume that they required, and he hesitated to pay the 35% to 40% discount that they demanded since this would involve a substantial increase in the retail price of his products:

When we first started in business, people did not buy ready-made furniture; they would have an upholstered piece, a sofa or a chair, made to order, and then they would have it recovered when the fabric became worn or soiled. As long as you did good work, you would have customers that would come back every 5 to 10 years, either to get a new piece to match the old one or to have the old one recovered and repaired. That is changing now. People buy their furniture from the big stores where they can look at maybe 100 different styles and pieces and fabrics. The big store won't recover it for them, so they put on slip covers, which look bad but they're cheap. Our daughter says that we're basically custom builders and that there's not much custom business left anymore. (Statement of Mr. Robinson.)

Mr. and Mrs. Robinson's daughter, Leonda, wanted her parents to open a small retail store in the suburbs. She was a recent graduate of Wellesley College in Wellesley, Massachusetts, which is a wealthy suburb of Boston. There she had met a black girl of approximately her own age who ran a furniture store on the main street of Wellesley for her uncle, who manufactured the furniture in Roxbury, a rapidly decaying section of downtown Boston. The suburban store was small, only 25 ft × 40 ft, and there was room to display only 3 sofas and perhaps 5 or 6 arm chairs, but they had sold approximately $200,000 worth of furniture there the previous year. One of the reasons for their success was that they were the only store in the area that offered a convertible arm chair that could be changed into a single bed, similar to the much more familiar convertible sofas that could be changed into double beds, but much smaller, more convenient, and more easily converted. Miss Robinson had described this convertible chair to her father, and he was certain that he could manufacture a similar line. The styles of the furniture sold in the Wellesley store were modern, with thin lines and either walnut, teak, or chrome-plated legs and arms and side-frames; Mr. Robinson was certain that he could imitate those styles. The fabrics sold in the Wellesley store were brightly colored, often with Merimekko patterns; Mr. Robinson was certain that he could obtain those fabrics. In short, the store in Wellesley appealed to younger people, often apartment dwellers, or others who had just purchased a small home and who wanted just a few pieces of good furniture. The Robinsons felt that there would be a similar market in the suburbs of Detroit and that they could manufacture the furniture that would appeal to this market. They were certain, however, that they would have to have a store in the suburban area and that they could not sell this line of furniture from their present, rather unattractive building in a poor section of the inner city.

> We've had three robberies in this building since we moved here, so now we have to keep the doors locked all the time. We have to send Leroy out to the bus stop with our workers in the evening to make certain that they are not bothered. [Leroy was a short, very heavy ex-stevedore from Mobile, Alabama who had worked for Mr. Robinson almost from the start of the business.] This is not the place for a retail store. (Statement of Mr. Robinson.)

Miss Robinson found a possible location for the retail store in the Somerset Mall, in Troy, Michigan, one of the northern suburbs, approximately 20 miles from the center of Detroit. This was a popular shopping area, particularly with younger people, for many of the existing stores emphasized the modern styles in clothing and home furnishings. There was another furniture store in the shopping area (large and apparently very successful), but it carried a full line of bedroom, dining room, and living room furniture and did not stress the upholstered lines. The problem was that the annual rental for this store, which was in a new and only partially finished area of the Mall, was $7.00 per square foot net, net, net, which meant that the renter had to pay for all taxes, utilities, and maintenance and that the owner would provide only shell space, with 3 concrete block walls, a steel girder roof, and a dirt floor. The renter had to install the front, pour the floor, decorate the ceiling and walls, and clean the entire store area, which would cost a minimum of $20.00 per square foot. The store was 25 ft × 48 ft, just the right size in the Robinson's opinion; the owner had intended it to be a jewelry store or stationery shop, but was willing to rent it as a furniture store provided the Robinsons quickly invested the money necessary to finish the building and stock the inventory and make a down payment of 6 months rent. Mr. Robinson approached the Woodward National Bank, where he had kept the company account since 1953, for a loan to rent, finish, and stock the new store, but his application was promptly rejected without explanation. The three members of the Robinson family felt badly about this rejection since they had been enthusiastic about the new store and about the prospect of working together:

> I went down to see Mr. Owen, the manager of the branch office of the bank just three blocks down from our factory building on West Fort Boulevard. He told me that he could not lend over $12,000, that we were over that already, and that I would have to go down to the central office. Well, I went down there and I saw a young fellow who didn't seem to know much about furniture. He told me that we didn't have enough capital. I know that we don't have enough capital; we would not have gone down to his bank if we had enough money to do this on our own. Then he said that the bank would not lend us the money.
>
> I don't like this present situation. I've been a customer of that bank for 18 years; I was one of the people they approached when they wanted to open an office down here on West Fort. I've always kept my money in that bank, and I've borrowed money from them before, for the truck and the car and for some machinery when we moved to the laundry, and then to keep the company going after the riot in 1967. I've always paid them back as soon as I was able to. Now they don't want to lend us the money we need to make this business a success and to set up our daughter out there in Troy. There are 100 shops in the shopping center in Troy, and you know that every one of them got a loan to finish the store and bring in the inventory. But that's all right; everyone of them is white. We're black, so they don't want to loan us the money.
>
> You know, my wife and I have seldom encountered prejudice in the past. It may seem strange to you, but we live in a black neigh-

borhood, we employ black workers, we trade with black people. I seldom see a white person, except when I go to the bank or the post office or the fabric supplier or when I drive out for a pick-up or delivery at a customer's home. Then, they're always polite, because they called and asked me to come out. It's better now than it was 15 to 20 years ago; then you couldn't go into a restaurant in downtown Detroit. But we didn't go out for dinner then, and we don't now. We have our own life and we live it our way, and we seldom encounter prejudice. But that bank is prejudiced. They loan money to whites; they should loan it to blacks. (Statement of Mr. Robinson.)

> Those white merchants don't want us out there in the Somerset Mall, but they're going to have us out there. We ought to go to another bank, one that is not so blatantly racist. (Statement of Miss Robinson.)

The vice president of the commercial loan division at the Woodward National Bank, also named Robinson but not related to the Robinson family, had a different view of the loan application and rejection:

> He came in one afternoon, without an appointment, talked to one of our trainees, and asked for as much money as we would give him. He was enthusiastic about his idea for a new furniture store, which evidently does have some degree of merit, but he didn't have a definite plan for the use of the money; he didn't have any idea when and how he could repay the money, and he didn't even know how much money he needed. We don't do business that way.
>
> Every time we turn down a loan to a white businessman, he says that we're interested only in big business, and every time we turn down a loan to a black, he says that we're prejudiced. We're not prejudiced and we're not interested only in big business, at least not in the commercial loan division which deals only with small and medium-sized companies in the metropolitan area, but we are conservative. We don't like to lose money.
>
> I'm not going to give you the lecture about our acting in a fiduciary capacity to protect our depositors' money. I don't think that many of us spend much time worrying about our depositors, but right now the cost of

money is about 6¼%, and we loan it out at 7¾%, and that's not much of a spread; we can't afford many losses. We are just not in the venture capital business. We are in the business of lending money to our customers so that they can improve their sales, production, and profits and repay our loan on a definite schedule. Then we can lend the money to somebody else.

We did not reject the loan for Mr. Robinson, although I will admit that we did not encourage him, given his present lack of information and indefinite plans. If he wishes to apply again, we will consider that application on its merits, just as we do for every other customer of this bank. Now, if you'll excuse me, I'm very busy this afternoon. (Statement of Mr. Robinson, vice president of the commercial loan division of the Woodward National Bank.)

ASSIGNMENT

Prepare a loan application for the Robinson Upholstery Company, requesting the funds necessary to open the proposed store in the Somerset Mall shopping center in Troy, Michigan. For assistance in preparing this application, Exhibit 6 gives standard ratios for the operations of a

EXHIBIT 6 Common operating and financial ratios for household furniture retail stores, by volume of retail sales.

	Under $500,000 annual sales	$500,000 to $1,000,000 sales	Over $1,000,000 annual sales
Sales	100.0%	100.0%	100.0%
Cost of merchandise, delivery	66.3	64.7	64.1
Margin on sales	33.7	35.3	35.9
Sales salaries and commissions	10.8	10.2	9.9
Rent/depreciation on building	5.3	5.6	5.8
Interest on loans	1.9	1.7	1.2
Heat, light, and power	2.1	2.1	2.2
Professional services	2.1	1.8	1.4
Insurance	1.9	1.7	1.2
Advertising	4.3	4.6	6.9
Administration	7.1	6.9	6.2
	35.5	35.4	34.8
Operating profit (loss)	(1.8)	0.1	1.1
Credit service charges	6.1	5.4	5.2
Net profit before taxes	4.3	5.5	6.3
Current ratio	1.4	1.5	1.9
Accounts receivable (days)	15.2	20.2	34.0
Inventory (days)	123.0	97.0	103.0
Accounts payable (days)	37.3	43.0	36.9
Return on equity (percentage)	17.2	18.4	16.6
Return on sales (percentage)	4.3	5.5	6.3
Debt/equity ratio	0.4	0.4	0.6

Note: Credit service charges on income statement or operating ratios represents the revenues less interest costs for financing customer purchases on installment loan contracts.
Source: Internal publication of the Woodward National Bank (disguised name).

EXHIBIT 7 Common operating and financial ratios for furniture manufacturing plants, by volume of wholesale sales.

	Under $500,000 annual sales	$500,000 to $1,000,000 sales	Over $1,000,000 annual sales
Wholesale sales	100.0%	100.0%	100.0%
Direct material costs	20.8	19.6	17.9
Direct labor costs	45.6	43.6	40.9
Indirect supervision and labor	6.2	5.7	5.5
Building rent or taxes/depreciation	4.7	5.8	6.9
Equipment taxes/depreciation	1.2	·1.6	1.8
Heat, light, and power	1.8	1.9	1.8
	80.3	78.2	74.8
Selling and administrative salaries	12.6	12.9	13.4
Selling and administrative expenses	4.3	4.6	5.6
Interest charges	1.7	1.4	1.3
Professional services	1.4	1.9	1.1
General insurance	2.4	1.9	1.7
	22.4	23.7	23.1
Net profit (loss) before taxes	(2.7)	(0.9)	2.1
Current ratio	1.8	1.8	2.1
Accounts receivable (days)	43.0	39.3	36.7
Inventory (days)	97.0	108.4	121.6
Accounts payable (days)	52.0	47.5	33.3

Source: Internal publication of the Woodward National Bank (disguised name).

furniture retail store, and Exhibit 7 gives the ratios for the operations of a furniture manufacturing plant. These, or similar ratios, are normally used by commercial banks in evaluation of loan requests. After preparing the application, consider the following questions:

1. What are the probabilities, in your opinion, that Mr. and Mrs. Robinson will receive the requested loan? What are the points in favor and against it?

2. Would these probabilities, again in your opinion, be increased by changing to a different bank, as suggested by Miss Robinson?

3. Could these probabilities have been improved by a different original approach to the Woodward National Bank?

Sawmill Machinery Corporation

The Sawmill Machinery Corporation was started in the fall of 1962 to manufacture modern processing equipment, such as log carriages, board edgers, and trim saws, for the lumber industry. Prior to the 1960s, sawmills in the eastern United States were built and operated with machinery that had not been basically redesigned since the late nineteenth century; steam was the common power source because the scrap lumber, sawdust, and planer shavings could be burned as boiler fuel. Manual labor was the usual material handling method, since the wage rates that were paid in the rural areas were low. Continual increases in the cost of logs, brought about by a growing scarcity of timber, the development of a market for the sawmill waste, which could be sold to local paper mills for use as pulpwood, and raises in the minimum wage rates, which were passed by Congress during the Eisenhower and early Kennedy administrations, brought very substantial changes in the economics of the lumber industry and in the practices of operating sawmills. Automatic machinery was required, with electronic control circuits and hydraulic positioning mechanisms, to reduce manpower and increase log utilization. The Sawmill Machinery Corporation was founded by Bradford and George Hoffman to take advantage of this industry need.

Bradford Hoffman was a graduate of the University of Pittsburgh in 1956 in mechanical engineering; his younger brother, George, had a degree in forestry and an M.B.A. from Pennsylvania State University. They were both interested in the lumber industry since their father ran a small sawmill in Wellsville, Ohio, in the "tri-state" area close to the West Virginia and Pennsylvania borders,

although neither worked for the family company. Both brothers wanted to return to Wellsville because they were disillusioned with large business practices and urban living conditions. Therefore, they were interested when their father during the Christmas holidays of 1961 told them both of the need for improved sawmill machinery and complained of the lack of available sources. They felt that this unfilled need might provide an opportunity for them to start a business in the local area. During the winter and spring of 1962 Bradford continued to work in Pittsburgh for one of the large steel companies, but he devoted evenings and weekends to the mechanical design of automatic machinery for the lumber industry, while George took a leave of absence from his job as a wholesale lumber salesman in Chicago to begin investigating the potential size and financial requirements of the sawmill machinery market.

You only had to look at the machinery that was available to the small or medium-sized Eastern sawmill to appreciate that a market existed for new products. Much of the existing equipment literally had not changed since the Civil War; many saw carriages [see Exhibit 5 for descriptions of the various sawmill machines] were still made with a frame of wooden timbers bolted together, and with cast iron operating parts mounted on bronze bearings. The argument for this form of construction was that the wood gave a little, and provided some resilience and flexibility when you rolled a heavy log onto the carriage so that the iron pieces would not break. This was true, but it also meant that you could not get any accuracy or speed in sawing. If you wanted to saw a 2-in. board, you had to set the saw for 2½ in. to allow for the lack of precision, and then you had to add another ½ in. to allow for the kerf (wood taken from the log in the form of sawdust to cut off each board) because the saw would wobble; the result was that 3 in. were taken from the log to get a 2-in. board. And the machinery was slow; it was all right as long as both logs and labor were cheap. When timber began to get a little scarce and the minimum wage started to climb, many of the mill owners began to think about improving their operations. (Statement of George Hoffman.)

George Hoffman visited over 150 sawmills in the Pennsylvania, Ohio, Indiana, and southern Michigan area during the spring and summer of 1962; he found that most mill owners were willing to talk to him about their operating problems and to describe the type of equipment they wanted.

The larger sawmills purchased their equipment from the West Coast, and there certainly were no wooden frames, cast iron parts, or bronze bearings in use out there in 1962, but the West Coast equipment was simply too big, too heavy, and too complicated for most of our Eastern sawmills. The typical mill in this area wanted machinery that was lighter in weight, less expensive, and less complex; we don't have the large logs or the large concentrations of timber to run a West Coast type sawmill here, except in a few special situations such as a paper company that has

ample timber holdings or a few special areas such as the Upper Peninsula of Michigan or the mountains of West Virginia. That was the reason people kept on using the older equipment; it was the only machinery that was available that was designed for local timber. My brother and I felt that we could offer a compromise, with automatic machinery of the West Coast type adapted to Eastern conditions. (Statement of George Hoffman.)

Using information he received during his market research study, George Hoffman developed a financial comparison that showed the very definite advantages that automatic machinery would offer the mill owners. The full comparison is given in Exhibit 6, but in summary the modernized sawmill would increase daily lumber production, and consequently lumber sales, approximately 75%, decrease labor costs more than 40% and, despite substantial increases in power, depreciation, and interest expenses, turn a loss situation into a profit.

All three members of the Hoffman family were encouraged by the reception that George had received during his travels to visit sawmill owners, and they were particularly pleased with the results of the financial comparison that George had prepared because it seemed to show the necessity of using automatic machinery in sawmill

EXHIBIT 1 Summary comparison of the financial results of operations between older sawmills with manual equipment and modern sawmills with automatic equipment.

	Older sawmill w/manual equipment	Modern sawmill w/automatic equipment
Revenues from lumber and pulpwood chip sales, per day	$ 1,200	$ 2,240
Log costs, per day	800	1,400
Labor costs, per day	240	150
Power costs, per day	20	40
Interest and depreciation costs, per day		120
General overhead and supervision costs	180	220
	1,240	1,920
Profit (or loss) per day	($40)	$320
Profit (or loss) per year	($10,000)	$80,000

operations. Mr. Hoffman confirmed that within his personal experience most sawmills were operating below the breakeven point during 1962 because of the high costs of labor and logs and that there was a general feeling throughout the industry that changes in sawmill methods and equipment were needed.

At a family conference held during June of 1962, Bradford Hoffman reported that he was absolutely confident that simplified automatic equipment could be profitably produced. His engineering drawings were, of course, not complete, but he had sketched out and roughly priced the major components, and he felt that the machinery for an automatic sawmill could be manufactured and sold for roughly $175,000, while the installation and start-up expenses for this machinery at each new sawmill would be in the neighborhood of $75,000. The total bill for an automatic sawmill would be, then, $250,000; this might seem high to most Eastern and Midwestern lumber companies, which were often small, family-owned concerns, but the after-tax earnings would be $50,000, depreciation would add $20,000, and the elimination of the loss would give another $10,000 for a total positive cash flow of $80,000. The Hoffmans felt that the return on the investment would be nearly 30%. Since there were more than 1,150 sawmills of the small and medium-size classifications registered (each sawmill must register with the Forestry Commission of the state in which it operates to ensure payment of the timber taxes and license fees) in West Virginia, Ohio, and Pennsylvania, the Hoffmans were certain that they had an excellent potential product and a huge potential market.

> I would recommend that anyone starting a business be absolutely certain that he has a product that no one else has and a market that no one else serves. The only thing that kept us going during the early years was the conviction that we were right and that eventually our customers would recognize this and come to us. You run into so many unanticipated problems that delay your development,

but you just have to keep on going. If we had not had a good product and a huge market, we would have folded. (Statement of George Hoffman.)

The brothers decided to start the company in the summer of 1962, as soon as Bradford could give notice to his employer and move his family to Wellsville. The initial capital was $12,000, with $10,000 invested by Mr. Hoffman and the balance provided by George in the form of expenses he had paid personally during his market research trips. In order to limit the financial liability of Mr. Hoffman, the legal form of the company was to be a corporation, with each member of the family owning one-third of the stock. Bradford was appointed the Vice President of Engineering and Production, George was the Vice President of Sales, and Mr. Hoffman was the President and Treasurer. Mr. Hoffman did not want to be active in the business, since he felt that he had to devote full time to his lumber company; so the actual division of responsibilities that was decided upon was the one that is common in many smaller companies: One founder is in charge of all inside activities and the other attends to all outside contracts. Policy decisions are made jointly.

Mr. Hoffman donated an old garage that was on the sawmill property for use as the manufacturing and assembly shop for the new company. A corner of this building was finished with wallboard to serve as the office. A used desk and drafting table were moved in, telephone service was requested, a sign was painted to go over the office door, and the new company was in business.

> I don't think that any other corporation was ever started as inexpensively as ours. We paid my cousin, who is an attorney in Cleveland, $100 for the Articles of Incorporation, but he sent the money back in the form of a good set of mechanic's tools that had belonged to his father. We bought an engine lathe from the junkyard and fixed it up so that it would run, and we got an old electric welding outfit and an acetylene torch from the manual training program at the local high school. (Statement of George Hoffman.)

The intention of the brothers was to build the sawmill carriage first, since this was the central piece of equipment in a modernized mill, and then to slowly expand their product line to eventually include the full range of automated sawmill machinery. Bradford had the preliminary design for the carriage nearly half completed when he arrived in August, and he immediately began working full-time to complete the engineering drawings. George went out to visit customers and find a mill that would be willing to install the first model.

The first time that I realized that we might have troubles came on those early sales trips. The mill owners who had been so enthusiastic when I asked for their opinions became very guarded when I asked for their orders. No one wanted to be the guinea pig and install the first unit, since they knew that there would be problems in the initial operation. They all said that they would come and look at it when we got one running somewhere else.

We had troubles at home too. It seemed that everyone wanted to keep our company from being successful. For example, the state fire inspector came by and found us cutting off parts with the acetylene torch and then putting together the steel frame for the carriage with the welder, and sparks were flying all over. Since the garage was an old wooden building with a timber floor that was just soaked in the oil that had been dripping off trucks for the past 40 years, he nearly had a stroke. We spent all of one afternoon listening to him. He kept telling us that we could not operate in the building, and we kept telling him that we didn't have any place else. Finally, it developed that he was mainly worried about emergency exits for the workers. Now, we only had one employee, a person who did the welding and machining for us, and there was a big truck door 12 ft wide by 12 ft high that was always left open, but that was not enough. It is a state law that a factory has to have exits on three sides, and since we were officially classified as a factory and since we obviously had only one exit, he would not let us go back to work until we cut fire doors on two more sides for our one man to go through.

There was no way to heat that building, of course, and it got cold working there dur-

ing the winter. Brad and I were doing the assembly, and we would work for about a half hour and then we would go into the office to get warmed up. The wind would blow right through the building; we used to work until 10:00 or 11:00 at night, and some nights it would get so cold that the coolant in the lathe would freeze, and we would have to thaw it out with a blowtorch. That winter was not a good time. (Statement of George Hoffman.)

The prototype of the carriage was finished in February 1963, but when no customer was found for the unit, Mr. Hoffman agreed to install it at his own sawmill.

Dad was reluctant to use our first carriage for the same reason that everyone else was; he was worried about breakdowns and the mechanical problems that are almost endemic in new machinery. You have to realize that most of the costs of a sawmill are fixed, so that it can be very expensive if the mill is forced to shut down for repairs. Further, since most of the smaller sawmills in our area had lost money over the past few years, they no longer had the cash reserves to withstand any additional losses brought about by equipment experimentation.

My father was absolutely certain that we were going to cause him problems, and I'm sorry to say that we did not disappoint him. That spring was not a good time either. (Statement of George Hoffman.)

The carriage had been installed early in March 1963; by the end of May most of the mechanical problems had been resolved, and the sawmill was producing steadily at the anticipated production rate and projected profit figures. Sales of the carriage were slow to develop, however.

We had thought that our troubles would be over as soon as we got our first automatic carriage running well enough so that we could demonstrate it to sawmill owners. It is a lot easier to sell a piece of machinery that is operating smoothly and easily than it is to sell a concept, however appealing. But it just did not work out that way. We did stir up a lot of interest, and we would have two or three people visiting Dad's sawmill each day, looking at the carriage, watching it run. But they still hesitated to place an order with us.

Part of the trouble was that the carriage was new, and they wanted to see if it would hold up in daily service. Another part was that we were new; my brother and I were both young and inexperienced, and our assembly shop did not look like much, so our customers probably wanted to see if we would hold up. Then, it takes more skill to run an automatic carriage than the old manual type, and they may not have been certain that their workers would be able to use and maintain the new machinery. Lastly, and I think that this was the most important point, it takes more than just a new carriage to have a modern sawmill. You have to have a new carriage drive and new carriage rails too, since the automatic carriage weighs so much more than the older manual type, and then you have to have new log conveyors to get the sawlogs to the mill, and you need new lumber conveyors since the boards come off the carriage so much more rapidly, and you ought to buy a new edger

EXHIBIT 2 Income statements and balance sheets for the Sawmill Machinery Corporation for the fiscal years 1963–1965.

Income statements for the years:	1963	1964	1965
Sales revenues	$15,210	$52,380	$204,030
Shop material costs	11,910	23,750	122,250
Shop labor costs	6,210	11,230	36,310
Shop overhead costs	920	3,730	14,310
	19,040	38,710	172,870
Selling expenses	9,420	14,270	15,440
Engineering expenses	12,360	16,060	15,870
Administrative expenses	2,850	9,020	10,890
	24,630	39,350	42,200
Net profit (or loss)	($28,460)	($25,780)	($11,040)

Balance sheets for the years:	1963	1964	1965
Cash	$ 40	$ 120	$ 320
Accounts receivable	460	6,480	23,460
Inventory	2,820	16,260	29,720
	3,320	22,860	53,500
Machinery and equipment	1,630	2,720	6,440
Building and improvements	240	740	2,420
Prepaid expenses	2,250	2,960	2,710
	4,120	6,420	11,570
Total current and fixed assets	$ 7,440	$29,280	$ 65,070
Accounts payable	$ 6,710	$12,670	$ 31,510
Loans from bank	—	—	20,000
Loans from stockholders	17,190	58,850	62,840
	23,900	71,520	114,350
Long-term debt	—	—	4,000
Common stock	12,000	12,000	12,000
Earned surplus (or deficit)	(28,460)	(54,240)	(65,280)
	(16,460)	(42,240)	(49,280)
Total current liabilities and equity	$ 7,440	$29,280	$ 65,070

and a new trim saw to prevent bottlenecks at those places too. Producing lumber is a system, and we were trying to convince our customers to replace just one component in that system. We sold only three carriages in 1964; that year was not much fun either. (Statement of George Hoffman.)

Sales began to accelerate in 1965 (10 carriages were sold, together with some of the auxiliary sawmill equipment needed for the modernized mill). Bradford Hoffman had continued engineering improvements on the carriage so that it was now easier and more profitable to build, and he had also worked on the design of the carriage drive and the various lumber conveyors to expand the product line of the firm. Nevertheless, company operations were still at a loss, and the financial position was critical. Exhibit 2 gives the income statements and balance sheets for the first 3 years of the firm, 1963 to 1965.

The company survived these early years because Bradford and George Hoffman worked long hours as designers, salesmen, and assembly shop workers at minimal salaries and because they advanced to the company all the money that they could borrow personally.

> By the end of 1965 we were borrowing funds every place we could find them. Our payables were stretched out over 90 days, and our suppliers were calling every day trying to get their money. Many of the suppliers refused to ship at all unless we paid cash in advance, and that really held up our production. We managed to get $20,000 from the bank, but only on the condition that Brad and I had to personally endorse the note. I don't know how much that endorsement was worth since we had already borrowed individually everything we could, against our cars and homes, to put into the company. Dad put in all the cash he could raise also; he mortgaged his retirement income to keep us in business. By this time we knew that the company would be technically successful, since we had 15 carriages running at various mills throughout the Eastern United States and we had lots of potential customers; we just did not know if we would be financially successful and be able

to get the money to keep going until we could earn substantial profits. (Statement of George Hoffman.)

The company reached the breakeven point in 1966, with sales of $427,000 and profits of $21,390. The financial position of the firm was still exceedingly tight, but the Wellsville bank agreed to finance needed machinery on a 3-year conditional sales contract and to extend their open line of credit to $40,000. Helped by this new financing, the company sales and profits continued to expand in 1967 and 1968. Exhibit 3 gives the income statements and balance sheets for the next 3 years of the firm, 1966 to 1968.

In 1967 a cement-block factory building, 120 ft x 50 ft, with an overhead crane for handling the heavy carriage frame and other steel weldments, was constructed. This building was financed by a mortgage contract arranged through the Industrial Development Commission of the State of Ohio. As a condition of the mortgage, the company stockholders had to agree to transfer their personal advances to the company from current loans payable to subordinated debentures and to arrange for the factoring (loans made by a bank or finance company against the security of a current asset) of their accounts receivable. The local bank participated in the negotiations leading toward the building mortgage and the accounts receivable loan and then agreed to increase the machinery financing available to the firm, though decreasing the open line of credit. As a further condition of the new sources of funds, which amounted in total to $180,000, the company owners had to agree to maintain the accounts payable and accrued taxes at "reasonable" levels, which was interpreted to mean no more than 30 days in arrears.

The new manufacturing facilities and working capital permitted a substantial increase in sales in 1968. Profits after taxes for that year were $92,780.

> The profits in 1968 brought our current ratio up to a reasonable figure (1.6:1) from the disastrous levels of 1964 and 1965 (0.3:1). We felt that our financial problems were over.

EXHIBIT 3 Income statements and balance sheets for the Sawmill Machinery Corporation for the fiscal years 1966–1968.

Income statements for the years:	1966	1967	1968
Sales revenues	$427,740	$603,210	$1,128,700
Shop material costs	214,110	296,090	478,940
Shop labor costs	127,020	176,120	313,500
Shop overhead costs	21,830	38,290	78,400
	363,960	510,500	870,840
Selling expenses	15,710	20,920	29,030
Engineering expenses	16,450	17,010	24,140
Administrative expenses	11,230	16,540	38,310
	43,390	54,470	91,480
Profit before taxes	21,390	38,240	166,380
Federal income taxes	—	—	73,600
Profit after taxes	$ 21,390	$ 38,240	$ 92,780

Balance sheets for the years:	1966	1967	1968
Cash	$ 1,170	$ 6,710	$ 15,440
Accounts receivable	59,840	96,510	203,160
Inventory	44,300	59,540	129,540
	105,310	162,760	348,140
Machinery and equipment, less depreciation	41,180	61,440	87,510
Building and improvements, less depreciation	5,610	137,520	139,750
Prepaid expenses	6,740	8,470	5,010
	53,530	207,430	232,270
Total current and fixed assets	$158,840	$375,190	$ 580,410
Accounts payable	$ 41,720	$ 26,110	$ 24,260
Income taxes payable	—	—	32,420
Loans from bank on open credit	40,000	20,000	20,000
Loans from finance company on accounts receivable	—	59,420	131,870
Loans from stockholders	80,350	350	—
	162,070	105,880	208,550
Equipment financing contract	28,860	54,210	67,380
Building mortgage contract	—	128,750	125,350
Stockholder subordinated debentures	—	80,000	80,000
	28,860	262,960	272,730
Common stock	12,000	12,000	12,000
Earned surplus (or deficit)	(43,890)	(5,650)	87,130
	(31,890)	6,350	99,130
Total liabilities and equity	$158,840	$375,190	$ 580,410

We knew that we were undercapitalized (4.8:1 debt/equity ratio), but we thought that we could look forward to a period of slowly expanding sales financed by retained earnings and that eventually we would get out from under our heavy debt charges. What we did not forecast was the huge sales increase in 1969. (Statement of George Hoffman.)

Sales orders during the first few months of 1969 increased more than 300% over the equivalent period of the previous year, and the order backlog of the company stretched out over 5 months. There were a number of reasons for this dramatic increase in sales:

1. The company had completed the design of all the machinery necessary for an automated sawmill and was now able to offer a nearly complete product line to the lumber industry. Bradford Hoffman, working with one other engineer and two draftsmen, had developed log and lumber conveyors and a high-speed edger and trim saw to complement the existing carriage and carriage drive. The company could now bid on a complete sawmill or any portion of the mill.

We made an investment in product design during the early years and it began to pay off in 1969. To sell sawmill machinery you have to have a complete product line. It does not take any longer to sell a new sawmill than it does to sell a new carriage since you first have to convince the customer of the benefits of automation and modernization, yet the order for the sawmill brings much greater revenues to the company. We began to get orders for complete sawmills, at $175,000 to $200,000 each, in 1969. (Statement of George Hoffman.)

2. The company had become well known throughout the lumber industry. George Hoffman, working with two others selling, had established contacts and made installations of carriages and other mill equipment in Maine, New Hampshire, Vermont, Massachusetts, New York, Pennsylvania, Ohio, Indiana, Illinois, Michigan, Wisconsin, West Virginia, Virginia, and North Carolina. The company now received inquiries and orders from the entire Eastern United States.

We made an investment in marketing also during the early years and that too began to pay off in 1969. To sell sawmill machinery you have to have equipment operating in the area that the customer can see; it is a tradition in this industry that sales are on a visual basis. We had to travel to get orders in 1966 and 1967, but by 1969 we had equipment operating in widespread locations and orders began to come to us. (Statement of George Hoffman.)

3. Adverse economic conditions had begun to affect the lumber industry. The business depression that began in 1969 brought increased competition for lumber sales and lower lumber prices but did not change either the costs of the saw timber or the wages of the mill workers. The sawmill owners were caught in a profit squeeze, and they began to look at equipment modernization as a means of economic survival.

The business slowdown helped our company. We had talked about the increased timber recovery and the decreased labor costs that were the primary benefits of sawmill automation to our customers for years, but the cost-price squeeze convinced them that we were right. We began to get orders in 1969 from people who had told us previously that they would never change their method of operations. (Statement of George Hoffman.)

The combined effects of the expanded product line, larger marketing area, and changed customer motivations brought a very substantial increase in the orders received by the company. As stated earlier, during the first 2 months of 1969 company orders were up 300% and the salesmen were in agreement that this trend would continue. There were 8,900 sawmills in the area now covered by the company, and an additional 5,200 in the Deep South (Georgia, Alabama, Mississippi, and Louisiana) and the Mississippi River Valley (Tennessee, Arkansas, Missouri, Iowa, and Minnesota) states that could be added easily to the company territory. The salesmen were mainly concerned that the company would be unable to make deliveries to these potential customers.

Bradford and George Hoffman felt that it

would be physically possible to triple production within their present plant facilities by concentrating upon assembly, subcontracting most of the weldments and machined parts, and by adding a second shift. Competent assembly workers were readily available in the area, which had suffered from high unemployment since the end of coal mining and river traffic in the 1950s; and suppliers who a few years previously had complained extensively about the credit practices of the firm were now very willing to provide weldments, contract machining, and purchased parts. The only concern of Bradford and George Hoffman was the cash required to finance the expansion.

The two brothers had prepared a pro forma income statement and balance sheet for 1969 which seemed to indicate an immediate need for $750,000 and a longer-term need for $560,000 in loans (see Exhibit 4).

The finance company loan, on factored accounts payable and inventory, was expected to be $560,000 at the end of the year, but it was also expected to peak at $750,000 in about 2 months as the company built up to the new sales level before the anticipated profits enabled partial repayment. Since the loan would be secured by the assignment of the accounts receivable and inventory, both brothers felt that their request for the additional funds would be granted, although they recognized that it represented a very considerable increase above the existing level of $131,870. Bradford made a special trip to Chicago to talk to the midwestern office of the finance company and to present their appeal for the additional funds.

> I had always heard that finance companies were direct in their dealings with customers, without the diplomacy and tact of banks, and that is certainly true. They would not even let me tell them about our plans. I had a nice little talk prepared, with charts and graphs, but the regional vice president just told me that they might go to $250,000 if their experience with us continued to be good, but that they had no interest in advancing us $750,000." (Statement of George Hoffman.)

The brothers then asked the local bank to arrange a meeting with its correspondent firm in Cleveland. The Bank of Wellsville was limited to $130,000 in loans by the state banking laws that restricted advances to any one customer to 10% of the bank's capital; to provide bigger loans to local customers most rural banks maintain a correspondent relationship with a much larger city bank in Cleveland, Chicago, or New York so that participatory loans may be arranged. The Bank of Wellsville had a correspondent relationship with the Hanna Trust Company of Cleveland and was able to arrange the requested meeting.

> We drove up to Cleveland to meet with the bankers there. They listened to our plans and were sympathetic to our problems, but they did not want to lend us any money. They felt that we were undercapitalized and that we had to get additional equity. One of them told us that we were lucky we had gotten $480,000 in loans on $12,000 in stock and that we should not push our luck much further. He was not accurate, for we had $70,000 in subordinated debentures and $86,000 in retained earnings in addition to the stock, but he was not going to change his opinion. (Statement of Bradford Hoffman.)

It appeared obvious to the Hoffmans that the company would have to raise equity capital to finance the planned sales expansion since the two major sources of loan funds were closed to them. Fortunately, the brothers had considered that possibility previously and had made various approaches to the venture capital market; these approaches, made by submitting a detailed history of the firm and their plans for expansion, had resulted in two contracts that might be developed fairly quickly into firm financing offers. The first contact, J. H. Abernathy and Company, specialized in private placements; the second, Markowitz and Trask, specialized in small public issues.

J. H. Abernathy and Company, a traditional venture capital firm, was founded in 1962 to manage a portion of the Abernathy family fortune; the intention was to manage the capital aggressively to overcome the dual threats of inflation and high taxes. It was a small firm, with a staff consisting of three executives, one of whom was a member of

EXHIBIT 4 Pro forma income statement and balance sheet for the Sawmill Machinery Corporation for the fiscal year 1969.

Income statement forecasted for the year:	1969 estimates
Sales revenues, at the increased rate for the full year	$3,000,000
Shop material costs, increased to 48% of sales for additional material	1,440,000
Shop labor costs, decreased to 25% of sales for reduced assembly	750,000
Shop overhead costs, constant at 7% of sales	210,000
	2,400,000
Selling expenses, for 3 persons plus travel costs	60,000
Engineering expenses, for 4 persons	45,000
Administrative expenses, for 2 persons plus interest costs	85,000
	190,000
Profits before taxes	410,000
Federal income taxes, at 52%	210,000
Profits after taxes	$ 200,000

Balance sheet forecasted for the year:	1969 estimates
Cash, at average balance of the previous year	$ 10,000
Accounts receivable, at average of 75 days because many customers are reluctant to pay before the machinery operates	625,000
Inventory, at average of 100 days because of the problems of scheduling many deliveries from new suppliers	400,000
	1,035,000
Machinery and equipment, with $12,500 additional investment required	100,000
Building and improvements, with no additional investment required	135,000
Prepaid expenses, at average balance of the previous year	5,000
	240,000
Total current and fixed assets	$1,275,000
Accounts payable, limited to 30 days by the loan agreement	$ 120,000
Loans from bank on open credit, at no change from previous year	20,000
Loans from finance company, on accounts receivable	560,000
Equipment financing contract, increased for new machinery	75,000
Building mortgage contract, decreased by annual payments	120,000
Stockholder subordinated debentures	80,000
	275,000
Common stock, at no change from the previous year	12,000
Earned surplus, increased by estimated profits from previous year	288,000
	300,000
Total liabilities and equity	$1,275,000

the founding family, a financial analyst, and three secretaries. Because the staff was limited, most of the investment proposals they received were rejected without investigation; it was said that the firm received over 1,000 proposals each year, looked at 30 to 50 fairly intensively, and invested in 3 to 5. As was true with most venture capital firms, the reasons for their interest in any specific investment proposal were seldom immediately apparent. The Hoffman brothers had submitted their written presentation to 8 firms and were quickly rejected by 7. The Abernathy firm was the only one to express interest, but this may have been due to the fact that the basis of the Abernathy fortune was in railroads and coal property in southeastern Ohio, near Wellsville.

J. H. Abernathy and Company was definitely interested. When it was contacted in February, it sent one of its executives and its financial analyst to Wellsville. They spent 7 days checking the records, investigating the management, looking at the products, and calling the customers of the company. They returned to New York, met with the other two executives of their firm, and then submitted a financial proposal with the following conditions:

1. J. H. Abernathy would purchase $500,000 in convertible subordinated debentures, at par, to be issued by the Sawmill Machinery Corporation.

2. The debentures were to be subordinated to all existing and planned debt, so that additional short-term loans could be acquired by the company to complete the financing of $750,000.

3. The debentures were to be convertible into 50,000 shares of stock of the company at the option of J. H. Abernathy. Prior to this conversion, the present stock of the company, which consisted of 1,000 shares equally divided among the three owners, was to be split on a 70:1 basis, so that the total owned by the Hoffman family would be 70,000 shares. The total shares authorized and outstanding after the stock split and debentures conversion would be 120,000.

4. The debentures were to contain restrictive covenants prohibiting the payment of dividends, the increase of executive salaries, or the repayment of executive loans without the permission of J. H. Abernathy.

5. The debentures were to include protective covenants specifying that J. H. Abernathy might assume control if the working capital dropped below $300,000 or if the current ratio dropped below 1.3:1.

6. The debentures were also to include the general provision that no additional debt or equity was to be privately placed without offering J. H. Abernathy first refusal and that no debt or equity was to be publicly sold without offering J. H. Abernathy the opportunity to participate in that sale.

7. The debentures were also to include the general agreement that a representative of J. H. Abernathy was to be placed on the board of directors of the firm and that a consultant nominated by J. H. Abernathy was to be hired at a minimum management fee of $20,000 per year.

8. The debentures were also to include the informal expectation that a public issuance of the stock of the company would be arranged within 5 years to enable J. H. Abernathy to recover its investment and realize its profits.

The offer by J. H. Abernathy and Company provided adequate funds for the expansion of the company, but a number of the provisions were considered burdensome by the Hoffman brothers. They disliked the interest charge, which amounted to $40,000 yearly in addition to the substantial interest and principal payments that were presently being made on the existing debt, and they did not wish to hire an unknown consultant or arrange a stock issuance at an unknown time for the benefit of the debenture holders. They were pleased to receive, therefore, another offer from Markowitz and Trask.

Markowitz and Trask was a small brokerage firm in Boston that had a reputation as a "Regulation A" house. Regulation A of the Securities and Exchange Act of 1933 allows a company seeking less than $750,000 (originally $300,000, but amended in 1962) in the public markets to use a short form of registration with the SEC. The short form is less expensive and takes considerably less time (2 to 3 months) than the full form (8 to 12 months). Firms that specialize in Regulation A issues are often regional companies with limited customer lists. Markowitz and Trask certainly fitted that description, but their customers had the reputation of being interested in the growth potential of smaller companies and of being willing to take risks for capital appreciation. Mr. Markowitz conducted an investigation of the company that centered on the potential size of the sawmill machinery markets. He then prepared a very different financial proposal:

1. Markowitz and Trask would purchase, for resale to the public, 100,000 shares, at $7.00 per share less a 10% brokerage commission, to be issued by Sawmill Machinery Corporation. Prior to this issuance, the present stock of the company was to be split on a 100:1 basis so that the total owned by the Hoffman family would be 100,000 shares. The total shares authorized and outstanding after the stock split and the public issuance would be 200,000.

2. Markowitz and Trask would charge the company for the legal and accounting costs associated with the registration and issuance of the stock; these costs were expected to be $30,000. It was stated that these costs might be capitalized as an organizational expense.

3. Markowitz and Trask would be issued warrants for an additional 20,000 shares; these warrants could be exercised by the payment to the company of $5.00 per share.

4. Markowitz and Trask would arrange for the immediate provision of a 90-day note for $100,000 by private investors whom they represented to enable the company to proceed with its plans for expansion during registration and issuance of the stock.

5. Markowitz and Trask would receive a commitment from the company that Markowitz and Trask would have first refusal on the future issuance of additional equity or convertible debt.

6. Markowitz and Trask would maintain an "orderly" market in the stock of the company, serving as specialists in the over-the-counter market.

7. Markowitz and Trask were to appoint two persons to the five man board of directors of the company to represent the new stockholders.

The Hoffmans felt that both financial proposals were costly in the amount of equity required and the percentage of control relinquished, but they also felt that it was unlikely that they could arrange better terms through other venture capital sources. They had contacted eight private investment firms, five brokerage houses, three small business investment companies, four banks, and numerous wealthy individuals by mail, telephone, and personal meetings and had been rejected, for various reasons, by all but two. They felt that if they were to expand their sales rapidly, they must accept one of the two proposals—the private purchase of the convertible debentures by J. H. Abernathy and Company or the public sale of common stock by Markowitz and Trask—but they disagreed strongly among themselves about the costs and benefits of each financing method.

George Hoffman, the Sales Vice President, was in favor of the private purchase of convertible debentures by J. H. Abernathy and Company. He felt that the Sawmill Machinery Corporation needed additional money quickly to counter competitive reactions that threatened the continued success of the firm, and he wanted to retain as much of the equity and control as possible among members of the Hoffman family.

All we've done so far is to prove that a market exists for sawmill machinery in the eastern United States and to demonstrate that it is a huge market. The equipment manufacturers on the West Coast are not dumb. Since this recession has really slowed down their normal business, they are looking in our direction. All they have to do is to change the size of their equipment and they can compete with us. All those companies, and there are four big ones, have moved salesmen into our area within the last 6 months, and I know that they are thinking about opening an office here or buying one of our old-line Eastern competitors to give them a manufacturing plant in our area. We have to move quickly to keep them out. We have an advantage now because we are known and because our equipment is running, but if we can't make deliveries, we will lose the business. It's as simple as that.

If we act now, we can double our sales each year for the next 5 years, up to an annual sales volume of $20 million to $30 million, and we can make so much money we'll never miss the equity we have to give up. We only have to give up 41% (50,000 shares out of 120,000 shares total) of the stock to Abernathy, so we keep control. I say that we ought to go that way now. (Statement of George Hoffman.)

Mr. Hoffman, the President and Treasurer of the firm, though generally inactive in the management, did not like the high interest and principal payments that the Sawmill Machinery Corporation was presently committed to make each year, and he did not want to add another $40,000 in interest charges on the Abernathy convertible debentures. He much preferred the Markowitz and Trask proposal for the sale of $700,000 worth of equity, since he felt that the proceeds of this sale might permit the repayment of some of the existing debt, and he was interested in establishing a market for the future sale of the company's stock.

Last year we paid $33,500 in interest ($131,870 finance company loan on factored accounts receivable at 9%, $20,000 bank loan at 6%, $67,400 equipment installment loan at 12%, $125,350 building mortgage at 6%, and $80,000 personal loans from the executives at 6%) and $18,800 in principal ($13,500 on the 5-year equipment installment loan and $5,300 on the 10-year building mortgage); I don't want to add another $40,000 in interest each year. I can remember very clearly periods of economic depression in the lumber business during which I was able to survive only because I kept the sawmill clear of debt, and I think that we ought to clear up this loan situation now.

I'm not much of a forecaster, but there is one thing I do know, and that is that at some time in the future business is going to turn down, and I don't want to be stuck with $91,000 in annual debt payments at that time.

Also, I just don't like owing money. I stopped by Cal's Esso [a gasoline station in Wellsville that serviced the company's trucks]

the other day, and Cal asked me if we couldn't pay him a little more promptly. Cal is a good friend, and he has looked after us. Now I think that we ought to look after him; we ought to pay him. We've borrowed money every place we could get it; now we ought to sell some stock and pay people back.

Then, I'm older and I want to be able to get some of my money back out of the company. I've put everything I have into it, and I'd like some of it back now so that I can think about retirement without wondering what my wife and I are going to live on.

One more thing, it would be good to have a market for the stock. When I die that stock is going to be in my estate, and it will be valued by the Internal Revenue Service if we don't have a market price. Last year we earned $92,000 and this year the boys are talking about earning $200,000 after taxes. If the IRS values the stock at just 15 times earnings, the company would be worth $3 million. I own one-third of the stock, so that means that my estate would have $1 million. There are exemptions for the widow, of course, but I don't know how my wife would ever pay the tax on $1 million unless there was some way to sell the stock. (Statement of Mr. Hoffman.)

Bradford Hoffman (Engineering and Production Vice President) objected to both financial proposals; he felt that he had worked too hard and too long to give up any considerable portion of the equity to new investors.

When we started the company, George and I used to work 14 hours a day, 7 days a week. We built the first carriage by hand, during the winter, and it was cold, miserable work. Then we had to prove that carriage at Dad's sawmill, and that was a lot of work. Then we had to prove that a market existed for the carriage, and that was a lot of work. George and I put in our own money, all that we had. We did more, in engineering, production, and sales, by ourselves than any company I've worked for could have done with 20 men. Now we're supposed to give over half of our company to a group of investors who aren't going to do anything except put in a little money. We've put in $178,000 ourselves ($80,000 personal loans, $12,000 common stock, and $86,000 retained earnings) and all the long hours, hard work, and good ideas, and those bastards want 54% of the company for $600,000. We can

EXHIBIT 5 Floor plan of an automated sawmill, with descriptions of the required equipment.

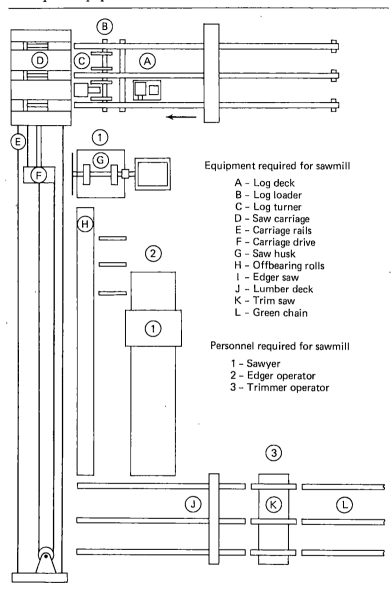

Equipment required for sawmill

A – Log deck
B – Log loader
C – Log turner
D – Saw carriage
E – Carriage rails
F – Carriage drive
G – Saw husk
H – Offbearing rolls
I – Edger saw
J – Lumber deck
K – Trim saw
L – Green chain

Personnel required for sawmill

1 – Sawyer
2 – Edger operator
3 – Trimmer operator

Log Deck. The log deck is a heavy chain conveyor, generally with a steel framework and either three or four strands of mill chain, that carries logs into the sawmill. Logs are placed on the deck by a forklift truck or tractor.

Log Loader. The log loader is a hydraulic unit, generally with four or more crescent-shaped steel arms mounted on a pivot shaft, that picks up one log at a time and rolls the log onto the saw carriage.

Log Turner. The log turner is also a hydraulic unit, generally with a heavy steel bar with projecting teeth that can be raised or lowered and

EXHIBIT 5 *(Continued)*

moved backward and forward; it is used to turn the log on the saw carriage and to push the log tightly against the carriage knees.

Saw Carriage. The saw carriage is the most complex portion of the sawmill. It consists of a heavy steel frame mounted on wrought-iron wheels that ride on the rails of the carriage track. On the frame are bolted three or four carriage knees, which are heavy steel weldments that slide in and out; each knee has a series of steel dogs, which are clamps that grasp the log. In operation, a log is rolled onto the saw carriage by the log loader and is then pushed up against the knees by the log turner; it is then held by the steel dogs, and the carriage knees are moved out toward the sawline. The carriage is pulled past the saw to cut off the first portion of the log; the carriage is then returned to the loading position. Here, the log may be turned, to make a square timber, or it may be advanced by the sliding knees toward the sawline to cut off a 1-in. or 2-in. board; the setworks is the mechanism on the carriage that advances the knees exactly (plus or minus 0.05 in. is the usual tolerance on an automatic carriage) the distance needed to cut the required lumber and to allow for the saw kerf (wood removed from the log by the saw).

Carriage Rails. Carriage rails are steel sections of track upon which the carriage runs; these rails are usually machined in a V-form and are very precisely positioned, so that the carriage runs accurately before the saw.

Carriage Drive. The carriage drive consists of a hydraulic unit that turns a drum with a steel cable wrapped around it; the steel cable runs to a pulley at each end of the carriage track and then is connected to the saw carriage. The carriage drive is used to pull the carriage back and forth in front of the saw. Each time the carriage is pulled past the saw, a board is cut off the log.

Offbearing Roll Conveyor. The offbearing roll conveyor consists of a series of powered steel rolls; boards that are cut off the log by the saw drop on these rolls and are carried either to the lumber deck or to the edger saw.

Edger Saw. Each board cut off the log (unless the log has been turned and cut four times upon the carriage, so that it is a square timber) is random width and has bark on the edges. The edger saw is used to cut these random width boards to the exact width needed for lumber and to square off the rough edges.

Lumber Deck Conveyor. The lumber deck is a short chain conveyor, generally with a steel framework and either three or four strands of mill chain, that gathers and stores the lumber coming from the offbearing rolls and from the edger saw and carries this lumber to the trim saw.

Trim Saw. The trim saw cuts off the ends of the boards to exact lengths for lumber and drops this lumber on the green chain.

Green Chain Conveyor. The green chain is a long chain conveyor, generally with a steel framework and either three or four strands of mill chain, that carries the lumber out of the sawmill and into the mill yard. The boards are pulled from the green chain, according to their grades, lengths, and widths, and are piled in the yard for air drying.

earn that sort of money in a couple of years if we just slow down and grow a little more slowly. (Statement of Bradford Hoffman.)

Eliot Vestal was deeply concerned by these statements. He was a recent M.B.A. from Ohio State University who had come to work for the company as comptroller and potentially as treasurer, just before the need for additional capital was determined and the two financial proposals were received. Mr. Vestal had never heard the owners of the business argue previously; indeed, he felt that one of the major reasons for the success of the firm was the apparent unanimity of opinion and easy working relationships that existed among members of the Hoffman family. Now they argued about the future of the company continually, to the exclusion of important operating decisions in marketing, engineering, and production. Mr. Vestal felt that he should prepare some means of evaluating the three alternative financing methods—debentures, common stock, or retained earnings—but he was not certain what factors should be included in this analysis, and he did not know how these factors should be compared.

ASSIGNMENT

Prepare an evaluation of the three alternative financing methods that are available to the owners of the Sawmill Machinery Corporation. Further data which may be helpful are included in Exhibit 5, which describes the sawmill machinery produced by the firm, and in Exhibit 6, which explains the economic advantages of operating this machinery, in comparison with the older and more traditional sawmill equipment.

EXHIBIT 6 Comparison of the revenues, costs, and financial results of operations between older sawmills with manual equipment and modern sawmills with automatic equipment.

	Older sawmill w/manual equipment	Modern sawmill w/automatic equipment
Production per day, in board feet of lumber	8,000	14,000
Lumber and pulpwood chip sales, per day	$1,200	$2,240
Log costs, per day	800	1,400
Labor costs, per day	240	150
Power costs, per day	20	40
Interest and depreciation costs, per day	—	120
General overhead and supervision, per day	180	220
Total costs of operation, per day	$1,240	$1,920
Profit (or loss), per day	($40)	$320
Profit (or loss), per year	($10,000)	$80,000

Notes on comparison:

1. Production per day. Lumber is measured in board feet (bd ft); each board foot is 1 in. thick × 12 in. wide × 12 in. long, or the equivalent of 144 cu in. of wood. An 8-ft long two by four, for example, contains nominally 5.33 bd ft (2 in. × 4 in. × 96 in./144 in. = 5.33 bd ft); lumber has a nominal measurement since the two by four is not actually cut 2 in. thick × 4 in. wide, but approximately 1⅝ in. thick × 3⅝ in. wide, depending on the industry standard of the area in which it is produced. Softwood lumber (pine, spruce, hemlock, etc.) is usually cut under the even inch; hard-

EXHIBIT 6   (*Continued*)

wood lumber (oak, maple, birch, ash, etc.) is usually cut over the even inch. An old-fashioned hardwood sawmill in the East or Midwest, sawing for grade on average-sized logs, will produce approximately 7,000 bd ft per day; a softwood sawmill, sawing for volume, will produce 10,000 bd ft. An average figure for Eastern and Midwestern sawmills, sawing both hardwood and softwood, is 8,000 bd ft per day. A modern sawmill, with automatic equipment, can be expected to increase production approximately 75%, to 14,000 bd ft per day.

2. Lumber and pulpwood chip sales. Hardwood lumber, at the date of the case, sold for approximately $175 per thousand board feet (mbf) as an average for all grades; softwood lumber sold for approximately $125 per mbf; the average sales price for Eastern and Midwestern sawmills cutting both hardwood and softwood was $150. The slabs and edgings, which are the waste product of a sawmill cutting round logs into square lumber, at a modern sawmill equipped with a log debarker and a wastewood chipper, can be sold as barkfree woodchips for pulpmill use. The sales price for these barkfree chips is $10 per ton, and approximately 1 ton is produced for every thousand board feet sawn. The total revenues per day for a modern sawmill would thus be $2,100 for 14 mbf of lumber and $140 for 14 tons of pulpwood chips.

3. Log costs per day. Logs at a sawmill are purchased by a scale that indicates the probable board footage in each log; at the date of the case, an average cost for hardwood and softwood logs, of all grades, was $100 per mbf.

4. Labor costs per day. An older sawmill, with manual equipment, requires 12 workers to produce, sort, and stack, ready for airdrying, 8,000 bd ft of lumber; a modern sawmill, with automatic equipment, needs only 7 men to perform the same operations for 14,000 bd ft of lumber per day. At the date of the case, a typical cost for sawmill workers, including both wages and employee benefits, was $20.00 per working day. The workers in the two types of sawmills are assigned tasks as follows:

	Older sawmill w/manual equipment	*Modern sawmill w/automatic equipment*
Log yard workers	1	1
Log deck workers	1	—
Log barker operator	—	1
Log turner	1	—
Sawyer (skilled position, paid $30 per day)	1	1
Saw tailer	1	—
Edger operator	1	1
Edger tailer	1	—
Trim saw operator	1	1
Lumber sorter	1	—
Lumber yard workers	2	2
	12	7

5. Power costs per day. An older sawmill, with manual equipment, requires approximately 100 hp; a modern sawmill, with automatic equipment, requires nearly 200 hp. At the date of the case, an average cost for either a diesel engine or electric motors was $0.20 per connected horsepower per day.

6. Interest and depreciation costs per day. The older sawmill in the East and the Midwest, at the date of the case, was generally 25 to 40 years old and was both fully paid for and fully depreciated, so that no interest or depreciation expense should be charged. A modern sawmill would cost approximately $250,000 installed and running; it could be legally depreciated over 12 years, with an annual charge of $20,000, and might be

EXHIBIT 6   *(Continued)*

financed over 10 years, with an annual interest cost, at 8% of the average value out-standing over the life of the loan, of $10,000. These annual charges could be converted into daily costs as follows:

	Older sawmill w/manual equipment	Modern sawmill w/automatic equipment
Depreciation charges, over 12-year life	—	$ 80.00/day
Interest costs, on a 10-year mortgage at 8%	—	$ 40.00
	—	$120.00/day

7. General and administrative costs per day. The general and administrative expense category includes supervisory, bookkeeping, and secretarial salaries (at approximately $20,000 per year), maintenance and insurance expenses (at $10,000 per year), local property taxes on the building, equipment, and inventory (at $10,000), and profes-sional services, both legal and accounting (at $5,000); these expense categories total $45,000 per year for the older sawmill. The modern sawmill will require an increase of $5,000 in local property taxes and an increase of $5,000 in maintenance and in-surance costs, for a total of $55,000 per year. These annual charges could be converted in daily costs (250 working days per year) as follows:

	Older sawmill w/manual equipment	Modern sawmill w/automatic equipment
Supervisory, bookkeeping, and secretarial salaries, per day	$ 80.00	$ 80.00
Maintenance and insurance expenses, per day	40.00	60.00
Local property taxes, per day	40.00	60.00
Professional expenses, per day	20.00	20.00
	$180.00	$220.00

Michigan Demolition
and Salvage Corporation

John Merriam, a 1968 graduate of the M.B.A. program at the State University of New York at Albany, returned to Detroit to accept a job with a real estate firm that specialized in constructing single-family housing on new development tracts in the northwestern suburbs of the city. Mr. Mer-riam, who also had an undergraduate degree in civil engineering, enjoyed his work and was good at it. By 1972 he had become responsible for the complete supervision of all construction activities of the company, from digging, forming, and pouring the foundations to landscaping the yards and finish-cleaning the homes prior to the retail sale. However, the adverse money market of 1974, during which funds for residential mortgages reached record interest levels, and then became unavailable at any interest rate, sharply reduced the activities of his firm. The company for which he worked was well financed, and there was no question of his being laid off, but the bonuses and commissions on which he had come to count as an expected portion of his annual income came to an end, and he began to look seriously for other jobs that might be available.

Mr. Merriam had 6 years of experience in residential construction, and he wanted to remain active in this field since he was certain that the single-family dwelling market would come back with the advent of easier credit policies. Moreover, he wanted to form his own company eventually, to take advantage of his experience and ability in home construction, but the depressed state of the home building industry, both in the Detroit area and nationally, seemed to leave no opportunity, just at this period when he had ample time to devote to planning. He looked about for opportunities in related fields for a new company but found that both commercial and industrial construction took too much capital and required too large an organization, and that residential repair and remodeling was too competitive. Mr. Merriam was about to accept a totally unrelated job, in industrial sales, which would make

use of his very apparent friendliness and openness of manner, and which offered a very high salary and commission structure because of the travel involved, when a friend suggested that he consider residential demolition, or tearing down obsolete and deteriorated housing. The friend explained that in his home state, Oklahoma, a much greater effort was made to save the used building materials, such as doors, windows, lumber, and bricks, and the used home appliances, such as plumbing fixtures, electrical units, and heating equipment, but that in Detroit the demolition firms seemed to concentrate on smashing the building as quickly as possible and then carting away the debris and rubble to the dump. Mr. Merriam explained that this was the result of the higher wage rates in Detroit that made the hand labor necessary to disassemble the house and save many of the components uneconomical, but then he began to think that the prices of most building materials and home furnishings had increased very substantially in the past few years and that perhaps the traditional relationship of labor cost to component salvage value was no longer true. Mr. Merriam decided to look seriously at residential demolition as a potential business.

First, Mr. Merriam found, by examining the county records, that building demolition was not a small industry and that approximately 8,000 homes were wrecked each year in the seven-county area of southeastern Michigan (see Exhibit 1).

The majority of the homes being de-

EXHIBIT 1 Buildings wrecked in southeastern Michigan by county, 1971–1973. (Source: Southeastern Michigan Council of Governments, Reports of 1971, 1972, and 1973.)

	1971	*1972*	*1973*
Livingston County	10	15	4
Macomb County (Detroit metro area)	256	205	238
Monroe County	3	0	2
Oakland County (Detroit metro area)	373	466	750
St. Clair County	183	67	118
Washtenaw County	102	92	103
Wayne County (Detroit metro area)	5,671	7,370	6,794
	6,598	8,215	8,009

EXHIBIT 2 Comparison of the indices of residential construction and residential demolition in southeastern Michigan, 1971–1973. (Source: Southeastern Michigan Council of Governments, Reports of 1971, 1972, and 1973.)

	1971	1972	1973
Index of residential construction (1971 = 100)	100	94	97
Index of residential demolition (1971 = 100)	100	132	130
Average mortgage rate	7¾%	8½%	8¼%

molished were in the Detroit metropolitan area, which is what Mr. Merriam had expected; homes outside the central city were usually remodeled or repaired, not destroyed. The second factor that was immediately apparent from the county records was that the amount of building demolition seemed to be independent of the rate of residential construction (see Exhibit 2).

The level of residential construction has traditionally been related to the mortgage interest rate, but according to the statistics gathered by Mr. Merriam, neither seemed to affect the amount of demolition in the area. In the spring of 1974 the requests for bids on demolition jobs were holding steady at approximately 150 per week, which certainly supported the earlier finding; demolition seemed to be an attractive business to enter at this time. In addition, 90% of the demolition contracts were for wrecking single-family and double-family homes; this made the business particularly attractive to Mr. Merriam since this was the form of construction he understood.

Mr. Merriam next spent some time observing the process of residential demolition. He knew that the city, in the case of abandoned property, or the owner, in the case of deteriorated or condemned property, advertised in a publication of the Detroit Construction Council for bids on wrecking. Sealed bids were submitted, usually by four or five companies, but Mr. Merriam quickly learned, through reading the bid tabulation sheet that was made public after each job was awarded, that the bids were not particularly competitive and that all were in the range of $0.75 to $0.80 per square foot. A member of the firm that had won the contract visited the site soon after the award and worked with representatives from the city water and sewer departments, the electric utility, and the gas company to disconnect these services, cap the pipes, and remove the entrance wires. During this visit to the site the company employee usually took away the "quick salvage" items, which were the nonstructural pieces that could be disassembled quickly and which had an immediate resale value, such as the doors, which could be taken off the hinges easily and sold for use as construction barriers, the plumbing fixtures, and some of the heating equipment. These items were carried away in a pick-up truck. The actual demolition of the house was performed with a large crawler tractor that had a hydraulically operated bucket-type loader on the front; a large tractor had to be used that would remain stable with the front-end loader extended to its full height, about 25 ft or 30 ft off the ground. The tractor was delivered to the job site on a flatbed trailer, pulled by a heavy twin-axle or triple-axle dump truck. After being unloaded from the trailer, the tractor approached the house at a right angle to the rafters (roof supports) and joists (floor supports). Starting with the roof, the tractor operator picked off large sections, each with three or four rafters and the attached roofing material, and deposited each section in the dump truck. Next came the attic floor, again pulled out in sections of three or four joists and the attached floor-

EXHIBIT 3   Types of buildings wrecked in the City of Detroit, 1972, 1973. (Source: Southeastern Michigan Council of Governments, Reports of 1971, 1972, and 1973.)

	1972		1973	
One-family dwellings	3,001	(3,001 apts)	3,583	(3,583 apts)
Two-family dwellings	1,345	(2,690 apts)	1,111	(2,222 apts)
Multiple dwellings	158	(1,014 apts)	142	(1,592 apts)
Rooming houses	1	(14 apts)	2	(4 apts)
Auto sales and service	4		2	
Banks	1		1	
Churches	6		19	
Commercial buildings	19		17	
Convents and dormitories	1		—	
Factories and shops	18		33	
Garages, commercial and repair	11		10	
Garages, parking	1		—	
Garages, private	98		38	
Gasoline stations	26		36	
Hospitals	—		1	
Hotels and motels	2		2	
Miscellaneous buildings	3		7	
Office buildings, major	—		1	
Office buildings, minor	6		17	
Public establishments	2		4	
Recreation buildings	1		1	
Restaurants	1		5	
Schools	5		6	
Storage sheds	4		—	
Storage warehouses	19		33	
Store buildings	119		94	
Store buildings with apartments	98	(114 apts)	60	(72 apts)
Terminals	—		1	
Theatres	1		2	
	4,953		5,216	

Note: Totals for buildings wrecked in the City of Detroit (Exhibit 3) may not agree with totals for buildings wrecked in Detroit metropolitan area (Exhibit 1) since the two geographic areas and political jurisdictions overlap but are not identical.

ing. After the attic floor was removed, the tractor pushed down the four second-floor walls and then started work on the first-floor ceiling. Sections of the house that were too large to be deposited in the truck were dropped on the ground, and the tractor ran back and forth over the material to break it into smaller pieces; these pieces were then loaded with the bucket scoop. When the truck was filled, the driver took the material to the dump; while he was gone, the tractor operator continued tearing down the structure, piling the material ready for loading when the truck returned. After the first-floor walls and floor were removed, the foundations were destroyed to 3 ft below the surrounding grade, all the remaining rubble and pieces of debris were scooped up and loaded, the cellar cavity was filled with sand and gravel, and then the entire surface of the lot was smoothed off.

To Mr. Merriam residential demolition

appeared to be a simple process; there was considerable skill required on the part of the tractor operator, who had to avoid damaging surrounding structures and who had to know the sequence of removing the various parts of the house, particularly in the case of the chimney and other heavy masonry parts, but it was not an impossible job to learn. The process also was quick—it took on the average only 2 days to wreck a typical two-story house—and it appeared to be profitable. Mr. Merriam was able to estimate the revenues from the bid tabulation sheets and the expenses from his own experience in construction (see Exhibit 4).

Mr. Merriam recognized that many of

EXHIBIT 4 Revenues and expenses for the demolition of a typical two-story frame residence performed by a contractor with owned equipment.

Revenues, which include the bid price charged to the city or owner for wrecking, and the sale of the "quick salvage" items.

Bid price charged for wrecking, usually at $0.75/sq ft	$1,500
Quick salvage items, including doors, plumbing fixtures, etc.	250
	$1,750

Preparation, which includes disconnecting and capping gas, water, and sewage pipes, disconnecting and removing electrical wires, preparing the site for machinery access, and removing the quick salvage items. Standard time is one worker for one day:

8 hours	laborer's wages at $7.00/hr	$ 56
4 permits	required for disconnect service from utilities at $10.00 each	40
		$100

Demolition, which requires the use of a crawler tractor with a front-end loader to tear down the structure and load the material onto dump trucks. Standard time is one tractor for 2 days.

16 hours	tractor operating costs at $18.00/hr	$288
16 hours	tractor operator wages at $12.00/hr	192
1 trip	movement of the machine to the site, at $100/trip	100
		$580

Removal, which requires the use of a twin-axle dump truck that has a 12-ton capacity to transport debris to the dumping site, and charges for dumping imposed by most cities and towns. Standard time is one truck for 2 days:

16 hours	12-ton dump truck operating costs at $9.00/hr	$144
16 hours	12-ton dump druck drivers' wages at $8.00/hr	128
8 loads	dumping charges at $20.00/load	160
		$430

Backfill, which involves the delivery of bankrun sand and gravel to fill the cellar cavity to ground level. Standard amount is 30 cu yd.

30 yards	gravel at $8.00/cu yd delivered	$240

Total variable costs of site preparation, building demolition, debris and rubble removal, and backfill for the foundation	$1,350
Total contribution to overhead and profit, per job	$400

Note: Operating costs on the crawler tractor and the 12-ton dump truck include fuel, lubrication, maintenance, insurance, and taxes, but not depreciation or interest charges.

the companies that specialized in residential demolition were small, often consisting of only two employees who owned the fully depreciated and paid-for equipment; under those conditions, and performing about 100 demolitions per year, the two owners could take out of the business about $70,000 each year in salaries and profits:

> Residential demolition can be very profitable. You often get two brothers who own their own equipment and who have worked in construction and demolition all of their lives. They work only 200 days a year and still make $35,000 or $40,000 apiece. One of the most famous wrecking companies in Detroit consists of a man and his wife; you might think that she would drive the truck but she doesn't; she drives the bulldozer, and he drives the truck. Together they work about 300 days a year and make well over $100,000. (Statement of Mr. Merriam.)

After looking further into the costs of residential demolition, Mr. Merriam discovered the reason for the lack of competitive bidding; success in this industry was dependent on owning the equipment, which had a new value of about $95,000 ($70,000 for the crawler tractor with a front-end loader, such as a Caterpillar #977K, and $25,000 for the twin-axle or triple-axle 12-ton dump truck), and which required over $60,000 for purchase in used condition. The high capital investment imposed a barrier on entry into residential demolition. The required construction equipment is available to rent, but the rental charges are so high that it is uneconomical to use rented equipment on demolition (see Exhibit 5).

Mr. Merriam recognized that he could not start a residential demolition company without owning the required equipment, but he also recognized that it would be difficult to

---

EXHIBIT 5 Revenues and expenses for the demolition of a typical two-story frame residence performed by a contractor with rented equipment.

Revenues, equivalent to demolition performed by a contractor with owned equipment (Exhibit 4)	$1,750
Preparation, equivalent to demolition performed by a contractor with owned equipment (Exhibit 4).	$100

Demolition, with standard times equivalent to demolition performed by a contractor with owned equipment (Exhibit 4) but with rental charges.

16 hours	tractor rental charges at $35.00/hr	$560
16 hours	tractor operator wages at $12.00/hr	192
1 trip	movement of the machine to the site, at $100/trip	100
		$850

Removal, with standard times equivalent to removal performed by a contractor with owned equipment (Exhibit 4) but with rental charges.

16 hours	12-ton dump truck rental charges at $20.00/hr	$320
16 hours	12-ton dump truck driver's wages at $8.00/hr	128
8 loads	dumping charges at $20.00/load	120
		$570

Backfill, equivalent to demolition performed by contractor with owned equipment (Exhibit 4)	$240
Total variable costs of site preparation, building demolition, debris and rubble removal, and backfill for the foundation performed by contractor with rented equipment	$1,760
Contribution to profit and overhead, per job	$10

pay for this equipment from earnings because the margins involved were low. These margins were substantial if the contractor could combine wages and profits, through doing much of the work himself, and if he did not have to meet interest expenses by using fully paid-for equipment; the margins were low if the contractor had to hire operators and drivers and then had to deduct his own salary and the equipment financing charges (see Exhibit 6).

Mr. Merriam felt that it would be possible to operate on a different basis from the other companies in the industry and thus increase the margins. He thought that it would be possible to disassemble, not demolish, each house and salvage a much greater portion of the building materials and contents. He knew that the older homes that were being torn down, both in Detroit and in the suburban cities and towns of southeastern Michigan, often contained heavy timbers and aged bricks that had an immediate market, copper water pipes, brass valves, and plumbing fixtures that had a high scrap value, and, occasionally, hardwood flooring, paneling, stairways, and trim that were irreplaceable:

> Homes were much better built 50 years ago than they are today. People used better materials then because they were not expensive, and they took more time with their work because wages were so low. Fifty years ago they put copper water pipes into a house, with brass fittings and valves; now we use plastic pipe. Fifty years ago they put hardwood door frames and trim into a house; now we use steel door frames and fiberboard trim. Obviously, I'm not talking about the tenement housing, which was poorly built even then, but they have been mostly torn down already. I'm talking about single-family and double-family residences, which form the majority of the housing being demolished today, and some of these residences, I estimate about 10%, have some very valuable contents.

> I was watching one of the wrecking companies tear down a house in a deteriorated section of Detroit, and I noticed that the wood in the walls of one of the rooms was really dark in color, almost black. After it had been smashed to pieces, I picked up a small chunk and, sure enough, it was black walnut; that wrecker was destroying $3,000 worth of millwork and trim. Now, you realize that wall of black walnut paneling was not oiled and burnished to a deep, rich glow. It had been put into the home about 1890, when it was built in one of the fine residential areas of the city; but about 1930, when the neighborhood began to deteriorate, someone painted it, probably to make the room more cheerful, and then someone else probably painted it in 1945 to cover up the dirt. It was painted three or four times during the 1950s and 1960s to seal in the cockroaches. Nobody could recognize the value underneath unless he knew what to look for. But you could strip off the paint, sand down the rough spots, and oil the wood, and it would be very attractive—and very valuable.

> I've seen solid cherry floors under worn linoleum, maple staircases covered with junk, and oak doors that were so dirty you could not recognize them. But these things are worth saving because you cannot replace them today. They are antiques and have a considerable historical value in addition to their intrinsic value.

> Probably the best story I know on the subject of unrecognized value concerns a house that was torn down in 1971 near the campus of The University of Michigan. The house had been used for 30 years by the faculty and students from the School of Architecture as

EXHIBIT 6 Estimated profits available for loan repayment in a residential demolition firm founded by Mr. Merriam.

Contribution from 70 jobs obtained the first year, at anticipated rate of $400 per job (Exhibit 4)	$28,000
Salary for Mr. Merriam, as manager and owner	15,000
Interest expenses on equipment loan of $60,000 at 12.5%	8,000
Cash flow available for loan repayment	$ 5,000

a place for small offices and drafting rooms; probably about every 5 years they put on another coat of paint to brighten up the walls. When the new building for the School of Architecture was completed, this old house was torn down. Every door in that house was solid walnut and every wall was paneled in walnut. There was $20,000 worth of antique millwork and trim loaded onto the wrecker's truck in small pieces. The faculty and students from the School of Architecture did not recognize the value and worth of what they were painting.

Hardwood millwork and trim are not the only valuable parts of older homes. There may be stained or leaded glass windows, and often there are well-made though standard doors and windows that ought to be saved. Also, there are the plumbing fixtures, electrical units, and heating equipment, some of which can be used again, and the copper water pipe and iron heating pipe and radiators that have a good scrap value; all of this material ought to be taken out prior to demolition.

Lastly, there are the used lumber and bricks which for years were not considered worth the trouble of saving. But the prices for new lumber and new bricks have increased so much recently that there is a definite opportunity for a company that is willing to try new methods in wrecking, that is, willing to disassemble a house instead of demolish it. (Statement of Mr. Merriam.)

Mr. Merriam examined about 50 houses that were scheduled for demolition. Most of them contained very few valuable items and very little salvageable material, but he estimated that 5 of them were definitely worth considering for his proposed process of disassembly. He expected a revenue per home of $3,200 (see Exhibit 7).

EXHIBIT 7 Expected revenues for the disassembly of a selected two-story frame residence.

Bid price charged to the city or owner for wrecking, at $0.60 per square foot, which is lower than the typical price of $0.75 in order to obtain the jobs that have salvageable materials	$1,200
Millwork, including doors, windows, hardwood flooring, paneling, trim, stairways, fireplace mantels, and built-in furniture	700
Hardware, including hinges, doorknobs, locks, closet hooks, etc.	50
Electrical fixtures, including lights, switches, outlets, heaters, entrance boxes, fuse boxes, and disconnect boxes	100
Plumbing fixtures, including toilets, wash bowls, bathtubs, kitchen sinks, laundry tubs, water meters, and shut-off valves	100
Heating equipment, including furnace, oil tank, or gas meter and piping, heating duct, or steam pipes	100
Copper water pipe and wiring, 200 lb at $0.90/lb scrap value	180
Steel and iron waste pipes, heating pipe and radiators, 500 lb at $0.20/lb scrap value	100
Used lumber, including rafters, joists, plates, studs, and siding, 4,000 mbf at $75/mbf reworked value (separated and nails removed)	300
Used bricks and cut stone, 2,000 bricks at $13.50 per 100 bricks reworked value (separated and mortar removed)	270
Wood chips, prepared from nonsalvageable lumber, 8 tons at $12.00/ton	100
Total estimated revenues for the disassembly of a selected residence	$3,200

Mr. Merriam next bid on one of the homes that had valuable contents and materials, won the award of the contract for demolition, and tried the disassembly process with rented equipment and temporary employees. He determined that it was possible to remove the nonstructural items, including the doors and windows, millwork, hardware, plumbing fixtures, electrical units, and heating equipment, with two laborers working for 3 days. He also decided that it would take three laborers working with the tractor for 2 days to separate the salvageable lumber and bricks from the sections of the house as they were torn down, remove the nails and mortar, and generally prepare the material for sale, provided the men were equipped with light air tools to make their work easier and provided conveyors were installed to carry away and stack the salvaged material, ready for loading on a truck, and to carry away and dispose of the unsalvageable lumber and masonry.

Mr. Merriam had an idea for a piece of equipment, which he called a "salvage trailer," that would combine the light air tools and the loading and disposal conveyors to make the process of salvaging used lumber and bricks much simpler and faster. He thought that the house would be torn down in the usual manner, by a crawler tractor equipped with a front-end loader, but that the sections of framing and masonry, instead of being loaded directly onto the dump truck or crushed under the tractor, would be placed on the salvage trailer. This would consist of a low flat-bed trailer, only 3 ft off the ground, with a large flat area for working, an air compressor and air tools, a conveyor on each side to take the recovered material to a truck, and a central conveyor running down the middle to dispose of the nonrecoverable material. He planned to have two salvage trailers: one for the framing sections and one for masonry. The trailer for the framing sections would have a large wood chipper at the end of the central conveyor. Two workers, using the air tools, would take apart the framing sections, pull out the nails, and trim up the ends of the salvage-

able lumber, which would then be placed on the side conveyors going to a truck. The lumber that was too broken or twisted to salvage would be pushed into the central conveyor leading to the chipper, which would reduce the boards to wood chips; these chips would be suitable for sale to greenhouses and plant nurseries for use as mulch at $12.00 per ton.

The salvage trailer for the masonry pieces would have a stone crusher at the end of the central conveyor. Since most homes had much less masonry than timber, only one worker would be required, also using air tools, to separate the bricks and cut stone, clean off the mortar, and place the salvageable material on the side conveyors going to a truck. Bricks that were too broken to save and pieces of mortar and cement would be pushed onto the central conveyor leading to the stone crusher that would grind the material down in size until it was suitable for use in the backfill.

Each of the salvage units was to be mounted on a low trailer so that they could be moved from one disassembly site to another. Each was to have a large diesel engine (75 hp for the wood chipper and 125 hp for the rock crusher) to power the conveyors and machinery. Assuming that these salvage trailers would be available, Mr. Merriam estimated the cost of disassembly and salvage at $1,700 (see Exhibit 8).

Mr. Merriam was certain that with his proposed process for partially automated disassembly and salvage he could tear down at least 100 residences each year; he was also certain that he could find at least 100 homes slated for demolition that had valuable contents and materials and that he could obtain the wrecking contracts on these homes by bidding $0.60 per square foot to the city or owner. One hundred homes per year would give him a pre-tax profit of $120,000 (see Exhibit 9).

Mr. Merriam felt that it would be easy to arrange financing since he could show a pre-tax return of approximately 100% on the required investment. By remortgaging their home, selling their car, ·and cashing in all

EXHIBIT 8 Estimated costs for the disassembly and salvage of a selected two-story frame residence.

Preparation, which includes disconnecting and capping gas, water, and sewage pipe, disconnecting and removing electrical wires, and preparing the site for machinery access. Estimated time is one worker for ½ day since no quick salvage items will be removed during this stage.

4 hours	laborer's wages at $7.00/hr	$28
4 permits	required for disconnect service from utilities. at $10.00/each	40
		$70

Recovery of nonstructural items, including doors, windows, hardwood flooring, paneling and staircases, plumbing fixtures, electrical units, and heating equipment, all of which can be taken out prior to demolition. Estimated time is two workers for 3 days.

48 hours	laborer's wages at $7.00/hr	$336
3 trips	2-ton truck to carry workers to the site and bring salvaged items back to the yard, one 40-mile round trip per day, at $0.25/mile	30
		$370

Disassembly, which requires the use of a crawler tractor with a front-end loader to tear down the structure and load the framing and masonry sections onto the salvage trailers. Estimated time is one tractor for 2 days.

16 hours	tractor operating costs at $18.00/hr	$288
16 hours	tractor operator wages at $12.00/hr	192
1 trip	flatbed trailer to bring the tractor to the job site at $100 per trip	100
		$580

Recovery of lumber, metal scrap, and wood chips through the use of a salvage trailer for framing sections; trailer to be equipped with light air tools, air compressor, sorting conveyors, waste conveyor, wood chipper, and 75 hp-diesel engine. Estimated time is two workers for 2 days.

16 hours	salvage trailer operating costs at $8.00/hr	$128
32 hours	laborer's wages at $7.00/hr	224
2 trips	2-ton truck to carry workers to the site and bring salvaged lumber back to the yard, one 40-mile round trip per day, at $0.25/mile	20
4 trips	2-ton truck to carry wood chips to customer location; two 40-mile round trips per day, at $0.25/mile, driven by one of the workers during the day	40
		$410

Recovery of bricks and crushed aggregate for fill through the use of a salvage trailer for masonry sections; trailer to be equipped with light air tools, air compressor, sorting conveyors, waste conveyor, stone crusher and 125-hp diesel engine. Estimated time is one worker for 2 days.

16 hours	salvage trailer operating costs at $8.00/hr	$128
16 hours	laborer's wages at $7.00/hr	112
		$240

	Backfill is not needed since the crushed aggregate from non-salvageable bricks, stone, concrete, and mortar will be used to fill the foundation.	
	Total variable costs for "full recovery" disassembly and salvage	$1,700

EXHIBIT 9   Estimated profits available for loan repayment in a residential disassembly and salvage firm founded by Mr. Merriam.

Revenues from 100 homes, at average income of $3,200 per home	$320,000
Operating costs for 100 homes, at average cost of $1,700 per home	$170,000
Contribution to overhead and profits	$150,000
Salary for Mr. Merriam, as manager and owner	$ 16,000
Interest expense on equipment loan of $110,000 at 12.5%	14,000
Pre-tax profits	$120,000

of their securities, Mr. and Mrs. Merriam could put together an equity investment of $15,000; Mr. Merriam felt that they needed a loan of $110,000 (see Exhibit 10).

Mr. Merriam prepared a detailed proposal for his bank, describing the proposed business, indicating the total need for funds by a monthly cash budget, and showing the expected repayment of the loan through quarterly pro forma income statements and balance sheets, but the loan application was rejected:

The loan officer at the bank told me that he liked my idea for the business and that he appreciated the amount of time I had spent in preparing the proposal, but that I was asking for an 8 to 1 debt/equity ratio. He told me that the bank seldom went beyond 1 to 1

EXHIBIT 10   Capital requirements for a residential disassembly and salvage firm founded by Mr. Merriam.

Two-ton open truck to carry workers to the job site and bring the salvaged items back to the yard; to be purchased new since Mr. Merriam felt that used trucks of this size were not reliable because of prior heavy usage	$ 7,800
Two-ton closed truck to carry workers to the job site and bring wood chips to the customer; also to be purchased new	$ 9,300
Crawler tractor with front-end loader, Caterpillar #977K, with a new price of $70,000 and a used price of $45,000; to be purchased used since Mr. Merriam was certain that he could find a serviceable machine because of the recent slowdown in construction activity	$ 45,000
Flatbed trailer for movement of the crawler tractor, with a new price of $13,500 and a used price of $9,000; to be purchased used since Mr. Merriam thought that he could buy this item with the tractor	$ 9,000
Salvage trailer for framing sections, with light air tools, air compressor, sorting conveyors, waste conveyor, wood chipper, and 75-hp diesel engine; to be constructed to order for Mr. Merriam	$ 18,000
Salvage trailer for masonry sections, with light air tools, air compressor, sorting conveyors, waste conveyor, stone crusher, and 125-hp diesel engine; to be constructed to order for Mr. Merriam	$ 22,000
Total equipment investment	$112,000
Working capital, with estimated 45-day collection period for wrecking contracts and sale of salvaged material; 6 jobs over that 45-day time period, at operating expenses of $1,700 per job, plus fixed charges	$ 12,200
Total equipment and working capital investment	$125,000

unless it knew its customer exceedingly well. That took care of the bank. (Statement of Mr. Merriam.)

Mr. Merriam then went to the Small Business Administration with the same proposal, but he was told that the SBA did not have funds available for direct loans and that all that it could do would be to guarantee 90% of the loan to provide additional collateral, if he could find a bank that would accept the loan on that basis. He could not find a bank willing to accept that loan either:

> I had already checked with my bank about the SBA. The bank had told me that the additional security provided by the 90% guarantee did not really change the adverse debt/equity position. That took care of the SBA. (Statement of Mr. Merriam.)

Mr. Merriam then went to three commercial finance companies that specialized in providing equipment financing for smaller businesses through either lease-purchase agreements or conditional-sales contracts; in each, the title to the equipment remained with the finance company until the complete payments on both interest and principal had been received. None of the finance companies wished to advance the money because of the specialized nature of the equipment:

> The finance companies also liked my idea for the business, but they did not like the specialized nature of the salvage trailers; they told me that if I went broke, they would be unable to sell these units to any other demolition contractor and that their title to the

equipment was really meaningless. That took care of the finance companies. (Statement of Mr. Merriam.)

Mr. Merriam lastly went to three venture capital firms. Two of them told him that the amount he requested, $110,000, was too small for them to consider since they usually invested in amounts of over $500,000. The third said that they were not interested in "start-up" situations:

> The last venture capital firm, an SBIC, said that they liked the idea, and that if I could get the company going and gain some experience, they would be interested in "reviewing the situation" after a year or 18 months. That took care of the venture capital firms. (Statement of Mr. Merriam.)

Mr. Merriam was discouraged; he had put together a business plan or strategy that would provide a 100% return on the invested capital, and yet he could not obtain the capital:

> I heard a talk by a professor at The University of Michigan who said that a successful small business had to have a "distinctive" strategy, or method of competition. Well, I have a "distinctive" strategy, but it's so distinctive that I can't get financing. That takes care of the academic advice. (Statement of Mr. Merriam.)

ASSIGNMENT

Prepare a financing plan for Mr. Merriam.

6

Product Development

Some of the most successful small companies owe their competitive positions primarily to their ability to develop new and improved products. This chapter focuses on the requirements for success in this activity, the decisions that must be made, and some of the special problems and opportunities encountered by small firms doing product development.

It should be recognized that product development may vary in the degree of technical advance and also in the extent to which new manufacturing and marketing knowledge is needed.

Product development often involves the improvement of existing products by lowering costs, improving performance characteristics, by correcting weaknesses leading to breakdowns and failure, and meeting shifting user needs. Some of these improvements result from great ingenuity, careful testing, and considerable expense. Some involve minor modifications to meet the needs of particular customers, for example, when "the customer wants it painted blue and with a larger motor."

Product development requiring major technical advance involves greater commitments and risks. If it is successful, however, it can be the basis for great growth and even new industries. When the first crude xerography machine was introduced in the early 1950s by a Rochester, New York producer of photographic paper, the Haloid Company, the process had been under development (first by the inventor Chester Carlson, then by The Battelle Memorial Institute, and then by Haloid) for about 13 years. It was not then obvious that the process would be so successful that Haloid would later change its name to Xerox and enjoy annual sales of over $3.5 billion.

REQUIREMENTS FOR SUCCESS

Not all small companies should try to develop new products. A strategy placing major emphasis upon product development should be adopted only if the following requirements are met:

1. There must be *innovation oriented management* willing to take the necessary risks and capable of making the stream of decisions associated with developing and introducing new products. Some managers are incapable of making these decisions, while others are unwilling to reduce current profits to invest in ventures that may or may not pay off in the future.

Functional managers in marketing, production, and finance must be willing to divert attention from smooth-running current operations to the intermittent headaches of pilot production runs, of test markets, and of continuing redesign. There must be a willingness to change, to coordinate across functional lines, and to make judgments based upon continually changing technical and market knowledge.

2. There must be *creative technical people*. Particularly if there is major technical advance, there must be people who can solve the technical problems and develop products that meet the desired cost and performance goals. Not all engineers are creative and attuned to market needs. Unless there are people who have real ability, the new products are likely to be unsuccessful, and the entire venture will be little more than a costly diversion.

3. Some *discretionary funds* must be available to support and exploit the development work. Product development requires cash for parts and prototypes, but mostly for salaries. If the technical development work is successful, then larger investments are needed for manufacturing and for market development.

SEQUENCE OF DECISIONS

The idea for a new product might originate anywhere in an organization, but the most likely places are the R&D and marketing departments. Salesmen may receive increasing requests for a product with particular characteristics or they may learn that a particular market segment is likely to grow. Sometimes a laboratory discovery or a new material available from suppliers will suggest a possibility.

Some executive then typically becomes the sponsor, the person who sees that information is gathered and that the proposal gets a hearing. In the small company, managers from marketing, production, and general management, as well as engineering, are normally involved in the early evaluations of a proposed project. Management may or may not make good decisions in a small firm, but there is likely to be communication within the company and common understanding of the assumptions on which decisions are based.

The decision on whether or not to undertake a proposed project should involve consideration of the following factors:

1. Technical Feasibility. Is it technically possible to develop the proposed product? How much will it cost to investigate the most promising technical approach?

2. Potential Market. Given the planned product attributes and selling price, what are expected sales? What actions can be taken to decrease uncertainty in regard to this critical factor?

3. Development Time and Cost. How much time may be required to develop the product (taking into account that most estimates should be multiplied by at least two to take into account all unanticipated problems) ? What would be the effect of delays on the firm's market position? Can development be financed, including the later more expensive stages associated with market introduction?

4. Manufacturing Compatibility and Cost. What are the expected manufacturing costs at various possible volumes of production? Can the manufacturing organization produce the product to the desired specifications and cost?

5. Strategic "Fit." What kinds of new products contribute to the firm's strategy and build upon its competitive strengths? What environmental changes, including industry trends and competitive actions, bear upon the decision?

A distinctive feature of product development decisions, particularly when there is considerable technical advance, is the great uncertainty associated with the key variables. Thus, the market for a proposed product may be difficult to assess, depending on its manufacturing cost and selling price, the performance characteristics that can be achieved, competitive reaction, and the response of users who may never have even thought about such a product before. Many of these factors are interrelated. The market might better be appraised if working models of the new product were available. Yet, the decision on whether or not to try to develop these working models depends on the size of that market.

Few management decisions are so fraught with risk. One study reported: "About seven out of every eight hours devoted by scientists and engineers to technical development of new products are spent on projects that do not reach commercial success."[1] Even when the products emerge from the laboratory, there is still substantial uncertainty. ". . . for every five products emerging from R&D departments as technical successes, there is an average of only one commercial success."[2] Given these risks, some observers question how small companies can commit substantial resources to product development and still survive.

Development is essentially a learning activity, with the investment of time and money hopefully bringing forth answers to technical questions, as reflected in test results, working models, blueprints, etc. These results hopefully permit better judgments to be made about factors such as probable manufacturing costs and product performance.

Uncertainty is greatest when a project is first undertaken. As development proceeds, uncertainty about factors such as technical feasibility, probable manufacturing costs, and probable performance attributes diminishes. Capable small firm managers typically keep their early investments low. In these early stages, a project can be investigated and dropped while the risks are still manageable.

One important class of decisions relates to resource commitments to a project. How much time should key people devote to the project? How should the project's priority be determined? Should funds be allocated to build a prototype, to order production tooling, or to produce an initial lot of production models for market testing? In a small firm the early commitments usually involve only part of the time of one or two key engineers.

Subsequent decision points that involve larger commitments may call for re-evaluation of the entire project. The resources needed to carry the project forward

[1] Management of New Products *(New York: Booz, Allen and Hamilton, 1960) , p. 3.*

[2] Ibid., *p. 3.*

must be balanced against the consequences for the company if the new product is unsuccessful. Clearly, the larger firm, with its greater resources, often has the advantage here. In the small firm it is sometimes necessary to seek joint arrangements with customers or suppliers, to delay development or seek additional funds, or to license the new product because the magnitude of resources required is greater than seems prudent or feasible to commit.

Another class of decisions relates to the attributes of the proposed new product. What should be the performance characteristics, taking into account the implications for development cost and manufacturing cost? Often, initial goals are modified as more is learned about technical feasibility and market preferences. It is particularly difficult to decide when the product is "good enough" to introduce to the market. Premature introduction may mean product "bugs" and loss of consumer confidence in the new product. Delays mean deferred cash inflows and possibly loss of market share to more aggressive competitors. Usually, development is continued even as the decision is made to introduce a version of the product to the market. There are then successive models or generations of the new product.

SPECIAL PROBLEMS

The small company faces special problems just because it is small. In addition to the problems already discussed, there are the following:

1. In terms of technical and market knowledge, most small companies have a relatively narrow focus. Within these areas, they may be more knowledgeable than even their largest competitors, but development projects may require that they draw upon unfamiliar technologies and explore unknown markets. Unlike the large firm, the small firm usually has no in-house metallurgist or analytical chemist or specialist in a relevant new technology to call upon.

Nevertheless, small firms may utilize external sources of assistance. Suppliers often will work to solve technical problems that may involve the use of their products. Consultants and contract research firms, although expensive on an hourly basis, have a breadth of experience that may enable them to be effective contributors.

2. In a small firm, major projects to develop new products are usually the responsibility of the same engineers who must solve the constantly recurring problems associated with production and special customer orders. If there is a great deal of this "fire-fighting," the long-term project may be continuously delayed.

One approach is for other engineers to assume some of the short-term responsibilities in order to permit more uninterrupted time to be devoted to the long-term project. If the technical people are personally excited about the project, they may "find time" for it, sometimes by devoting time on evenings or weekends.

3. It is difficult for the small company to survive many new product failures. The Ford Motor Company could absorb the failure of the Edsel; du Pont could lose $100 million on Corfam; both could survive because there would be other, successful projects.

Small company managers must control their development expenditures closely, particularly in the later stages when commitments can be large. Very large projects may be beyond the reach of the small company. Many small companies, however, are so successful in creating cost consciousness that they can develop new products at less cost than their larger competitors.[3]

4. If the small company is successful in developing and introducing a new product, it may subsequently face formidable competition. Larger competitors may then recognize the potential and bring their massive resources to bear in competing with the small company that has borne the pioneering risks. Sometimes the smaller companies are "shaken out" as the field matures. For example, within the electronic calculator field great pressure has been brought to bear upon smaller competitors as companies like Texas Instruments have emphasized policies of cost and price reduction.

Patents and technological know-how sometimes provide protection from competition. Management can choose to develop products for relatively small markets in order to minimize incentives for larger competitors to challenge their established position. If the new product is consistent with the small firm's strategy, building upon its technological and market strengths, then the company is in the best position to withstand future competition.

OPPORTUNITIES

The small firm also has real advantages in product development, for example:

1. The size of the management team provides a degree of cohesiveness and mutual understanding that is difficult to achieve in the departmentalized structure of a larger firm. The decision makers usually have an intimate understanding of the technology and market. This understanding comes from personal experience instead of from reading reports. It is usually not necessary to have to "sell" projects through successive echelons of management. The entire management team can be assembled quickly and reach agreement about undertaking a project, or changing its focus, or introducing a product to the market.

Some authors have emphasized that the organizational structures and formal performance measurement systems of large companies cause managers to be willing to take risks only if their decisions are fully supported by reports that can be used to justify their actions if the project is unsuccessful.[4] The informal decision processes of the small firm can result in ill-considered commitments, but there is the opportunity to move ahead while the large company is still trying to decide whether or not to put the proposal on the agenda for the next meeting of the New Product Committee.

2. The initial market for new products is often small and reflects the crudeness and high costs that are so often characteristic of new technology. Large firms, with their high overhead rates and policies oriented toward mass production and distribution, often find small markets unappealing. The performance

---

[3] *Arnold C. Cooper, "R&D Is More Efficient in Small Companies,"* Harvard Business Review *(May–June 1964)*, *pp. 75–83.*

[4] *Donald A. Schon,* Technology and Change *(New York· Delacorte Press, 1967)*.

measurement systems of large companies usually penalize the divisions nursing new products which have low sales. Smaller companies, however, are often oriented to serving small markets and may find profitable opportunities associated with the early stages of new products.

3. Small companies usually have less commitment to the status quo. A new product may achieve some of its sales at the expense of existing products. Firms whose existing products have strong market positions have less incentive to assume the risks and to make the investments needed to develop new products. Smaller companies, and particularly new companies, have less investment in traditional technology and have more incentive to try to revolutionize their industry.

The public usually associates modern technology with large firms. It is true that many small companies do very little product development, that they are primarily technical followers. Nevertheless many of the most important inventions of the twentieth century originated with independent inventors or small companies. The developers of these new products were sometimes not successful financially, but they demonstrated the extreme creativity possible in the small firm environment. Their inventions have included magnetic recording, xerography, air conditioning, the ball point pen, polyethylene, and catalytic cracking of petroleum.

Most new products are not this revolutionary, and do not lead to the establishment of new industries. Within many industries, however, small companies have built and maintained strong competitive positions by developing new and improved products.

Maryland Electronic
Instrument Corporation

The Maryland Electronic Instrument Corporation was founded in 1959 by three members of the research and development division of a large Eastern airframe manufactur-

This case was prepared by Associate Professor LaRue Tone Hosmer, with the assistance of Andrew F. Lawlor, as a basis for class discussion. It was copyrighted (1974) by The University of Michigan and is not to be quoted or reproduced without the permission of the authors.

ing firm; they rented a small factory in Hagerstown, in the Allegheny mountain region, an area with surplus labor and conscientious workers, and they concentrated upon the design and production of very sophisticated electronic instruments and inspection systems for the aerospace industry. The timing of their move could not possibly have been better; the early years of the 1960s were a period of almost constant experimentation and development in the field of space exploration funded by the substantial federal grants of the Kennedy and Johnson administrations, and the company grew rapidly, from 3 employees in early 1959 to just under 300 in 1969, and from less than $80,000 sales the first year to approximately $13,000,000 in the last year. By the end of the 1960s the company had established an excellent reputation with both the Department of Defense and the National Aeronautics and Space Administration because of its ability to take an electronic development program from first concept to final design and manufacture with complete system integration and reliability and because of its experience with very advanced remote sensing and detection technology in the IF, UV, FUV, and X-ray wavelength regions.

IF, UV, FUV, and X-ray are all terms that refer to electromagnetic radiation. The complete spectrum of electromagnetic emissions is subdivided into seven regions which, in the order of decreasing wavelength and increasing wave frequency, are named: radio waves, radiant heat, infrared radiation (IF), visible light, ultraviolet (UV), far ultraviolet (FUV or Millikan), X-rays, and gamma rays. Electromagnetic radiations in all of these regions have basically identical characteristics; the only differences are in the wavelengths and frequencies. The wavelength of a radio broadcast, for example, may be a few thousand meters long, while the wavelength of a gamma ray is $0.000,000,001$ centimeters, or $1 \text{ cm} \times 10^{-9}$; the frequency of each wave is a constant reciprocal of the length, with the length of the wave in centimeters divided into the speed of light in centimeters. The relatively small portion of the frequency spectrum that is visible to the human eye extends through the wavelengths that give the subjective effect of the colors red, orange, yellow, green, blue, indigo, and violet. Infrared radiation is a somewhat obsolete term that refers to waves below the red portion of the visible light spectrum in frequency; ultraviolet means waves beyond the violet portion. Electromagnetic waves on each side of the visible light spectrum have known characteristics of emission, refraction, and penetration on various materials, and therefore they can be used for inspection and detection; all that is required is a system for generating electromagnetic energy in a given frequency, receiving the reflected or nonabsorbed waves, and converting the reception to a visible pattern or a decimal equivalent. Maryland Electronic Instrument Corporation specialized in the design, development, manufacture, and testing of inspection and detection systems that utilized electromagnetic radiation on each side of the visible light spectrum.

The hardware units that the company had designed and manufactured for their electromagnetic inspection and detection systems were mostly one-of-a-kind or, at the most, a few-of-a-kind models, such as on-board inspection instruments for analyzing moon conditions on each of the Apollo missions, or airborne detection equipment for mapping earth resources or locating pollution causes by aerial surveys. Innovative scientific concepts and advanced technical competence were primary characteristics of the design of these units, since they were developed to perform functions that had never been accomplished previously, particularly under the obvious constraints of size, weight, power supply, and environmental conditions. Reliability was a primary requirement of the performance of the units, since they could not be repaired or replaced once the intended operation had begun. Redundancy, back-up capability, and component quality were all part of the original design. Continual inspections and rigid tolerances were part of the manufacturing process. As might be expected under these conditions, price was not a major factor in contract awards; instead, most of the company's products and systems were sold on a cost-plus-fixed-fee basis, and financial success was based on accurate cost collection and justification, not on revenue and expense forecasting and budgeting procedures. The company's accounting system emphasized cost allocation between contracts, not cost responsibility among management, and even the bookkeeping system was constrained by federal auditing standards that were designed to monitor government contracts, not profit or loss ventures. The government contracts were obtained by submitting research and development proposals directly to procurement authorities in either NASA (National Aeronautics and Space Administration) or DOD (Department of Defense). These research proposals were prepared usually in response to a request from one of the defense or aerospace agencies, or occasionally on the initiative of one of the engineers or scientists within the company; they generally contained a highly technical description of the proposed product or system, together with graphs of potential performance characteristics, but they seldom specified prices. Estimates of the cost and parameters for the performance of the system were negotiated after the contract was awarded, and then often renegotiated during the course of the contract, by the company engineers and the procurement agency personnel. Maryland Electronics, in brief, was an engineering firm in which the conceptual and scientific values of the engineers took precedence over the more commercial aspects of pricing, marketing, manufacturing, finance, and accounting, but it was a successful engineering firm because of the innovative ability and technical competence of the staff, which provided an unquestioned reputation for the firm, and the availability of space exploration and defense system contracts, which offered an assured market for their products.

In 1968 the company began to explore the possibility of transferring their scientific and technical expertise from government procurement to commercial ventures. The three original founders foresaw the end of the space exploration contracts because the Apollo moon missions would soon be completed and there would be reduced interest in aerospace on the part of the Nixon administration. They expected reduced defense expenditures with the end of the Vietnamese war and the public distrust of military research. The founders formed small study groups within the company, usually consist-

ing of two or three engineers and scientists, together with one representative from the corporate marketing staff and one person from the production department. These groups were assigned the responsibility of investigating commercial opportunities for electromagnetics within the nongovernmental sectors of the economy. They looked, in very broad terms, at the four following general areas of potential applications:

1. Electromagnetic analysis systems for process controls, with particular emphasis on the nondestructive analysis of various chemical compounds. Electromagnetic radiations of a given frequency, when applied to a chemical specimen, incite different fluorescent emissions, depending on the chemical elements present within the specimen to be analyzed; these emissions can be portrayed on a spectrum and then automatically analyzed to determine the qualitative and quantitative content of the specimen. The process, termed electromagnetic spectrometry, is parallel to the more common optical spectrometry, in which a portion of the specimen is burned, but it is considerably more precise and, of course, nondestructive.

2. Electromagnetic testing systems for quality controls, with particular emphasis on the nondestructive testing of the composition, strength, and physical characteristics of materials, fabrications, and laminates. Electromagnetic radiation of a given frequency has different penetration and absorption curves, depending on the nature and density of the item to be tested. Voids, and the consequent weak spots, can be detected in metal castings, structural weldments, and fabric or plastic laminates. The thickness, density, or porosity of any material can be gauged very precisely. In addition, microelectromagnetics can define, through magnification, the crystalline structure of the various metals, such as germanium and silicon, used in electronics, and the phase structure of the various alloys, such as tool steel, used in metal working.

3. Electromagnetic diagnostic systems for health care. The chemical analysis and structural testing capabilities of electromagnetic radiation can be used in the diagnosis of many pathological conditions. The common medical and dental x-rays are basically just a fairly simple form of nondestructive electromagnetic testing; medical and dental X-rays are, of course, an established field with very limited potential for a new company, but there are many additional diagnostic and treatment possibilities in the health care area for electromagnetic systems.

4. Electromagnetic processing systems for the chemical industry. Electromagnetic radiation can assist in the mixing, diffusion, or precipitation of various chemical compounds and can act almost as a catalyst in various chemical reactions, for the pharmaceutical, petroleum, and heavy chemical industries. A dramatic example of the application of electromagnetics to chemistry is the strengthening, by a factor of 10, of synthetic polymers in the plastics industry.

The company process of looking for commercial opportunities for electromagnetic capabilities within many different industries was not particularly successful. The study groups found many interesting and challenging possibilities, but each seemed to require extensive research to determine if the potential application were technically feasible, and then lengthy development to design the system and debug the hardware. The money to fund this research and development activity was apparently not available from the potential customers. It was decided, therefore, to change the direction of the search and to ask the study groups to find industrial applications for existing products and systems:

We originally felt that it would not be difficult to go from the ultrahigh quality hardware of the space program to the "commercial" grade instruments for the industrial market and that it would be both a challenging and profitable change to look for opportunities for our scientific and technical skills in the civilian area. We found a lot of opportunities, but we didn't find much funding: I guess that we had been spoiled by the federal support of R&D projects in aerospace and defense.

We also found that our scientific and technical leadership did not automatically carry over into the industrial market. That market is not a vacuum. There are numerous firms already there offering laboratory equipment, testing and inspection devices, process controls, and cybernetic systems in all of the manufacturing and service sectors of the economy. Their hardware might not be as sophisticated or as reliable as ours, but it was a lot less expensive and very well established. We could go into research and development, using our own funds, to develop new applications, but then there was no guarantee that there would be a market for the new system. I think that we are pretty good at evaluating the technical feasibility of a product, but we have had no experience at evaluating the market potential. We decided to study market evaluation, but to study it using our existing products and systems. We felt that we modify these products slightly for commercial use, but that we would not redesign them for new uses since that was simply too expensive.

New products are important for a small company such as ours because the obsolescence rate in electromagnetics is very high. We can expect that there is going to be increasing technical competition in our industry since there are so many firms similar to our own that are planning to switch from aerospace and defense contracting to the civilian market. We have a head start on them now, but we have to learn now to manage the R&D function for commercial product development in order to stay ahead.

I think that there are two obvious choices in commercial product development. You can say, "I've got a market need. Is it technically feasible?" or you can say, "I've got a technically feasible product. Is there a market need?" The first choice is very expensive in R&D, and you never really know that you have the market until after you design the product and show it to a few customers; and the second is much less expensive and much more certain, for you can demonstrate what you've got right at the start, but it is also much more pedestrian. That is, IBM and Xerox would not be the exceedingly successful firms they are today if

20 years ago they had sat around demonstrating their existing products. Their scientific and technical innovations lifted them above the competition and gave them the cash flow to continue original product development. I'm not certain which is the optimal route generally, but I do know that we have to try looking for market applications for existing products, since we have to learn more about market evaluation. (Statement of company executive at the Maryland Electronic Instrument Corporation.)

Maryland Electronics had one existing system that certainly seemed to be suitable for their planned investigation of the commercial market applications for established military and aerospace products. This was a portable X-ray unit that had been developed as an outgrowth of classified inspection contracts for the Department of Defense during the late 1960s. The complete unit consisted of a short-pulse X-ray generator and receiver set, only 6 in. square × 17 in. long, with a weight of approximately 16 lb, and a battery pack for remote operation. In use, an object was placed on a glass slide or frame between the generator and the receiver, and pulsed, and the resultant X-ray shadow image was recorded on Polaroid film that could be developed on the site in about one minute. It was a simple and convenient unit that admittedly did not have adequate power or capacity for the nondestructive testing of

castings or weldments, but it did have very definite applications for the quality control of thinner and less dense materials, such as plastics and fiber compositions. The distinctive features of the product were the use of Polaroid film in the receiver, which offered a very simple and accepted means of recording test results, and the design of the short-pulse generator, which greatly reduced radiation leakage and health concerns. Each pulse, or burst of radiation at X-ray frequency, was only 40 nanoseconds (1 nanosecond $\doteq$ 1 billionth of a second) in duration. The advantage of this short pulse was that it was safe, even in an unscreened and unprotected operation; the leakage exposure to the operator was less than 1/1,000,000 of the exposure of the typical dental X-ray and 1/10,000 of the permissible weekly exposure established by the National Bureau of Standards (see Exhibit 1).

Starting in January 1971 three demonstration models of the ME-1 portable X-ray unit were manufactured and tested and then shown to electronic wholesalers, industrial equipment suppliers, testing laboratories, and precision part fabricators, but the reception and sales did not meet company expectations:

> Some of the national distributors added the product to their line of testing hardware, but there was less interest than we had ex-

---

EXHIBIT 1 Exposure standards of the Bureau of Radiological Health within the National Bureau of Standards. (Source: company records.)

10,000 Roentgens $\}$ Radium therapy	
1,000 Roentgens $\int$	
100 Roentgens	—
10 Roentgens	Routine dental X-ray exposure
1 Roentgens	Routine chest X-ray exposure
0.1 Roentgens	Permissible weekly exposure
0.01 Roentgens	Radium wristwatch daily exposure
0.001 Roentgens	—
0.0001 Roentgens	Cosmic ray daily exposure at sea level
0.00001 Roentgens	ME-1 portable X-ray (specimen exposure)
0.000001 Roentgens	ME-1 portable X-ray (operator exposure)

pected. It is pretty clear now, however, why this happened: Our portable X-ray unit was not powerful enough to test metal parts or fabrications. Any small plastic part or fiber composition that needed nondestructive structural analysis could easily be carried to a permanent X-ray installation. Also, since most small plastic or fiber compositions are inexpensive, the simple analytical method is statistical sampling and destructive testing: You just pick out a few pieces and cut them apart to see how your process is running. There wasn't much of an industrial market, but we got quite a bit of interest from public safety and law enforcement agencies. (Statement of company executive at Maryland Electronic Instrument Corporation.)

In late 1971 the Department of Defense asked the company to develop a "real-time" inspection system based upon the ME-1 portable X-ray unit; they wanted a package inspection system that would display the X-ray image on a video monitor, rather than on film, so that they could have instant information feedback. The officials at the Pentagon wanted to improve building security (because of the continued existence of bomb threats), and they expected to examine all personally carried packages and briefcases at the entrances to the building. The X-ray inspection unit with Polaroid film took too long and made each individual carrying a package wait a minimum of 60 seconds for clearance. The proposed real-time system, with instant feedback capabilities, required a more complex receiver and display device than the existing unit which depended on Polaroid film, but it was not impossible to build. All that was needed was an electrooptic assembly, which could amplify and then scan the shadow image on the X-ray receiver screen, a storage unit that could hold the amplified shadow image for a short period of time, perhaps two minutes, and a video screen to display the stored picture. The complete system is, as stated previously, complex but not difficult to design and manufacture:

> I could give you a technical description of the equipment, but I think that would probably be meaningless to your students. Instead,

think of the X-ray image on the receiver screen as a grid, with very minute horizontal lines and vertical sectors. If you could accurately judge the gray level for each square in that grid and then accurately reproduce that gray level on each square of a different grid, you could accurately reproduce that X-ray photography. Electronically you can do that fairly easily, with an amplifier to magnify the differences in the gray levels, and a line scanner to record them. Our electrooptic assembly has those amplifying and line scanning capabilities. It is not quite similar, but it is close to the way black and white television broadcasts work.

The storage unit, which is the next component in the system, is needed because of the short-pulse nature of the X-ray generator. We couldn't use a direct receiver screen, electrooptic amplifier and scanner, and an output video screen system since the original X-ray pulse lasts for only 40 nanoseconds. If we had used a direct system, the electronic impulses would have gone all the way through the system. We could have said that it worked, but the operator could not have examined the contents of the package or briefcase in 40 nanoseconds; as a matter of fact, he would not even have been able to recognize that there was a momentary flash of light on the screen. So we had to store the image and then reproduce it from storage on the video screen; then, the operator would have time to inspect the X-ray photograph and look for suspicious outlines and forms. The simple way to store information is in the digital form. The storage unit converts the gray levels of each square in the grid reported by the line scanner equivalents and then stores that data.

You might explain to your students that if you kept on the X-ray generator for longer than 40 nanoseconds, perhaps for 3 seconds so that you could get a direct look at the contents of the package, without using the storage unit, you would multiply the X-ray emission exposure by 750 million times. That, for fairly obvious reasons, is simply not acceptable.

Our real-time inspection system, then, consisted of our ME-1 portable X-ray generator and receiver screen, with an electrooptic amplifier and line scanner, a digital storage device, and a video tube. We designed the system using "off-the-shelf" components from other manufacturers, except for our own generator and receiver, put together a prototype in our own shop, and it worked.

We delivered the prototype to the Pentagon, and they were apparently happy with it, although they never set up the complete building security system they had planned because of objections from the senior officers, and they only used our hardware for the inspection of occasional packages and other items carried by unauthorized personnel. (Statement by company executive at Maryland Electronic Instrument Corporation.)

Corporate officials at Maryland Electronics were pleased with the design of the real-time inspection system and the performance of the prototype. They instructed the members of the study group to accelerate their analysis of the potential market. As a consequence of this decision, two additional prototype models of the unit, now termed the Maryland Electronics SearchR Inspection System (Model ER-2), were put together and taken on a marketing research tour of the country, to introduce the product and to demonstrate its capabilities. Each demonstration unit consisted of the four modular components described previously, without integrative housing or cabinetry. They were assembled by members of the demonstration team in major cities throughout the country and were shown to representatives of police departments, security guard firms, customs agencies, airline companies, airport authorities, etc. The tour was well organized; invitations had been sent in advance, and both hotel room simulations of possible inspection applications and on-site examples of security testing were performed. As an example of the latter, the carry-on luggage for two trans-Atlantic airline flights was checked, and three weapons were found. Overall, members of both the product study group and corporate management could not help but be pleased with the results of the tour: Attendance was good, the equipment worked well, and the response was as positive as could be expected from an audience who related X-rays to doctors' offices and dental visits. When the tour was completed, the summary of an internal management report stated that

the company had achieved its three major market research objectives:

1. We have succeeded in making first contact with representatives of the organizations on our prospective customer list, and we will be welcomed back for a more concentrated one-on-one demonstration with all of them.

2. We have successfully combined initial market research with on-site product testing; the system performed well in isolating objects hidden within packages that were volunteered by visitors to the demonstrations, and it held up well on a rough cross-country tour.

3. We have determined the priority of our prospective customers' concerns. Safety is foremost for product acceptance; the customers do have fears about high-dose radiation exposure, as well as concerns about possible damage to photographic film. Ease of operation is next; they frequently state that they do not have technically trained personnel to operate the unit. Availability of maintenance is third; again, they frequently express concern that they do not have electronic technicians to repair the system. Consequently, we may need to offer a service contract as part of each sale. (Statement in management report of Maryland Electronic Instrument Corporation.)

After the results of the marketing research tour were analyzed (in May 1972), the members of the study group, who were now much more active in product management than product development, proposed a definite 6-month plan for the balance of the year. Some of the engineers assigned to the study group would work on system reliability testing since the X-ray tube within the generator had shown a somewhat shorter life than expected; some would work on defining potential applications for the ME-2 system; and others would work on the promotion of the general concept of real-time X-ray security inspection. This last group prepared pamphlets and advertising brochures that showed the advantages of the system and stressed the safety and the ease of operation, which were the two major concerns of potential customers discovered during the market research tour:

The system operator, even if standing directly in the X-ray beam, would receive less exposure from 100,000 inspection pulses than from a single dental X-ray. It is impossible for an operator to stand in the X-ray beam; consequently, the operator can receive only leakage exposure, and this would not approach the National Bureau of Standards' weekly limit, even if the operator were on duty for 24 hours each day for 7 consecutive days during that week. The radiation from the single-pulse inspection system is so low that it will not even harm photographic film in the package or briefcase being examined. (Statement in advertising brochure of the Maryland Electronic Instrument Corporation.)

No special instruction is required; the Maryland Electronic SearchR Inspection System can be operated easily by the present personnel of police departments, security agencies, building guards, or airport authorities without technical training. All that is needed is a short demonstration, showing the characteristic outlines and forms of hidden weapons and other contraband as they appear on the video monitor. The controls are simple (on–off and pulse), and the operation is automatic once the "pulse" control is activated." (Statement of advertising brochure of the Maryland Electronic Instrument Corporation.)

Concurrent with the general promotion of the product, representatives from the corporate marketing staff prepared lists of individual prospective customers and rated each according to sales potential in number of units, sales requirements in conditions of use, probability of the order capture by Maryland Electronics (did the ME-2 system meet the expected conditions of use), and probable date of the first order. The list was arranged by first order dates since company officials and members of the directing study group felt that it was important that Maryland Electronics take the first few orders so that they might establish a dominant market position at the outset. There were five classifications on this priority list:

1. The Department of Defense headed the prospective customer list; building security officials at the Pentagon wanted to purchase 15 to 20 automated systems, with conveyors to speed up the flow of items to be inspected, since they felt that it was necessary to examine all parcels, packages, and hand luggage entering the building. The Department of Defense was the customer that Maryland Electronics knew best, and since the Department of Defense already had experience with the prototype model of the ME-2 inspection system, company officials were reasonably confident of receiving this order.

2. The U.S. Capitol complex and other federal office buildings in the Washington area were second on the list. Security officials at the Capitol wanted to complement their closed-circuit TV system with something more efficient, less embarrassing, and less time-consuming than hand search of the visitors' purses and packages, and they liked the concept of real-time X-ray inspection. Company officials expected the security agencies at the Capitol and other federal office buildings to buy after examining the experience at the Pentagon. Again, the company was reasonably confident of receiving the order, which could amount to 25 or 30 units.

3. Banks and corporate office buildings in major U.S. cities were next on the list; bomb threats and actual bombings had occurred frequently during the summer of 1972, particularly in New York City. Company officials expected the security agencies that provided guard services for many of these headquarter buildings to start package inspections the way the federal government was doing.

4. Airport authorities and airline companies were fourth on the list. They were considered to constitute the largest potential market, since each airport might require 10 or more units, and they had the most visible need, because of the series of airplane hijackings and bomb threats that had started in the late 1960s, but company officials felt that this market would be very slow to develop. The problem was that the FAA (Federal Aviation Authority), the airlines, the airport authorities, and the security companies that pro-

vided guard services at the airports could not agree on who was to purchase and operate the inspection systems. Each pointed at the others, and all disclaimed responsibility when the topic of improved inspection and security was mentioned. The reason for this apparent evasion was economic; due to the large number of passengers at most airports, many of whom traditionally carried personal luggage aboard the airplanes, the cost of inspection would be substantial. Company officials, therefore, expected to maintain the contacts already established with airlines, airports, and the FAA, and they intended to continue their educational efforts on the advantages of X-ray inspection, but they did not anticipate immediate sales from this market segment.

5. The U.S. Treasury, for import customs examination and drug control programs, and international airlines and foreign governments were also considered to be potential customers, but they placed lower on the priority list. Company resources in personal selling and product promotion were to be directed at the first four groups of potential customers. The last group was to receive only long-range marketing efforts.

While members of the corporate marketing staff were examining potential customers, a team of engineers was assigned the task of looking at possible competitors. Three major competitors were identified, and their equipment was evaluated by the engineers:

1. American X-ray Corporation had a direct view inspection system, with an extended energy pulse at very low intensity that created a shadow image on a fluorescent screen. The unit produced very considerably higher radiation than the ME-2, but it still was below the weekly emission exposure allowed by the National Bureau of Standards, and the inspection process did not damage photographic film. The system was one of the few for which a firm price had been announced, at $18,000. It was felt that this machine, which was slower and difficult to automate, might appeal to some of the smaller airlines and to security agencies at some of the less heavily trafficked office buildings and banks.

2. Eastern Engineering Associates had an X-ray inspection system with a flying spot scanner, which is a pencil beam that travels quickly over rows of ionized crystals on the receiver, a line at a time, to create a pattern that is then held and displayed on a video monitor. Radiation leakage was not high because the focus of the X-ray beam was very narrow, but it did cause damage to photographic film, and the displayed shadow image was not as clear as on the ME-2, due to the inherent size problems of the ionized crystals on the receiver. No price had been announced for the unit, but it was expected to be competitive, around $30,000, since the company was known for aggressive marketing and product promotion. This machine was fast and could be automated; it was expected to provide substantial competition for Maryland Electronics.

3. Indiana Instrument Corporation produced a slow but inexpensive system that consisted of a high-intensity and extended duration energy pulse that was shielded to prevent unacceptable emission leakage. In essence, the item to be examined was placed in a lead-lined box, the cover was closed, and a direct X-ray picture was taken that appeared on a viewer similar to a medical photofluoroscope. The process was quicker than might be expected, though it could not be automated, but it did produce a very clear shadow image. Again, no price had been announced, but it was expected to be just slightly over $20,000.

The engineering group concluded that the Maryland Electronic SearchR Inspection System was technically superior to all the competitive units since it combined a very clear video image with very low radiation exposure and rapid processing, but they also felt that it was likely to be the most expensive. Cost, however, was not felt to be a major factor with the first two customer groups on the priority listing, the Pentagon and the U.S. Capitol, and it was believed that if these groups purchased the ME-2, other customers would tend to follow because the system's reputation would be enhanced and its market position would be established. Corporate management agreed with this belief and instructed the study group to continue the customer contacts with the governmental agencies that, it was hoped, would result in a number of actual sales and permanent installations by the end of the year.

On August 10, 1972, however, all of the corporate plans relative to the introduction of the EP-2 X-ray inspection system were thrown into a state of disarray by an FAA announcement that effective January 5, 1973 all airlines must inspect 100% of all carry-on luggage; the airlines were to be allowed to pass on to each passenger the costs of this inspection in the form of a surcharge of $0.375 per flight, or $0.75 per roundtrip ticket. The airline market was going to be the first to develop and it was going to develop very quickly and very dramatically.

Representatives of the corporate marketing staff and members of the directing study group quickly organized a second cross-country tour in late August that was aimed directly at carry-on baggage inspection procedures. Fortunately, personnel from Maryland Electronics were already in close contact with the corporate executives, industrial engineers, and purchasing agents at all of the domestic U.S. airlines as a result of their earlier market research and market education efforts. They were able to contact these people quickly and talk with them candidly about inspection problems, and they demonstrated the capabilities of the EP-2 inspection system in actual use. The EP-2 equipment was portable, of course, and the original method in these demonstrations was to move the unit from gate to gate, but members of the engineering staff who accompanied the marketing personnel on these trips quickly noted that there was often one place in each airport that people had to funnel through to get out to the airplanes. They established

the concept of the sterile concourse. This concept definitely appealed to the airlines since fewer pieces of equipment were needed and since customer delays occurred during the walk out to the concourse and not right at the moment of boarding. The central engineering staff was instructed to prepare passenger flow and inspection time studies for all the major U.S. airports which, when completed, supported the validity of the sterile concourse concept.

As a result of customer comments from the larger U.S. airlines during the hurried market research trip, and as a result of the passenger flow studies at major U.S. airports during the equally rushed engineering tour, it was decided that there were five major factors that would determine the eventual purchasing decision by the airlines for X-ray inspection systems.

1. Speed of Operation. The airline companies were concerned about the speed of the inspection system because positioning the inspection process at the entry to the concourse rather than at the gate to the aircraft imposed much higher operating rates. Maryland Electronics decided, therefore, to offer an automated model, with a conveyor that would bring luggage to the X-ray generator and receiver, stop for the pulse and inspection, and then continue automatically unless the operator wanted an additional inspection. The conveyor was to be designed with a variable speed feature and a maximum inspection rate of one item every 2 seconds.

2. Warranty of the Equipment. The airline companies were concerned about the reliability of the inspection system, since the models offered by all of the competitors were new and unproven. Maryland Electronics decided, therefore, to offer a 90-day warranty on the system and a warranty of 100,000 pulses or inspections on the X-ray tube. The tubes that had been tested by the engineering group assigned to work on system reliability had shown an average life of only 30,000 to 50,000 pulses, but some had gone far over

100,000. Consequently, it was felt that the short life was a production defect and not a design defect and could be corrected prior to delivery. The three competitive manufacturers of X-ray inspection systems offered warranties that went beyond 100,-000 inspections, but they used different technologies and more proven tubes.

3. Price of the Equipment. The airline companies were concerned about the price of the inspection system since they were limited by the FAA to a charge of $0.375 per inspection to pay for the wages of the operator and the depreciation and maintenance of the machine. Maryland Electronics decided on a price of $28,000, based upon an examination of the cost of the components. This price was acknowledged to be considerably higher than that of two of the competitive manufacturers, but it felt that the Maryland Electronics system was considerably faster and, therefore, more valuable.

4. Maintenance of the Equipment. The airline companies were concerned about the repair and maintenance of the inspection system since they did not have personnel experienced in electromagnetic instruments. Maryland Electronics decided, therefore, to offer a 1-year maintenance contract for $4,700; this optional contract would apply after the 90-day warranty period and included $1,700 for parts and $3,000 for service personnel.

5. Delivery of the Equipment. The airline companies were not as concerned about delivery of the inspection system as they were about the other factors in their purchase decision since they could institute hand search on January 5, and so comply with the FAA order. Because hand search was expensive, they wanted some reasonable promise of delivery. Maryland Electronics decided, therefore, to order parts for 50 systems and to offer 2- to 4-month deliveries.

Written proposals were prepared for all major U.S. airlines. The proposals suggested the location of the Maryland Electronic SearchR Inspection System at all the airports served by the carrier, specified the passenger flow at that site for different time periods over the week, and then listed the speed of operation, the warranty, the price, the optional maintenance contract, and the expected delivery. These proposals were followed up by personal visits of combined marketing and engineering teams to answer questions and to reassure doubts about the operations of the inspection systems. The combined marketing and engineering effort was intensive, since it was the opinion of corporate management that the customers had to be sold quickly or else lost forever to competitive units. Members of the sales teams worked 7 days a week during the fall in an effort to secure the first orders.

By late November it was apparent that the intensive marketing campaign would be successful. The FAA ordered 2 units for testing, and Trans-Continental Air Lines ordered 2 units for installation in their Washington terminal, and then 12 more for other terminals. In December Global Air Lines ordered 6 units, and Worldwide ordered 10. By January orders from smaller airlines were coming at the rate of 3 per month. March was the month that highlighted Maryland Electronic's complete dominance of the market; their proposal for 30 units was formally accepted by Northern Air Lines, and Global ordered an additional 25 systems. The Northern and Global proposals had been extremely competitive and had included special quantity discounts that provided a full year of on-site service at no cost, but company personnel were pleased to have received over 80% of all orders for X-ray inspection systems since they believed that this early success would result in continued market dominance and sales that might average $3.5 million per year for the next 3 to 5 years. Corporate management felt that the study group organization, combining representatives from engineering, marketing, and production, had been able to compress the traditional product development cycle and had been able to carry an existing product design through to commercial success in a rapidly developing market in less than one year. They were certain that this could be done with other existing product designs, which would ensure the continued growth and profitability of their firm.

ASSIGNMENT

Review the product development program at Maryland Electronics Instrument Corporation and consider the two following questions:

1. As a management consultant at the date of the case, would you make any spe-

cific recommendations to improve the product development program at this company?

2. As an owner of the company, and one of the three original founders, what conclusions could you draw about the product development program 18 months after the date of the case, when the SearchR Inspection System sales resulted in losses of more than $4,000,000 and when the company had to file for bankruptcy as a result of the decisions described in this case. What, in your opinion, went wrong, and what should have been done to prevent the overwhelming financial losses and eventual bankruptcy?

Space Components, Inc. (A)

In March 1961 Space Components, Inc. was slightly over 2 years old and had total personnel of 30. The company specialized in developing and producing transistors,[1] particularly transistors that had not previously been developed by any other companies in the industry. At this time management was preparing to introduce to the market a radically new product—the "field-effect transistor." The product represented the culmination of 8 months of development effort by Space Components. According to management, the field-effect transistor had been predicted in the early 1950s, but despite considerable money spent by other companies in an effort to develop such a product, Space Components was the first company to develop successfully a commercially practical field-effect transistor.

[1] *A transistor is a device used to control and amplify electrical currents.*

Although Space Components was one of the smallest companies in the transistor industry, it had apparently succeeded in developing a field-effect transistor where others had failed. This series of cases focuses on the decisions made by management in the development of this product.

COMPANY BACKGROUND

In 1958 the plans had been laid for the founding of Space Components. Thomas Jablonski and Richard Morton were engineers doing development work on transistors for a large electronics company located in the Greater Los Angeles area. Both were dissatisfied because of what they considered to be a lack of dynamism on the part of their large employer. Also, being interested in managing their own efforts and in realizing the financial fruits of successful entrepreneurship, they decided to found their own transistor firm.

The two engineers made up a proposal that described the transistor company they wished to start. They showed this proposal to a number of people and to companies that appeared interested in backing the new company. Finally, agreement was reached with two other parties who became joint owners, together with the two engineers, in the new enterprise.

In February 1959 Space Components was founded with Mr. Jablonski and Mr. Morton as the only employees. These two men each received one-sixth of the outstanding stock in the new company. The total cash invested in the new company was $40,000, $30,000 of which was furnished by a wealthy private individual who received one-third of the stock. The remaining one-third of the stock was owned by a firm that conducted metallurgical research on a contract basis, chiefly for the government. This company furnished $10,000 in cash and was expected to provide $40,000 in services to the new company. These services were to include a rent-free room (located in the metallurgical company's building), secretarial service, managerial advice, etc. The exact nature of these services and the way in which they would be valued were not spelled out in detail at that time.

Space Components was housed in a single room on the second floor of a building occupied by the metallurgical firm. It was an old frame building standing in the shadow of a giant gas storage tank in an industrial section of Los Angeles, California.

In August 1959, 6 months after the company was founded, the two engineers were still concentrating on developing the company's first product. It is called a nonsymmetrical silicon transistor and is described in greater detail below. There had been no sales and the company's cash balance had declined, mainly because of the development expenses and the salaries of the two engineers. At this time, the individual who had invested $30,000 in the company was dissatisfied because the company apparently

had nothing to show for the time and money already invested. This investor thought that if the new product really were any good, Space Components should have been able to get some firm orders. A short time later this investor sold his interest to another private individual for $50,000, taking a $20,000 profit on his initial investment.

The two engineers continued to concentrate their development efforts on the nonsymmetrical silicon transistor. This product was very similar to a transistor that was being produced by the electronics company for which they had formerly worked. At the time they decided to develop this transistor as Space Components' first product, they knew that the demand for these transistors was considerably greater than the supply. In fact, the government was even allocating these transistors to various defense projects.

About November 1959 Space Components introduced the nonsymmetrical silicon transistor to the market. Management found, however, that the product was considerably more difficult to sell than anticipated. Several other transistor companies had also entered the market and these companies, with their established reputations and large sales organizations, were formidable competitors. The fact that it had not been easy to procure these transistors some months earlier had had an adverse effect on the market; many engineers had designed their circuits to use other transistors that were more easily available. Also, Space Components found prospective customers saying, "Why should we buy this product from an unknown and unproven company when we can get it from established suppliers?"

Mr. Morton said that at that time they made a decision to concentrate their future development efforts on products that had not been developed before.

Although the new product was not as successful as anticipated, enough units were sold to support operations while additional products were being developed. During the first year of operations, total sales were about $15,000 and a loss before taxes of about $40,000 was shown.

In April 1960 David Stewart joined the company to supervise production. He had 8 years of experience in managing the production of transistors; the production department that he had most recently supervised had over 100 personnel. Several months later, as the result of a verbal agreement reached at the time he joined the company, Mr. Stewart received 10 shares of stock in the financial reorganization which is described below.

Friction continued to develop between the investors and the managers. Management chafed at the restrictions imposed by outside investors. For instance, all checks had to be signed by the president, who was one of the outside investors and rarely there. Management felt that the investors were quick to criticize but slow to come up with helpful alternatives. Finally, Mr. Jablonski and Mr. Morton indicated to the outside owners that they did not think they could continue to be productive under the existing agreement. They asked the outside investors, who owned two-thirds of the stock, how much they wanted for their shares.

These investors indicated they would accept $150,000 for their 66⅔ shares. In addition, of the funds they had invested in the company, $12,500 was recorded as a loan; they indicated they would expect immediate repayment of this loan. Mr. Jablonski and Mr. Morton contacted a lawyer who assisted them in arranging for a change of ownership in the company.

Through this lawyer they contacted a small electronics company that was interested in acquiring an equity interest in Space Components. A series of negotiations culminated in the electronics company's purchasing the 66⅔ shares of stock held by the two outside investors for $150,000. The electronics company also assumed the $12,500 debt owed by Space Components to the former owners. The lawyer originally contacted, as well as another lawyer who assisted in the negotiations, each received 5 shares of stock in exchange for their services. The electronics company then gave to Mr. Jablonski and Mr. Morton 16⅔ shares of stock. Mr. Jablonski and Mr. Morton then each gave Mr. Stewart 5 shares of stock; Mr. Stewart made no cash payment for these shares. Thus, the ownership of Space Components was as follows:

Electronics company	40 shares
Two lawyers	10 shares
	(5 shares each)
Mr. Stewart	10 shares
Mr. Jablonski and	40 shares
Mr. Morton	(20 shares each)

Subsequently, Mr. Jablonski, Mr. Morton, and Mr. Stewart made the principal decisions associated with managing the company. The electronics company was represented on the Space Components' Board of Directors, but, as of March 1961, the Board had met only to satisfy legal requirements and had not been active in shaping company policy.

By March 1961 the electronics company had had several offers to sell its shares in Space Components at a profit. In addition, the management had been contacted on a number of occasions by parties interested in investing in the company. Mr. Jablonski commented, "We are polite and listen to their offers, but we don't want more money now."

As of the end of March 1961 the company's sales and profits for the 2 years and 2 months of operations to date had been as follows:

	Sales	Profits before taxes
1959 (11 months)	$ 15,000	$41,000 loss
1960	$250,000	$18,000 profit
1961 (3 months)	$ 95,000	$30,000 profit

MANUFACTURING

Manufacturing skill is a critical requirement for success in the transistor industry. Mr. Stewart supervised nine girls who made up the Space Components production department.

According to Mr. Stewart, there are two basic methods of producing transistors: the alloy method and the diffusion method. The objective of both methods is to introduce a very small but carefully controlled amount of a particular impurity (such as aluminum) into certain parts of the semiconductor crystal. Space Components used the alloy technique, in which a silicon crystal was sandwiched between two tiny discs of aluminum and placed in an oven, which was held at a temperature of about 1,000°C. During the heating process, a carefully controlled amount of aluminum is alloyed into the silicon crystal.

The diffusion method, which was originally developed by Bell Laboratories, was used by most transistor companies. It produced impurity layers in crystals of silicon or germanium by heating them in an atmosphere containing gaseous impurities (such as aluminum). Mr. Jablonski estimated that 90% of silicon transistors were made by the diffusion method. According to Mr. Stewart, the diffusion method lent itself to certain mass-production techniques particularly suitable for large companies, but the alloying method did not. In addition, the diffusion method could be carefully controlled, and the extensive experience of the many companies using this method had led to a considerable degree of sophistication in its use.

Neither the alloying method nor the diffusion method was patented, but both methods involved a tremendous amount of "know-how." Mr. Jablonski and Mr. Morton had acquired considerable experience in working with alloying techniques while they were working for their former employer. Since founding Space Components they had added considerably to this experience and they now felt that they knew as much about alloying techniques as anyone in the industry. They considered their knowledge of diffusion techniques to be much less extensive. If Space Components were ever to produce transistors by the diffusion method (on other than a laboratory basis), they anticipated that considerable time and money would have to be spent in acquiring the necessary experience.

A particular transistor produced by alloying would have different electrical characteristics than the same transistor produced by diffusion—in effect it would be a different product. For many applications, transistors produced by either technique would be suitable. For certain applications, particularly involving higher frequencies, transistors produced by diffusion had a clear performance advantage. Another somewhat smaller area of application was particularly suited to transistors produced by alloying.

Space Components produced only silicon transistors. David Stewart, commenting on the relative difficulty in producing silicon transistors, said, "Producing germanium transistors is a picnic by comparison. Everything goes according to the theory. With silicon nothing works out as it is supposed to." In general, silicon and germanium transistors did not compete directly with each other for the same applications; each was more suitable for certain uses.

The production of Space Components' transistors took place in a room about 20 ft $\times$ 50 ft; inspection of the transistors took place principally in an adjacent room which was slightly larger. The first step in production was assembling parts in jigs. A jig was about 10 in. long and looked a little like a cribbage board. In each of the 100 holes in a jig, a girl assembled the parts of a transistor. She put down a disk of aluminum, then a wafer of silicon, and then another disk of aluminum with tiny arms projecting from it. The arms would later be used to position the transistor within the "stem.") This stacking process was repeated until the jig held 100 "sandwiches" ready to be baked, one in each hole. Each transistor measured about 0.2 in. by 0.15 in., with certain dimensions being critical to 0.0001 in.

The jigs were then placed in an oven and baked at about 1,000°C. This process caused the aluminum to adhere to the silicon and a certain number of aluminum atoms to penetrate into the silicon crystal. The temperature and time of baking were carefully controlled.

Each transistor was then fastened to a "stem," which was a metal cup with wire leads protruding from it. The transistor was carefully positioned by welding the protruding arms to appropriate wires. Wires that were to carry the current were soldered to the correct places on the transistor. Both the welding and soldering operations were performed under a microscope.

The transistors were then cleaned by being soaked in an "etching bath." This bath contained an acid that removed various impurities that could affect the electrical characteristics of the transistors. After being cleaned, the transistors were placed in an oven where they were heated to drive off moisture.

The dried transistors were then subjected to the first of many tests. In a dry-box, in which the relative humidity was held to less than 1%, the transistors were tested for certain electrical characteristics (only a few of the many electrical parameters were investigated at this point). This test resulted in the rejection of about 50% of the transistors. These rejected transistors were sent bank to the etching bath, then to the oven, and then back to be tested again. About 50% of these "repeats" passed the first test on the second try.

After being tested, the units were hermetically sealed (a protective cap was placed over the transistor). The transistors were then sent to the inspection room.

Each transistor passed through a series of tests, including measurement of 15 different electrical parameters. The transistors also had to display an ability to operate under difficult environmental conditions. Before undergoing additional tests, each transistor was heated in a pressure cooker and then baked for 300 hours at 165°C.

Each test resulted in the rejection of a certain number of transistors. In addition, certain of the tests served as the basis for separating the transistors into different product categories; two transistors which were assigned to different categories would be identical mechanically, but different in regard to certain electrical characteristics. Thus, for example, 100 transistors started through the production line might result in 25 being thrown out at the first test station and 25 others failing various later tests. Of the remaining 50 transistors, only

10 might be of top quality, i.e., having electrical characteristics that would command the highest price. The remaining 40 transistors might fall into various other categories; they would be suitable for certain uses and be offered to the market at lower prices. The yield was based upon the prime quality transistors that were produced. Thus, in the above example the yield would be 10%.

On the transistors that Space Components had been producing for some time, the yield averaged about 20%, with some lots being lower and some higher. A new product first being put into production might have a yield as low as 1%. Gradually the yield would be increased through discovering the optimum processing conditions for the particular transistor. For instance, David Stewart might hold all other variables constant and vary the temperature in the oven. In other cases, he might improve the yield by slightly changing the dimension of a particular component. Space Components had never achieved a consistent yield above 20% for any transistors. Mr. Stewart said that the highest yield he had heard of, even with the easier-to-process germanium, was about 60%.

According to Tom Jablonski, there were some manufacturing savings from larger production volumes, chiefly through purchasing discounts. Some of the larger producers, particularly those that used the diffusion method of production, had invested in certain automatic equipment, but since the industry changed so rapidly, companies were reluctant to invest in equipment that might soon become obsolete. The primary factor affecting manufacturing cost was yield.

Space Components kept its entire inventory, valued at about $100,000, in a two-door metal filing cabinet. Before any order was shipped, every transistor in that order was completely inspected again (meaning that the company used 200% inspection). Records were kept on the test performance of every transistor shipped. Management emphasized the importance of maintaining a reputation for good quality. A single missile might contain 5,000 transistors; if one transistor did not work, the missile might fail.

One other factor of particular importance in the company's production organization was the way in which production and development worked closely together. If, in trying to improve the yield on a particular transistor, David Stewart thought it might be useful to change a particular dimension on the product, he would simply walk into the next room to discuss the change with Richard Morton. If that particular change did not improve the yield or if it adversely affected the product's performance, they wasted no time in trying to decide who was responsible for the suggestion; instead, they tried something else. David Stewart said that most of the large transistor companies with which he was familiar handled product changes in a much more formal manner. In these organizations, the production department would formally request a particular change in a transistor's design; this change would then have to be authorized by the product evaluation group, which was always responsible for the product. In order to protect themselves, the members of the product evaluation group would sometimes be reluctant to authorize the change; then delays would result while they investigated the change more thoroughly.

SALES

Space Components' products were sold by 22 manufacturing representatives; these 22 organizations had a total of about 50 to 60 men in the field. All of these companies also handled other noncompetitive electronic components. The effectiveness of these manufacturing representatives seemed to vary widely. In general, management thought that the company's sales organization was not as strong as those of most competitors.

Mr. Jablonski, as time permitted, visited various prospective customers and the company's manufacturing representatives. He said that these visits permitted him to keep in touch with what the market wanted and also, to a limited extent, to advise prospective customers and the manufacturing representatives how to use the Space Components' products.

It was typical in the industry for a new transistor to be introduced at a very high price, sometimes over $100 per unit. Then, as the yield increased, as production volume increased, and as competitors came out with their own versions of that particular transistor, the prices dropped drastically. A typical example is the price history of a Philco high-performance switching transistor. "Introduced in sample lots at $100 each in 1956, it came on the market in May 1957, at $60. By September of the same year it was down to $19, and in February of 1960 it could be had in lots of 1,000 for $6.75 apiece."[2] In 1959 the average industry price was $2.50 per transistor; in 1960 Space Components' average price was about $22.00 per transistor.

When a new product was introduced, it was typical for sales to follow the pattern below.

The first sales were normally made to laboratories. Then sales would drop off as the electronic engineers of the prospective customers evaluated the new transistor and perhaps designed it into the circuits of new products. Some months later sales would begin to increase as the transistor was used in production models.

The management of Space Components

[2] *L. S. Silk,* The Research Revolution *(New York: McGraw-Hill Book Company, 1960), p. 84.*

Sales

Time

reported that it was much easier to get a transistor designed into a new product than it was to get it designed into an existing product to replace a transistor already being used. They said that design engineers were loath to spend the time and money necessary to evaluate a new transistor and to design it into a circuit if there was an existing transistor already doing the job.

Some of the larger companies in the industry announced new products with full-page advertisements in the various electronics publications. Although Space Components had never advertised in this way, it had gotten considerable publicity for its various new products. Management thought that this was because Space Components' products had been newsworthy, for they were (with the exception of the company's first product) unique developments.

The literature that Space Components had prepared on its products could be left with the design engineers of a prospective customer. This literature contained test data that showed the electrical and mechanical characteristics of the product. In the past, Space Components had prepared a single data sheet (printed on both sides) for each of its products. By contrast, some larger companies provided booklets of test data for design engineers. Tom Jablonski had said that Space Components had always been so short of cash and management time that management did not think the company could afford more elaborate data sheets.

Some competitors provided considerable engineering design assistance to prospective customers. For example, an engineer who was designing a particular part of a control system would specify a transistor from Texas Instruments because he knew that the supplier had already designed a circuit to take advantage of the particular electrical characteristics of that transistor. By specifying "pre-engineered components," circuit engineers could avoid a considerable amount of costly design time. In addition, some of the larger producers of transistors had sales engineers who spent considerable time in the customers' plants working with the customers' design engineers on problems involving the utilization of transistors. Space Components had not been able to provide these services, and, in fact, had not even been able to afford free samples for prospective customers—a common practice in the industry.

ORGANIZATION

In March 1961 the oldest man in the organization was 32. Tom Jablonski and Richard Morton had B.S. degrees in engineering. They said they did not consider their lack of advanced degrees to be a handicap because they believed that it was very difficult for a man in school to gain the specialized knowledge and experience useful in developing and producing transistors. All the members of the executive team had had extensive experience in the transistor industry.

Management emphasized that the organization was very informal and that in a typical day any member of the organization was likely to be concerned with problems in several functional areas. Richard Morton commented that he was rarely able to spend a whole day on development. A problem might arise on the production line that would require his assistance. Then he might be needed in the shipping department and after that to talk to a vendor.

PRODUCT DEVELOPMENT POLICIES

Tom Jablonski said that Space Components could not compete with its larger competitors on the basis of reputation. (Most prospective customers did not even know of this new firm.) He thought that the company did not have the finances and manufacturing sophistication that would permit it to compete on the basis of large-volume, low-cost production of transistors. He also thought that the company could not compete through superior selling because it lacked a strong sales organization and also the money to compete in offering engineering service, elaborate data sheets, and eye-catching advertising.

Therefore, he thought that Space Components had to concentrate on the one thing it could do best—product development. He thought that the company should concentrate on developing radically new products, products that would command a large margin because they were significantly better for certain uses than any other products on the market. Noting the industry pattern in which an innovation was often quickly followed by competitors, he thought that the company should also concentrate on developing products for relatively small specialized markets, markets that would probably not appeal to large companies. Summing it up, he said, "We've got to come up with products that are hard to develop and are intended for relatively small markets."

In March 1961 Space Components offered four lines of transistors to the market, each of which was offered in several different categories—the natural result of the distribution of products resulting from a production run. Three of these product lines were unique. One of the products had been designed into a missile that was being produced in large quantities. Sales of the transistor, intended for use in this particular missile, accounted for 40% of company sales in 1960. Because the prime contractor had ordered these transistors from Space Components on a sporadic basis, management had found it difficult to forecast the company's sales.

Richard Morton, assisted by one technican, did most of the product development work. Tom Jablonski and David Stewart frequently made suggestions and Tom sometimes worked in the lab in the evenings to try out ideas of his own. Management had found that if a transistor could be made in development, then it could usually be made in production, since production was regarded more or less as a glorified development laboratory.

Tom Jablonski maintained that Space Components could usually achieve working models of new transistors in a matter of days or weeks after a project was undertaken. (Nevertheless, delays sometimes did occur because the company did not have machine shop facilities to construct needed components.) In contrast, he knew of one large company that required an average of 8 months to go from idea to first working model. Space Components followed a policy of trying to proceed straight from an idea to a model; the approach was very pragmatic. In large companies the attempts to build models were usually preceded by extensive theoretical studies. He had observed that new transistors built according to the theory rarely worked and usually required a re-examination of the theory and the building of subsequent models.

He said, "The large company usually has a good enough theoretical understanding to explain why their initial models don't work." He added, "We rarely can explain with as much confidence why our models *do* work." Because of Space Components' emphasis on a pragmatic approach and also on investigating concepts at the lowest possible cost, he thought that the company enjoyed a tremendous cost advantage in development when compared with its larger competitors. Space Components' line of symmetrical silicon transistors had been developed at an estimated cost of $30,000 (including Richard Morton's time); management thought this same development job would have cost a large company $250,000.

ORIGIN OF THE IDEA FOR A FIELD-EFFECT TRANSISTOR

In keeping with its policy of trying to develop radical new products for small markets, management was considering, in July 1960, undertaking a project to develop a transistor that would be especially suitable for switching very low-level currents. Management, because of its familiarity with the electronics industry, knew that the transistors then being used for this purpose were not very satisfactory. According to management, this was not a very remarkable discovery and many engineers were well aware that rapid switching of low-level currents presented problems. One use of such switches would be with the radio transmitters carried aboard missiles.

Such transmitters had to send thousands of pieces of information per minute back to the ground. This information came from many different sources on the missile (fuel gages, air speed indicators, etc.), and it was necessary to switch very rapidly so that each source could use the transmitter in turn.

In order for it to be particularly suited to low-level switching, management conceived of trying to develop a transistor with no "offset voltage."[3] The achievement of a transistor with no offset voltage would be a unique development, and one of particular significance for low-level switching purposes. In many cases, it would make possible considerably simpler circuits that would be both cheaper to design and to manufacture.

Management thought it was theoretically possible to develop a transistor with no offset voltage and extremely fast switching characteristics. Richard Morton had some ideas he thought might work and he was eager to try them. Management thought that some of the larger companies had done development work in this area, but had not been successful in overcoming the various technical problems involved. Management believed that from a theoretical point of view the proposed product could most probably be achieved through using alloying techniques and silicon, and management believed that its competence in this particular area of transistor technology was as great as that of any other company in the industry. However, the technical problems seemed formidable, with the transition from theory to practical achievement appearing very uncertain. Even if a crude model of the new transistor could be achieved, the practical problems of improving the various electrical characteristics, of improving the yield, and of working with the very small dimensions involved might well keep the product from ever getting out of the laboratory.

Since management was so familiar with the industry, it had no doubt that a potential market existed for such a product, provided

it could be offered at a reasonable price. The company's previous development experience had been that the manufacturing cost of a new transistor could be brought down drastically if the product could only be achieved in the laboratory; therefore management was not too concerned over the problem of offering the product to the market at a reasonable price. Management anticipated that the potential market for a transistor developed primarily for low-level switching would be about $2 million to $3 million per year. In management's opinion, this would probably be a market large enough to attract some competitors, but still small enough so that it would not seem attractive to many of the large companies in the industry.

Although management was absolutely confident that a market existed for such a transistor, it did not think that this market would automatically develop with the first appearance of the product. Some engineers might already be solving a problem with existing components, albeit in a rather clumsy manner. Even if Space Components were to develop a more suitable product, one aimed specifically at solving certain problems, the engineer might not be willing to invest the time and money necessary to investigate the new transistor and to design it into the circuit.

It would be necessary for Space Components to seek out actively those uses for which the new transistor would be particularly suited. It would be necessary to develop test data illustrating the potential uses of the new product. It might even be necessary to assist in designing certain circuits that could use the new product.

Management made no attempt to estimate the time it would take to develop such a product. Richard Morton anticipated trying various approaches to see if the new transistor could be achieved in the laboratory. If he were not successful, the project could be dropped after a few weeks of work. Management anticipated trying to make the transistor by using the manufacturing techniques with which the company was already familiar. Therefore, management thought

---

[3] *One of the parameters of a transistor that is of particular importance when input voltages are low.*

that no new equipment would have to be bought to develop the product or to produce it if development efforts were successful. The company also had a stock of components on hand which were used in the company's other lines of transistors. Insofar as possible, management planned to use these components in the laboratory work.

Underlying all of these plans was management's feeling that it was absolutely necessary to keep the development cost down in these early stages when the gamble seemed greatest. Management thought that such limitations would not defeat the purpose of the research as, for instance, in not being able to achieve a working transistor solely because of a policy of using existing materials and facilities in development. Management anticipated that the early development would be directed toward only one question, "Is it possible to achieve a working model of the new product?"

Management estimated that the out-of-pocket cost of this early development work would be no more than a few hundred dollars, principally for components that would be needed in attempts to build working models. In addition, the time of Richard Morton and one of the technicians would be invested in the project, although Richard Morton would not be able to drop all of his other responsibilities to concentrate on this project. He would continue to supervise the shipping department, to assist David Stewart on production problems, and, in accordance with the company's very informal organizational structure, to "give a hand" wherever it was needed. These day-to-day matters could not be ignored, and, as had been the case in the past, Richard Morton would probably have only about 10% to 20% of his time free for development. Essentially, management was considering whether or not to invest this "time available for development" in a project to develop a transistor suitable for low-level switching.

Another factor bearing upon management's decision was the company's financial position. In July 1960 Space Components' cash-plus-receivables-less-current-liabilities to-

taled about $8,000. Tom Jablonski commented that Space Components probably had less capital than any other company in the industry. At this time, management did not want to obtain additional funds from outside investors, partly because it might lead to losing control of the company. Management thought it had enough resources to develop and market the new product, particularly since no new production equipment was anticipated. However, as Tom Jablonski said, "We had the usual worry of whether our sales would hold up to support our various expenses." Management was somewhat concerned because 40% of sales were of one product to one customer. Although this fact introduced additional uncertainty in trying to forecast whether the company would be financially able to complete any development project which it had begun, it also introduced an additional incentive to develop new products that would make the company less dependent on this one customer relationship.

Management did realize that the company's limited financial position would preclude extensive investigation of various manufacturing methods for any new product that might be developed. Tom Jablonski said, "We could easily spend $20,000 in developing more sophisticated production techniques for any new product we might develop. We will have to be satisfied with relatively crude methods of production."

Limited financial resources had also meant that the company did not have the extensive test facilities common in many transistor laboratories. However, management thought that various prospective customers and a large technical university in the area would probably let Space Components borrow certain testing equipment for a limited time.

The nature of transistor development was such that an engineer could not always be sure that he would end up with what he started out to develop. For example, a new transistor design intended for certain uses might turn out to have certain electrical characteristics that would make it more suitable for entirely different uses. In some cases the product that was actually developed would be more salable and more profitable to produce than the product originally envisaged; of course, sometimes the reverse would also be true.

Management said that there were no other development projects being considered seriously at this time. Richard Morton had previously done some development work on a product called a "power transistor," which management thought would be a unique product for solving certain problems not then being met by any existing transistors on the market. Just as with the low-level switching transistor, management thought that the power transistor could best be developed by using alloying techniques with silicon and that Space Components' considerable experience in this area of technology gave the company a unique advantage in developing such a product.

Richard Morton had previously achieved some models of a power transistor that "showed life," but the technical problems still remaining seemed formidable. Furthermore, considering the development already done, management thought that a considerable investment would have to be made in additional equipment for development and production before the product could be introduced to the market. Management had not made a careful study of the technical problems remaining and of the potential market existing for a power transistor because the product had not really excited management.

In essence, Richard Morton had done some preliminary development on the power transistor, but there were some important technical problems remaining as well as the need for considerable funds to complete development and to introduce the product to the market. At about this time, management had conceived of the possibility of developing a transistor suitable for low-level switching. A very preliminary consideration of such factors as the technical problems involved, the funds needed for development and production, and the potential market indicated that the development of a transistor for low-level switching looked like a more promising way to invest development time than did the power transistor. Therefore, management decided to investigate this seemingly favorable alternative more thoroughly. Essentially, the decision was made to select an alternative for more thorough investigation.

A POINT OF DECISION

Tom Jablonski, Richard Morton, and David Stewart had made a preliminary decision to investigate the development of a transistor suitable for low-level switching. They had devoted some time exploring the various factors bearing upon this possible application of development time. Having spent some time in evaluating the proposal, they now had to decide whether or not to undertake the project.

The project might result in another "hard to develop product for a small market," just the kind of product management preferred to develop. However, the company's financial resources were small, and the technical uncertainties associated with this project appeared to be great. Management wondered whether or not it was an unnecessary risk of the company's limited resources to *pursue* a project so fraught with uncertainty.

ASSIGNMENT

What should the management of Space Components do? If additional information is desired, indicate how it should be obtained and used.

Space Components, Inc. (B)

INITIAL DEVELOPMENT

In July 1960 Richard Morton started to devote part of his time to trying to develop a transistor suitable for low-level switching. He had been thinking about the technical problems involved for some time. After further thinking, he ordered some special materials and components he thought would be needed to achieve the desired design. About a month passed before the components were delivered. During that time he tried various other approaches to the problem that utilized components already available in the laboratory.

After the needed components arrived, Mr. Morton worked with one technician in making up batches of transistors and then testing them. Each batch of about 10 transistors was varied in some way—materials, geometry, or processing conditions. He had a plan for trying to achieve the new product, but he modified it as testing proceeded. For about 2 weeks every batch was unsuccessful and there was no indication that the product in mind was even feasible. Nevertheless, Mr. Morton had had such extensive experience in the development of transistors that lack of success on initial efforts did not discourage him unduly. He knew that very small details, for example, the temperature of baking, could make a big difference—might even make the difference between whether a batch of transistors showed "signs of life" or not.

Finally, in the third week, the needle on the testing dial began to show the desired movement. In showing "signs of life," it indicated that Richard Morton's approach to the technical problem was probably feasible.

A new kind of transistor had been in-vented, and Richard Morton proceeded to investigate its electrical properties more fully. A very important discovery resulted. Mr. Morton found that the product's electrical characteristics were somewhat different from those that had been anticipated. As intended, the product had no offset voltage, making it uniquely suited for certain uses involving low voltages; in addition, it had certain other electrical characteristics that made it suitable for amplification as well as switching. Further investigation disclosed that the product had the characteristics of a "field-effect transistor."[1]

Management considered this a tremendous discovery. Field-effect transistors had been predicted by leading transistor scientists since the early 1950s, but, despite development efforts (reputed to have cost several million dollars) by several large transistor companies, no practical field-effect transistor had ever been developed. It was management's understanding that some of these other development efforts had resulted in crude laboratory models that worked but that had performance characteristics so poor that the products had not even approached market introduction. The field-effect transistors that had been achieved in the Space Components' laboratory had very poor performance characteristics, and considerable development work would be required before they would be marketable. Insofar as the

[1] *A type of transistor having certain unique electrical characteristics. It has electrical characteristics similar to a vacuum tube, so that it might be directly substituted for vacuum tubes in many circuits. (Other transistors, although often performing the same function as a vacuum tube, differ from the vacuum tube in various electrical characteristics.)*

theory was concerned, however, management thought that Space Components was in an excellent position to overcome the remaining technical problems. Other companies had worked primarily with diffusion techniques and germanium; the management of Space Components felt that, from a theoretical standpoint, the best field-effect transistors could be made by using alloying techniques with silicon.

Further testing of the new product indicated that it was not suited for high-speed switching, the job for which it was originally developed. Richard Morton found that its switching speed was much slower than that originally envisaged, but this finding did not bother management, because the successful development of a field-effect transistor would open much wider markets. In general, management explained that a field-effect transistor would have certain electrical characteristics not possessed by any other transistor and would compete directly for many uses which previously had been the sole domain of the vacuum tube.

Management decided, without hesitation, to proceed to a second stage of development, a stage of perfecting and improving the product. This discovery appeared to be the biggest thing that had ever happened to Space Components, and management was confident that if the performance and yield of the product could be improved, the product could then be marketed profitably.

A consideration of the electrical characteristics found in the first working models of the field-effect transistor led management to a decision to develop the product primarily for use as an amplifier rather than as a switch. Management thought the price per unit for amplifiers would be considerably greater than for switches. The technical problems were such that management thought the cost and time of development would be about the same regardless of whether amplifying or switching characteristics were emphasized. In addition, management thought that the market for a field-effect transistor would be considerably larger if the product were developed to give good amplifying characteristics.

As Richard Morton made successive batches of the new transistor, the electrical characteristics showed steady improvement. Originally, the transconductance (which is related to amplifying power) was only 25, compared to 1,000 for an equivalent vacuum tube. Gradually this was improved to about 100. Many of the other electrical characteristics were improved simultaneously.

During the fall of 1960 management made a decision on the product goals required before the product would be introduced to the market. It was decided to try for a transconductance of 500, about one-half the transconductance of an equivalent vacuum tube. Management thought that this would provide performance sufficiently high so that the new product would attract favorable attention. Management also believed that a "sufficiently" large market would await such a product. Basing their opinions upon the technical performance to date, Mr. Jablonski and Mr. Morton believed that this was a realizable goal. If, however, after several more months of development, they found themselves against a stone wall, they thought they would probably introduce it at a lower transconductance, whatever that might be. This decision would not be made for several months and would depend, to a considerable extent, on the opinions of prospective customers.

Contrary to expectations, Richard Morton found it necessary to secure certain additional equipment to aid in the production of sample field-effect transistors. The cost of this equipment was only several hundred dollars, and, for the most part, he found it possible to use existing equipment and production methods. One excursion from this policy of using existing production techniques occurred when Richard Morton made some sample field-effect transistors using the diffusion method. (The diffusion method was used by most companies in the industry. Space Components' experience was with the alloying method.) After only a few days of making and testing such samples, he decided to concentrate on alloying techniques in making field-effect transistors. He had known that Space Components lacked sophistication in using diffusion techniques. He had found that field-effect transistors made by diffusion techniques raised certain technical ·problems (in regard to the performance of the product) that appeared to be more serious than those encountered when the product was made by alloying. .

About this time Space Components began to familiarize some of its sales representatives with the new product. These sales representatives, as well as Space Components personnel, began to mention to prospective customers that the company was developing a field-effect transistor. Subsequently, a number of electronics companies ordered samples from Space Components to test in their laboratories.

Space Components had set a price of $30 each on these samples and had also mimeographed a very simple "lab bulletin," giving some of the electrical characteristics of the product. The fact that Space Components claimed to have developed a field-effect transistor created a great deal of interest, and as a result a number of laboratories ordered samples in order to keep informed on this latest technical development. During the fall of 1960 and the first 2 months of 1961 Space Components sold about 200 samples of the field-effect transistor at $30 each.

Management said that these samples were sold to prospective customers at that time for two reasons. The first and most important reason was that management wanted the opinion of other engineers. As Tom Jablonski said, "After all, we may have been kidding ourselves." Management wanted the engineers of prospective customers to test the new product, to play with it, to see what it would do. Neither Space Components nor any other company was really familiar with the field-effect transistor, and, in fact, the management of Space Components was not even certain what electrical characteristics should be measured and improved. The company wanted the opinions of experienced electronic circuit engineers on how good the field-effect transistor really was; the company also wanted to know how much the product would have to be improved in order to meet the needs of prospective customers.

Space Components' second reason for sending out samples at this time was that the company wanted to develop market contacts and to begin to familiarize circuit engineers with the new product. Thus, when the new product was finally improved to the point where it could be introduced to the market, management hoped there would be less delay before customers started ordering the product.

Management admitted that placing samples in the field was a form of "tipping their hand" to competitors. In particular, management thought that competitors might hasten their own projects to develop a field-effect transistor if they knew that working models had already been developed by Space Components. The management of Space Components did not feel that these samples would aid others in solving technical problems even if they fell into competitors' hands. This was because the specific know-how involved in producing the new product was not obvious from examining a sample.

Although the transconductance had been brought up to about 100, further improvement proved elusive. In further efforts to improve the performance, a number of technical changes were tried, none of which was very successful.

Meanwhile, some of the companies that had bought samples for testing began to comment on the new product. One very large company indicated that it considered these field-effect transistors, even at existing performance levels, to be very suitable for certain uses—better than anything previously available. These favorable comments caused management to decide to introduce the product to the market even if a transconductance of 500 could not be achieved within the next few months.

It was in this context that in December 1960 Richard Morton achieved what was virtually a "breakthrough" in the design of the field-effect transistor. It involved a change in the geometry of the transistor, so that one layer of the "sandwich" was shaped like a ring. This small change resulted in a surprising improvement in the transconductance; many of the transistors made in this way had a transconductance of 500, and some had a transconductance of 1,000.

Management had previously been concerned over the "noise"[2] of the field-effect transistor, and, in fact, one prospective customer had tried to persuade Space Components to concentrate development effort on decreasing that noise. The design change that produced the remarkable improvement in transconductance also drastically reduced the noise. Tests on the new field-effect transistors indicated that the transistors produced less noise than any other transistors on the market.

Management later said that at this time, after the remarkable improvement in product performance had been achieved, it was confident that it had a highly successful product.

The major focus of development efforts now shifted to increasing the yield of prime-quality field-effect transistors. Mr. Morton approached this problem by trying variations in the materials, the geometry of the product, and the processing conditions. By January he had improved the yield to about 10% on some days, although on other days the yield remained much lower.

In regard to performance characteristics, Richard Morton was devoting a portion of his development time to one parameter—the frequency of the signals that could be handled. The field-effect transistor, as it then existed, was limited to rather low frequencies, principally below 5 megacycles. In management's opinion, applications at these lower frequencies represented but a fraction of the potential market for the new product. Theoretically, the dimensions of the aluminum ring that made up one layer of the transistor sandwich were of critical importance. Mr. Morton tried to obtain smaller rings than those he had been using, believing that this change would give the product a capability in the higher frequencies as well as in the lower frequencies where it now operated. The extremely tight tolerances of the desired component, however, made it

difficult to obtain samples for testing. One supplier who had promised delivery of a small number of the needed rings within a few weeks finally, after several additional weeks of delay, admitted that he could not produce the needed rings.

Management continued to contact various suppliers in an effort to obtain aluminum rings of the desired dimensions in a quantity sufficient for testing. Management said that if Space Components had had the necessary machine tools, the company itself would have tried to make up some samples, but since the company lacked these facilities, it continued to try to find a supplier. The company had great confidence that this change in the product's dimensions would bring about the desired improvement in frequency capabilities; it was also confident that eventually it could find a supplier to make the desired parts.

In January 1961 Mr. Morton was concentrating his efforts on trying to increase the yield of the field-effect transistor; he was also spending some of his time on trying to increase the frequency capabilities of the product. At this time the management team considered whether or not the new product should be transferred to production so that David Stewart might begin trying to increase the yield on the production floor.

Mr. Morton favored leaving the product in development longer. He thought they didn't know enough about how to produce the field-effect transistor and that additional development time might result in marked increases in yield. He also favored waiting until he had had a shot at solving the frequency problem. He pointed out that it was important for Space Components to introduce a product of high quality, one that would command the respect of the scientific community and one that could be produced at a yield sufficiently high so that the product would not be unrealistically priced. He emphasized that Space Components should not do anything to damage the reputation of this product, which was so new that most engineers had not yet even formed an opinion of it.

[2] *Extraneous signal introduced by the device.*

In regard to the fact that the field-effect transistor was now limited to low-frequency applications, Tom Jablonski and David Stewart thought that this might be a blessing in disguise. They thought that the field-effect transistor represented such a significant technical advance that it would probably be designed into some circuits in a fairly short time. They knew that Space Components' resources were limited; the company was then producing only a few hundred transistors of all kinds each day. Management was somewhat concerned over what to do if a large customer ordered 1,000 field-effect transistors per month. Considering the nature of the product, they thought this was entirely possible. Of course, since there was usually a delay of several months to a year from the time a transistor was purchased for laboratory testing until it was purchased for production, they anticipated that they would have some advance warning that would permit them to build up their production organization. Tom Jablonski was confident that Space Components had the nucleus of an organization that could be expanded, with each man carrying considerably more responsibility than at present. "Yet," he said, "we're not really business men. We're not even sure what problems we'll encounter if we find ourselves managing a much larger organization in only a few months."

This concern over whether or not the company might grow too fast was one reason why Tom Jablonski did not mind that the initial models of the field-effect transistor would be suitable only for low-frequency applications. This represented just a small share of the market that would exist for a transistor with broader frequency capabilities.

He thought that this smaller share of the market could supply enough orders to keep Space Components busy initially. Later, after Richard Morton had solved the frequency problem, the field-effect transistor could be modified to handle higher frequencies.

In regard to increasing the yield, management anticipated that the yield would drop when the product was first transferred to production. It was always that way while the girls were learning how to make a new product. Past experience showed that there would be a succession of minor changes in the production process that would then result in a steady increase in yield.

It was possible that certain rather basic changes in the product or in the production method (e.g., different kinds of silicon, etc.) would bring about much higher yields than were possible with the present product configuration and production methods. These improvements were more likely to result from the development performed by Richard Morton than from the more minor modifications tried by David Stewart.

Management did not anticipate purchasing any additional production equipment to produce the new transistor. It had been designed with the company's existing production methods in mind, a natural occurrence since Richard Morton had formerly supervised production himself. Furthermore, if the product were now turned over to production, there would be no investment in this particular product configuration that would commit the company to the present design (no production tooling, no extensive employee training, etc.).

The timing of market introduction was an important consideration in this decision. Management said that its biggest concern at this time was that some competitor might introduce a field-effect transistor to the market before them. Space Components did. Management knew that at least one large competitor had achieved field-effect transistors in the laboratory, for management had been told that when this same company learned of Space Components' success, it had put its project on a crash basis. One prospective customer who had tested samples of field-effect transistors produced in the laboratories of both Space Components and this competitor indicated that the Space Components' product was far superior; the transconductance of the models produced by the competitor was almost as low as the units that Space Components was rejecting because of inadequate performance.

This competitor was apparently trying to produce the field-effect transistor by using the diffusion method. The management of Space Components believed that even if this competitor were able to make rapid progress in improving its field-effect transistor, the product would still have characteristics different from the Space Components product because of having been produced by a different method. In regard to some parameters, although Richard Morton thought that the competitive field-effect transistor might have certain performance advantages, he thought that the Space Components product, because of the method by which it was manufactured, would have advantages in regard to other parameters.

There were various reasons why management hoped that Space Components would be the first company to introduce a field-effect transistor. One was publicity. The pioneer would receive a great deal of free publicity, both through industry trade publications and at industry conventions. Many companies that had never heard of this tiny company might remember it as the company that had been first to develop a field-effect transistor. The publicity would be valuable in introducing the new product, particularly since management thought that the company could not afford to do much advertising. In addition, the publicity might aid the other products in the company's line.

The company that would be first to introduce the new product would probably also have advantages in getting it designed into the circuits of the products of prospective customers. According to Mr. Jablonski, engineers in almost all companies in the industry were interested in obtaining samples of new components because it permitted them to be knowledgeable on what was new in the industry. The first producer to introduce a new component to the market had the advantage of getting the electronic engineers in various companies to spend their time in evaluating this component and designing it into their circuits. If another company then introduced a similar component to the market, these same engineers were loath to spend time and money in

evaluating it since the component which they had already evaluated might be solving their problems. The company that had first introduced the product to the market would try to bring its prices down and provide good service in order to minimize the incentive of the engineers to investigate the components of other suppliers.

Management, however, realized that the companies that were first in development did not always have the market to themselves. One of the most successful companies in the industry had a reputation for almost never being first with a new product but of then doing a good job in producing transistors at a low cost.

Management also thought that the limited financial resources of the company constituted a strong incentive to begin selling the product as soon as possible. Samples had been sold to various laboratories for testing, resulting in about $6,000 in additional revenue. The company's cash balance was only a few thousand dollars, and management indicated that it would feel much more secure if this balance could be built up through immediate sales of the field-effect transistor.

Closely associated with whether or not to transfer the field-effect transistor to production at this time was a related decision concerning the amount of test data to be gathered on the new product. The company now had a limited amount of test data on the performance and reliability of the field-effect transistor; this information had been mimeographed and sent out to prospective customers who had purchased samples of the product the previous fall. The product had been improved considerably since that time and the earlier data sheets did not indicate the extent of the present product's performance advantages. Management could transfer the field-effect transistor to production and announce it immediately to the market. Another alternative would be to spend from 1 month to 6 weeks in gathering detailed performance data on the new product; this information could then be incorporated into a sales booklet on the field-effect transistor, similar to the booklets issued by some of the larger companies in the industry. This information could be gathered during February, regardless of whether or not management decided to transfer the product to production at the end of January.

While management was considering this additional decision on gathering test data on the new product, it expressed the greatest concern over its effect on the timing of market introduction. It would be tragic if market introduction were delayed for 6 weeks in order to permit additional testing, only to find that a competitor introduced a version of the field-effect transistor during the same time period.

If the decision were made to get additional test data, someone in the organization would have to be freed from other duties during that period in order to conduct the testing. This job would require considerable skill, and the only man in the organization who was qualified and who could be freed was the company president, Tom Jablonski. Mr. Jablonski said he would be willing to do this, even if it meant that he would have to work longer hours and slight the job of president a while.

There was also the possibility of adding another man to the organization who would be qualified to perform the testing. Management knew of a young man who was working for a large transistor company in the area, primarily in the testing and quality control area. Management thought that he could be induced to join Space Components. If he could, he could immediately apply his experience to testing the new field-effect transistor. For some time management had felt the need to add a man to the organization who would be responsible for testing and quality control, but management hesitated to add to the company's fixed costs. As Tom Jablonski said, "The larger your organization becomes, the more imperative it becomes to get additional orders." Management was not sure that it relished acquiring these pressures to obtain additional business.

In considering whether or not to undertake additional testing of the field-effect transistor at this time, management placed particular weight on the general impression

that it anticipated the publication of extensive test data would make. As one executive said, "Many companies in this industry make sweeping claims that do not hold up. If we introduce a field-effect transistor that is backed up by extensive test data, the circuit engineers are going to have more respect for our claims. We can't afford to give away free samples of the product, but we can give away data sheets that will provide substantial support for our claims." In addition, detailed test information might stimulate circuit engineers to find applications for the new product which would otherwise be overlooked.

Against this argument management considered the effect of timing and the possibility that a competitor would beat Space Components to the market while testing was being conducted. There was also the matter of cost; the added testing would take about 4 to 6 man-weeks in addition to several thousand dollars for the cost of printing the data sheets.

Space Components had done all right in the past without furnishing elaborate data sheets; prospective customers that were interested in particular parameters of Space Components' products had performed the necessary testing themselves. With an exciting new product such as the field-effect transistor, management thought prospective customers might be very willing to do their own testing.

A POINT OF DECISION

In January 1961 the field-effect transistor had been developed to the point at which management was considering introducing the product to the market. Although it was limited at this time to low frequency applications, the product appeared to have excited considerable interest on the part of prospective customers. Management realized that the production yield was still very low and that the company lacked extensive test data on the product's performance. Management was considering three alternatives:

1. Keep the product in development until the yield could be significantly in-

creased, meanwhile working on the problem of operation at higher frequencies.

2. Transfer the new product to production. While David Stewart was working to improve the yield, gather the desired test data. Withhold announcement of the product until this information was assembled to provide support for the claims for the product.

3. Transfer the new product to production, perhaps continuing development efforts to improve the performance at high frequencies. Immediately introduce the product to the market without gathering further test data at this time.

A critical factor bearing upon the decision was whether or not a competitor was likely to introduce a field-effect transistor in the near future. Management thought that no company was ready to do so but admitted that it could not be sure.

ASSIGNMENT

Develop recommendations for the management of Space Components.

Space Components, Inc. (C)

FURTHER DEVELOPMENT

David Stewart immediately began to produce the field-effect transistor. As expected, the yield on the new product was initially much lower in the production department than it had been in development. Then, as the production department gained experience in producing the field-effect transistor and as various improvements in the manufacturing methods were worked out, the yield climbed. By mid-March the yield had reached 10% to 12%, with indications that further increases would probably be possible. Existing production equipment and techniques were being used although management realized that exploration of other production methods might make even higher yields possible.

In making changes in the production method or in the configuration of the product, David Stewart worked closely with Richard Morton and Tom Jablonski. Usually, they discussed proposed changes, and, since

all three were intimately familiar with the production process, useful ideas might come from any of them. If a particular change were not successful, they accepted it as part of the development process and tried something else.

Meanwhile, the new man in charge of testing was gathering test information on the various parameters of the new product. He conducted these tests on equipment owned by several organizations, including (1) a nearby engineering school, (2) the electronics company that owned a part interest in Space Components, and (3) another electronics company that was very interested in utilizing the field-effect transistor in certain of its circuits. This test equipment was valued at several thousand dollars and was kept in the buildings of the owners where he went in order to conduct the tests. Space Components made no payment for the use of the equipment provided by the various organizations because of these organizations' interest in the test data being generated. Some of the parameters were measured at the suggestion of prospective customers who had been testing samples of the product for several months. Other parameters were chosen because management knew that these were characteristics that normally interested design engineers.

Test data were gathered by the end of February. An eight-page pamphlet, more elaborate than Space Components had used for any product previously introduced by the company, was printed. Management chose this more elaborate method of presenting the data because management thought that this was a product so spectacular that it deserved full and professional presentation.

Additional testing of the product developed data that brought out performance characteristics of the new product that were not fully evident before. The field-effect transistor appeared to be ten times more resistant to radiation than any other transistor. It also appeared to have lower noise than any vacuum tube or transistor ever offered to the market before. These performance advantages were "bonuses" because development had not been directed toward achieving these characteristics.

Management's fear of what competitors might do proved groundless during this period. As of mid-March no competitor had introduced a field-effect transistor to the market. Although management knew that one large company was placing great emphasis on trying to rush the development of a field-effect transistor, management was not too concerned, because it had seen samples of this competitor's field-effect transistor and these samples appeared to be about the same quality as the transistors that Space Components was rejecting because of poor quality. In addition, the competitor was using a diffusion method of production that gave the product certain characteristics different from the Space Components alloyed transistor.

Management now estimated the immediate market for a field-effect transistor at $10 million with the expectation that the market would be expanded considerably as the product was improved, as the manufacturing cost was brought down, and as various engineers in the industry searched for applications for the new component. Management anticipated that other companies would follow Space Components into this large and growing market, particularly since Space Components had demonstrated that a field-effect transistor was technically feasible. Some of these future competitors were large companies that had the resources and experience to drive the manufacturing cost down. The management of Space Components looked with some trepidation upon the prospects of such future competition.

In March 1961 the sales literature was ready and distributed to the company's 20 sales representatives. Several industry trade publications indicated interest in publicizing the new product and the company. In addition, management prepared to introduce the product at the annual Institute of Radio Engineers Convention to be held in New York City in late March 1961.

Initial reaction to the new product exceeded expectations. Salesmen rapidly exhausted their supplies of the sales booklets and contacted the company to obtain more. Orders for samples quickly depleted the company's inventory of about 400 field-effect transistors (built up through the production of the first few weeks). An article describing the field-effect transistor appeared in one leading electronics publication and broke all records for number of inquiries received in regard to an article.

Space Components was quoting prices of $72 to $30 per unit, depending on the volume purchased and on the quality classification of the unit. Some prospective customers asked whether or not Space Components planned future price decreases. Management replied that there could be no promises, but that there had always been price decreases on new products in the past. Several prospective customers indicated no concern over the price but were primarily skeptical of whether or not the field-effect transistor could actually perform in the way the test data indicated.

Although initial orders had depleted the inventory, management expected to be able to meet future orders without undue delay. Yield was steadily increasing and management expected sales to drop off after the initial sales to laboratories had been completed. If it seemed likely that substantial orders for production would result, management anticipated that the present Space Components production organization could easily be expanded severalfold.

In thinking back over the project, management was very pleased for it appeared that a calculated risk had paid off. Management's major concern was over the effects of competition when competitors came out with their versions of a field-effect transistor. The company's past experience had been almost entirely in producing and selling products that no one else produced. The field-effect transistor, however, was something big enough to attract the largest companies in the industry. Management feared that Space

Components was doomed to be driven from the market by these larger competitors after only a few months or years of enjoying the fruits of being the first to develop the new product. The company wondered whether or not the successful development of the field-effect transistor might well change the basic nature of the company, orienting it more toward manufacturing and selling and less toward development. If this were to be the future nature of the company, management wondered what steps should be taken now in order to prepare the company for future competition in a mature market against seasoned competitors.

ASSIGNMENT

Evaluate the sequence of decisions leading to the field-effect transistor. Develop a program for exploiting the product, including contingency plans for dealing with the entry of major competitors.

7

Organizational Management and Control

No matter how skilled the founder, the firm's potential will be determined by the quality of the people who subsequently join the company and whether or not their efforts can be effectively organized and controlled. When the organization is very small, these problems are among the least of the founder's concerns, but with growth the founder must give careful attention to how to structure and control the organization.

In many respects, these issues are more complex in large companies in which there are multiple organizational levels, broad and sometimes diverse product lines, and geographic separation of operations. The growing small firm, however, also faces difficult problems that are often not foreseen by the founder. This chapter focuses on some of these, including the changing role of the founder, problems of delegation, and the establishment of more formal methods of transferring information and controlling operations.

GROWTH STAGES

Companies usually go through identifiable stages as they grow. They encounter change along dimensions other than simply sales and profits. The stages do not automatically occur at a given size but depend on the complexity of the business, the kinds of people in the organization, and the management style of the founder. Some typical growth stage characteristics are the following:

1. Direct Founder Operation. At inception the president (and other co-founders) may be personally involved in every activity, including producing the product, purchasing, keeping records, recruiting, training and supervising personnel, selling, and sweeping the floor. He performs service calls, raises money, injects cash from personal bank accounts into the operation, negotiates legal arrangements, and plays a prominent role in development and modification of the company's product and/or service.

2. Early Growth. As the first half dozen or so employees are added, it becomes impossible for the founder to handle everything personally. Delegation becomes necessary—to the bookkeeper for preparing statements, to someone in the shop for keeping track of the work of different individuals, to some other person or representative for contacting customers and taking sales orders, to someone else for keeping track of inventory and contacting suppliers to replenish stocks, and so forth. As more people "get into the act," problems arise, for example, tasks are not done as the president would do them, people do not arrive on time or do not complete work accurately and on schedule, and possibly there is a shortage of money to finance inventory and receivables. Customer complaints that top management did not anticipate begin to arise and demand attention.

3. One-Layer Middle Management. Subsequently, it becomes necessary not only to delegate tasks but also to delegate tasks through others. A middle layer of intermediate managers is established. To an increasing degree this involves delegation of operating decisions. The introduction of this layer separates the founder from direct contact with the first level of activity—be it production, or sales, or engineering. When this first layer is introduced, the chief executive must use different methods from those he used in the early growth stage. To avoid undermining authority of the intermediate manager, the chief executive must stop "meddling" directly in some of the company's activities and must begin to work "through channels." The organization becomes more formal.

4. Multilayered Management. When the number of middle managers in a company reaches the point at which the chief executive cannot attend to them all personally, a second layer of management, typically in the form of a general manager and/or executive vice president, is needed. Other officers, possibly including a treasurer and a vice president of marketing, may also occupy this management level. The president works directly with these people rather than meeting formally with first-line supervisors. Advantages of this inescapable detachment are that the president can devote more time to long-range planning and to dealing with vital outside connections, for example, sources of capital. Disadvantages are that it becomes easier for the chief executive to lose touch with vital events on the line, for distortive politics and waste to enter the company, and for the leader's impact on operations to be dissipated through intermediate managerial layers before it reaches the line. These advantages and disadvantages grow in strength as the number of people in the intermediate layers increases.

Somewhere along the growth spectrum the company changes from small to medium-sized and then to large. It may evolve from one to several plants, from single to diverse product lines, from one to several divisions, and from national to multinational sales. The later stages of growth are beyond the scope of this book, but important changes in the key functions of the executive can be traced through all stages.

INCREASED SPECIALIZATION

In the early stages of a new firm most of the small work force is able to perform many functions. Someone from the production line answers the phone or walks to the front of the shop to serve as receptionist when no one else is there to do it.

The bookkeeper may walk back to the shop to help unload a supplier's truck or to pack some goods for shipment. The president may, in the same day, work on engineering design, help make some of the parts, go out and call on a potential customer, and then help straighten up the shop at quitting time before settling down to some financial analysis.

As the organization grows, however, shifting and interchanging of roles must diminish if confusion is to be avoided. Individuals in the company must become more specialized. The process may be accelerated by the formation of a union, which may prohibit engineers from doing carpentry and carpenters from helping with plumbing work.

ROLES OF THE FOUNDER

The stages of growth described above have important implications for the founder. These influence the nature of the nonmanagerial contributions of the founder and the way he spends his time. In the beginning, most of the time is involved in "doing," with little time for managerial activities. If the founder is not extremely good in the critical activities that determine the company's competitive strength, he may never confront the problems of growth. Thus, the new retail business may grow primarily because of the skills of the founder in purchasing and personal selling, with most of the time being devoted to these activities.

With growth, the sheer volume of activities compels the founder to turn some duties over to others. There is, however, the question of which duties to delegate and which duties to retain. Typically, growth brings a substantial change in the role of the founder, with "doing" activities largely delegated and the job becoming more and more managerial in character.

Sometimes this shifting role permits the founder to concentrate on the managerial activities in which he or she gets the greatest satisfaction and can make the largest contribution.

However, when the founder has been uniquely good at a critical task, for example, product development or selling, the transition can be difficult. The business may suffer in two ways. First, the unparalleled skills of the founder may be replaced by only average skills in the hired engineers or salesmen. Second, the founder who was unusually good in product development may be only an amateur manager who lacks skill or even relish for the difficult tasks of managing a growing organization.

A particular difficulty in both stable and growing small firms is what could be termed "unbalanced management." In terms of managerial skills, the management may be good in some areas, for example, in marketing, but abysmally weak in other areas, for example, in accounting and finance. Growth can make these problems either more or less severe. If the founder recognizes his deficiencies and hires people to add support in activities where he is weak, the company can be strengthened. Unfortunately, founders sometimes either do not recognize their own weaknesses or shrink from adding competent people.

DELEGATION

Some founders find delegation extremely difficult, and they postpone it as long as possible. Some entrepreneurs appear to delegate, but do so more in form than in substance, for they constantly "look over the shoulders" of their subordinates. Symptoms of failure to delegate include an overworked and harassed president, as well as slow and faulty decision making because subordinates compete to get some of the president's time.

A number of factors may impede delegation. Early employees may have been hired for their technical skills rather than for their managerial potential. Measures of performance and the reward system may be so fuzzy that there is no incentive for employees to "stick their necks out" and accept increased responsibility.

Many founders have characteristics that make it difficult for them to allow others to make decisions and to occupy key positions. They may have started their firms, in part, because of a desire to receive direct feedback on the results of their personal efforts and to lessen their reliance on others. Because of all the time and money they have invested, they think of the business as their "baby," and they hesitate to allow others to make mistakes that might harm it. In their struggle to succeed, they may have developed so much confidence in their own abilities that it is only "their ideas" or "their way of doing things" that seem right.

Less frequently, the founder may delegate too much too soon and then essentially withdraw from the business to engage in civic activities or golf.

What is required is careful thinking about where the president can contribute most effectively. This should be coupled with a plan to hire or develop capable subordinates. As will be discussed below, more formal methods to keep management informed and the development of carefully considered policies make meaningful delegation feasible in the growing organization.

CONTROL

Growth increases the number of employees, the number of managers, and eventually the number of levels of management. First top management and then succeeding layers of middle management must deal with subordinates through other people. This requires the development of skills different from those used in dealing directly. Some small company managers fail to adapt to the change, and either they cause substantial problems for their companies and/or they have to be replaced as their companies grow.

One of the distinguishing characteristics of the very small firm is the president's direct contact with employees, with products, and customers. Knowledge of production problems, of customers' complaints and satisfactions, and of the status of new products is not based upon reading reports, but rather upon first-hand experience and direct involvement. The development of a level of middle managers separates the president from this first-hand experience. Thus, in a growing organization, the president may say, "I used to know every employee and every customer, but I don't any more." Needed information flows haphazardly and may be impressionistic and unreliable. The president may thus "lose touch," with the result that cost control, quality, delivery, and customer satisfaction may suffer.

The growing small company must institute more formal ways to keep management informed. Better accounting systems, budgets, regular reports, and scheduled meetings to discuss plans and problems are usually required. Management, however, must develop skill in using these methods of keeping informed. This can be difficult for the entrepreneur who lacks experience in interpreting written material and who is most comfortable in developing a "feel" through first-hand experience.

In order to interpret the information received and to direct the efforts of subordinates, standards must be developed. Thus, cost accounting variances for waste may replace the old method of visually noting the scrap level in a trash container. Sales goals may be developed to replace an intuitive reliance upon the judgment and effort of the salesmen involved. More formal standards and more explicit measures of performance can aid coordination, add to a sense of fairness, and permit better monitoring of progress.

The very small firm has great flexibility, for instance, in meeting the special requests of customers or of employees. As both the volume of decisions and the number of decision-makers increase, policies must be developed to ensure coordination and increase efficiency. These can be thought of as contingent decisions. For instance, if an employee has worked for the company for 2 years, he or she is entitled to 2 weeks of paid vacation.

One part of the growing process that is especially difficult for some company founders is the need for increased formality. Entrepreneurs often leave larger companies and start their own because they wish to escape from what they regard as the stultifying effects of written job descriptions, communication through memoranda, organization charts, and rigid performance goals. The idea of reintroducing these ingredients as their companies grow is therefore repulsive. Furthermore, if the company has achieved growth and some success, there may be resistance to breaking up a successful pattern. The president and other members of the management group may find it difficult to operate in a more formal environment, and, therefore, change may be postponed as long as possible. The firm, however, can make the error of introducing excessive formality too early, for formality can add to costs and stifle the flexibility and entrepreneurial spirit that may have been one of the key strengths of the growing firm.

Moves toward increased systematization and formality do not occur at a single point in the firm's development, nor should they. Some of the governing factors include the following:

1. The style of managing can vary widely, with some managers being much more comfortable with formal information systems, performance standards, and written policies.

2. Management succession can bring into the organization executives who lack the experience of having grown up with the business. They typically feel a need for more formal methods of control.

3. The nature of the business may determine the extent to which tight control versus flexibility and creativity should be emphasized. For instance, a wholesaling business, competing on the basis of low costs and dependable service, may require more formal controls than a management consulting firm would.

4. The president may be intimately involved in some aspects of the business, but he may be separated from others by several layers of management. Thus, in a company in which most of the sales go to a few major customers, the president may handle most of the customer contact and the negotiations personally. At the same time, manufacturing may involve several layers of management, with substantial emphasis on formal systems.

EXTERNAL ASSISTANCE

The managers of small companies are often good, even exceptional, at some activities, but they are exceptionally weak at others. Because the small firm, particularly in its earlier stages, cannot support a wide range of specialists, the firm reflects, to a marked degree, the strengths and weaknesses of a few managers.

The small firm is also characterized by having relatively few managers to review and re-examine proposals. For instance, the president of one small firm, who had previously been an executive at General Electric, commented, "Here, I don't have any peers or superiors with whom to discuss plans. My subordinates are available, but I spend much of my time teaching them, and I don't feel that they're experienced enough yet to give me the advice I need."

Small companies can supplement their internal management from several outside sources. Professional advisors, for example, accountants, lawyers, bankers, and consultants, can, if carefully chosen and worked with closely, provide many of the advantages of in-house specialists.

A particularly important group to the aspiring small company can be its board of directors. Possible members include other entrepreneurs, consultants, executives of larger companies, and sometimes retired executives who have special expertise and connections that may be useful to the growing firm. Care must be taken to choose people who can contribute the needed skills or perspectives that the company lacks internally. They should be sufficiently interested in the company to make the effort to understand it well and to think carefully about its needs, problems, and opportunities. The president should be able to relate well to each member and have confidence in his judgment. Directors who are interested only for prestige reasons should not be chosen. Company employees, except for the president and perhaps one other officer, are usually not good candidates because their input is available to the president already.

Capable board members whose judgment is respected by the president can help to maintain objectivity. This can be especially difficult to maintain in a company that is prospering and growing because people will be impressed with such performance and tend to lionize the top executives. "Everybody begins telling you how great you are," recalled one entrepreneur whose company went from a rapid rise into a quick decline and receivership, "and it's very easy to start believing them unless someone, like your wife and a solid board of directors, helps keep your head down to size." What is needed is a group that will take a detached and yet informed, competent, and interested view of the company and present it objectively to the president.

Hampfel-McFarland Company

The Hampfel-McFarland Company was founded in Grand Rapids, Michigan in 1933 by George Hampfel and Joseph McFarland. Both were sheet metal workers who had been laid off during the Depression; they formed the new company so that they might bid directly on jobs that involved the repair or replacement of the sheet metal ducts and piping that were used for fume or dust control in industrial plants. Grand Rapids at this time was the center of the furniture industry within the United States. Production of furniture requires various cutting, shaping, sanding, and finishing operations; these operations create dust and exhaust fumes that must be removed from the plant both for worker health and to prevent the possibility of explosion and fire. (Fine sawdust particles suspended in the air can explode, particularly when mixed with the alcohol and lacquer vapors from the finishing operations.) The company specialized in the manufacture and installation of components for the dust and fume control systems needed by the furniture industry and was quickly successful through offering day-and-night repair service at reasonable charges.

> Since there were two of us in the company, one of us could work during the day making the parts and the other could work at night putting them up. The furniture companies liked that service since it meant that they could get their machines back in production quickly and save some money. During the Depression it was important to save some money for your customers. (Statement of George Hampfel.)

By 1938 the two partners had been so successful that they were asked by a local bank to purchase the assets of their previous employer at a bankruptcy sale; as part of this arrangement, which enabled the bank to close out a loan which was totally in default, the two partners were granted additional working capital. With the new machinery, the larger building, and the expanded financing, they were able to start to sell complete new emission control systems; as the long depression of the 1930s came gradually to an end, the new installation service, as opposed to the previous replacement and repair, came to be the major portion of their business.

Over the next 35 years, from 1940 to 1975, the changing industrial base of the region, coupled with the increased prosperity of the country and the growing concern over working conditions and environmental pollution, led to a continual expansion in the breadth of the company's product line and the dollar volume of the company's sales. By 1975 the company produced and installed emission control systems for the metal casting, metal plating, wood working, electronics manufacturing, and spray painting industries. Major applications included smoke control from industrial furnaces and ovens, fume ventilation from spraying and plating operations, dust collection from cutting, buffing, and sanding machines, and pollution abatement from cement plants, iron foundries, and steam boilers. The company operated throughout southern Michigan, northern Indiana and Illinois, and eastern Wisconsin, and the company sales approached $6,000,000 annually.

Company profits, however, had not kept pace with the increase in sales revenues. Mr. Hampfel felt that this was at least partially because his partner, Mr. McFarland, had retired from the day-to-day marketing, production, and installation functions of the firm and was in complete control of the financial records. Mr. McFarland, who had taken a few evening courses in accounting during the 1950s in an effort to improve the cost control and financial forecasting performance of the firm, had gradually become increasingly concerned with the details of bookkeeping and journal entry. By 1970 he had hired five bookkeepers and three secretaries who were segregated in a second-floor office at the main plant and who kept very meticulous records of the company's revenues and expenses. At the conclusion of each fiscal year, on December 31, Mr. McFarland would send to his partner a written slip of paper with an estimate of the annual profit or loss; approximately 3 months later, at the conclusion of the yearly audit, Mr. McFarland would meet his partner in the office of the bank that had provided the original financing for the firm, confirm his earlier estimate of the financial results (profit or loss) for the prior year, announce the line of credit (maximum amount of short-term loans) desired by the company for the coming year, ask if there were any questions, and return to his office. No other financial reports, either written or verbal, were distributed during the year.

> I didn't want to fight with him (Mr. McFarland) because of the old days. Many a time, he and I worked right straight through the night to finish a job and keep a customer happy. He was a very skilled worker, a very hard worker, and a daredevil. In the old days we didn't have much safety equipment, and it was dangerous to climb 50 ft or 60 ft high on an iron smelter cupolo to put in a new section of blower pipe. But he was always the one to say, "Let me do it." I'm not going to be the one now to tell him that he can't do the accounting. (Statement of George Hampfel.)

In the middle of June 1975, Mr. McFarland died suddenly of a heart attack. Mr. Hampfel immediately asked his son, George Hampfel, Jr., who was a recent graduate of the M.B.A. program at The University of Michigan and an employee of a major ac-

counting firm in Chicago, to come back to Grand Rapids and assume the position of treasurer. The older Mr. Hampfel told his son that he had concluded an arrangement with the widow of his ex-partner to purchase her interests in the company, and he explained that he would be willing to give this ownership position to his son provided George Jr. was willing to provide the sort of operating and financial information that the company needed. George Hampfel, Jr. understood the problem that the company faced and the need that his father had for more current and detailed management information, since he had known Mr. McFarland personally.

> Accounting became an obsession to the old man [Mr. McFarland]. He would talk to me when he would not talk to my father or anyone else in the company, because I was taking the accounting courses at The University of Michigan, so he felt that I was one of the elect. He didn't understand much accounting, but he was fascinated by the concept that the books must balance. He had an almost mystical belief that if at the end of a full year, after tens of thousands of individual journal entries, the total debits equaled the total credits, then everything was all right.
>
> They kept the original books of entry in incredible detail. They recorded the receipt of each box of capscrews, and then they deducted the use of those capscrews through shop requisition slips, but they never allocated the costs against any job; instead, they just wanted to keep track of the number of capscrews they had at any given time. They would not even tell the purchasing agent how many capscrews of a given size there were in inventory; they would let him figure it out for himself. It was totally financial accounting, with no element of managerial accounting whatever.
>
> My father wants managerial accounting reports, but, of course he doesn't call them that. If I accept his offer, and I think that I shall, we will have to start from scratch to develop an information system and a control system. It will be an awful job, but I think that it could be an immeasurable help to the company also. The primary problem is that my father thinks that I can just sit down and write out the reports that he needs from the

existing records, and the secondary problem is that he really doesn't have any idea what reports he does need.

I would have to develop, totally, the information system and the control system and tie the reports to the structure of the company and the needs of the business. I think that I would like some help on that. (Statement of George Hampfel, Jr.)

In order that students may be able to offer meaningful consulting assistance to George Hampfel, Jr. in his new position as treasurer and partial owner of the Hampfel-McFarland Company and help in the design of the new information and control systems, the balance of this case provides information on the product descriptions, marketing plans, production methods, installation requirements, organizational structure, and current problems of the company.

PRODUCT DESCRIPTIONS OF THE HAMPFEL-MCFARLAND COMPANY

The Hampfel-McFarland Company manufactures, sells, and installs complete emission control systems, repairs and modifies existing systems, and produces unrelated sheet metal products. Company sales in 1974 were just slightly under $6,000,000, with complete systems accounting for 54% of that total, repairs and modifications 37%, and miscellaneous unrelated products 9%.

The complete systems for dust and/or fume control vary, of course, by size and complexity, depending on the requirements of the productive process they are designed to serve, but generally each system consists of a number of roughly similar components. These similar components are the collector hoods, the collector pipes, the header pipes, blower pipes, separator units, blower fans, and special units.

1. Collector Hoods. Collector hoods are sheet metal forms that cover the grinding machines, heating furnaces, plating tanks, spraying booths, and other pieces of equipment that produce the dust, fumes,

waste products, or pollutants that are to be removed by air. The collector hoods are generally designed individually for each application, but some new pieces of equipment are now delivered with the collector hood as an integral part of the unit; other commonly used machines have standard collector hoods that we have built many times in the past, so they do not require redesign.

2. Collector Pipes. Collector pipes are sheet metal sections of piping that convey the dust, fumes, waste materials, or pollutants from the collector hoods on the individual machines, furnaces, etc. to the header pipes. The collector pipes are generally made in smaller diameters, because of the limited air required, and are usually produced from lighter gauge steel, because of the limited amount of wear. Common diameters for collector pipes are 4 in., 5 in., 6 in., 7 in., 8 in., 10 in., 12 in., and 14 in.; they are made in both straight sections and elbows of 30°, 45°, and 90°.

3. Header Pipes. Header pipes are sheet metal sections of piping that join the collector pipes from the individual machines, furnaces, tanks, etc. to the main blower pipes that carry the dust, fumes, waste materials, or pollutants to the central separator units. The header pipes are generally designed individually for each application since the number, the location, and the diameter of the collector pipes and the size of the main blower pipe will usually differ for each system; however, some of the more common units, such as a header pipe that will accommodate four 6-in. collector pipes and connect to a 12-in. blower pipe, have been built many times in the past and can be made from existing drawings.

4. Blower Pipes. Blower pipes are sheet metal sections of piping that carry dust, fumes, waste materials, or other pollutants suspended in air from the collection point at the header pipe to the processing point at the separator unit. Blower pipes tend to be in the larger diameters, because of the volume of air required, and they often are made of heavier gage steel, because of the wear involved. Common diameters for blower pipes are 16 in., 18 in., 24 in., 30 in., 36 in., 42 in., 48 in., 60 in., 72 in., and 84 in.; the larger pipes are obviously for very large systems. Blower pipes are also made in straight sections and elbows.

5. *Separator Units.* Separator units are sheet metal units that are used to separate dust, fumes, waste materials, or other pollutants from the air that is used to transport the materials and then to discharge the clean air at the top and the pollutants at the bottom. There are four major types of air separator devices:

(a) Cyclone air separators are the familiar cylinder and cone-shaped units that are seen on factory roofs. They operate on the principle that since they are very much larger in diameter than the incoming blower pipe, the air will slow down as it enters the cyclone, and suspended particle matter such as sawdust or planer shavings will settle out of the air stream at the slower speeds. Cyclone collectors vary between 5 ft and 12 ft in diameter; they are generally used for coarse or heavy particle matter, but they do not work well on fine dust. They do not work at all for smoke or fumes.

(b) Bag filter separators are simple enlargements of the common vacuum cleaner. Industrial bags are made of different materials, depending on the particle matter to be collected, and may be from 16 in. to 48 in. wide and from 10 ft to 30 ft long. They are usually hung from the top, with the exhaust air forced into them from the bottom. Several bags are used in parallel; periodically the air stream to a single bag is cut off, and the bag deflates, depositing the particle matter in a hopper. Bag filter separators are often used for fine dust, but they do not work at all for smoke or fumes. The bag filters are not 100% effective for very fine dust, and, consequently, they are seldom used whenever clear air laws are stringent.

(c) Wet scrubber separators are thought to be more efficient collectors of the smaller pollutant particles, such as very fine cement dust or coal dust, than either of the first two units, and they will even separate some of the vapor pollutants. The dirty air stream comes into the collector where its speed is greatly increased, either by reducing sharply the diameter of the pipe or by installing a powered fan. The air, now moving at 135 to 175 miles per hour, is sprayed with water, producing an atomized mist. The dust particles adhere to the water droplets, and some of the vaporized chemicals are dissolved in the water; the air stream then enters a cyclone which separates the slurry (watery mixture) by gravity. The slurry falls to the bottom of the cyclone where it collects in a hopper; it may be then either taken or piped to a settling pond where the water evaporates, leaving the dust and chemicals behind.

(d) Electrostatic precipitator separators are the most technically advanced collectors of the smaller pollutant particles. The precipitator is a large unit, often 20 ft high × 10 ft wide × 5 ft thick, so that the air stream slows down as it enters the separator. The dirty air first passes through a series of copper plates where the dust particles are given a positive electrical charge. The air then passes through another series of negatively charged copper plates and, like iron filings attracted to a magnet, the dust particles adhere to the electrostatic plates. Periodically, the air flow and the electrical currents are shut off and the plates are shaken, dropping their built-up layers of dust into a hopper below.

6. *Blower Fans.* The blower fan or power unit consists of a purchased fan, mounted on a steel shaft with low-friction bearings, encased by a sheet metal housing, and driven by an electric motor. The air flow within the emission control system is determined by the size and speed of the blower fan. Blower fans are available in sizes from 24 in. to 84 in. in diameter and

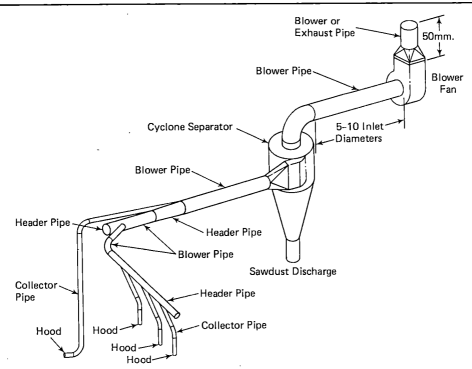

EXHIBIT 1 An emission control system for sawdust collection and separation at a furniture manufacturing company. (Source: company records.)

are driven by motors that range from 5 hp to 75 hp.

7. Special Units. Special units are occasionally required because of the corrosive nature of the fumes or the high temperatures of the air to be carried within the system. These special units are usually made of stainless or alloy steel and are designed to neutralize the corrosive fumes by chemical action or to cool the heated air by a heat exchanger or water spray. The smoke and fumes from a smelting furnace, for example, would be at a temperature of 600°F; this would melt the usual galvanized steel used for collector hoods and blower pipes. A heat exchanger, made of a high-temperature alloy steel, is used with an inner and outer sleeve; the furnace smoke and fumes are in the outer sleeve, with cool air in the inner sleeve. The cool air is heated to about 400°F, which, of course, reduces the temperature of the furnace emissions; the heated air is then blown into the furnace to support combustion and to conserve fuel.

An example of a simple system is shown in Exhibit 1. This particular system has been designed for sawdust collection within a furniture factory, and it operates like a giant vacuum cleaner, drawing the sawdust and wood shavings in from the various machines within the factory (saws, planers, jointers, sanders, etc.) via the collector hoods and the collector pipes to the header pipes and then transporting the waste material through the blower pipe to the cyclone separator. The collection, transportation, and separation of sawdust in this manner requires an air speed of 4,000 ft per minute. This velocity must remain constant throughout the system, since insufficient speed causes clogging and since excessive speed produces wear. (The means of calculating the air speed for all parts of a system are described in the marketing and customer engineering section of this case.)

The material composition of the various components within each system is determined by the abrasive nature of the material or the corrosive nature of the fumes the system is designed to handle and by the temperature at which the system is designed to operate. Components may be fabricated from galvanized steel, alloy steel, stainless steel, and glass or ceramic coated steel, although 85% of the work is with galvanized (zinc coated) steel. Material thicknesses range from 22 gage to $\frac{3}{8}$-in. plate, though again 85% of the work is with standard weights of sheet metal for each size components, i.e., 36-in. blower pipes are normally made from $\frac{3}{16}$-in. sheet steel.

MARKETING AND ENGINEERING SERVICES OF THE HAMPFEL-MCFARLAND COMPANY

The initial customer contact usually originates through a letter or telephone call requesting either a price estimate or engineering assistance on the fabrication and installation of a new emission control system or the modification and repair of an existing system. The Hampfel-McFarland Company has never advertised and has never performed missionary sales work, but Mr. Hampfel feels that the company is well enough known so that it is asked to bid or assist on "a goodly portion" of the available emission control business within the area. After receiving the request, a salesman is sent to interview the customer. The company has five salesmen who are called "sales engineers," but none has extensive engineering training; instead, all are long-term employees who have worked in the shop on sheet metal fabrication and in the field on air system installation, so that they have extensive practical knowledge.

On approximately 30% of the calls, the salesman is told that the proposed or modified system has been entirely designed by the customer's engineering department or by an engineering consultant, and Hampfel-McFarland is asked only to submit a formal bid on the fabrication and installation, as described in the drawings and specifications that are given to the salesman. Most of the larger systems, with a value from $250,000 to over $1,000,000, are sold in this manner. For the smaller systems, which represent perhaps 70% of the calls, the company is asked to recommend the design and then bid on the fabrication and installation. In these cases, the salesman will estimate the volume and weight of the dust or waste materials to be moved, will establish the location of the sources generating these materials, will sketch the dimensions of the collector hoods covering these sources, will measure the distance the material is to be transported, and will recommend the type of the separator and the size of the blower fan to be used.

The drawings and specifications, if available, or the information on the requirements of the system are then brought back to the Grand Rapids office and given to the engineering staff. Again, the formal engineering training of the designers and estimators is limited, but all members of the department have had extensive drafting and practical experience. The designers convert the information recorded by the salesmen to the specific components needed for the system. Exhibit 2 illustrates this conversion for a dust control system being designed for a foundry using sand shakers to form the molds for casting; for brevity, only the first few components of this system are listed.

The designer generally selects the components in order to roughly balance the total duct area throughout the system; that is, the four 7-in. collector pipes, each with an area of 0.267 sq ft, or 1.068 sq ft in total (4 × 0.267) connect to a 14-in. header pipe with an area of 1.069 sq ft. If two 14-in. header pipes came together, representing 2.136 sq ft in total, the designer would con-

EXHIBIT 2 Components for dust control system for foundry sand shakers in molding department. (Source: company records.)

No.	Component name	Duct area (sq ft)	Pipe straight	Pipe elbow	Pipe entrance	Total length
4	Shaker hoods pattern #8713	1.335	—	—	—	—
4	7″-collector pipes	0.267	12.6′	90° × 2.0′	30° × 2.6′	17.2′
1	14″-header pipe with four 7″ × 30° junctions	1.069	26.0′	—	—	26.0′

nect them to a 20-in. blower pipe, with an area of 2.1817 sq ft.

After selecting and sizing the components, the designer looks up within published tables the resistance factor, the friction that the air and the conveyed material will encounter against the sides of the piping. The resistance factor is a function of the weight and nature of the material to be carried and the number and angle of the bends in the pipe; it is expressed as a resistance per 1,000 ft of the component. The air volume is then computed based upon the size and speed of the blower fan and the number and size of the divisions within the piping leading back to each component. Lastly, the air speed is computed by using the following formula: Air velocity = air volume/duct area × resistance (see Exhibit 3).

The resultant air velocity and hood suction at each dust or waste material source is compared to a standard needed to pick up the material. If the air velocity at the pickup points is not great enough, the designer increases either the size or speed of the blower fan and calculates the air velocities once again.

After the air velocities have been determined and after the size of each component has been definitely set, the list is given to an estimator for bidding. Technically, the estimator is to compute the material and labor needed both to fabricate and install each piece. (The material used at installation consists of supports and braces for the piping and other components.) Actually, since many of the pieces have been made many times in the past, standard costs have become accepted for these units. All collector pipes and blower pipes in standard sizes and all other components that have a pattern number (the pattern number refers to the template that is used to lay out the cutting and forming dimensions on the sheet metal) indicating previous manufacture, now have standard costs that are used in bidding; no

EXHIBIT 3 Air volume and air speed calculations for dust control system for foundry sand shakers. (Source: company records.)

No.	Component name	Duct area (sq ft)	Resistance factor	Resistance component	Air volume	Air speed
4	Shaker hoods pattern #8713	1.335	—	—	929	718
4	7-in. collector pipes	0.267	0.0841	0.001447	929	3590
1	14-in. header pipe with four 7″ × 30° junctions	1.067	0.0337	0.000875	3717	3478

EXHIBIT 4   Labor and material cost estimates for dust control system for foundry sand shakers. (Source: company records.)

No.	Component name	Fabricate material	Fabricate labor	Install material	Install labor	Total costs
4	Shaker hoods pattern #8713	$26.87/ea		$14.00/ea		$163.48
4	7-in. collector pipes with 90° elbows × 17.2′	$41.17/ea		$10.00/ea		$204.68
1	14-in. header pipe with four 7″ × 30° junctions	$21.41	$117.43	$4.17	$20.00	$163.01

calculations on labor or material are performed. The estimator computes the labor and material costs only for the nonstandard components (these are often the header pipes) within the system (see Exhibit 4).

The estimator totals the costs for all the components required within the system and then multiplies by 1.5 to allow for both manufacturing and administrative overhead. The full report for each system, consisting of both engineering calculations and cost estimates, is then given to George Hampfel, Sr., who studies it for a short period of time and adjusts the total price upward or downward depending on his "feel" for the situation. All seven members of the engineering department were in agreement that Mr. Hampfel had an uncanny ability to estimate costs accurately. One member of the department stated that, "When a bid goes out of here, it is right; Mr. Hampfel won't be off more than $5 on a $250,000 job." Only the final price for the system, as adjusted by Mr. Hampfel, is sent to the customer; no supporting details are included in the bid.

Bids are sent to customers at fairly regular intervals throughout the year, but a majority of the orders are received in the late spring for shipment over the summer. Approximately 60% of the dollar volume of annual billings usually fall in the 4-month period from June to September. This seasonality is partially due to the weather, since outside installation is easier during the summer, but it is primarily due to the model changes of the automobile and home appliance industries. The installation, modification or repair of an emission control system often requires the shutdown of the productive equipment, and this work is usually scheduled for the annual plant shutdown for the model changes.

PRODUCTION AND INSTALLATION FUNCTIONS OF THE HAMPFEL-MCFARLAND COMPANY

When an order is received for the fabrication and installation of a new emission control system or for the modification or repair of an existing system, a job order is prepared by the engineering department listing the customer, delivery date, and required components. Engineering drawings are completed for the new items, particularly header pipes, for which no existing patterns are available. The job order and the related prints are then sent to the shop foreman.

Production of the sheet metal components for an emission control system within the shop can be broken into three major operations:

1. Layout. Sheet metal layout involves descriptive geometry. This is the process of unfolding and drawing the three-dimensional shape of the finished component onto the one-dimensional surface of the sheet metal prior to cutting, bending, and rolling. A straight section of pipe is a fairly simple example, since it requires only a rectangular sheet of metal of the proper dimensions, but an elbow or entrance section requires a triangular piece with two curvilinear edges. Some of the more intricate components, such as collector hoods or header pipes, involve very complex geometric analysis. Patterns, the results of this analysis as performed for prior jobs, are used when available. In 1975, the company had 1,105 patterns; each pattern can be visualized as a template that is laid over the sheet metal to assist in marking out the required shape for cutting and bending. Almost every job sent to the shop, however, involves one or two components that have never been made by the company previously and, consequently, have to be laid out from the blueprints by a skilled worker.

2. Fabrication. After being laid out, either by pattern or by hand, the sheet metal is cut to the required shape and dimensions by powered shears. The flat piece is then formed into the three-dimensional shape through the use of both hand tools and powered machinery; a brake bends sheet metal at a sharp angle; rolls produce a gradual curvature.

3. Assembly. Assembly is the process of joining the fabricated shapes into finished units through welding or riveting and then combining the units into a complete component. A collector pipe or blower pipe, for example, is usually assembled in 4-ft lengths (the standard width of galvanized sheet metal), and then the 4-ft sections are welded or riveted, with elbows or entrances as required, into the desired lengths, up to 20 ft.

Miscellaneous products, for example machine guards, motor covers, part baskets, and hydraulic tanks, which together represent 9% of the total company revenues, are manufactured by the same process of layout, fabrication, and assembly that are used for the emission control systems.

Installation of the completed components for a new or remodeled emission control system outside the shop requires delivery and placement:

1. Delivery. The company operates a fleet of seven trucks of different sizes to carry the system components to the job site; some of the trucks are equipped with a light crane to make installation easier.

2. Placement. The company normally sends a crew of workers to set the components in place and to erect the supporting structural steel. Electrical components (motors and control switches) are mounted, but not wired. Placement requires the use of hand tools, portable welders, and, occasionally, light cranes.

The production shop of Hampfel-McFarland occupies the entire ground floor of an older brick building in the industrial section of Grand Rapids. The work flow is from an extensive sheet metal inventory to 7 layout benches, then to 4 shears, to 5 brakes and 2 sets of rolls for fabrication, and finally to 11 welding benches for assembly. Finished units are stored near the loading dock ready for shipment to the customer.

The work force of Hampfel-McFarland is entirely unionized; all employees are members of the United Brotherhood of Sheetmetal Workers. Wage rates are the major component of production costs; Mr. Hampfel estimated that the total cost structure of the company could probably be broken down into 60% wages, 15% material, 15% shop overhead, and 10% general overhead and profit. Wage rates in 1975 averaged $9.76 per hour.

The wage rates in sheet metal fabrication and installation are high since the workers are considered to be skilled tradesmen and receive 4 years of training through a union run apprenticeship program. The apprenticeship program combines on-the-job training with classroom instruction; particular emphasis is placed on the descriptive geometry needed for sheet metal layout. The program, however, concentrates on the layout, fabrication, and assembly of heating and air conditioning duct systems, work that involves much lighter metals and much simpler components than those used by Hampfel-McFarland. For this reason, recent employees tend to be of a much lower skill level than the older workers.

The work force fluctuates in response to demand. There are approximately 70 full-time employees who work straight through the year, and there are an additional 50 part-time employees who are hired for the peak demand period during the summer months. Seasonal employees are available through the union hiring hall.

The employees can be separated into four major classifications, although there is considerable movement back and forth between the assignments, depending on the order volume and the level of skill required:

1. Layout Men. Layout is considered to require the highest degree of skill in sheet metal work. Even though 90% to 95% of all layout work uses patterns, the balance involves very complicated analysis, calculations, and projections. The layout men tend to be the oldest employees in the company. They have worked both inside on fabrication and assembly and outside on delivery and installation and have selected this job as the most desirable. The layout men, however, often work on other tasks, such as the fabrication and assembly of nonstandard and complex components.

2. Leadsmen. Leadsmen are considered to be the second highest skilled group in the company; they are the foremen of the installation crews. Each crew, which may vary between two and seven men, usually takes one of the company trucks, which is equipped with portable welders, hand tools, and other field equipment, and drives to the job site. For small jobs, the components are usually loaded on the company truck; for larger systems, the components are shipped by either contract or common carriers. The leadsman on each job is responsible for the entire installation phase; he communicates with the shop foreman requesting additional material shipment, required design changes, or closer adherence to tolerances. During slack periods the leadsmen also work on tasks inside the shop, such as fabrication and assembly.

3. Fabrication and Assembly. The workers assigned specifically to fabrication and assembly are usually older men who wish to avoid the travel required for field installation but lack the skill or seniority required for full-time layout work. They fabricate and assemble the components and do some of the simpler layout tasks.

4. General. The largest group of workers includes all of the seasonal employees and perhaps 25 to 30 additional full-time men. They work inside on fabrication and assembly and outside on the installation crews.

All job assignments and production scheduling is set by the foreman; he starts the various components into production based upon his perception of the time required for completion, the delivery date for the completed system, and the present loading on the shears, brakes, and rolls from other jobs. Individual work assignments are made on an availability basis. When an employee completes an assigned task, he reports to the shop foreman to receive another job. The foreman attempts to match individuals and their particular skills with specific tasks, again in light of the workload on the available facilities. Tasks assigned to layout men often include both layout and fabrication operations, but no assembly. Other individuals are assigned to complete the assembly of components begun by the layout men or to initiate and complete components from start to finish. In addition to job assignment and production scheduling, the shop foreman is responsible for sheet metal ordering and inventory control, design modifications, component tolerances and quality control, final shipment of the completed systems, and supervision of the installation crews.

Problems in the shop production include

bottlenecks that continually develop around the shears and brakes. Considerable setup time is required for each new operation on these machines, and workers with an assigned job are often idle waiting to utilize the units. Component orders for large systems can monopolize the available machine time, and the smaller jobs and emergency repair orders are either forced to wait or to break into an established sequence of operations, which substantially increases the setup costs and machine downtime. The machines are expensive (a new shear capable of cutting ⅜″ steel plate would cost $28,000 installed) so

that while the company has room for additional equipment, Mr. Hampfel has been 'reluctant to make the investment. The foreman estimates that 5% of shop time is wasted as a result of these bottlenecks, and he has repeatedly asked for additional machines.

Problems in field installation revolve about the coordination between marketing, engineering, and production. Often, an additional collector pipe or blower pipe is needed above that estimated by the engineering department, and occasionally new elbows or pipe bends are required to avoid an obstruc-

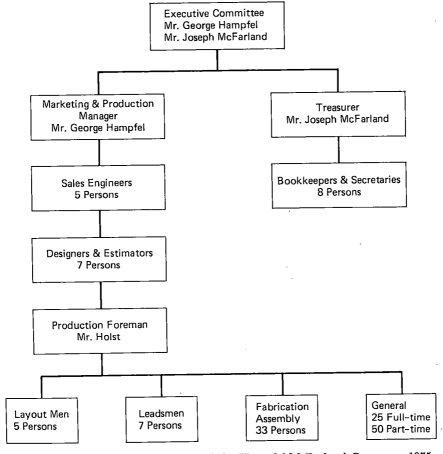

EXHIBIT 5 Organizational structure of the Hampfel-McFarland Company, 1975, prior to the death of Mr. McFarland. (Source: George Hampfel, Sr.)

tion in the customer's plant, that was not recorded by the salesmen. Lastly, since errors often occur in sheet metal fabrication and assembly, it is not uncommon for the components to require extensive reworking in the field in order to be joined together. All of these problems are magnified when the installation crew is a considerable distance (up to 300 miles) from the shop and either has to wait for additional materials or return to rebuild a single component. Some of the leadsmen estimated that the total hours lost were in the range of 7% to 8%.

George Hampfel, Jr. recognized the inherent problems and opportunities in the Hampfel-McFarland Company since he had worked in the shop and on installation crews during summer vacations while he was in college and the M.B.A. program, but he was not exactly certain how he should set up the management information and control systems for the company.

ASSIGNMENT

The existing management information and control system for the Hampfel-McFarland Company consists of a single figure (annual profit or loss) written on a 3-in. × 5-in. piece of note paper. What improvements would you recommend? Exhibit 5 shows the existing organizational structure of the company.

Dakota Fertilizer Equipment

"In most fields, if you bust your tail you'll make it. You can't just work 8-to-5 or sit back and glide." The speaker, Bob Speake, was not chatting idly. It was 8:00 p.m. on a Monday in 1975's mild autumn as he neared the end of his workday as owner of Dakota Fertilizer Equipment. Although he planned to work his usual 70-hour week, Bob took a few minutes to discuss the record and prospects of the fertilizer equipment firm he had founded in 1962. In 1975 its net sales surpassed the $1 million level and Dakota's plant, adjacent to the railroad in Lennox, South Dakota, was "snowed under with work."

With assembly operations literally overflowing Dakota's buildings, Bob Speake had

decided to build a second plant in Albert Lea, Minnesota, about 190 miles northeast of Lennox. He also planned Dakota's first significant trade advertising, and he was considering franchising dealers in several other regions of the United States. Now in the midst of his planning, he had just been contacted by the former marketing manager of the nation's largest seller of fertilizer equipment. This man offered, in conjunction with a multimillion dollar distributor in Illinois, to buy a 40%-interest in Dakota. He also proposed that he might become an officer of the company and build its distribution network.

Bob Speake believed that Dakota had grown successfully beyond the limits of one-man management in part because of the increasing skills of his subordinate managers, Dave Koslo and Karl Spooner. Even so, he felt overtaxed: there were still too many things for one man to do.

> I was hoping for a coasting year with sales off from 10% to 15% so I could concentrate on the Albert Lea expansion. In every business there are peaks and valleys, but we're busting right along. If we're not careful, we could go to $2 million next year. I think 15% is a more normal, healthy growth rate."

Keeping Dakota's growth orderly was particularly important to his long-run personal goals. Although he was only 43 years old, he was already planning an early retirement from Dakota. Childless and with a chronically ill wife, Bob Speake felt little need to increase his wealth. Instead, he sought to realize his gains while young and healthy. Looking ahead, he said, "I hope that 10 years down the road I'll be through with this."

COMPANY HISTORY

Dakota Fertilizer Equipment was the product of detailed research Bob Speake conducted in 1961–1962. At that time he was in his fourth year with Carlson Brothers, a Missouri manufacturer of dry fertilizer spreaders.[1] Although he had been hired as an accountant, Mr. Speake's duties in the small company included advertising, purchasing, sales, service and repair, and even an occasional repossession. His experience with Carlson Brothers convinced him that he could earn large profits as a Carlson Brothers distributor in Nebraska, South Dakota, North Dakota, and Minnesota. The company had no distributor in these states, but it had received inquiries from established dealers. Preferring to keep Mr. Speake in the parent company, Oscar Carlson offered him a raise and a profit-sharing plan. Bob Speake stuck to his entrepreneurial plans, though, and Carlson Brothers acceded to his request.

From the outset, Carlson Brothers agreed that he could sell liquid fertilizer spreaders, as did many of the company's distributors.[2]

His research had shown Mr. Speake that although Illinois and Iowa farmers used more fertilizer than did farmers in Nebraska and the Dakotas, Nebraska and the Dakotas offered better prospects for sales growth. Typically, a manufacturer of fertilizer spreaders sold through its own salesmen within 300 miles of its plant. Beyond that radius, it relied on truck body distributors who carried agricultural equipment in addition to dump, grain-carrying, or delivery van bodies for truck chassis. There were no manufacturers in Nebraska or South Dakota and there was little competition from specialized distributors.

Further examination of transportation, employment, and wage rate data convinced Bob Speake that Lennox would be a good site. Its rail connections would provide one-week delivery from the Missouri manufacturer, and its bus and truck lines offered more rapid delivery on small parts.

Dakota Fertilizer Equipment modestly began its corporate history in 1962. Having less than $10,000 to establish the company while his wife's teaching salary supported them, Bob Speake avoided early commitments of funds for fixed assets. He used his apartment as an office and its basement for storing the few, most frequently needed parts he carried in inventory. He worked mainly at selling Carlson spreaders, which he then ordered and prepared for delivery. Not until sales outpaced his ability to prepare the equipment did he hire anyone or obtain a permanent plant.

From $198,000 in its first full year (1963), Dakota's net sales passed $300,000 in 1966. In this period Bob Speake hired workers and acquired machinery. As it grew, Dakota stocked an increasing number and range of spare parts and accessories. The company also undertook the manufacture of replacement parts, using a power steel saw, a thread-

---

[1] *Dry fertilizer spreaders were basically large bins with augers or other controls to regulate the rate of outflow. They were mounted either on trucks or on trailers.*

[2] *Mr. Speake expected liquid spreaders to provide at most 30% of his sales.*

ing machine, milling machines, and presses. Bob Speake hired an experienced shop tool draftsman to make prints of all spreaders manufactured by Carlson Brothers. He later explained his actions:

> This gradual buildup of knowledge and machinery was not done with the intention of competing with our supplier. That wouldn't be ethical. But I had to protect the past 4 years of hard work. What if they had a strike or a fire, or if there should eventually be a disagreement between Dakota and them?

By 1967 Dakota Fertilizer Equipment had become a small-scale manufacturer as well as a distributor. It accepted old, rusted spreaders on trade and then reconditioned[3] and sold them. Bob Speake, the draftsman, and a few key employees did most of the manufacturing work. Dakota's manufacturing expanded in 1967 when Mr. Speake and an employee developed and marketed the first hydraulic sprayer for truck-mounted liquid fertilizer units.[4] The unit was well-received, winning Mr. Speake an invitation to show it in Denver at the convention of the National Fertilizer Solutions Association.

Dakota's net sales grew modestly to $340,000 in 1970, rose by 67% in the following 3 years to $568,000 in 1973, and then rose by another 42% in 1974. See Exhibits 1, 2, and 3.

EXHIBIT 1 Net sales and net income.

	Net sales	Net income after taxes
1970	$ 339,800	$19,600
1971	$ 409,600	$25,800
1972	$ 514,400	$24,200
1973	$ 567,700	$31,700
1974	$ 806,600	$32,400
1975	$1,036,400	$48,000

---

[3] *Reconditioning comprised sandblasting, repair, and spray repainting.*

[4] *The hydraulic sprayer permitted a more even distribution of liquid fertilizer because the rate of spraying varied with the vehicle's speed.*

THE COMPANY IN 1975

Despite its rapid growth, Dakota Fertilizer Equipment remained essentially an assembler of purchased parts rather than a fabricator of those parts. The major components of its finished products were the truck bodies on which spreader or sprayer units rested. Customers frequently brought their own trucks to Dakota for installation or customization of units. In other cases, Dakota purchased and carried truck bodies. The bins, tanks, and most accessory parts were purchased, mainly from Carlson Brothers. Dakota's primary function was the assembly, including customization, of spreader and sprayer units. Parts and service also provided revenues, as indicated in Exhibit 4. Purchased parts generally consumed about 65% of Dakota's net sales dollar.

Product Line. As noted earlier, Dakota's products fell into two basic groups—dry spreaders and liquid sprayers. There were three "pull spreaders," which were hauled by tractors or pickup trucks, and two truck-mounted models. The pull spreaders held 4, 5, or 6 tons of fertilizer; the truck-mounted models held from 6 to 13 tons of fertilizer or 13 tons of lime and they used twin distributor fans controlled by a hydraulic governor. Liquid sprayers were harder to categorize. According to the Dakota catalog, they were "manufactured on an individual basis allowing the applicator full options of pumps, tank sizes, nozzle spacing, boom length, and color." Tank capacities ranged from 300 to 1,500 gallons.[5]

Dry spreader prices began at $2,400 but were commonly more expensive because few customers chose the simplest, least adorned model. A combination of optional features for both performance and appearance[6] boosted the average price to the same range as an intermediate-sized automobile. Liquid

---

[5] *Different manufacturers' models varied little in performance, style, or price.*

[6] *In the latter category were custom paint jobs with mixed-to-order colors.*

EXHIBIT 2   Balance sheet July 31, 1975 (unaudited).

ASSETS

Current Assets:*

Accounts receivable		$ 21,073.69	
Merchandise inventory		215,488.65	
Total current assets			$236,562.34

Fixed Assets:

	Cost	Depreciation	Net	
Leasehold improvements	$ 19,885.86	$ 2,420.14	17,465.72	
Machinery equipment	29,945.28	17,437.09	12,508.19	
Automotive	80,131.21	18,971.55	61,159.66	
Furniture and fixtures	16,973.89	9,261.35	7,712.54	
Leased equipment	25,287.12	8,939.35	16,347.77	
Airplane	22,403.89	13,190.33	9,213.56	
Totals	$194,627.25	$70,219.81		124,407.44
Total assets				$360,969.78

LIABILITIES and SHAREHOLDERS' EQUITY

Current Liabilities:

Bank overdraft		$ 5,581.92	
Accounts payable		15,789.32	
Accounts payable, officer		2,630.20	
Note payable		10,000.00	
Accrued taxes		6,860.69	
Accrued salaries		14,500.00	
Total current liabilities			$ 55,362.13

Long-Term Liabilities:

Note payable		40,000.00	
Less current, above		10,000.00	30,000.00

Shareholders' Equity:

Common stock issued		45,444.43	
Retained earnings		230,163.22	
Total shareholders' equity			275,607.65
Total liabilities and shareholders' equity			$360,969.78

* At this date cash was essentially zero. Inventory was at a level about $100,000 higher than normal. This had resulted because the company had placed large orders with many suppliers during the preceding months when parts were difficult to obtain. The subsequent flood of deliveries depleted cash and built up the inventory level.

sprayers were so thoroughly customized that prices varied widely.

Sales from a $75,000 inventory of 6,000 different parts constituted one-quarter of the company's net sales. These parts ranged from common bolts and fittings to stainless steel nozzles costing $25 apiece. Some were low-turnover items, with only one or two units in inventory, which sold at markups as high as 75%. Other parts were salvaged and rebuilt from trade-in units. Neither new nor rebuilt parts were subject to ob-

EXHIBIT 3 Income statements for the years ending July 31, 1974 and July 31, 1975.

	1974	1975
Gross sales	$895,800	$1,155,500
Less: Discounts and allowances	89,200	119,100
Net sales	806,600	1,036,400
Cost of sales	556,100	722,900
Gross margin	$250,500	$ 313,500
Wages, salaries, and benefits	$115,600	$ 142,700
Selling expenses*	7,900	11,300
Travel and vehicle expenses	21,500	28,600
Depreciation	14,300	27,600
Operating supplies	5,900	6,100
Rent	4,800	4,800
Telephone	4,500	6,000
Interest	2,700	2,500
Repairs and maintenance	600	2,000
Social security	6,000	7,100
State and local taxes	8,800	10,800
Dues, subscriptions, contributions	500	900
Administration and overhead†	12,500	13,300
	$205,600	$ 263,700
Net operating income	$ 44,900	$ 49,800
Other income	2,300	11,000
Net income before taxes	$ 47,200	$ 60,800
Federal income tax	14,800	12,800
Net income after taxes	$ 32,400	$ 48,000

Selling expenses include sales commissions, entertainment, sales meetings, trade show expenses, advertising, warranty expenses, and freight and delivery.
†*Administrative and overhead expenses include legal and accounting, office supplies, insurance, utilities, and outside services.*

EXHIBIT 4 Composition of sales revenue, August 1975.* (Source: Bob Speake's estimates.)

	Revenue	Percentage
Finished units	$27,000	68
Parts	11,000	27
Service	2,000	5
	$40,000	100

The company was closed for annual vacation for half the month.

solescence because changes in spreader and sprayer products were infrequent. Limitations on product lines were physical rather than technological: many of the fertilizers and chemicals were highly corrosive. Depending on its uses, a spreader or sprayer typically lasted from 3 to 10 years.[7]

Production and Operations. Dakota's dozen employees all were working a 5½-day, 49-hour week as Mr. Speake strove to keep pace with burgeoning demand. The employees were not unionized and shifted freely among tasks as needed. Of the non-supervisory jobs, only spray painting was regularly assigned to particular personnel.

Despite these efforts and the use of outdoor space for production work during clement weather, Dakota quoted a 120-day delivery time. A typical unit assembled from purchased components required 3 days' work: one each in assembly, the paint room, and "finishing up." Its 3,500 sq ft building included 2,700 sq ft of assembly and production space where 2, or sometimes 3, units could be accommodated.[8]

The past year's output of 300 new units (250 dry spreaders and 50 liquid sprayers) and 25 refurbished trade-ins had left little slack time. During infrequent lulls Dakota had built some units mainly from parts that it produced itself, averaging about a week's work per unit. These respites from regular production also had freed manpower for improvements in the company's plant and offices. Because Dakota's 1974 and 1975 sales had been far less seasonal than those of past years,[9] production continued fairly steady throughout the year. Even if the pace of orders faltered, limited storage space hampered production for inventory.

[7] *Stainless steel equipment, costing roughly 80% more than steel or iron, lasted longer. Dakota sold both types.*

[8] *There was also a 400-sq ft paint room and a two-level office and storage area.*

[9] *The relative difference between peak and slack sales months was only one-half of what it had been in earlier years.*

In 1973 Mr. Speake experimented for 3 months with a second shift, but he abandoned it because of friction and inefficiencies resulting from dual responsibilities for production. For example, he found that the night shift often left work partially completed or unchecked and that the day shift either overlooked or redid the work. Either the product or the efficiency of production suffered. He had similarly dropped a flexible working hours[10] plan when he found himself driven to work the full day lest he lose his close control over operations.

Marketing. Relatively few farmers owned equipment such as Dakota's. Instead, they rented spreaders and sprayers from cooperatives, grain elevators, or fertilizer dealers. The company's sales reflected this: 93% were to such organizations and only 7% were to farmers. Thus, a typical customer owned several units and offered the prospect of repeated sales over the years.

Bob Speake had once been Dakota's salesman. Now, one full-time and one part-time salesman did almost all selling. Mr. Speake handled a few key accounts that he had established, but he added none to his group.[11] Nevertheless, the company's selling philosophy remained the same: meet a customer's demands on timing or special features if at all possible—it is better than losing the order (and perhaps future orders) to a competitor. Thus, an order might be filled by working all night or on Sunday or by disrupting prior production schedules. This flexibility did not extend to pricing, though. Unlike most competitors, Dakota granted a 30% discount to most customers, but planned its prices to allow the discount. Large orders, ranging upward from $25,000, were granted an additional 5% discount.

[10] *A flexible working hours plan typically allowed employees to work 8 hours within a given longer workday. Presence during some "core time" was required.*

[11] *In 1975 sales to these accounts were 15% of the company's total. Mr. Speake actively sought to turn the accounts over to Mr. Koslo or Mr. Spooner.*

But Bob Speake would not budge on his prices to cooperatives that wanted to resell spreaders and sprayers: they wanted additional 10% price reductions—revenue he believed that Dakota could capture itself through direct sales.

Ninety-five percent of the company's sales were made in Nebraska, North Dakota, South Dakota, and Minnesota. With only the company's salesmen and no distributors, it had never seriously sought sales outside these four states; it did no advertising and its brochures featured a four-state map. In 1975 Bob Speake estimated that Dakota had a 40% market share in these states and that the company's sales growth exceeded the market's growth.

Mr. Speake believed that the keys to Dakota's success were its service and its parts inventory. Equipment failures could be disastrous because fields had to be treated at particular times. Therefore, Dakota would make emergency visits to repair defective units but not to units suffering normal wear and tear. Repair parts were also of urgent importance. These advantages permitted Dakota to maintain net prices about $50 above those of its competitors on most equip-

ment and to offer the standard trade discount of 10%/10 days on parts.

Bob Speake's Role. His 70-hour workweek in 1975 was not as tough on Bob Speake as the 80-hour weeks he had devoted to Dakota as recently as 1972. Then, as in earlier years, he had worked alongside his production workers, manufacturing replacement parts and customizing purchased truck bodies and spreaders.[12] He also had done most of the direct selling and convention presentations. In 1975, though, he had nearly eliminated his personal involvement in production work, reduced his sales activities, and taken his first extensive vacation since founding the company. (Bob Speake's typical workweeks in 1970–1972 and in 1975 are described in Exhibit 5.)

The time he no longer spent in production and sales work afforded him an opportunity to handle long-term planning and daily administration of Dakota's office. Long-term planning included developing plans for the Albert Lea plant and for a network of

[12] During the company's infancy Bob Speake had often spent the night helping his employees load or unload freight cars at the plant siding.

EXHIBIT 5 Bob Speake's typical work weeks in 1970–1972 and in 1975.

Activities	1970–1972	1975	1970–1972	1975
	Percentage of time		Hours per week	
Field or phone sales and conventions	40	30	32	21
Production and production supervision	40	5	32	3½
Daily office and shop administration	⎫	43	⎫	30
Long-term planning	⎬ 20	10	⎬ 16	7
Purchasing*	⎪	8	⎪	5½
Walk-in customers	⎭	4	⎭	3
	100	100	80	70
Annual vacation			1 week	12 weeks

* In 1975 Mr. Speake's involvement in purchasing consisted mainly of conferring with Dave Koslo.

liquid sprayer distributors. Office administration comprised every sort of daily activity in Dakota's operation. In the past week, for example, Bob Speake had telephoned a truck dealer to inquire about an unannounced $500 increase in a truck's delivered price, filled the purchasing and marketing roles of Mr. Koslo or Mr. Spooner during their separate sales trips, and continued his practice of reading all incoming mail. Of the latter, he said "I like to open the mail. That way you can check up before anything gets covered up."

In anticipation of a much larger organization and operation, Mr. Speake was strengthening the company's control systems. These already included a perpetual inventory record and an invoice file that was cross-indexed by order number and customer name. Now he was considering a computer time-sharing system for inventory control. The parts inventory had always been recorded on a FIFO (first in, first out) basis, despite the added costs incurred through taxation of the resultant inventory profits created by recent years' inflation. He thought that the costs of changing to LIFO (last in, first out) and of maintaining the additional requisite records probably would exceed any tax savings.

Virtually every Dakota financial and accounting document passed through Bob Speake's hands. He assiduously double-checked all outgoing sales invoices (and sometimes spotted errors worth hundreds of dollars), although Dave Koslo was nearly prepared to relieve him of this responsibility. Routine items, such as the monthly telephone bill, never escaped Mr. Speake. One area of financial control with which he was not satisfied was cash management: He lacked the time to exploit fully the company's cash balance, now about $100,000. Although he often had the money placed in overnight loans, Bob Speake thought that he could do better if he had more available time.

The continuing development of Dave Koslo and Karl Spooner had freed still more of Mr. Speake's time. Each worked about 55 hours a week, including sales visits. They each performed nearly every general management task at some time, but Mr. Koslo concentrated on purchasing and Mr. Spooner on sales. With an eye toward preparing them for eventual control of the company, Bob Speake had had both men scheduling pickups and shipments and preparing purchase orders. At this time, though, he still checked their schedules and orders before effecting them. Both men carried more of the daily office burden, too, particularly in handling walk-in customer relations.[13] Their advancement had permitted Bob Speake to take 12 weeks of vacation in fiscal 1975—weeks that he used to plant and harvest crops at several farms he had acquired in northern Iowa. He also found time for more pheasant hunting, swimming, and flying than in recent years.

During Bob Speake's unprecedented absences for vacation Dave Koslo and Karl Spooner divided office responsibilities, depending on which man was available. Price quotations proceeded normally, even on large orders, and purchases were uninterrupted. Some items accumulated on Mr. Speake's desk to await his return. These items included license plate applications and documents requiring his signature. He telephoned Mr. Koslo or Mr. Spooner a couple of times a week, but Mr. Speake never had to return prematurely for business reasons. In his judgment, the vacation arrangements worked very well.

His young assistants' success had pleased Mr. Speake. He had recruited each man in the hope that he would become a reliable manager for Dakota. They were graduates of his alma mater, Prairie State University, and had rural backgrounds. Mr. Spooner, raised on a Wyoming ranch, joined Dakota immediately upon being graduated in 1972.

---

[13] *Bob Speake preferred relative anonymity when he was in the public area of Dakota's offices. In fact, he chose "Dakota" as the company's name precisely because it did not identify an owner or boss. "It deters people who always want to see the boss or always want to buy from the boss," he explained.*

Mr. Koslo was an Indiana farmboy and had worked a year in sales and assembly for an International Harvester distributor in Ohio before Mr. Speake hired him in 1971. Mr. Spooner was a 25-year old bachelor; the 28-year old Mr. Koslo was married and had two children.

PREPARING FOR
FURTHER GROWTH

In the last year Bob Speake had taken several steps to prepare the company for the higher volume he foresaw. The most notable step was undertaking the Albert Lea plant, which would add between 6,500 and 7,500 sq ft to Dakota's production area. The Albert Lea City Development Corporation would finance the plant through sale of $200,000 in tax-exempt $7\frac{1}{2}\%$ bonds. Mr. Speake himself or Dakota would purchase some bonds and an Albert Lea bank would take the rest. On repaying the debt, Dakota would receive title to the plant. Mr. Speake planned to assemble dry spreaders at Lennox and liquid sprayers at Albert Lea and to stock a full range of parts for both in each plant. Accounting and purchasing would be centralized at the existing home office.

Dave Koslo was being groomed for the manager's position in Albert Lea. To ensure his complete dedication to the new endeavor, Mr. Speake planned to make the Albert Lea plant nearly autonomous and to base Mr. Koslo's compensation on its profitability. For his part, Mr. Koslo was eager to accept the challenge and responsibility and had made several trips to meet a major Dakota customer whose company was in Albert Lea.

While awaiting the final plans for the new plant, Mr. Speake moved Dakota to a more aggressive promotional strategy. He increased the company's participation in conventions and trade shows to about a dozen a year, at a total cost of $7,000 to $8,000. To broaden its appeal, he dropped the four-state map and localized copy from Dakota's sales brochures. He was planning

the company's first national advertising, too: $3,600 worth of ads in specialized trade publications would promote Dakota's liquid sprayers.[14] Bob Speake was quick to emphasize that $3,600 really bought very little advertising, but he also noted that it was a tenfold increase from Dakota's 1975 expenditure.

Not all of the company's growth was planned for its current geographic market. To reach new territories, Mr. Speake was sounding out potential distributors for Dakota's liquid sprayers in Iowa, Illinois, Indiana, and Ohio. The sprayers were essentially proprietary products that utilized the valves, hoses, and technology developed by or for Dakota. Unlike the dry spreaders, which were sold by other Carlson Brothers distributors in these states, the sprayers posed no ethical or competitive problems for Dakota's own distributorship. Mr. Speake believed that distributors would agree to the standard 20% to 25% discount on the liquid sprayers.

None of Bob Speake's expansion plans had reached a crucial decision point by December 1975. Then, unexpectedly, Ralph Cook, the recent marketing manager of the industry's sales leader contacted him. Under his leadership that firm had grown to $13 million in annual sales since its founding in 1967. Mr. Cook wished to arrange a meeting to explore his joining Dakota as an officer and a stockholder. A major distributor of his firm, with annual sales of $3 million, also would be at the meeting to discuss shifting to become a Dakota distributor. Their tentative proposal was that they would buy 40% of Dakota's equity (30% for Cook and 10% for the distributor) as part of a total package in which they would "build your sales and take you national." Mr. Cook said that he had an idea for an improved spreader and had good contacts throughout the industry. Bob

[14] *The ads would be one-eighth of a page and would cost $200 per insertion. They would run in all six annual issues of three of the five leading magazines in the liquid fertilizer field.*

Speake didn't doubt their ability to make Dakota grow rapidly from what they termed its "sleeper spot" as the industry's tenth or eleventh largest firm. To him the critical question was not "Can we grow?" but "Do I want to grow anymore?"

As he explained to a business friend, he was already wealthier than he had ever expected to be. He hesitated to take risks and assume headaches just to pay higher taxes. Yet, he also hesitated to stand still and thought that he should consider the proposal carefully.

ASSIGNMENT

What should Mr. Speake do? Appraise his current plans and develop recommendations in regard to the problems and opportunities he faces.

8

Formation

Essentially, there are three ways to enter small business employment: go to work for someone else's small company, acquire a small company, or start a new company. Which approach an individual takes tends to depend heavily on opportunity and external pressures. But desire and preparation can also play major roles. The purpose of this chapter is to describe briefly what is involved in starting a new company.

MECHANICS

The formal procedures for setting up the shell of a company, whether a proprietorship, partnership, or corporation, depend on the state in which the company is formed and the type of business it is to be. Typically none of the steps is difficult, although many may be involved. The way to learn specific procedures in a particular locality is to call nearby governmental agencies (city hall will do for a start) and ask about the requirements. The agencies will either send an applicable list or refer the call to other agencies from which information can readily be obtained. There is no charge for this information.

Typical steps in bringing a company formally into being include the following:

1. Choose legal structure. (The appendix to this chapter discusses the options of proprietorship, partnership, and corporation.)

2. Choose location. (Possibly obtain post office box.)

3. Choose and register company name with appropriate governmental agency.

4. Obtain business license from city hall.

5. Obtain any other licenses, such as seller's permit, from other governmental agencies depending on location and type of business.

6. Set up system of keeping records of financial transactions, correspondence, taxes, licenses, and other required formalities.

7. Select logo and purchase letterhead stationery and business cards.

8. Take out whatever business insurance, or bonds are needed, as determined by discussions with two or more insurance brokers.

9. Pay applicable taxes.

Virtually anyone can mechanically proceed through these steps to become the founder, owner, and manager of a new business. Even incorporation can be handled without a lawyer, and thereby the founder can attain the self-created position of corporation president. All this is relatively easy and can be inexpensive, but having the company operate, transact profitable business, and produce income is something else again—and much more difficult.

REQUISITES FOR OPERATION

The mechanics of setting up the business are in most cases *not* the first steps in the process of forming a new venture, although they can be. Typically the mechanics are intertwined with other requisite start-up actions requiring more time, effort, money, and thought, actions needed to marshall the following five key elements for bringing the company truly into operation:

1. "Line" or technical *know-how* in such things as performance of the service or design, manufacture and application of the product, its procurement, sales, and so forth.

2. *Connections* with people outside the business whose assistance will be needed, for example, suppliers, bankers, lawyers, accountants, advertising agencies, middlemen, and others.

3. The *idea* or *concept* of the particular product or service the company is to offer, which must include some unique advantage to enable it to compete with existing products and services on which future customers are currently spending their money.

4. *Resources* both of a physical nature (selling and office space, plant, equipment, tooling and inventory) and of inside people to make the company go. Both of these resources may have to be acquired with a third resource, money.

5. *Customer orders* for what the company is in business to sell.

It might be expected that there would be a "best" order in which to obtain these five key elements. In fact, histories of successful start-ups reveal that although the above order is most common, any one of the five elements may occur first, and many different ensuing sequences of the other four may follow. There are no specific required amounts of these elements. Some entrepreneurs start with small amounts of any or all; others start with large amounts of some and less of others. Other factors may play important roles at times, for example, the psychological makeup of the particular entrepreneur, advantages of the local environment, economic developments at a certain point in time, and "luck," which has been characterized as the "coincidence of preparation with opportunity." Exceptions can be found wherein such other factors are missing in start-up but the five listed above appear virtually always to be present before a venture achieves sustained operation. Moreover, if these five elements are present and the entrepreneur has a desire to start a business, they will be sufficient to get it going.

KNOW-HOW

Technical know-how regarding the particular product or service is what most company creators have to begin with. This know-how is usually in either sales or engineering and, generally, it comes mainly from work experience. For example, an entrepreneur who is an ex-salesman could know the market needs that were not being adequately met, who the potential customers would be, what they would be likely to buy, and how they could be reached and persuaded to buy and at what price. An entrepreneur who has engineering experience would be aware of the state of the art in the particular technology, what capabilities that art might have to produce a next generation of products, and how to create those products. Other kinds of work experience with which entrepreneurs might start would be (1) operations, which could have given them an awareness of how to produce the same product or service at lower cost or in a way more satisfactory to customers, and (2) finance in which the entrepreneur could have learned about sources of available money plus investment opportunities to which such capital might be applied. In the mid-1960s many companies were formed as "conglomerates" by people whose experience was in finance. Their strategy was first to amass enough capital to buy controlling interest in one or two small companies, then trade stock in the holding company to acquire other companies, and then amalgamate them to form a larger company.

Before it comes fully into operation, any new company will somehow have to acquire several of these experience elements. Studies of start-ups have shown that success comes more frequently to entrepreneurs who have had experience in two or more of these different functional areas,[1] but most start without all of these work backgrounds—some without any. One personal strategy could be to seek out such experience before embarking on a new venture, perhaps deliberately working through several different jobs in order to become "rounded" in experience. A second approach could be to plunge ahead and acquire the experience as part of the start-up process. Possibly the start-up will be a failure, but it will be an educational one that will provide better footing for the next try. A third approach could be to seek out a team of founders whose backgrounds complement each other. A number of studies have confirmed the fact that companies started by teams tend to have higher odds of success than those started by solo founders.[2]

There is also the know-how associated with the process of forming new companies, and some people even make careers out of starting new business ventures. Usually, some of their ventures succeed and others fail, but these "career entrepreneurs" learn from both. They become good at spotting opportunities to pull together the elements of a venture and at "jelling deals"[3] that get the ventures

[1] *William M. Hoad and Peter Rosko,* Management Factors Contributing to the Success or Failure of New Small Manufacturers *(Ann Arbor: Bureau of Business Research, The University of Michigan, 1964)* .

[2] *Jeffery Susbauer, in A. C. Cooper and J. Komives,* Technical Entrepreneurship: A Symposium *(Milwaukee: Center for Venture Management, 1972)* , *p. 45.*

[3] *Orvis Collins and D. G. Moor,* The Organization Makers *(New York: Appleton-Century-Crofts, 1970)* , *p. 141.*

into motion. Part of this art includes a familiarity with the mechanics of start-up mentioned before. Other important parts become knowledge of whom to contact for particular kinds of aid and skill in negotiating for what is needed. It is not uncommon for these "starters" to have several ventures and other potential ventures in process at one time and to sell them off as they either fail or begin to expand and offer a sellout profit that can be plowed back into new start-ups.

Study of entrepreneurship can provide (1) an awareness of the kinds of know-how that may be needed for different ventures, (2) practice in thinking through the sorts of problems faced by new ventures and, consequently, increased skill in making good venture decisions, (3) the beginnings of know-how about the business aspects of start-ups and about where additional know-how and assistance can be obtained, and (4) knowledge of how a few ventures began, which may add insights into how opportunities can arise or be found and exploited.

CONNECTIONS

One of the least studied aspects of management and yet one of the most important aspects, particularly in the start-up of new companies, is the executive's connections with people outside the company who can help the company. From these connections often come the motivation to start a company, an idea for what the company should sell, resources, customer orders, and necessary expertise. The company formation process cannot proceed very far without establishing connections with outsiders for advice, supplies, recruitment of people, operating space, advertising, or sales channels. One would-be entrepreneur chose a deliberate strategy of contacting people as a way of getting his own company. He made it a regular practice each day to contact at least one person who might be useful in a start-up. Within 2 years he had acquired a partner and the two had begun an "after-hours" venture in engineering consulting. Within 4 years the entrepreneur was president of his own manufacturing company that sold a sophisticated bio-medical product line that he had obtained from his contacts.

Some connections who may be helpful and some of the ways they may be able to help include the following:

1. Other Entrepreneurs. Information on recently formed local firms can be gathered from a number of sources, for example, bankers and lawyers. A more convenient source may be the financial section of the local newspaper, where new companies are typically announced. A visit to the editor's office should yield a number of leads immediately. Then the entrepreneurs who founded the companies can be contacted. Most will be willing to talk about their experiences to a student or would-be entrepreneur. They may also be able to tell about new venture opportunities.

2. Salesmen and Engineers. These can be sources of new product and service ideas. They can be met by socializing and by "asking around." Some may be potential partners for a new company.

3. Bankers. It will be most advantageous for the new company to have the services of an alert, able, imaginative banker who is experienced with small companies and who is resourceful in helping them. Although there tend to be few bankers like this, they can be found by asking other entrepreneurs whom they have found to be most helpful. One justification for following up with visits to check out these leads can be to ask bankers about other venture opportunities they may know about. They may also be aware of companies for sale. Banks themselves sometimes fall heir, either through default on a loan or through death of the owner, to companies they would like to sell. Commercial loan officers and trust officers can be good sources of information on these.

4. Lawyers. Several types of legal expertise can be important, and no single lawyer can cover them all, although a large law firm may include as members specialists in all of them. Patents, copyrights, trademarks, and secrets are a highly specialized field of law. Taxes are another specialty. Forming a corporation or partnership need not be complicated, but it is best to have a lawyer who has handled many corporation or partnership agreements. It is accepted practice to ask a lawyer how many agreements he has handled. Other fields of law that may become important to the entrepreneur are contracts and (hopefully not) bankruptcy. One way to locate experienced lawyers in these specialities is to pick the largest law firm in a metropolitan area. A second way is to ask other entrepreneurs and bankers who perform these different types of legal work for them.

5. Other Professionals. There are several categories of professionals who may not be needed until the company is in motion but who can be identified beforehand to save time later when time will be more difficult to spare. A CPA firm can help design a simple and economical bookkeeping system that will have the capacity to grow as the firm grows. If the company is to go public at some stage there may be need for a history of audited statements. (For example, going public requires audited statements for 3 years or since inception.) Venture capitalists often require audited statements before they will invest in a company.

The insurance that the company will need will depend on the kind of work the company performs. General brokers usually carry full lines of insurance. Instead of dealing with a broker whose business is homeowner and automobile insurance, it is better to deal with a broker whose business is largely commercial firm insurance. Similarly, there are real estate firms that specialize in commercial property instead of residential property. These firms can help when the company needs space that complies with its business needs and with the city zoning requirements.

Advertising agencies, personnel recruiters, public relations specialists, venture capitalists, and credit bureaus may also be needed at some points during the start-up. It is most advantageous to learn which ones to use before starting a business. The best way to find these professionals is to ask other entrepreneurs and then to visit and interview two or more of each. At the very least, it would be well to develop a list of some who have been recommended because they have performed services for other new companies.

6. Governmental Contacts. Depending on the type of business to be performed, different governmental connections can be necessary. All ventures must have some sort of business license and all ventures must make tax payments. Offices in city hall can provide information on them or advise where to go for more information. State departments of commerce may be more helpful with special requirements, such as environmental impact statements, that may apply to particular types of companies.

7. *Suppliers and Sales Channel Connections.* These will clearly depend on the particular type of business to be entered. Suppliers' problems will be how to obtain trade credit and get delivery. With sales channels—which may include wholesalers, manufacturers' representatives, retail dealers, and so forth—the problems will be how to persuade them to take on a line and push it instead of other lines they might choose to push which might yield more return for less effort than a new line. Although it will not be possible to know which of the above will be needed in advance of choosing the type of business, there would be no harm in contacting raw material suppliers and manufacturers' agents and wholesalers selected from the Yellow Pages to ask how they work and what is required to get their help in doing business, particularly how to get supplies at favorable prices and credit terms.

VENTURE IDEA

The element most influential in bringing a new venture into focus is usually the idea or concept for what the company will buy or produce and sell. In order to make headway against the tide of established competition, the concept must include some sort of advantage, for example, an innovation in product or service, lower price, higher quality, better service, a more convenient location, or more effective selling. Sometimes a market can be found in which existing companies have grown flabby and can be outclassed or in which rapid expansion of demand has created needs, but existing companies have not grown fast enough to meet these needs.

Where do these concepts for new ventures come from? Most often they are from the entrepreneur's prior work activity. Care must be taken not to steal from the employer things to which the entrepreneur is not entitled. For example, it would be illegal to remove drawings of products, lists of customers, or written descriptions of processes or procedures unique to the employer's operation and use them to compete with the employer. If the employer's products are patented, they cannot be copied by anyone. If the employer has trade secrets (just what constitutes trade secrets can sometimes be complicated to determine), the employee must have the employer's permission to use the trade secrets in starting a new company. If there is an agreement between the employee and employer that the employee will not go into competition within a specific time period or within a specific geographical radius after leaving the employer, the agreement must be adhered to. Nevertheless, it is still very possible to find ideas arising out of employment that suggest new customers to serve, new products to make, or new ways to operate with a new company. This is obvious because there are so many new start-ups.

Another source of ideas for new ventures is from among the connections discussed above and from among acquaintances, friends, relatives, and business associates. Many companies have begun with the social formation of a small group of would-be entrepreneurs who agree to meet together at regular periodic intervals, such as one or two evenings per week and jointly search for venture opportunities. Many others have come from simply exchanging ideas with acquaintances about business ideas, opportunities, and desires. Still others have emerged from hobbies and avocations. Almost never have they come from solo "brainstorming" by would-be entrepreneurs, although many have come from chance observations of people's needs. Deliberate search and brainstorming by would-be entrepreneurs may increase sensitivity to such needs.

The variety of possible ventures is virtually limitless, as can be seen by looking through the Yellow Pages or a manufacturers' directory or by driving through business districts. The *Standard Industrial Classification Code,* prepared by the federal government for classifying types of businesses, lists over 900 categories. An entrepreneur may be able to invent a new product or service in one of these categories, devise improvements on one that already exists, join forces with someone else who has conceived an invention, acquire rights and tooling from another company that is not exploiting a product it already possesses, become a middleman for someone else's product or service, or acquire someone else's company.

Criteria for checking a product or service idea will vary, depending on the product or service involved and the resources and inclinations of the entrepreneur, but the following questions should usually be asked:

1. Will it work? Sketches, drawings, and other pencil and paper analysis can help test it, as can expert advice from people familiar with that sort of thing. If a product is involved, a breadboard, mock-up, and/or prototype may have to be made, either in the entrepreneur's own shop or else by a custom manufacturer or local job to test feasibility.

2. What will it cost? Presumably this will depend on volume and options in the design.

3. Who will buy it? Why? How much will they pay? How many will they buy? Experts such as wholesalers, retail store buyers, mail order house buyers, and other middlemen may give helpful opinions. Trying the idea on people may also help, but this can be misleading because people tend to react one way when they are asked by a stranger to hand over money and react another way when they are asked by a friend what they think of a potential new product or service idea.

4. How great will the margin be? To earn a profit, products typically must sell at retail for four to five times manufacturing cost and services must sell for between two and one-half and four times labor and materials. Allowance must also be made for unforeseen developments as well as for competitive price cutting.

5. How great an investment will be required? Large investment needed for setup, plant, or tooling tends to raise the risk and the required profit. Return on investment must be considered. Ability to get by with very low investment, however, may mean that it will be relatively easy for competitors to enter and will depress margins and lower profitability.

If the product or service shows sufficient promise after being tested by the above questions, it may be worthwhile contacting an attorney to obtain legal protection. A product idea may be protectable with a patent that theoretically provides monopoly rights for 17 years. Patents usually take from 3 to 5 years to be processed and issued, but during that time others may copy the product. After that time, competitors still may be able to design around the patent. If they openly violate the patent, expensive legal action, possibly costing more than the royalties that may be extracted if the suit is won, will be needed to crack down on the culprits. For this reason, patents have sometimes been called the "rights to bring suit." Consequently, many inventors do not bother to obtain patents. If the venture idea involves written material, it is easy and inexpensive to obtain a copyright by following procedures that can be obtained through writing to the Library of Congress. Copyrights are valid for 28 years and may be renewed once. If the venture idea includes a unique name or label, a trademark may be obtained which lasts 20 years and may be renewed any number of times.

RESOURCES

Virtually any enterprise needs money to start. This money is commonly referred to as *seed capital*. Early expenses will include costs of letterhead, possibly incorporation costs or legal costs of drafting partnership papers, taxes, office equipment, a post office box, travel expenses, possibly secretarial assistance and accounting help, patent expenses, prototype fabrication costs, and so forth. Seed capital costs may range from $200 to $25,000 or more before the company can claim to be in business in any substantial way. If the entrepreneur takes time off from a regular job to perform the founding activities, there will be an additional cost in lost salary or living expense, depending on the point of view.

Seed capital is not available from venture capital firms, banks, or outside investors generally because there is no going concern to invest in. From a bank's viewpoint, there is essentially no collateral against which to lend. From an investor's or venture capitalist's viewpoint, there is no tangible evidence that the company exists and can be expected to make a profit. Consequently, seed capital must be obtained from personal savings and from that of friends and relatives. House mortgages have provided seed capital for many startups. Sometimes customer advances against orders can be obtained, but not often.

As more and more money is needed for such things as market research, initial plant, equipment, tooling, prototype testing, and market testing there may be ways to extend seed capital. One option for a married entrepreneur is to have a spouse who is employed. Another option is to bring in partners who contribute capital or who retain their jobs to provide shared living income while the company gets started.

New companies often find ways to cut corners on spending and minimize the seed capital needs. Used equipment and office furniture cost much less than new. Many items of equipment can be leased instead of purchased. Equipment can also be bought on time, or financed through chattel mortgages. Some lawyers will take stock for legal services, and sometimes machine shops will take stock as payment for tooling and prototypes. "Moonlight" labor and work by housewives or GI's if there is a military base nearby can be obtained at low rates, although care must be taken that the time costs of organizing a fractionated work force not exceed the savings of lower hourly rates. Shop equipment may be available in the entrepreneur's garage or in a friend's garage. Some employers allow employees to work in company shops during the evenings, and many junior colleges and technical schools offer courses at low cost in which shop equipment can be used. Alternatively, particularly at the start, it may be advisable to have products made by custom manufacturers instead of setting up shop before products are proven. It costs more to manufacture that way, but the risk is lower. If profits are not possible above the costs of custom manufacturing or subcontracting, it may be a sign that the margin potential of the new product is too slim anyway.

Still further strengthening of the company's ability to recruit seed capital will come when customer orders begin to arrive. Then bankers and investors alike will begin to have faith in the company's promise for doing business and making money. On some orders it may be possible to obtain progress payments. Many companies have been started with money raised against military contracts and even by obtaining advances from the government and large companies that served as seed capital.

As the company takes on substance, suppliers will become willing to extend trade credit, and other forms of capital will become available for expansion, as discussed in the section on financing the small firm. Most of these sources, however, will require some sort of "track record" of performance. It therefore makes sense for a would-be entrepreneur to embark on a savings program early and to avoid buying goods on credit or investing in risky schemes that may wipe out the stake needed later for venture start-up.

CUSTOMER ORDERS

The most convincing sign that a company is truly coming into existence is the arrival of orders from customers. To bring this event about, there can be many options, including the following:

1. Selling directly through salesmen, mail order, government contract bidding, or establishment of retail outlets. The advantage in this approach is that middleman complications and commissions are minimized. Retail sale has the added advantage of minimizing the need to carry accounts receivable.

2. Selling through commissioned agents such as manufacturers' representatives who also carry other lines. Advantages in this approach are that fixed costs of selling are minimized, for commissions are paid only after sales are made, and that the company can have its product or service offered as part of a full line carried by the representative. Start-up selling time can be minimal because the representative has already established customer contacts. There is no way, however, to push the representative to sell for the company because the representative is a free agent. The agent will generally work hardest on lines that make the most money most easily, and these often are the established lines, not the product of a new company.

3. Selling through distributors. An advantage is that distributors will stock the product and thereby enable the company to sell in larger quantities and not have to carry as much inventory. Moreover, the geographical spread of distributors' inventories may allow more rapid servicing of customer orders in distant localities. From the customer's point of view, the source of supply thereby becomes closer. The price paid for this advantage is the discount that must be provided to the distributor or wholesaler.

A typical pattern in manufacturing companies is to start first selling through manufacturers' representatives. Then when sales grow large enough to support company salesmen, the representatives are dropped in favor of hiring full-time sales departments in order to allow better control.

But how does it all begin? Where do the very first sales come from? How are the manufacturers' representatives engaged? The following examples illustrate some of the many possible variations:

1. A manufacturer of aircraft radios took a mock-up of the product, before a working model had been produced, to distributors. He explained a new service policy under which a pilot would receive an exchange radio immediately if his radio failed so that his aircraft would not be grounded for radio repair. He also offered a larger discount than other existing manufacturers did. The typical reaction of distributors was, "Where do I sign?" Before the first unit was produced orders were already rolling in.

2. A laid-off aircraft worker designed a fish smoker for himself. He also made some as presents for friends. These friends asked to buy some for their friends. He took some units to sporting goods stores and immediately received orders.

3. A graduate student earning his way through school by repairing TV sets devised a very powerful hi-fi amplifier (700 watts). Friends asked him to make units for them and then other people began calling him. Soon dealers were asking and orders were coming in.

4. The designer of a new hobby product asked if he could demonstrate the product in a discount supermarket. He rapidly sold out his stock and started making more. The market offered to stock the product and he went to other markets, building sales.

5. An inventor of a new type of bicycle lock approached the buyer for Sears, Roebuck. When Sears agreed to carry his product, he was in business.

6. Three aerospace engineers devised a new solid waste disposal concept. They began contacting government agencies until they found one that was interested. Their first sale came in the form of a government contract.

7. A hi-fi speaker maker began by running the following classified ad in the newspaper: "For Sale: Engineering Prototype Hi-Fi Speakers." He then opened his own retail outlet by renting a storefront.

8. An employee found that his employer was having trouble obtaining screw machine products locally. The employee contacted a machine dealer, bought his own screw machine, and obtained orders from his former employer.

9. A college dropout bought photographic enlarging equipment for a hobby and taught himself how to use it. When a friend offered to buy the first print, the young man decided to ask drugstores if he could make high-quality prints for them. They gave him orders and he was in business. Later, at the suggestion of a friend, he tried advertising his service in a photo magazine. Within 2 years his sales were over a million dollars annually through mail order.

10. A man who was manufacturing plastic shrunken heads in his garage rented a booth at the county fair. Soon he was sold out, and shortly after that he had the opportunity to sell his garage operation to a larger company for a substantial profit.

PLANNING

If the company is to continue, these first sales must only be the beginning of a continuing automatic pattern of sales. The first products or services may be handled personally by the founder but eventually the products or services will have to be handled by people who are unfamiliar with them. This means both that the workers must be trained and that action must be taken on the problems that are likely to result. Products that work well in the prototype stage can exhibit all sorts of problems when they are first made on the production line by people other than those who designed them.

Customers' complaints about the "bugs" in the new products or services must be handled. Avenues must be set for servicing, providing replacement parts, and reworking. It will be necessary to keep ahead of competitors who are likely to enter if the new company begins to show promise. This may mean that the company will have to expand rapidly in order not to lose important segments of the market to new entries. Expansion requires capital, and if capital is not being generated fast enough internally, the founders may have to obtain more on the outside.

This capital search, however, may take time away from other important work needing to be done in running the company. Thus, the entrepreneurs will be faced with how best to allocate their time and energy. This points to the desirability of planning ahead insofar as possible. If the capital needs for expansion have been estimated in advance and those from whom capital will be sought put on notice that they may be needed, then less time will have to be taken from other things to get the capital later. If the company's product has been more fully analyzed and tested before being put on sale, there will be less drain on the company later for coping with dissatisfied customers. If the manpower needed to expand operations has to some degree been sought out in advance, less energy will be taken away from operations to recruit when people are needed for growth.

Planning and pre-testing are very helpful and can begin with the construction of prototypes and with pencil and paper analysis. Then testing (both in physical terms and in terms of soliciting review and advice from outsiders) can proceed. Searching for outsiders can be a way of developing connections that may be helpful to the company and of locating resources that may later be needed. Thus, planning and pulling together the key elements needed for start-up can work together. The would-be entrepreneur should bear in mind (1) that all the key elements discussed in this section will be needed and must be located somehow and (2) that things begin to happen only after action is taken. Company formation is not a process of academic contemplation but rather one of search, personal encounter, negotiation, commitment, and action.

APPENDIX—PROPRIETORSHIPS, PARTNERSHIPS, AND CORPORATIONS

Three choices are open to most businesses in choosing what legal form to become. The largest number of small companies start as proprietorships, or "one person" companies. In this type of firm the owner owns the business by personally possessing all the assets used in the business, and bills owed by the business are personally owned by the owner. If there are two or more owners who personally possess the assets and owe the bills, the business is a partnership. Many small businesses, all law firms, most accounting firms, stock brokerage firms, and real estate syndicates are partnerships. The third type of legal form, the corporation, is one in which the assets for doing business are owned by the corporate entity, which is in turn owned by those who hold its stock. Unlike proprietors and partners, the stockholders of a corporation are not liable for bills owed by the business, unless they make a separate agreement to become so. Virtually all large companies in the United States are corporations, although there are no size requirements and there are many small ones as well.

Proprietorships. To form a proprietorship can be as simple as setting up a lemonade stand. "You just start doing business," was the comment of one entrepreneur whose action to establish a proprietorship was simply to buy space in the Yellow Pages advertising himself as a home remodeling firm. Sometimes cities and/or states additionally require acquisition of a business license, which is usually very simple and cheap to obtain by a visit to the local city hall.

Advantages of the proprietorship (sometimes called "sole proprietorship") form include:

1. It is simple and cheap to set up.

2. There is no need for the owner to clear business decisions with anyone, such as partners or corporate directors.

3. Profits belong to the owner and need not be shared.

4. The owner's personal income tax is the only one that need be paid on profits.

5. Expenses and losses of the business are directly tax deductible for the owner.

6. "Red tape" is minimal. No lawyer is needed for setup. No corporate reports or inspections are required. There are no restrictions on the type of business to be performed, which can be changed at will by the owner. Termination of the firm is as simple as startup.

Disadvantages of the proprietorship form include:

1. Any liabilities of the business apply to the owner personally. If someone sues the business and wins, it is the owner personally who must pay. If the business fails, the owner must personally pay its bills.

2. The single owner may not be as likely to succeed going solo as compared to bringing in resources and talents of others.

Partnerships. To form a partnership can be as simple as setting up a proprietorship. If two people contribute money or other assets to the venture and agree to split profits a partnership automatically exists, regardless whether there is any written agreement. It is therefore very easy to "fall into" a partnership without realizing it, and because either partner can make the other liable for debts of the business it can also be dangerous. If there is no written agreement of the partnership and the partners decide to split up, courts will typically divide assets of the business "down the middle," even though one partner may claim to have been entitled to more than a proportionate share of ownership by verbal agreement. Because of such pitfalls it is easy to find many examples of partnerships which became unhappy relationships. The importance of seeing a lawyer first is greater with partnerships than with any other form of business. To find a good lawyer, don't use the Yellow Pages. Ask other entrepreneurs. Ask bankers what lawyers they use. Pick one with experience in the particular field.

It should be possible to save on lawyer's fees by first thinking through what should be included in the partnership agreement, possibly even "roughing out" an agreement in advance. Some likely items to include are:

1. Names and addresses of partners, and of the business.

2. Type of activity business is to perform.

3. Amounts of money and/or items contributed by each partner.

4. Salaries and withdrawals each partner is entitled to.

5. How profits or losses should be divided.

6. Duties, responsibilities, and restrictions, if any, on authority of each partner.

7. Provision for admitting new partners.

8. Provision for access to the firms and/or its records by partners.

9. Provision for division of assets on dissolution.

10. Procedure in event of death or disability of a partner, such as provision of life insurance and method for computing value of interest in the partnership.

11. Procedure to be followed in event partners disagree.

A *Limited Partnership* provision can also be included. This creates two classes of partners. One class is that the *General Partner,* which is entitled to vote but must also assume liability for any debts or obligations incurred by the business. This general partner can be a corporation. The other class includes *Limited Partners,* who can be excluded from liability for the company's debts but are not entitled to vote. Formation of such a partnership requires state registration and more "red tape" than ordinary partnerships.

Advantages of the partnership form for a business include:

1. It can be simple to enter.

2. It is a way that more talent and capital can be brought into a business.

3. Tax advantages are like those of the proprietorship.

4. Once formed, reporting and government interaction are minimal.

Disadvantages of the partnership form include:

1. Personal liability may be unlimited. One partner can bind another or be bound by others without agreeing or even being informed of it.

2. Because each partnership agreement tends to be "custom" and personalized rather than standard, it can be hard to avoid legal "bugs."

3. Death or withdrawal of a partner automatically causes legal dissolution.

4. Sharing ownership with others or raising additional capital can be awkward. Absent a specific agreement for it, a partner cannot sell or assign his interest without consent of all partners.

Corporations. To form a corporation a set of rules set up by the particular state must be followed. Any state can be chosen for the filing, and for those choosing to file outside their state of residence the one most often chosen is Delaware, but generally it is more convenient to file in the state of residence, and most corporations do so. Most corporations are set up with the help of lawyers, whose fees typically range from $200 to $500 depending on the complications involved, but it is not necessary to use a lawyer, and a person can choose to do the job personally without one. Standard forms are available at legal stationery stores, and information about filing can be obtained from the state capital and legal references.[4]

Advantages of the corporation as a legal form include:

1. Stockholders are not personally liable for debts or obligations of the company. (Knowing this, however, lenders and suppliers often require owners of small corporations to sign personally on notes so that the owners' assets do back up corporate obligations.)

2. Transfer of any fraction of ownership is relatively convenient, simply by transferring shares of stock. When money is short, it can be possible to pay people with stock, although taxes on such transactions can in some circumstances be complicated.

3. Raising capital through sale of stock, or issuance of options, possibly contingent upon certain performance or conditions, can sometimes be advantageous. Care must be taken, however, to learn about and observe "blue sky laws." These require that full disclosure of risks be made to buyers of the stock and that such sales be made only to people capable of understanding what they are getting into, "sophisticated investors." There are also many legal limitations regarding how many potential investors can be approached under what conditions, where stock can be sold, what kinds of stock can be sold, and so forth, which apply depending upon the circumstances. Consequently, although setting up a corporation with a few investors can be fairly easy and uncomplicated, the raising of capital through broader stock sales should never be undertaken without first consulting the Securities and Exchange Commission, the appropriate state agency, and a lawyer.

4. More tax options are available to corporations than to proprietorships and partnerships. Although tax deductible pension plans can be set up under either, more flexibility is possible under the corporate form.

5. Corporate regulations require the discipline of explicitly stating what the nature of the business is to be, who the directors and officers are and what

---

[4] *Nichols, Ted,* How to Form Your Own Corporation Without a Lawyer for Under $50, *Enterprise Publishing, 1000 Oakfield Lane, Wilmington, Delaware 19810.*

their authorities and responsibilities are. Control can be concentrated even with widespread ownership.

6. Because it has its own existence, the corporation can more easily be continued if its owner (s) die.

Disadvantages of the corporate form can include:

1. Money and effort are required to form it. If a lawyer is used, there will be a fee ranging upwards of $200. (Sometimes lawyers accept stock). There will be state filing fees, possibly around $100, and in some states a minimum capital requirement. (Possibly $1,000, though some states, such as Delaware, require none.) The same kinds of provisions listed above under partnerships need to be thought through and stipulated for a corporation.

2. More "red tape" is required for maintaining it. Records must be maintained, formal meetings held, and reports filed with the authorities. The corporation must confine operations to what its charter provides (which is an argument for writing a very broad charter) or else go to the trouble of formally amending the charter. Geographic operations in other states require filing with them for legal permission. More fees and regulations then result.

3. More taxes apply. States levy capital stock taxes scaled according to size. The federal government requires payment of income taxes by the corporation on its profits. If the profits are then passed on to shareholders as dividends, the shareholders must pay personal income tax on them, so that taxation is double. Attempts to circumvent dividends by either paying very high executive salaries to reduce profits or keeping the cash in the corporation are discouraged by penalties aimed directly and effectively at preventing such tactics.

It is possible to reduce some of the federal tax disadvantages, however. Under some conditions a corporation can elect what is known as a "Subchapter S" form, under which income in the corporation passes directly to shareholders as in proprietorships and partnerships without a double tax. If during its formation the type of stock issued is designed as "1244 stock," moreover, it is permissible for stockholders to deduct any capital losses incurred in the corporate investment from ordinary income. These two provisions are often desirable in small corporations and consequently should be investigated before a new corporation is established.

Arthur Hanan

In late 1975 Art Hanan, an M.B.A. student in his final year of study was reconsidering how he should proceed in the search for a suitable business venture. He had already embarked on a deliberate formal search, and over the preceding 30 weeks he had devoted approximately 500 hours to it on top of carrying a job and going to school. In that period he had looked at roughly 30 ideas in some depth, plus another 50 in less depth. In an effort to manage the search effort rationally, he had kept records of his progress, and at intervals paused to make attempts at improving them. Recently, he had been able to learn of the experience of three other people who had also performed deliberate searches for ventures. It seemed to him that before proceeding further in his present pattern he should both reconsider the results it was producing and evaluate the new information about others' experiences. Then he thought that he should recast his plan with the benefit of this additional experience and get on with the search.

Art Hanan, 29, married, father of five children, held an undergraduate degree in business administration, an associate arts degree in digital electronics from community college, and was completing his masters in business. He had been employed full time throughout his studies, both as an aerospace company computer programmer and currently as general manager of the Lecture Notes enterprise at a large Los Angeles area university, which provided "Phi Beta Notes" and syllabus materials to students on a break-even, nonprofit basis. The Lecture Notes firm employed from 90 to 110 students on a part-time basis for this work under the direction of the full-time manager. He had also worked as a household products salesman and as a computer technician. He estimated his total assets, mainly house equity and auto, at $10,500, his outstanding debt, aside from mortgage, at $4,000, and the monthly amount needed for living at $700 minimum, $1,100 for moderate circumstances, and $1,400 up for comfortable circumstances.

INITIAL THREE IDEAS

At the outset Art had three ideas that he intended to explore in depth. He planned to proceed with implementing the best of the three. The first was a personalized letter service for children to which parents would subscribe. A computer would be fed data on each child and then would write appropriate letters at intervals. The idea had been triggered by Art's observation that his own children delighted in receiving letters. He spent nearly 100 hours over the next several weeks learning computer assembly language and setting up to write the letter, but then he concluded that the costs of operation would be triple his initial estimates, largely because of the heavy computer demand, and would require an unacceptably high price to users. He later learned of a California company that used a simpler approach to write personalized children's books.

His second initial idea was to start a classified advertising newspaper that would focus on a limited population area and be given away free in local stores. Its commercial advertising would be limited to sale items only. Many of the advertisements, he believed, could be computerized with "canned" programs, and by contacting a printer he learned that compatibility between computer and typesetting machines was not a problem either technically or union-wise. The venture was shelved after roughly 20 hours of effort mainly because he believed that several thousand dollars plus considerable learning about advertising technology, neither of which Art could immediately afford, would be needed to start.

Art's third idea was for a campus sandwich shop that would make food available at sites on the widespread university campus not presently served by existing food services. His research indicated that 76,000 student lunches per week were bought off campus and that the existing sandwiches available from university food services could be improved upon. He planned to manufacture the sandwiches at one site and sell them both through roving sandwich men with baskets and other coffee and donut stands already operating. Recruiting a second MBA and drafting his own partnership agreement, Art wrote a prospectus for the venture, lined up approval from various university agencies, and approached two banks for loans. One turned down his request for a $5,000 advance, the second for a $2,000 loan. Consequently, he shifted his approach to arranging for payment for needed supplies and rent out of percentages of receipts and persuaded key suppliers to go along with him. This left him, after investing an estimated 200 hours in this venture, with the need for approximately $800 for initial setup and equipment plus a need for money to live on while getting started.

EXTENSION OF SEARCH

Although he had initially intended to confine his investigation to the three initial ideas, Art found as he researched these ideas and thought about problems of starting a venture that his mind kept suggesting other alternative venture ideas as well, and he decided to make a deliberate exploration beyond the initial ideas in an effort to find a more ideal venture. "In developing ideas for examination," Art said, "I usually made a conscious effort toward the different and offbeat. The ordinary small business such as laundromats had no appeal to me, since I felt them to be typically limited in potential and large in start-up costs." He found that sometimes ideas would emerge when it was impossible for him to investigate them immediately. Sometimes he would have several ideas before he had an opportunity to study even one of them. Exhibit 1 illustrates this overlapping pattern with reference to some of the ideas on which he spent the most time. He also found that because of his job and family commitments, the amount of time he could spend on the venture search varied considerably. His overall sequence appears in Exhibit 2.

In the first 3 weeks of the project Art's job took most of his time, though a little was spent on his original three projects. Then around the fourth week other ideas began to occur, as Art described it. (Numbers refer to sequence following first three ideas.)

4. Cleaning company to bid on government work. Paperwork on window washing for Downey CSA warehouse consisted of 26 pages. After talking to professional cleaner acquaintance, estimated 15 days clear weather for 2 people. Contemplated partnership so work rules wouldn't apply. Use student labor, bid low, take 20% for arranging deal, plus deduction for tools and materials I would own. Drawbacks: jobs too infrequent; large performance bond needed. Procrastinated and missed it.

5. Similar company for private jobs. Students would be only competitive edge, and there would likely be labor problems with students on such work.

6. "Woman's World" shopping center with classes, day care, kiddie movies, and other refinements. Time and money requirements too large.

7. Gas bill provoked idea of buying blower and insulating homes. Many prob-

EXHIBIT 1 Timing of some ideas (numbers in parentheses indicate approximate hours spent).

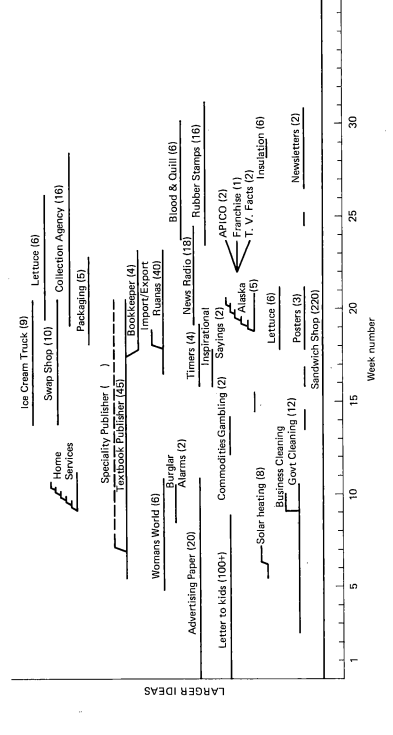

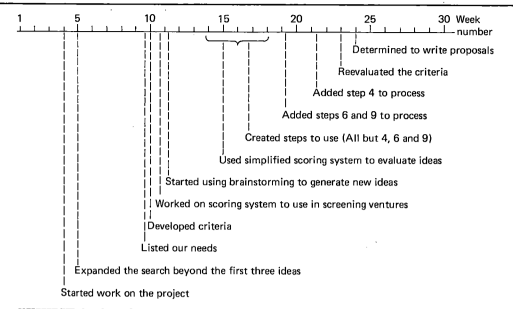

EXHIBIT 2 Overall sequence of the development of the selection model.

lems, lack of money, how to do good job (professional told me hard to make it even after rafter beams covered), respiratory system danger, and could not see cheap way to get clients.

8. Maybe solar heating for homes. Located some units that might work well. But hard to sell in a warm climate.

9. Noticed a garage sale, by the same person, several times in a row. Compete with Goodwill? Not suited to interests.

10. Job problems at Lecture Notes triggered idea of entering publishing business. Few universities have text publishing capabilities, and 17 geographical areas lack lecture note operations. High return on capital possible. Rejected because of time needed to reach profitability, start-up capital needed, and requirement to leave home area to start.

11. Research on printing costs revealed gap in market between high quality slow and fair quality quick work. Why not fair quality slow at lower prices? Estimate of costs showed could cut lowest price in

town by one-third. Capital requirement of $10,000 killed idea.

12. Found that some shops in midwest perform as above by mail order. High shipping costs, but small run prices save 15%. Maybe broker to people unaware of this service. Profit too low.

13. Reupholstering business? Another of those "nothing" ideas.

DEVELOPMENT OF CRITERIA

In addition to the above ideas, many others occurred to Art which, like the reupholstering business, he considered not worth considering and rejected out of hand. He began listing his needs as venture ideas occurred and around the tenth week developed them into a formal set of criteria. The needs and desires he listed were:

I. Time at home. Although the start-up phase might draw time heavily, and although he recognized 16-hour days continuously might pay, Art believed no degree of success could compensate for failure at home. By 1½ years after start-up he thought that he should have weekends and most evenings available for his family.

II. Flexibility in hours, to allow for children's violin lessons, preschool, church functions. . . . "It means much to a child when her father comes to see her school play Tuesday afternoon."

III. High probability of satisfactory income. Venture should probably be "moonlight" during start-up.

IV. Interesting and fun to start and run (unless with hired manager).

V. Prefer Pacific Coast location.

VI. Personal preferences—not heavy personal selling, status is unimportant, new problems and challenges.

From this list and from his reactions to the different venture ideas Art developed a list of "ideal" criteria, intending it only for screening ideas. He found, however, that it also guided his search. These were:

A. Low initial investment and high positive cash flow.

B. High income per unit time expended.

C. Some monopoly features.

D. Flexibility in personal time.

E. Challenge that extends own knowledge and abilities.

F. Not tied to one customer or supplier, rather many.

G. No unethical or dishonest characteristics.

H. Continuous need by customers (recession proof).

I. Not need partners or financial backers.

J. No heavy personal selling required by myself.

K. Service rather than product (wave of the future?)

L. Easily taught to assistant.

M. Preferably franchisable.

N. Not geographically tied, suitable for urban or suburban.

O. Interesting and enjoyable to me.

P. Industrial rather than consumer product or service.

Q. Original, with new twist to it.

R. Prestigious for its owner.

S. Allow long vacations without collapsing.

T. Features allowing retention of control even after growth.

U. Not dependent on my personal skills to run.

V. Resistant to unionization.

W. High potential for growth.

As he continued his search, Art at first tried looking only for "perfect" ventures and also tried to apply a quantitative scoring system. "Unfortunately," he said, "I quickly discovered I could not do it. Interactions between criteria, their relative and shifting weights, and the complete subjectivity of some criteria all combined to create a problem I could not even define rigorously, let alone solve. After a trial pass at filtering I decided it was not essential for an idea to pass all the criteria (in fact, some are contradictory). I did, for a while, use a simplified scoring system, tallying up plus and minus points for each idea, and it proved helpful, so long as I did not attach too much significance to the score without looking at the entire idea.

Ideas that continued to emerge included the following:

14. Wife's wanting carpets cleaned triggered idea of rug and wall cleaning firm when I thought about how much it would cost us to have our carpets cleaned.

15. Manufacture burglar alarms cheap enough to sell in supermarkets. An article said another alarm maker found high percentage of sales went to people recently robbed. Maybe check police blotter for sales leads. Capital needed too high.

16. Recalled that as scoutmaster I had set up a drive to collect waste computer printout paper. Advantages: commands price twice that of newsprint, sources concentrated in few firms big enough to offer volume but too small to have own

salvage. Troop produced over 400 lb per week at 1¼¢/lb. Decided good for charity operation, but not for business.

BRAINSTORMING

In the thirteenth week of the project Art began trying the approach of brainstorming, but working alone rather than with others. This quickly yielded another 14 ideas he considered worth noting plus many others which in his opinion were not.

17. Large-scale letter shop, combined with printing.
18. Computer programming services (using own skill) for small business.
19. Sight of ice cream trucks triggered thought of using trucks, driven by high schoolers, to sell groceries.
20. Cutting and selling firewood, which is available free in forested lands.
21. Sight of abandoned orange trees gave thought of making and selling dried fruit.
22. Rent metal detectors at beach concession stands.
23. Develop plot of land for city residents to farm.
24. Start a trout or salmon farm.
25. Sell devices which capture for home use the methane gas produced by backyard compost.
26. Print, package, and sell books by professors.
27. Publish short summaries of different areas of learning to serve as refreshers called, "Snap Shots." Sell in student bookstores.
28. Friend suggested Colombian ruanas (ponchos) might sell well on campuses. Some sold in department stores for $80 and in local stores "cheap" for $35. Asked store owner for quantity bid and estimated his cost at $5–$10. Contacted brokers and air freight offices. Took sample to U.S. Customs Office. Learned "wool" in ruanas was 50% acrylics and "handmade" character was probably the result of a maladjusted semiautomatic

loom; violated customs labeling requirements, Wool Products Act, and Textile Labeling Act. Could be expensive to correct.

29. Investigated import/export business in general, but began to feel like a "sheep among wolves."
30. Grocery home delivery service by high schoolers. Couldn't get the numbers to work out in financial estimates.

The search was interrupted by Art's regular job from the fourteenth week through the sixteenth week. Then, during the seventeenth week, another 21 ideas emerged as follows:

31. Pachinko machines bought rebuilt in Japan for $9 each and imported by a service friend might be retailed in the U.S. Something like pinball, the machines sold in Japanese mail order catalogs for $150 and up.
32. Executive timer coupled with small notebook could be programmed to buzz at key times during the day as reminders of important things to do, meetings, etc.
33. Inspirational sayings display: "paragraphs ranging from religious sayings to salesmanship boosters and ego builders to philosophical quotations . . . many offices use such signs."
34. Calendar-adage gadget, like wheel with three concentric circles of printing, (1) days, (2) months, and (3) saying for each date, to be mailed monthly to subscribers, who insert, according to their choices.
35. News format radio: combination of tape machines, preparing the news offline, and presenting it with a sequencer. Newscaster could key in a code designating time, type of news, and priority. Messages on separate cassettes would be merged by computer overseen by an engineer. Commercials similarly inserted.

"This was another example of my prematurely chasing trivia," Art recalled. "I spent time trying to determine the flux requirements for analog and digital tapes and the start and stop times for recorders before realizing it was too big a project. Even then I toyed with the idea of developing and selling the idea."

36. Renting typewriters or selling typing to students in finals "crunch" or maybe through phone hookup to businesses; possibly coupled with printing services.

37. Cable car mass transit idea. ("Incredibly poor for me.")

38. Selling legally piratable recordings. ("Legal, but not moral.")

39. Kiddie shows in shopping center movie houses timed to match the average woman's shopping trip.

40. Friend's venture in earthworms was intriguing, but because the earthworms doubled their population every 90 days they spilled over into his backyard.

41. Convert a school bus for commuters.

42. Poster sales through a central organization that would drop ship to around 100 campuses.

43. Friend's hydroponic garden gave idea of selling lettuce to the University, which buys $75,000 worth per year. Net of $20,000 estimated possible. Needs half acre hothouse, and University bureaucracy sometimes takes 6 months to approve contracts. Farm workers might demonstrate.

44. Received mass mailing circular and thought of doing same for local merchants.

45. Buying nails in small packages at hardware store at very high markup suggested bulk buying and packaging. Somebody makes high margins on this, but I couldn't find out who.

46. Conversation with farmer suggested mink breeding.

47. High cost of replacing own windshield suggested opening outlet to resell junkyard windshields.

48. Abandoned service station prompted idea of renting workspace and tools for do-it-yourself car repair. Maybe hire one mechanic to help guide patrons.

49. Conversation with shopowner friend suggested idea of starting collection agency. Existing ones charge up to 50% for collection of small accounts and alienate customers. Began thinking about series of letters to replace door pounding, legal action, and garnishment. Legal requirements hurdles turned out to include $200 license, $5,000 surety bond, plus $5,000 bank balance for all such agencies started since 1973. Talked to attorney general about eliminating this obviously anticompetition clause, but no hope.

50. Learned advertising agencies make no charge for many services, but take markup on media clients use (typically 15%) and shun small accounts (less than $50,000). Alternative might be to service smaller accounts on a fee basis for services rendered and share media discount with clients. Could operate with low capital by collecting cash and utilizing media credit terms. Offer additional services through freelancers and students.

51. Construct vacation homes, seeking out ways to shave costs through bypassing some of the more archaic building codes.

FORMULATING A SEARCH PROCEDURE

The need to filter the substantial number of ideas that were occurring plus impatience with himself for spending so much time investigating details of ideas that did not work out prompted Art to work further on his screening procedures. He consequently began to work out a sequence of steps, as follows:

A. Generate ideas by brainstorming or other observation of potential.

B. Filter through judgment criteria as before.

C. Modify rejected ideas to correct deficiencies, once at most, then return to step B.

D. Investigate troublesome areas in depth and optimistic aspects with care.

E. Accept the idea if it gets this far,

and either work further on it or "store" it for future work.

F. Begin work on most appealing ideas. "In reality," Art said, "this was both a final step in the search process and the first implementation step, since I dropped several concepts after running into unanticipated problems. This was a concession to my impetuous nature, since I could not help starting work on some schemes, even though I had not thought through the angles carefully."

Armed with this somewhat more formal scheme, Art returned to the process of idea generation, but not until after a 2-week interruption. He commented:

> 52. Week 19 was consumed by a flurry of Alaska ideas, any number of schemes in which I could supply some part of Alaska's needs and make gobs of money. One that I thought about longer than most was that of building small (35-ft) mobile homes in Seattle with heavy insulation and towing them to Fairbanks in time to rescue (at generous rents) those thousands of pipeline hopefuls who could not find housing.
>
> 53. Become a coordinator for local print shops. Average out load for each, using agreed upon algorithm. Possible problems: expertise, union, antitrust, cheating.

Art shortly found it desirable to add two more steps to his search procedure. Following step D (investigate troublesome areas), he added: based on the information turned up in step D (filter the idea through the criteria again). At the end of the procedure, following step F (begin working), he added another step: Reassess the idea in light of all information gathered to date. Evaluate its chances for success and use the filter once more to see how closely it still fits the ideal venture. Then write a formal proposal. With these modifications to the list of screening steps, the search continued:

> 54. Friend who sells to 70 Northwest health food stores mentioned that many home fruit dryers are being sold. Price gap existed between $50 "cheapie" and $100+ fancy models. Estimated could produce intermediate model for $20 cost.
>
> 55. Thought of several possible mail order products. Art said, "I viewed the entire mail order field as basically one venture idea, since a plethora of ideas and products are sold in almost exactly the same manner. I decided that this field, though 'perfect' for me in many ways, was not likely for initial success and shelved it until better able to spend time and withstand losses on some products."
>
> 56. Annoyance at filling out name, number, address, and zip for each library book led Art to look for a rubber stamp. He figured if 1,200 students (3.5%) bought one the first quarter and 250 per quarter after that he could pay for a vulcanizer. Finding none locally, he checked suppliers. Their price, $6, led him to request mail order house quotes. None came.
>
> 57. Sell blood and quill pens (sterilized and anticoagulated) for people to write blood letters, pay taxes, etc. Problems: packaging, obtaining quill pens, government approvals on blood sales.
>
> 58. Flower party, similar to Tupperware. Wife is doing it; early results are promising.
>
> 59. Passing glance at restaurant ideas prompted thought of a site analysis service. Restaurant Association members would be sent glamorous pitch for such a computerized service; apparently just a multiple regression package, easy to imitate. Different applications might include market segmentation and new product line analysis.
>
> 60. Newsletter idea had occurred several times since reading *Weaver's You, Inc.* Ego appeal high, but failed on criteria.

Art's final step in the search procedure was to fit the following between steps C and D: Get reactions from friends and acquaintances. "A negative reaction or confusion on their part was to be taken as an indication that I had not thought through some phases," he said. "As it turned out, their comments were more perceptive than expected, and several modifications were made based on their suggestions."

61. "Franchises looked appealing in advertisements, but their luster evaporated upon closer investigation," he said. One called APICO claimed only $2300 was needed as an initial investment to sell auto parts. But potential problems revealed by study included unknown product quality, firm unheard of by Better Business Bureau, and too broad a product line to carry adequate inventory.

62. Big name fast-food franchise. Attempted meeting with vice president who was coming to town. He never came.

63. TV *Facts* magazine franchise owner in nearby city willing to sell for $13,000. Free magazine; revenue from advertisement sales. Owner performed own layout work, ad design, and typesetting, "so main office would not mess up his customers." Pressed his wife and unsuspecting friends into delivery service. "He quoted averages for other such operations around the country showing great profits," Art recalled, but (grudgingly) revealed data indicating the best he did was $400 gross per week against expenses of $550."

64. Find tasks like house painting, moving, curb lettering, and gardening for college students in summer.

ANALYSIS

The first part of filtering was supposed to be discarding thought that would obviously be of no use to me. After that, I was supposed to be relentless in carving the ideas into three piles, those that met most criteria and had no obvious fault, those that had one or more problems but were possibly salvageable, and those for which I had no hope. In fact, the first two received almost all entries. I fared much better in eliminating other people's ideas.

Although the pretty model I devised made each step a clean break from the one before it, I found the process blurred considerably. It proved impossible to talk about realism in the third step without doing some of the in-depth investigation that was supposed to occur in the fifth step. The investigation itself often turned out to be implementation, since I often jumped in with both feet.

I was especially proud of the idea of getting the reactions of others, but found two problems in this step. First, I tended to sell the project, shielding tender areas I knew to be weak. Second, I did not get each person to probe in depth. I just spent a few minutes talking about any idea with any one person, and then went on to another person, giving the same basic points and getting the same superficial reactions. One benefit I had discounted was the value of ideas I would get from others, which was in error.

In-depth analysis was intended to apply to only a few ideas, but my failure to prune the list before reaching this point clogged up the system so I wound up working on up to six ideas at once. Most of the ideas were mine, and it seemed my inner self hated to admit some of them were crummy. I feel that this clogging also impeded generation of new ideas, since there were always some in the mill. Still, even when I tried to halt the flow and concentrate on analysis, other ideas kept trickling in. (Statement of Art Hanan.)

65. Set up a manufacturing operation to make imitation sausage and other meats using bulgar wheat.

66. Haul loads of fruit, vegetables, and hay from San Joaquin Valley and sell them in bulk to consumers.

67. Start a new enterprises magazine or newsletter.

68. Considering high costs of mail, why not have newsboys deliver it, using computer to match paper routes with addresses?

69. Create monthly home-study series on "natural living," for example, how to make your own soap, etc. Maybe sell key materials.

70. Custom manufacturing: solicit ideas from businesses for products they would like, then produce for them.

71. Become a manufacturers' representative.

72. Portable computer service from a truck.

73. Market research service for firms.

74. Agency to hire out part-time workers (not temporary employees).

75. Homemaking package for students who are "batching," to include plates, pots, utensils, etc.

76. Company that matches products created by one company with a company more interested in producing them.

77. Greenhouse kits with attached solar traps for year-round operation in colder climate.

78. Sell services of midwest printing firms locally.

79. Advertising agency using student skills and labor for sandwich boards, mimes, paintings on cars, etc.

80. Home canning supplies shortages and fears of home canning dangers prompted idea of canning service for city residents.

81. Sell and/or manufacture dehydrated foods.

82. Fishing pole with detachable line and spool would allow fishermen to have several lines in water for each pole in boat.

83. Commuter service to blood bank for donors; charge bank for recruitment.

84. Hand plows and other "ancient" equipment for urban farming.

85. Manufacture wood and coal burning stoves that can be hooked to ducts of central heating systems.

86. Rent garden tractors. Employ heavy promotion.

87. Run tours to local entertainment spots; charge the entertainment spots.

88. Tape cassettes of bible readings with commentary, inspirational materials, and pep talks.

89. Newsletter analyzing correlations between politicians' promises and voting of politicians.

90. Rent motorcycles, especially for those whose own motorcycles cannot pass noise laws.

91. Buy and operate radio station.

92. Anti-eavesdropping "bug detector," camouflage sound-maker to conceal speech, crypto device for phones, etc.

93. Small area newspaper.

94. Advertise and drop ship $40-mimeograph machine that few people are aware of.

95. I worked out a method (in block form) to make a supercheap computer terminal. Couldn't find way to turn profit on the idea.

96. I plagiarized the idea of a "rent-a-thief" that a businessman could hire and then fire as an example for the other employees.

CONCLUSIONS

The one idea that Art followed through with by developing a full written proposal was for a campus sandwich shop, the third of his initial three ideas, which he had worked at off and on throughout the project. He felt that several other ideas would be worth further work as soon as time allowed.

I discovered that my bank-proposal type of writeup was definitely not an operations plan for implementing a venture. The small things you are able to skip over when writing your lofty financial and marketing analysis will return to haunt. For example, in writing the financial analysis you always assume that your cash flow is channeled through a bank. But which bank? How do the funds reach the bank? Have you controlled for pilferage and for outright theft of the cash box? (You have included a cash box in your list, haven't you?)

An even bigger problem was working with other people and finding the right ones to talk to. In the rubber stamp project, for instance, I had planned a smooth progression of events that became stymied by lack of the right contacts for obtaining the product. I looked in vain, finally learning about such references as *Thomas Register* that they never told me about in school. Having information about contact is extremely important. I also found that as my communications with others grew, I tended to generate ideas that required even more contacts to make them work. My first few schemes were ones I could implement alone, while later ones tended to require more political interactions and multiple suppliers.

Working with partners was intended to solve two problems: procrastination and going in too many directions at once. To some extent it worked, because after taking in a fellow M.B.A. on the sandwich project I found that making commitments to him forced me to keep working toward a single goal. At other times it worked less well, as when I spent a lot of time trying to sell an idea to another potential partner who was to provide money and salesmanship. He proved to be more a talker than a doer, and he wasted my breath. In another case, I took in partners who held me up rather than helping me move forward, so I was worse off than I would have been alone. I will think several times before entering another partnership, though I may do so. (Statement of Art Hanan.)

EXHIBIT 3 Partnership agreement.

This is a mutual agreement between Arthur Hanan (Art) and Thomas Hitson (Tom) for the purpose of establishing a business.

The business to be started will be engaged in the general business of manufacturing and wholesaling sandwiches at or near the University campus, plus any additional projects that will be developed in the future.

It is agreed that there shall be 2 partners, Art holding 50.01% of the business. No additional partner shall be admitted, nor will either partner's interests be transferred without agreement by both partners.

If one partner should desire to sell out, the other party shall have first opportunity to purchase his interests.

It is agreed that the business shall incorporate as a California corporation as soon as cash flows permit. The name of the new corporation shall be "Edible Inc." There shall be 999 shares in the first offering, with the following division of shares: Art, 499 shares; Tom, 498 shares; Art's wife, 1 share; Tom's wife, 1 share. The offering shall be so constructed as to obtain Subchapter S standing under IRS rules.

Both parties agree that they shall not engage in or be part of any food sales operation at, or in the immediate vicinity of, the university campus (other than this business) from this moment until 2 years after exiting from this partnership agreement.

Each party shall input up to $500.00 in cash, in establishing this business on a dollar-for-dollar basis. In addition, both persons agree to input as much time and labor as is possible in implementing the program. This is construed to mean at least 40 hours per week if the party has not obtained full-time employment elsewhere, and 30 hours per week if he has full-time employment in the Los Angeles vicinity.

Under both the partnership arrangement and the future corporation, profits shall be dispersed in the following manner: 15% to Art; 15% to Tom. The remaining 70% will be allotted in various manners, depending on actual circumstances. The following cases have been determined to be most likely and are herein presented. Should a different situation apply, the specifics will be decided upon by agreement or by arbitration.

Scenario 1: One partner works full-time while the other works part-time. The full-time partner receives an additional 55%, the part-time person 15%.

Scenario 2: One partner works full-time, the other not at all. The working partner receives the full 70%.

Scenario 3: One partner oversees a hired supervisor. The overseeing partner receives 15%, while 30% goes to the employee. The remaining 25% is made available to the employee (based on a formula including longevity and achievement bonus). Unearned bonus will be divided equally between the partners.

Should there arise an argument between the partners, both parties agree to binding arbitration as specified by AAA rules. After incorporation, this section shall not apply.

A copy of the sandwich shop partnership agreement that Art drafted personally appears as Exhibit 3.

SUBSEQUENT DEVELOPMENTS

Recently, Art encountered another student, Dave Latona, who had also attempted to conduct a methodical search for venture ideas, but he used different methods. Dave had discontinued his search, partly because of financial and family pressures and partly because he had just encountered a job opportunity that offered him a substantial advancement. He still hoped eventually it would be possible for him to develop his own business, however, and he welcomed the opportunity to exchange experiences with Art. A description of Dave's search appears in Appendix I.

Among the entrepreneurs Art had encountered in his investigations it seemed that most had come upon the ideas for the ventures they entered largely as a result of chance combined with their work activities rather than as a result of methodical searching. Two, however, had utilized deliberate searching procedures, and he thought he should consider their experiences in reviewing and developing his plans. One of these two said that he had followed up a number of advertisements in the "business opportunities" section of a metropolitan newspaper. "Most of them were just taverns, restaurants, motels, and gas stations," he said, "but I did run across one interesting idea in which I invested, a product developed by a jockey for training horses. We will be entering manufacture of it shortly." The other approach this man had tried had been to run classified advertisements himself saying "capital and management help available for new ventures. Send ideas." This method had yielded mostly what he called "kooky" responses, but the number and variety he received, 20 within a week, surprised him. "I finally concluded that the most interesting deals I was going to find would come through my job, and I would have to find one that my employer would not want to exploit and would let me take it and run myself," he said. "So far it has not come."

The second man had used still another method. After deciding that he wanted to have his own company, he began a deliberate campaign in which he would try to contact at least one person each day through mail, phone, or visit, who might be able to help him get a venture. It could be a potential partner, supplier, financier, another entrepreneur, inventor, or any number of others. He made these contacts during lunch and coffee breaks and after work, and in addition he took every opportunity to attend entrepreneurially oriented training programs such as university symposia and small business administration courses. Within 2 years he had joined with a partner and the two had undertaken some small development contracts in their spare time for other companies. After another 2 years, they had identified an attractive licensing opportunity for a product developed by a university under government contract. Their licenses gave them exclusive rights in return for a royalty, and they were in business, with sales of $500,000 in their second year and looking toward twice that in the third year.

> "The key in my opinion," this second man observed, "is contacting people. They are the ones with the answers. You should start with people lower on the ladder technically, the salesmen in the field who know what people want; then as you learn from them begin to contact people whose technical knowledge is deeper—the engineers. Finally, when you really know what the product is about technically and what you can do with it, you are ready to talk with higher executives to see where a new company might be able to fit in and serve needs that they either cannot or don't want to bother with. I think you can start a company in just about any industry with that approach if you really want to."

On this optimistic note, Art decided that he would continue looking for an attractive venture. The sandwich shop, even on a 30,000 student campus, he felt might be too small for his long-run needs. But were any of the other ideas he had come up with better? If so, which? If not, then by what procedure should he continue his search?

ASSIGNMENT

Evaluate the approach taken by Art in searching for venture ideas, and recommend two alternative plans of action for him: (1) a plan by which to implement whichever of his ideas you think has most merit, and (2) a plan by which he could continue his search to find still better ideas.

Appendix I
Dave Latona's Search

The venture search performed by Dave Latona began with a review of several books dealing with innovation and starting new ventures. His search consumed approximately 228 hours over a 10-week period, generated roughly 37 ideas from brainstorming, reviewing legislation, attending meetings, and conversing with individuals plus well over 100 other ideas from reading books about ideas. Approximately 11 of these ideas were regarded by Dave as "good," but none of them proved sufficiently promising to invest in seriously.

Dave Latona, 41, married, the father of five children, was Director of Management Engineering for the Southwest Hospital Association. His job required long hours and kept him on the road traveling around the state much of the time. In 1959 he earned a bachelor's degree in electrical engineering, and since then his work had ranged from logical design through computer systems design, programming and sales, to industrial engineering and management training. For 9 years he had been employed by IBM as a systems engineer. For 2 years prior to his present job he had worked for Battelle Institute in its systems program for hospitals. He assisted administrators, department managers, and head nurses with improving the quality of service and with utilizing resources. While with Battelle he had seen friends who worked on technical projects with the Institute develop new ventures around their projects by obtaining licenses from the Institute and then forming companies to exploit their ideas. Another friend had sought out a business to buy and thus become self-employed. These developments were part of the stimulation that prompted Dave to begin his own venture search, although he noted that the friend who bought a business had found it necessary to spend 6 months looking full time to find one.

PRIOR INVESTIGATION

In an earlier paper for an entrepreneurship course Dave had studied the problem of entering business through acquisition of a going concern. He had interviewed several bankers, an accounting firm executive, and an IBM salesman to learn how acquisitions might be found and purchased. Sources of leads, he found, included:

Banks
    Branch managers
    Trust department managers
    PR and business development offices
    Bank internal newsletters
Accountants—but not large firms
Lawyers
Commercial realtors
Direct contact of desired companies
Newspapers
Business brokers

Two suggestions that came from several of the courses and that he found persuasive were: (1) Choose one or a few types of companies most desired and visit all of that type in the area to inquire which are for sale. (2) Talk to as many people as possible to maximize the odds of finding the desired venture. He was informed that small companies that are for sale seldom reach the marketplace, because they are first picked up by a friend, another similar business, an employee, or a relative. At the same time, it was also pointed out that small company owners frequently do not plan for succession in the business and, consequently, may have to sell in haste or may die with no arrangements, in which case the business may fall to heirs or a bank trust department who are inclined to sell it. Active and persistent search may reveal these opportunities. Therefore, he decided to search for both new venture ideas and acquisition opportunities, but he found that the same sources of information generally did not apply to both, although one conversation in search of ideas turned up a ski resort for sale. Because he spent so much time concentrating on the new idea search, he found that there was no time left for an acquisition search.

NEW VENTURE IDEA SOURCES

After reading several books about innovation and starting new ventures (listed in Exhibit 1), Dave drew up a list of symptoms pointing to situations where opportunities might exist:

1. Existing company weaknesses, such as high costs, slow service, product deficiencies, poor location, ineffective marketing, or customer dissatisfaction.
2. Voids, shortages, or surplus in products, services, materials, talents, capital, etc.
3. Undesirable tasks, because they are boring, hazardous, or socially unfashionable, or because they cause discomfort, etc.
4. Upheaval or changes: political, technological, social, population, regulation, demand, or supply.
5. New combinations, inventions, talent, locations, etc.

Awareness of such opportunities, he read, might be triggered by many possible sources. These he sorted into the following categories, recognizing that many possibilities overlapped:

1. Studying. Industries, organizations, area, groups, individuals, products, services, properties.
2. Creative Thinking Techniques. Forced association, morphology, synthetics, brainstorming, attribute listing, scenario forecasting.
3. Government Agencies. SBA, Patent Office, Department of Commerce, Department of Agriculture, foreign trade commissions, state and local governments, chambers of commerce, economic development groups.
4. Universities and Colleges. Students, professors, theses.
5. Printed Materials. New product lists, idea books, trade publications, technical journals, consumer magazines, professional magazines, corporate publications, newspapers and newsletters, advertisements, new product reports, business directories, library reviews, franchise lists.
6. Organizations. R&D organizations (Battelle, G. E., Bell Labs), search companies, patent lawyers, private foundations, public institutions, information and service groups, associations.
7. Gatherings. Trade shows, invention expositions, conventions, professional meetings.
8. Individuals. Entrepreneurs, inventors, engineers, suppliers, customers, customers of customers, consultants, professionals (doctors, dentists, accountants, lawyers), technology brokers, patent agents, bankers, financiers, friends, relatives, work contacts in other organizations.

Noting the large number of possible sources, Dave decided to narrow his search mainly to two fields, health care and information process, and to concentrate on trying five types of sources: universities, meetings, printed materials, creative thinking methods, and discussions with individuals. In each of these categories he felt that he could explore only one or a small number of approaches.

University Doctoral Dissertations. The two avenues for locating university ideas which Dave considered were talking to people, such as students and professors, and doctoral dissertations. The first of these two he regarded as part of the "individuals" category, which left the "university" category with one option, doctoral dissertations. Visiting a nearby University Medical School Library, he began looking through doctoral dissertations, starting with the "A's" and proceeding alphabetically. Six hours and 289 dissertations later he abandoned this approach. He recalled:

> This was a very boring and unproductive procedure. Out of 289 items investigated, only one, an analysis of one particular type of artificial kidney, appeared to offer any information that might lead to new business possibilities. All the others seemed too superficial, were not oriented toward subjects that lend themselves to new business opportunities, or were too technical for me to understand enough to discern business leads. In general, I felt this approach might be useful for experts in that field. Also, maybe dissertations in some other field, such as engineering, might have offered more ideas.

Meetings. Dave went to four gatherings where he hoped to encounter ideas. Two were conventions, one sponsored by the hospital chapter of the American Institute of Industrial Engineers and the other by the American Hospital Association for Hospital Management Engineers. These took 5½ days total, and although he found them interesting, Dave concluded that they were unproductive:

> After touring the Queen Mary in Long Beach and visiting Marineland in Palos Verdes, I thought that perhaps some other city could support similar attractions, but no unique ideas occurred. An old horse-drawn fire truck converted to sell popcorn and hot dogs outside the Queen Mary and netting around $300 per summer day suggested that such concessions might be more profitable than I had thought. Some shops with an English village theme, gas lanterns, and cobblestone walks suggested that shopping centers with strong themes and atmosphere can also be profitable.

Eight hours spent at the Southwest Hospital Association midyear meeting also failed to suggest what Dave regarded as new opportunities, except during one conversation in which the need for a good means of solid waste treatment and disposal was mentioned. Nor did four hours spent at a recreational vehicle show suggest any ideas that were not already being exploited by others. He did gather the impression that a series of campgrounds or recreational vehicle parks strategically located around the state might be a promising investment. He also thought that a computerized reservation system for independent campgrounds and vehicle parks might possibly be worth trying and that there might be a place for a management and construction organization to spot likely locations, develop, and possibly manage them. He concluded that the main benefit of attending meetings in search of venture ideas was the opportunity it gave for talking with others expert in the field, and he also concluded that perhaps trade shows might be more productive of ideas, especially for manufacturers.

Printed Materials. Two types of literature, in addition to the dissertations mentioned earlier, that Dave investigated were what he characterized as "ideas books and those dealing with starting new businesses" (listed in Exhibit 2) on which he spent approximately 45 hours, and pending state and federal legislation related to hospitals and health care, on which he spent approximately 12 hours. The first of these two he found highly enjoyable, observing, "It's great fun reading about the experience of others; in fact, it appears to be habit forming." It also gave him an enormous number of ideas, so many that it became difficult to investigate even a small fraction in depth. "It opened up so many general areas where ideas might be found," he said, "that it was difficult to decide which to pursue further." The main difficulty, however, was that it seemed to him that all the ideas generated by this approach had either had their day or else never would. Since the ideas were available to all readers, he concluded that whatever ones had not been used by others must be unfit. The habits of thought cultivated by practicing this type of search, however, he thought might prove useful, particularly if applied in a person's own area of interest and skills.

> Only one specific idea from these books seemed to fit my interests and inclinations. It was Harvard's Information Gathering Service in which student employees would gather information, research new products, write speeches, develop computer programs, translate materials, and so forth, for a price. Another more general idea that came from reading these books was that many really good products can be found by experimenting with common chores and activities. An example would be a friend of mine who has recently developed a new lightweight newspaper carrier bag that can be seen at night. He has been doing well marketing it nationally to newspaper firms who in turn sell it to their boys.

Reviewing pending legislation on health care began with looking through the Federal Register plus Hospital Association newsletters from across the country. Eight ideas emerged from 12 hours' work in these materials, most of them within the first 2 hours. These ideas included organizing centralized services shared by several hospitals for biomedical engineering, microfilming, industrial engineering, credit and collection services, and so forth. Other service ideas triggered by this literature were for home health care for the ill, aged, or injured, training programs for home health care personnel and for long-term health care facility employees, and both individual and community health care planning services.

CREATIVE THINKING METHODOLOGY

After reviewing books on creative thinking, Dave experimented with the approach of trying mentally to convert items he saw during work travel around the state into income-producing ventures by putting them together in different combinations, moving them to different localities, or applying them to different uses. He also drafted lists of unrelated items and tried putting them into different combinations to generate useful ideas. The first of these approaches he found generated three ideas; the second, none. His conclusions after approximately 11 hours of working with these approaches were that possibly more time spent on them would have improved the payoff and that they might have worked better had he used them in collaboration with other people of different backgrounds. Their main value then, he thought, might be in stimulating communication with other individuals, a source he considered particularly promising.

INDIVIDUALS

"Talking with individuals," Dave said, "was by far the most interesting and productive approach I tried." The people he chose included relatives, hospital managers, and professional associates, and he found that from 86 hours applied to this approach he was able to identify 20 ideas, of which 8 he regarded as "fairly good." These included:

> 1. Auditing shipping invoices from the past year for business firms to detect use of incorrect rates. Apparently, because of the complexity of rate schedules, goods are often shipped at higher rates than they should be and the difference will be refunded if caught within one year.
> 2. Establishing a microfilm systems design and brokerage service. An expansion of this would be specialization in hospital microfilming problems with rapid turnaround for in-state hospitals.
> 3. A mobile car repair service or boat repair service that would not require owners to take their car or boat to a shop. Instead, the shop would be brought to them.
> 4. Buying and selling computer time by using available time on systems installed in various commercial or institutional organizations around the area. In other words, this would be matching two needs for a fee.
> 5. Development of a simulation model for school finances combined with special

skills in conducting public discussions to assist school districts in communicating with the public, with other governmental agencies, and with teacher organizations. This idea could possibly be expanded into other community planning activities, for example, health planning.

6. Combining a typewriter and addressograph machine so that two operations can be accomplished at once.

Dave noted that none of his idea search conversations had been with inventors, development engineers, professors, or technicians. He thought that perhaps they might be even more helpful than the ones he had already talked with.

In reflecting on the idea search experiment overall, Dave commented:

This project proved much more difficult than I expected. Fewer ideas than I anticipated were uncovered and those that did turn up were of poor quality. The time required in just locating ideas did not leave enough for systematic investigation as I had originally planned. My findings indicate that talking to individuals and creative thinking, especially related to specific activities or problems, are the most productive approaches to finding new business opportunities. Investigating legislative changes may also work, though it did not for me. The main finding is that it appears much harder to come up with good new ideas than to find good going concerns that might be purchased as a way of entering business.

EXHIBIT 1 Dave Latona's initial information sources.

Allen, Louis L., *Starting and Succeeding in Your Own Small Business.* New York: Grosset and Dunlap, 1968.

Bunn, Verne A., *Buying and Selling a Small Business.* Washington, D.C.: Small Business Administration, 1969.

Dible, Donald M., *Your Own Organization.* Santa Clara, Cal.: Entrepreneur Press, 1971.

Heidingsfield, Myron S., anl Frank H. Eby, Jr., *Marketing and Business Research.* New York: Holt Rinehart and Winston, 1962.

Karger, Delmar W., and Robert G. Murdick, *New Product Venture Management.* New York: Gordon and Breach, 1972.

Kay, Edith W., and Walter F. Shaw, *How to Start Your Own Business.* New York: Ziff-Davis Publishing Company, 1945.

Kelley, Pearce C., Kenneth Lawyer, and Clifford M. Baumback, *How to Organize and Operate a Small Business.* Englewood Cliffs, N.J.: Prentice-Hall, Inc., 1968.

Lasser, J. K., *How to Run a Small Business.* New York: McGraw-Hill Book Company, 1963.

Liles, Patrick R., *New Business Ventures and the Entrepreneur.* Homewood, Ill.: Richard D. Irwin, Inc., 1974.

Mueller, Robert Kirk, *The Innovation Ethic.* New York: American Management Association, Inc., 1971.

Murphy, Thomas P., *A Business of Your Own.* New York: McGraw-Hill Book Company, 1956.

Newman, William H., and James P. Logan, *Strategy, Policy, and Central Management.* Cincinnati: South-Western Publishing Co., 1971.

Slocum, Donald H., *New Venture Methodology.* New York: American Management Association, Inc., 1972.

Steiner, Gary A., ed., *The Creative Organization.* Chicago: The University of Chicago Press, 1965.

WWWWW Information Services, Inc., *Buyerism—How to Buy a Franchise or a Small Business.* Robert A. Fowler, 1970.

Wayne, William, *How to Succeed in Business When the Chips Are Down.* New York: McGraw-Hill Book Company, 1972.

EXHIBIT 2 "Idea books" Dave read.

Cossman, E. Joseph, *How I Made $1,000,000 in Mail Order*. Englewood Cliffs, N.J.: Prentice-Hall, Inc., 1963.

Cossman, E. Joseph, *How to Get $100,000 Worth of Services Free Each Year from the U.S. Government*. Rev. Ed. New York: Frederick Fell, Inc., 1975.

Editors of Fortune, *Adventures in Small Business*. New York: McGraw-Hill Book Company, 1957.

Editors of Fortune, *100 Stories of Business Success*. New York: Simon & Schuster, Inc., 1954.

Getty, J. Paul, *How to Be Rich*. Chicago: Playboy Press, 1965.

Hicks, Tyler G., *Magic Mind Secrets for Building Great Riches Fast*. Los Angeles: Parker Publishing Co., 1971.

Payne, Jack, *The Encyclopedia of Little-Known Highly Profitable Business Opportunities*. New York: Frederick Fell, Inc., 1971.

Sandman, Peter, and Dan Goldenson, *How to Succeed in Business Before Graduating*. New York: The Macmillan Company, 1968.

Walton, Sidney, *How to Start Getting Rich*. Profit Research, Inc., 1963.

Witt, Scott, *How to Make Big Money at Home in Your Spare Time*. Los Angeles: Parker Publishing Co., 1971.

Camping Resorts of Puerto Rico

By May 1971 David Simmons had been developing plans for a proposed new business for several months. He hoped to develop and operate a series of campgrounds in Puerto Rico in which he would utilize permanently installed recreational vehicles on leased land in seaside parks. While he was investigating the project and developing the business plan shown on pages 301–324, he was also supporting himself. He was eager to raise venture capital, but he did not know what further actions he should take at this time.

David Simmons received his B.S. in industrial engineering in 1969 and his M.S. in

industrial administration in 1970 from the University of the Midwest. While a graduate student, he was head of a student group that sought to find job opportunities in small businesses for masters students. Upon graduation he declined offers from several larger firms to join Leisure Systems, Inc., a new company being established by Leonard Hoyle, a stockbroker and entrepreneur in St. Louis.

Leisure Systems had been organized to pursue a number of entrepreneurial ventures conceived by Mr. Hoyle, and David Simmons was the first full-time employee. Mr. Hoyle had sold stock in the corporation to a number of his brokerage customers. David joined the company in October 1970, with the expectation of investigating and possibly managing one or more of the ventures. Initially, he investigated campground franchises, including a specific location in the Ozarks that had high tourist traffic.

Subsequently, his efforts focused on the concept of campgrounds in Puerto Rico, with permanently installed recreational vehicles on site for tourists who would fly to the island. It appeared that parkland might be leased from the Recreational Development Corporation (RDC) of the Commonwealth of Puerto Rico. David Simmons and Leonard Hoyle flew to Puerto Rico to negotiate for the lease of parkland near Humacao on the east coast of the island. Subsequently, negotiations were broken off by RDC. It appeared to David that RDC officials had taken a dislike to Mr. Hoyle who had negotiated in a brusque manner.

By January David had become disillusioned about the managerial ability and the ethics of Mr. Hoyle. Mr. Hoyle disclosed that he was planning to dissolve Leisure Systems. When David asked whether he might personally pursue the Puerto Rican camping resort venture, Mr. Hoyle indicated orally that he would not object.

In February 1971 David left Leisure Systems. His wife taught in the local schools and he accepted an offer to teach one night course in a local university. He devoted the remainder of his time to developing plans for the camping resort. He began a detailed investigation of the market, investment requirements, and operating expenses.

David sought help from a number of people, including a professor at The University of the Midwest, the treasurer of a small technical consulting firm, and an entrepreneur who had been successful in franchising. Each of these introduced him to others who provided information and assisted in identifying factors that needed further investigation. David and his wife were able to meet their living expenses and the cost of some travel to gather information. However, David did not feel that he could afford to go to Puerto Rico for on-site investigations and for negotiations with RDC. Furthermore, he hesitated approaching RDC before he had made some preliminary arrangements to raise capital.

One banker told David that he should not pursue the idea until he was older and had developed a "track record" as a successful businessman. The more deeply David investigated the proposed camping resort, however, the more optimistic he became about its potential. He had recently completed the business plan (shown on pp. 301–324) and hoped to move ahead quickly before potential competitors saw the opportunity.

Proposed Camping Resort for Humacao, Puerto Rico

INTRODUCTION

The purpose of this report is to introduce a proposed venture developing a series of camping resorts in the Commonwealth of Puerto Rico. These resorts will be in cooperation with a private branch of the Puerto Rican government and will be available to both tourists and native Puerto Ricans.

PUERTO RICO

Puerto Rico, "Rich Port," is located just off the eastern tip of the Dominican Republic, 550 miles due north of Caracas, Venezuela, 1,600 miles southeast of New York, 1,050 miles southeast of Miami. It is the smallest of the Greater Antilles Island group and is a rectangle 100 miles long by 35 miles wide, or nearly the size of Connecticut. The mountainous central portion, which constitutes three-quarters of the island's terrain, is bordered by a broad coastal plain trimmed with palm-lined beaches meeting the turquoise waters of the Caribbean Sea on the south and the Atlantic Ocean on the north.

A land of great scenic beauty, Puerto Rico provides a distinctive and most agreeable style of life, blending its own Spanish heritage with the most modern conveniences in supermarkets, shopping centers, and health and housing facilities. Puerto Rico offers a next-to-perfect climate; the average yearly temperature on the island is 79°F (76°F in winter and 83°F in summer). The island averages 360 days of sunshine each year and has a steady breeze to moderate the warmth of the tropical sun. There are no flies, mosquitoes, snakes, or other pests commonly associated with the summers in the continental United States.

The most efficient means of reaching the island is by air; a more leisurely approach is to take a Caribbean cruise on one of the many steamship lines. Some sample *round-trip* air fares are: New York, $132; Chicago, $230; Miami, $100; Detroit, $213.

THE PROJECT

The project under consideration is a series of deluxe camping resorts to be located throughout the island. The land used will be leased (35-year lease) from the Recreational Development Corporation (RDC) of the Commonwealth of Puerto Rico. The RDC is a government established corporation charged with developing recreation throughout the island.

Since there is no camping in Puerto Rico today, the RDC decided to turn to private enterprise for assistance. The promoter has been in continuous contact with the RDC concerning the rental of the land. This company is highly enthusiastic about this project and is willing to grant the initial developer the option to develop all the campsites throughout the island. The RDC wishes to reserve the right to approve all rates charged

by the developer or concessionaires for accommodations, facilities, and services. The reasonableness of such rates will be judged primarily by comparison with those currently charged for comparable accommodation, services, or goods furnished or sold in other areas under similar conditions with due allowance for such factors as difficulties involved and risk of operation. Rates, when approved, remain in effect until amended with the approval of the RDC.

In regard to the lease terms, the RDC has proposed as guidelines for the initial development a monthly rent of either $500 per month or 5% of gross income. This final rent figure will have to be negotiated. Juan Rodrigeuz Diaz of McConnell, Valdes, Kelley & Sifre law firm of San Juan, Puerto Rico, is in the position to advise the promoter of any changes in the RDC's position concerning the campgrounds.

The first resort will be located on an existing public beach near the city of Humacao. Humacao is located 40 miles southeast of the city of San Juan. It can be easily reached from San Juan by taking highways 1 and 30. These highways are four-lane interstates except for a section of approximately 3 miles near the city of Juncos. The initial development will consist of 200–250 campsites located on the beach of the Caribbean Sea on a former coconut palm plantation. This particular location is ideal for camping because the palm trees are laid out on a grid pattern with 30-foot centers. The actual site has approximately one-half mile of existing beach and the land extends inland one-quarter mile from the beach to highway 3. At this site are some parking facilities plus limited facilities for electricity, water, and sewage. Because of these existing facilities and to keep the initial investment low, Humacao was chosen for the first development. See accompanying maps.

Since there is no camping on the island, the developer will want to start a rental operation to lease camping and related equipment. This should be done because it appeals to both the native Puerto Rican market and the tourist market. Leasing allows the

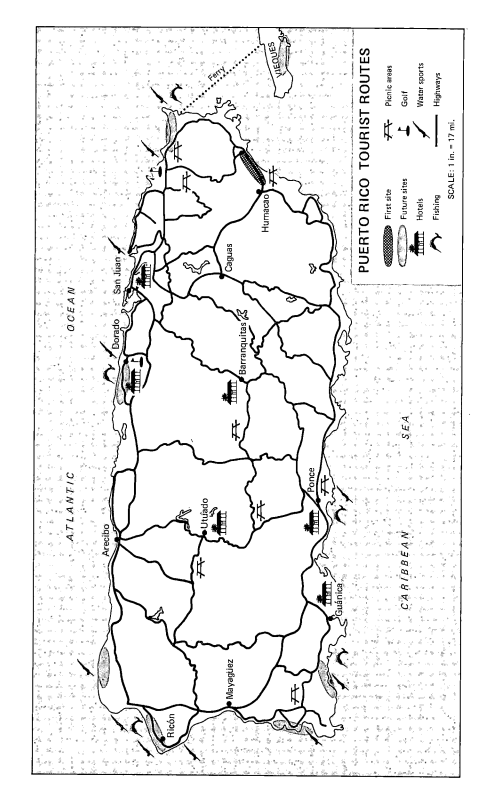

PUERTO RICO TOURIST ROUTES

First site
Future sites
Hotels
Fishing

Picnic areas
Golf
Water sports
Highways

SCALE: 1 in. = 17 mi.

VIEQUES

Ferry

ATLANTIC OCEAN

CARIBBEAN SEA

San Juan
Dorado
Arecibo
Humacao
Caguas
Barranquitas
Utuado
Ponce
Guánica
Mayagüez
Ricón

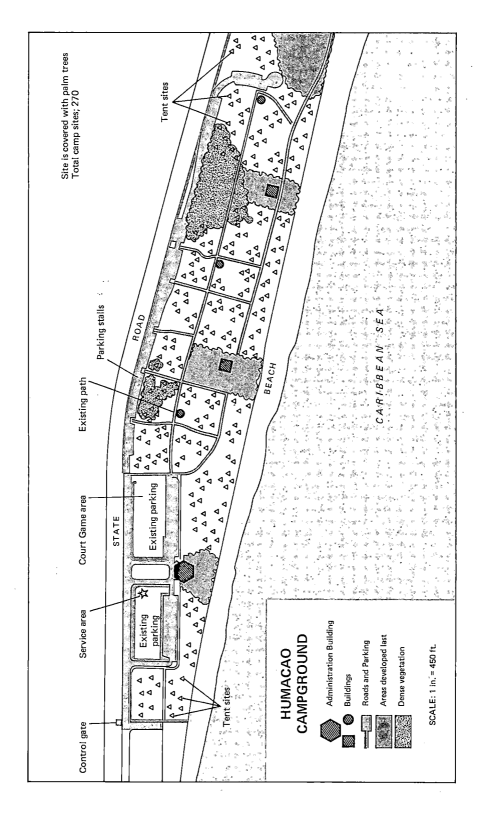

HUMACAO CAMPGROUND

Site is covered with palm trees
Total camp sites; 270

Control gate

Service area

Court Game area

Existing parking

Parking stalls

Existing path

STATE

ROAD

Existing parking

Tent sites

Tent sites

BEACH

CARIBBEAN SEA

Administration Building

Buildings

Roads and Parking

Areas developed last

Dense vegetation

SCALE: 1 in. = 450 ft.

native Puerto Ricans to rent equipment at the site and thus eliminates the problem of storing the equipment in their already over-crowded cities. This leasing operation will also be an advantage to tourists because it will eliminate the costly process of transport-ing private equipment to Puerto Rico. The leasing market will be stressed by the devel-oper because it is felt that this is where most of the financial reward will be found. Any-one who wishes to purchase equipment may do so, and anyone who wishes to rent a campsite may use his own gear.

MARKET POTENTIAL

There has been a great growth in camping in the United States: 300,000 in 1960 to 23,000,000 in 1969 (see Exhibit 1).* One of the reasons for this boom is the decided cost advantage, not only relating to the cost of lodging, but also to the preparation of meals. Camping has allowed people in the United States to take vacations at approximately one-half the cost of staying in motels or hotels. This cost savings advantage is often combined with a desire to be out-of-doors.

Camping in Puerto Rico will be highly appealing because of both the ideal climate and the high cost of hotels. As can be seen from Exhibit 2, 67% of all nonresident hotel visitors' expenditures in Puerto Rico in the fiscal year 1968–1969 was spent on food and lodging. The proposed camping resort will allow us to provide a camping trailer for $10 a night as opposed to the $40 per night double occupancy charged by the island hotels (this does not include meals).[1]

This camping trailer will compare favor-ably to a modest hotel room without a shower; deluxe shower facilities will be within a short walking distance. The camp-ing trailer could house as many as six people, thus further reducing the cost per person. The camper will also be able to purchase his food in a supermarket, three miles away in Humacao, which is similar to

those found in the United States—another cost savings. For the convenience of the campers a camp store will be located on the grounds to sell many of the items needed for camping, such as food. Many successful campground operators in the United States have found that the camp store provided an income equal or greater than that of their site rental income.[2] The savings to native Puerto Ricans would also be substantial al-though not as great as the savings for tour-ists. The Economic Development Adminis-tration has estimated that the native Puerto Ricans spend 50% of each vacation dollar for food and lodging. The reason for the lower cost is because Puerto Ricans use the hotels in the summer when reduced rates apply. The campground in Humacao will be ideal for both Puerto Ricans and tourists because it will provide a low-cost beach vaca-tion that will rival any beach cottage and be at a much lower cost than the hotels found on the island.

The temperature at Humacao averages 76°F per year and Humacao has a rainfall of 64 in. per year concentrated in brief after-noon or late evening showers (see Exhibits 3 and 4). This allows a camping resort to have a 360-day season as opposed to the typical 120-day season found in the United States.

UNITED STATES MARKET

The following should be noted when con-sidering the United States market:

1. Tourist travel from the United States to Puerto Rico has been increasing at the rate of 11% per year (see Exhibit 5).

2. Bruce Jones of the Economic Develop-ment Administration of Puerto Rico (Chi-cago Office) reports that he receives an average of 25 requests per month from travel agents seeking information on camping fa-cilities on the island of Puerto Rico for their clientele. This information is usually re-quested for groups of people. It should also

---

* *Note: Exhibits begin on p. 311.*

[1] *Source: Bruce Jones of the Economic Develop-ment Administration of Puerto Rico, Chicago Office.*

[2] *Source: Dick Sandy, editor,* Campground and R. V. Park Management.

be noted here that the Chicago Office is but one of several offices of the EDA located in the United States.

3. Despite dramatic growth in available hotel rooms (from 3,000 in 1960 to 8,700 in 1969), the year-round occupancy rate averages 75% (see Exhibits 6 and 7).

4. A camping operation exists in the Virgin Islands at Cinnamon Bay on St. John's Island. It is run through the cooperation of the National Park Service. A phone call to the camp at Cinnamon Bay on February 12, 1971, revealed the following:

a. There was a 100% occupancy level for the 58 tent sites from December 18, 1970 through May 31, 1971.

b. There was a 100% occupancy level for the 10 existing cabins from December 18, 1970 through August 1971.

c. An advance reservation system is used, and, in addition to (a) above, the tents are 80% filled as of February 12 for June through August; they are usually filled to capacity during these months. It was also learned that they have a 50% occupancy level from September through December 15. Using the above information one can estimate their occupancy level for an entire year to be 85% (see Exhibit 8).

d. A person is limited to 14 days of camping in the campgrounds in any 365-day period.

e. The cost for 4 people is $11 per night for tents and $14 per night for cabins.

f. The market is entirely made up of tourists from the United States.

g. The only available restroom facilities are pit toilets.

h. No electricity is available.

i. Available facilities at the campgrounds are tents, cots, blankets, water jugs, lanterns, and some cooking utensils.

j. A very limited variety of food can be purchased on the island, such as bread, eggs, milk, beer, and a few cold meats.

k. The campground highly recom-mends to its campers that they visit Puerto Rico to take advantage of the many tourist attractions on the island.

The campers at Humacao shall have far superior eating and sleeping facilities, a more substantial food supply, and easy access to San Juan and the rest of Puerto Rico.

PUERTO RICAN MARKET

The following facts are considered pertinent when studying the potential Puerto Rican campers:

1. There is a growing middle class of people in Puerto Rico who have money to spend for vacations. Often their tastes have been influenced during their college days in the United States. Because of the expense of leaving, Puerto Ricans tend to take their vacations on the island. As can be seen from Exhibits 9 and 10, Puerto Ricans occupy up to 50% of selected hotel rooms during the year. This is especially true during the summer because they can take advantage of lower summer rates. Random discussions with native Puerto Ricans indicate a great deal of excitement and interest in the camping resort.

2. At the present time there are no camping facilities in Puerto Rico. The nearest approximation is a group of 80 cabins located on the beach near Boqueron and operated by the RDC. These cabins are approximately 20 ft by 25 ft and are very plain. It is known from the RDC that these cabins maintain almost a 100% occupancy for an entire year and have a waiting backlog of 3 to 4 months.

3. In 1969 the population of Puerto Rico was 2.8 million. It is known that 10% of the population of the United States are campers and their median income is $8,000. Using this information, one should note that if 1.3% of the Puerto Rican people stay at the campground one night in any given year, they alone would provide an occupancy rate of 50%.

MARKET APPROACH

A well-planned advertising and reservation system will help smooth the way for the camping resort. It is anticipated that a substantial number of native Puerto Ricans will be attracted to camp on weekends. It is also anticipated that tourists will generally stay from 1 week to possibly 2 weeks at a time. To this end the following is pertinent:

1. The RDC has agreed to insert our advertising literature whenever they have to turn down people for cabins at Boqueron.

2. Missouri House Advertising Agency is a wholly owned subsidiary of Smithfield Industries, Inc., Smithfield, Missouri. Smithfield is the largest manufacturer of recreational vehicles in the United States and Missouri House does all of its advertising. Missouri House estimates that $25,000 will more than cover the initial required publicity within the United States.

3. In conversations with Katherine Lord (Missouri House Advertising), Jane Floss (well-known recreational writer), David Andrews (Recreational Park Management), Recreational Vehicle Institute, and various other editors and writers of the news media, it was learned that we can obtain a great deal of "free ink" in various magazines and publications throughout the United States. Some of these articles would be designed to appeal to the woman reader and would appear in such publications as *Red Book* and *McCalls*.

4. Royal Smithfield Estates, a new and successful camping resort in Tampa, Florida, has a full-time publicity girl whose services they would be willing to share. The cost would be her salary during the time she is working for us and, of course, any operating expense incurred on our behalf.

5. Airlines such as Eastern have indicated considerable interest in this project, although no written agreements exist at this time.

a. The airlines did express an interest in a cooperative advertising program in which the airlines would furnish brochures and pay the fee of travel agents for the booking.

b. The possibility exists that the developers, as long as they are limited in number, may have passes on the airlines when their work requires them to travel between Puerto Rico and the United States.

6. A new car leasing operation, A&I, has also expressed a great interest in this project. A&I is willing to lease a Chevrolet Vega or similar car at the rate of $35–$40 per week. Terms have not been worked out, but they did indicate that lower rates could be arranged if justified by volume.

7. It is very possible that a vacation package could be worked out with the airlines and the car leasing operation.

8. Hotels on the Gold Coast of San Juan receive many requests from guests for excursions to the remaining areas of the island. Bruce Jones of EDA, who works with these hotels, expressed great optimism that a package could be worked out with the hotels, allowing people to take 2 or 3 days during their stay to go out to the "out island" and do some camping. This could help alleviate a drop in occupancy during the week days.

INVESTMENT

The required investment for the resort campgrounds in Puerto Rico would depend on the scale of initial facilities. For simplicity, the investment requirements will be broken into two sections: The first section is that of 100 campsites; the second section is that of 200 campsites (see Exhibit 11).

The following items should be noted for the investment requirements and are so designated in Exhibit 11.

1. Land Improvements. These estimates were provided by Millard Cook of the St. Louis Branch of Howard Bond and Associates, Landscape Architects. The figures were prepared using data supplied by their branch

office in Puerto Rico. The land improvement for 200 sites is more than twice that of 100 sites because the 100-site development takes advantage of existing water, electrical, and sewage facilities. The expansion to 200 sites would require complete installation of these facilities.

2. Administration Building, Restrooms, and Shelter. The number of buildings was determined by using the Standards for Certification of the State of Missouri; the estimated cost was then provided by Howard Bond and Associates. There would be 1 restroom for 100 sites and 2 for 200 sites.

3. Advertising. These estimates were provided by Miss Rosalie Corson, General Manager, Hoosier House Advertising Agency, Middlebury, Indiana.

4. Working Capital. This is the estimated capital required. The estimate was based on the judgment and opinion of persons experienced in campground operations. A listing is found in the section on operating expenses.

5. Tent Trailers, Tents, and Related Equipment. The figures provided include all costs, such as shipping, from the manufacturing plant to their arrival at Humacao. The estimates were obtained from information provided by:

    a. Viking Boat, Middlebury, Indiana.

    b. Hobo Manufacturing, Edgerton, Ohio.

    c. Camel Manufacturing, Knoxville, Tennessee.

    d. Sears, Roebuck, Chicago, Illinois.

    e. Sealand Services, Inc., Chicago, Illinois.

    f. TransAmerican Trailer Transport, Chicago, Illinois.

6. This is an estimate of the resale value of tent trailers based on discussions with manufacturers and tent trailer dealers. Although promising, this is somewhat uncertain at this time and therefore not included in ROI calculations.

Please note that the *investment has assumed only equity financing with no initial debt.* It is believed that favorable borrowing terms can be obtained (see section on financing). This would decrease the amount of equity required and substantially increase the return on investment.

OPERATING EXPENSES

It has been very difficult to obtain accurate information on the operation of a campground in the United States because this information simply is not available. Most campground operations today are "mom and pop operations" which do not keep very accurate records of their operating expenses. Various people were contacted to obtain the best estimate possible for operating expenses of a campground. Among them are:

    a. David Andrews, Editor of *Recreational Vehicle Park Management.*

    b. Lester LaRue, Royal Smithfield Estates, Tampa, Florida.

    c. Harold Comings, Recreational Supplies, Minneapolis, Minnesota.

    d. Safari Campgrounds International, Chicago, Illinois.

    e. *Recreational Vehicle Park Management and Design* provided and written by Ira P. Lykes.

    f. Dr. Doug Smitson, The University of the Midwest, Williamsburg, Missouri.

    g. George Dawson, The University of the Midwest, Williamsburg, Missouri.

It should be noted that the estimated revenue does not include any provision for a camp store, etc. Successful promoters earn approximately the same amount in income from their camp store as they do from the rental of their various sites. It could, therefore, be reasonably assumed that the income provided will be approximately one and one-half times as great as that shown on the attached pro formas. Similarly, the rates of return would be approximately one and one-half times as great since it is anticipated that the operation of a camp store will not cause the operating expenses to increase from the estimates given.

The following should also be noted in terms of the pro forma operating statements and are noted in Exhibits 12 through 15.

1. Personnel. The personnel figures were arrived at by using the figures obtained from that of the St. John's campground in the Virgin Islands. Three men are used per 69 campsites to operate this campground. The wage rates provided in the attached pro formas were estimated from a publication entitled "New Life for Your Business in Puerto Rico," published by the Economic Administration. Actual wages may be a great deal less.

2. Depreciation. The schedule of depreciation for the buildings and grounds was worked out with the cooperation of Millard Cook of Howard Bond and Associates. The estimates for the life of the leasing equipment and depreciation allowances were worked out in cooperation with manufacturers of the said equipment (see the section on investment).

3. Rent. The terms for rent were those that had been provided as guidelines by the RDC. The conditions and terms, however, are subject to final negotiation.

TIMING

Estimates of time needed to implement this project are given in Exhibit 16.

TAX EXEMPTION

No Federal Taxes. Puerto Rico is part of the United States. The currency, banking, and postal systems are the same. It enjoys a tariff-free flow of all goods and services to and from the United States plus full protection under the constitutions, laws, and courts of both the United States and Puerto Rico. However, income earned in Puerto Rico is not subject to federal taxation.

100% Local Tax Exemption. Under Puerto Rico's Industrial Incentive Act of 1963, an individual, partnership, or corporation that manufactures a product in Puerto Rico that was not produced on a commercial scale in Puerto Rico before January 2, 1947 or operates tourist and commercial hotels is eligible for tax exemption.

Companies eligible under the Industrial Incentive Act can be given complete exemption from all taxes on corporate earnings, real and personal property taxes, municipal taxes, and license fees for a period of 10, 12, 15, or 17 years. Humacao exemption is 15 years.

Investor Exemptions. The same exemptions apply to dividends paid by tax exempt companies to:

1. Stockholders who are bona fide residents of Puerto Rico.

2. Nonresident stockholders who are not taxed on such dividends outside Puerto Rico or who cannot take the tax imposed in Puerto Rico as a deduction from or a credit against the tax payable in their jurisdiction.

SUPPLEMENTARY FINANCING
(Source: EDA)

The following are supplementary sources of equity capital that can be tapped in order to reduce the equity capital required.

Sources of Debt Capital. 1. The Government Development Bank. If a company cannot secure money on reasonable terms from a private financial institution, the GDB may provide loans through mortgages on buildings and chattel mortgages on machinery and equipment for extended periods of times.

2. Puerto Rico Industrial Development Company. A secondary source of capital through second mortgages, personally guaranteed loans, minority equity capital investment.

3. Federal Economic Development Administration. This program under the United States Department of Commerce provides financing up to 25 years to eligible industries locating in underdeveloped areas.

As much as 90% of the value of fixed assets may be obtained as follows:

    a. 65% from federal EDA at 5¼% interest on a second mortgage basis.

    b. 5% from local government as equity capital or on a third mortgage loan.

    c. 29% from the GDB or from private lending institutions on a first mortgage basis.

    d. 10% from the applicant.

This agency can also guarantee up to 90% of a working capital loan made by a private lending institution to a borrower establishing or expanding an operation, provided he is also an applicant for a fixed capital loan. Grants for feasibility studies plus grants and long-term loans for public facilities related to the industrial projects are also available.

4. The Small Business Administration. The SBA provides funds to "small businesses" to finance fixed assets and working capital (depending on the SBA size standards applicable to particular fields of operation) at a normal prevailing interest rate of 5½%.

Sources of Equity Capital. 1. Local Entrepreneurs. Local investors, who in addition can provide local know-how, ready-made markets, business connections, and knowledge of Puerto Rican laws, people, and living conditions, will invest private capital.

2. Small Business Investment Companies. The SBICs, regulated by the Small Business Administration, provide equity capital and long-term loan funds to small businesses as is done in the States.

3. Joint Ventures. More flexible long-term financing for fixed assets and working capital is provided by the Puerto Rico Industrial Development Company for joint venture projects between United States or foreign and local capital in which Puerto Rican residents participate with 50% or more of the capital. (In this type of venture, incentive grants may also be used for marketing and engineering assistance in addition to the cited uses.)

Cash Incentive Grants. Cash incentive grants are available to assist during the start-up period. The amount of the grant varies according to the number of workers, the capital invested, and the location.

FUTURE

The RDC has set aside a *minimum* of six areas throughout the island that will be devoted to camping. The developer of the first area will be given the right to develop all of the remaining areas; at present, this would be at least from 2,500 to 3,000 sites.

Based on the Virgin Islands' campground, discussions with various travel agencies throughout the eastern part of the United States, and an assessment of the potential market, it is felt that the occupancy rate for the camping resorts could easily exceed 55%. If this becomes the case and if proper business judgment is used, the financial rewards, as were shown, are exceedingly great.

ASSIGNMENT

Appraise this opportunity. Develop a detailed plan of action for David Simmons in regard to how he should proceed from this point.

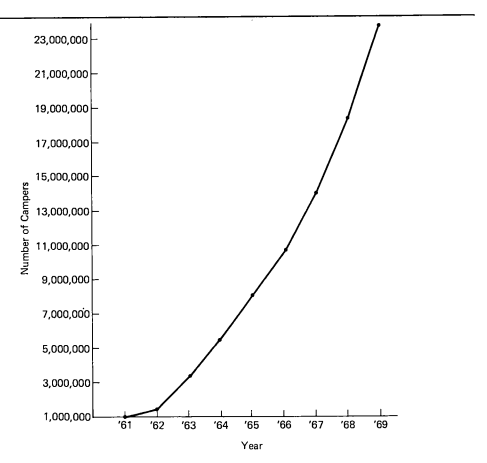

EXHIBIT 1 Estimated campers in the United States. (Source: Recreational Vehicle Institute.)

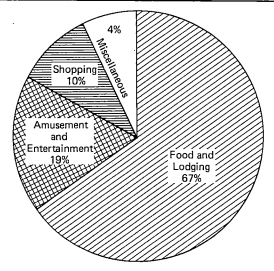

EXHIBIT 2 Distribution of the nonresident hotel visitor expenditures, Puerto Rico, Fiscal Year 1968–1969. (Source: Economic Development Administration of Puerto Rico, Department of Tourism.)

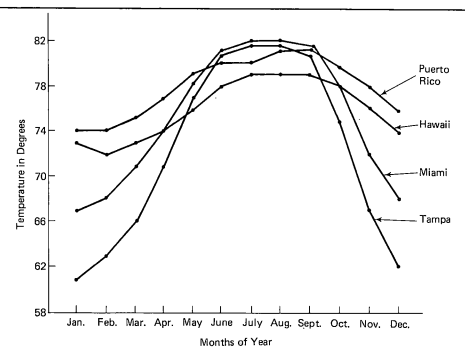

EXHIBIT 3 Average monthly temperatures of selected areas. (Source: National Weather Records Center, ESSA, U.S. Department of Commerce.)

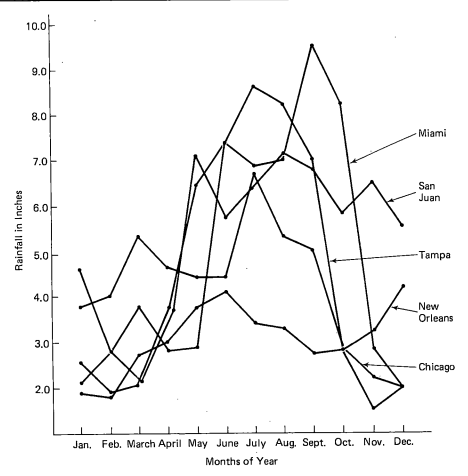

EXHIBIT 4 Average monthly rainfall of selected areas. (Source: National Weather Records Center, ESSA, U.S. Department of Commerce.)

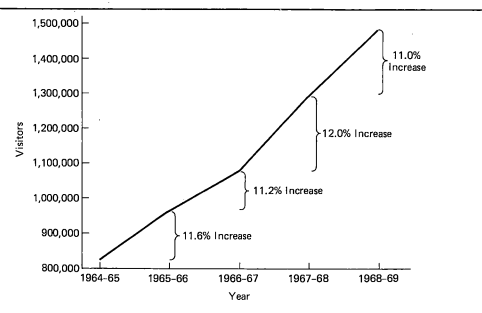

EXHIBIT 5 Visitors from the United States to Puerto Rico, 1965–1969. (Source: Economic Development Administration of Puerto Rico.)

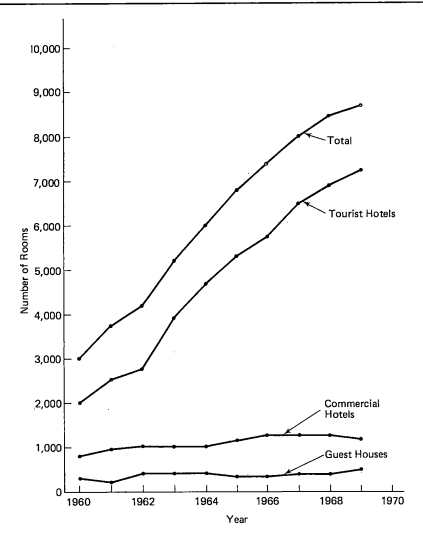

EXHIBIT 6 Number of rooms available in June of each year.
(Source: Economic Development Administration of Puerto Rico.)

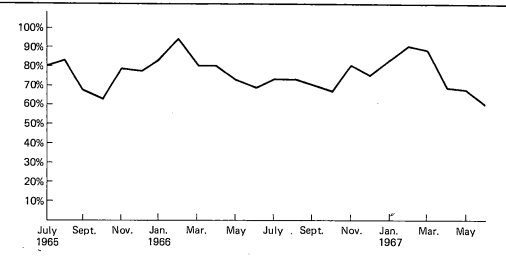

NOTE: Total rooms available in July 1966 – – – –7,300.
      Total rooms available in June 1967 – – – –8,100.

EXHIBIT 7 Percentage of rooms rented of those available. (Source: Economic Development Administration of Puerto Rico, Office of Economic Research, General Economics Division.)

EXHIBIT 8 Estimated yearly occupancy level, St. John Campground. (Source: Phone call to St. John, February 12, 1971.)

Month	Days possible per month	Occupancy level (%)	Days filled
January	30	100	30
February	30	100	30
March	30	100	30
April	30	100	30
May	30	100	30
June	30	100	30
July	30	100	30
August	30	100	30
September	30	50	15
October	30	50	15
November	30	50	15
December	30	75	22.5
	360		307.5

$$\frac{307.5}{360} = 85.5\% \text{ occupancy for year}$$

Sample calculation for full days:
   Note: 30 days at 10% occupancy is equal to 3 days at 100% occupancy for sites rented.
September–November: (30 days) (50%) = 15 full days.
December: (15 days) (50%) + (15 days) (100%) = 22.5 full days.

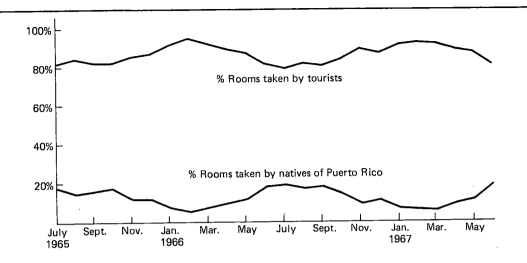

NOTE: For total number of rooms available, see Exhibit 6.
For rooms rented, see Exhibits 6 and 7.

EXHIBIT 9 Of motel rooms rented, registrations by residence. (Source: Economic Development Administration of Puerto Rico, Department of Tourism.)

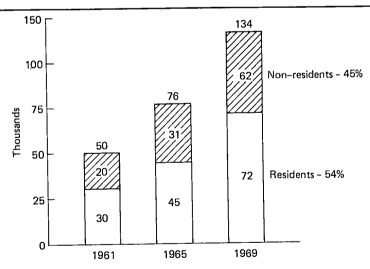

EXHIBIT 10 Hotel registrations by residence, selected island hotels (fiscal years). (Source: Economic Development Administration of Puerto Rico, Office of Economic Research, General Economics Division.)

EXHIBIT 11

INVESTMENT

100 Sites			200 Sites	
Average	*High*		*Average*	*High*
$ 32,423	$ 52,100	Land improvements[1]	$ 97,980	$158,720
50,000	70,000	Administration building[2]	50,000	70,000
20,000	30,000	Restrooms[2]	40,000	60,000
15,000	20,000	Shelter[2]	15,000	20,000
25,000	35,000	Advertising (initial) [3]	25,000	35,000
25,000	35,000	Working capital[4]	25,000	35,000
22,500	30,000	(25) Tent trailers (50) [5]	45,000	60,000
7,500	9,400	(75) Tents[5] (150)	15,000	18,750
$197,400	$281,500	Total (this figure was used for rates-of-return calculations)	$313,000	$457,500
—22,500	—30,000	Less recovery of capital	—45,000	—60,000
$175,900	$251,500	from sale of used tent trailers after 3-years use[6]	$268,000	$397,500

Note: Superscripts are explained in investment section.

EXHIBIT 12 Pro forma operating statements.

	200 Sites—$10 maximum 50%		Combined fee 75%		90%	
INCOME						
Site rental	($4/site)(.50)(200 sites)(360 days) = 144,000		($4/site)(.75)(200 sites)(360 days) = 216,000		($4/site)(.90)(200 sites)(360 days) = 259,200	
Equipment rental	($6/site)(.50)(200 sites)(360 days) = 216,000		($6/site)(.75)(200 sites)(360 days) = 324,000		($6/site)(.90)(200 sites)(360 days) = 388,800	
Total	360,000		540,000		648,000	

EXPENSES	*Low*	*High*	*Low*	*High*	*Low*	*High*
Rent[3]	6,000	18,000	6,000	27,000	6,000	32,300
Salaries						
Manager	10,000	15,000	10,000	15,000	10,000	15,000
Ass't Manager	5,000	7,000	5,000	7,000	5,000	7,000
Secretary (s)	2,500	4,000	5,000	8,000	5,000	8,000
Maintenance Men[1]	(6)* 18,000	36,000	(7)* 21,000	42,000	(8)* 24,000	48,000
	35,500	62,000	41,000	72,000	44,000	78,000
Depreciation[2]						
Land Improvements	11,000	17,600	11,000	17,600	11,000	17,600
Buildings	5,500	7,000	5,500	7,000	5,500	7,000
Rental Equipment	12,000	20,000	12,000	20,000	12,000	20,000
	28,500	44,600	28,500	44,600	28,500	44,600
Operating Expenses						
Office Supplies	1,580	2,000	1,800	2,300	2,200	2,800
General Supplies	3,160	4,000	3,600	4,600	4,400	5,500
Maintenance and Repair	8,000	11,000	10,000	15,000	13,000	18,000
Utilities	10,000	13,000	12,000	16,000	15,000	20,000
Insurance	3,500	4,600	4,500	6,000	5,000	7,000
	26,240	34,600	31,900	43,900	39,600	53,300
Advertising	5,000	10,000	5,000	10,000	5,000	10,000
TOTAL EXPENSES	101,240	169,200	112,400	197,500	123,100	218,200
Profit	$258,760	$190,800	$427,600	$342,500	$522,900	$429,800
Return-Average Investment	83%	61%	137%	109%	167%	137%
Return-High Investment	57%	42%	93%	75%	114%	94%

Note: Superscripts explained in section on operating expenses.
* Number of maintenance men.

319

EXHIBIT 13 Pro forma operating statements.

	100 sites—$10 maximum 50%		Combined Fee 75%		90%	
INCOME						
Site Rental	($4/site)(.50)(100 sites)(360 days) = 72,000		($4/site)(.75)(100 sites)(360 days) = 108,000		($4/site)(.90)(100 sites)(360 days) = 129,600	
Equipment Rental	($6/site)(.50)(100 sites)(360 days) = 108,000		($6/site)(.75)(100 sites)(360 days) = 162,000		($6/site)(.90)(100 sites)(360 days) = 194,400	
Total	180,000		270,000		324,000	
EXPENSES	*Low*	*High*	*Low*	*High*	*Low*	*High*
Rent³	6,000	9,000	6,000	13,500	6,000	16,200
Salaries						
Manager	10,000	15,000	10,000	15,000	10,000	15,000
Ass't Manager	5,000	7,000	5,000	7,000	5,000	7,000
Secretary (s)	2,500	5,000	2,500	5,000	2,500	5,000
Maintenance Men¹ (4)* (5)* (6)*	12,000 29,500	24,000 51,000	15,000 32,500	30,000 57,000	18,000 35,500	36,000 63,000
Depreciation²						
Land Improvements	4,150	7,100	4,150	7,100	4,150	7,100
Buildings	4,000	6,000	4,000	6,000	4,000	6,000
Rental Equipment	6,000 14,150	10,000 23,100	6,000 14,150	10,000 23,100	6,000 14,150	10,000 23,100
Operating Expenses						
Office Supplies	700	1,500	900	1,800	1,000	2,000
General Supplies	1,200	1,800	1,800	2,800	2,000	3,000
Maintenance and Repair	3,200	5,000	4,000	5,500	4,500	6,500
Utilities	3,600	5,400	4,800	6,000	5,800	7,500
Insurance	1,400 10,100	2,200 15,900	2,000 13,500	4,000 20,100	2,500 15,800	4,500 23,500
Advertising	5,000	10,000	5,000	10,000	5,000	10,000
TOTAL EXPENSES	64,750	109,000	71,150	123,700	76,450	135,800
Profit	$115,250	$ 71,000	$198,850	$146,300	$247,550	$188,200
Return-Average Investment	58%	36%	101%	74%	125%	95%
Return-High Investment	41%	25%	71%	52%	88%	67%

Note: Superscripts explained in section on operating expenses.
* Number of maintenance men.

320

EXHIBIT 14 Pro forma operating statements.

	200 Sites—$7 maximum 50%		Combined fee 75%		90%	
INCOME						
Site Rental	($3/site)(.50)(200 sites)(360 days) = 108,000		($3/site)(.75)(200 sites)(360 days) = 162,000		($3/site)(.90)(200 sites)(360 days) = 194,400	
Equipment Rental	($4/site)(.50)(200 sites)(360 days) = 144,000		($4/site)(.75)(200 sites)(360 days) = 216,000		($4/site)(.90)(200 sites)(360 days) = 259,200	
Total	252,000		378,000		453,600	
EXPENSES	*Low*	*High*	*Low*	*High*	*Low*	*High*
Rent[3]	6,000	12,600	6,000	18,900	6,000	22,600
Salaries						
Manager	10,000	15,000	10,000	15,000	10,000	15,000
Ass't Manager	5,000	7,000	5,000	7,000	5,000	7,000
Secretary(s)	2,500	4,000	5,000	8,000	5,000	8,000
Maintenance Men[1]	18,000 (6)* 35,500	36,000 62,000	21,000 (7)* 41,000	42,000 72,000	24,000 (8)* 44,000	48,000 78,000
Depreciation[2]						
Land Improvements	11,000	17,600	11,000	17,600	11,000	17,600
Buildings	5,500	7,000	5,500	7,000	5,500	7,000
Rental Equipment	12,000 28,500	20,000 44,600	12,000 28,500	20,000 44,600	12,000 28,500	20,000 44,600
Operating Expenses						
Office Supplies	1,580	2,000	1,800	2,300	2,200	2,800
General Supplies	3,160	4,000	3,600	4,600	4,400	5,500
Maintenance and Repair	8,000	11,000	10,000	15,000	13,000	18,000
Utilities	10,000	13,000	12,000	16,000	15,000	20,000
Insurance	3,500 26,240	4,600 34,600	4,500 31,900	6,000 43,900	5,000 39,600	7,000 53,300
Advertising	5,000	10,000	5,000	10,000	5,000	10,000
TOTAL EXPENSES	101,240	163,800	112,400	189,400	123,100	208,500
Profit	$150,760	$ 88,200	$265,600	$188,600	$330,500	$245,100
Return-Average Investment	48%	28%	85%	60%	106%	78%
Return-High Investment	33%	19%	58%	41%	72%	54%

Note: Superscripts explained in section on operating expenses.
* Number of maintenance men.

321

EXHIBIT 15 Pro forma operating statements.

	100 Sites—$7 maximum 50%		Combined fee 75%		90%	
	Low	*High*	*Low*	*High*	*Low*	*High*
INCOME						
Site Rental	($3/site)(.50)(100 sites)(360 days) = 54,000		($3/site)(.75)(100 sites)(360 days) = 81,000		($3/site)(.90)(100 sites)(360 days) = 97,200	
Equipment Rental	($4/site)(.50)(100 sites)(360 days) = 72,000		($4/site)(.75)(100 sites)(360 days) = 108,000		($4/site)(.90)(100 sites)(360 days) = 129,600	
Total	126,000		189,000		226,800	
EXPENSES						
Rent³	6,000	6,600	6,000	9,900	6,000	11,800
Salaries						
Manager	10,000	15,000	10,000	15,000	10,000	15,000
Ass't Manager	5,000	7,000	5,000	7,000	5,000	7,000
Secretary (s)	2,500	5,000	2,500	5,000	2,500	5,000
Maintenance Men¹ (4)*	12,000	24,000	(5)* 15,000	30,000	18,000	36,000
	29,500	51,000	32,500	57,000 (6)*	35,500	63,000
Depreciation²						
Land Improvements	4,150	7,100	4,150	7,100	4,150	7,100
Buildings	4,000	6,000	4,000	6,000	4,000	6,000
Rental Equipment	6,000	10,000	6,000	10,000	6,000	10,000
	14,150	23,100	14,150	23,100	14,150	23,100
Operating Expenses						
Office Supplies	700	1,500	900	1,800	1,000	2,000
General Supplies	1,200	1,800	1,800	2,800	2,000	3,000
Maintenance and Repair	3,200	5,000	4,000	5,500	4,500	6,500
Utilities	3,600	5,400	4,800	6,000	5,800	7,500
Insurance	1,400	2,200	2,000	4,000	2,500	4,500
	10,100	15,900	13,500	20,100	15,800	23,500
Advertising	5,000	10,000	5,000	10,000	5,000	10,000
TOTAL EXPENSES	64,750	106,600	71,150	120,100	76,450	131,400
Profit	$61,250	$ 19,400	$117,850	$ 68,900	$150,350	$ 95,400
Return-Average Investment	31%	10%	60%	35%	76%	48%
Return-High Investment	22%	7%	42%	24%	53%	34%

Note: Superscripts explained in section on operating expenses.
* Number of maintenance men.

322

EXHIBIT 16

Months Following Signing of Contract	1st Month	2nd Month	3rd Month	4th Month	5th Month	6th Month	7th Month	8th Month	9th Month	10th Month	11th Month	12th Month
Land Preparation	Receive Bids		Construction									
Building Construction	Receive Bids		Construction									
Advertising			Lead Time Needed for Placing of Advertising in Magazines									
Personnel							Running Ads & Interviewing / Hiring / Training					
Equipment			Place Order	Manufacturing and Shipment to U. S. Port		Port to Port		Port to Site				

This chart assumes opening the campground on the ninth month after signing the contract.

———— Expected Time

━━━━ Longest Time

EXHIBIT 17

DAVID C. SIMMONS

ADDRESS

605 State Street
New Castle, Missouri

EDUCATION

M.S. Industrial Administration, August 1970; The University of the Midwest Graduate School of Industrial Administration.

B.S. Industrial Engineering, June 1969; The University of the Midwest. Course work emphasized production and manufacturing engineering.

Education financed through summer work, part-time work during school year, scholarship, and college loans.

EXHIBIT 17   *(Continued)*

WORK EXPERIENCE

Leisure Systems, Inc., St. Louis, Missouri, October 1970–February 1971. Vice-President Puerto Rico Development. Due to circumstances not relating to Puerto Rico and beyond my control, this company has liquidated.

General Foods Corp., Battle Creek, Michigan; June 1969–September 1969. Building Engineer; responsible for all engineering work relating to the "Post Toastie Corn Flake Process."

Continental Can Corp., Elkhart, Indiana; June 1968–September 1968. Production Line Foreman.

Continental Can Corp., Elkhart, Indiana; June 1967–September 1967. Industrial Engineering Trainee.

INTERESTS

Water and snow skiing, scuba diving, hunting and camping, independent baseball and basketball, coaching little league baseball.

Crain's English Pig & Whistle, Inc.

INTRODUCTION

Mr. Stephen Kyle was graduated from Purdue University's School of Agriculture in 1946. Prior to 1968 for some 10 to 15 years he had been in the business of raising turkeys and hogs near Pine Village, Indiana. His farm was located within 30 miles of West Lafayette, Indiana, home of Purdue University. In early 1968, because of decreasing agricultural margins and the gradual disappearance of small farmers, he was contemplating a change. Mr. Kyle's deliberations were influenced by the condition of his health. In 1964 he was stricken by multiple sclerosis, and this had caused him to consider quitting the turkey business which had become both a physical and psychological burden for him. Although he was still physi-

This case was prepared by Mr. John F. Uhles of Purdue University. Reprinted by permission. Copyright © Purdue Research Foundation, 1975.

cally able to perform the work on the farm, Mr. Kyle's doctors had recommended that he develop outside interests to relieve some of the psychological pressures and to provide an alternative should his condition deteriorate. As a result of his search, Mr. Kyle's attention had focused on Crain's English Pig & Whistle, Inc. and the possibility of investing in one of their franchises.

Crain's English Pig & Whistle had been in operation in West Lafayette since February 1967. It served beer and sandwiches in a pub styled in the Old English tradition. Mr. Kyle felt his lack of experience in this business might be a disadvantage and was wondering if this would be counterbalanced by the experience and other advantages offered by the Crains under their franchise. The West Lafayette establishment had been very profitable, and Mr. Kyle was anxious to make a final decision about the franchise he had been offered.

BACKGROUND OF THE
FRANCHISE RELATIONSHIP

According to the International Franchise Association (see Appendix A at the end of this section) there were nearly 350,000 franchisees and 1,500 franchisors in the United States by 1964, including such corporations as Ford, Pepsi Cola, Standard Oil, Burger Chef, and Mary Carter Paints. An estimate of the number of franchises in various industries is included in Appendix A. Since World War II franchising had become increasingly popular and this growth can be attributed, in part, to the advantages for both parties of the franchise agreement. Among these advantages for the franchisor are: increased distribution of his product with relatively low capital investment, participation in the risk of the enterprise, and local managers who can react to local conditions. From the franchisee's point of view, the advantages include national (or regional) promotion by the franchisor, the experience and advice of the franchisor, volume buying, and proven products.

A workable definition of a franchise might be "the right to do or use something granted to the franchisee by the franchisor." Considering the scope of franchise operations today, this definition might further include that a franchise is a continuous arrangement in which both parties receive benefits from their union. In order to be successful, the agreement should be viewed as similar to a partnership in which each party contributes mutually beneficial talents and assets. A copy of the International Franchise Association's Code of Ethics is reproduced in Appendix B.

This arrangement proves attractive to many small investors who don't have extensive knowledge of the specific aspects of the enterprise because they can rely on the services offered by the franchisor. The franchisee buys a "package" for marketing the product or service from the franchisor. This package may include a building style, advertising copy, promotional material, and national brand promotion among other aids. He also receives supplies, a method of production, opportunities for financing, and a management technique. These services have usually been tested and proven by experience; consequently, some franchisors claim that their franchises are profitable from the first week of operation.

The franchisor, in turn, usually receives a percentage of the franchisee's business in addition to a flat fee for the franchise rights. In addition, the franchisor is able to expand his business through the franchisees while avoiding the problems of creating a large centralized organization. With this arrangement, the franchise can maintain the advantages of smallness and close community contact as well as those of large-scale purchasing and advertising. Since the responsibilities for a successful operation are shared by both parties to the agreement, both are working to achieve the same goal.

Some studies, however, have shown that problems still exist in some franchises. William G. Fitzgerald, a franchise consultant, has described one of the major problems—a lack of mutual cooperation:

> . . . We feel that new concepts have not yet been devised for better franchising, only better applications of existing principles, e.g., to select the best franchisee and continue to motivate him to maximum efforts requires a relationship that is not one-sided, as is too often the case. As we see it, it's a case of attitude. . . . There exists in a number of franchise programs a mutual distrust, or suspicion, between franchisees and the franchisor. The franchisor takes the position of "I'm the boss and what I say goes; my franchisee's trouble is due to his not following the book; he's not pushing the line sufficiently; and in some cases, he's not paying all the royalties due me, etc." In other words, the franchisor in this example, regards himself as having an exclusive right on wisdom and virtue. On the other hand, the franchisee feels, in some cases, that he's being compelled, or coerced, by the parent company, that too much is expected of him, and he pays too much to receive too little. The upshot is bad rapport, poor communication, and misunderstanding. (Statement of Mr. Fitzgerald.[1])

[1] Partners for Profit *(New York: American Management Association, Inc., 1966)*, *p. 20.*

THE ORIGINAL CRAIN'S
ENGLISH PIG & WHISTLE, INC.

The original Pig & Whistle, or "The Pig" as Purdue students call it, opened its doors in February of 1967 and averaged sales of approximately $22,000 each month between then and September 30 of that year. An income statement for that period is shown in Exhibit 1. In the first 7 months of operation, the cost of sales averaged 44% of sales as compared to 57% for the industry in 1962. General information on the industry as a whole is included in Appendix C. Jim Crain, the corporation's vice president, gave several reasons for these results. He said, "It may look as though we were simply lucky in doing so well, but this is not quite true. My older brother, Dick, who is our corporate president, and I have gained invaluable experience by working with our father who owns two restaurants here in West Lafayette; besides that, while we were both students at Purdue we could see that an operation like 'The Pig' might be very successful. Nothing at all similar to it was in existence in the area when we started, and our present success seems to prove that our basic ideas were sound."

West Lafayette and the neighboring city, Lafayette, had a combined resident population of approximately 60,000 in 1968, and

EXHIBIT 1 Crain's English Pig & Whistle, Inc. statement of income for the seven months ended September 30, 1967.*

	Food	Bar	Total
Sales	$72,192.70	$80,414.66	$152,607.36
Cost of sales	34,498.51 (47.7%)	32,781.30 (40.7%)	67,279.81 (44.0%)
Gross margin	$37,694.19	$47,633.36	$ 85,327.55
Operating expenses			
Salaries			$ 28,999.20 (19.0%)
Employee meals			746.66 (.4%)
Supplies			6,592.75 (4.3%)
Utilities			1,995.58 (1.3%)
Taxes, Indiana gross income			763.49 (.4%)
Taxes, payroll and other			2,020.55 (1.3%)
Insurance			1,406.96 (.9%)
Repair and maintenance			1,638.70 (1.0%)
Advertising			2,053.70 (1.3%)
Peanuts			7,003.49 (4.5%)
Equipment rental			365.47 (.2%)
Laundry			676.07 (.4%)
Music			279.28 (.1%)
Depreciation, equipment			1,769.01 (1.1%)
			$ 56,310.91
Profit before occupancy and administrative expenses			$ 29,016.64 (19.0%)
Occupancy expenses			
Land			$ 3,360.00 (2.2%)
Property taxes			500.00 (.3%)
Depreciation, building			1,955.69 (1.2%)
			$ 5,815.69 (3.8%)
Profit before administrative expenses			$ 23,200.95 (15.2%)

An audited statement by our accountants is available to substantiate this statement.

Purdue University, located in West La-fayette, added about 25,000 to the local population. Jim Crain observed, "The Pig & Whistle has become a favorite student meeting place, but it has also proven to be rather popular among the local businessmen and townsfolk."

At the time Crain's Pig & Whistle opened, there was only one other establishment within the same distance to the University which had a beer license. It was a small bar serving packaged foods like potato chips, pretzels, and various sandwiches in addition to beer. Mr. Crain cited the food, space, decor, and proximity to the University as reasons for the immediate profitability of their establishment.

The decor of "The Pig" included their menu executed in Old English lettering, English tavern signs, pithy sayings typical of Old English landlords and innkeepers, and tables of deck planking atop oak barrels. The Crains and Mr. John Hudson, the cor-poration's second vice president, added a log fireplace in the middle of the room, and free peanuts provided the carpet on the floor. Many of these features were patterned after the informal atmosphere found in a typical English pub.

> Simplicity is the basic operating philosophy behind the Pig & Whistle. This is exemplified by our menu. We have six basic sandwiches, one soup, onion rings, French fries, and two draft beers from the barrel. Each item was chosen for its proven popularity, ease of prep-aration, and profit margin. The sandwiches, for example, were chosen because a poll showed them to be among the most popular of all sandwiches. We also considered the ease of storage, preservation, and service when making our selections.
>
> The customers come to the bar to order and pick up their food. They then seat themselves wherever they wish. Because of this, we've re-duced the number of service personnel to four people per shift. Another advantage of this ease of operation is the time taken for training —in most cases it takes only 10 to 15 minutes. Because we are located near the University, we never lack for job applicants.
>
> In keeping with this basic simplicity, we're even using a cash register that helps in keep-ing the inventory records. This enables the manager to spend more time on other matters and it makes his record-keeping duties less complicated. (Statement of Jim Crain.)

THE FRANCHISE

After 3 months of operation, the three of-ficers of the Pig & Whistle decided that they would like to expand into other Midwestern cities, especially concentrating on areas where colleges or universities were located. They felt that a good way to do this would be through franchising. Therefore, they con-sulted the legal firm of Sonnenschein, Levin-son, Carlin, Nath and Rosenthal of Chicago. This was the firm that had organized the MacDonald's Hamburger franchise. Sub-sequently, an advertising program was begun by P. J. Finnerman & Company from In-dianapolis, and potential locations were in-vestigated. Many local people had inquired about the investment opportunities, and shortly after the decision to offer franchises, an advertisement was placed in *The Wall Street Journal* to stimulate further interest. It is reproduced in Exhibit 2.

In February 1968 construction was under-way on four sites: South Bend, Bloomington, and Muncie in Indiana, and Champaign in Illinois. Several other locations had been selected and were secured with options or down payments. The Crains planned to keep half of these sites, while the remaining locations were to be sold to franchisees or other investors who would then lease to the franchisee.

In no case was there a requirement for the franchisee to own the land or building. The land could be leased from the owner of the land by the franchisee. The time period might vary with the location, but the Crains were using a 15-year period in their contracts. The building was constructed in such a way that it could be easily converted into a variety of operations, thereby provid-ing protection for the landowner.

The costs of the franchise consisted of a $10,000 basic fee and a continuing fee of 3.1% of the gross receipts of the business. In addition, there were several other costs

EXHIBIT 2   Franchise ad from the *Wall Street Journal.*

If
you've
the bloomin' ambition . . .
we've
the bloody
answer!

Actually, it's not exactly a new idea. It has been a smashing success in England for hundreds of years.

We call our happy American innovation "Crain's English Pig & Whistle."

After all, how can one go wrong with draft beer and six kinds of sandwiches? Old English Pub atmosphere, American ingenuity and market know-how? Modern up-to-date service and inventory control? Virtually no labor problems?

There are already eight "Crain's English Pig & Whistle" franchises in operation or under construction in the midwest.

We are now accepting inquiries for franchises from interested businessmen. For complete details about how you can own & operate a franchised "Pig & Whistle," write our headquarters at:

Crain's English
Pig & Whistle, Inc.
University Square - Suite
1-A - U.S. 52 - West La-
fayette, Indiana   47906

Join the
"Inn" crowd.

---

associated with opening the business which the franchisee would be expected to meet. These costs are detailed in Exhibit 3. The services to be performed by the franchisor are described in Exhibit 4. Jim Crain felt that one of the key services was that of training the managers. Either the franchisee or the Crains would select the manager. Then the manager would be trained 6 days a week for 3 weeks. After the franchisee had opened his unit, there would be follow-up training for the manager as well.

We want to train the manager in every facet of the operation, since our success and that of the franchisee often depends on him. Besides getting acquainted with our own organization, Anheuser-Busch and Swift both provide 2-day schools where the trainees are taught how best to market their respective products. The remainder of the time is spent working in the West Lafayette unit where the prospective manager's duties range from preparing the menu items and using the equipment to learning the auditing procedures. At the end of the 3 weeks, he can be sent to his own establishment.

EXHIBIT 3 Crain's English Pig & Whistle, Inc., estimated franchise costs.*

	March 5, 1968
1. Building: bar bases and tops, painting, tables, fence, brick	$28,400.00
Electrical	4,300.00
Mechanical and plumbing—air conditioning, heating, hood for fireplace, gas lights	15,000.00
Sewers, site prep, black top, etc.	10,000.00
	$57,700.00
2. Land cost	Varies
3. Down payment on equipment†	$ 8,000.00
Rest room equipment	130.30
Leased signs, deposit	200.00
Time clock and cards	275.00
Cash registers (leased) deposit	300.00
Inside signs	1,021.00
Office equipment	308.43
Beefeater guard	35.00
Wall clocks (est.)	50.00
Opening cleaning and paper inventory	552.00
Opening food inventory	1,408.54
Opening beverage inventory	825.30
Banks to operate, petty cash	1,000.00
First weeks payroll	1,500.00
Fire extinguishers	82.00
3-M music system	66.70
Player piano, used	300.00
Dart board and darts	10.00
Soft water equipment plus installation charge	301.56
Utilities, deposit	100.00
Gas logs	100.00
Safe	150.00
English pub signs	25.00
Accounting and bookkeeping	101.50
Advertising manual	100.00
	$16,942.33
Franchise fee	$10,000.00
	$26,942.33

* *Items 1 and 2 are usually met by an investor. The building and land are then leased from the investor.*
† *This represents one-third of the value of the equipment. The remainder is secured by a note.*

EXHIBIT 4

Crain's English Pig & Whistle Franchise Fee
Covers the Following Costs and Services:

1. Assistance in site location and negotiation of the lease.
2. Obtaining of all building permits, supplying of a site plan, and complete building plans.
3. A complete 3-week management training course.
4. Supervision during pre-opening and a management team of two persons during the first week's operation.
5. Complete purchase and specification program.
6. Advertising kit and radio tapes.
7. Trademark protection.
8. Payroll and bookkeeping instruction.
9. All food and beverage costs at invitational opening.
10. A fully comprehensive operations manual.
11. Full assistance in obtaining beer and wine license.

Crain's English Pig & Whistle 3.1% Franchise Royalty
Maintains the Following Services:

1. Weekly management supervision.
2. Bulk purchasing and national price advantages.
3. New product research.
4. Test marketing.
5. Record control assistance.
6. Relative performance records.
7. Continuous management training.

We like to work closely with the franchisee for about 3 or 4 weeks after he opens to help iron out any problems that may develop. After all, our success depends on how well each of our franchisees performs. This is especially important during the early part of the operations. (Statement of Jim Crain.)

SELECTION OF THE SITE

In the case of the Pig & Whistle franchise, the Crains and Mr. Hudson perform an analysis of the market of an area, find available land, make their selection of the site, and search out potential investors for the building and land. After this is completed, the total "package" is then presented for the franchisee's approval. The early popularity of the West Lafayette Pig & Whistle with the Purdue students caused the Crains to adopt the policy of considering cities that contained sizeable colleges or universities, at least for their initial franchises.

The site that Mr. Kyle was considering was in Lexington, Kentucky. Lexington had a population of approximately 62,000 in 1968 and is the location of the University of Kentucky (1967–1968 enrollment of 17,-000). The purchase of three-fourths of an acre of land was arranged by the Crains, and an investor from Lexington had agreed to buy the site, construct the building, and lease it to the franchisee with a co-signature from Crain's English Pig & Whistle. The agreement was to last 15 years with monthly rental of $1,000 to be paid by the franchisee.

Mr. Kyle was favorably impressed with the location when he traveled to Lexington with Jim Crain. It was across the street from a woman's dormitory and only four or five blocks from the downtown area. Thus, the location was convenient for city shoppers and for businessmen during the lunch hour as well as the University. Although Lexington has a number of bars and nightclubs, including three bars near this site, the Pig &

Whistle would be the only one serving sandwiches and free peanuts.

> Even though Lexington is approximately 250 miles from the Pine Village area, I would plan to continue living on my farm and fly down to Lexington every week or so to see how things are going. I'd probably get rid of most of my turkeys and hogs, so I don't think finding the time would be any problem. Of course, this means I'll have to find a manager for the place, but with the Crains' help, I don't anticipate any problems. (Statement of Stephen Kyle.)

THE CONTRACT

Mr. Kyle realized that many well-conceived franchises collapse because of the restrictions placed on the franchisee. In some instances, these could prevent the franchisee from catering to local tastes, but the franchisors felt that these controls were necessary for their own protection. Mr. Kyle had spent a number of hours studying the Pig & Whistle contract in an attempt to avoid any condition that might lead to future problems. Jim Crain summarized the main provisions of the contract:

> The three main areas of most franchise agreements are as follows: (1) territorial designation and the franchisee's right to a defined geographical area of operation; (2) Franchisor–franchisee relationship with respect to dealing in or the purchase of goods, products, or services supplied by the franchisor; and (3) termination provisions. Our contract contains a section on each of these, and since Steve and I have gone over it several times, I think he would know what to expect if he signed the contract.

After his study and several talks with Jim Crain, Mr. Kyle felt that he had a clear understanding of what the Pig & Whistle contract entailed. He explained what he thought the benefits would be in such a relationship:

> The Crains sell their franchise only after the location has been selected, so defining a geographical area of operation would be unnecessary. The only question in my mind regarding this section of the contract concerns that of establishing a second Pig & Whistle in the area after I've been successful with mine. Their contract provides me with the first option on a new unit, but if I decided not to purchase it for some reason, the Pig & Whistle Corporation could go ahead and find another franchisee for the new unit or run it themselves. I know I do have first choice, but something like that could cut my business drastically. I'm sure that they wouldn't consider such a move now that they're still small and want me to succeed too, but with both Lexington and the University increasing in size, as they're doing right now, I'm afraid the chance for some money might overshadow their present concern for me and my unit.
>
> Since the land is leased by me, it is my responsibility, but since the Crains would co-sign the contract, they can assume complete control of my unit if I can't pay the rent. The owner of the property has no real control over me except for seeing that no excess wear and tear occurs on the building and land . . . and, of course, I have to see that he gets the rent.
>
> When I asked Jim about what products to buy, he said that certain articles must be purchased from the franchise—things like napkins, mugs, signs, etc.; also, I can't add anything to the menu without approval. I will be charged the same price as all the other franchisees for these products because of the Robinson–Patman Act. Jim cannot specify brand names, but since he has accounts and agreements with several companies that distribute nationwide, it might be worthwhile to continue with those brands. Besides, those products have proven successful in West Lafayette. The other things, such as signs, would be leased to me under the franchise agreement. I would be able to use any building contractor I want or buy any type of equipment as long as they meet the franchise specifications and standards.
>
> The termination provisions of the agreement mostly concern a breach of contract by either party. Jim gave an example of the case where I might want to add pizza to the menu. If I went ahead and did it without consulting them, this would constitute a breach of contract and they could take over my unit without paying me anything. I guess I can see their point, since I did pay for their ideas, and it all bears their name. Also I can, with their agreement, sell the franchise rights to someone else if I find it is not working out for me.

EXHIBIT 5 Crain's English Pig & Whistle, Inc.'s statement of estimated cash receipts and disbursements.*

	Price to Opening	Accounting Period†												
		1	2	3	4	5	6	7	8	9	10	11	12	13
Sales														
Food		8,700	9,800	9,900	9,500	7,900	8,700	8,000	19,900	9,900	9,900	8,000	8,000	9,500
Bar		12,200	10,800	10,700	9,500	7,900	8,900	6,300	13,500	13,500	13,500	6,300	6,300	9,500
Total		20,900	20,600	20,600	19,000	15,800	17,600	14,300	23,400	23,400	23,400	14,300	14,300	19,000
Cash disbursements														
Franchise fee	10,000	600	600	600	600	500	500	400	700	700	700	400	400	600
Equipment down payment	9,000													
Opening inventory, etc.	10,000													
Food purchases‡		4,100	4,600	4,600	4,500	3,700	4,100	3,700	4,600	4,600	4,600	3,700	3,700	4,500
Bar purchases		4,900	4,300	4,300	3,800	3,200	3,600	2,500	5,400	5,400	5,400	2,500	2,500	3,800
Salaries														
Manager	500	500	500	500	500	500	500	500	500	500	500	500	500	500
Other		3,600	3,500	3,500	3,200	2,700	3,000	2,400	4,000	4,000	4,000	2,400	2,400	3,200
Other§		3,200	3,200	3,200	3,200	3,200	3,200	3,200	3,200	3,200	3,200	3,200	3,200	3,200
Total disbursements	29,500	16,900	16,700	16,700	15,800	13,800	14,900	12,700	18,400	18,400	18,400	12,700	12,700	15,800
Excess of receipts over disbursements	(29,500)	4,000	3,900	3,900	3,200	2,000	2,500	1,600	5,000	5,000	5,000	1,600	1,600	3,200
Opening cash balance		(29,500)	(25,500)	(21,600)	(17,700)	(14,500)	(12,500)	(10,000)	(8,400)	(3,400)	1,600	6,600	8,200	9,800
Ending cash balance	(29,500)	(25,500)	(21,600)	(17,700)	(14,500)	(12,500)	(10,000)	(8,400)	(3,400)	1,600	6,600	8,200	9,800	13,000
Excess of receipts over disbursements	(29,500)	4,000	3,900	3,900	3,200	2,000	2,500	1,600	5,000	5,000	5,000	1,600	1,600	3,200
Occupancy Costs‖														

* This presentation is based upon a March 1 opening.
† Periods 1–8 are based upon actual operating results from West Lafayette. Periods 9–13 are estimates. The accounting period is 4 weeks long.
‡ We are assuming all bills are paid currently.
§ See Exhibit 1 for breakdown.
‖ Occupancy costs should include land and building rent (or mortgage payments) and equipment rent.
N.B. Since the printing of this material periods 9–12 have been completed and have shown total sales and excess of receipts over disbursements above the projected estimates.

Another situation was interesting to me. There's always the possibility that the franchisor would go under financially; in that case, my unit would belong to me, and I would not owe the Crains anything. Under the franchise agreement, I pay 3.1% of the gross receipts to the Crains, and if they should decide to advertise nationally, that would increase to 4.1%. If they failed, I wouldn't have to pay this any longer and I would not be liable for any of their debts. All things considered, I suppose we both would be about equally protected.

They would also set the prices I could charge, which might vary between units. I'm certain these would be fair prices; besides, with their experience, they should know what to charge. I think that covers the most important provisions of the contract.

I have the money for the investment. I am impressed by their success in West Lafayette and their projections for franchisees. (A copy of the forecast cash flow is included in Exhibit 5.) Since franchising is becoming increasingly popular, it must be worthwhile for many people. I would still like someone to go in with me though. Maybe my manager would be interested.

THE SITUATION IN MARCH 1968

In March Stephen Kyle was still trying to make his final decision. He considered keeping his turkey and hog business, but he hoped to find something that would provide him a good income and return on his investment and that would not be such a burden as the farm. He thought that the franchise might be very profitable as well as interesting for him. He was also aware that other opportunities might exist but they might be difficult to find and he needed to decide on the franchise. Besides, he didn't want to "spend forever searching and never doing."

Mr. Kyle briefly reviewed his situation:

You know, I might end up paying $10,000 for nothing but a name and an idea when I could be able to do just as well if I devoted some time to thinking about it. I am not really

sure that a franchise is the thing for me and I still haven't worked out all the right answers.

I've done some checking and the whole restaurant business appears to be a rather tricky affair (see Appendix C). Also, the West Lafayette unit might not be a good example of what I can do, since it is the only establishment of its kind in that area.

Another thing is that success or failure might just hinge on what kind of manager I would be able to employ. The provision in the contract states that his salary is up to negotiation. It also allows him 1% of the net if he keeps his costs under a certain level. I could possibly get someone who really knew his business, but his price wouldn't be cheap and he might not want to be restricted to a franchise operation. The Crains say that the management is so simple that their training program insures success, but I don't really know for sure.

Then, of course, since I am not really very familiar with the sale of food or beer, I'd be learning as I went along. I know I can depend on the Crains and Mr. Hudson for their advice and experience, but it is *my* money that is on the line. I know how it is to have a bad year—once I lost $100,000 on my turkeys and it took me a very long time to recoup that loss.

I've been meaning to devote closer study to their figures on projected sales and costs, but Lexington could be a very different situation. And then because there is always the possibility of my paying the 4.1% of the gross if they should decide to advertise nationally, my estimations would be pretty vague anyway.

I don't think they're trying to sell me a bill of goods, especially when I see that they are not having any trouble finding people to buy the other franchises. They have been very nice about leaving the door open for me, but they would like me to make up my mind before May so that they can go ahead with their plans.

ASSIGNMENT

Appraise this opportunity from the point of view of Stephen Kyle.

APPENDIX A   Indication of size of the franchise industry, 1964.

Sales ($ billions)	Industry	Number of outlets
$35.0	Automobiles and trucks	33,000
14.2	Gasoline and automobile service	206,302
2.0	Soft drink bottlers	4,000
5.9	Food service outlets (including grocery stores)	40,590
2.1	Miscellaneous	54,759
$59.2*	Total	338,651

* $59.2 billion represents approximately 35% of total retail sales in the U.S. in 1964.
Source: International Franchise Association.

APPENDIX B   Code of ethics, International Franchise Association, adopted 1960

Each Member Company Pledges:

1. To properly and effectively serve the needs of the ultimate user or consumer of the company's products or services.

2. To provide a professional, competitive and successful program that will establish and maintain a franchising enterprise to distribute the company's products or services.

3. To establish terms of franchise, license contract, or similar agreement completely and clearly set down in print. All terms of said agreement are to be fair to the franchisee and fully understood by him prior to signing. The franchisee shall in all cases be furnished with a complete and accurate signed copy of the agreement. The company shall abide by its franchise agreement in letter and in spirit.

4. To always provide complete information to prospective franchisees concerning the cost of entering into such business. No company shall minimize, diminish or in any way disguise or withhold the amount of necessary capital, work, or qualifications necessary to commence and maintain ordinary operations as a franchisee.

5. To advertise or communicate to any person or company, by conversation, correspondence, newspapers, magazines, radio, television or any other means of communication:

   a. Factual information only concerned with the growth of the company or its number of operating outlets at the time of communication.

   b. Realistic or average yearly profit projections that can be reasonably expected by franchisees. Reasonable net profit figures are to be ascertained by using known average figures for comparable cities and/or operations. Overstated or exaggerated figures are to be eliminated.

   c. True and proper representation of all policies, products and any other important information which has influence on the enterprise.

   d. Ethical consumer advertising, to avoid any misleading claims such as, but not limited to, false comparisons, untrue, unproven or exaggerated statements, trick photography or omission or pertinent facts.

6. That all products furnished and sold to franchisees through, by, or upon the recommendation of the company shall be as represented, and manufactured with ingredients or materials of acceptable standards approved by the applicable trade, profession, or industry.

7. That distribution of the company's exclusive franchise products, services or equipment under more than one name in order to obtain business through more than one outlet in a franchised area without disclosure to the franchisee, shall be a violation of the spirit and/or letter of the franchising agreement and shall be prohibited.

8. That it shall completely avoid by demonstration and action, and shall encourage its franchisees to avoid, illegal practices of any sort.

9. That it shall respect all contracts, pay all obligations, maintain good credit rating and in other respects follow the highest standards of business conduct.

10. That it shall not in any way copy or represent the trademark, or other distinguishing marks, of other companies with intent to mislead the public.

11. That it shall assume the moral obligation to conduct continuing research in its field to increase the knowledge of its franchisees with respect to all phases of their business operation to assist them in maintaining competitive position, achieving better performance and obtaining maximum profits.

APPENDIX C   "Restaurant failures."*

CHART I   Failure rate (1960–1966).

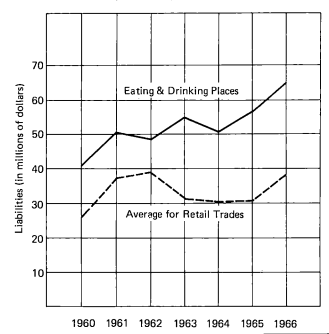

Underlying causes	Percent of failures
Incompetence	39.2
Unbalanced experience	19.9
Lack of managerial experience	19.8
Lack of experience in the line	12.4

Source: Dun & Bradstreet, Inc., Statistical Abstract of the United States, 1967.
* *From* Washington Report, *Marketing Research, 10, no. 16 (April 17, 1967).*

APPENDIX C *(Continued)*

CHART II Failure rate—liabilities.

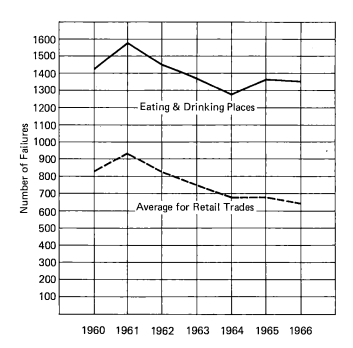

Source: Dun & Bradstreet, Inc., Statistical Abstract of the United States, 1967.

APPENDIX C (Continued)   "Costs—restaurant industry."*

TABLE I. Operating cost trends—individually owned eating and drinking places† (1961–1963).

Item‡	1963	1962	1961
Sales	100.00%	100.00%	100.00%
Cost of goods sold	56.24	56.71	56.53
Gross profit	43.76	43.29	43.47
Salaries and wages	13.94	13.51	13.39
Rent	3.62	3.44	3.44
Interest		.59	.58
Taxes	3.03	2.61	2.56
Bad debts	.05	.05	.05
Repairs	1.12	1.04	1.05
Depreciation, amortization	2.83	2.88	2.79
Net profit§	7.62	8.30	8.20

TABLE II. Operating cost trends—eating and drinking place partnerships† (1961–1963).

Item‡	1963	1962	1961
Sales	100.00%	100.00%	100.00%
Cost of goods sold	43.91	49.92	50.94
Gross profit	50.09	50.08	49.06
Salaries and wages	17.66	17.99	17.52
Payments to partners	1.66	1.56	1.29
Rent	3.44	3.51	3.46
Interest	.65	.55	.49
Taxes	3.38	3.18	2.96
Bad debts	.03	.04	.04
Repairs	1.14	1.12	1.04
Depreciation, amortization	2.76	2.75	2.80
Net profit§	10.63	10.23	10.05

Sources: Internal Revenue Service, Statistics of Income, U.S. Business Tax Returns; NRA.

Note: Not all operating costs are shown; therefore, net profit cannot be obtained from the subtraction of operating costs in this table.
† Includes all proprietorships whether or not they show a net profit.
‡ See text.
§ Before Federal Income Tax.

* From Washington Report, Marketing Research, 10, no. 16 (April 17, 1967).

TABLE III Comparison of costs—restaurants and other businesses, 1962.

	Proprietorships						*Partnerships*					
Kind of business	*Cost of goods sold %*	*Gross profit %*	*Salaries and wages %*	*Rent %*	*Taxes %*	*Net profit %*	*Cost of goods sold %*	*Gross margin %*	*Salaries and wages %*	*Rent %*	*Taxes %*	*Net profit %*
Apparel and accessories	68.29	31.71	7.78	4.08	1.27	8.16	66.61	33.39	9.71	3.80	1.45	8.40
Drug and proprietary stores	68.40	31.60	10.31	2.08	1.58	10.30	66.28	33.72	9.99	2.13	1.71	11.07
Eating and drinking places	56.71	43.29	13.51	3.44	2.61	8.30	49.92	50.08	17.99	3.51	3.18	10.23
Furniture and home furnishings	66.89	33.11	7.81	2.30	1.39	8.37	64.98	35.02	10.15	2.27	1.56	8.71
Gasoline service stations	79.54	20.46	6.03	2.05	1.01	4.78	76.69	23.31	6.47	2.07	1.28	6.81
General merchandise	74.56	25.44	4.64	1.68	1.31	7.74	73.56	26.44	7.68	1.68	1.54	6.42
Grocery and other food stores	84.47	15.53	3.56	1.02	.91	3.98	81.62	18.38	5.49	1.05	1.12	4.76
Hotels	29.13	70.87	16.06	7.88	5.12	4.74	17.41	82.59	18.50	6.72	6.49	5.55
Tourist courts and motels	13.24	86.76	9.45	1.02	5.68	8.92						

* *From* Washington Report, *Marketing Research, 10, no. 48 (November 27, 1967)* .

Wheels of the World

WHEELS OF THE WORLD
6749 East Marginal Way South
Seattle, Washington 98108

Offers

250 Convertible Bonds due December 15, 1981, $1,000

Par Value, 8% Coupon

The conversion privilege will be exercisable on or after December 15, 1972 to and including December 15, 1976 at a rate of one hundred (100) shares of common stock per bond converted. The Company reserves the privilege of calling these bonds with ninety (90) days notice on or after December 1, 1972 to and including December 1, 1976.

THESE SECURITIES HAVE NOT BEEN APPROVED OR DISAPPROVED BY THE SECURITIES AND EXCHANGE COMMISSION NOR HAS THE COMMISSION PASSED UPON THE ACCURACY OR ADEQUACY OF THIS OFFERING CIRCULAR OR ANY OTHER SELLING LITERATURE.

	Offering price	Proceeds to the company
Per bond	$ 1,000	$ 1,000
Total	$250,000	$250,000

There is no established public market for these bonds or the common stock available upon conversion. The offering price has been established by the management of the Company.

The Company reserves the right to reject any subscription agreements tendered in response to this Offering Circular. Further the Company may terminate the offering at any time before all securities are sold.

The effective date of this Offering Circular is December 1, 1971.

All inquiries and communications with respect to this offering should be directed to the Company at 6749 East Marginal Way South, Seattle, Washington 98108, telephone 206-762-5525.

No salesman or other person has been authorized to give any information or make any representation not contained in this Offering Circular in connection with the offer made by this Offering Circular. If given or made, such information or representation must not be relied upon as having been authorized by the Company.

Neither the delivery of this Offering Circular nor any sale made hereunder shall, under any circumstances, create an implication that there has been no change in the affairs of the Company since the respective dates as to which information is given hereunder.

INTRODUCTORY STATEMENT

Wheels of the World Inc., the "Company," was incorporated under the laws of the state of Washington on June 10, 1971. The Company proposes to engage in the business of building high quality, lightweight ten-speed bicycles.

At the present time only one manufacturer in the U.S. builds a high-quality lightweight ten-speed bicycle. All other high-quality ten-speed bicycles are imported from Europe and Japan. These imported high-quality ten-speed bicycles and the model made in the U.S. are primarily racing bicycles. The Company plans to build an adult recreation bicycle which incorporates the lightweight features of the racing bicycle and the convenience features necessary for enjoyable riding on U.S. roads.

RISK FACTORS

In analyzing this offering, prospective investors should consider the following factors:

1. Neither the Company nor any of its current management has previous experience in the bicycle industry. However, the distributor for the Company is the largest importer and distributor of quality bicycles on the West Coast and has agreed to supply the necessary initial expertise.

2. The frame materials and assembly procedure represent new technology in the bicycle industry. This technology is subject to both production and market impediments. The reasons for the innovations are, however, supported by extensive market information and are designed to both differentiate the Company's product from existing quality ten-speeds and fulfill the important attributes of such bicycles as perceived by the current market.

3. The single most crucial constraint facing manufacturers of ten-speed bicycles is a shortage of component parts. The Company has minimized this risk through access to a portion of a long standing and recurring order available to Bicycle Products Development International, a division of our distributor, the West Coast Cycle Supply Company.

4. The current quality ten-speed bicycle market is dominated by imports, mainly from England, France, Italy, and Japan. There is only one U.S. manufacturer that has a quality model; therefore, the market currently has a preference for imports. However, most imports are sold, not marketed. It is the opinion of the Company that the proper use of promotions and advertising will enable us to overcome the current market preference.

5. Bicycle sales in the U.S. are growing rapidly among all age groups. Bicycles are, therefore, a known commodity, and the Company's product does not differ enough from existing quality ten-speed bicycles to cause difficulties at entry or necessitate a reeducation of the market.

DESCRIPTION OF DEBENTURES OFFERED

The debentures are $1,000 par value, 8% coupon, convertible bonds due December 15, 1981. The conversion ratio is 100 shares of common stock per bond. The bonds may be converted from or on December 15, 1972 to and including December 15, 1976.

The company may elect to call any of these bonds with 90 days written notice. During the period the bonds are eligible for conversion they may be converted into 100 shares of common stock. The call price shall be $1,000.

USE OF PROCEEDS

The proceeds from this offering will be used to finance initial development costs, accounts receivable, inventories, and plant and capital investments and to purchase materials and components until the proceeds from sales provide the cash required for these purchases.

DESCRIPTION OF CAPITAL STOCK

The Company's authorized capital consists of two hundred and fifty thousand (250,000) shares of common stock having no par value. Each share of stock is entitled to one vote per share. There are no preemptive rights with respect to the stock of the Company.

CAPITALIZATION

The following table sets forth the capitalization of the Company as of September 30, 1971 and as adjusted to give the effect of this offering before and after conversion of the debentures.

	Number of shares
September 30, 1971	
Authorized	250,000
Issued	25,000
Reserved for warrants	19,000
Upon completion of this offering with no debentures converted	
Authorized	250,000
Issued	25,000
Reserved for warrants	19,000
Reserved for conversion	25,000
Assuming exercise of all warrants and conversion of all debentures	
Authorized	250,000
Issued	69,000

SHAREHOLDERS

The initial subscribers to stock in the Company and the number of shares and warrants purchased are shown below:

Name	Number of shares purchased at $.80	Number of warrants to purchase shares at $1.00 purchased for $.05 each
William A. Leber	5,000	5,000
Robert W. Howard	5,000	4,000
William G. Powell	5,000	4,000
Norman D. Wall	5,000	3,000
Joseph L. Parker, Jr.	5,000	3,000
	25,000	19,000

DIVIDEND POLICY

The management of the Company does not anticipate that any dividends will be paid on present or converted stock within the foreseeable future. It is the view of management that earnings of the Company should be retained for capital improvements and expansion in the business activities of the Company. In the event there are retained earnings in excess of an amount deemed by management necessary for such purposes, dividends may be declared at a future time.

INDUSTRY

The Company will be in the bicycle industry in general, and it will compete in the light-weight ten-speed segment specifically. This is the fastest growing segment of the industry, and bicycling is the fastest growing outdoors activity in the United States. Total bicycle sales in the U.S. have grown from 7.1 million units in 1969 to close to 8.0 million units in 1970 (retail sales of $400 million) and are progressing at a rate estimated sufficient for sales of 8.5 million units in 1971.

The lightweight segment of the industry includes three-, five-, and ten-speed bicycles. This segment has grown from 10% of unit sales in 1968 to approximately 50% in 1971, and the ten-speed portion of the lightweights has been the major contributing factor in the current bicycle boom. Ten-speed bicycles now comprise approximately 50% of the lightweight sales, thus accounting for close to 25% of the total U.S. bicycle market.

The main contributing factors to the rapid growth in ten-speed bicycle sales have been (1) young bicycle riders who have been moving away from "high-rise" bicycles to ten-speed lightweights and (2) an increase in bicycle sales to adults. The adult market has increased from 5% of unit sales in 1966 to an expected 25% of unit sales in 1971. This increase has been mostly in the ten-speed lightweight category. The reasons for the trend into ten-speed lightweights include: (1) an appreciation of the advantages of ten-speeds over "high-risers," (2) a national emphasis on ecology, (3) the aware-ness of the importance of proper, consistent exercise, (4) traffic congestion and driving-related expenses, (5) increased leisure time, and (6) recognition in the United States of bicycling as a competitive sport.

The market share of ten-speed lightweights is expected to increase substantially as more of the 20.6 million potential bicycle riders between the ages of 9 and 14 continue the trend away from the "high-rise" bicycle and as the percentage of bicycle riders among the 129.4 million between the age of 14 to 65 years old increases.

COMPETITION

The quality ten-speed lightweight market in the U.S. is currently dominated by imports. As early as 1963 imports constituted close to 25% of the total U.S. bicycle market, declining in magnitude to around 11% in 1965 as the "high-rise" bicycle captured close to 70% of the U.S. market. By the end of 1970 imports had again risen to 25% of unit sales, and they are expected to increase to 33% by the end of 1971. This increase is primarily the result of the trend in the United States toward lightweight bicycles.

U.S. bicycle manufacturers are currently reallocating productive capacity toward lightweights—mostly ten-speeds. Murray Ohio Manufacturing Company, the U.S. volume leader, produced 40% lightweights in 1971, and Schwinn Bicycles (number three by volume), having doubled its lightweight production to 45% of unit output in 1970, increased it again to 72% in 1971. But despite the increase in lightweight bicycle production by U.S. manufacturers, only Schwinn produced a model that could be defined as a quality ten-speed lightweight bicycle.

Most of the quality ten-speed imports come from England, France, Italy, and Japan. Raleigh (England), perhaps the best known of the imports, increased its lightweight shipments to the U.S. by 28% in 1970 while Peugeot accounted for about 50% of the imports from France. Gitane, also from France, is another ten-speed bicycle which has increased shipments to the U.S. and has become well known. American Eagle is the best known of the Japanese imports. In addition, there are numerous other imports, most newcomers to the U.S., all with very small portions of the market, and most with very little marketing support.

THE COMPANY'S MARKETING PLAN

The Company has established a twofold marketing objective: (1) to produce a line of competitively priced, quality ten-speed bicycles which appeal to the knowledgeable bicycle buyer and (2) to achieve a brand identification that differentiates our product line from existing quality ten-speed bicycles. The product line will initially contain two models—a touring bicycle and an "around town" bicycle. Each will have components appropriate to the use and will be available in three frame sizes. The touring model will be available with a choice of tubular (sew-up) or clincher tires.

Differentiation will be achieved by the innovative use of new metals in frame construction, the effective use of promotions and advertisements, and visual characteristics of the bicycle. The anticipated brand name is "Titan."

The Company feels that the combination of increased purchases by young cyclists, increased publicity, governmental attention, and increased competitive bicycling will contribute to a market more knowledgeable about the important attributes of and distinctions between ten-speed lightweight bicycles. The Company plans to build a bicycle that has the attributes perceived by the market to be desirable for riding in the U.S.

Initial sales will be made through the West Coast Cycle Supply Company in Los Angeles, who will distribute the Company's bicycles to approximately 175 quality bicycle retail outlets throughout California (140 outlets) and parts of Arizona, Washington, Oregon, Nevada, Texas, Utah, New Mexico, Hawaii, and New Jersey. This distribution will give the Company access to a population of about 26.6 million people, or nearly 13% of the total U.S. population. On a per capita basis, this marketing area would support total annual sales of 273,000 ten-speed lightweight bicycles. It is the opinion of the Company and West Coast Cycle Supply Company that the Company can conservatively make one sale per outlet per week, or 700 bicycles per month, thus capturing 3% of the market in West Coast Cycle Supply Company's area of distribution. The 3% market share must be qualified as a probable overstatement because on a per capita basis California supports a disproportionately high level of bicycle sales. In 1967 California had approximately 9% of the U.S. population and close to 15% of total U.S. bicycle sales.

Sales for 1972 will start at 250 bicycles in February, advance to 500 in April, 750 in August, and stabilize at 1,000 bicycles per month in September for the remainder of the year. Pending successful prototype development, West Coast Cycle Supply Company will issue a purchase order for the first year's production.

The Company plans selective expansion into new geographic markets. No sales are anticipated through discount or department stores, and no corporate sales force is envisioned during the first year of operations.

MANAGEMENT

The Directors and Executive Officers of Wheels of the World are:

Name	Position
William A. Leber	President and Director
William G. Powell	Vice President and Director
Robert W. Howard	Secretary and Treasurer and Director
Norman D. Wall	Director

The resumes of all officers and directors follow:

Management and Directors

William A. Leber has a Bachelor of Mechanical Engineering from Purdue and a Master of Business Administration from the University of Washington. He served three years in the USMC as an artillery and personnel officer. He has 6 years of experience with duPont in research and development, consulting engineering, production assistance, and recruiting.

Robert W. Howard has a Bachelor of Science in math and physics from the University of British Columbia, a Master of Science in

aeronautical science from the University of California, and a Master of Business Administration from the University of Washington. He worked for Boeing on the SST Aerodynamics staff and is President of Fireside Lodge Corporation.

William G. Powell has a Bachelor of Arts degree in history from Stanford University and a Master of Business Administration from the University of Washington. He has worked in an industrial sales capacity in the management training program at the Gardner-Denver Company, and he served 2 years as an operations officer in the U.S. Army.

Norman D. Wall has a Bachelor of Arts in business administration from the University of Washington. He served in the U.S. Marine Corps as a supply officer. He has worked in sales management for Proctor and Gamble. He was the general manager of Unique Zipper Company and is now the director of sewing notions for the Vogue Butterick division of American Can Company.

REMUNERATION OF OFFICERS

There are no director's fees or other compensation for services as a director. Officers' annual salaries are as follows:

Office	Name	Salary
President	William A. Leber	$15,000
Vice President	William G. Powell	13,800
Secretary/ Treasurer	Robert W. Howard	6,900

No other form of compensation is presently authorized for the officers. When Company operations warrant, salaries may be expected to increase in accordance with the guidelines established by the government. Additional salaried officers may join the Company, and other forms of compensation may be authorized in the acceptable lawful manner.

PRODUCTION

The frames for the Titan bicycle will be built using titanium tubes and high-quality steel lugs. Special adaptors have been developed to bond the titanium to the steel. These adapters will give the same effect as double butting on steel tubing, and they can be used to stiffen the frame at selected points. After assembly the frame will be painted to the Company's specifications by an outside firm.

The wheels will be spoked and trued in local handicap and shelter workshops. The Company has designed and built a special stand to facilitate wheel spoking. In-plant facilities will be maintained to check and correct the tolerances on all wheels.

The Titan will be assembled and tested by a skilled craftsman. Each craftsman will have a work area, and assembly/test stand, and storage facilities for about one day's supply of parts. The craftsmen will be assigned in teams of two so that they can assist each other with a few of the assembly and test operations. For every four craftsmen there will be a person who will bring frames, components, and packaging materials to the craftsmen and substitute for a craftsman if necessary.

There will be some minor disassembly before packaging the bicycle so that it will fit in a compact shipping container. None of the critical adjustments made during assembly will be altered by the disassembly for shipping. It should take the retail dealer about 5 or 10 minutes to unpackage and set up the Titan (it takes about an hour to unpackage and set up an imported ten-speed bicycle).

ASSIGNMENT

Evaluate this company as a prospective investment. Evaluate the presentation of the company as given in the prospectus. Develop recommendations for both the company and a prospective investor.

EXHIBIT 1   Product description.

Titan Touring

Frame	Titanium tubing, double butted, Prugnat or Bocama lugs
Finish	Acrylic or polyurethane
Weight	About 22 lb
Sizes	21 in., 23 in., 25 in.
Tires	Clement or Soyo tubular or clincher
Rims	Fianne or Araya tubular or light alloy with stainless double-butted spokes
Hubs	Shimano or Sunshine high-flanged with quick release
Crank	Sun Tour Magic Compe light alloy cotterless 42/54
Rear cog	Shimano or Sun Tour 14/34
Shifters	Sun Tour power or double lever mounted on the down bar
Gear range	33–104
Rear derailleur	Sun Tour GT
Front derailleur	Sun Tour
Brakes	Dia Compe or Weinman center pull
Handle bars	Maes pattern light alloy
Stem	Forged Gran Compe
Pedals	Pro Ace light alloy road with toe clips and straps
Extras	

Titan Around Town

Frame	Titanium tubing, double butted, Prugnat or Bocama lugs
Finish	Acrylic or polyurethane
Weight	About 26 lb
Sizes	21 in., 23 in., 25 in.
Tires	27 × 1¼ clinchers
Rims	Araya light alloy with stainless steel double-butted spokes
Hubs	Shimano or Sunshine high-flanged with quick release
Crank	Very light alloy cotterless 36/52
Rear cog	Shimano or Sun Tour 14/34
Shifters	Stem mounted Sun Tour power shifter
Gear range	29–100
Rear derailleur	Sun Tour GT
Front derailleur	Sun Tour
Brakes	Dia Compe or Weinman center pull with safety levers
Handle bars	Maes pattern light alloy
Stem	Forged light alloy
Pedals	Pro Ace light alloy track
Extras	ESGE kickstand, spoke protector, chain guard

EXHIBIT 2 Comparison to competition.

	Price (approx.)	Weight (lb)	Frame and finish	Tires rims hubs	Gear range	Derailleurs	Brakes	Crank and pedals
Titan: Touring	$250	22	Titanium lugged Acrylic	Tubular tires Light alloy rims QR hubs	33–104	Sun Tour GT	Center pull	Light alloy Cotterless w/toe clips
Titan: Around Town	$200	26	Titanium lugged Acrylic	Clincher tires Light alloy rims QR hubs	29–100	Sun Tour GT	Center pull w/safety lever	Light alloy Cotterless
Schwinn: Sports Touring	$200		Steel welded Enamel	Clincher tires Light alloy rims	28–104	Compy Gran Tourisimo	Center pull w/safety lever	Light alloy
Gitane: Professional Tour de France	$195–$219	21½	531 double-butted and lugged Enamel	Tubular tires Light alloy rims QR hubs	44–104	Simplex Criterion	Center pull	Light alloy Cotterless
American Eagle: Semi-Pro	$190	28	Double-butted and lugged Enamel	Clincher tires Light alloy rims QR hubs	38–95	Sun Tour GT	Center pull w/safety lever	Light alloy Cotterless
Peugeot: Professional Competition Racer	$195	21	531 double-butted and lugged Enamel	Tubular tires Light alloy rims QR hubs	53–100	Simplex Prestige	Center pull	Light alloy Cotterless
Raleigh: International	$289	Estimated at 25	531 double-butted and lugged Enamel	Clincher tires Light alloy rims QR hubs	50–100	Compy	Center pull	Light alloy Cotterless
Compania: Professional	$230	Estimated at 24	Double-butted and lugged Enamel	Tubular tires Light alloy rims QR hubs	25–101	Sun Tour GT	Center pull	Light alloy Cotterless
Crescent: Special Racer	≈$190	Estimated at 24	531 double-butted and lugged Enamel	Tubular tires Light alloy rims QR hubs	50–100	Compy Valentino	Center pull	Light alloy Cotterless

EXHIBIT 3 Legal counsel.

Legal opinions in connection with this offering and corporate legal counsel are provided by the firm of Karr, Tuttle, Campbell, Kock and Campbell.

Patent and trademark counsel are provided by the firm of Seed, Berry, Dowrey and Cross.

EXHIBIT 4

EVERETT D. OHLUND
Certified Public Accountant

SUNSET 3-6824
5809 15TH AVENUE NORTHWEST
SEATTLE, WASHINGTON 98107

October 20, 1971

The Board of Directors,
Wheels of the World, Inc.,
Seattle, Washington.

We have examined the balance sheet of Wheels of the World, Inc. as of September 30, 1971 and the related statement of income (loss) and deficit for the period from inception, June 10, 1971 to September 30, 1971. Our examination was made in accordance with generally accepted auditing standards, and accordingly included such tests of the accounting records and such other auditing procedures as we considered necessary in the circumstances.

In our opinion, the accompanying balance sheet and statement of income (loss) and deficit present fairly the financial position of the Wheels of the World, Inc. at September 30, 1971, and the results of its operations for the period then ended, in conformity with generally accepted accounting principles.

Everett D. Ohlund

Certified Public Accountant

EXHIBIT 5 Wheels of the World, Inc., Balance Sheet, September 30, 1971.

ASSETS

Current Assets:

Cash		$5,583.13
Inventories (Note A*) :		
Components	$ 179.55	
Materials	450.74	630.29
Prepaid expenses		43.50
Total current assets		$6,256.92

Furniture and Equipment (At cost, less

accumulated depreciation, $49.60)	658.80

Other Assets:

Unamortized organization expense	492.60
	$7,408.32

LIABILITIES AND STOCKHOLDERS' EQUITY

Current Liabilities:

Trade accounts payable	$ 510.03	
Accrued wages payable	290.00	
Total current liabilities		$ 800.03

Stockholders' Equity:

Common capital stock (authorized $50,000.00, 250,000 shares of no par value, resulting in a 20¢ per share valuation) :

Issued, 12,500 shares	$ 2,500.00	
Subscribed but not issued, 12,500 shares at		
80¢ per share (Note C)	10,000.00	
Warrants issued and outstanding, 19,000		
(Note D)	950.00	
	$13,450.00	
Less uncollected subscriptions	10,000.00	
Common capital stock	$ 3,450.00	
Capital paid in on purchase of stock in excess		
of 20¢ per share valuation	7,500.00	
	$10,950.00	
Less operating deficit	4,341.71	
Stockholders' equity		6,608.29
		$7,408.32

* *See notes to financial statements.*

EXHIBIT 6 Wheels of the World, Inc., statement of income (loss) and deficit, from inception, June 10, 1971 to September 30, 1971.

Gross Sales		None
Expenses		
Salaries to officers	$1,615.00	
Selling expenses	30.00	
Travel	590.13	
Graphics and printing	65.89	
Office supplies and telephone	410.14	
Rent of office	87.50	
Research and development (Note F*)	1,199.82	
Miscellaneous	143.96	
Taxes: payroll and excise	114.51	
Amortization	35.16	
Depreciation	49.60	
Total expenses		$4,341.71
Net income (loss) and deficit (Note G)		($4,341.71)

* *See notes to financial statements.*

EXHIBIT 7 Wheels of the World, Inc., notes to financial statements, from inception, June 10, 1971 to September 30, 1971.

Note A—Inventory Pricing Methods:
Inventories are valued at cost or market, whichever is lower.

Note B—Depreciation:
Depreciation is determined on a declining balance method at rates adequate to depreciate the applicable assets over their expected average useful lives.

Note C—Capital Stock Subscriptions:
On July 16, 1971 25,000 shares were subscribed for at 80¢ per share, with 12,500 being paid for and issued. Payment for the remaining 12,500 subscribed shares will be due December 31, 1971.

Note D—Stock Warrants:
19,000 warrants were issued July 16, 1971 at $50.00 per 1,000 and will expire July 31, 1976. Warrants can be exercised in multiples of 1,000 on a one to one basis for common stock at $1.00 per share.

Note E—Purchase Commitment:
A commitment for the purchase of materials and components for inventory was outstanding at September 30, 1971 in the approximate amount of $25,000.00.

Note F—Research and Development:
The company has elected to write off research and development expenses in the current year. This election will also be made for income tax reporting purposes.

Note G—Net Loss per Share:
The net loss per share was 49¢. This amount was computed by using the treasury stock method.

EXHIBIT 8 Sales projection.

1972	Jan.	Feb.	Mar.	Apr.	May	June	July	Aug.	Sept.	Oct.	Nov.	Dec.	Total
Market Mix (bicycles)													
Touring	0	125	125	250	250	250	250	500	500	500	500	500	3750
Around Town	0	125	125	250	250	250	250	250	500	500	500	500	3500
Sales	0	$30,875	$30,875	$61,750	$61,750	$61,750	$61,750	$95,750	$123,500	$123,500	$123,500	$123,500	$898,500

1973		*Quarter 1*		*Quarter 2*		*Quarter 3*		*Quarter 4*		*Total*
Market Mix										
Touring		1,750		2,250		2,250		2,250		8,500
Around Town		1,500		2,250		2,250		2,250		8,250
Sales		$404,500		$ 555,750		$ 555,750		$ 555,750		$2,071,175

1974		*Quarter 1*		*Quarter 2*		*Quarter 3*		*Quarter 4*		*Total*
Market Mix										
Touring		2,250		3,000		3,000		3,000		11,250
Around Town		2,250		3,000		3,000		3,000		11,250
Sales		$555,750		$ 741,000		$ 741,000		$ 741,000		$2,778,750

1975		*Quarter 1*		*Quarter 2*		*Quarter 3*		*Quarter 4*		*Total*
Market Mix										
Touring		3,000		3,750		3,750		3,750		14,250
Around Town		3,000		3,750		3,750		3,750		14,250
Sales		$741,000		$ 926,250		$ 926,250		$ 926,250		$3,519,750

1976		*Quarter 1*		*Quarter 2*		*Quarter 3*		*Quarter 4*		*Total*
Market Mix										
Touring		3,750		4,500		4,500		4,500		17,250
Around Town		3,750		4,500		4,500		4,500		17,250
Sales		$925,250		$1,111,500		$1,111,500		$1,111,500		$4,260,750

EXHIBIT 9 Pro-forma cash flow statements, 1972.

	Jan.	Feb.	Mar.	Apr.	May	June	July	Aug.	Sept.	Oct.	Nov.	Dec.
Cash receipts												
Cash at beginning	5,165	9,665	9,715	8,900	4,275	6,155	2,605	3,205	4,205	7,655	17,285	23,815
Cash from business	—	—	30,875	30,875	61,750	61,750	61,750	61,750	95,750	123,500	123,500	123,500
Cash from outside sources	60,000	27,500	20,000	30,000	5,000	—	20,000	45,000	20,000	0	0	—
Total receipts	65,165	37,165	60,590	69,775	71,025	67,905	84,355	109,955	119,955	131,155	140,785	147,315
Cash disbursements												
Inventory	33,300	11,750	38,750	48,000	50,500	50,500	66,250	83,750	90,000	90,000	93,000	95,500
Assembly labor	—	2,500	2,500	5,000	5,000	5,000	5,000	7,500	10,000	10,000	10,000	10,000
Plant rent and maintenance	400	400	400	400	400	400	400	500	500	500	500	500
Plant supervision	—	—	—	—	—	—	—	—	500	900	900	900
General and administrative	7,000	8,050	7,200	9,200	7,900	8,300	8,400	9,750	10,300	11,700	10,900	11,000
Interest	150	550	740	900	1,070	1,100	1,100	1,250	1,500	1,670	1,670	1,670
Capital investment	14,650	4,200	2,100	2,000	—	—	—	3,000	—	—	—	2,000
Federal income tax	—	—	—	—	—	—	—	—	—	—	—	—
Total disbursements	55,500	27,450	51,690	65,500	64,870	65,300	81,150	105,750	112,300	113,870	116,970	121,570
Cash at end	9,665	9,715	8,900	4,275	6,155	2,605	3,205	4,205	7,655	17,285	23,815	25,745
Cumulative cash needs from investors	82,500	110,000	130,000	160,000	165,000	165,000	185,000	230,000	250,000	250,000	250,000	250,000

EXHIBIT 9 Pro-forma cash flow statements, 1972 (Continued).

	1973				1974			
	Quarter 1	Quarter 2	Quarter 3	Quarter 4	Quarter 1	Quarter 2	Quarter 3	Quarter 4
Cash receipts								
Cash at beginning	25,745	16,775	60,105	85,590	104,974	82,260	65,980	106,865
Cash from business	370,500	528,000	555,750	555,750	555,750	679,250	741,000	741,000
Cash from outside sources	45,000	30,000	—	—	—	—	—	—
Total receipts	441,245	574,775	615,855	641,340	660,725	761,515	806,980	847,865
Cash disbursements								
Inventory	335,500	405,000	405,000	410,500	448,500	540,000	540,000	545,500
Assembly labor	32,500	45,000	45,000	45,000	45,000	60,000	60,000	60,000
Plant rent and maintenance	1,500	3,000	3,000	3,000	3,000	3,900	3,900	4,200
Plant supervision	2,700	2,700	3,000	3,000	3,000	6,000	6,000	6,000
General and administrative	37,200	50,800	45,900	46,500	50,600	52,950	52,950	54,000
Interest	5,070	6,400	6,600	6,600	6,600	6,600	6,600	6,600
Capital investment	10,000	0	3,000	3,000	3,000	13,000	3,000	3,000
Federal income tax	0	1,770	18,765	18,765	18,765	13,085	27,665	27,660
Total disbursements	424,470	514,670	530,265	536,365	578,465	695,535	700,115	706,960
Cash at end	16,775	60,105	85,590	104,975	82,260	65,980	106,865	140,905
Cumulative cash needs from investors	295,000	325,000	325,000	325,000	325,000	325,000	325,000	325,000

EXHIBIT 9 Pro-forma cash flow statements, 1972 (Continued).

	1975				1976			
	Quarter 1	Quarter 2	Quarter 3	Quarter 4	Quarter 1	Quarter 2	Quarter 3	Quarter 4
Cash receipts								
Cash at beginning	140,905	126,445	117,631	167,106	211,031	202,106	205,581	187,371
Cash from business	741,000	864,500	926,250	926,250	926,250	1,047,750	1,111,500	1,111,500
Cash from outside sources	—	—	—	—	—	—	—	—
Total receipts	881,905	990,945	1,043,881	1,093,356	1,137,281	1,251,856	1,317,081	1,298,871
Cash disbursements								
Inventory	583,500	675,000	675,000	680,500	718,500	810,000	810,000	810,000
Assembly labor	60,000	75,000	75,000	75,000	75,000	90,000	90,000	90,000
Plant rent and maintenance	4,200	4,200	4,200	4,200	4,200	5,100	5,100	5,100
Plant supervision	6,000	6,000	6,000	6,000	6,000	6,000	6,000	6,000
General and administrative	64,500	68,850	69,150	70,200	79,050	87,750	88,050	88,050
Interest	6,600	6,600	6,600	6,600	6,600	6,600	6,600	5,010
Capital investment	3,000	10,000	4,500	3,500	9,500	4,500	4,500	4,500
Federal income tax	27,660	27,664	36,325	36,325	36,325	36,325	44,460	44,460
Total disbursements	755,460	873,314	876,775	882,325	935,175	1,046,275	1,054,710	1,053,120
Cash at end	126,445	117,631	167,106	211,031	202,106	205,581	187,371	245,751
Cumulative cash needs from investors	325,000	325,000	325,000	325,000	325,000	325,000	250,000	250,000

EXHIBIT 10 Pro-forma balance sheets.

	1971	1972	1973	1974	1975	1976
Assets						
Cash	5,165	25,745	104,975	140,905	211,031	245,751
Accounts receivable	0	123,500	185,250	247,000	308,750	370,500
Component inventory paid for but not yet received	5,200	22,750	30,000	39,000	48,000	54,000
Component inventory on hand	0	60,000	90,000	120,000	150,000	180,000
Lugs paid for but not yet received	5,000	18,750	25,000	32,500	40,000	45,000
Lugs on hand	0	5,000	7,500	10,000	12,500	15,000
Other assets gross	2,204	30,155	46,154	68,154	89,154	112,154
Less accumulated depreciation	(170)	(6,750)	(15,770)	(27,570)	(41,170)	(56,670)
Net	2,034	23,585	30,384	40,904	47,984	55,484
Total assets	17,399	279,330	473,109	630,309	818,265	965,735
Liabilities						
Accounts payable	214	214	214	534	214	214
Notes	0	0	75,000	75,000	76,000	0
Bonds	22,500	250,000	250,000	250,000	250,000	250,000
Tax	0	1,770	31,850	55,324	72,650	88,919
Total liabilities	22,714	251,984	357,064	380,858	397,864	89,133
Assets–liabilities	(5,314)	27,346	116,045	249,451	419,081	876,602
Equities						
Paid-in capital	20,950	20,950	20,950	20,950	20,950	20,950
Retained earnings	(26,265)	6,395	95,095	228,501	399,451	605,652
Owners equity	(5,314)	27,346	116,045	249,451	420,401	876,602

EXHIBIT 11 Pro-forma statements of income.

	1971	1972	1973	1974	1975	1976
Gross sales	0	898,500	2,071,750	2,778,750	3,519,750	4,260,750
COGS	0	735,500	1,699,400	2,286,000	2,890,800	3,493,500
Gross margin	0	163,000	372,350	492,750	628,950	767,250
Less						
Salaries	11,285	45,750	51,000	56,400	61,800	67,800
Office expenditures	359	11,550	17,550	20,400	24,000	27,600
Management	533	2,050	4,100	6,000	6,000	6,000
Selling	30	1,100	1,950	3,300	5,400	10,500
Travel	1,790	5,100	4,700	6,000	6,000	8,400
Legal	675	1,200	2,100	3,300	4,500	8,100
CPA	975	1,600	2,600	2,900	3,900	6,000
Freight	0	14,500	38,000	52,350	74,250	104,700
Warranty	0	3,300	9,900	13,050	17,250	20,400
Ads and graphics	1,690	12,000	25,000	24,000	43,800	57,600
R&D	8,688	8,650	17,800	16,800	19,800	19,800
State and local tax	0	2,000	5,700	6,000	6,000	6,000
Interest	70	13,370	24,670	26,400	26,400	24,810
Depreciation and amortization	170	6,400	9,200	11,800	13,600	15,500
Total	26,265	128,570	214,270	248,700	312,700	383,210
Profit before tax	(26,265)	34,430	158,080	244,050	316,250	384,040
Federal income tax	0	1,770	69,380	110,644	145,300	177,839
Profit after tax	(26,265)	32,660	88,700	133,406	170,950	206,201

EXHIBIT 12 Earnings/share.

	1971	1972	1973	1974	1975	1976
Shares currently outstanding (25,000)	(1.05)	1.31	3.55	5.34	6.84	8.25
Shares to be outstanding after exercise of warrants (44,000)	—	0.74	2.02	3.04	3.89	4.69
Shares to be outstanding after exercise of warrants and full conversion of bonds (69,000)	—	—	1.29	1.93	2.48	3.00

EXHIBIT 13 Extent of distribution through West Coast Cycle Supply Company.

State	Cities		Outlets
California	All major cities		140
Washington	Seattle	4	
	Vancouver	1	
	Bellingham	1	6
Oregon	Portland	2	
	Beaverton	2	4
Arizona	Scottsdale	1	
	Phoenix	4	
	Tempe	1	
	El Mirage	1	
	Youngtown	1	
	Flagstaff	1	
	Glendale	1	
	Tucson	3	13
Nevada	Reno	1	
	Las Vegas	1	2
Texas	Dallas		1
Utah	Salt Lake City		1
New Mexico	Albuquerque		1
Hawaii	Honolulu		1
New Jersey	Brielle		1
Mexico			2
			172

EXHIBIT 14 U.S. bicycle market, 1960–1971 (number of bicycles).

Year	Domestic Production	Imports	Apparent Consumption
1960	2,592,910	1,186,596	3,779,506
1961	2,579,093	1,087,298	3,666,391
1962	2,954,215	1,267,329	4,221,544
1963	3,118,260	1,294,905	4,413,165
1964	4,082,563	1,010,035	5,092,598
1965	4,618,743	1,058,884	5,657,627
1966	4,829,122	927,223	5,756,345
1967	5,180,352	1,117,246	6,297,598
1968	5,966,184	1,534,138	7,500,322
1969	5,089,023	1,970,528	7,059,551
1970	6,000,000	2,000,000	8,000,000
1971	6,200,000	2,300,000	8,500,000

EXHIBIT 15 Bicycle costs.

Cost category	Costs	
	Touring (dollars)	Around town (dollars)
Completed frame	30	30
Components	70	50
Assembly labor	5	5
Post assembly labor	5	5
Total	110	90

Revenue per bike.

Bicycle model	Cost	×	Markup	=	Revenue (dollars)
Touring	110		1.235		136
Around town	90		1.235		111

9

Purchase of
a Smaller Company

One route to small company ownership is to buy an established firm. This chapter considers some of the advantages and disadvantages of purchasing a small company, the steps that might be taken to find and acquire a suitable business, and the alternative ways of structuring the purchase.

ADVANTAGES AND DISADVANTAGES OF PURCHASING A FIRM

The advantages of purchasing an existing business include the following:

1. A "going concern" is acquired; it has an organization, methods, customers, and hopefully orders. (Of course, it is possible for a business to be moribund and barely "going.")

2. There is a record of tangible performance that can be evaluated. Industry conditions may change, and the new management may be more or less capable, but there is a record. (In contrast, the costs, needed investment, personnel required, and expected sales for a new venture must be based upon estimates that may be highly speculative.)

3. The acquired firm is eliminated as a competitor. If an entrepreneur starts a second furniture store in a town, there are then two stores competing for the market; if, instead, the entrepreneur buys the first store, he has the market to himself.

4. Existing businesses may sometimes be purchased at attractive terms, possibly at less than replacement value.

5. The existing business may have contractual relationships, distributors, patents, leases, tax-loss carry forwards, etc., that would be difficult or impossible to duplicate.

358

The potential disadvantages of purchasing a company include the following:

1. The right business may not be available. If the entrepreneur primarily has an idea for a new product or a service not previously offered, then a new venture may be the most logical vehicle.

2. The acquired business may have serious problems. If the organization, facilities, and reputation reflect poor previous management, the acquirer inherits the seller's problems.

3. The terms at which a business is available may be unattractive. If, for example, the seller is under no pressure to sell, the price may be unrealistically high.

STAGES IN ACQUIRING A FIRM

The four stages of searching for and acquiring a firm are (1) identification, (2) screening, (3) evaluation, and (4) negotiation.

There is no one best source of information on candidates for acquisition. If the entrepreneur has developed very specific ideas about the kind of business to be acquired, then this obviously narrows the focus of the search. Useful sources of "leads" on businesses for sale include the following: (1) commercial bankers, (2) lawyers who have substantial corporate or estate practices, (3) public accountants, (4) investment bankers, (5) business brokers, (6) management consultants, (7) realtors, (8) insurance agents who do estate planning for business owners, (9) trade association executives, and (10) advertisements in newspapers and trade publications. Personal introductions are helpful and should be utilized whenever feasible. Some sources will expect a commission or finder's fee for sales culminating from leads they have provided.

Unless the entrepreneur is only considering very specific opportunities, there should be no difficulty in generating leads. There are a surprising number of businesses, of all sizes and degrees of profitability, which might be purchased. The suitability of these opportunities, however, may vary widely. This leads to the next stage—screening.

SCREENING OPPORTUNITIES

Unless the entrepreneur wishes to make a career of searching for a suitable business, he must be able to screen the mass of possibilities efficiently. Criteria should be developed that can be applied so that each situation does not have to be investigated in detail, thereby permitting attention to be focused on the more promising situations.

In developing criteria for screening purposes, the entrepreneur should first consider his goals, his resources, and his skills. What can he do well? What contacts and industry knowledge does he have? How much money can he raise? How much time is available to find a suitable business? (Time pressures can be both financial and psychological.) Does he want a stable, profitable business, perhaps one that he can purchase from a retiring owner? How willing is he to take on a high-risk venture? What are his preferences for industry, for location, and for degree of control?

The entrepreneur must be prepared to modify his thinking, as he becomes aware of what is available. He must be flexible, without wasting time on ventures which are clearly unsuitable. If a suitable venture does not turn up quickly, the entrepreneur must not panic and pursue inappropriate businesses in order to justify his decision to search for a company.

EVALUATING COMPANIES

Once the entrepreneur has selected a company for detailed evaluation, he should consider all the factors that bear upon its future profitability. Almost any list of factors could be expanded; furthermore, many of the factors are interrelated. For instance, expected sales depend on product price and quality, reputation, the distribution systems, and the competitive environment. Here are some of the most important questions to ask:

1. Product (or Service). Does the product line enjoy competitive advantages because of its quality, price, etc.? What trends may affect the future sales of this product?

2. Competition. What are the relative strengths of the competitors? Are any major changes anticipated? (The seller may not go out of his way to point out that a major new competitor is entering the market.)

3. Facilities. What are the capabilities and expected further life of the major facilities? How do they compare with newer equipment that has become available?

4. Organization. How capable are the people? If key people leave, can they be replaced? How critical to the success of the business are the skills of the current owner?

5. Financial Position. Are current financial statements available? Are balance sheet values justified? (Accounts receivable may be overstated because the allowance for bad debts is inadequate; inventory may be obsolete; fixed assets may have been poorly maintained.) Are there redundant assets that can be sold or can excess funds be withdrawn without hampering operations? Conversely, must additional investments be made? (In "turnarounds" the funds needed for working capital may be greater than the company purchase price.)

6. Expected Sales and Profits. Can the purchaser make the business more profitable by improving efficiency or by pursuing unexploited opportunities? Has management compensation, including perquisites, been unreasonably high or low, and would it be changed after the business is purchased? If substantial changes in operations are anticipated, as, for example, in turnaround situations, then forecasts are usually less certain.

Some sellers are honest; some are not. Most sellers would see no reason why they should point out to the buyer that certain assets may be overvalued or that the company's major market faces a bleak future. The prospective buyer should be skeptical, he should cross-check with other sources, and he should independently verify all important facts. If the evidence suggests that the seller is untrustworthy, the buyer should be extremely vigilant or cease consideration of the opportunity. Many entrepreneurs have purchased businesses which, like used cars, proved unable to live up to their former owners' glowing claims.

The "value" of the business to the purchaser depends on the future stream of earnings that the business will generate. For the entrepreneur, these might be realized as cash, for example:

1. Dividends.

2. Interest income or repayment of principal on loans made to the corporation.

3. Future sale of the business, possibly to an acquiring corporation.

4. Sale of some of the entrepreneur's stock, possibly in a secondary offering to the public.

5. Salary and perquisites that may be set at levels higher than the entrepreneur would realize if he were working for others.

Valuations based upon assets can be useful in evaluating the possible point of view of the seller, the risk exposure for the purchaser, or alternative options for the buyer or seller.

Book value is the easiest measure of value to determine and can be a tangible starting point. It can, however, be markedly affected by accounting practices and may bear little relation to the earning power or market value of the assets. The seller may feel that book value is important, believing it to be what he has invested in the business.

Liquidation value should reflect what might be realized if the assets were sold and all of the liabilities were paid off. It may seem to lack relevance if the purchaser plans to operate the business as a going concern. Nevertheless, liquidation does represent one alternative for the seller, who presumably would not accept less than this amount. It may also roughly represent what might be realized if the business is unsuccessful and the entrepreneur is forced to liquidate; of course, if there are some months of unprofitable operations, liquidation value could erode substantially.

Reproduction value of assets would be pertinent particularly if the entrepreneur has decided to enter a particular business and is evaluating the alternatives of purchasing an existing firm versus starting a new venture.

The corporation may have redundant assets that would not be needed for current operations. Presumably, these assets could be sold. The market value of redundant assets should be added to the value of the business based upon expected earnings in order to arrive at a total value of the business.

In estimating value based upon expected earnings, the entrepreneur must estimate future profits under his leadership. These may differ substantially from historical earnings and from future earnings under the current owners. Not only must changes in industry conditions be considered explicitly, but the plans and abilities of the purchaser must also be considered. In analyzing the value of the business, the entrepreneur should assume salary and perquisites at a level that would be paid if a hired manager were to replace the previous owner. (Of course, the purchaser may plan to take less out in salary and perquisites because of the financial needs of the business, or he may plan to take more out to avoid the double taxation associated with dividends.)

Expected earnings should be capitalized at a rate that takes into account both stability of earnings and expectations of future growth. The entrepreneur should, if possible, study comparable firms whose stocks are traded publicly because the price–earnings ratios of those stocks may suggest the multiple that might be used. Of course, comparability should be considered carefully because firms in the same industry may differ substantially in growth prospects and in the level of risk.

A sophisticated analysis would involve estimating the cash flows by year and discounting these at a level appropriate to the risk involved. This might include negative cash flows in the early years associated with the purchase price, further investments for working capital, and the owner's taking a lower salary than he could earn working for others. In later years, cash might be withdrawn through dividends, much higher salary and perquisites, and possibly eventual sale of the business.

NEGOTIATING THE PURCHASE

It is important for the purchaser to recognize the point of view, the objectives, and the particular concerns of the seller. Particularly in a stable business whose owner has management succession problems, non-economic factors may be important. Often the owner who has spent a lifetime building a business has conflicting emotions about letting someone else take it over—it is almost like putting a child up for adoption. The seller may be concerned about whether or not the reputation of the business will be maintained, about how the employees will be treated, and about whether or not there will be an opportunity for him to continue to contribute to the business and to feel useful. Here, economic considerations may be less important than convincing the seller that the buyer is trustworthy and the "right kind of person."

The bargaining positions of both the buyer and seller should be considered carefully. Pressures on the seller may be particularly severe if the business has been losing money. Estate taxes, financial pressures from other business ventures, disagreements among the present owners, or a desire to diversify financial holdings may motivate the seller. Of course, the extent to which both the buyer and the seller have other attractive alternatives is important.

The purchaser should approach negotiations with a bargaining strategy in mind. This strategy should include carefully considered positions on what the business is worth to the purchaser, the relative importance of various factors that might be conceded in bargaining, and a decision on whether to open negotiations with an offer that might be substantially modified or to open with something approaching "our best offer."

This is no time for the purchaser to scrimp on good legal advice. An experienced lawyer can be helpful in drafting clauses to protect the purchaser and meet the particular concerns of the seller. Some of the most common clauses are:

1. Representations and Warranties. The seller may guarantee certain representations in writing, for instance, specifying that clear title is held to the assets to be sold and that the corporation faces no impending legal suits.

2. Escrow Arrangements. Funds may be placed in the hands of a disinterested third party, such as a bank, to be transferred to the seller if certain conditions are met. The agreement might specify that the amount of uncollectable accounts receivable or any liabilities not recorded on the balance sheet and later becoming evident would be subtracted from the funds held in escrow.

3. Noncompetition Agreement. The seller may agree not to engage in the same line of business for a specified period or within a given region.

4. Management Contract. The seller may provide certain management services over a given period and receive specified payments during that period. Sometimes the payments are excessive for the services provided and might be viewed as part of the purchase price.

Payments may be in cash, in notes, in stock, or in some combination thereof. Management contracts and contingency payments (based upon future profits) can also be used. The available funds of the purchaser, tax considerations, and the goals of the seller are major determinants of the instruments used. Presumably, the purchaser is willing to pay more if payment can be made over time—in essence, paying for the business out of its own profits.

STRUCTURING THE PURCHASE

There are several ways that an entrepreneur may arrange to buy a business. Exploring alternatives may reveal approaches that meet the particular needs of both buyer and seller. Since tax and legal considerations are very important in structuring the purchase, it is essential to obtain a very capable attorney.

If the business is a corporation, the purchaser might buy either the common stock of the corporation or its assets. Some of the implications are the following:

Buying Common Stock. If the entrepreneur buys a corporation, he takes over a legal entity with all of its existing contracts, including leases, license agreements, purchase agreements, labor union contracts, sales orders, and possibly tax-loss carry forwards. A common concern is that there may also be undisclosed liabilities, pending lawsuits, or other claims on the corporation associated with actions of the previous owner. Also, unless there is some sort of prior spin-off or sale of assets, the purchaser gets all of the assets of the corporation; this may include some assets not desired.

If there are minority stockholders who do not wish to sell their stock, the buyer may choose to live with them. Another alternative would be first to obtain control, then to vote to liquidate, and finally to sell the assets of the company to a new corporation that he has formed. The minority stockholders would then receive cash, the amount being based upon an independent appraiser's assessment of the value of their shares of the sold assets.

Buying Assets. The purchase contract may specify the particular assets that are to be purchased, possibly including fixed assets, inventory, accounts receivable, customer lists, rights to use patents and the company name, etc. Some corporate assets may not be included. Certain liabilities may be assumed by the purchaser as part of the purchase contract. From the standpoint of the purchaser, hidden liabilities are avoided and unwanted assets may be excluded. Desirable contractual arrangements and tax-loss carry forwards, however, may be lost.

It is necessary to assign values to each asset included in the purchase. This has tax implications for both buyer and seller. Presumably, the seller wishes to assign higher values to those assets upon which gains would be taxed at a capital gains rate, such as fixed assets. Assets upon which gains would be taxed at ordinary rates, such as inventory, should be valued at a lesser amount from the standpoint of the seller. Of course, the purchaser normally has the opposite point of view and would prefer to minimize immediate taxable income by assigning higher values to inventory and as little as possible to assets that cannot be depreciated, for example, land and good will.

The simplest way to purchase a business is for cash. From the standpoint of the seller, there is the advantage that the transaction is complete and that the cash is received immediately to invest or spend as desired. However, the purchaser may not have enough cash. Furthermore, in regard to taxation, if the seller realizes a profit on the sale, the full amount of taxes on the profit is due in the current year.

An installment purchase can involve both cash and notes. For the purchaser, less cash is required and the business can, in part, pay for itself. If the payments received by the seller during the initial year of sale are less than 30% of the total selling price, there are tax advantages for the seller. The profit from the sale of the business can be reported over the period of years during which payments are received, thereby permitting the seller to avoid being thrust into such a high tax bracket in any given year and also permitting delaying the payment of taxes.

In an installment purchase, the purchaser normally would not wish to make the note a personal obligation that he would owe the seller. Not only would this make the purchaser personally liable, but there would also be tax disadvantages. In order to repay the note, the purchaser would have to take cash out of the business, presumably as salary or dividends. Because he would have to pay personal income taxes on this income, less after-tax cash would be available to repay the note.

There are two possible approaches to this problem. The entrepreneur could organize a new corporation that would buy the stock of the old corporation for cash and notes. If the new corporation were to own more than 80% of the stock of the old corporation, then dividends could pass from the old company to the new company without income taxes on the exchange. The new corporation could then repay the note. It would also be possible to have a plan of liquidation in which the old corporation would be liquidated into the new.

Another approach would be to utilize only the old corporation. The purchaser would buy some of the stock from the seller, possibly for cash. The corporation would then buy back the remaining stock and give the seller a note or cash and a note. The note would then be an obligation of the corporation and the purchaser would own all the outstanding stock.

If the seller would be willing to accept stock, it would be possible to structure the purchase so that no taxes would be owed by the seller. In essence, the seller would exchange stock in the old corporation or its assets for other securities. Although there are several kinds of such "reorganization," stock in the buying corporation is the most common means of payment. The seller does not owe taxes until he sells the stock received. Since there are many aspects of these transactions that must be considered, the entrepreneur should seek excellent legal advice.

Coldwater Container Corporation

George Arnold was a graduate (1966) of the M.B.A. program at The University of Chicago. After graduation, he worked for 6 years in the comptroller's office at the Ford Motor Company; at first he was very enthusiastic about his job, but in later years he became increasingly dissatisfied and discontent:

When I first came to work for Ford, I looked upon my job as one of providing the cost information and the financial projections that were necessary for informed, professional decisions by upper management. But it just doesn't seem to work that way in large corporations. I might develop detailed cost data and financial returns on a given project, but instead of going to upper management, the report would be distributed to middle management people in all the various divisions who would then go into a room and question the figures, argue about the project, and propose alternative plans. I might just as well not have done the work. It was not so bad on styling decisions, on the appearance of the car, since then you would just have people from product planning and vehicle engineering in the meeting, and as long as I kept providing the costs of the proposed alternatives as a percentage increase or decrease over existing models, they would eventually, after 14 meetings and 27 hours of dialog and diatribe, reach the compromise that was obvious in the first 30-minute conference. It seemed that these people were just playing a game; it seemed that they had to defend their departmental positions and accuse their organizational opponents of a lack either of basic competence or of essential understanding of the market for the project or the strategy of the firm before they finally got down to business and made a reasonable decision.

Styling decisions on the appearance of the car were a game; functional decisions on the suspension, steering, braking, power plant, or drive train elements were a war. In functional meetings you would get product planners, vehicle engineers, assembly engineers, component engineers, safety engineers, representatives from the basic manufacturing and production divisions, and some poor financial analyst from the comptroller's office. The way the control system was set up, each division wanted something different. Since the production plants were charged for warranty expenses, they wanted the part to be reliable; since the basic manufacturing divisions were charged for tooling, they wanted the part to be the same as that used last year or the same as that used on another vehicle in the product line. Since the vehicle, assembly, and component engineers were charged for intentional weight and cost overruns, they wanted the part to be lighter and cheaper, but the safety people wanted it to be heavier and more expensive. Corporate management provided the product planners with a Program Description Book (Blue Book) that had very general and subjective guidelines, such as a "10% improvement in noise, vibration, and harshness" or a "significant gain in sports car performance and handling characteristics," all at an "improved product cost, car weight, and profit projection," and they expected the product planning people to achieve those objectives through an endless series of meetings, conferences, and telephone calls. The product planners were the best paid middle management people in the company, and they deserved what they got because they had an impossible job. Since there was no compromise that would satisfy all the different interests, they just kept proposing alternatives, all of which had to be costed by the financial representative, who usually had to work late at night to get the data ready for the next day's meeting, until they could wear down their opponents. Eventually, as the deadline for building the prototype and planning the factory production of the car drew near, everyone started to ignore the financial information and gradually narrowed down the alternatives to one or two designs that would work, regardless of the cost. Previously, they had ignored the safety and environmental considerations, but they couldn't do that anymore after 1971, so they just began to ignore the numbers. My boss kept climbing on me, since unplanned cost overruns are charged against the comptroller's office, but there was nothing I could do. It was not very pleasant to be both ignored in the decision process and condemned for the decision, but it happened to all of us in the financial area all the time, so that I was not alone.

Since I didn't enjoy my work under those conditions, I began looking for a smaller company that I could buy. I thought that most smaller companies failed because they didn't keep track of their costs and because they didn't plan the financial consequences of their decisions. Since those were my strong areas, I was certain that I could be successful in managing a smaller firm. The only problem was to find one that was for sale at a price that we could afford to pay. (Statement of George Arnold.)

Mr. Arnold was certain that purchasing a successful smaller company would present no financial problems, within limits. He had been well paid while he worked at Ford; his base salary was over $20,000 and was supplemented by paid overtime and an annual bonus. Mrs. Arnold worked as a music teacher in the Livonia school system. Together they had been able to save more than $12,000 each year. In addition, Mrs. Arnold had inherited approximately $40,000 from the estate of her parents who had been killed in an automobile accident in Florida. The Arnolds had realized very considerable capital gains from the investment of these funds in the stock of the Ford Motor Company, which went from $40 per share in early 1966 to $70 per share in the middle of 1972. From all sources Mr. and Mrs. Arnold had a total net worth in 1972 of $172,000. Mrs. Arnold wanted to retire from teaching because she felt that her students had become too disruptive in the classroom. They were both in agreement that they would use this money to buy an established business:

We had more money than most people our age (29 years old) because we had both

worked and because we had both saved. We didn't spend our money on vacation trips or on new cars or clothes; instead, we lived quietly and planned for the future. Also, it helped that we invested in Ford; they pay a good dividend, and we got a nice capital gain. We decided to use that money to buy a small company that would provide us with a good return on our investment and with compatible employment. (Statement of George Arnold.)

Mr. and Mrs. Arnold decided that they would conduct an extensive search so that after they purchased a company they would not feel that they might have found a much more attractive opportunity with just a little more effort. They were determined to conduct an intensive investigation of each opportunity so that they would not be disappointed with the company they finally decided upon. In January 1973 Mr. Arnold resigned from his position with the Ford Motor Company, Mrs. Arnold took a leave of absence from the Livonia School System, and they began their search process. As a start, they wrote letters to both loan officers and trust officers at the major Detroit banks and to the staff at the local SBA office. They also contacted attorneys, business consultants, public accountants, and professional business brokers. In their letters and in their initial contacts they emphasized that they wanted to purchase a successful smaller company in an expanding industry and that they were particularly looking for an established manufacturing or distributing firm with an older owner or group of owners who wanted to retire; they concluded by saying that they felt that they could contribute both equity financing and managerial capability. They specifically asked for the names of companies available for purchase. Both Mr. and Mrs. Arnold expected to receive a number of suggestions from these initial inquiries; they were disappointed when they received only a few brief and noncommittal replies. Nevertheless, they followed up their letters with telephone calls, appointments, and meetings, and then they started to receive a number of suggestions and recommendations on smaller companies that were for sale. These suggestions and recommendations, however, did not seem to supply the company for which Mr. and Mrs. Arnold were looking:

We planned our search very carefully, and I think that we ought to tell you about it, even though it did not work out as well as we had expected. We found the company we were looking for, but only after a good many false starts and blind alleys.

First, we contacted the loan officers at the large Detroit banks and the staff of the local SBA office since we felt that these people would be good sources of information about smaller companies that were available for purchase throughout the state; we found, however, that they tended to tell us about companies that had fairly substantial financial problems in the Detroit area. We did not object to buying a company that had problems, and we did not object to buying a company in the metropolitan area, but the problems had to be resolvable and the neighborhood had to be reasonable. One bank sent us to look at six tool and die firms. Now, tool and die work was very profitable in the 1950s and early 1960s when there was a scheduled model change in the automobile industry every 2 years that was as regular as clockwork. The tool and die companies bought a lot of expensive machinery in those days to do the model change work, but for the past 5 years style changes requiring extensive tooling have been minimal since this was one place that the automobile companies could keep costs constant in a period of rising prices. The volume of the potential tool and die work in Detroit is now probably 40% of what it was earlier. The surviving firms bid for this remaining business on a cutthroat basis, and they are all out looking for additional work in Cleveland, Pittsburgh, and Chicago to cover the high fixed costs of the very expensive machine tools they purchased 10 years before. Even the best managed tool and die shops lose money now. There seemed to be nothing we could do to reverse the adverse trends in this industry. The banks and the SBA also sent us to look at local businesses in the center of Detroit, but most of these were service firms, such as clothing stores or dry cleaning shops or insurance agencies in deteriorating neighborhoods; again, there did not seem to be much that we could do to reverse these social and economic changes. We did not get many valid leads from

loan officers at banks or the SBA. I think that both groups tend to suggest companies to whom they have just refused a loan. There has to be something basically wrong with the situation when neither the bank nor the SBA will advance money to an established business.

Next, we contacted a number of lawyers who specialize in trust work, and we also talked to trust officers at the larger banks. We thought that these people could tell us about family businesses that were for sale because the founder or the principal owner had died. They did tell us about a number of smaller firms in this condition, but all of them seemed to be in either dead or dying industries. We looked at a foundry that cast steel switch and crossing parts for railroads, and we looked at a milling company that ground flour for local consumer sales; both companies were still profitable, but both were about one-fifth the size they had been in 1929. Since we felt that there was little future in either railroad track construction or home baking, we did not follow up on these or on the other older firms that we heard about. I think that trust people have an established market and a limited marketing process for the younger, growing firms that come under their control as part of an estate, and that it is only the older companies in the stagnant basic processing industries that are offered for sale to the general public. It's too bad, but that seems to be the way it is.

We also went to business consultants and CPA firms, again thinking that these people could tell us about companies that were for sale throughout the state. The consultants wanted us to hire them on a professional fee basis, but we were not willing to spend our money on that. The accountants did not seem to know as much about the intentions of their clients as you might expect. One of the partners in a public accounting firm told us about a heating and air conditioning contractor in one of the northern suburbs of Detroit who had been very successful, but he was now 78 years old and getting feeble. When we called to ask him if he were interested in selling his business, he became very angry and ill-tempered; he said that he was going to keep on working until he was 100 and that we just wanted him to die like all the rest of his family did. The other people we called at the suggestion of public accountants were not as rude, but they said they had no current intentions of selling. It seemed as if all the accountants retire before they reach 60 years of age, and they expect everybody else to retire then also, but, of course, most of them don't.

We also contacted a number of business brokers who specialize in arranging the sale and purchase of smaller firms, generally for a 5% or 7½% commission. Many of these people are also real estate salesmen; they tend to know about drugstores, hardware stores, gift shops, etc., whose owners want to sell the building, the fixtures, and the inventory as an entity. Neither Jane nor I wanted to be in a retail business, though we did look at a gift shop in East Lansing and a hardware store in Grayling. Some brokers claim to represent more substantial manufacturing and wholesale firms. We probably should not complain too loudly about these people since one of them did recommend the firm we finally purchased, but we always had the feeling that these brokers just listened to our description of the type of business we wanted to buy, went through an industrial directory, and called companies that matched our requirements. The problem is that many owners of smaller businesses, when asked if they want to sell, say that they are willing to talk about it, but what they really want is to find out what their companies are worth. So, you drive up to see an owner, you look at the records, you check the inventory and the receivables, and you learn about the product, the market, and the production process. When you make an offer, he says he wants more. You can waste a lot of time examining businesses that aren't really for sale, except for an exceptional price. Warn your class about this difficulty. (Statement of George Arnold.)

To Mr. and Mrs. Arnold screening and evaluating each opportunity seemed to be fully as troublesome as finding the opportunity in the first place. Some businesses could be quickly rejected because the product was obsolete, the market was limited, or the financial condition was impossible, but many others required intensive investigation before a negative decision could be reached. Still others needed continued work in order to estimate a fair price and to prepare a firm offer. Mr. Arnold quickly learned that the financial examination had to be on the most basic level since the accounting records of many firms were incomplete, inaccurate, or misleading, and he also learned that the

product evaluation had to be equally careful since the market forecasts of most firms were overly optimistic, if not deliberately falsified:

When we first started this search, we looked at a drug wholesaling firm in the western part of the state that seemed to be old-fashioned but profitable. There seemed to be considerable opportunities for improvement and expansion, and it was located in a lovely town right on Lake Michigan. We were very excited about it and almost ready to close, when I noticed that the cost of goods sold as a percentage of sales was much lower than the industry average. When I asked the owner, he hesitated for a minute but then told me that the reason was that he had excellent relationships with his suppliers. Well, I called one of the suppliers and was told that this wholesaler never seemed to pay its bills completely; the supplier said that this started about 6 months ago and that some bills were now 6 months past due, but others were paid within 10 days. I checked further and found that the past-due invoices were just never entered in the accounts payable journal. Warn your class that this is an easy way to make a company look a lot better than it is. If you buy the company, you are responsible for the unrecorded amounts, but you don't know about them until one of the suppliers calls you or attaches your bank account.

Another account to check carefully, of course, is inventory. We looked at a steel fabricating firm near the Indiana border that built prefabricated bridges. It seemed to be a profitable and a good opportunity for us, but I noticed that the firm had a high inventory relative to sales. When I asked the owner, he told me that you need a high inventory in the steel business because of the strikes and delays in delivery. When I looked at the physical inventory, I found that it consisted mostly of short bars and I-beams that were valuable only as scrap, at less than $0.01 per pound. Bridge beams are heavy and are useless in short lengths, for no one really wants an 8 ft or 12 ft bridge. The form had over $200,000 of worthless steel listed in its inventory account.

You have to check the fixed assets and the depreciation schedule, and you have to revalue the R&D, patent, and good-will amounts. You even have to confirm the cash balance. It takes a lot of time.

You have to be just as careful when you

look at the characteristics of the product, the potential of the market, and the costs of production. We were very interested in a large florist in Grand Rapids; the company had extensive greenhouses and grew their own flowers, but we found that it is now much cheaper to grow flowers in the tropics of Central and South America and ship them north by air than it is to grow them locally in greenhouses. Careful product, market, and production evaluation also takes a lot of time. (Statement of George Arnold.)

After careful financial examination and intensive product, market, and production evaluation, Mr. and Mrs. Arnold found three companies that appeared to meet their requirements for purchase, but in each case the owner did not accept their initial offer. Instead, he requested a considerable premium in the purchase price. These last-minute obstructions were particularly discouraging to the Arnolds:

> You have to get the leads, screen the opportunities, evaluate the companies, and then negotiate an agreement. It all takes time, and we can guarantee you that you'll get discouraged since nothing seems to go the way it should and since no one seems to be interested in helping you to find and examine and buy the company you want. You might think that it's a buyer's market, but it isn't; it is a confused and disorganized market, and the buyer has to find his own way around in it. It's fairly discouraging. (Statement of George Arnold.)

Mr. and Mrs. Arnold were discouraged in the late spring of 1973 since their search seemed to be taking more time than they had expected, to be requiring more study than they had planned, and to be producing fewer alternatives than they had anticipated. But one evening in May a business broker called and described a company that seemed to be very attractive. The company was the Coldwater Container Corporation, located in Coldwater, Michigan, a small city of just under 10,000 population that was 20 miles south of Battle Creek. The company produced cardboard boxes and corrugated shipping containers for the small manufacturing companies and the fruit and vegetable farms

in the south-central portion of Michigan and the north-central section of Indiana; it was a successful firm, with sales in 1972 of $850,000 and with profits after taxes of $71,000. The owner had set a firm price of $240,000, which was only 3.3 times earnings. This seemed to be low to Mr. Arnold, but the broker explained that the owner had told him that 1972 was an exceptional year, that the average profits for the past 5 years were $40,000, and that he had set the price at 6 times these average annual profits. The owner had also told the broker that the company had never lost money, although it had some lean years when it started in 1961, and that it now had a net worth of slightly under $300,000. Lastly, the broker said that the owner, Fred Etzel, had been aware of the interest of Mr. and Mrs. Arnold in purchasing a company for some time, but that he had delayed contacting them until he had the certified statements for 1972. Mr. Etzel now had these statements, and if the price were not higher than Mr. and Mrs. Arnold were willing to pay, he would be glad to meet with them at their convenience and to arrange to have the accountant who had prepared the audited statements, a partner in a very respected CPA firm in Jackson, drive down for that meeting. Mr. and Mrs. Arnold made an appointment for the next day since they were very pleased with the description of the company and the approach of the owner:

> Well, after all the false leads and blind alleys we had traced down, and particularly after all the inaccurate financial statements we had studied and the indefinite prices we had been quoted, this seemed almost too good to be true. Also, we had both been in Coldwater and knew that it was a very attractive town in a farming area with light manufacturing industries. We were very excited when we went to bed that night.
>
> Next day we drove over to visit the company to meet the owner and the accountant. I knew as soon as we drove into the parking lot that this was the company we were going to buy. The building was a simple concrete block structure, about 50 ft × 200 ft, but it was well-made, the trim was painted, the windows were clean, and the lawn was mowed; it just

gave the appearance of a neat, orderly, well-managed, and profitable company.

The office was just as neat and orderly as the outside. The secretary was friendly and obviously efficient; she was typing a few letters, but she stopped as soon as we came in to take our coats and tell Mr. Etzel that we were there. Mr. Etzel took us back to his office and after the usual preliminaries about the weather and the trip were over, he told us about starting the company and the problems that he had had for the first few years.

He had been a salesman for a large corrugated box firm in Detroit, but because he wanted to live in Coldwater, he started the firm here. He said that everyone told him when he started the company that it could not be successful in a rural area and that it had to be in a large industrial center such as Chicago or Detroit. Nevertheless, he had been certain that there was a good market for boxes and shipping containers in the middle of the state, between the two industrial centers, and fortunately he had been right. He wanted us to understand that his company could never be as big or as profitable as those in Chicago or Detroit, but that it was pleasant living here and much more pleasant dealing with the local customers. He described his market as a circle with a radius of about 50 miles around Coldwater and said that it included the small manufacturing firms, farmers, and wholesalers who were not large enough to buy from the big box companies. He also said that he tried to keep his prices closely competitive so that he would not cheat his customers, but that they seemed to be willing to pay a bit extra for prompt service and smaller quantity orders.

He went on to explain that he and Mrs. Etzel had talked about retiring for some time, although they were only in their early 50s. Their children were now grown and a warm climate would be much better for Mrs. Etzel's health. They planned to go to St. Petersburg, Florida where Mr. Etzel, who was a lay preacher, could work with the older members of a local church and where, he confidentially admitted, he also planned to spend some time fishing and relaxing in the sun.

He explained that he wanted it to be understood that the price of $240,000 was firm. He said that he had set the price at 6 times earnings and 80% of the net worth in order not to take advantage of anyone, but in return he did not want to bargain. He knew that he could get a higher price from a pulp and paper company since they were integrating forward into corrugated box manufacture, but that he much preferred to have the company owned by local people who would continue to treat his employees well. He said that he had already refused an offer at a higher price from a competitor in western Michigan who had planned to move the machinery and consolidate all the operations in Grand Rapids because he felt that he had an obligation to keep the company in the town.

His last comment was that he wanted to be paid in cash, not by a note with periodic payments or a percentage of the earnings. He wanted us to take as much time as we wanted to look at the books, the plant, the machinery, the employees, and the customers, and he was willing to give us as much advice and help as we wanted until we took over, but that on the day we took control he wanted to receive a check and be able to leave for Florida, without having to worry about the company anymore. He said that he had worried about the company for 12 years, and that if he had to worry about it in the future, he was going to keep on owning it in the future.

Following the preliminary discussion, Mr. Etzel took Mr. and Mrs. Arnold on a tour of the plant. The box and container manufacturing process was a very simple but well-organized operation. Two rolls of heavy kraft paper, called liner board, were fed into the top and bottom of a fairly long machine, while a third roll of lighter paper, called corrugating medium, was fed in between the two outer rolls; the corrugating medium was folded in accordion fashion and glued between the top and bottom liner boards to form the very familiar corrugated board. The width of the corrugated board was determined by the width of the paper rolls on the infeed end of the machine; the length was determined by an automatic shear on the outfeed end that cut the board into rectangular blanks. These blanks were then taken to another machine that notched the corners, folded the board, and taped the seams. The finished boxes and containers were then ready for shipment to the customers.

Each size box required a different width and length of corrugated board for the blank. Mr. Etzel said that one of the secrets of success of the company was to maintain a large raw material inventory on hand so that the right widths of liner board and corrugating medium were always available to keep the waste to a minimum and that another secret of success was to make some boxes for finished goods inventory to keep the machinery set-up costs and downtime to a minimum. He explained that (1) he had a formula to balance the best width of paper and length of production run for each box size and (2) he also had standard costs for material, labor, and overhead on each box size for these optimal production runs. Mr. and Mrs. Arnold were impressed with the obvious care and attention that had gone into the design and control of the production process:

> The plant was very orderly and well-run. Mr. Etzel explained that the machinery was perhaps 25 years old (he had bought it second-hand when he started the company) and that it was considerably slower than the modern equipment available now, but that it was perfectly adequate for the small runs of the local market. The machinery was newly painted and very well-maintained; the plant was spacious and very clean; and the employees were cheerful and very hard working. We were impressed. (Statement of George Arnold.)

Mr. Etzel next introduced Mr. and Mrs. Arnold to Mr. Cooper, the accountant, who had set up the books at the start of the company in 1961 and who had supervised the annual audit every year since that time. Mr. Cooper said that the company had been successful since it had been run with strict attention to economy and control of the overhead expenses. He said that Mr. Etzel had only the secretary–bookkeeper and the shop foreman to help him, both good, competent people, but that he had done all the selling, production scheduling, cost control, and purchasing work himself. He said that corrugated box manufacture was a low margin business in which a person could do very well provided he was able to combine volume production with low overhead. He said that Mr. Etzel had achieved this volume because he gave his customers good service and excellent quality and that he kept the costs down by doing so much of the work himself. Mr. Cooper said that he was explaining this because he felt that Mr. and

Mrs. Arnold should not buy the company unless they planned to do much of the work themselves. Mr. and Mrs. Arnold said that they were certainly in agreement with that philosophy of management. Then Mr. Cooper showed them the accounting records:

> The books of account were in excellent shape. Mr. Cooper showed us the cash journal and the supporting monthly statements from the bank. He showed us the accounts receivable subsidiary ledger and the confirming letters that had been sent to customers for the annual audit. He showed us the inventory records and then took us out into the shop for a physical inventory; he would identify a roll of corrugating medium or liner board and then show us an invoice from the supplier to confirm the value. He showed us the machinery ledger, which identified each piece of equipment by number, and then listed the original cost and the depreciation schedule. Lastly, he showed me the accounts payable journal and the confirming monthly statements from the suppliers. He then let me spend the rest of the day going over the financial records, and that night I understood how the company ran. It was a high fixed cost, low margin business that could make a lot of money provided the volume remained high.
>
> The next day Mr. Etzel took me to visit with his banker, who was very cordial and said that he was sorry to lose such a good customer and friend, but that he could assure me that the container company had always been very successful and could remain very successful with good management. Then, we spent 2 days visiting customers. Mr. Etzel was well liked; he would chat with the customers and then give me a chance to ask about the quality of the boxes and the promptness of the service. We saw probably 20 customers, and none of them said that they were dissatisfied, and 8 of them said that they would like to buy more from the company, but that Mr. Etzel had never wanted to add a second shift. Mr. Etzel always smiled at this and said that they would talk to me in a few months about increased orders; he explained that I was younger and willing to work longer hours. Driving back the last night, Mr. Etzel said that it would not be easy to increase production since it would be difficult to get good people to work at night and it would also be difficult to supervise them, but he recognized that the company could be very profitable if those problems

could be worked out and a second shift added. (Statement of George Arnold.)

Mr. and Mrs. Arnold went home to think over the proposal. They had told Mr. Etzel that they would give him their decision in a week, but after just 2 days they were so certain that this was the best company that they could find, and so certain that they could manage it profitably, that they called Mr. Etzel and told him that they wanted to buy his company for $240,000:

$240,000 was a little bit more money than we wanted to spend, but we borrowed the extra funds from my parents since we could pay it back so quickly from earnings.

We went to Coldwater and rented an apartment until we could find time to look for a house. We both went to work for the company and helped Mr. Etzel for the next 2 weeks. We learned everything we could about the marketing and production of corrugated boxes. When everything seemed to be going well and when we seemed to know enough about the company, we gave Mr. Etzel a check for $240,000, and he and Mrs. Etzel said goodbye and left for Florida.

We decided not to change anything for at least 3 months, since I remembered that the behavioral courses at The University of Chicago always emphasized the problems of change, but about 2 weeks after Mr. Etzel left I had been asked so many times by customers about increasing production that I thought that we should start to build up our inventory of raw material, and perhaps add a partial second shift. I called the manufacturer of the liner board and corrugating medium, the Northern Kraft Corporation, and talked to the sales vice president. I shall never forget that conversation. He told me that he had personally called all of his customers, including Mr. Etzel, about 4 weeks previously to advise them that because there was a shortage of wood pulp, shipments of both liner board and corrugating medium were being reduced 20% effective immediately and that this reduction would probably go to 30% by the end of the year. He also said that this conversation had been confirmed by a registered letter.

I called all other producers of kraft paper in the country, but we couldn't get shipments from any of them. The problem is that since kraft is the lowest profit margin product in the paper industry the companies are using their available wood pulp for higher margin products such as newsprint, printing papers, and household products (paper towels, napkins, etc.). Some people say that the paper companies are using this shortage of kraft paper to squeeze the independent converters and box manufacturers, while maintaining full production at their own converting plants. I don't know if those allegations are true, but I do know that we will just barely break even at a 20% production reduction and that we will lose about $50,000 per year at a 30% reduction.

We were cheated. This company is not worth a fifth of what we paid for it. We can't sell it now; we can't sell the machinery; and we can't operate it at a profit. We've lost the money we worked so hard and saved so long to get, and we've lost the money that we borrowed from my parents. My parents say that they are sorry to hear about our problem, but they still don't understand. My mother asked Jane just the other day when we can pay them back since they need the money for their retirement. Jane doesn't understand either; she thinks that I should have discovered this before we bought the company, but I don't know how.

Mr. Etzel cheated us. He did it very legally and very efficiently, but he still cheated us. When he got the call from Northern Kraft, he knew exactly what it would mean to his company. He called the broker, who had called him a month or two previously, and made up the story about waiting for the completion of the audited statements. We fell for his story. We can't sue him, and, as a matter of fact, we can't find him; he did not go to St. Petersburg. The church there has never even heard of him, and that particular denomination said that it did not have lay preachers. I still don't know where we went wrong. (Statement of George Arnold.)

ASSIGNMENT

Consider better means of finding, screening, and evaluating smaller businesses that can be purchased and specifically identify the errors in the search process that Mr. and Mrs. Arnold used.

Kassel Manufacturing

"I have to sell my business soon and I could use some help. I don't have the strength or the inclination to go on running it, and I need to draw cash out faster than the business can bring it in. My accounts payable are already stretched about as far as they can go, and the suppliers are putting the heat on us to pay up faster or they'll put us on COD. Do you think that I should bring in the auctioneer and tell him to put my equipment on the block?"

In mid-December 1973 Frederick Kassel was talking to a consultant friend who happened to be in town for the Christmas holidays. His company, Kassel Manufacturing, of Alhambra, California, manufactured a line of commercial kitchen bussing carts made of aluminum tubing and stainless steel, aluminum coat racks, and portable vault ladders sold mainly to banks. Four men were employed in the shop, and there was one woman in the office who handled orders and kept the company books. Sales had totaled $140,911 in 1972 and $139,544 for the first 11 months of 1973. Mr. Kassel had drawn $12,000 from the company in 1972 resulting in a loss for the year of $5,451, and the figures were expected to be similar in 1973.

BACKGROUND

As an engineer at a large Detroit auto maker, Mr. Kassel had risen rapidly. One of his inventions had been the pressurized auto radiator cap used in virtually all liquid cooled cars. Another had been the mechanism to allow locking a car door without using a key. Others had dealt with muffler systems. He noted that patents on his designs had made millions of dollars for the company, but by

company policy his employment agreement required that he sell each patent to the company for one dollar. Promotions and praise had been his main rewards, but because of the freeze on wages in the World War II period it had not been possible for the company to raise his pay commensurate with his rank, and this irritated him immensely. It also aggravated him that he had to submit to supervision and had to clear all significant decisions with higher officials of the company. "I was sure that I could perform better and make a lot more money if I were out of the company and on my own," he recalled.

In 1943 at age 35, with a wife and four children to support and no particular job in view, he announced his resignation. Several higher executives tried to persuade him to stay, and one of his superiors even offered to increase Mr. Kassel's income by sharing some of his own salary if he would stay. Others expressed surprise that he would leave a relatively high position—he had become executive engineer at the auto company with 500 engineers under his direction—so soon in his career. "It was funny," he observed, "some people started coming to me quietly and telling me they thought I might be crazy to quit, but they wished they had the nerve to do it too. They felt they just had too much tied up in the company and at the same time they were afraid to quit without first having something lined up on the outside. They didn't see what else they could do but stay with it."

He packed his family into a trailer, sold his house in Detroit, and drove to Southern California where he rented space in a seashore trailer camp. Through acquaintances and referrals to local people from his friends in Detroit, he began to search for a company he could own and run independently. After 6 months of looking in a 100-mile radius around Los Angeles at companies ranging from manufacturing to automobile dealerships, he located a job machine shop with 30 employees in East Los Angeles. The company produced parts, chiefly out of aluminum, for the warplane industry and was one of several small firms owned by a local entrepreneur. Since skilled manpower was scarce because of wartime manpower conscription, the entrepreneur welcomed the chance to take Mr. Kassel in as a partner to run the shop while he concentrated his own attention on his restaurants and other ventures. Mr. Kassel invested his personal savings and took charge. By the time the war ended he had bought out the former owner and changed the name from the C.Z.I. Machine Shop to Kassel Manufacturing.

When termination of defense work at the end of the war drastically reduced orders, Mr. Kassel found himself in possession of an inactive shop with a large inventory of aircraft aluminum tubing. He had anticipated such a decline and had devised an electric cart powered by auto batteries and electric starter. "I thought seriously about developing a business in such vehicles," he said, "but decided it would take a lot more capital than I could raise." He was able to patent some aspects of the vehicle, however, and later received royalties on the control system from other companies which used it in electric golf carts patterned after his design. With his own company, however, he concentrated on applications for the aluminum tubing and devised a wide range of products, including desks, bedroom furniture, and the institutional equipment that came to be the company's product line. For his own children he devised a pogo stick that eventually became a fad in the early 1950s and produced rapid sales growth. Competitors quickly entered pogo stick production with cheaper versions. "Compared to our product, theirs were junky," he recalled, "but since they could make them for a lot less, they took our

sales away." The institutional furnishings of tubing continued.

PRODUCTS

The company's products were divided into essentially four lines, all of which utilized aluminum tubing for main structural members. These were bussing carts, tray stands, costumers (vertical pole coat racks), and step stools (vault ladders). Illustrations of these appear in Exhibit 1. All were put together with screws, which allow replacement of any parts which broke, and all were noted for durability. "A salesman was telling me," the secretary commented, "that the trouble with our products was that they were too well made, so they just last and last. If we made them flimsier, there would be more replacement business, and if we welded them together instead of using screws, more people would throw them away when they broke, instead of fixing them."

Since none of the designs had been patented, competitors copied them in many forms, some virtually identical, and others with variations such as skimpier materials, welded instead of screwed construction, or stainless steel (which was stronger) instead of aluminum (which Kassel believed was fully strong enough) frame material. "Shortly after we came out with our carts and they began to sell well, some other companies in the midwest started copying them," Mr. Frantz recalled. "One of them even had the gall to put one of our own carts on display in a trade show as their own new product while they were tooling up to manufacture it."

Mr. Kassel had designed home furnishings using aluminum tubing as frame material complemented by wood and plastic. His home contained such items as sturdy folding TV trays on casters, a bar, bureau, and desk of such construction. "But the department stores wouldn't buy it," he said. "They told me it looked too much like it had been made in a machine shop." He had also designed a drinking fountain for attachment to a home refrigerator. The one in his own

EXHIBIT 1 Kassel products.

DEALER DISCOUNT 50%

PRICE LIST

EFFECTIVE NOVEMBER 1, 1973

CATALOG NO.	DESCRIPTION		SHIPPING WEIGHT	LIST PRICE
	## *UTILITY CARTS*			
C-16x24-2 S	2 STAINLESS STEEL SHELVES		27 LBS.	$ 94.00
C-16x24-2 C	2 CHROME-PLATED SHELVES		27 LBS.	82.00
C-16x24-3 S	3 STAINLESS STEEL SHELVES		34 LBS.	108.00
C-16x24-3 C	3 CHROME-PLATED SHELVES		34 LBS.	96.00
	OPTIONAL EQUIPMENT			
	RETAINING RAILS — 7/16" ALUMINUM ROD	per shelf	1 LB.	10.00
	4" PLATE CASTERS ON CROSS CHANNELS		6 LBS.	11.00
	SIDE BRAKES ON TWO CASTERS			5.00
	4 DO-NUT TYPE RUBBER BUMPERS ON CART FRAME			4.00
C-21x33-2 S	2 STAINLESS STEEL SHELVES		42 LBS.	153.00
C-21x33-2 C	2 CHROME-PLATED SHELVES		42 LBS.	134.00
C-21x33-3 S	3 STAINLESS STEEL SHELVES		51 LBS.	179.00
C-21x33-3 C	3 CHROME-PLATED SHELVES		51 LBS.	157.00
	OPTIONAL EQUIPMENT			
	RETAINING RAILS — 7/16" ALUMINUM ROD		1 LB.	13.00
	ENCLOSED THREE SIDES WITH STAINLESS STEEL		13 LBS.	90.00
	SIDE BRAKES ON TWO CASTERS			5.00
	4 DO-NUT TYPE RUBBER BUMPERS ON CART FRAME			4.00
	## *TRAY TRUCKS*			
TT-4	4 STAINLESS STEEL SHELVES		65 LBS.	185.00
TT-5	5 STAINLESS STEEL SHELVES		79 LBS.	200.00
TT-6	6 STAINLESS STEEL SHELVES		88 LBS.	220.00
	4 DO-NUT TYPE RUBBER BUMPERS ON CART FRAME ARE STANDARD EQUIPMENT			
	## *EKONO-KARTS*			
EK-2 C	2 CHROME-PLATED SHELVES		23 LBS.	66.00
EK-3 C	3 CHROME-PLATED SHELVES		28 LBS.	76.00
EK-2 S	2 STAINLESS STEEL SHELVES		23 LBS.	76.00
EK-3 S	3 STAINLESS STEEL SHELVES		28 LBS.	86.00
	OPTIONAL EQUIPMENT			
	4" SWIVEL CASTERS		2 LBS.	6.00

EXHIBIT 1 *(Continued)*

CATALOG NO.	DESCRIPTION		SHIPPING WEIGHT	LIST PRICE
	## *DELUXE SERVING CARTS*			
C-27-2	2 NATURAL WALNUT FORMICA SHELVES		30 LBS.	$82.00
C-27-3	3 NATURAL WALNUT FORMICA SHELVES		37 LBS.	98.00
	OPTIONAL EQUIPMENT			
	4" PLATE CASTERS ON CROSS CHANNELS		4 LBS.	11.00
	## *HI-BOY STOCK TRUCKS*			
HB-2	SOLID 21X33" TOP SHELF — TUBULAR BOTTOM SHELF		48 LBS.	80.00
HB-3	SOLID TOP AND 20X27" BOTTOM SHELF		58 LBS.	94.00
	OPTIONAL EQUIPMENT			
	5" HEAVY DUTY CASTERS		3 LBS.	14.00
	STAINLESS STEEL TOP SHELF			11.00
	## *LO-BOY STOCK TRUCKS*			
LB-1			34 LBS.	71.00
LB-1HD	SAME AS LB-1 EXCEPT WITH EXTRA HEAVY DUTY 5" CASTERS		37 LBS.	86.00
	OPTIONAL EQUIPMENT			
	(EITHER MODEL) ZINC PLATED SOLID STEEL BED COVERING TUBULAR FRAME		13 LBS.	9.00
	## *TRAY STANDS*			
R-1	FOLDING TRAY STAND		3½ LBS.	14.00
R-3	FOLDING TRAY STAND WITH LOWER CROSS BARS		4 LBS.	16.00
	## *LUGGAGE STANDS*			
R-2	FOLDING LUGGAGE STAND		4 LBS.	14.00
R-4	FOLDING LUGGAGE STAND WITH WALL PROTECTOR		5 LBS.	18.00
	## *COSTUMERS*			
HC-1	72" HIGH, DURAL		19 LBS.	40.00
HC-3	68" HIGH, DURAL		18 LBS.	38.00
HC-4	68" HIGH, CHROME-PLATED		22 LBS.	40.00
HC-5	72" HIGH, REVOLVING HEAD, CHROME-PLATED		27 LBS.	52.00

EXHIBIT 1 *(Continued)*

CATALOG NO.	DESCRIPTION	SHIPPING WEIGHT	LIST PRICE

STEP STOOLS

CATALOG NO.	DESCRIPTION	SHIPPING WEIGHT	LIST PRICE
UV-1	1 STEP	6 LBS.	$27.00
UV-2	2 STEP	12 LBS.	50.00
UV-3	3 STEP	19 LBS.	73.00
UV-3 HR	3 STEP WITH HAND RAILS	27 LBS.	94.00
UV-1 SC	1 STEP WITH SPRING CASTERS	9 LBS.	46.00
UV-2 SC	2 STEP WITH SPRING CASTERS	16 LBS.	71.00
UV-3 SC	3 STEP WITH SPRING CASTERS	21 LBS.	92.00
UV-3 SCHR	3 STEP WITH SPRING CASTERS AND HAND RAILS	29 LBS.	122.00

OPTIONAL EQUIPMENT

FILING SHELF FOR HAND RAILS		22.00
HAND RAILS FOR UV-2 OR UV-2SC — ADD		30.00

REPLACEMENT PARTS LIST
(List Prices Shown)

16x24" STAINLESS SHELF $20.00
16 x 24" CHROME PLATED SHELF 15.00
21 x 33" STAINLESS SHELF 30.00
21 x 33" CHROME PLATED SHELF 25.00
1" DURAL FRAME FOR 16 x 24" SHELF 30.00
  (Specify 2 or 3 Shelf)
1" DURAL FRAME FOR 21 x 33" SHELF 40.00
  (Specify 2 or 3 Shelf)
1" DURAL FRAME FOR TRAY TRUCK 55.00
  (Specify 4, 5 or 6 Shelf)
7/8" DURAL FRAME FOR EKONO-CART 28.00
  (Specify 2 or 3 Shelf)
7/8" DURAL FRAME FOR C-27 SERVING CARTS 28.00
  (Specify 2 or 3 Shelf)
4" STEM CASTERS W/SOCKETS ....4.00 ea.
4" PLATE CASTERS ....6.00 ea.
5" PLATE CASTERS ....8.00 ea.
5" PLATE CASTERS WITH SIDE BRAKE ....10.00 ea.
3" STEM CASTER W/SOCKETS FOR EKONO-KART ....3.50 ea.
5" EXTRA HEAVY DUTY CASTERS FOR LB-1HD ....12.00 ea.
  (Specify Swivel or Rigid)
RUBBER DO-NUT BUMPERS 2.00
16 x 24" FORMICA SHELF ASSEMBLY FOR MODEL C-27 CART 20.00
STRAP WITH SCREWS FOR ALL TRAY & LUGGAGE STANDS (MINIMUM ORDER 24 EA.) .... 1.00 ea.
STRAP MATERIAL IN BULK FOR ALL TRAY & LUGGAGE STANDS (MINIMUM 50 YD. ROLL) ...... 1.00 yd.
CRUTCH TIPS FOR TRAY & LUGGAGE STANDS (MINIMUM ORDER 48 EA.) ....20 ea.

house included a faucet for ice water and a springloaded step so that small children could reach the fountain spigot. This item, however, was complicated to install because it required cutting holes in the refrigerator case and inserting heat exchange tubing inside to cool the water. Consequently, none of these household items was manufactured by the company as of 1973. The pogo sticks had long since been dropped from the line.

The most profitable product had been a test stand control panel for the Nike rocket manufactured in the late 1950s. Mr. Kassel had bid on the prototype and put a great deal of effort into the design, which had won the bid. A follow-on production contract brought the company to its best year, in which earnings had been $159,000 before taxes. A subsequent contract, however, went to another company to produce the identical design that Mr. Kassel had originated. He had subsequently not much pursued government subcontract work. From time to time he had been approached by invention services, some asking if he had designed products that he would like to license (through the service) to other manufacturers, as illustrated in Exhibit 2, and others asking if as a licensee he would like to manufacture some of the products others had developed. A list of the inventions he had received appears in Exhibit 3. He had not, however, undertaken such arrangements.

SALES

Another company, Phantasmo Products Corporation, acted as the sales agent for Kassel and received a 7% commission. The Phantasmo plant was located directly across a freeway with a clear view of the Kassel plant, although driving between the two required a half-mile trip because there was no nearby cross street. Phantasmo handled lines of several manufacturers so that it was able to offer a full catalog of equipment for restaurants and offices, including tables, chairs, booths, cabinets, silverware, and kitchen utensils. One of the men in the Kassel shop pointed out that their products included carts similar

to those made by Kassel as well as Kassel's.

Phantasmo had handled Kassel's products for about 2 years. Previously, the line had been handled by another organization, Link, but Mr. Kassel had grown dissatisfied because he did not think sufficient effort was applied by their salesmen. When he had expressed this discontent to another business associate, who happened to own the building in which Phantasmo's plant was located, the man introduced him to the co-owner of Phantasmo, and the change was made. "There aren't many choices for obtaining representatives in this business," Mr. Kassel observed. "The big manufacturers of products like ours tend to carry their own full lines and have their own sales forces. But we could not afford to have our own salesmen in other cities around the country where we sell."

Kassel did sell directly to a few large accounts that were regarded as "house accountants." These included a large hotel chain that bought its luggage racks from Kassel; a large grocery chain that used Kassel carts in its meat department (not shopping carts—these were regarded as very high production items that Kassel was in no way equipped to manufacture) and Kassel costumers in their offices; and a large bank chain that bought Kassel step stools for its bank vaults. One house account was a company that had recently contacted Kassel Manufacturing to inquire whether or not one of the Kassel carts could be adapted for carrying portable room partitions which the other company made for hotels. The foreman in Kassel's shop modified a cart by adding protrusions to the sides of the cart for such applications. Kassel subsequently enjoyed an increasing volume of business with this customer. A breakdown of sales volume by product appears in Exhibit 4.

Also included among house accounts were customers outside the seven western states served by Phantasmo. Kassel did not solicit in these areas, but a thin scattering of customers reached as far as the East Coast. These customers had been obtained in the early days of the products before other manu-

EXHIBIT 2   Letter from patent attorney.

1300 Liberty Square
Reno, Nevada

Mr. Frederick Kassel
21 Bay Street
Long Beach, California

Dear Mr. Kassel:

As a manufacturer of restaurant equipment, your company may
have developed items falling outside your area of market interest,
but within the product areas of one or more of six corporations
which I represent.

A list of represented corporations and the involved product
areas is enclosed.

Whirlpool, for example, would be interested in considering
items which may have been developed solely for restaurant use, but
which might, with suitable modifications, be adapted for domestic
use. In view of Whirlpool's outlets, both through RCA-Whirlpool
dealers and the Sears, Roebuck stores, a licensing arrangement
covering such an item, particularly if protected by patent, might
prove worthwhile. Wisconsin Wire Works is interested in considering outdoor barbecue equipment and the like, and perhaps you have
no interest in that type of market.

Should you feel that at least an exploratory discussion might
be warranted, I could arrange to come to your office when next in
the Los Angeles Area in early January.

Very truly yours,

Enclosure

EXHIBIT 3 Invention sales company letter copy.

UNIVERSAL INVENTION SALES
A Complete Professional Service for Inventors

478 South Main St.
Marion, Ohio
2-0262

September 24, 1958

Mr. Frederick Kassel
21 Bay Street
Long Beach, California

Gentlemen:

We represent the inventor of a very versatile cart that may be used for a variety of things around the house, office, hospital, restaurant, warehouse, hotel, or any other place where a wheeled cart could be of use. The cart is designed with two large wheels, and one much smaller wheel which swivels for greater ease of manipulation. It is very lightweight because it is constructed of tubular aluminum. However, the cart will support many, many times its own weight with ease.

The construction is simple, though very rugged, the operation is troublefree and foolproof, it is easily handled, turned, stopped, and it may be used for carrying any item or items from one place to another quickly with the expenditure of very little effort. The manufacturing cost is very low, and this cart will easily pay for itself in convenience and time and labor saved.

We shall be glad to provide complete details without obligation to interested manufacturers. Your comments and suggestions are invited and appreciated. In the event this device is unsuited for your manufacture, perhaps you could suggest someone who would be better qualified for its submission, in which case we would be most grateful.

Cordially yours,

UNIVERSAL INVENTION SALES

Managing Director

FC/pm

EXHIBIT 3 *(Continued)*

MOST OF OUR INVENTIONS ARE PATENTED. OTHERS HAVE PATENTS PENDING. PATENTS INSURE PROTECTION FOR ALL.

Magnetic Force Demonstration Device. An educational apparatus for demonstrating the force of magnetism. Clearly demonstrates the three laws of magnetic force. Invaluable for classroom demonstration. Low cost to manufacture. Operation foolproof and troublefree. Patented with strong patent of recent issue. Should be investigated for full disclosure. MATHIESEN

Lightning Arrestors. For use with wire fences. Keeps livestock safe from lightning during storms. Low manufacturing cost. Wide range of prospective buyers. Simple to install with easy process developed by inventor. Pay for itself in livestock saved. Patent Pending. HANEY

Flashlight Circuit Tester. Quickly and easily test flashbulb, batteries, and contacts before taking pictures with flash cameras. More satisfactory and troublefree than testers now available. Accurate, foolproof, low cost, no special operating technique. Real seller. LAJARA

Little Gem Coin Machine. Small and easily handled for separating, counting, and packaging coins. Invaluable for school lunch counters, savings accounts, hot dog stands, churches, and the like. Separate parts may be used individually. Simple, accurate, speedy, portable. STILLE

Knight Watchman. A very apt title for a device that hangs on the doorknob, instantly ready for use. When door is locked, guard is fitted through the hole in key. Impossible to unlock or dislodge key till guard is removed. Adaptable in any home for any door, with the exception of Yale locks. Low cost, volume sales, safety feature, premium item for lockmakers. HEILAND

Fisherman's Third Hand. To attach artificial flies to fine leader, chiefly nylon. Simple, quick, and easy with this device. No larger than ball point pen. Can be any required size. Low cost, foolproof, metal or plastic. Assured sales in quantity when shown. JESNESS

Split Exhaust Type Muffler. Novel; for use with V-type engines. Makes eight- and six-cylinder cars sound like twice that. Eliminates over 90% of back pressure. Increases gas mileage from 3 to 5 miles per gallon. No new dies or jigs required. Satisfactory use. KLUDT

Retrieve-O-Matic. To be attached to any type rod and reel. Can be retrieved immediately if dropped overboard. No loss. Small buoy immediately goes into action—floats to surface; simple matter to secure rod and reel. Saves money and tempers. Preliminary search in Patent Office reveals nothing close to this. Potential market is terrific. Show it, sell it! BOND

"Make It Yourself" Crossword Puzzle. Essentially a game of board type. Separate white and black squares fit on a marked board. Letters and numbers on white squares; black squares are blank. Professional puzzle makers will go for this in creating new puzzles; educational; solve any diagramless puzzle; cardboard or plastic. Great appeal for old and young. LOVELESS

Cupid Auto Signal. Directional signal apparatus for cars. Kewpie doll design lights up and points the way for turn signals. Terrific novelty and ornamental appeal, particularly for the younger generation. Metal or plastic. Could be used on toy cars. A hot one! HOLCKER

COMPLETE DETAILS ON ANY INVENTION IN OUR FILES WITHOUT OBLIGATION. GET DETAILS TODAY!

INVENTIONS FOR PROFIT   *PROGRESSIVE INVENTIONS*

Device Operating a Pneumatic Jack. Carries a supply of compressed air in a tank for emergency use in inflating tire or raising a jack. Valves fit tires and may be filled from any filling station air hose. Small and compact; gage indicates degree of compression. Especially useful for female drivers. Years of use. A real value and seller. PROVOST

Mason's Mortaring Tool. A great improvement over three-cornered trowel used for smoothing and laying up mortar. Even a novice can accomplish professional results. Professional mason and helper can increase speed and efficiency 50% to 100%. Few working parts to go out of commission. Will sell itself. Just show it, that's all you need to do. COOK, SR.

"Multi-Drive" Farm Tractor. Departure from present types of tractors. Superior, four-row tractor. Tested and used under actual conditions. Performs efficiently. Four-wheel drive, four-wheel steering.

EXHIBIT 3 *(Continued)*

Operates in either direction. Used with any other farm tool. Only two-wheel tracks. Performs perfectly on rough hilly ground. Control without use of brakes. Check this one. SCHMELTZ

Luxury Seat. For all passenger cars, trucks, trains, buses. Suspension of seat in either of two ways allows for 3 to 4 feet movement from side to side and up and down. Reduces fatigue, sore and tired back; does not affect seat adjustment. Nominal manufacturing cost; efficient. Auxiliary or standard equipment on any of the aforementioned vehicles. COGGIN

Combination Driving Light and Fog Light. For use in fog. Sealed beam lights contain two bulbs operated by separate switches. Newer cars with separate lights for dim use the fog light in conjunction with dim light. Very low cost; vital safety feature. STARR

Board Jack. For carpenters. Patent applied for. Provides novel means for straightening and tightening siding, flooring, etc., so that it may be nailed to joists or studs with ease and efficiency. Minimum effort. Simple, compact, portable, rugged. Get details! PEARCE

Star Separator for Tumbling Mills. Makes mills more accessible by elevating them. Interliner separates jacks from iron. Iron dumped directly into hoppers. Saves manpower and time, therefore money! Low cost; rugged; pays for itself with use. Patented. Write! SHAFER, JR.

Clothesline Support and Tensioning Device. Adaptable for use with any backyard clothesline post. Ratchet means for tightening lines quickly, easily; no tools needed. Locks into position; releases at a touch. Detachable for easy storing. Leave backyard free for full utilization. Rugged; easy to operate. Will delight the housewife! Patented. HAMRICK

Mail Box Clip for Outgoing Mail. Attached to any type mailbox. Securely and firmly holds outgoing mail in accessible position. Prevents loss and soiling by being blown away. Metal or plastic; attractive in appearance. Foolproof and troublefree. Variety store item. EVANS

Mechanism for Bicycle. Novel arrangement for pedaling a bike. Source of power is leverage; much easier to pedal. Less weight needed; more speed obtained. Contrivance designed to be installed as new equipment or used with bikes now in use. Unusual, clever. DAVIDSON

Cleanrite. A cleaning solution for glass windows, windshields, showcases, mirrors, and all other glassware. Small amount needed for all windows in house. Also used for porcelain stoves, freezers, refrigerators, kitchen cabinets. Excellent germicide. Easy on hands. LONGLEY

COMPLETE DETAILS WITHOUT OBLIGATION TO INTERESTED MANUFACTURERS. WRITE TODAY

INVENTIONS   *INVENTIONS*

Broom Duster. Skirt-like design attaches around handle of broom. Dust-absorbing material; dusts floors without changing from broom to dust mop. Two jobs in one operation. Time saving; very low cost; novelty item. Volume sales assured. Efficiency is astonishing. COWAN

Self-Leveling Device. Entirely eliminates rolling and pitching of sections or portions of ship. Absolutely retains level status. Used for beds, chairs, dining tables—gives the effect of being on dry land. No motor, no wires, no mechanical means of operation. Relies on gravity alone. Beautiful in design. Low cost. Patented. Write about this one! SMITH

The Thawer. For thawing frozen locks on autos, etc. Saves money, time, and tempers. Small, compact, efficient. Attaches to car under hood or near license plate holder. Small wire plugged into thawer; ground to lock on door; less than a minute to thaw. See it. RICHARD

Zing Cap Shooter. Designed for the smaller of the "small fry." Relies on rubber band for power. Easy to shoot for small hands; easy to replace. Metal and wood construction for pistol. Lightweight. Troublefree. Hours of fun; easy on parents, too. Novel. A seller! TOWNSEND

Multiple Radius Bending Apparatus. For bending rods, tubes, and the like. Reinforcing rod, electrical conduit, and plumbing lines may be bent on location with this device without dismantling or altering the apparatus. Saves time, labor, money. May be made in any size—large, power driven; or smaller and hand operated. Patented. Economical. See it. HART

Improved Flashlight. Eliminates switch trouble completely. Batteries are separated and connected by wiring through a switch. Direct disconnection and connection. Can replace worn switch without buy-

EXHIBIT 3 *(Continued)*

ing new flashlight. Patented. Eliminates all insulation, shorting caused corrosion, dampness, wearing or breaking of circuit members. Less expensive. ALEXANDER

Pressure Power Unit. May be made in any size depending on amount of power to be developed. Any shape. Liquid, air, steam for power source. Atomic power possible source of energy. Power developed is enormous. Cost is negligible. Simplifies transmission. Possibilities are absolutely endless. Factories, autos, machinery, appliances all use this. EPP

Wheel Bearing Tool. Eliminates tedious work of removing wheel and drum from car. Bearing and seal left on spindle and not damaged in any way. No mess, no muss, no fuss. Clean whitewall tires are undamaged. Cuts time in half. Tested under pressure. Great! REYNOLDS

Mechanic's Hand Adaptor. For assembling and disassembling any type of mechanical motor. Crank case, spark plugs, fuel pump, cap screws, etc., are simple to assemble. Acclaimed by mechanics as most versatile. Universal favor. Low cost; troublefree. Show it, sell it. ROSENE

Cat Napper, Dog Dozer. Bed for cat or dog; in smaller version can be used as a camp stool. Consists chiefly of tubular frame over which cover is fitted. Any material for cover; device is small, compact, rugged, and firm; any size, lightweight; years of use. Details! MORRIS

WRITE—TELL US WHAT YOU NEED—WE ARE CERTAIN TO HAVE IT—DON'T DELAY— WRITE TODAY!!!

PROGRESS, PROFITS, INVENTIONS, UNIVERSAL—THE NATURAL ORDER OF EVENTS!

Attachment Cable Cutter. Patented attachment for any size hydraulic portable ram for cutting electrical cables, wire, rope, etc. May be separate or as part of complete unit. Quick, efficient action; saves time and money. Cuts waste to minimum. Electricians, dockyard workers, dredging crews, oil well crews, mining companies, logging companies, commercial fishing craft, aircraft. List is endless for uses for this patented attachment. Write today! RABY

Easy Pipe Filler Lifter Tab. Simplicity of design and convenience are surprising. Remove inner wrapper from can of tobacco with ease and no effort. Neater; handier; no waste. Cost to manufacture is infinitesimal; no radical change in present design. Sales appeal. TEMPEL

Headlight Adjustment. No need for leaving the driver's seat of the car. Quick, easy, no tools needed. Small variations corrected immediately. Full range of adjustability to compensate for heavy vehicle loading. Not a dimmer. Invaluable for bad weather. Patented. GOFF

Back Support. Designed particularly to strengthen and support the back against strain and fatigue of stooping, bending, etc. Used by men, women, and children. Good for weak backs. Worn with ease and comfort; easily adjusted; distributes reinforcing tension uniformly. Unobtrusive, yet effective. Low cost, readily washable materials, patent pending. MYLRS

Sani-Penser Toothpaste. For use with dispenser type tube for toothpaste, shaving, and hand creams, etc. Cap never need be removed. End of tube automatically kept closed until paste is needed. Never drips. No mess. No extra cost. Sanitary. Savings. Novel. GOMES

Pressure Paint Roller. Applies paint under pressure. Patent applied for. Surpasses now prevailing types. Full control of paint flow at all times. No dripping or splattering. Paint more evenly applied; efficient; low cost; pressurized with hand pump. See it! WICHERN

WRITE—TELL US WHAT YOU NEED—WE ARE CERTAIN TO HAVE IT—DON'T DELAY— WRITE TODAY!!!

EXHIBIT 4 Unit sales history of Kassel Products.

Model	Description	Total sales in number of units 1967	1968	1969	1970	1971	1972
C16x24-2-S	TWO stainless steel shelves						60
C16x24-2-C	TWO chrome-plated shelves						3
C16x24-3-S	THREE stainless shelves						68
C16x24-3-C	THREE chrome-plated shelves						10
		360	200	207	155	120	141
C21x33-2-S	TWO stainless steel shelves						96
C21x33-2-C	TWO chrome-plated shelves						12
C21x33-3-S	THREE stainless steel shelves						357
C21x33-3-C	THREE chrome-plated shelves						73
PC							75
		711	718	487	614	457	613
TT-4	FOUR stainless steel shelves						0
TT-5	FIVE stainless steel shelves						4
TT-6	SIX stainless steel shelves						7
		14	22	24	22	18	11
EK-2-C	TWO chrome-plated shelves						19
EK-3-C	THREE chrome-plated shelves						20
EK-2-S	TWO stainless steel shelves						28
EK-3-S	THREE stainless steel shelves						20
		298	431	368	271	154	87
C27-2	TWO walnut formica shelves						302
C27-3	THREE walnut formica shelves						97
		412	456	447	402	270	399
HB-2	Solid top shelf						3
HB-3	Solid top and bottom shelf						33
		46	63	42	49	41	36
LB-1	Low bed stock truck						31
LB-1-HD	Low bed stock truck w/ HD casters						17
		110	109	78	101	47	48
SS-100	Simple Simon cart						7
R-500	Lugs for above						45
		102	106	157	142	51	52
R-1	Tray stand						2,915
R-3	Tray stand w/lower cross bars						1,635
		4,853	4,856	4,672	4,028	3,902	4,550
R-2	Luggage stand						24
R-4	Luggage stand w/wall protector						589
		701	609	951	521	450	613
HC-1	72″ costumer, Dural						117
HC-3	68″ costumer, Dural						165
HC-4	68″ costumer, chrome						63
HC-5	72″ costumer, chrome w/revolving head						121
		2,748	1,861	1,679	1,070	511	466
UV-1	ONE step stool						15
UV-2	TWO step stool						117
UV-3	THREE step stool						238
UV-1-SC	ONE step stool w/casters						6
UV-2-SC	TWO step stool w/casters						137
UV-3-SC	THREE step stool w/casters						127
UV-3-HR	THREE step stool w/hand rails						0
UV-3-SC-HR	THREE step stool w/casters and handrails						63
		560	522	595	560	616	703

facturers had copied the products. A few customers remained loyal, but the number had steadily declined over the years. The company currently listed approximately 200 accounts in its active file, with two or three times that number in the inactive file.

Mr. Kassel noted that sales were no longer as high as they had been once, and attributed this to severe competition from his imitators. "They have more complete lines, and that lets them have their own sales force. We just have to hope our agents will choose to push our products rather than some of the other things they handle. Because they have fuller lines, our competitors are able to offer package deals in which for the same freight they can tuck in items that ride along free. From what I hear, I gather they give special discounts, rebates, price breaks, and all sorts of things we can't afford. Since their production runs are longer, they may also give cost advantages in manufacturing, but I'm not sure."

In a letter dated February 24, 1971, Mr. Kassel expressed additional views about what he regarded as unsatisfactory sales: "Our total 1970 sales were up slightly over 1969, but were no ways near what they should be. I believe that the following are the main reasons for this:

1. Intense competition from a couple of large manufacturers that have many more products to offer.

2. We have not put forth much effort recently to add new or redesigned products.

3. Our sales representation is not as effective as it should be. It is human nature for the boys to spend more time on selling items that have larger sales and commission potential."

A student at the University of Washington in Seattle (one of the cities in which Kassel sales had declined) had done a study in mid-1971 of the cart market and how it worked. Excerpts from this study appear in Exhibit 5.

More recently, the consultant friend of Mr. Kassel visited a large office furniture store in the Los Angeles area and inquired about Kassel products. "I knew this store handled the line," he said, "because they were included in recent company billings. But when I asked one of the senior salesmen in the store about Kassel products, he said he wasn't sure whether they still handled the line or not. When I asked him why, he said because the products they now handled were better, but he could in no way whatever tell me why they were better. I noticed the selection of costumers along one wall and among them was a Kassel. The pole on it was loose because it had apparently not been assembled correctly when they unpacked it to use as a demonstrator. So I tightened it, which was a simple matter. All sloppy as it had been, the absence of a label was probably lucky for the Kassel reputation."

The consultant also visited some restaurant supply stores in another city and visited with the Phantasmo representative. The representative confided that the incentive to push Kassel products was somewhat lower than on other lines because on Kassel products he had to split his commission with Phantasmo, whereas some others he carried direct, mostly to hospitals. He said he had not done much business in Kassel products thus far, but expected there would be more in the future. Visits to some of the local restaurant dealers in his territory turned up the fact that some had not received current literature or price lists. All spoke well of the Kassel products, which they recalled as being among the first to become available and of high quality. One, however, said that his customers prefer all-stainless construction to combination aluminum and stainless because they believe the former is more durable. "Some of the old-time customers still insist that they will have nothing but Kassel though," he said. "So we order it for them." None of these dealers carried any samples of Kassel products on the floor. Dealers also commented that Lakeside offered more product variety and that Bloomfield in some cases offered substantially lower prices for carts that appeared similar to Kassel's.

1. Large Hotel Supply Company. Franchised dealer for Bloomfield line, primarily all-stainless carts. Main retail market is restaurants, institutions, schools, and hospitals. Typical produce life is 5 to 10 years, depending on use. In recent years the emphasis has shifted to bussing systems, and selling analytical service, not just products, through factory representatives as restaurants move to more assembly line types of operations.

2. Restaurant Equipment Supplier. Saw this industry as becoming cutthroat. Too many distributors are entering the market and cutting bids, sometimes out of ignorance, to survive. Distributor buys through factory rep, then has to floor models, provide floor salespeople and field salespeople to take orders, and arrange delivery. Because few exclusives are given on products any more, the margins are squeezed. "I would not recommend this business to my son," was the comment. This man saw distributors being wiped out in the future as more manufacturers sell direct to large institutions and chains rather than through middle men.

3. Small Hotel Supply Company. There are from 10 to 15 bussing cart makers in the country, most of which are divisions of larger companies. All but Lakeside make other things besides carts. Ninety percent of the carts sold are all stainless. One company, Fiber Glide, has been trying to introduce fiberglass carts. Bloomfield is the biggest company in the industry. Standard costumer sales are declining because emphasis is now on blending better with decor.

4. Medium-Sized Hotel Supply Company. Shellymatic makes high-impact plastic products and regards itself in conveyor business. It makes carts, belts, chain conveyors, and other devices that move things in the food industry. Variety of sizes in carts has diminished and salesmen now become key to differentiating products. Distributor is seen as becoming more a systems expert helping customer devise ways to reduce work and, most importantly, breakage of dishes. This firm takes a retainer for working with the architect who designs the restaurant and returns part to the customer if he buys from them. They see the industry, which now has many distributors, changing to a few distributors like themselves, with factory reps replacing the rest. Hat racks are becoming more important as coat-checking gets too expensive, but pole type is declining because it is unsightly. Closet-type with shelves is taking over because the materials fit the decor. Typical life is 5 years for racks and 2 to 5 years for carts. "Our industry is wide-open. We have no place to go but up."

5. Food Facilities Planning Manager, Large Hotel Chain. About 90% of carts are sold from catalogs, and 5% to 10% are custom. Industry is increasing in competition with increasing emphasis on aesthetics. Sometimes equipment is too well built and hence expensive. Each branch of the military has its own specifications, as does the General Services Administration for the rest of the U.S. government. Cart must last for at least 10 years. Industry trend is toward more options and more variations of each model. Plastics and fiberglass may increase in importance. Independent kitchen consultants are introducing systems concepts which tend to counteract advantages of full-line companies because the systems designers pick and choose from many different suppliers as needed.

   Manufacturers used to sell only through distributors, but increasingly they sell directly to large users. Personal selling by representatives is important. Salesmen need experience as food facilities managers and as floor salesmen. Representative should have a bankroll of $25,000 to start, because purchasers expect him to entertain, dress well, and stay in good hotels. He must also take time out to attend such shows as the National Restaurant show in Chicago, the Hotel Show in New York, or others in San Francisco, Los Angeles, etc., each year. One thing not discussed in the industry is fee splitting by salesmen with customers when direct sales are made.

6. Government Hospital Dietician. Parts of the country differ in sophistication of buyers. She says hospitals in the Northwest would buy anything, whereas the East Coast, where she was before, has better trained salesmen and is more demanding on manufacturers. Northwest data, she said, should be highly discounted as unrepresentative of the nation.

7. Northwest Representative for Kassel Products. His own specialty is selling to hospitals; he used to sell for a dealer before becoming an independent representative. No complaints about Kassel products, no other cart makers are located in Northwest. His other lines overlap slightly with Kassel; Phantasmo offering a similar cart, though he wasn't sure how prices compared. (Turned out Phantasmo was $85 versus $71 for Kassel.) Recently lost a bid with Kassel luggage racks at $5.50 to Technabilt at $4.00. Toughest cart competition is Lakeside, which doesn't have men on the road but does lots of advertising. Bloomfield recently introduced cantilever carts at $37 which are hard to compete with. Main reason Kassel hasn't sold better, he said, was that his predecessor did not sell hard enough. He also said the 50/50 split he must give Phantasmo on commissions is unusual. On most of his lines—and he has a big, thick catalog—he gets it all.

OPERATIONS

Manufacturing consisted mainly of bending pipe, drilling holes, assembling, and crating. Aluminum pipe was passed through an automatic sanding machine to give it a burnished finish. It was then cut to length and bent in a hydraulically operated machine which was set to the special dimensions required for the parts to fit together. The stainless steel trays and customer bases were purchased from suppliers which used Kassel-owned dies to form them to the proper shapes. Casters were also purchased. Pneumatic screwdrivers were used for inserting the screws that held the parts together. Finally, the Kassel label was attached and the finished product packed in a carton. Costumers were packed with the bases separate for easier shipment.

Although the company shop included a full line of standard machine tools, such as lathes, mills, etc., only a few of them were used in most fabrication. A somewhat antiquated but serviceable screw machine, for instance, was only used for making plugs to assemble tubing, a process only performed at intervals of several weeks. No goods were produced for inventory in anticipation of orders. Consequently, most of the company's inventory consisted of raw materials that could be used for various combinations of products. Purchasing was performed by the bookkeeper as needed, but she commented that lately there had been some difficulty in obtaining supplies. She felt that this was partly because supplies had become tight nationwide and partly because Kassel had become slow in paying. The company's supply of casters, for instance, was running low, and replacements had been on order for over 2 months.

The plant was situated in a building leased from the Southern California Edison company. It had once belonged to Mr. Kassel but had been sold to generate cash. The current lease was scheduled to expire in April 1974, but officials of the utility had indicated likely willingness to renew on some basis.

Four men worked in the shop. Their duties, skills, and time with the company were as follows:

Foreman: had designed much of the shop tooling and was the only person in the shop skilled in repairing, setting up, and adjusting the screw machine; with the company since 1951; paid $16,640 per year.

Shipper: in charge of inventory, packing, and shipping; also performed assembly work; with the company since 1954; paid $10,920 per year.

Driver of the delivery truck: also performed assembly work; with the company since 1953; paid $7,800 per year.

Assembler: with the company since 1965; paid $7,280 per year.

All the men knew how to make the products and all could run the pipe bending machine that made the frames. The main times when all were needed were when heavy loads of materials arrived from suppliers and when there were sudden calls for larger orders. "We'll have it fairly slack for a while, and then there will be a big rush with all of us going hard to fill some order a customer wants yesterday," one of them observed. Mr. Kassel's consultant friend observed that lately the work had been relatively light. He noted that one of the men was rebuilding his own auto transmission on one of the company benches and that the two other men were off somewhere in town, apparently on errands.

One of the Phantasmo employees commented that he thought discipline was too lax in the Kassel shop. "I saw one of them drinking a beer on the job the other day, for instance," he said. "And I just don't think that leads to good work. Frankly, I think they have one or two too many men over there for what they produce. If they just told customers to come and pick up their own orders the way we tell ours to, they could lay off one man right away." One of the Kassel employees, however, commented to the contrary. "When orders come, we all are needed here. I wouldn't want to work on unloading some of the heavy stuff that comes in here with fewer men either. If one of us gets laid off here, I think we should all go, and I think the others would agree."

"I think that our efficiency is no worse than it ever was," Mr. Kassel commented. "It's just that the volume is down at the moment. I would estimate that we could increase output by roughly 50% with the same work force if we just had the orders. If we added the maximum work force on one shift operation, we could probably double the output with this plant. I let a consulting firm that gave us a great pitch about what it could do come in and analyze the company about 10 years ago. The consultant put in 27 hours at $25 an hour before I cut him off. He analyzed the plant operations, confirmed my own conclusions about our needs, but came up with essentially no useful solutions for us." A copy of the consultant's report appears in Exhibit 6. Mr. Kassel said methods had changed relatively little since.

OFFICE

The company bookkeeper (with the company since 1968, salary $7,800 per year) handled orders, bookkeeping, payment of bills, purchasing, and the files. Although she was not a typist, she also wrote letters for Mr. Kassel and took care of company correspondence. In spite of this broad variety of activities, she often found time on her hands, and when Mr. Kassel called the shop to dictate a letter, he would sometimes jokingly ask her if it was all right to interrupt her game of solitaire.

> At one point he told us we should all get out and sell if we wanted to keep the company going so that we would have jobs. So we tried. I called customers on the phone, and each of the boys in the shop tried putting on a suit and going out to make calls. But it didn't work. They're just not salesmen, and I'm a bookkeeper, period.
>
> This company really needs full time from a professional. Mr. Kassel is a wonderful man, but he has really almost totally neglected the company since I've been here, and I gather

for at least 5 years before that. We have all fallen way behind in pay, but we know there just isn't any more money to go around. I need the income because my husband is ill, but I wouldn't dream of leaving Mr. Kassel now that his own health has given out and he can't come in here and hold things together. Phantasmo seems to be giving sales a fair try; they must have spent a couple of thousand dollars on brochures to advertise our products. But that is not enough. We're all just holding on. (Statement of company bookkeeper.)

Lately, the company's cash had run short and accounts payable had become extended, with adverse effects on relations with suppliers. Most were calling the bookkeeper and requesting payment soon. Some were becoming slower on making deliveries, and although none had as yet threatened to put the company on COD delivery, she was worried that some might. "The boys in the shop wish we had more inventory so they would have more to work on, but we just can't afford it. Mr. Kassel cut his own draw down to $1,000 per month a year ago, but now it's hard for the company to come up with even that. Comparative statements for the company appear in Exhibit 7.

> Trying to hold the finances together has really been making me lose sleep at night. So far I have been getting along fairly well with suppliers. My approach is just to be open and honest with them, and I think they appreciate that. I tell them when I expect we will be able to send them some money and how much. Since I always keep my word, I think they trust me. At the same time I make it a point to tell customers how much I appreciate their paying promptly, and if they get behind they know they will get a call from me and also that we won't fill their next order until they've paid. They appreciate the fact that we fill orders fast and will deliver right to their plant, and they know we have good products. So they are pretty good about paying.
>
> But now we're stretched about as far as we can go, and I don't know what will happen next. I don't think Mr. Kassel realizes how tight things are getting, although of course he personally is liable for all the bills, since we're not a corporation. Because his health is so poor I haven't had the heart to tell him how

EXHIBIT 6 Consultant report.

Management Service Progress Report
No. 124 319 - 1

December 15, 1960.

KASSEL MANUFACTURING
Long Beach, California

Gentlemen:

As stated in the "Authorization for Management Service Development and Method of Payment," this is one of the series of Progress Reports our executive staff will give to you in order that at all times our engagement will be entirely under your control. It summarizes current and cumulative attainments and outlines future plans, thus keeping you fully informed as to the development of our work on your assignment. We ask that this report receive your most careful consideration, particularly in view of the need for your close cooperation as set forth in Paragraph 3 of the "Authorization for Management Service Development and Method of Payment," which reads as follows: "Recognizing the achievements realized from Management Service work depends upon many factors, including human aptitudes and the cooperation of your staff, which factors are not within the control of the Consulting Company, it is understood and agreed that no express or implied warranty of any general or specific results shall apply to the work done under this agreement."

REPORT

Following a brief opening conference on Monday, December 12th, Staff activity was devoted through Monday and Tuesday to an analysis of departmental costs and expenses with the object of determining:

      A. Average wage rates for Machine and Assembly operations.
      B. The operational Overhead Burden factor applicable to productive
         labor in the Shop and Assembly areas, respectively.
      C. The sales level at which the individual operational departments
         would be in a position to establish competitive prices.

and an interview with the Sales Representative in the local area.

Information available for the fiscal year 1959 was used to either compute, prorate, or estimate departmental costs and expenses for an average operational month.

With an average monthly sales volume of $19,120.00 during 1959, the Shop overhead burden of approximately 182% (after adjustment of wages to reflect the recent termination of one machinist) compares unfavorably with a norm for production shops of less than 100%. The Assembly Department burden factor is slightly high as compared with a norm of 75% to 80%. The "Rental Factor" used for analysis represents $1\frac{1}{4}\%$ of the estimated current re-sale value of Land and Buildings ($825.00 per month) which is generally accepted locally as a standard. The "Reserve" item included as operational expense represents 15% of the acquired value of the Equipment utilized in each operational area, Year end balance of Inventories (Warehouse only), and the year end balance of cash and receivables pro rated to revenue producing areas in direct proportion to departmental sales attainment . . . distributed over 12 months.

To bring departmental overhead burden factors into line, competitively at present wage rates—$3.13 per hour in the shop as compared with a norm of approximately $2.75–$2.83 per hour in Assembly as compared with a norm of $2.00 for comparable skills in similar industries, it would be necessary to attain an overall annual volume of about $340,000.00. This would also be our Staff's estimate of sales attainment utilizing the full capacity of the present plant and existing facilities.

EXHIBIT 6 *(Continued)*

The fact that the Screw Machine and other items of machine equipment were utilized to only a small proportion of their respective capacities was noted at the opening conference and the possibility that these units might be more fully utilized on a "jobbing" or Subcontract basis has been carefully considered. However, the current burden factor applicable to shop labor would make it necessary to quote on machine estimates at $6.00 per hour or more in order to insure even a token operating profit and, even though increased volume might make it possible to quote a low enough rate to get supplementary work, it would not be compatible with present production and would definitely interfere with any program designed to develop projects requiring a relatively large proportion of processed tubing production.

Observation of several production operations—bending, fabrication of costumer posts, etc.—indicated excellent planning with respect to setups and methods. Bending operations observed averaged approximately 8 bends per minute during continuous operation. The multiple operation on costumer posts—pressing in base plug, pinning, and drilling hangar holes—required about $1\frac{1}{2}$ minutes during repetitive operations. Polishing costumer bases, however, was handled intermittently and the time per unit was not consistent. Manual assembly of cart components utilized only hand tools and was not set up on a production basis. However, the employee doing the job explained that it was a "fill in" operation intended to utilize otherwise unproductive time.

Our Staff's interview with the local Sales Representative indicated that sales contacts are concentrated primarily among relatively small institutional suppliers—Restaurant Supplies, Beauty Shop and Barber supply houses (local), local Stationers, etc. Sales of C-16x24 and C-21x33 carts should total approximately $200,000.00 in the Western States (annually) and the sales forecast for 1961 (institutional sales) should be approximately that figure for these two items. Use of repetitive direct mail to the purchasing agents of large institutional users of utility carts and chains, such as Mannings, etc., was discussed with possibly a separate commission (or discount) arrangement set up to protect local dealers and encourage them to solicit volume business. The format of mailing pieces was also discussed.

A retail consumer version of the C-27 cart can be produced with adequate control of departmental costs and expenses (Overhead factors) which would be a far more saleable item than the poorly constructed units now being sold in retail stores at prices from $10.00 to $30.00. The suggested retail price, however, would have to be below $30.00. Sturdy folding tables similar to the pilot model already developed but utilizing less expensive and more attractive tops (with respect to retail consumers). The profit factor on these items produced in quantity for retail consumption would probably not exceed 5% with shop and assembly burden factors established at less than 100% and 75%, respectively. However, reduction of burden factors with respect to production of institutional items would considerably increase the profit factor in that area.

The need for simplification and revision of accounting procedures in order to provide the current operational information required for departmental cost and expense control was discussed during the recent survey. With adequate information provided on a current basis and attainment of a reasonable proportion of potential sales volume there is no reason for departmental burden factors to exceed those of comparable industries.

Although pilot models of consumer items would be desirable, production costs can be developed on the basis of experience with similar institutional items and projection of the wage, cost, and expense factors that must be realized to insure an adequate profit. With detailed specifications, illustrations of optional styling and decoration, and tentative prices, we would immediately be in a position to approach prospective buyers in both the San Francisco and Chicago areas either directly by utilizing the contacts that various members of our staff maintain in the retailing field or through your present Sales Representatives.

Efforts are being made to procure either a sample or illustrations of a line of folding tables and servers which, tentatively, will be introduced in the spring of 1961. The units incorporate imported hardwood and pressed wood trays in natural finishes and with hand decoration. The price range will be from $10.00 to $25.00. As soon as costs can be projected, direct contacts should be made with several large office supply Wholesalers either through our staff or your Sales Representatives to

EXHIBIT 6   *(Continued)*

thoroughly explore the possibility of producing items such as vault ladders, clothes hangers, tubular racks, and costumers under the Wholesaler's trade name. Through this method of distribution individual items could be manufactured to supplement existing lines rather than attempt to promote individual items in competition with sales organizations that handle complete "lines."

SUMMARY OF COST REDUCTIONS

Development of a limited number of volume production items (tentatively for retail consumption) will serve to generate the sales volume of approximately $340,000.00 required to minimize and stabilize operational costs and expenses and accomplish greater utilization of existing production facilities. As nearly as can be estimated without further market research, an operating profit slightly exceeding 5% can be realized on quantity production items. The addition of these items, however, will make it possible to maintain a Profit Factor approximating 18% on the type of institutional items currently produced and still maintain a highly competitive price position. Annual dollar profit should approximate $55,000.00 as compared with a projected profit of slightly over $30,000.00 for 1960 without additional investment in plant and equipment.

TOTAL $ _____

SUMMARY OF ACCOMPLISHMENTS, METHODS, AND PROCEDURE IMPROVEMENTS

Respectfully submitted,

EXAMINED, ACCEPTED, AND APPROVED

COMPANY: Kassel Manufacturing

BY: _____

Date: Dec. 15, 1960

EXHIBIT 7(a) Kassel Manufacturing—comparative income statements.*

	1968	1969	1970	1971	1972
Net sales	$142,812	$146,102	$151,748	$127,216	$140,911
Cost goods sold					
Materials purchased	54,548	48,200	52,136	30,939	48,671
Inventory decrease	177	2,141	(4,287)	5,599	1,424
Packing materials	3,142	2,437	3,329	2,233	3,008
Freight incoming	181	454	200	148	214
Direct labor	20,019	20,660	20,507	22,308	22,290
Subcontract labor	7,619	6,843	10,730	4,030	7,689
Shop burden					
Indirect labor	14,957	15,140	15,125	15,860	15,860
Shop supplies	608	955	1,970	676	659
Rent	35	35	5,154	6,855	6,855
Maintenance	432	2,077	365	409	548
Utilities	942	984	860	935	1,016
Payroll tax	1,578	1,577	1,536	1,729	2,008
Insurance	2,775	2,809	2,514	3,370	3,634
Depreciation	3,187	2,361	1,143	534	261
Small tools	123	164	241	107	25
Selling expense					
Travel expense	224	95	241	136	136
Auto expense	1,910	1,998	2,494	1,755	2,495
Freight outgoing	919	1,237	2,557	2,169	1,863
Sales commissions	6,936	6,218	5,941	4,932	3,433
Truck driver salary	1,300	1,325	1,250	1,300	1,301
Entertain and advertising	842	540	138	280	72
General and administrative					
Owner's salary	12,000	12,000	12,000	12,000	12,000
Other office salary	7,218	6,925	7,041	6,390	7,384
Office supplies	1,268	548	1,366	399	1,013
Tel. and Tel.	1,418	1,050	1,311	1,026	1,009
Postage	316	450	429	295	394
Taxes	2,176	2,020	1,156	1,055	1,309
Welfare	272	430	526	546	431
Legal and Accounting	60	65	75	510	65
Miscellaneous, including janitor	1,236	956	1,298	1,200	365
Other					
Interest	16	38	13	158	168
Bad debts	387	15	389	549	575
Customer discounts	1,195	1,176	1,890	917	1,085
Profit (Loss)	$ (7,004)	$ 2,173	$ 610	$ (4,133)	$ (5,451)

* Figures taken from individual years' statements prepared by accountant and put into comparative form by case writer.

it's getting with suppliers. (Statement of company bookkeeper.)

DECISION TO SELL

Taking out a pencil and paper, Mr. Kassel added up the current cash balance of the business plus the figure for accounts receivable. From this he subtracted the current liabilities, which he noted gave a minus $10,000.

That number is a meaningful one to me. I don't know how to make it go to a plus, and even if I did, there isn't enough physical strength left in me to do it. So I have to sell out and pay off these bills. I don't have any big psychological problems with selling this

EXHIBIT 7(b) Kassel Manufacturing—comparative balance sheets.

	1968	1969	1970	1971	1972
Assets					
Cash	(801)	(9,411)	1,068	(7,481)	(8,380)
Receivables	10,877	14,008	13,133	15,755	15,087
Raw materials	10,855	10,571	10,398	6,116	7,513
Parts in process	3,524	2,411	4,269	3,510	3,589
Finished goods	2,614	1,870	4,472	3,914	3,862
Shipping supplies	500	500	500	500	500
Prepaid insurance	369	317	156	191	76
Total current	27,938	20,266	33,996	22,505	22,247
Building	38,764	38,764			
Machinery and equipment	26,636	26,636	26,636	26,636	26,636
Small tools	3,110	3,110	3,110	3,110	3,110
Furniture and fixtures	8,788	8,788	8,788	8,788	8,788
Vehicles	5,949	5,949	5,949	5,949	5,949
Less depreciation	(51,296)	(53,941)	(42,431)	(43,108)	(43,450)
Total fixed	31,951	29,306	2,052	1,375	1,033
Total assets	59,889	49,572	36,048	23,880	23,280
Liabilities					
Accounts payable	6,146	1,791	8,922	3,348	6,198
Taxes payable	1,542	1,743	1,891	1,313	1,517
Commissions payable	2,268	2,887	442	2,557	373
Bad debt reserve	750	750	750	750	750
Total current	10,706	7,171	12,005	7,968	8,838
Net worth	49,183	42,401	24,043	15,912	14,442
Total liabilities	59,889	49,572	36,048	23,880	23,280

business. I lost interest in it over 10 years ago and have just neglected it ever since, and it has finally fallen apart.

The question is, where do I go from here. My health won't let me spend any more time at the plant. How do I find someone to buy it? What price do I ask, or what sort of terms? What should I do while I'm waiting for a deal to develop? Should I take some sort of action down at the shop, or should I just leave it alone until somebody buys? Should I tell the people in the plant that the company has got to be sold or we'll have to shut down? Either way it may mean that they will lose their jobs, and suppose that knowledge leads them to quit before it's sold? Then what should I do?

What I figure I need personally is to get the bills paid off and to keep an income equivalent to the draw I've been taking. After I'm gone, my wife will continue to need the income. So the question is how things can be best handled with the company to provide something as close as possible to that. I guess that depends a lot on what kind of person or company might be interested in taking over and what they should be able to do with the company. What sort of offer should I indicate I'm prepared to consider?

ASSIGNMENT

Analyze the situation of this company, and make recommendations to Mr. Kassel regarding the deal he should seek for sale of the company. Tell how he should go about finding a buyer.

Lay out a plan of action to be followed by a new owner of the company.

10

Consolidation of a New Company

The period of time between starting a business and reaching a break-even level of operations is of critical importance. A promising business can fail during this time without ever testing its potential.

This dangerous early period is usually characterized by cash flowing out but very little cash flowing in. Obviously, this cannot continue indefinitely and the key question is whether the business can reach a cash break-even point before its initial resources are exhausted. This is also a time when the company's basic strategy is being tested for the first time in the market place. Management must interpret the early market response to determine whether or not the strategy should be changed.

CASH MANAGEMENT

The length of time that a company can exist before either reaching break-even or failing depends on (1) the initial capital available; (2) the rate of cash outflow; (3) the rate of sales buildup and cash inflow. One dilemma is that although more initial capital buys the business additional time to reach the break-even point, this start-up money is relatively expensive because of the unproven nature of the new venture. If the same amount were raised after the firm is operating profitably, it would cost less. Yet, if the company starts with too little capital, it may be unable to survive early misfortune or it may appear so unimpressive and marginal to prospective customers that its sales never develop.

Early cash outflow is primarily for fixed assets and for operating expenses, including wages, raw materials, and monthly expenses such as rent and utilities. The amounts spent and the timing of the outflows must be of critical concern to the entrepreneur. This is the time to be diligent, even fanatical, in conserving cash. Later, when the business has a positive cash flow, the entrepreneur can indulge in paneled offices, rarely used equipment, or a larger staff than is absolutely necessary.

Businesses vary widely in the investment needed to get started. Some businesses, such as those engaged primarily in selling, in consulting, or in producing hand-crafted goods, can start on very little; in fact, the concept is often tested on a part-time basis. By contrast, if a new building or substantial equipment is necessary, it may require half a million dollars just to open the door and see if there are any customers or to produce the first product for shipment.

There are several approaches to minimizing the initial investment in fixed assets. Buildings can be rented instead of built; time can be bought on equipment owned by others; used equipment can be renovated; and operations can be subcontracted. The entrepreneur should also consider the possibility of expansion in stages. For instance, in the Camping Resort of Puerto Rico case in this book, the entrepreneur was considering a first stage of site development which, although not benefiting from scale economies, would have a lower break-even point and require less investment than a full-scale development.

The wages of the first employees, including the founders, can be a major cash outflow. A new business faces a wide range of problems and at one time or another it needs almost the full array of skills to be found in a large, established company. A large organization, however, cannot be supported financially. The entrepreneur can deal with this dilemma in several ways. Key employees may be persuaded to work for less current income than they could draw elsewhere, with the enticement of stock ownership and the chance to be "in on the ground floor." Professional people, such as lawyers and accountants, may be willing to postpone compensation, both because of anticipated future income and the excitement of being involved in a new venture. Friends may be persuaded to donate time. During this period the founders themselves usually withdraw much less than they could earn elsewhere, living in part off their personal savings or the wages of spouses. This is also a time of heavy personal commitment that requires long hours and physical stamina. When there are multiple founders, the cash outflow is sometimes minimized through having "early founders" and "late founders," with the latter continuing in their old jobs and donating their evenings and weekends to the new venture until it can support them full time.

The development of sales and particularly the timing and magnitude of cash receipts are critical. The unknown new company faces special problems in trying to get distributors to carry its product and in developing consumer awareness. By contrast, the established firm has a reputation, bargaining power, experienced marketing personnel, and the ability to "last out" disappointing initial sales. The timing of cash receipts is affected by policy decisions on terms of sale and the extent to which credit is granted. Although generous credit terms may aid sales, the new firm, thirsting for cash, can rarely afford to compete on this basis.

Some new firms are started for the purpose of developing technically advanced products, often for growing markets. If the products are successfully developed and are attuned to market needs, the companies may enjoy outstanding growth as they exploit their unique product positions. Product development can be plagued by delays, however, and it is not uncommon for development cost and time to be several times what was originally estimated. This can be disastrous for a new company that has no cash flowing in from the sale of other products. The initial capital that may have seemed sufficient to see the company through to break-even operations may erode away; the entrepreneur must then seek additional funds, often under very difficult conditions.

One approach is for the founder to do as much of the product development as possible during evenings and weekends before quitting his old job. This, however, can lead to conflicts of interest with his employer. Another approach is to have a two-phase strategy in which the initial emphasis is on generating cash by consulting, acting as a sales representative, or performing on government R&D contracts. A proprietary product is then developed on a part-time basis, and the company shifts into phase two when the new product is successfully marketed.

A new venture is fragile and often unable to survive bad luck or unfortunate timing. Promising new businesses have failed because newspaper strikes cut off their advertising, highway construction diverted traffic flows, or local recessions depressed demand. The entrepreneur should study seasonal demand, recognizing that a new business opened in the "off season" may have to survive many months with little revenue. New companies are not the only ones affected by these factors, but they are particularly vulnerable because of their narrow focus, lack of reputation and customer loyalty, and limited financial resources.

What if the venture seems likely to run out of money before reaching the break-even point? Cash outflow can be lessened by releasing employees, persuading them to work for less, cutting back on facilities, or persuading suppliers to wait for payment. Sometimes the founder will take another job or work part-time to try to bring in cash. If there are several founders, this may be a time of great strain on the founding group. Some may lose heart or lack family support and decide to give up the struggle. Sometimes additional funds can be raised from banks or sources of venture capital. However, the entrepreneur whose earlier plans have not been realized may have lost credibility, to say nothing of bargaining power, in seeking to negotiate for additional capital.

EVALUATING THE INITIAL STRATEGY

The initial strategy of the business is usually based upon a concept that has not been fully tested. Can a planned product (or service) be sold to a particular market in the volume and at the prices planned? When the company opens for business, evidence begins to accumulate on whether or not the concept is sound. Orders and reorders may (or may not) develop. Cost data begin to accumulate. Competitors may react. The entrepreneur learns what is really involved, hour after hour, in running a particular business.

Sometimes the initial sales are disappointing or costs prove to be much more than planned. The entrepreneur must then try to assess whether or not the assumptions underlying the company's strategy are sound. This is somewhat like trying to assess one's own child; it is difficult to be objective. Can the founder psychologically accept and use unfavorable information? Some founders deny negative feedback, but others seek out any facts, however unfavorable, that would help them improve their businesses.

Sometimes it appears that the initial strategy will not work and that the prospects of reaching the break-even point are dim. The only chance for survival may be to develop and implement an alternative and hopefully more successful strategy before the funds are gone. One advantage a new firm has is its great flexibility. With relatively few people to convince, with almost no commitment to an existing reputation or customer group, with few distractions associated with other products or markets, the organization can literally "turn on a dime." Furthermore, there is the dedication of committed people who realize that their jobs depend on the company's survival. There have been no research studies focusing on the number of new firms that change their strategies during this time, but the number is not insignificant. Ice cream parlors have changed to steakhouses, electronic component manufacturers have changed to subcontractors, and producers of test equipment have changed to testing laboratories.

The period of time until break-even is probably the time of greatest strain on the entrepreneur and the entrepreneur's family. It is during this time that the founder must work very hard, withdraw the least cash, have the least organizational support, and sometimes wake up in the middle of the night wondering whether or not the business will succeed. An entrepreneur needs energy, stamina, and optimism, but most of all he needs an understanding and supportive family.

Traffic and Safety Control Systems, Inc.

By late August 1971 Traffic Safety and Control Systems of Seattle, Washington had been making shipments of its new Miles per Gallon (MPG) Meter for one month. Six units had been operating for an aggregate total of about 4,500 miles on cars of company employees. The performance was generally satisfactory, but a few "bugs" had become evident. The instruments told drivers continuously and instantaneously the gas mileage they were getting as they drove, something management hoped increasing numbers of drivers would become interested in as availability of the new instrument became known. Advertising information on the product appears in Exhibit 1.

How fast we should try to expand is a tough question we face today. As we add employees and as buyers in distant parts of the country begin making their own installations, we may run into difficulties we didn't foresee. It's not easy to decide whether we should push hard for sales to break even sooner and support further new product development or let them come slower to be sure we don't get a reputation for flawed products. (Statement of Chuck Wurster, company president.) Financial statements for the company appear in Exhibits 2 and 3.

BACKGROUND

The company was originally formed in March 1968 to manufacture a patented fiberglass illuminated curbing for streets. An early company prospectus described the company's intentions as focused in two principal areas: (1) development of new products to increase safety and control of vehicular traffic on streets and highways, with particular emphasis on increasing capacity of existing arterials to handle increased traffic loads and (2) development of existing "urban hardware" such as street lights, traffic signs, stop lights, sidewalks, gutters, and pedestrian crossings. An advertisement showing the initial product appears in Exhibit 4.

Through this prospectus a public stock offering of 28,000 shares at $10 each was made in June of 1969, netting $252,000 to the company. The prospectus further characterized the company as an "extremely high risk" investment and pointed out that zero sales had been made to date. Use of the proceeds was planned for 18 months as $87,-000 for administrative salaries and expenses, $55,000 for marketing and promotion, $20,-000 for R&D of new products, $50,000 for

EXHIBIT 1

Linear MPG Meter

Model 10A

A unique new performance instrument that instantly and accurately displays miles-per-gallon vehicle performance. Both fuel flow and vehicle speed are continuously measured to instantly tell the driver the effect upon mpg performance caused by smallest changes in accelerator pressure, speed, engine tuning, type of gasoline, load, size, etc.

Model 15A   Model 25A

Features:

- A precision measuring instrument with 120° dial face calibrated in miles-per-gallon.
- Easy installation, full installation instructions and mounting hardware included.
- For all vehicles with 12 volt negative ground electrical system and standard SAE 7/8" - 18 thread speedometer takeoff on transmission housing. Fits all U.S. made vehicles since 1967. Ford vehicles having sleeve - end speedometer cables require adapter kit.
- Low profile, black leather textured, scuff-proof housing with hooded bezel, and indirect illumination.
- Easy to read white on black numerals and graduations, fluorescent red pointer.
- Zinc die cast footing swivels a full 280° permitting meter head to be mounted easily above or below dash, on console or steering column.
- Solid-state circuitry and rugged, vibration-proof, magnetically shielded meter movement assures long life, and unfailing accuracy.

Linear Flow Transducer (Patents pending): Connects easily into the fuel line near the carburetor using fittings provided

and fuel line hose. Meets laboratory standards for accuracy with linear output signal accurate to ±1.5% for flow rates to 20 GPH. Flow transducer cannot clog nor affect fuel flow; pressure drop is below 0.5 PSI at 20 GPH. Simple electrical connections with three color coded wires. Zinc die cast unit is cadmium/dichromate plated to provide years of service even near salt water. Flow transducer uses a bladed rotor breaking a light path to signal flow rate to the dial instrument. Only part to replace is standard automotive bulb.

Speed Transducer: Fits between standard 7/8" - 18 thread speedometer takeoff on transmission housing and end of speedometer cable. This rotary cam switch has a minimum 50,000 mile rating and runs cool at 100 MPH. Unit has threaded ground connection and is cadmium/dichromate plated. Single wire connection to dial instrument is provided.

EXHIBIT 1 *(Continued)*

Mounting Details

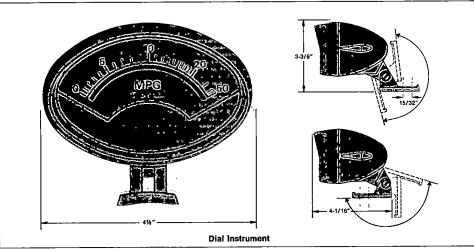

Dial Instrument

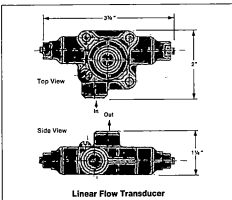

Top View

In Out

Side View

Linear Flow Transducer

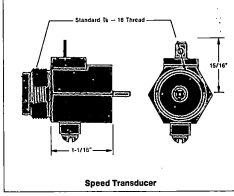

Standard ⅞ — 18 Thread

Speed Transducer

Statement of Warranty

We warrant to the original purchaser these units to be free from defects in material and workmanship under normal use. Within six months from date of purchase we will repair or replace at our option, F.O.B. Seattle, any part which proves upon inspection to be defective. This warranty does not cover defects resulting from accident, improper use, alteration, tampering, failure to follow installation instructions or water damage.

FloScan Instrument Company
3016 N.E. Blakely St., Seattle, Wash. 98105
(206) 524-6625

EXHIBIT 2 Traffic and Safety Control Systems, Inc., balance sheet, July 31, 1971.

ASSETS		
Current assets		$ 10,001.69
Cash	$ 6,232.07	
Marketable securities	3.50	
Accounts receivable	2,885.27	
Prepaid insurance	555.85	
Prepaid rent	325.00	
Equipment		61,592.78
Manufacturing	62,406.55	
Office	1,136.38	
Automotive	225.00	
Less depreciation	(2,175.15)	
Inventory		26,508.23
Purchased parts, Curblite	5,568.00	
Purchased parts, MPG Meter	20,940.23	
Intangible assets		7,026.36
Organization expense	602.00	
Patents	5,623.13	
Copyrights and trademarks	801.23	
		102,129.06

LIABILITIES AND STOCKHOLDERS' EQUITY		
Current liabilities		49,915.68
Accounts payable	11,097.00	
State sales tax payable	7.46	
Withholding payable	659.80	
FICA payable	151.42	
Notes payable	35,000.00	
Junior subordinated convertible notes		
payable		31,750.00
Stockholders' equity		26,463.38
Common stock	39,105.00	
Additional paid-in capital	224,673.24	
Common stock warrants	20.00	
Deficit	(237,334.86)	
To 3/31/71 209,274.50		$105,129.06
From 3/31/71 to 7/31/71 28,060.36		

working capital, and $30,000 for reserve. Manufacturing was to be by subcontract.

The company had been formed with limited private capital to develop Curblite product prototypes, and the public offering, contingent upon hiring a full-time manager, was to build a company. Chuck Wurster had recently left as assistant managing director of a large fertilizer company in South Africa and was looking for new employment in the

EXHIBIT 3 Traffic and Safety Control Systems, Inc., income statement for July, 1971.

Revenue—Sales		$ 1,756.17
Expenses		11,111.27
Office	30.55	
Advertising	1,648.47	
Legal	383.50	
Freight-in	34.06	
Freight-out	23.73	
Consumables, manufacturing	115.85	
MPG development	1,281.88	
Travel and entertainment	24.35	
Automotive leasing and operating	278.85	
Rent	315.00	
Telephone	158.19	
Reproduction	45.68	
State excise tax	13.08	
Seattle B&O tax	6.55	
Salaries	5,149.20	
Social security	75.71	
Dept. of Licenses and Inspections	(6.80)	
Insurance	116.00	
Miscellaneous, Leasehold improvements	417.42	
Audit	1,000.00	
		$9,355.10

Northwest, preferably in a small company. He had previously studied industrial administration at Yale and obtained an M.S. in industrial management at MIT. He then worked in a major oil company, first in economic planning and later in setting up and running the fertilizer subsidiary. Traffic Safety seemed to him an ideal opportunity. He joined it in June 1969 and persuaded his former chief mechanical engineer from the fertilizer company, Wilfried Baatz, to join him in September.

A letter to stockholders dated December 5, 1969 announced the hiring of Mr. Baatz as technical manager. It also said that "Curblite products have the best profit potential of the various profit making possibilities considered to date," that those products had been improved, prototypes tested, manufacturing arrangements with subcontractors made, and production delivery scheduled for March 1, 1970. Arrangements for selling to state and local governments for roadways and also to motels and other businesses that might use illuminated products were being made, but the letter pointed out that "it will be mid-1970 before exposure and market response to the general concept and to our specific designs will be adequate to provide a basis for accurate evaluation of Curblite's profit potential.

As Mr. Baatz worked on technical problems of Curblite and as Mr. Wurster tried to sell the product, its promise steadily diminished. A company memorandum later stated, "Although unique and useful product designs were developed which have resulted in basic patents being granted, the product was not successful because there were persistent difficulties in manufacturing the necessary fiberglass parts. Repeated attempts with three experienced fiberglass fabricators and technical backup from Owens Corning Fiberglas failed to achieve a satisfactory product."

EXHIBIT 4

Standard Shapes for Compatibility

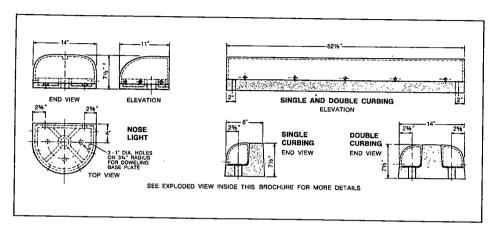

SEE EXPLODED VIEW INSIDE THIS BROCHURE FOR MORE DETAILS

TYPICAL SPECIFICATIONS

Nose Light

Nose light shall be 7½" high, 14" wide, and 11" long. The base shall be cast ductile iron. The lens cover shall be compression molded fiberglass. The incandescent fixture shall be capable of direct connection to ½" incoming conduit and shall contain a double socket for S-14 incandescent bulbs.

Single (double) Face

Single (double) face illuminated curbing shall be 7½" high, 8" wide (14" wide) and 52⅛" long. The base shall be reinforced pre-cast concrete. The one (two) lens cover(s) shall be compression molded fiberglass and shall key into concrete base. The illuminating fixture(s) shall be capable of direct connection to ½" incoming conduit and shall (each) contain six sockets for S-14 incandescent bulbs (alternate: shall contain fluorescent lampholders for High Output (Rapid Start) or Slimline lamps).

Catalog Number	Description	Fixture Type	F.O.B. Price (1)
NI	Nose Light	Incandescent, Two S-14 Sign Lamps	$ 95
SI	Single Curbing	Incandescent, Six S-14 Sign Lamps	$130
SF	Single Curbing	HO Fluorescent, One F48T12/HO Tube (2)	$130
DI	Double Curbing	Incandescent, Twelve S-14 Sign Lamps	$203
DF	Double Curbing	HO Fluorescent, Two F48T12/HO Tubes (2)	$203

NOTES: (1) Net F.O.B. factory price to Contractors excluding cost of freight, lamps, and remote ballasts. Precast concrete bases shipped from the factory in Washington, California or Arizona nearest jobsite. Other components shipped in single carton from assembly points in Seattle and Los Angeles.

(2) Fluorescent fixture incorporates ELSCO 60/60S recessed double contact sockets for outdoor use. Optionally available with Weather Resistant Slimline sockets.

Write for further information

Traffic and Safety Control Systems, Inc.
1422 Northern Life Tower · Seattle, Washington 98101

©1970 Litho in U.S.A.

EXHIBIT 4 (*Continued*)

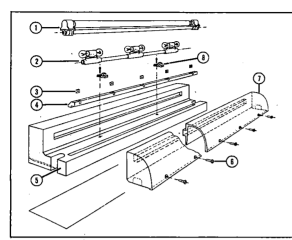

1. Fluorescent fixture, weather-resistant lampholders High Output (Rapid Start) or Slimline fluorescent lamps

2. Incandescent fixture, using six 11- to 25-W, S-14, long-life sign lamps

3. Heavy duty machine nuts, stainless steel

4. Die molded fiberglass fastening key

5. Pre-cast reinforced concrete base

6. Machine screws, ⅜" stainless steel

7. Compression-molded fiberglass cover

8. Corrosion resistant conduit clamps

FAST INSTALLATION... MINIMUM MAINTENANCE

Curblight is fastened to the roadway with standard epoxy adhesive. Incoming electrical conduit or UF cable connects for simple installation. Curblight's key-in design and stainless steel fasteners permit re-lamping in minutes.

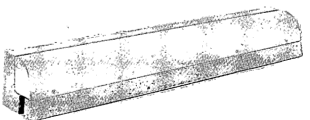

STANDARD FEATURES

- Close tolerance manufacturing for complete interchangeability of parts
- Illumination options ... long life incandescent bulbs, High Output (Rapid Start) or Slimline fluorescent lamps
- Meets National Electrical Code Standards

- Flexible installation ... accepts rigid conduit or UF cable at either end
- Corrosion resistant metal parts
- Deep base design permits at least one resurfacing
- Patents pending

The MPG Meter development began in May 1970 while fiberglass experiments were still in progress; by autumn the two men were convinced that it deserved primary attention in the company.

THE MPG METER

As shown in Exhibit I, the MPG Meter was a gage that could be mounted on the steering column, dashboard, or floor of a car to allow the driver to read directly the number of miles per gallon of gasoline his car was delivering as he drove along. The three parts of the instrument were as follows:

1. A speed switch that was attached between the car's transmission and the speedometer cable. A cam in this part opened and closed the points as the speedometer gear rotated, thus giving a series of electric pulses whose frequency was proportional to the speed the car was traveling. In effect, this indicated the "miles" for computing miles per gallon.

2. A flow meter that was inserted in the fuel line between the fuel pump and carburetor. This meter contained a tiny paddle wheel which was spun by gasoline flowing through the line at a speed directly proportional to the amount of fuel flowing. A light beam shone through the paddles to a light sensor so that it was interrupted each time a paddle passed by, thereby sending a series of electric pulses whose frequency was proportional to the "gallons" used in computing miles per gallon.

3. An indicator that was mounted in the car. An electronic circuit in the unit received the pulses from the speed switch and the flow meter to compute miles per gallon which then showed on the dial read by the driver. Neither the indicator nor the speed switch was considered patentable, but the flow meter was. Consequently, patents on the flow meter were applied for. Although other types of flow meters existed, it was considered very difficult to measure flow as accurately or inexpensively with them as could be done with the company's unit.

Installation required no special tools. To attach the speed switch, it was necessary to unscrew the speedometer cable connection at the transmission, screw the speed switch in its place, and then reconnect the cable to the speed switch. Since the flow meter had to be inserted in the fuel line between the pump and the carburetor, it was necessary to cut the line and run two flexible hoses from the cut ends to the two sides of the meter wherever it could be mounted on the body or frame of the car. The indicator was mounted to either the dashboard or floor inside the car with two self-threading screws. Six wires were used to connect the three parts of the system. These wires were fastened with metal clips that could be crimped on with pliers after cutting the wires to proper length. Tuning or adjustment of the instrument was not required after installation. Engine performance was not affected by the presence of the flow meter in the fuel line.

In operation, the gage needle would rest at zero as the engine was started and while the car was sitting still. As the car began to roll, the needle would move up to around 5 miles per gallon in a typical full-sized U.S. car during acceleration; it would then level off between 10 and 20 miles per gallon on level road. During coast or deceleration the needle would rise still further as pressure was removed from the accelerator. Because fuel flow into the carburetor was regulated by a float (similar in principle to toilets), the amount flowing could be affected by sloshing in the float bowl. Consequently, the reading of the instrument was influenced by sudden starts or stops, although normal bumps and turns did not affect it appreciably. By electronic damping in the instrument circuit the needle was restrained from responding suddenly with jerky movements and tended to "average" its reading. The most accurate reading, however, was obtained in straight, level, smooth driving.

Since the speed sensor obtained its signal from the speedometer cable, the key to accuracy of the overall instrument was the flow meter, which was accurate to within 2% at normal operating speeds. Since the company was applying for patents on the flow meter, the company expected that copying would be difficult or impossible. Instruments using other principles had to the company's knowledge been offered by two other companies as MPG meters, but Mr. Wurster described them as substantially inferior in appearance, durability, and accuracy. Literature had just been received, however, on a new competitive unit that used a small voltage generator to sense speed, a float resistance principle flow meter, and simpler gage circuitry than that of Traffic Safety. This company was offering custom prototypes at $150.00 each and announced that production units would be offered at $29.95 each in November 1971.

Traffic Safety heard of this new unit almost a year earlier, but the announced date of its offering was continually moved back, suggesting to Mr. Wurster that the company was having trouble with it. He further pointed out that the company developing it was small like Traffic Safety and principally concerned with microwave electronic products. Although the company had referred to a $29.95 mail order price before, in recent months there had been indications that the trouble they were having could increase its price. He felt that it would be unlikely that the competitive instrument's manufacturing cost would be lower than Traffic Safety's because the lower electronics cost of the competitor would be at least offset by the greater cost of its purchased meter movement. In other respects, costs would be comparable. The limited technical information that Mr. Wurster had on the new meter appears in Exhibit 5. Mr. Baatz expressed admiration for the simplicity of the circuit, but he doubted that the flow meter would be accurate to within 5% because it was based on a principle of operation that had been used in flow meters for many years.

EXHIBIT 5 Milomax MPG Meter description.

The instrument consists of three components: a speedtransducer, a flowtransducer, and indicating ma-meter. The speedtransducer is a DC-generator that generates voltage proportional to the speed of the car and is inserted between the speedometer and the speedometer cable. At 1,000 rpm of the speedometer revolutions (corresponding to 60 mph for standard U.S. cars), the voltage generated by the speedtransducer is 1 volt and is linearly proportional to speed. The flowtransducer generates resistance proportional to gasoline flow and consists of a lamp No. 53 and of a photocell. The indicating instrument is a DC-ma meter with 1 ma full scale.

CALIBRATION

The Milomax was calibrated at the factory with a precision flowmeter of ± 2% accuracy, using gasoline with specific gravity of 0.715. Battery voltage is 12 volts nominal (corresponding to 14.1 volts actual for fully charged battery).

ACCURACIES OF ACTUAL UNITS BUILT

Actual gas mileage (miles per gallon)	Indicated gas mileage (miles per gallon)
6	5.5
10	9.8
12	12.0
15	15.1
20	20.0
24	23.0
30	N.C.
40	N.C.

PRODUCTION

Outside manufacturers accounted for much of the Traffic Safety MPG Meter fabrication. Electronic components were purchased and sent to Mexico where the foreign subsidiary of another U.S. company assembled the circuit boards and wiring harnesses. Many of the mechanical parts were injection molded with dies provided by Traffic Safety. Stampings of sheet metal parts and painting of the instrument dial were also done outside. Mr. Wurster explained that the company had profited by the current economic slump in the Seattle area in having tooling made at an exceptionally low cost ($35,000 total). The company had been able to select suppliers carefully for dependable work and further economies had been realized by using "family" dies in which many parts were made at once rather than separate ones that required more labor to use.

Only drilling and tapping, all of which was done on a single drill press, winding of electric coils for the gage, and assembly of the pieces and packaging were done in the company plant, which occupied approximately 1,000 sq ft (difficult to estimate because the rooms were shared by another unrelated company), roughly half of which was used for offices. In addition to the president and the chief engineer, there were a secretary who also kept the books and a woman whose sole task was assembly. The company also employed (on a part-time basis) a graduate student who did the few drill press machining functions.

All components of the instrument had been designed by the chief engineer, Mr. Baatz, so that it would not be difficult for unskilled people to assemble the instrument. He had also designed and built the jigs and fixtures that were used in the company plant for drill press machining, holding the partially completed assemblies during fabrication, and squeezing together on an arbor press the parts of the flow meter. The most expensive piece of manufacturing equipment in the plant was the coil winder which cost about $500, had a capacity of 8 coils per hour, and was operated by one person. The $300 drill press could process 250 units per 40-hour work week, according to Mr. Wurster, and the $75 arbor press approximately 60 units per hour. Assembly and testing of the instrument, which utilized special apparatus costing around $450, could be done by one experienced person at 5 to 10 instruments per hour. It was estimated that production facilities could be doubled in the existing floor space. Suppliers were believed able to produce up to 10,000 units per month with present tooling. Typically, $2\frac{1}{2}$ months lead time was required for delivery from suppliers of ready-to-assemble components which represented about one-third of the total direct cost of the instrument.

When units were completed, they were packaged and mailed individually at a cost of $1.00 per unit. The total cost of direct labor and materials was $17.50 per unit. As of the end of August 1971, there were 50 units completely assembled and ready for shipment. All outstanding orders had been filled. Parts for another 650 units were on hand and in various stages of partial assembly. Some key parts of the instrument beyond this first "batch" had been partially redesigned to improve performance, facilitate assembly, and increase durability. A small number of these new parts were also on hand for testing. Their incorporation was not expected to greatly affect either the performance or manufacturing cost of the instrument. Mr. Wurster had prepared an estimate of direct materials and labor costs for different sales volumes as shown in Exhibit 6.

SALES

The two selling channels used as of late August 1971 were direct mail and a manufacturer's representative who dealt primarily with distributors serving recreational vehicle outlets in the Northwest. Selling efforts for the MPG Meter had begun in September 1970, with a trip to California and visits to custom auto equipment suppliers.

> They weren't much interested. We had no finished product, just a prototype in Seattle, and no reputation in the business. I guess

EXHIBIT 6 MPG Meter manufacturing cost summary.

	Lot size		
	1,000	*5,000*	*10,000*
Material			
Instrument	350.7	300.6	286.7
Cable harness	101.1	91.7	84.9
Electronics	433.3	392.9	378.7
Flow meter	226.6	167.9	151.7
Switch	92.0	63.5	56.9
Packaging	85.2	56.9	47.2
Subtotal	1288.9	1073.5	1006.1
Scrap loss @ 2%	25.7	21.5	20.1
Freight @ 2%	25.7	21.5	20.1
Subtotals, material	1340.3	1116.5	1046.3
Labor			
Instrument	—	127.0	—
Flow meter	—	67.0	—
Switch	—	44.0	—
Packaging	—	21.0	—
Subtotal, labor	259.0	259.0	259.0
Subtotal, labor and material	1599.3	1375.5	1305.3
Contingency @ 5%	80.0	69.0	65.0
Cost per hundred	1679.3	1444.5	1370.3
Unit cost	$16.80	$14.45	$13.70

those firms are accustomed to stories about wonderful new auto gimmicks from new companies that promptly fold up. They were interested enough in the concept of our product to give up appointments when we called them "cold turkey" on the phone, but in the interviews they'd just say "come back and see us when you have a finished product." So we didn't get any orders. (Statement of Chuck Wurster.)

At the suggestion of a Seattle speed shop, a manufacturer's representative in the local area was contacted who expressed great enthusiasm for the product. He was engaged in November at the customary 7½% commission, but he failed to produce orders among his connections who sold primarily to speed shops. A second representative was engaged in March who had a longer record of experience and sold mainly to distributors serving mass merchandizing outlets such as chain auto stores and discount houses. Orders for over 100 units were shortly received from stores in Seattle and Portland. The company promised delivery by May 1, but because of engineering problems and delays by suppliers who were having difficulty in completing tooling and because of a machinists strike, it was not possible to ship until mid-July. Some orders were canceled during the delay. Others were filled, but no reorders followed. "Without advertising, the instrument just didn't move off the stores' shelves," Mr. Wurster commented.

"Meanwhile, we had been thinking about selling to the recreational vehicle market. We had a booth at the rec vehicle show in Seattle during May and were impressed by the interest vehicle owners showed in the instrument at our booth, although only *four* of them actually bought units. We figured that if they were that interested, there must be some way to get their suppliers to carry the product." A representative who sold primarily to distributors of recreational vehicle supplies in Washington and Oregon was consequently engaged August 1, 1971. Although the other representative shortly resigned, this new man brought in orders for over 100 units within 2 weeks and persuaded 3 distributors to carry units, one who sold to trailer supply dealers throughout the Northwest, a second who sold to truck and new car dealers locally, and a third who sold to a number of recreational vehicle outlets in Spokane, Washington.

To stimulate direct-mail sales and also to interest other possible dealers, an advertisement offering the MPG at an introductory price of $39.95 was placed (one-sixth page costing $750) in *Popular Mechanics* (circulation 1.7 million) to appear in the July issue that came out during the last week of June. One month later a second advertisement was placed in *Trailer Life* (one-third page costing $450, circulation 200,000) for a selling price of $44.95 per instrument. "We thought of other promotion ideas, like offering units as door prizes in vehicle shows and advertising through camper clubs, but our initial attempts in these directions produced no results," said Mr. Wurster. In addition, new product releases were sent to 50 leading consumer and trade magazines in automotive and recreational fields. Mr. Wurster explained that the typical cost for mailing a brochure plus price and delivery information sent either as advertising or in response to mail inquiries from interested consumers was about 16¢ per letter which included 6¢

for the one-page color description (from which Exhibit 1 was made), plus 2¢ for a price sheet and envelope plus 8¢ for mailing.

It's hard to know just how to price an item like this. To get an independent auto store or speed shop to offer it at $44.95, we'd have to sell it to the distributor for $21.50 who would sell it to the store for $29.25. A discount store or mass merchandizer might sell it for $37.95. But what price will consumers pay? There may be some price below which volume is fairly insensitive to price and above which people just won't buy. If so, we'd like to know what it is, but we unfortunately don't. (Statement of Chuck Wurster.)

Retail prices of other dashboard instruments typically available appear in Exhibit 7.

There were approximately 71 million motor vehicles in the U.S. in 1971, and according to company information, the total automotive aftermarket (products installed after manufacture) was $14 billion in 1970, half of these sales being made by "traditional" marketers such as wholesale parts distributors, jobbers, parts stores, and gas stations. The rest went through some 50,000 mass merchandiser and mail-order outlets. Tachometer sales by volume marketers, for instance, amounted to around $7 million in 1969, and were growing at around 15% per year. There were approximately 2.5 million recreational vehicles on the road in 1970, including travel trailers, pickup campers, and motor homes (bus-type vehicles

EXHIBIT 7 Instrument retail prices.

Automobile			
Tachometers	$15.95	$ 24.95	$ 41.95
Oil pressure	5.49		
Ammeter	4.89		
Vacuum gage	10.49		
Boat			
Tachometer	$26.99	$ 38.00	
Speedometer	12.99		
Compass	10.97	13.50	17.99
Depth/fish finder	89.00	119.00	149.95

Source: Sears Catalog, *Summer, 1971.*

EXHIBIT 8　Sales Record.

Shipments	Instruments Shipped			
	Mail order		Distributors & dealers	
	Washington	Other	Washington	Other
July	4	8	57	5
August	44	15	110	24

Complaints
August　6. Excessively low reading, cause unknown.
　　　　11. Excessively low reading, cause unknown.
　　　　23. Leak in flow meter, defective assembly.
　　　　24. Vapor bubble problem on two motor homes because of fuel heating.
　　　　27. No reading because of defective transistor.
　　　　30. Excessively low reading on Mr. Wurster's own car. Components check out
　　　　　　perfectly in shop. Cause unknown.

Backing
　　As of the end of August all orders have been filled. Neither dealers nor distributors (who numbered 20 in total) reordered. No orders came during the past week.

Guarantee Form
　　A total of 16 forms (to be sent back by purchaser within 15 days of purchase to validate 1-year guarantee) were returned by retail customers.

---

furnished like trailers), and annual production exceeded 400,000 units.

Mr. Wurster estimated that approximately 75 mail inquiries had come from the *Popular Mechanics* advertisement and another 250 from the one in *Trailer Life*. A summary of orders, shipments, and complaints to date appears in Exhibit 8. He further observed that four local direct sales had resulted when friends had observed the instrument operating in his family car. "Some of them were not even particularly mechanically inclined or all that interested in mileage," he said. "But they said, 'gee, that sure is a swell looking instrument,' and bought one anyway." The most favorable letter received so far from a user appears in Exhibit 9.

Two other magazines had tested the instrument as the possible subject for articles. One had used it on a pickup truck with satisfactory results and was expected to publish the news in late October. The second had tried using it in a motor home but had not been able to get the instrument to work

properly. "Because the engine compartment was so poorly ventilated the flow meter kept getting too hot, causing the gas to vaporize so that the meter wouldn't work properly and gave a very high mileage reading," Mr. Wurster recalled. "We tried everything we could think of at the time, but we couldn't fix it. When the same problem arose on conventional cars, we were able to cure it by mounting the flow meter on the fender away from the engine and connecting it with extended rubber hoses. But in motor homes this isn't sufficient to solve the problem. So Wilf Baatz has been thinking about trying to develop some sort of vapor bypass to cure the problem."

ENGINEERING

Mr. Wilfried Baatz joined the company as technical manager with responsibility for product design and engineering in September 1969. He had received his education in mechanical engineering in German schools and prior to joining Traffic Safety he had

EXHIBIT 9   Example of favorable user response.*

August 3, 1971

Floscan Inst. Co.

Dear Sirs,

I have misplaced the guarantee card for my M.P.G. Meter. The number is 179.   The meter is installed on my Chevi Nova SS 350 engine, 1969.   After installing the meter I was sure there was something wrong with the meter, it read 6 mpg.   After many changes in gas line hookup I eliminated the vapor bubbles; then it read 8 mpg. Then the carberator was cleaned and it went to 10 mpg.   Not satisfied, I put in new distrubutor points and timed the engine.   Believe it or not, the meter now reads 20 mpg to 25 mpg in city driving.   Thanks to you for a very necessary instrument.   They should be stock on all new cars.

(signed by an Ohio user)

* Copied verbatim from handwritten original received by the company.

worked under Mr. Wurster as mechanical engineer for the fertilizer company. He had been project engineer for the construction company which built the $30 million fertilizer plant and had been hired by Mr. Wurster to stay with the factory. Mr. Wurster described him as having not only great inventive ability and analytical competence in mechanical engineering but also as being versatile and able to work well with electronic gear, production tooling, and even styling. He not only conceived the MPG Meter and developed the basic prototypes, but he also did the production tooling and much of the design of the box in which the instrument was shipped and displayed, an item on which the company had received compliments from virtually everyone who saw it.

Upon joining Traffic Safety, Mr. Baatz observed that the existing curblite design was woefully deficient and should be completely redone. The whole product was entirely redesigned and the fiberglass shield forming the curb and enclosing the light bulb was greatly strengthened, but it was not possible to make the shield as strong as fully desired without unduly diminishing its translucence. The company had, however, obtained state approval for the system, obtained distributors for it, and invested over $30,000 in tooling to make it by September 1970. By then, however, interest had shifted to the MPG Meter, a prototype of which was operating, and diminishing effort was spent on pursuing elusive sales of the curbing. By November Mr. Wurster and Mr. Baatz concluded that the wrong choice of fiberglass fabricating process had been made on the curbing but it was not worthwhile starting again to correct it. Instead, efforts should become entirely concentrated on the MPG Meter.

Development of the meter had been begun by Mr. Baatz in May 1970, after consideration of several possible alternative products, including a laser printer, trailer equipment, and exploitation of some patents that the Boeing Company was willing to

license. After Mr. Baatz conceived the basic concept for operation of the MPG Meter, he set to work on fabrication of mechanical components for a prototype unit. Two electronic technicians at the University of Washington were engaged on a consulting basis to work out the electronic circuitry. Within 4 months an experimental apparatus to test the principles of operation was working. By November the decision had been made to order production tooling and solicit sales orders for the meter.

By late August 1971 there appeared to be four alternative directions for application of Mr. Baatz' talents:

1. Debugging of the existing instrument. The two main problems seemed to be (1) formation of vapor bubbles in operation under high temperatures and (2) excessively low mileage readings in some installations. The first of these difficulties occurred in motor homes and occasionally in autos that had been driven under hot conditions and then allowed to sit or operate at low speed so that heat under the hood was not blown out, but warmed the gasoline excessively. This caused excessively high mileage readings. The cause of occasional readings that were too low was still a mystery. No other chronic problems had appeared.

2. Developing adapters for products of the Ford Motor Company and foreign producers. Because Ford speedometer cables fastened with a snap-on device rather than with threads, the MPG speed sensor would not fit on Ford transmissions. Another adapter would have to be made. Foreign cars created difficulties not only in attaching the speed sensor (Volkswagen speedometers are driven from the front wheels rather than the transmission), but also in computing miles per gallon from revolutions of the speed sensor since their speedometers did not translate from revolutions per mile to vehicle speed by the same ratios as did American cars.

3. Design of fuel consumption meters

(gallons per hour) for boats and stationary engines. A gage could be made using just the flow meter. It would be basically simpler than the MPG Meter because it would not need the speed sensor. It was estimated that Mr. Baatz could accomplish the adaptation in about one month of his own time. Mr. Wurster pointed out that although it would have fewer parts and simpler electronics, such a unit might be able to sell for a higher price because boat owners were accustomed to higher priced accessories than were most car owners. Although he considered the unit basically safe, he expected there might be considerable "red tape" to overcome in having it certified by appropriate government agencies.

4. Develop other products. Mr. Baatz had a number of ideas for other new products, including some that had been considered before the MPG Meter, and the prospect of carrying more of them through to completion appealed to him. Less appealing was the prospect of further developing Curblite, which he estimated might take from 9 to 18 months of his time plus another $30,000 for tooling and $6,000 for testing.

MANAGEMENT

The financial affairs of the company were handled by Mr. Wurster with the aid of a secretary who was trained in double-entry bookkeeping and who answered the phone, kept books, did the billing, and managed files for both Traffic Safety and the small construction company which also shared the building. In spite of all these responsibilities, she was not unduly busy. Annual audits and formal statements were prepared by a national accounting firm. "I maintain a 2 months' cash forecast against which I check expenditures," Mr. Wurster said, "but since until the last 2 months there have been zero sales, aside from checking on expenses there hasn't been much need for other management reports."

Beyond the public offering in mid-1969, the company went through two rounds of additional financing by the end of August 1971. In June 1971 the company coffers were empty. Mr. Wurster spent the better part of a month preparing a comprehensive financial proposal in the hope of obtaining an SBA guaranteed bank loan or interesting SBICs or venture capitalists in equity participation. A few nibbles resulted in nothing because the MPG Meter was an unproven product. The company finally obtained a normal bank loan by means of personal guarantees. The end of August saw the procedure repeated and again the same response. With capital requirements for inventory buildup temporarily at an end and sales beginning to develop, the company's net cash requirements appeared small enough that a few individuals could perhaps supply the needed capital through November.

Near the end of August the case writer visited a local stockbroker and inquired about underwritings of smaller companies that had been made during the past few years. One of these mentioned by the broker was Traffic Safety. The broker described this particular stock as one of the less interesting possibilities and said that he did not recommend it for investment because the company had done nothing but lose money and the stock was held by so few people (approximately 100) that the stock could be difficult for any investor who bought it to sell. He estimated that shares could be obtained if the casewriter were interested for around $5 per share. There were currently 39,000 shares outstanding.

As Mr. Wurster was contemplating these issues, two very interesting orders arrived in the mail. One was from the Hurst Performance Corporation which not only manufactured speed equipment, but also installed equipment (on a subcontract basis) on the major auto manufacturers' special models. Hurst ordered two MPG Meters, one to be installed on their custom Gran Prix Pontiac and the other on a new version of the minicompact Chevrolet Vega shortly to be offered in custom form through auto dealers. A few days later an order for three MPG Meters was received from testing laboratories of the General Motors Technical Center in Warren, Michigan.

> We're not sure what these orders mean. If meters were suddenly ordered in large volume by auto companies, we couldn't possibly fill them. On the other hand, if they did the manufacturing in volume, they could probably cut our costs by at least half. Presumably we should then expect some sort of royalty arrangement. Then there would be the question of what sort of terms we should seek. Possibly they are just testing the gage to keep abreast of developments and won't be interested in using it as an option on their cars or trucks. I'm wondering what our plans should be with all these uncertainties in the wind and what action we should be taking meanwhile.

> I'd like to see us become a medium small company with from 200 to 300 employees based on products that have a unique technical proprietary edge plus low manufacturing cost. But I'd rather not have to cut quality to get that cost. I don't want a company in which there are so many people that everyone is looked upon as a digit and employees are regarded as a means to reach human goals. As we grow I'd like to have us add more creative people like Wilf and give them lots of freedom to develop new products. Then as they "score," they should be rewarded with stock options and other remuneration so that they can become financially independent to pursue their own creative interests as Wilf would like to. (Statement of Chuck Wurster.)

Smalltren Engineering, Inc.

Joseph Small, owner and president of Smalltren Engineering, Inc., was concerned about the future of his company in the fall of 1970:

> I've got some very important decisions to make. There are all these opportunities that I have to act on or they will start disappearing. How am I going to take advantage of them and still keep Smalltren running properly? (Statement of Mr. Small.)

Smalltren Engineering, Inc. was a job order machine shop in Rockland, Massachusetts, a town of 15,000 people, approximately 20 miles from Boston. The company employed 18 people. Its sales, consisting of machined metal parts made in small quantity to customer order, were at an annual volume of about $180,000. The shop and offices were in a single-story, 40-year-old,

This case was prepared by Robert Lund. Copyright © 1971 by the President and Fellows of Harvard College.

5,600-sq-ft building. This building and an adjacent 3,000-sq-ft parking lot were owned by Smalltren.

The shop comprised a number of general-purpose machine tools, including engine lathes, milling machines, grinders, punch presses, and welding and brazing equipment (see layout in Exhibit 1). The only specialized machines in the shop were two electrical discharge machining (EDM) tools used in forming complex holes in electrically conductive material.

At one side of the main shop area were workbenches for hand operations and assembly. A room at the front of the building served as the foreman's office, as a parts inspection area, and as the place where finished jobs were kept prior to delivery. Mr. Small's large, comfortably furnished office and a reception room were adjacent to the shop and the foreman's office.

Mr. Small began his company in October

EXHIBIT 1   Smalltren Engineering, Inc., plant layout, November 1970.

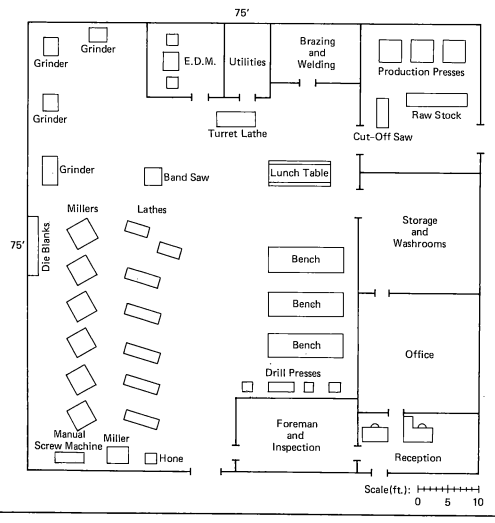

1961 in the basement of his home. At that point he was a highly skilled machinist, having worked for 5 years in a large machine shop of the Raytheon Company and for 4 years in a small, privately owned job shop. When Mr. Small told the owner of the job shop of his decision to start out on his own, he was told, "You're crazy. How do you expect a Black to get work when a white man can't?"

At the start, Mr. Small had only a hand-operated screw machine, a specialized lathe used for turning and boring small parts in quantities of 100 to 5,000 pieces. The early years were difficult, particularly because it was difficult to get profitable jobs. Mr. Small frequently took work on subcontract from other machine shops. "When you get that kind of job, the profit is all gone before you get your hands on the work," Mr. Small recalled.

In spite of problems of discrimination and limited profits, the company managed to grow. As Mr. Small added machines, he moved from his basement to a storefront building (where he had to jack up the wooden floors periodically to level his machine tools), and then to the fourth floor of a vacant textile mill.

By 1964 Mr. Small had two milling machines, four lathes, and several drill presses. In addition to himself, he employed one full-time machinist and one half-time machinist. It was at this point that he had a chance to lease a 3,000-sq-ft building in Rockland. Although it would have been an improvement, Mr. Small felt that occupancy costs would have increased his overhead beyond the point where Smalltren's income could handle it. The owner of the building, impressed by Mr. Small's shop, offered to help cover the rental costs by having Smalltren make some of the parts which he sold in his sign and display business. On this basis, Smalltren moved into the larger quarters. Mr. Small expected to sublet half the area, but within 6 months he had expanded into the entire building. He added one more man full time. At the end of a year he arranged to buy the property; within 4 years he had constructed an addition to the building and had outgrown that. In 1968 Mr. Small purchased the building that is the present home of Smalltren, and he sold the smaller plant.

In 1970 there were 14 hourly paid machinists in the shop. Eight worked for Smalltren full time and the other six each worked an average of 18 hours a week. The normal full-time workweek averaged 48 hours. Pay ranged from $2.40 to $3.90 per hour, averaging $3.15.

The work force was supplemented by Mr. Small and Paul Chinn, the foreman. Both men spent an appreciable part of their time working at the machines. Mr. Small, Mr. Chinn, and a semiretired journeyman tool and die maker who worked half-time were the most highly skilled of the group. Mr. Chinn felt that the availability of other highly skilled machinists was low:

> It's hard to get good machinists these days. Youngsters don't want to go into this kind of work. With skilled machinists' rates down

around $4.00 an hour, they see construction trades paying $7.00 an hour, and they go into those trades. (Statement of Mr. Chinn.)

Mr. Small made all of the customer contacts and arranged for the work that was subcontracted from other shops. He spent about 40% of his time on the road in one or the other of these activities, 40% of his time working in the shop as a machinist, and 20% in general administrative functions.

Mr. Chinn was the second in command to Mr. Small. He supervised the men in the shop, ordered materials and supplies, did most of the job estimating, assigned work to the machinists, and inspected finished work before it was delivered to the customer. These duties consumed about 50% of his time, and the balance was spent working in the shop.

The two staff people in the organization were Mrs. Mahoney, Mr. Small's secretary, who acted as receptionist and secretary, and Mr. Fogg, recently hired to handle accounting and order control. Mr. Fogg had worked for the previous tenants of the building and "really knows the overheads," according to Mr. Small. Mr. Fogg was expected to dispatch all jobs to the shop, set up and maintain records on each job, and establish and maintain a cost control system for the company. Until Mr. Fogg was hired, Mr. Small followed some of the jobs in the shop and Mr. Chinn kept track of others, but record keeping had been very informal and incomplete.

Information needed for tax matters was handled by a public accounting firm, which maintained a set of accounts at its office for Smalltren on the basis of monthly information supplied by Mr. Fogg. Mr. Small received an interim income statement every 4 months and a year-end income statement and balance sheet from this firm. Their services cost $1,200 in 1969.

Smalltren handled a wide variety of machined-part fabrication. An order typically was for 1 to 20 pieces, with an average unit value of approximately $10.00 and an average order value of $150.00. Occasionally an order would be received for 500 to 5,000 pieces, but the average unit value then was normally less than $1.00.

Most orders were received on the basis of firm bids; a customer would send an engineering drawing, and either Mr. Chinn or Mr. Small would estimate the work and submit a bid price to the customer. If the bid were accepted, the drawing and a job report showing the operations sequence used in preparing the estimate were given to one of the machinists. Typically, the job would require operations on two or more different types of machines. The machinist responsible for the job would list on the job report the operations he performed and the number of hours (to the nearest half-hour) he spent on each operation. The completed parts, the drawing, and the job slip were returned to the foreman, Mr. Chinn, who inspected the pieces, checked the times reported on the job card, and arranged for the shipment of the finished parts to the customer.

A consistent "bread and butter" source of income (30% of sales volume) was the fabrication of steel die sets which were used in punch presses to form the outline of a part or to make holes of various shapes in sheet material. The die block, which contained the hole into which the mating die punch was driven by a punch press, started out as a "blank," or steel cylinder formed on a lathe. The blank was then set up on an EDM machine, and the hole was literally "eaten away" by electric spark erosion, using a graphite electrode machined to the shape of the hole.

The blank for the die punch was also turned on a lathe. The finished shape might have been produced on a milling machine, lathe, grinder, or a combination of all these machines. The two parts of the die set were sent out for heat treating, which hardened the metal, and then brought back for finish grinding, inspection, application of a protective wax coating, and shipment to the customer.

The shop had a small heat-treating oven, but it was seldom used. Jobs requiring heat treating (approximately 25% of all jobs) were usually sent out to a larger firm which

had ovens in continuous use and which could certify the temperatures used and the degree of hardness attained. This firm maintained instruments and records of tests that provided some insurance in the case of a customer complaint.

There were a limited number of die sizes used by most punch presses. For this reason, it was possible to make up a small work-in-process inventory of die blanks and also a finished inventory of die sets for frequently ordered standard-sized holes. This inventory normally consisted of about 500 pieces divided among 12 different sizes, and it was worth about $10,000. The inventory varied considerably, however, because the making of die blanks was used as a fill-in job whenever business was slow.

As of November 1970, capacity utilization on the EDM machines was approximately 50%, on a one-shift basis. Sales of die sets were made in several ways. Some orders were obtained in the course of Mr. Small's visits to customers. An additional amount was ordered by telephone and mail by customers who had initially been reached by mail advertising. Mr. Small had bought from Dun and Bradstreet a listing of all potential customers for die work in Connecticut, Rhode Island, Massachusetts, and New Hampshire. He had sent to each of these a brochure and price list on the standard die sets and a group of diagrams to assist the customer in describing special shapes. A third source of die set sales for the past year had been a machinery sales representative in Waltham, Massachusetts. This had proved to be a growing source for larger-sized orders. Mr. Small had also been in touch with two manufacturers of punch presses; both firms were interested in subcontracting the die orders they received. Mr. Small believed that he could obtain enough work to completely fill the EDM capacity from this source, but he was sure that the prices he would be able to charge would give him a very small margin over shop costs. A die set for which he would normally charge a customer $38.00 would bring about $17.00 from the punch press manufacturers. The sales representative would sell the same die set for $36.00 and was billed at 75% of his selling price.

Although Mr. Small had not recently obtained actual unit cost figures for standard punch and die sets, his best estimate of the direct costs in a typical $38.00 die set was approximately $13.30 (see Exhibit 2).

Pricing for contract machining, not punch and die sets, was prepared by estimating the expected number of machine hours required and the weight of the amount of raw material required. These were then priced at a rate of $3.50 per hour for labor on the lathe, milling machine, or grinder and $15.00 per hour for labor on the EDM machine, and at the appropriate price per pound for the material. Although material costs varied from job to job, experience showed them to average 9% of the job price. Shop overhead was then applied at the rate of 80% of the sum of the direct labor and direct material. To the total shop cost for labor, material, and overhead, 40% additional was added to cover administrative and selling expenses and profit. As a rough check of the correctness of an estimate, or to prepare a quick bid, the price of a job was figured by multiplying the estimated number of hours by $12.00 per hour. Jobs requiring electric discharge machining were priced to yield a higher return, about $25.00 per hour, for time spent in setup and operation of the EDM machine.

A major factor in being able to secure work, Mr. Small realized, was the differential between Smalltren's rate and the rates of $15.00 to $20.00 per hour that were charged by shops in larger companies. During tight times, when excess machining capacity existed in other shops, this differential shrank, and a lower rate had to be used if Smalltren were to continue to get business. During the business slowdown in early 1970, for example, large companies placed a greater share of their work in their own in-house shops, and cost reduction pressures on their buyers caused them to sharpen up their practices. The resulting competition among job shops for the available work depressed prices severely. Some of Smalltren's bids had to be made at the equivalent of an $8.00 per hour price, and a few were priced as low as $6.00 per hour just to get work into the shop.

As the end of 1970 approached, Mr. Small felt that Smalltren was established and that he could expect to have a steady volume of business as long as he maintained close contacts with his customers and competitive prices. The slowdown in business volume in

---

EXHIBIT 2 Estimate of direct costs in a standard die set for Smalltren Engineering, Inc.

Operations, in sequence	Machine type	Machine hours	Machine rate	Total cost
Form punch and die blanks	Lathe	0.50	$ 3.50	$ 1.75
Form graphite electrode for die	Lathe/miller	0.25	3.50	0.88
Preliminary machining of die	Lathe/miller	0.17	3.50	0.58
EDM machining of die	EDM machine	0.33	15.00	5.00
Form punch	Lathe/miller	0.25	3.50	0.88
Finish machining	Grinder	0.50	3.50	1.75
				$10.84
Material cost, alloy steel for punch and die blanks				2.00
Subcontract cost, heat treating for punch and die sets				0.50
				$13.34

Note: Machine rates include allowance for average wage ($3.15) of operator, plus depreciation and electrical power required for each machine.

early 1970 had led him to feel that he might have been overextended, but the volume of work was picking up again by the end of the year, and he expected that total sales would be approximately $180,000. Mr. Small was concerned, however, since company operations in 1969 had produced a loss of $11,850 on sales of $156,800, and he felt that the increase in business in 1970, which was less than he had projected at the start of the year, might not be enough to insure profitable performance. The income statement and balance sheet for Smalltren Engineering, Inc. for 1969 are given in Exhibits 3 and 4.

EXHIBIT 3 Income statement for Smalltren Engineering, Inc., for the fiscal year ending December 31, 1969.

Sales		$156,837
Cost of goods sold:		
Purchases, material	$13,684	
Purchases, subcontract heat treating and machining	6,682	
Direct shop labor	70,603	
Direct shop overhead	12,040	—103,009
Gross profit		$ 53,828
Overhead expenses:		
Administrative expenses	23,227	
Taxes on real estate	4,422	
Depreciation on building and equipment	5,698	— 33,347
Owner's salary and commissions:		
Salary for Mr. Small	18,200	
Commissions for Mr. Small	14,131	— 32,331
Loss for the year:		($ 11,850)

EXHIBIT 4 Balance sheet for Smalltren Engineering, Inc., for the fiscal year ending December 31, 1969.

Cash (account overdrawn)	($ 6,745)		Accounts payable	$11,641
Accounts receivable	19,364		Equipment loans due	13,682
Depository receipts	300		Payroll taxes due	8,698
Finance charges prepaid	3,304			34,021
Inventory, raw materials	16,854			
Inventory, finished goods	3,619		Equipment loans, long-term	16,035
Advances to employees	1,835			
	38,513		Capital stock	4,000
			Retained earnings, 1968	55,470
Machinery and shop equipment	60,403		Less loss for 1969	—11,850
Office furniture and equipment	3,171			47,620
Vehicles (2)	10,475			
Reserve for depreciation	(16,658)			
	57,391			
Miscellaneous assets	1,772			
	$97,676			$97,676

In addition to the possibility of continued losses for fiscal 1970, Mr. Small was concerned about the demands of the business on himself. He felt that he had to continue making the rounds of customers' plants in order to get jobs; he would have liked to be out getting orders 3 days a week, but 2 days a week was closer to the average:

> I'd like to be out much more because you'd be surprised how much business you get just because you happen to be at the buyer's office at the right time—and how much you lose if you don't keep making the calls. I have visited a buyer to tell him what kind of work we can do, and he has said, "I don't have anything for you right now, but I'll call you as soon as something comes up." The next time I happen to be in his office, he'll say, "Gosh, do I wish you had come in yesterday; we had a hot job that would have been a natural for you, but we let it out to someone else." (Statement of Mr. Small.)

Half of the jobs in the shop were obtained by Mr. Small's routine personal contacts. He felt that it was essential that the person making the calls be an experienced machinist; Mr. Smith recalled that when he had been asked to advise a sheet metal firm that was having trouble getting business, he had found that the salesman did not even' know how to read blueprints. He had advised the manager of that firm to send his shop foreman out as the salesman, and business had started to increase. Mr. Small, however, did not want to spend too much time away from his own company; he felt that the pace of work slackened when he was not there:

> When I am in the shop, I can keep two or three machines going. I can see if someone is having trouble getting a job set up, and I can help him so that he doesn't waste a half-day trying to figure it out. I can hear how we are doing. If someone is using a dull tool, I can hear it from across the shop and get him to sharpen it before he ruins the job. And I can make sure that jobs are completed and delivered so that they don't hang around in the shop. (Statement of Mr. Small.)

Mr. Small was also concerned that it was difficult for him to get a close feel for the financial performance of the company. Until Mr. Fogg's recent arrival, Smalltren had existed with only part-time bookkeeping assistance. The lack of records, the need for both Mr. Small and Mr. Chinn to perform much of the highly skilled work in the shop, and the relative inexperience of both men in the use of records for control purposes all contributed to Mr. Small's qualms. The $12.00 per hour rate had been established only a few months ago; the previous rate had been $10.00. Mr. Small recalled how difficult it was to know what rate should be charged:

> Every week I would ask my secretary, "How are we doing?" Sometimes she would tell me there wasn't enough cash in the bank for next week's payroll. Then I would go through the accounts receivable and pick out invoices on which I was sure I could get quick payment. I would call the buyer and ask if he could send a check. Sometimes when Friday afternoon came, the checks were not in yet and I had to pay the men out of my own pocket and make out an I.O.U. from Smalltren. I was busy trying to get work for the shop; the secretary was just taking care of the checkbook, and neither of us had any real idea of just what was going on.
>
> This went on for months. Then one night I sat up in bed and said, "Dammit, something has to be wrong!" I got dressed, drove down to the office, got out all the records, and studied them. In the morning I called the accountant and the secretary and told them I wanted to know immediately just where I stood. They went to work and when they were through I found that I was covering less than half (43%) of my overhead with the volume of work I was getting out of the shop. We changed the bidding rate to $12.00 per hour, and I went out to the shop and called the men together. I told them that they just had to get more work through the shop or I would have to let some of them go. They had been slowing down because they felt that there were fewer jobs coming in. After I talked to them, things started to improve somewhat.
>
> You have to know how to make money. Take this big job we just got. Paul Chinn wants to give this lots of attention so that it gets finished and delivered. But you have to keep the small jobs going too, because they have to produce the cash to meet the payroll

each week. The other day I found a job just waiting for deburring and packaging. I told Paul to get that job out right away. We needed the $913.00. It is hard for others to have the same feel for priorities that the owner has. (Statement of Mr. Small.)

Mr. Small's concern for the financial performance of his company was magnified by his awareness of new opportunities that were available to him during the late fall of 1970. There were four major alternatives among these opportunities; some of them seemed to be logical extensions of Smalltren's present business, but others would involve significant changes and increased risks:

1. Sheet Metal Fabrication in the Existing Shop. Mr. Small felt that a sheet metal fabricating capability would complement his machine shop and permit him to take on a broader range of jobs that he could handle in-house. Smalltren had three stamping presses that could be used to cut and form light sheet metal into various shapes, and it had an electric arc welder and oxyacetylene brazing equipment. The major pieces of equipment that would be needed were a brake and a shear (a brake is used to bend sheet metal, generally at 90° angles, to form a square or rectangular unit; a shear is used to make a straight cut across sheet metal) ; Mr. Small felt that he could buy used equipment for about $20,000. He could then hire a skilled sheet metal worker to handle the jobs and would add people only as the work increased. Since press, brake, and shear operations can be performed by relatively low-skilled people, he would be able to hire apprentices or trainees who could start in the shop on these jobs when volume permitted.

Smalltren was already handling some sheet metal jobs by farming the work out to others. Because the customers for sheet metal work were often the same firms who now purchased machined parts, and because their buyers were often the same men whom Mr. Small now visited, the amount of additional sales time re-

quired to obtain sheet metal fabrication orders was considered to be fairly low.

2. Sheet Metal Fabrication in a Separate Shop. Expansion in the Rockland shop was limited to three or four more machines because zoning regulations prohibited additions to the existing building. An alternative being considered by Mr. Small was the establishment of a sheet metal shop in Roxbury, a community in metropolitan Boston having a high Black population and a high proportion of unskilled and unemployed people. Mr. Small, who was born and grew up in Roxbury, had two partners in a liquor store venture in that area; one had a full-time job as a draftsman and the other managed the liquor store. Both wanted to get into manufacturing, but they lacked experience in shop operations. Mr. Small believed that the two men had the ability to manage a shop similar to his if they could obtain the necessary experience.

By locating a shop in or near Roxbury, Mr. Small could provide training and job opportunities to disadvantaged people and receive financial support from the government for doing so. Smalltren had already been asked to participate in one such program at the Rockland plant. This was in the JOBS programs of the National Alliance of Businessmen, a voluntary organization of about 30,000 firms assisting the U.S. Department of Labor in finding jobs and providing training and promotion opportunities for disadvantaged people. A proposal for five trainees in an Entry Program for machine operator positions had been prepared in the summer of 1970. Approximately $2,700 per trainee would have been awarded to Smalltren for the training program, with the beginning rate paid to the trainees set at $2.50 per hour minimum. This proposal was still being weighed by Mr. Small as of November 1970, but the 18-mile distance from Roxbury to Rockland was considered a barrier. About one-half of his present labor force lived in Roxbury, but Mr. Small realized that a skilled machinist with a steady job was better able to afford this transportation.

There was some indication that Mr. Small would be able to obtain financial support for the separate business in the form of loans from banks, backed by a 90% guarantee by the Small Business Administration. A considerably larger proposal, made by Mr. Small in 1969 in connection with an acquisition bid for another company, had been well received by Boston banks.

Since setting up a new shop meant a steep increase in overhead costs, a corresponding increase in total sales volume would be needed. The inexperience of the potential managers of the new shop meant that the venture would absorb a good portion of Mr. Small's time. Equity funds for the new venture would have to come in large part from Mr. Small or from Smalltren. These factors, plus the financial and legal work necessary to set up the operation, were some of the difficulties Mr. Small anticipated.

3. Contract Assembly of Prototype Machines. As a consequence of the aggressive efforts of a major U.S. manufacturing corporation to purchase more goods and services from minority-owned businesses, Smalltren had recently been awarded several orders for complete prototype machine assemblies. One such order, in the amount of $9,100, was for a precision liquid metering and dispensing unit for an electronic assembly line. The unit had 500 separate machined parts, and tolerances were as close as 0.0005 in. This was the first time the unit had been made; if the prototype model worked successfully, it was possible that as many as six additional units would be ordered.

To qualify as a bidder on a contract assembly job such as this, Smalltren was visited by an appraisal team from the company. Small, single-part jobs were then sent to Smalltren for bids. Over a period of 2 months, Smalltren successfully bid for and completed a number of these jobs and then was awarded the prototype assembly work:

> I knew that they were checking me out on the nickel-and-dime stuff, but I began to wonder when I was going to get a decent-sized job from them. Then one day I got a call from the buyer, who said, "Joe, we have inspected each job you have sent us, and I want you to know that you have passed our performance requirements. You can expect to get some larger jobs now. We will be flying up to see you tomorrow with a job we think you may be able to handle. (Statement of Mr. Small.)

The buying team, a buyer and a design engineer, went over detail drawings with Mr. Small and explained the process of bidding on the job. The buyer left with Mr. Small a copy of a written procedure for making an estimate. It took 3 days for Mr. Small and Mr. Chinn, working separately, to make up estimates, which they then compared. When they were reasonably sure that they were in agreement, Mr. Small called the buyer and told him their tentative price. The buyer indicated that his estimate for the job was in the same vicinity, and the price was agreed upon. Delivery was set for 8 weeks.

Mr. Chinn set up a large table in the center of the shop and put out on it the drawing for each part in the assembly, the work record sheet for that part, and the raw stock required to make the part. He then issued jobs to the machinists from this table. After inspection, the machined parts were returned to the table to await assembly.

Assembly, however, was difficult because there were tolerance and clearance problems that are endemic in building a new machine. Mr. Small got prompt assistance from the customer's buyer on these problems; the buyer would either get an answer for him or have one of the design engineers on the project fly to Boston to work out an answer on the spot. One week before the completed unit was to be delivered, two of the customer's engineers arrived with 12 additional changes that were needed to make the parts fit together. Many of these changes were simple relocations of holes, but two pieces had to be completely made over:

There are always changes in a prototype model because there are engineering problems, but you can't blame the engineers; it is difficult to foresee all the troubles. The company agreed to allow extra money for the changes and to allow an extension of the delivery date, but hoped I could stick to the original date. (Statement of Mr. Small.)

One week after the original delivery date, the unit was still in the shop. Because of a final design fault, some of the pneumatic fittings had interferences with the front of the cabinet. Mr. Chinn had consulted with the design engineer and had gotten agreement to rework the fittings; a list of the changes required and their costs had been set up. An invoice for the job had been sent to the customer on the scheduled delivery date, but it was not clear that this would be paid until actual delivery was accomplished. The amount of the invoice was $1,650 higher than the contract price, and it was expected that additional costs would be billed at shipment.

Jobs like these would increase, Mr. Small felt, if Smalltren demonstrated that it could handle the initial orders capably. He realized that his inspection equipment was barely adequate to handle jobs of this complexity and that he would have to purchase an optical comparator (a device that projects a precisely enlarged profile of the part to be inspected on a ground glass screen for measurement of critical dimensions) for $3,000 to $5,000 and additional gages for an equivalent amount.

4. *Government Procurement of Fabricated Items.* As part of its program to assist minority businesses, the General Services Administration (GSA) has set aside a portion of its normal procurement funds to be used in buying items that could be made by minority enterprises. If a capability to make an item at a reasonable price could be demonstrated, the

procurement would be directed to the minority firm through the Small Business Administration. Mr. Small had visited the regional GSA Supply Depot to see items that he might be able to make. He found several small assemblies which the government bought in quantities of 100,000 or more per year which he believed he could make. One of these was a metal looseleaf calendar holder, consisting of an enameled sheet metal base, a formed wire retainer, and four rubber inserts. Another was a magnetic display board clip, consisting of a piece of flexible magnetic plastic material, a rivet, washer, and a spring clip. Mr. Small believed that he could design and make all the necessary tooling to form the metal pieces and that he could easily buy the plastic and rubber items. No additional machine tools would be required, but a small assembly area would have to be set up and inexpensive riveting, cementing, and packaging stations would be needed. His cost estimates showed that he could quote prices comparable to those now paid by the government. Because procurement would be directed to Smalltren on a noncompetitive basis, the bids did not have to be lower than the prices which the government now paid.

Mr. Small felt that he should decide quickly about these new opportunities, but he was not certain what decision he should make on the future direction of his firm.

ASSIGNMENT

Design a strategy or method of competition for Smalltren Engineering, Inc. Be certain that you include both explicit goals and objectives for the firm and the major functional policies and plans in marketing, market research, production, finance, R&D, and the organizational structure and systems to achieve these goals and objectives in a consistent and distinctive strategy.

11

Expansion of a Smaller Company

Sometimes you will hear "a business must grow or die." It's not that simple. As pointed out in the introductory chapter, some businesses are in lines of work, such as shoe repair or flower sales, in which expansion is very unlikely, perhaps impossible. Others may have a choice. Some restaurants, for example, have expanded into chains although they could alternatively have confined themselves to one location and continued to do well. Similarly, some manufacturers have deliberately kept from expanding into broader lines or reaching to more distant geographical markets while others have parlayed the same lines into much larger empires. Finally, there have been some lines of work in which companies have either had to grow large or perish; examples are the manufacture of medium-priced automobiles, airplanes, and household detergents. Small companies that embark on trajectories of sales growth, either by choice or necessity, reap benefits and encounter special management problems that deserve careful attention and forethought to circumvent disasters and make the most of opportunities.

ADVANTAGES AND DISADVANTAGES OF GROWTH

Whether or not a company should grow is in part a function of the kind of business it is. It is also very much a function of executive and owner choice, reflecting their attitudes toward risk taking, how hard they want to work, and their drives for profits and achievement.

Some of the advantages of growth include the following:

1. Profits usually increase with growing sales. For stockholders, this can mean increased dividends and appreciation of the value of the stock.

2. A growing organization creates opportunities for employees to move up faster to higher responsibilities and pay. Without growth, it may be impossible to attract and keep ambitious younger managers.

3. For executives, growth means challenge, more capacity to affect the world in which the company finds itself, and the opportunity to build something of lasting importance.

4. If growth is carefully managed, it can mean greater security as the company lessens its reliance on a small number of managers, customers, and products. Large firms are less at the mercy of their environments and hence less likely to fail.

5. Growth can preempt opportunities and prevent competitors from growing stronger. The manager who chooses not to grow when his firm serves a growing market is inviting competition.

Growth does not automatically confer these benefits. Some profitable small firms have become unprofitable larger ones. Some companies that have failed would still exist had they not placed such extreme emphasis upon growth.

In Chapter 7 on organization management and control, some of the specific problems associated with developing and controlling a growing organization were examined. These included the changing role of the founder, the necessity for increased specialization and delegation, and the problems of developing more formal methods of keeping informed and controlling a growing organization.

Management must not only be sensitive to these problems, but it must also guard against the following threats associated with growth:

1. Impersonality, which tends to come with larger size, can lead to higher employee turnover. Possible antidotes include deliberate efforts to pay more attention to individuals through evaluation and review procedures, personnel training programs, house periodicals, recreation programs, pension and profit sharing plans, and other fringe benefits.

2. Impersonality may also work its way out to contact with customers, causing poor service, alienation, and loss of sales. Measures to combat impersonality include spot-checking by managers in the field, surveys of customers to assess satisfaction, solicitation of customer comments on service through mail campaigns, and careful analysis of and response to complaints, unexpected dips in sales, or losses of formerly loyal customers.

3. Cash liquidity can be imperiled by any rapid bursts of expansion. Such a "cash crunch" can unnerve suppliers and lenders, causing them to "crack down" by calling loans or putting the company on C.O.D. delivery, which in turn can slow production, cause delays in delivery, lose sales, and put an end to the growth or even to the company itself. The best remedy is careful financial forecasting and use of cash budgets to anticipate needs and prepare for them in advance.

4. Increases in direct costs are very likely to occur as it becomes necessary to add new people and train them. This will introduce some mistakes and inefficiencies. These should diminish with time as the "learning curve" takes effect and as the company is able to introduce economies of scale through expanded production. If they do not diminish, something is probably growing slack in the organization and needs to be tightened up.

5. Creeping overhead increases constitute a continuing pressure as the company grows. Parkinson's law makes itself felt through any number of reasons to add staff to perform more functions. (Does the company really need departments for public relations, market research, employee relations, and data processing yet?) Pressure also develops to add various assets and outside services, all of which increase overhead costs unless continual review and vigilant emphasis on cost control are maintained. (How about redecorating the president's office? Should a janitorial service firm or an industrial design firm be put on retainer?)

6. Executive time demands multiply as the company grows. In order to take on required new contacts and activities, some of the old ones will have to go. Great fractions of time can be consumed by conversations with old customers and employees who call up or drop in. Reading reports, newspapers, magazines, and trade publications can also become great "time sinks." A logical antidote is to keep a record in half-hour intervals of where time goes for a week or two and then analyze the record in relation to things that most need to be done. The manager can then formulate a new time pattern and work on habit changes needed to implement it. This may be the point where a small company executive decides not to become a big company executive but rather to withdraw into some more appealing role as the company grows and as it demands different executive disciplines. Examples of other roles include chairman of the board, R&D consultant, or founder of a new subsidiary of the original firm.

Management must not only consider whether or not to grow, but it must also consider the optimal rate of growth. It is sometimes difficult to limit growth, particularly if the firm is trying to maintain market share in a rapidly growing market or meet the expanding needs of a major customer. Growth, however, can often be controlled by the amount of promotion, by the rate at which new customers and orders are sought, by pricing policies, and by decisions about introducing new products. For every business, there is probably an optimal rate of growth that is related to cash flows, the availability and skill level of prospective employees, and the ability and willingness of management to change and develop new skills.

STRATEGY

For both stable and growing firms, management must think carefully about strategy. Strategy refers to what kind of company a given firm is and what it seeks to become. Explicit consideration of strategy is particularly important in the growing company. Such firms have an increasing number of new managers, all of whom are making decisions based upon assumptions about the direction of growth and change for the firm. A growing firm is also more likely to be changing because it has new customers, new markets, and possibly new methods of competing.

A way to state the firm's strategy is to answer briefly the following questions in a one paragraph summary profile. By generating alternative fictional answers to these questions for some future point in time it is possible to explore different kinds of companies it could seek to become, from which should be selected the one most appropriate.

COMPANY PROFILE

The [*name of company*] company produces [*what product or service?*] as part of the [*what is the general industry it is in? It should be possible to state several different ways, each of which will have different implications for strategy*] industry. It employs [*how many people of what general skill levels?*] and is located [*where? For some types of business, such as retailing, this can be much more important than others such as musical instrument making*]. Its customers are [*what types of firms or individuals?*] who are located [*where— local or widespread?*], and who make their buying decisions on the basis of [*what?*]. The company sells through [*what channels?*], has annual sales of [*how much?*], and competes with [*what other firms?*]. Its main selling appeal in contrast to competitors is [*what?*]. The company has approximately [*what fraction?*] of this market while [*how many?*] of its competitors have larger fractions than this. The company president holds [*what fraction?*] of the company ownership, other officers hold [*what fraction?*] and other employees [*what fraction?*]. It operates on a total equity of $[*how much?*], and earns $[*how much?*] in profit plus a draw to the owner of $[*how much?*] with a debt-equity ratio of [*how much?*]. Owners' objectives are to see the company progress in the direction of [*what main goals?*].

A goal that has much to recommend it for many companies is to achieve the largest share of the particular market in which it specializes. History has demonstrated that the firm that manages to attain this position tends to have the lowest per unit cost of production and hence the highest profit margin. These lowered costs are derived from the effect of learning curves (those who practice more perform better) and from economies of scale (larger volume allows greater investment in cost-cutting measures and machinery, and larger volume spreads R&D, advertising, and selling costs thinner, etc.). As a result of the greater margin and sales, the company is able to cut prices lower than competitors, thereby driving marginal producers that have small market shares out of business to increase its market share still further, and so forth. Industries are continually seeing this Darwinian process of competitive survival occur, and it is one of the strongest arguments for a small company to seek to grow.

How can a small company have a large market share? The answer depends both on the definition of the market and on the focus chosen for the company's work. For example, General Motors has the largest share of the total U.S. auto market (and the highest profit margins of the large auto makers), but there are smaller companies that specialize in pieces of that market, such as Midas which makes only mufflers and smaller companies which manufacture only speed equipment. The reason that some very small companies are able to prosper in the auto industry, while even large ones such as Chrysler and American Motors, because of their small market shares relative to the leader, General Motors, have trouble surviving, is that the small companies are highly specialized and concentrate on smaller portions of the overall market in which they can enjoy market shares that are large in relative terms. Thus, the *best* strategy for a small company is likely to include a high degree of specialization so that the company, however small, can be dominant in those things it does.

Some things a small firm can seek to capitalize upon in reaching for market share include the following:

1. Quickness. When unanticipated opportunities arise, management in a small company can decide quickly to take advantage of them without the delays of clearing with committees and following standard procedures that slow down less alert or more bureaucratic competitors.

2. Exceptional Quality. While a company is small its top management can pay closer attention to performance of employees at the operating levels and thereby ensure quality.

3. Geographical Closeness. By concentrating on those customers to whom it is closest a small company may be able to give closer attention, greater convenience, and quicker service than can its competitors headquartered farther away.

4. Customized Treatment. By concentrating on a smaller number of customers a small company can more easily make exceptions to tailor products or services to their needs than can competitors who are larger and have to be more standardized.

5. Innovativeness. Although larger companies can support more research and can better tolerate the investments and lead times needed for bringing new ideas to market, small firms can more easily attempt incremental changes because their investment in the status quo is less.

6. Low-Volume Markets. Bigger companies cannot afford to proliferate their products or services to serve very small markets, such as wall-sized television receivers or surgical bone drills. Thus, these markets are left for small companies to exploit.

By concentrating on strength in one or more of these special characteristics in which smallness is an advantage, a smaller company can in effect select a market in which it can achieve a dominant share. This in turn can provide a base from which to grow larger either by (1) penetration into still further share of that market, (2) geographical expansion, nationally and perhaps internationally to similar markets, or (3) vertical integration to become its own supplier and/or its own distributor as well as producer. Diversification is a fourth possibility, either through expansion into broader lines, related lines, or unrelated lines. Caution must be taken in this approach, however, not to go in new directions where the company's market share will not have a chance to become large or where it does not have some justifying competitive advantage. There have also been many entrepreneurs who have developed small companies successfully in several different fields, sometimes simultaneously.

Strategy formulation is necessarily a circular process, which may cycle through the following steps to pick what seems to be the best direction for the company to take:

1. Existing Strategy. What is the company's present profile as suggested above? What does it seem to be aiming toward?

2. Performance Trends. How well has the company been doing in terms of profits, comparison of products or service to the competition, rate of growth, market share, employee morale, and so forth? How have these been changing over time?

3. External Environment. What trends and changes have been taking place in the industry and what others could happen or might reasonably happen? (Note that declining industries sometimes present excellent opportunities because they are an anathema to large companies, which sometimes give them up to go in directions with larger potential future sales volumes.) What are competitors doing?

4. Company Strengths and Weaknesses. What is the company's market share in different areas? Where is it largest? How does what the company offers compare to what competitors offer? (Listing characteristics of the product or service down the side of a page and competitors across the top and then comparing them point by point can help.) What is the company's capability to take on new programs in terms of financial and people resources?

5. Threats and Opportunities. Considering the company's strengths and weaknesses in relation to its external environment, what dangers does it face and in what directions can it choose to move ahead? Creative thinking should be applied in this exploration and many possibilities should be considered, even some that are "far out." The company portrait should be recast in fictional terms, two or more different ways. This is done simply by inventing different answers to fill in the blanks of the portrait described earlier, answers which illustrate how the company might become rather than how it presently is. These answers connected together will present alternative future portraits which the company might seek to achieve.

6. Performance Targets. According to whichever future portrait appears best, goals should be set and elaborated on as targets for the various parts of the company, sales, production, finance, R&D, and management. Plans should be laid and policies established to accomplish these targets.

The formulation of these targets and the analysis of policies are necessarily highly judgmental and subjective processes. Utilization of formalized procedures such as flow chart sequences, though sometimes helpful, may also be more of an encumbrance than an aid in this process, and blind reliance on these formalized procedures rather than on careful thought and common sense can be disastrous. Once an analysis has been made, however, it may be worthwhile to check the analysis with the aid of a list of things to look for (see Exhibit 1). This list is not a "recipe" for performing strategic analysis. Trying to use it as one is likely to cause difficulties. The list should be used for seeking ways to improve on the analysis *after* it has been performed.

TRANSLATION INTO ACTION

Most often in small companies the plans are mainly in the head of the owner/manager, but as the company grows larger, it becomes important to involve other people in working out plans and to develop plans in more formal detail, preferably written. This is not to say that the plan should be rigidly adhered to. In fact, it

EXHIBIT 1   Checklist for review of company strategy analysis.

1. Have we presented a paragraph portrait describing the "as is" of the company briefly?

2. Have we offered at least a one paragraph portrait of how the company should be at some definite point in the future?

3. Have we appraised the company's financial status and trends of performance as a basis for developing action ideas?

4. Have we shown consideration of external trends, circumstances, and likely future developments and related them to the company?

5. Have we shown an examination of the company's internal strong points and competitive advantages?

6. Have we been complete in spotting problems and listing weak points in all areas of the business?

7. Have we listed advantages of the company's competition?

8. Have we been imaginative in listing many possible opportunities for the company? Are both separate actions and strategic packages of actions considered?

9. Have we indicated orders of importance and which problems and opportunities deserve the most attention?

10. Have we been comprehensive and even reached "far out" in order to generate possible answers to solve the problems and exploit opportunities?

11. Have we considered the cons as well as the pros in making decisions among alternatives?

12. Have costs of most likely actions been projected?

13. Have we prescribed action in terms that make it clear who is to do what and with what resources?

14. Is there a clear indication of time phasing of the recommended action?

15. Have we indicated what results to look for from the action?

16. Have we considered "what if" (suppose the action fails) questions?

17. Have we wrapped up our thoughts in a clear and interesting presentation that includes financial projections, appropriate use of tables, diagrams, etc.?

18. Have we given the presentation to other knowledgeable, interested, and objective parties to obtain feedback and cross-checking of facts, assumptions, ideas, and reasoning?

should not. But, nonetheless, it will help the company by (1) testing the feasibility of achieving the intended strategic goals, (2) increasing the ability to anticipate needs that have long lead times, such as obtaining some types of governmental permits, amassing capital, and so forth, (3) keeping company personnel better informed about what the aims of the company are so that they can better work toward those aims, (4) stabilizing management against being pulled one way and another by premature responses to short-term events and giving it a rational basis from which to think through more appropriate responses, and (5) providing a record against which to check and measure company progress over time.

The plan should tell what is to happen, how it is to be brought about, who is to bring it about, and when it is to happen. It should also consider contingencies and what is to be done if events don't work out as hoped? A practical method of laying out the sequences of events and the timetable is to use a flow diagram on a large sheet of paper showing activities and events, particularly those that depend on one another, and how they fit together. Tables accompanying the flow chart should include a listing of manpower needed in different skill categories and financial forecasts including funds flow statements and pro forma balance sheets and income statements. Over time this plan should be expected to change. The original draft is likely to be wrong, but only subsequent developments can reveal in what ways. The discovery of errors will, of course, make changes necessary.

The plan should explicitly state the policies of each of the functional areas—product development, marketing, credit, personnel, production, inventory control, purchasing, accounting, borrowing, and so forth. These policies form the set of "rules" that everyone in the company should obey in order to propel the company toward its goals. The rules need not be rigid and they need not be permanent, but they should be dependable enough that employees will not have to ask for guidance because the rules are not clear. If the company's policy is not to reach for sales beyond a certain geographical area, or not to be first with new designs but rather to copy what has been worked out by others, or to record inventories on a FIFO basis, or to make only certain parts and buy others, then these policies must be made clear so that people will not waste time arguing about how to handle individual cases, so that policies will not be violated, and so that the company will not be hindered from reaching its goals.

Implementing policies in the early stages of company growth is typically very informal ("Hey, Frank. If any more customers whose bills are more than 90 days overdue call in an order, tell them we have to see some of their money before we can ship, O.K.?"). As the company grows, however, informality will become impractical. There will be an increasing need to discuss the policies with other people in the company and to express the policies more formally, often through written memoranda and policy manuals. Many styles of leadership are possible for getting the policies into action. Typically, smaller companies are more autocratic, with employees doing "what the boss says" and sometimes "what the boss wants," even though it has not been said. As most companies grow, they tend to become less autocratic. Decisions are made more by teams and committees and are carried out more through mutual deduction of what is to be done.

There is still a range of degrees of directiveness within which management can choose its operating style. Within a given company there is also typically a range of opinion, varying with the perceptions of each individual, as to just how autocratic the management in that company in fact is. Management of a growing company must work out its most effective methods for implementing policies.

It is more likely to be successful in doing so, however, if it remembers that since new pitfalls as well as opportunities tend to develop as the company grows, the managers' habits and methods of operating will also have to change.

Radair Incorporated

"The big decision facing me now is whether or not to expand to a full line of products." Richard Heckmann, 27, President of Radair Incorporated was absorbed with this question as he left the Minneapolis–St. Paul airport late one fall evening in 1970. Radair manufactured a line of six electronic instruments for general aviation (light planes) cockpits. Sales were made through a nationwide network of independent distributors, and the largest of these was Van Deusen Air, which also carried products of the two industry leaders, King Radio corporation (annual sales $25 million) and Narco Avionics (annual sales $50 million). Earlier that evening William Carolla, President of Van Deusen, had said that these two clients had expressed displeasure that his firm had taken on Radair.

It pleased Dick Heckmann that the two industry giants had acknowledged the presence of tiny Radair. He inferred from the rest of his conversation with Mr. Carolla that Radair's recent publicity and growing reputation were beginning to embarrass the industry leaders. Near the end of the evening Mr. Carolla dominated the conversation as he explained why he had asked Dick to make the special trip to Minneapolis. He preferred to have his company handle full lines rather than partial ones like Radair's and consequently he would like to see Radair immediately begin to add a series of new products. Mr. Heckmann recalled his comment to the effect that "Narco and King don't like our carrying Radair, but I have

such a high regard for the products your company makes that I'll jeopardize my relationship with them if you can promise me a full competitive Radair line."

Mr. Carolla seemed to think that now would be a good time to make the expansion. The current economic recession had reduced general avionics sales and consequently Narco and King were fighting for every dollar and were unlikely to take immediate action against distributors. Dick's intuitive feeling was that the recession would continue for another year or so, which meant he would have less than 2 years to complete the expansion. He guessed that the cost of the new development might be in the range of a quarter million dollars.

RICHARD HECKMANN

Dick Heckmann had spent 4½ years in the Air Force hoping to attend the Air Force Academy, but repeated delays including a tour as helicopter pilot in Vietnam had outworn his patience, and he resigned to complete his bachelor's work in political science, begun on a part-time basis in the service, at the University of Hawaii. To buy a car in college, he answered a want-ad for a part-time job selling Fuller brushes, and from this selling experience he formulated two philosophical observations. The sales trainer who accompanied him the first day told him that one out of ten calls would, on the average, land a sale. But his own first day and a half landed him nothing but discouragement. Then suddenly when he was just about to quit, a woman bought $80 worth of brushes.

His first philosophical observation was that "if you make enough calls you will find somebody who will buy." The second was that "every time someone says 'no' to your sales presentation, you should rejoice, because you are one person closer to a sale." He also formulated a definition of a self-starter as "a person who realizes that when things seem to be getting at their worst, they are bound to improve if you just keep plugging."

One of the doors he knocked on happened to belong to the Hawaiian general agent for the New England Life Insurance Company. Dick studied evenings for his life insurance license, and after his college graduation he took a 1-week insurance sales course to become a representative. He found that his philosophy about the importance of making large numbers of calls applied equally well to insurance, and he formulated an additional observation as well: "You can take a new product into an old market that you understand and make money, or you can take an old product that you understand into a new market and make money. But you're in trouble when you take a new product that you don't understand into a new market that you don't understand."

Choosing his calls with care, making large numbers of calls, and refining his sales presentation, within a year he became the leading salesman for New England Life in Hawaii. A year later, in 1967, he married, and because his wife preferred the mainland he transferred to the New England office in Portland, Oregon, where he placed over $2,500,000 worth of insurance his first year there to become the leading New England Life salesman in the Pacific Northwest.

THE PARENT COMPANY, UNIWEST

Radair was closely connected with the investment company that owned it, Uniwest Incorporated, which had been formed by Mr. Heckmann and two of his life insur-

ance customers. One was Charles H. Morse, IV, heir to an eastern manufacturing fortune, who worked for the Weyerhaeuser Lumber Company; the other was J. Michael Nolte, a practicing Portland attorney. The relationship began socially around interest in golf, business, and "having a good time." One frequent topic of conversation was the currently successful entrepreneurial career of James Ling and others who started from humble beginnings and by clever financial operations acquired companies to build "conglomerates."

The decision to form their own investment company emerged almost as casually as their friendship.

> We sat down for a couple of drinks one afternoon in the latter part of 1968 after a round of golf. I mentioned that again this week I had made some calls on executives who seemed successful in their own businesses (he was by now specializing in corporate insurance and pension funds) but did not project themselves as super individuals. Nolte commented that he often provided legal help to small and medium-sized companies that seemed to succeed without impressive managerial talent. Morse suddenly said, "Let's quit talking about it. Let's start our own conglomerate. I'll put up $5,000 and buy the first round of drinks for a toast." (Statement of Richard Heckmann.)

The other two matched Morse's ante, and Uniwest was formed that afternoon in the clubroom.

The following Monday at the suggestion of Mr. Nolte they made their first investment, purchasing convertible bonds of SCI Corporation, a client of his law firm which needed additional capital while it prepared to make a public offering. The convertible notes were for a period of 1 year, bearing 7% interest and convertible into common stock at $.90/share prior to December 1, 1968, at $1.80/share thereafter until April 1, 1969, and at $3.00/share thereafter until paid. A prospectus offering 400,000 shares at $3.00 was expected to be made public in November of 1968. They converted their bonds into 16,666 shares of common stock prior to December 1, 1968 and completed selling the stock over the counter at an average price of $10.00/share by March 1969. A similar experience during the same time period resulted from an investment in Trailer Dyne which allowed them to double their money in 90 days.

Their success at part-time investing was tempting and in early 1969 they agreed to terminate their respective jobs, incorporate Uniwest, and become serious investors. They rented an office, hired a secretary, and began inquiring about business investment opportunities with bankers, lawyers, and other business acquaintances. They also watched the local papers and *The Wall Street Journal* for leads. Their objective was to guide Uniwest Incorporated into a large Northwest conglomerate by purchasing other companies. They planned to use Nolte's experience as a securities legal expert to purchase companies in glamorous industries, dress them up, take them public, and then use the proceeds to repay the debt used to buy the companies and finance further acquisitions.

RADAIR BACKGROUND

The first company acquired, Radair Incorporated, had been formed in 1966 by Robert Florence, a draftsman by training, in his Denver basement. He developed what he regarded as a better exhaust gas temperature gage for general aviation aircraft. He then sold the gages to fellow pilots. He was joined shortly by an unemployed engineer, John Holoway, who invested $5,000 plus a year without pay to develop an aircraft strobe light that improved visibility for night flying. Because there was little aircraft industry in Colorado, the company was moved to Seattle, where another engineer, Mr. Blattman, joined the company, bringing with him a third product, a VHF direction finder that would give pilots a visual and aural indication of whether or not the aircraft was on course. The company also produced a position light flasher to blink aircraft navigation lights 72 times per minute and a

solid-state ice detector to notify a pilot of carburetor icing.

Mr. Blattman had also suggested an emergency radio beacon for downed aircraft, but Radair lacked capital to bring it to fruition, and, consequently, he began a capital search. Through an attorney friend in Portland he was put in touch with Uniwest. Radair's 1968 financial statement showed no net worth and showed a loss for the year of $1,700 on sales of $218,000, 90% of which came from the exhaust gas temperature gages and engine analyzers. However, the company had expensed all research and development costs for obtaining over 250 FAA and FTC design approvals and patents which Mr. Florence estimated had a replacement value of over $311,000.

The owners of Uniwest felt that Radair was an attractive potential acquisition for Uniwest because the above products could be associated with the electronics industry in a manner that would look good in a future public stock offering prospectus. This opinion they confirmed through conversation with Hughbanks, Inc., a local Seattle stock brokerage firm. Their investigation indicated that the general aviation industry (mostly light planes, excluding airliners and military aircraft) had been one of the fastest growing segments of the United States economy in the late 1960s. Aircraft shipments had increased from 7,628 units with an estimated retail value of $217,000,000 in 1963 to 14,418 units valued at $558,000,000 in 1968. The big five general aviation manufacturers (Aero Commander, Beech, Cessar, Moody, and Piper) forecasted 1969 sales approximately 20% to 25% greater than 1968 sales. These five estimated 1969 shipments at about 18,000 units. An aircraft owner normally purchased his airplane with a minimum of extras and then gradually upgraded the aircraft as finances would permit. As of December 31, 1968 estimates showed the retro-fit market potential at over 105,000 single-engine aircraft and 16,000 multi-engine aircraft.

The chief uniqueness of Radair's existing products at the time was that they were the highest quality obtainable with correspondingly high prices. An agreement was made in early 1969 to acquire Radair for 26,000 shares of Uniwest stock, which the founders valued at $17 per share. The agreement provided that if Uniwest could not properly support Radair, Mr. Florence would retain control.

Disputes shortly began to arise. There were charges of deliberate production slowdowns, and Uniwest was unable to obtain current financial statements from Radair as sales failed to meet projections and capital became tight. Consequently, in mid-1970 an agreement was reached in which Uniwest bought back its shares from Mr. Florence along with a 6-year agreement that he would not enter competition with Radair. Mr. Florence received a payment of $390,000 with $113,000 down and a balance over 6 years at 8% interest. Dick Heckmann became Radair's new president.

For the first 9 months after the Radair acquisition Heckmann and Nolte studied the aviation industry while Florence ran Radair. They let the company run largely unchanged, and it stayed slightly below break-even while they snooped around the general aviation industry, traveling constantly, asking questions, looking behind closed doors, and listening. "We did, and still do, a lot of homework," Heckmann observed. "Our aim was to approach the competitors like Patton approached Rommel. I liked the scene where Patton was watching his tanks chew up the Panzers and George C. Scott as Patton said, 'Rommel, you magnificent bastard, I read your book.' We tried to read every competitor's book."

Heckmann and Nolte concluded that the industry consisted of two publicly held giants, King and Narco, plus 20 other small unorganized companies. Nolte recalled from business school that industries dominated by few companies can sometimes be particularly vulnerable to competition. "We were surprised to find," Heckmann commented, "that although their line of business was directed at small aircraft pilots and

that industry was headed for high growth, they were doing all their dreaming about things like collision avoidance systems for airliners, which are another market entirely." Nolte and Heckmann also learned that large companies such as RCA and General Electric were doing research in avionics, but they too appeared to be ignoring small private aircraft.

DART EMERGENCY TRANSMITTER

Work had continued on the development of the emergency radio transmitter for locating downed aircraft, although the costs of roughly $25,000 for design plus an additional $12,000 for tooling to produce the impact-resistant plastic case were substantial. Heckmann appreciated from his Vietnam helicopter flying of 72 missions the value of such a product. During the 9 months he and Nolte had spent learning the industry, however, he was surprised to find that few general aviation pilots carried such a device. Pilots told him that radio beacons had been on the market for over 15 years but were expensive, costing around $1,500, and unreliable. Rescue beacons, he concluded, were regarded like auto seat belts—good for the other guy. Moreover, apparently the more experience a pilot had, the less he considered a beacon necessary.

These seemed flimsy excuses to Heckmann. Expense and reliability were, he felt, certainly factors, but the real reason appeared to be that pilots regarded the beacons as "tombstone markets." This Mr. Heckmann considered a marketing problem instead of a technical problem. The answer, he decided, was to design a beacon that would allow voice transmission as well as sending a tone signal. Then the pilot would feel that he could aid in his own rescue. If his regular transmitter failed, he could use the beacon unit to communicate.

Other manufacturers argued against voice capabilities for the following reasons:

1. When the microphone is used, it drains the flashlight batteries at a rate that

is four times as fast, cutting the life of the rescue device considerably.

2. Downed pilots may give inaccurate information that would delay the rescue crew for several hours.

Competitors' complaints of the new device were loud enough that an FAA committee agreed to hear arguments from both sides. Dick was not successful in his attempt to have the regulation specify that voice communication be part of rescue beacons; however, the outcome of this attention was a new regulation requiring that rescue beacons with or without voice be carried in all aircraft.

California was the first state to require a rescue beacon and the Dart II was the first to win approval in that state. Heckmann noted, "We had six saves in the first 7 months of production."

"From the beginning, the marketing philosophy for the Dart II," stated Heckmann, "was give the customers what they wanted." Features he regarded as important, in addition to the voice capability, included a "lexan" case that would withstand 400°F temperature and a 38-caliber bullet fired point-blank. Tests showed that the Dart II would work after being dropped from 2,000 ft and would withstand 5 G's acceleration. The piano wire antenna on the Dart II was permanently extended. Those of competitors were not. Dart II's retail price was $195, one-half the cost of the cheapest competitive unit. The first order received was for 500 units. Dart sales reached almost $200,000 in 1969 and were running at a $350,000 annual rate by October 1970.

DEVELOPMENT OF THE RADAIR 10-CHANNEL RADIO

As the Dart II design work neared completion, Dick Heckmann was worrying about how the Radair engineers' time should be used next. He looked over the instruments in a cockpit and asked where the biggest dollar volume market was. He noticed the communication radio and was struck by the thought that it was an instrument every aircraft needed, and was therefore high in sales volume.

Questions came to mind: How many companies are making radios? Not very many. And what was the price spread of radios? Not much. They were all priced around the same and that price really seemed awfully high. We took apart a couple of the existing radios on the market and looked at them. We couldn't understand why they were priced the way they were, until we figured out that it was the sweetest little cartel we'd ever seen.

We spent a lot of time going over annual reports on the industry leaders and buying drinks for conversations with branch managers of distributors. With four or five drinks in him we'd ask a man, "By the way, how many Narco and King radios did you sell last month?" He's proud of his sales volume, so he says, "I sold 50." Then we'd multiply that times the number of such branches. We quickly knew the market volume.

What we found supported the theory that says the biggest companies in an industry are likely to have the most marginal customers, making the market vulnerable to entry. For 27 years two companies had controlled the general aviation radio market, and they had taken on an attitude that if people didn't like the way they did things there was not much they could do about it. As a result, there were a lot of customers and middlemen who hated them and would love to find an alternative. At the same time, that alternative had to be attractive in its own right, if we were going to get people to buy something like this that their life depended on. We felt we needed not just one, but several distinct competitive advantages if we were going to break into this market and survive. The next question was what could we offer that they could not compete with. We wanted a marketing strategy so completely different from the leaders that they couldn't possibly react fast enough to stop us.

We decided to forget about the OEM (original equipment maker) market and concentrate on the retro-fit market. The OEM's are almost impossible for a small company to sell to because they are afraid they might spend $100,000 to test the new product and get it through all the red tape of certification only to have the small company go under and leave them with nothing to show for it. A lot of guys in big companies have lost their jobs for making contracts with small suppliers that went under.

The retro-fit market is a lot easier to contend with. They take whatever gives them the easiest selling job and the best margin. Unlike the OEM buyers, they don't go through all the checkout and testing. If it looks like it works, they buy it. The demonstrator we took around to them was just an empty box with a voltage regulator inside it to glow. As it turned out, the deal we came up with for them was so attractive that they were giving us orders for the product before we had a model with real insides in it to show them—before it actually worked at all. (Statement of Richard Heckmann.)

Existing radios carried 90, 200, and 360 channels, but Dick knew from his own flying experience and from his study of the industry that this number was many more than most general aviation pilots needed. He talked to Mr. Carolla, president of Radair's largest distributor, and asked him to estimate the minimum number of channels needed for safe operation. Mr. Carolla guessed around 20. Dick continued to question him about which 20 were needed and when Mr. Carolla began to list them the number shrank to 10, which meant that the radio could be smaller, lighter, and cheaper to make. When Mr. Carolla jokingly began referring to himself as "the father of the 10-channel radio," Dick concluded both that there was need for such a product and that his distributor was already sold on it.

Because of this reduction in the number of channels, the radio could be smaller and lighter and it could be made less expensively. Technical design of the radio circuitry was not regarded by Heckmann as a particularly difficult problem. "I guess radio circuits are pretty well worked out and straightforward," he said. Our engineers had never designed radios before, but they knew circuit design. Since they were all pilots, they knew what was needed, and since we had already taken everybody else's radio apart, we knew how they were made."

A leading New York industrial design firm, Walter, Darwin, Teague, was hired to work out external styling of the radio. Heckmann commented, "We said, here is everything in the cockpit. Design something that will turn somebody on and make them want to buy it. And they did. It cost us $16,000 but it was worth the price. They came up with something a pilot would look at and say, 'It's different, I like it, and I want it in my cockpit.' You have to give the customer an excuse to buy, maybe because of looks. Maybe something else. But he has to want it."

In their visits among dealers and customers, Heckmann and Nolte had found that a source of dissatisfaction was existing warrant policies. Both leading companies handled warranties through radio repair shops. If a radio failed, it had to be taken to the shop for repair. While it was there, the pilot had no radio in his airplane.

We decided to give a warranty the industry had never heard of. We didn't have the money to write repair manuals, and we were not big enough to set up repair stations in the field, and we didn't know how to do either of these things anyway. So we figured that it would be cheaper just to offer new radios instead of repairs for old ones. This takes the distributor and the dealer out of the warranty claim business, which is a headache for them. The customer is better off because he doesn't have to wait with his plane on the ground while his radio is in the shop. He brings in the defective radio and we give him a new one. We take the radio in, fix it, put a new cover on it, and sell it again. This way of working also gives us quick feedback on how to improve the product. The customer gets an even more reliable circuit because it's been "burned in." But the main advantage of our policy is that it gets around the argument of distributor dealers and customers that a new product is likely to cause them a lot of trouble.

This way they know we're completely behind it, and they can get it fixed right away. We even had one come in with a tire mark across the top of it. The radio still worked, but it was squashed out of shape so it wouldn't fit in the hole of the instrument panel. We took it back and gave them another, just as we promised. (Statement of Richard Heckmann.)

From a combination of the existing high margins of the industry and the fact that their simpler radio would be much cheaper to produce but not correspondingly lower in retail price, the Radair management decided they could offer distributors and dealers approximately double the margins they were making on existing products.

> Now we were in a position to really blitz the competition. They can't turn their production line around fast when they're geared to produce $60 million a year. They aren't likely to go in and chop up their distribution system just to compete with some little newcomer. They aren't going to take 27 years of experience in the warrant business and throw it down the tube. So what can they do? While they're trying to figure it out they are taking up to 4 months on deliveries while we offer immediate service.
>
> Some people have told us, of course, that we're crazy, smoking pot or dropping LSD. They say there's got to be a reason why the competition grew so big doing it their way. And sometimes we say to ourselves we hope there isn't something they know that we don't know. But it's starting to look like the competition is being stupid enough to ignore us and let us break in on them. We tell our own people that the moment they hear about a couple of guys trying to start a competing company in their garage to let us know about it, so we can run them out before they get a toehold like we're doing. (Statement of Richard Heckmann.)

Orders for the new radio were given by dealers when they were shown the mock-up and told about the warranty policy, delivery schedule, and discount schedule, before the Radair 10 was in production. By October 1970 sales were approximately $40,000 per month and rising at an annual rate of 400%. New uses for the product were cropping up. It was reported that one executive bought the Radair 10 to install in his boat allowing him to have communication with the company airplane during his leisure time. The radio that had cost $50,000 to develop was introduced at a retail price of $389 plus $69 for the optional battery pack. One distributor remarked, "Those little radios don't do a lot, but what they do, they do well and they have certainly opened up a new market not available to the $795 90-channel radio."

ENGINEERING

Radair's entry into the avionics market with the Dart II and Radair 10 took off faster than Uniwest's management expected, but Heckmann explained that he felt that it was a "classic case of bringing together several young, goal-oriented people who get a lot of satisfaction out of what they are doing. The average age of our 63 employees is only 27 years." He commented, "I can recruit any man for any job and money is usually not the drawing card; in fact, every one of Radair's top engineers took a pay cut to work for this small company. Salesmen are motivated by money, but engineers seek challenge and a chance to be recognized for their talents. Whenever the company gets publicity for its products or design of new equipment, I try to pass the credit on to the engineer and mention his name." The company employed two former NASA engineers, Dan Blattman and Don Quist, whom Heckman had recruited. Blattman held the patent for part of the warhead on the Shrike missile (a heat-seeking antiaircraft missile). Prior to joining NASA he had worked for the FAA. He designed the Dart II which was technically simple compared to a radio and started design of the Radair 10 which Quist finished. In Dick's opinion, Blattman's main contribution to Radair was his ability to work with the FAA to get certification. He understood FAA procedure, knew what they considered important, and most of all, he had a previous relationship with many FAA executives.

Heckmann described Quist as an engineer's engineer. He was 27 when he came to work for Radair. He has a Ph.D. in physics and is already credited with a major part of the design for fusing underwater mines. He had a nagging sense of morality that finally made his government job impossible. "Don just got tired of building things that kill people," Heckmann explained. Quist was not only a pilot, but also a former lightplane owner and an instrument instructor.

> A lot more high-risk engineering is needed in the general-aviation area, and we plan to do it in the next decade. General aviation is riding on the coattails of 20-year-old electronics engineering, and there is no reason radios have to be built the way they are. (Statement of Don Quist.)

> One of our strong points is that none of us has ever built avionics before. The stuff our people were building at NASA is a great deal more sophisticated than what they are building now so that was no great problem. But we had no preconceived ideas about size, cost, or weight. We did not design to beat the competition, but to meet our own standards of performance. (Statement of Richard Heckmann.)

> By having a person build something he's never built before, he can approach it with an uncluttered attitude. It is an advantage to be unhampered by any bogus requirements to do things the old way, just because "that's the way it's done." And there's so much room for innovation in general aviation. (Statement of Don Quist.)

Heckmann admitted that he and Quist had some conflicts over the design of a certain piece of equipment versus the marketability of that equipment. As an example, Don was very excited about the design of a challenging new idea that would allow instrument landings at fields without omni's. The new gear would electronically move a nearby omni to the desired field. Dick postponed any design on the project because he felt that market was too small to warrant production at that time. Dick felt that Quist lacked the flexibility required in a small company. Don did not like to be rushed in the design of new products and he did not cope well with production problems. Dick had mentioned to Quist that he would like to set up an R&D avionics laboratory sometime in the future. This captured Don's attention, but Dick doubted

Don could tolerate the uncertainty of a small company long enough for the R&D facility to become reality.

OPERATIONS

Radair had been able to design and put the Dart II transmitter into production in its 35-member organization in 90 days. Standard purchased circuit components, such as resistors, transistors, etc., were assembled by the company's all-female production group. The main difficulty with this new product had been designing tooling to make the "lexan" (high-impact plastic supplied by General Electric) case. Two outside tooling makers failed, but a third managed to design workable tooling. The final cost of the tooling, $12,000, was double Radair's estimate. All assembly of each Dart II circuit board was done by a single woman from start to finish. The board was then stamped with a code indicating the date, assembler, and final tester.

The new 10-channel radio also entered production at a development cost of $50,000, but without major problems. The design used existing avionic technology. Assembly was facilitated by ample room in the case, since the radio was allowed the same cockpit space as models with many more channels. One difficulty encountered was during the first test transmission. From the Radair plant they called the nearby Boeing Field tower. After a brief pause came the reply: "We read you two by two with a loud squeal in the background." (Two by two meant that the signal was weak and poor). However, the problem was quickly remedied by minor adjustments.

When electronic components fail, they usually do so within the first 10 hours of use. Radair consequently did extensive pre-testing, using such equipment as a 14-ft long former delicatessen beer cooler heated to 125°F in which each radio was played continuously for 48 hours. Each radio was also given 5 hours of testing on a vibrating platform plus 5 hours of constant receiving, with transmission cycles every 15 seconds. This factory testing uncovered approximately 20% of incipient failures. Warranty records indicated that most returns were the result of improper installation and that the lowest percentage were the result of design deficiencies. Most problems in the sets themselves were caused by assembly mistakes, such as cold soldered joints, tiny spicules of solder bridging gaps, shorted wires, and component failures.

Radair, like most avionics manufacturers, did not make its own circuit components, such as resistors, capacitors, and switches, but bought them from suppliers. Ideally, each component would be tested when received by operation in a radio, but this would be too expensive. "The only alternative is selective testing of something like one out of every hundred," Dick Heckmann observed, "but selective is really a synonym for hit-or-miss. And the ones we miss are the ones that hit us back." Consequently, the company had developed a twofold solution. The extended testing and "burning-in" was to identify unreliable components before shipping. At the same time a time-sharing computer terminal at Stanford's Business School was used to predict reliability curves and forecast components most likely to fail on the basis of warranty returns. Radair then performed 100% inspection on those components.

As with the Dart II, each assembler built a circuit board from start to finish. To minimize assembly mistakes, Dick Heckmann emphasized the role of engineering design. "You can't build in quality; it has to be designed in," he commented. "But then you have to make sure your manufacturing process is good enough to build the quality that is called for by the design. As our sales orders grow, it seems to be getting harder to keep the production quality up and also to schedule it. The competition all make dealers wait 3 and 4 months for delivery, which lets them schedule their production better. It gives us a sales advantage to be able to offer almost immediate delivery, but it also makes it difficult to coordinate production to meet the orders."

Accounting in Radair was run by an accounting major who took the job upon receiving his degree in the summer of 1970. He seemed to Dick Heckmann to have some difficulty with tasks such as pressing for payment of receivables and haggling with suppliers about payables, perhaps because this was his first full-time job and he was not yet accustomed to it. Heckmann found it necessary to handle financial emergencies, such as finding payroll money in tight moments, himself and was uneasy at times about whether or not the accounting system would give him adequate warning when cash problems arose.

SALES

There were 22 national distributors in the Aviation Distributors and Manufacturers Association (ADMA), which according to Radair management had, in effect, a marketing monopoly in the general aviation industry. Sales were made directly to distributors who stocked the products. Manufacturers representatives were not used in these sales. Less than 1% of sales were in Washington State. The largest markets were in Los Angeles and Miami, while 18% were in foreign countries. Distributors in turn sold to retail dealers and repair shops, and thus they removed from manufacturers the responsibility of screening and making collections from these dealers. Following introduction of the 10-channel radio, Radair became the only avionics manufacturer to have its product on the shelves of all 22 ADMA distributors. Dick Heckmann attributed this feat to a combination of the wider distributor discount offered by Radair, to its exceptional warranty policy, and to a heavy effort in advertising.

> The starting point with a product like this is to go out and personally sell it to dealers yourself. You have to be able to prove to distributors that the dealers will buy it. Otherwise, the distributors won't spend any time on it. Why should they spend time on a new unknown product when they can spend the same time on things they know people will buy?

If, however, you prove that it will sell, very soon everybody will want to get on the bandwagon, and you'll get distributors who are really eager.

So our first step in getting sales was to get on airplanes and travel around to every dealer. We'd show them the radio and tell them, that this is our product and this is what it will do. Here are the brochures. This is how much you make on every one you sell. Whatever we can do to help you, we will. We kept talking to them every week with phone calls and letters, and we kept advertising to create the pull, and they bought it. Actually, the first demonstrator we showed them was just a box with a voltage regulator inside it, so we could plug it into the wall and the light would go on. The dealers were placing orders for it before it ever worked. (Statement of Richard Heckmann.)

Radair was currently spending $12,000 per month on advertising. Management decided that in order to give the new company an image that would compete with the established competition, it would be advisable to outdo the competition in advertising, for example, by placing full-page, full-color ads in the inside covers of magazines like *Flying*. Competitors presented only black-and-white advertisements on inside pages.

We've found that you can do a great sales job on advertising agencies. Agencies want accounts. If you turn them on with your product line and approach, they think it will work to give them ultimately a big client, and they will carry the company for a while on credit. Currently, we're getting 90 days from them, figuring that will be time enough for us to get our money back through sales to pay them.

A mistake some people make in advertising is to think that if they don't get instant results, they should either quit or change the ad. But I figure that when you get tired of an ad, you should run it another year. You get bored with it because you saw the program conceptually, you saw the first run, got advance copies of the magazine, you've shown it to your bankers, your kids, your neighbors, and everybody else, and you're tired of it. But the public will not even have noticed it yet. You have to keep hitting them. If you don't believe it, just try

to make a list of the ads you saw in a magazine last week. You probably won't be able to list many, even though many of the ads haven't changed in the past 5 years.

By keeping our advertisements running, we hope that people will come to regard Radair as a well-established company. The dealer will put our radio on his shelf, and the customer will come in and say, "Oh yeah, I remember seeing their ad on the inside cover of Flying." Since the distributors and dealers are going to make an exceptional profit on it, they will back it up with a good pitch: "Sure, I've been out to the Radair plant, and they have about 800 people working there." The customer will buy a radio, even though it has no formal government certification.

Advertising should also get the pilots talking about it. The average pilot is a conceited guy who likes to show off how much technical knowledge he has. He will do this at the airport where he meets other pilots. They will talk about radios and how good this one or that one is. When our ads get through, one will talk about Radair, and the others will say they know about it too. Then they will all notice it at the dealers, and because it is designed to appeal, hopefully they will buy it. (Statement of Richard Heckmann.)

MANAGEMENT TEAM

Advertising firms can be very difficult to control, though, and if you don't watch them they will start telling you how to run your whole marketing system. It's very necessary to have consultants and advisors, but they have to be used in areas in which they are strong and you are weak. Marketing is not my weakness. Since everything else is my weakness, I need lots of help on many things, but not on marketing, and not from an advertising agency on things other than advertising. The trouble is that too many specialists act as if they are experts on everything.

The same thing goes for lawyers and accounting firms. I consider myself a marketing man, and I am very weak from a financial point of view. I wanted an accounting firm that would tell me what the products cost, what the administrative costs are, and what all those other numbers mean. So to find one that would give us good information on those things but not give us gratuitous advice on everything else, we went around and talked to all of them, just like you might shop for a car or a new suit. We tried to find ones that would really get involved, ones that would come out and learn our business.

We changed bankers because we had one who wouldn't get involved. He would come around sometimes, but he was chicken. He wouldn't get into an airplane, and that is the only way to understand our products. Instead, he would just keep asking to look at the financial statements. That's no way to appreciate a company because the statements are always a big lie. They overstate the receivables and inventory, and they understate the liabilities. The most important thing you have, and the thing that makes or breaks the business, are your people. But they don't show up on the financial statements at all.

So we found a banker who will go flying with us. He's even started taking flying lessons. Apparently, our account is one that is always coming up in the loan committee, so he *has* to know about us. When our largest distributor came to town recently, we had the banker up to meet him. We have the banker go out with us and talk to customers, so that he can see what our products are doing and what the competition is doing and really understand the business. This is important to us, because we essentially don't have any money except what he'll let us have. We've already hocked everything we have, including all our personal assets. If it weren't for bank support, I'd probably soon be out selling Fuller brushes again like I was the day I received a bachelor's degree in political science.

It still isn't easy by any means. Going to the bank for money is sort of like trying to climb a big pile of sand. You can't get anywhere; so the thought occurs that maybe we should bring in another partner, one with lots of money. But that's one thing we won't do. Unless he's strong at something we're weak at, he would be second-guessing us all the time. We'll make some good decisions and some bad ones, but when we make the bad ones that second-guessing would just kill us.

We go through tremendous battles now every time we try to second-guess each other, and we've already learned that's no good. For example, we had two very strong engineers. Both were circuit designers, and both considered themselves experts on the same things.

Any argument they got into ended in a deadlock. So we had to ask one of them to leave. To survive, a small company must have someone in authority to settle arguments.

Another danger we're aware of is having people tell us how great we are. Every time our sales go up, more people come in telling us what a great job we're doing and trying to sell us on something or other. I believe one of the things we have to do in a company like this is stay out in the field and find out where we're not doing the job we should be doing. We can't ever let ourselves get isolated from the field, sitting back in our office letting everybody tell us how smart we are. The competition is like a big dinosaur out there, and we're hacking away at one of its front legs. We think soon we'll get it to stumble a little bit. But there will still be a lot more animal left out there to hack up. I expect to travel about 120,000 miles visiting customers this year. (Statement of Richard Heckmann.)

NEW PRODUCTS

The new products that Radair had been urged by Mr. Carolla to add to its line are listed in Exhibit 1. Although no formal design work had begun on any of these Quist, Radair's chief engineer, and Heckmann had discussed several possible product innovations, many of which involved technical advancements in the state of the art of avionics. For instance, Quist already had some design sketches for a 360-channel "com" radio that would feature solid-state electronic tuning and a digital synthesizer employing only three crystals to generate all frequencies. Narco and King used an older analog design employing 16 or 17 crystals to produce the 360 frequencies. While Quist was explaining the advantages of a radio with a digital design, it reminded Dick of a digital clock he had noticed in a cocktail lounge the previous week. The digital display consisted of electronically illuminated numbers rather than a mechanical device and was easy to read in the dark. Dick thought a radio with digital tuning and an electronically illuminated digital display would attract immediate attention and be easy to market. Quist said there would be a reliability advantage in the

EXHIBIT 1 Proposed product line additions.

	Estimated prices and current annual volumes by company						Estimated development costs
	Narco		King		Others		
Product	Price	Units	Price	Units	Average Price	Units	
Navigation radio, 200-channel	$495	7,000	$ 795	3,000	$ 495	500	$180,000
Communication radio, 360-channel	495	8,000	795	4,000	895	2,000	combined
DME (distance measuring equipment)	795	1,000	1,000	500	1,495	200	$35,000
ADF (automatic direction finder)	595	1,500	895	1,000	995	200	combined
Transponder (radar)	395	15,000	595	10,000	595	5,000	$35,000
Glideslope indicator	695	2,000	995	1,500	895	500	$35,000
Omni direction finder	395	7,000	500	3,000	495	500	combined

442

design of an electronic digital display. Such a system might be electronically linked to the digital synthesizer to guarantee that the display always gave correct frequencies. Competitors' displays system involved a mechanical linkage which he said could break or slip out of adjustment. Quist also suggested that the digital tuning system could also be designed to accommodate future regulations requiring 720-channel radios. He predicted the 360-channel radio with 100 KHz spacing between channels would be obsolete within the next 5 years as the demand for air traffic control communications increased. Normally, 360-channel "coms" and 200-channel "navs" were sold as a set. Quist felt that once they got the 360-channel com designed and working satisfactorily, it would be easy to build the companion navigation radio.

Looking further into the future, Heckmann and Quist also discussed the possibilities of a data transmission system from ground to air using light-emitting diodes (LED) to spell out air traffic control transmissions. Heckmann explained, "If you use DME (distance measuring equipment), you're in constant electronic contact with a vortac, and it should be possible to set up an LED data display through the vortac instead of using voice communication. If this were done, air traffic control would become a silent traffic cop, stepping in only when needed." They also believed they had a remarkably simple electronic scheme for a collision avoidance system and an unusual idea for an airborne telephone system. These ideas for equipment of the future were the type of things that Quist dreamed about working on in R&D environment, but Heckmann thought that should Radair build a base as an avionics manufacturer before it could afford the luxury of an R&D facility.

ANTICIPATED PROBLEMS

Although both Quist and Heckmann assumed that there were likely to be some technical problems with new designs, neither thought that they would be serious. For the most part, they expected to parallel designs of existing products on the market, improving on accuracy and reliability and with a few innovations, but drawing on the company's experience in new designs to avoid major pitfalls.

Both felt that the idea for a digital synthesized radio had so many advantages that it was amazing nobody had introduced it to general aviation already. One possible explanation was thought to be economics. It might cost too much to change from the analog design to the new digital. Or it was possible that the integrated circuitry required for the synthesizer was too expensive. Another possibility was that neither Narco nor King had the technology expertise in advanced electronics to design a working digital radio. The Radair engineers were accustomed to the digital synthesizer design from their work at NASA and one problem they anticipated was an internal hum generated by the synthesizer. This had never been a problem when Quist had worked at NASA because NASA had enough room to separate the synthesizer from the transmitter and receiver. Quist expected that if the hum problem existed, they could solve it by building a "can" to isolate certain parts from the rest of the radio. This would require a carefully planned layout.

Layout and production engineering had been separate functions at NASA and the design engineers concentrated only on design. After the design was perfected, layout engineers modified the design for easy assembly and took care of production problems. Quist mentioned, "I have asked Dick to hire a NASA layout engineer several times, but he refuses on the basis that Radair's volume does not justify it. Just the same, I'd prefer to do only design and leave the layout and production problems for others." Quist could see one possible advantage to the old analog design that Narco and King used. If one of the 16 or 17 crystals fail, only part of the radio went dead. In the digital design using only 3 crystals, the entire radio was dead if one crystal failed. Crystals were very reliable, but if one should fail it would be serious and not representative of the reputation Radair wanted to build for quality. That was a design problem, however, and Quist felt confident that he could design circuitry providing for emergency service from the radio on any 2 crystals.

Other product development problems Dick anticipated concerned the electronically illuminated digital display they would probably use (LEDs). He could not anticipate exactly what the problems would be but felt that they were probable, simply because the LEDs had not been used in that application before. Quist added, "Usually in developing new products, the worst problems are the ones that you don't expect at all."

Another risk associated with the minimal time allowed for design and production of new products was ordering the initial inventory. It was possible that because there was a 3-month lag between placing and receiving an order of electronic components from Japan, Radair would have to make a commitment for the initial inventory prior to the time that the newly designed unit had been fully tested by the engineers. If they waited until everything was tested, there would be a delay in starting production, but it was possible that if they ordered in advance and a serious design error was discovered, they might end up with unusable components. Heckmann had estimated that development of the additional products would cost approximately $225,000 over a 10-month period. "The biggest problem would be if we were to get behind schedule," he said. "Every month of delay would cost us something like $20,000 extra in design expenses."

The possibility of developing only part of the line instead of all of it had been considered, but only briefly. Mr. Heckmann pointed out that the navigation, communication, and omni direction finding units would all have to be ready simultaneously because they had to be sold together by practices of the trade. These units made up the bulk of the estimated R&D program. Moreover, once

the program was geared to a capacity at which it could produce these three units simultaneously, it would, he argued, make sense to keep it rolling long enough to produce the other items as well rather than cutting back and laying off technical people prematurely. Estimated development costs of the various units generated by management appear in Exhibit 1.

OTHER DEVELOPMENTS AT UNIWEST

In August 1969, Morse, Nolte, and Heckmann steered Uniwest into real estate by buying a Portland land development company in exchange for 7,500 shares of Uniwest stock. This acquisition they renamed Uniwest Development, Inc. Rights to two parcels of land 10 minutes from downtown Portland were obtained, the first of which was to be used for town houses. Four town houses were immediately built and sold for an average of $40,000 each. This success encouraged the trio (under the direction of Morse whose family was experienced in real estate holdings) to construct 30 more town houses. During construction, however, the housing market dipped leaving UDI with properties that could not be sold and were difficult to rent.

At the same time, UDI ran into difficulties on their second parcel of land, a 60-acre tract on which they proposed a fully planned unit development, including large office buildings and other commercial buildings. This land had been purchased at an attractive price with the understanding that it was not zoned for their intended use. Although UDI had no experience in land development, it seemed to management that money was made in real estate by buying property with problems at the right price, solving those problems, and then selling or developing the land for a handsome profit. UDI's request for a zone change met difficulties when Multnomah County (Oregon county surrounding Portland) discovered sewage problems resulting from the county's rapid growth. The county's answer was that no zoning requests would be considered that might add to the sewage problem until the existing problem was under control and plans for future expansion were completed.

In October 1970 UDI was struggling with nearly 30 luxury town houses for which there was no market and a 60-acre site of prime development land that could not be properly zoned. UDI's property tax and mortgage interest amortized on a monthly basis was in excess of $2,000. Morse stated, "The future of UDI is uncertain. We must find some way of stopping the negative cash flow even if it means selling at a loss." Morse, who came from a wealthy family, explored the possibility of providing more money for Uniwest ventures himself. His estate, however, was in custody of a trust, and although he had visited the banker in Chicago who served as trustee, he was unable to persuade the banker to invest any of the money in Uniwest ventures.

In August 1970 Uniwest acquired a third company, Continental Controls of Albany, Oregon for 5,000 shares of Uniwest stock. Although Continental manufactured its own line of environmental controls, Uniwest's primary interest was to acquire a base of operations from which to utilize exclusive rights to manufacture and distribute controls patented by Sauter of Switzerland. Sauter was Europe's largest manufacturer of environmental controls, such as themostats, and had often looked at the American market, but Nolte, who was put in charge of this acquisition because he knew German, explained, "Sauter was deterred from entry because language barriers in Europe required labels with graphics like pictures of the sun and the moon, which don't sell here." Consequently, the Uniwest group engaged the Walter, Darwin, Teague firm to redesign the Sauter products for the U.S. market. The cost of this work turned out to be double the $6,000 the trio had expected during negotiations with Sauter.

By October of 1970 the environmental control division had been moved to Seattle and the name changed to Imperial Controls. The imported thermostat proved to be of superior quality and sales rose to 7,000 units per month; unfortunately, the gross margin was low because the costs of importing and final assembly were high. Management believed that it could not stand any price competition from national manufacturers such as Minneapolis Honeywell, Johnson Services, or Robertshaw. During the economic recession of the late 1960s the price competition among the major manufacturers forced Imperial Controls into a negative cash flow situation.

Nolte felt that Imperial Controls would be stuck in the negative cash flow situation until the economy turned up and competitive prices returned to normal. Uniwest's management agreed that the environmental control division was for sale if a likely buyer came along. Morse expressed some interest in purchasing Imperial Controls himself if a more qualified buyer, willing to pay Uniwest's price equal to the investment of nearly $130,000 did not appear, and if he personally could raise the money. Morse felt that he could change the products and aim for a low-volume specialty market that would not be so vulnerable to competition.

The Uniwest founders had initially planned to go public within the first 2 years by selling 15% of the company for around $3 million. However, their investment bankers said the new issues market had gone sour and this was not possible. The brokers advised them to run their acquisitions until they had established respectable "track records" and the new issues market, which was showing no signs of early recovery, had bounced back. The three men also discussed the possibility of re-incorporating Uniwest under the Radair name. Nolte suggested that there were advantages in making a new offering under Washington's securities laws instead of under Oregon's securities laws. He further proposed that if this transaction were planned carefully, it could be done in a manner so that the new corporation would not lose any of the other company's tax loss carry forward provisions. He suggested that they merge Uniwest, Imperial Control, Uniwest Development (all Oregon based corporations), and Radair (a Colorado corporation) into a newly formed Washington finance and holding company called Uniwest Acceptance Corporation. Then, in the same transaction the name of Uniwest Acceptance Corporation would be changed to Radair, Inc., a firm incorporated under the Washington State securities laws. A diagram of the organization plan for Uniwest appears in Exhibit 2. Financial statement information for Uniwest, including Radair, that management had available appears in Exhibit 3.

As Dick Heckmann weighed the new product decisions of Radair, he thought that he should consider both the status and over-

all plan for Uniwest as well as Radair itself. Another key factor seemed to be the current economic situation. Aerospace layoffs were hitting the Seattle area hard, with Boeing company employment down 50% in a year from its high of 105,000 Seattle employees. Someone had posted a sign on the outskirts of Seattle saying, "Will the last person out of Seattle please turn out the lights." Heckmann noted that other companies in the general aviation business were not introducing any new business and seemed to be contracting defensively.

This is turning into the worst slump that general aviation has seen, and a lot of people

EXHIBIT 2 Organization plan.

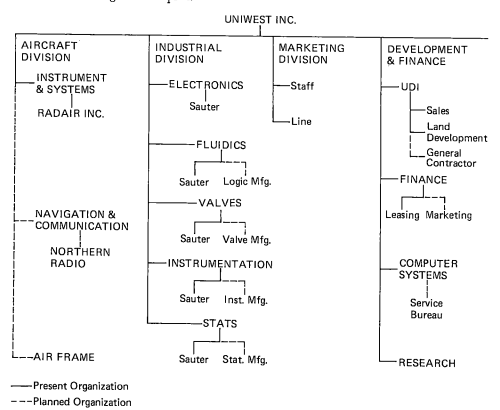

——Present Organization

– – –Planned Organization

EXHIBIT 3(a) Uniwest Incorporated, statement of income, ten months ended October 31, 1970 (unaudited).

Income	
Net sales	$753,161
Other income	9,218
Total income	762,379
Cost and Expenses	
Cost of products sold	$302,604
Depreciation and amortization	20,325
Selling, general and administrative	361,789
Interest	10,357
Other	3,341
	698,416
Income before federal income taxes and extraordinary amortizations (Note 1)	63,963
Federal income taxes and extraordinary amortization	13,335
Net income	$ 50,628
Net earnings per share of common stock (Note 2)	$.49

Note 1. The company does not anticipate the payment of any income taxes for 1970 because of prior years operating losses available for carry forward for federal income tax purposes.

Through October 31, 1970 the company has a total of $13,335 of extraordinary amortization. See note 5 to the balance sheet.

Note 2. The computation of net income per share is based on the actual number of shares outstanding as of October 31, 1970.

EXHIBIT 3(b) Uniwest comparative consolidated balance sheets (unaudited).

	July 31 1969	Oct. 31 1970	Notes
Current Assets			
Cash and deposits	$134,752	$ 19,069	
Accounts receivable, trade	26,603	264,032	
Notes receivable, officers	40,000	37,000	
Inventories	40,227	241,932	
Prepaid and other	6,015	27,756	
Total current assets	247,597	589,789	
Fixed Assets			
Machinery and equipment	16,536	19,141	
Office furniture and equipment	3,208	6,506	
Aircraft	32,194	32,194	
Automobile	5,244	5,244	
Boat	8,087	8,087	
Leasehold improvements	3,364	3,627	
Total	68,633	74,799	
Less depreciation and amortization	15,089	11,870	1
Net	53,544	62,929	
Land	136,000		
Total net fixed assets	189,544	62,929	

Investments and Other Assets			
Organization expense less amortization	8,966	29,024	
Option on land	2,000		
Investments, Sauter, Inc.	8,384	193,055	2
FAA and FCC designs and approvals	311,310	311,310	2
Deferred R&D less amortization	18,530	108,682	3
Other subsidiary investments		174,712	3
Covenant not to compete, less amortization		196,167	4
Total investments and others	349,190	1,012,950	
Total assets	786,331	1,665,308	
Current Liabilities			
Notes payable, bank		157,500	5
Notes payable, stockholders		47,946	
Accounts payable	36,521	223,255	
Accrued taxes and interest	6,411	18,545	
Current portion of long-term debt		63,855	
Total current liabilities	42,932	511,101	
Long-Term Debt	287,707	358,304	5
Stockholders' Equity			
Common stock	182,690	426,648	6
Paid-in-surplus	311,310	311,310	
Retained earnings	(38,308)	57,945	
Total liabilities	$786,331	$1,665,308	

EXHIBIT 3(c)   Notes to balance sheet.

1. *Depreciation and amortization*

The Company provides for depreciation and amortization by charges to income based upon manufactured or acquisition cost and estimated useful lives of individual property items using the straight-line method for book purposes. Estimated useful lives are as follows:

Machinery and equipment	2 to 10 years
Office furniture and fixtures	6 to 10 years
Leasehold improvements	Terms of lease

Expenditures that materially increase property lives are capitalized. The costs of maintenance and repairs are charged to expenses as incurred. When depreciable property is retired or disposed of, the related cost and accumulated depreciation are removed from the accounts, and any gain or loss is reflected in income.

2. *Acquisitions and principles of consolidation*

The financial statements include the accounts of Uniwest Incorporated and its former subsidiaries Radair, Inc. and Imperial Controls Corporation, both of which have been merged into the Company effective October 31, 1970.

The Company owns 100% of the stock of Uniwest Development Inc. ("UDI"), all of which was acquired in August of 1969. The Company records its investments in UDI at underlying book value. Upon completion of sale of the six remaining town houses located in Portland, Oregon, the Company intends to dissolve UDI.

The Company owns 100% of the stock of Continental Controls Corporation, all of which was

EXHIBIT 3(c)   Notes to balance sheet (*Continued*).

acquired in August of 1970. The Company records its investments in Continental as an amount equal to the sum of all monies advanced by the Company to Continental since its acquisition. The Company intends to dissolve Continental upon completion of the sale of the remaining Continental inventory of thermostats and related products.

	Investment	*Advances*
Uniwest Development, Inc.	167,112	—
Continental Controls Corporation	—	7,600
	167,112	7,600

3. *Other assets*

Certain of the expenses incurred by the Imperial Controls Division of the Company are attributable to obtaining and implementing an exclusive long-term license to distribute, modify, and in some cases to manufacture in the United States the entire line of products of Fr. Sauter A.S. of Basel, Switzerland. Through October 31, 1970, a total of $193,055 has been attributed to this license.

For periods prior to January 31, 1969, the Radair Division of the Company has followed the practice of expensing research and product development costs as incurred. Much of this research and product development cost was incurred by the Company to secure over 250 FAA and FCC approvals in the form of Type Certificates, Technical Standard Orders, and other required approvals that entitle the Company to produce and distribute certain FAA and FCC approved airplane instruments and navigation–communications equipment. At the time the Company acquired Radair, Inc., prior management carried management's estimate of the replacement value of these certificates on their books at $311,310. The Company intends to commence amortizing this value in 1971 on a straight-line basis over a 10-year period.

For periods subsequent to January 31, 1969, the Radair Division of the Company has capitalized certain nonrecurring research and development costs and is amortizing these costs on a straight-line basis over a 5-year period. The amount capitalized during the period January 1, 1969 to October 31, 1970 is $113,619 and the amount amortized through October 31, 1971 is $19,275.

4. *Covenant*

On April 29, 1970 the Company purchased 26,000 shares of the Company's common stock, no par value, and a Covenant Not to Compete from Robert E. Florence, the former owner of Radair, for a total of $390,000. The down payment was $113,000 with the balance to be paid over a 6-year period together with interest at the rate of 8% per annum.

The first annual installment of principal and interest is $58,785. This is payable in the amount of $37,855 on January 1, 1971, which includes interest from May 1, 1970 through January 1, 1971 in the sum of $14,772 and principal in the sum of $23,083. The remaining balance of the first annual installment in the sum of $20,929 is payable on July 1, 1971.

The balance is payable in semi-annual installments of $29,392, including interest, which installments are payable on each January 1 and July 1. The Company has established a sinking fund of $4,500 per month to be utilized to make the semi-annual installment payments.

Of the $390,000 purchase price, the Company has allocated $209,500 to a Covenant Not to Compete. The Covenant covers all existing products and certain products expected to be developed in the future. The Covenant is for a period of 6 years. The Covenant is being amortized at the rate of $32,000 in the first year and $35,500 each year thereafter. The amount amortized through October 31, 1970 is $13,335.

5. *Borrowing*

The bank loan arrangement provides for borrowings on demand notes with interest at 9%–9½% per annum. The Company's accounts receivable and inventory are assigned as collateral for borrowings from the bank. In August 1969, the Company was given a line of credit from the bank in the amount of $150,000 at the rate of 9% per annum. Borrowings under this line reached a

EXHIBIT 3(c)   Notes to balance sheet (*Continued*).

maximum of $131,159 and, as of November 30, 1970, had been reduced to $112,000. As of January, 1971, the Company will commence repaying this loan at the rate of $3,000 per month, plus interest, until such time as the loan is repaid.

A summary of long-term debt as of October 31, 1970, is as follows:

Notes to bank	$126,159
Notes for acquisition of Company stock	277,000
Total	403,159
Less portion maturing within 1 year	63,855
Long-term portion	$339,304

The Company has issued 12-month convertible subordinated debentures in the amount of $171,050 with interest of 8¾%. These debentures are convertible into shares of common stock of Uniwest, Incorporated, as follows:

Converted:	July 1, 1970	$ 9.75
	November 1, 1970	14.00
	Thereafter	17.00

At October 31, 1970 all of these debentures had been converted into common stock except $19,000.

6. *Stock Options*

As of October 31, 1970, under the Company's Qualified Stock Option Plan, options to purchase an aggregate of 9,325 shares were outstanding under the plan, having been granted by the Company to 9 key employees. The options expire in each case, 5 years from the date of grant and are exercisable at the rate of 25% of the stock subject to the option annually beginning 1 year from the date of grant. All such options are exercisable at $9.75 per share.

Warrants to purchase up to 5,130 shares of common stock of the Company at a price of $17.00 per share exercisable at any time prior to January 1, 1973 have been issued in conjunction with previous financing.

are questioning whether Seattle will stay in business, let alone a little company like Radair. They tell us we'd be crazy to invest in a lot of new products now. But the distributors tell us the opposite, that it's now or never. Salesmen are depressed and saying if they only had something new maybe sales would pick up. After things finally do pick up, the competition will begin adding things, and then it may be too late for us. So if we're going to develop a full line, the next few months may be our only chance to break in. (Statement of Richard Heckmann.)

ASSIGNMENT

Analyze the circumstances of Radair as of the end of the case and develop a plan of action for the president Richard Heckmann.

Laboratory Resources Corporation

"I expect it will be 2 or 3 years before we begin thinking about entering another business," commented Ralph Ersten, Chairman of Laboratory Resources Corporation (LRC). "What we learn in building this one will give us the know-how to do it all over again someday. But this has to be a success first."

Laboratory Resources was founded in November 1968 by three Oakland men. By March 1, 1971, it included 5 divisions, employing 185 people, with sales of $1.3 million for the 6 months ending December 31, 1970, made through independent representatives on a 10% commission basis with 85% of the total in the eastern half of the U.S. This growth was accomplished by acquisition of 4 companies and purchase of the patent rights of another. LRC stock was traded over-the-counter with bid prices ranging from $1.00 to $1.75 in 1969 and $1.60 to $4.25 in 1970.

Two of the acquired companies manufactured cages for laboratory animals; one of these also produced devices for setting broken animal bones, and the other also produced materials-handling equipment such as bread racks for commercial bakeries. A third company bred beagle dogs and guinea pigs for research, and the fourth provided contract research services in Western Germany. Consolidated financial statements appear in Exhibit 1, and comparative statements for the four acquisitions are in Exhibit 2. An organization chart as seen by the company president, Nat England, is given in Exhibit 3, and a discussion of the industry is given in the Appendix.

HISTORY

Ralph Ersten and Simon Hughes, investment analysts for the mutual fund owned by a large Oakland insurance company, and Jason Marne, vice president of the fund, had witnessed what they regarded as phenomenal growth in high-technology industries such as electronics, medical sciences, and research. Over a period of 6 months they frequently discussed the idea of forming a company, until one evening over a beer Ersten said, "I've got the name—Synerco." "That's it," Hughes and Marne agreed. "We weren't sure what we would be, but we knew that was the name," Ersten later recalled.

The conversation continued: "Let's incorporate. We need a lawyer. I'm familiar with equity. Simon, you know bonds, and, Jason, you're a CPA. We need someone in policy and administration." The three agreed to think about who might fill the gap. A professor Ersten had met in graduate school at the University of California, Ned Williams, was contacted for expertise in the policy area and he referred them to an attorney, Richard Anston. The five donated a total of $900 to start the company.

Their initial plan was to raise $1 million by finding a company priced below book value that they would sell for a higher figure. They found Wyoming Grain Corporation, with a book value of $48 selling at $15 per share, but they were unable to reach terms with controlling stockholders after several months of negotiations. Because of possible conflict of interest with the insurance company employing him, Mr. Marne resigned. The other four continued to meet monthly, but began to question their strategy for raising money. Ersten began using the initial capital to trade in high-technology stocks.

In mid-1968, Ersten met the term, "life science industry." In researching stocks for the mutual fund, he noticed Charles River, a supplier of research animals, which had

451

EXHIBIT 1 Laboratory Resources Corporation's comparative financial statements, consolidated LRC.

INCOME STATEMENTS

	June 30, 1970	Six months, ending December 31, 1970
Sales (net)	$ 86,576	$1,288,892
Cost of sales	164,476	920,154
Gross profit (loss)	(77,900)	368,738
Operating expenses	139,184	344,818
Net income (loss)	(217,084)	23,920

BALANCE SHEETS

Current assets		
Cash	$ 138,746	$ 248,841
Receivables (net)	260,833	721,780
Inventory	263,665	532,744
Other	5,187	33,592
Total current	$ 668,431	$1,536,957
Contract receivables	2,895	170,000
Fixed assets (net)	609,830	574,646
Other assets	171,334	375,504
Total assets	$1,452,490	$2,657,107
Current liabilities	339,597	798,017
Deferred federal income taxes	35,555	35,555
Long-term debt	1,042,334	989,071
Shareholders equity	35,004	834,464
Total liabilities and shareholders equity	$1,452,490	$2,657,107

grown 30% annually for several years and recently gone public. Simultaneously, while scanning the Oakland Yellow Pages for high-technology companies that Synerco might buy, he noticed one called Mackin Research and Development Company. He phoned to learn what it was and was told the company produced an automated rat housing cage. To learn more about the industry supplying laboratory animals, he checked Standard and Poor's but found no such industry described. Simon Hughes could find nothing in the library on the subject. Ersten contacted his former finance professor, Dr. Hermann Constantin, at the University of California, who became interested and agreed to suggest study of the subject to a team of students under his supervision.

Peter Mackin operated the company Ersten had called in his spare time while employed as systems engineer with a national electronics firm. Previously, Mackin had owned a small business making training aids for the police, and he had also worked on rat cage development for the University of California. His cage fed the animal and cleaned the cage automatically by electronic timing. Advertisements in psychology trade journals between 1965 and 1968 brought orders for 25 cages at $2,200 each. By mid-1968, however, orders slackened, causing Mackin to close his small shop and move the fabrication equipment to his garage. Still, he felt that the product was promising and that with more money the product could be developed to profitability.

EXHIBIT 2 Comparative financial statements, LRC acquisitions.

	Westerman		Setworth		Inbifo		Blatner	
	12 months 3/31/69	12 months 3/31/70	12 months 6/30/69	12 months 6/30/70	12 months 11/30/69	12 months 11/30/70	12 months 9/30/69	12 months 9/30/70
INCOME STATEMENTS								
Sales	354,781*	416,648*	100,245	96,116	235,884	279,459	1,595,170	1,822,536
Cost of sales	196,338	258,604	78,534†	85,370†	146,968	148,833	1,208,568	1,283,256
Other expenses	118,058	118,721	10,509	6,745	55,470	78,650	293,838	267,671
Net income	40,385	39,323	11,202	4,001	33,446	51,976	92,764	271,609
BALANCE SHEETS								
Current Assets								
Cash	17,612	31,239	NOT PREPARED	1,000	60,520	29,599	85,951	161,003
Receivables	103,441	61,644	BY PREVIOUS	128,865	32,255	81,952	266,728	413,545
Inventory	29,507	31,824	OWNER	134,308	4,696	8,670	189,271	188,350
Prepaid expenses	7,447	3,618		30	920	1,092	9,507	15,846
Tax reserve		1,071						
Total current	158,007	129,396		264,203	98,391	121,313	551,457	778,744
Contract receivables	87,000					454		
Investments	28,167							
Property and equipment (net)	88,788	112,648		299,090	46,999	38,004	52,964	103,303
Brood stock‡				65,986				
Other	260	260		1,870				
Total assets	362,222	242,304		681,149	145,390	159,771	604,421	882,047
Current liabilities	62,558	62,240		74,525	58,392	31,818	216,155	342,357
Long-term debt	163,398	21,373		74,859	65,710	71,291		35,799
Shareholders equity								
Paid-in capital	45,000	45,000		5,582,255	16,061	6,575	58,214	87,860
Retained earnings	91,266	113,691		(71,490)	5,227	50,087	330,052	416,031
Total equities	362,222	242,304		681,149	145,390	159,771	604,421	882,047

* Westerman sales 1969: Surgical 35%; cages 53%; misc. 12%.
                    1970: Surgical 34%; cages 63%; misc. 03%.
† Direct cost of care of animals.
‡ Animals for breeding.

EXHIBIT 3 Laboratory Resources Corporation, organization chart, March 1, 1971.

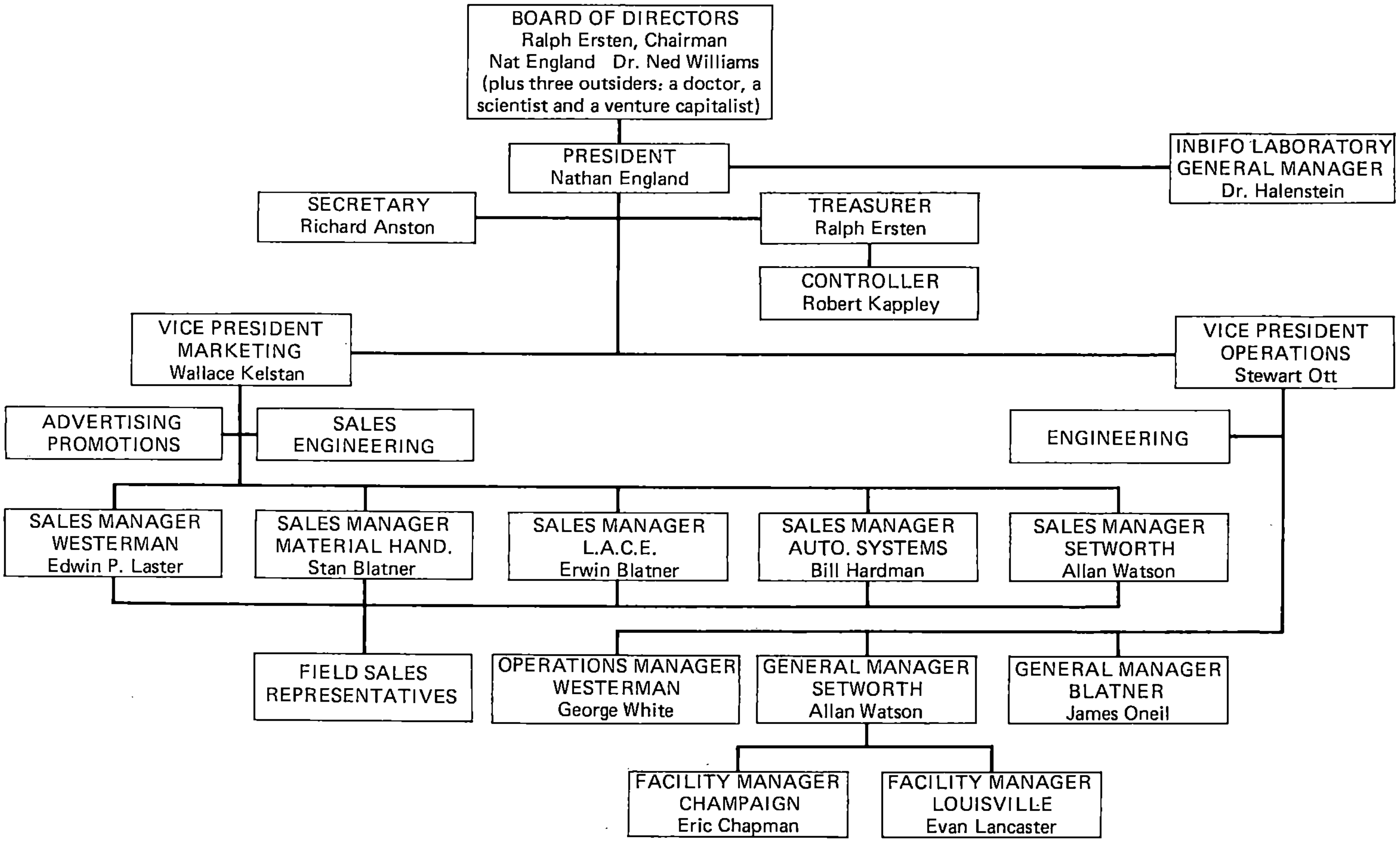

BOARD OF DIRECTORS
Ralph Ersten, Chairman
Nat England Dr. Ned Williams
(plus three outsiders: a doctor, a
scientist and a venture capitalist)

INBIFO LABORATORY
GENERAL MANAGER
Dr. Halenstein

PRESIDENT
Nathan England

SECRETARY
Richard Anston

TREASURER
Ralph Ersten

CONTROLLER
Robert Kappley

VICE PRESIDENT
OPERATIONS
Stewart Ott

ENGINEERING

SALES MANAGER
SETWORTH
Allan Watson

SALES MANAGER
AUTO. SYSTEMS
Bill Hardman

SALES MANAGER
L.A.C.E.
Erwin Blatner

OPERATIONS MANAGER
WESTERMAN
George White

GENERAL MANAGER
SETWORTH
Allan Watson

GENERAL MANAGER
BLATNER
James Oneil

FACILITY MANAGER
CHAMPAIGN
Eric Chapman

FACILITY MANAGER
LOUISVILLE
Evan Lancaster

VICE PRESIDENT
MARKETING
Wallace Kelstan

SALES
ENGINEERING

SALES MANAGER
MATERIAL HAND.
Stan Blatner

FIELD SALES
REPRESENTATIVES

ADVERTISING
PROMOTIONS

SALES MANAGER
WESTERMAN
Edwin P. Laster

454

In February 1969, after 6 months of discussions with Ersten about building a company using his product, Mackin accepted 60,000 shares of LRC stock and an option on 65,000 more at 10¢ per share in return for his product and $6,000 of assets, mostly machine tools which had been mutually appraised by Ersten and Mackin. He also received an 18-month contract as general manager of LRC with the understanding that someone else would be found to run the business while he developed the product. LRC was capitalized with $17,500 from Synerco, with Ersten as president. Operations continued in Mackin's garage.

By May 1969 Ersten said that the concept of the company was starting to change. The Constantin study had estimated sales of $33.9 to $39.2 million for experimental psychological research equipment, increasing annually at 14.4%. Approximately 25 small firms, averaging 14 years of age, were providing for these needs, but none was attempting to do so on an integrated basis. Ersten saw LRC as perhaps a single company to amalgamate the industry rather than one of several small Synerco companies. "To grow that way I didn't think I should stay president, because I didn't have the background to run a company," he said. "I'd never even worked for a manufacturing company. I preferred to be creative in finance." A new president was hired, Nathan England, 32, a Harvard M.B.A. and acquaintance of Dr. Williams. He had served 6 years as special assistant to the president in charge of acquisitions for a nearby manufacturing company.

While the new president was being hired, Ersten, who had parted from the mutual fund in June 1969, was looking for an electronics engineer. Through a mutual acquaintance, he met Jack Wilson, an M.S.E.E. with his own small shop and who built small components primarily for the University of California. Pete Mackin also visited Wilson and reported that Wilson's skills would be useful in automated cage development. In July 1969, he joined LRC. Another new employee at the time was Stewart Ott, a graduate mechanical engineer and M.B.A. student at the university. Ott was given charge of the cage development over Wilson and Mackin.

Through stock trading, the original $900 of Synerco had grown to $44,000 by February 1969. The latter sum, combined with $6,000 in assets from Mackin, brought the LRC capitalization to $50,000. Anticipating sales of $100,000 by the end of 1969, the founders decided to raise $100,000 for operations, plus $100,000 to buy another company. Through an intrastate offering in California, Ersten, from contacts developed as an investment trader, was readily able to sell 200,000 shares at $1 per share.

During the summer of 1969, workspace was rented in a Concord, California warehouse to continue development of Mackin's product and prepare for production. England and Mackin attempted to sell cages by displaying an operational unit at a Vancouver, B.C. psychologists' convention. It seemed to them that visitors paid considerable attention to the display and asked numerous questions indicating interest. Two orders were received shortly thereafter, and England predicted break-even by December. By that date, however, no more orders had come. Potential customers explained reluctance to buy with such statements as, "It's twice as expensive as a conventional cage." "It hasn't been tested yet, has it?" "I don't have the money right now." "We just bought cages last year." "What we need are cages for rabbits and dogs, not rats." And, "We want cages that are individually removable." Even government institutions expressed reluctance to invest $100,000 for automated cages.

Ersten spent the summer of 1969 on stock market transactions and seeking new acquisitions for LRC in "tomorrow" growth industries, not necessarily restricted to life sciences. The search took him through abandoned mink ranches, a surgical sales company in Albany, an animal farm in San Jose, and a nearby electronics company. Occasionally, he simply drove through the local industrial area looking for companies.

At the Laboratory Animal Science Convention in Dallas, attended by England, Ott, and Ersten in October 1969, contact was made with Erwin Blatner, whose company, according to Constantin and others in the field, was a leading maker of animal care equipment. Ersten got the impression that the Blatners were interested in selling. On a sales trip in Des Moines in December, Ersten called Erwin Blatner and asked to visit the plant and talk about business. In discussion over lunch the following day, Mr. Blatner at first denied interest in selling, but later he said that he and his brother might consider it. Both Blatners expressed concern over selling to a new and unestablished company, and no action was taken for several months. LRC continued to show interest, however, through numerous visits to the Blatner plant.

In November through a business friend Ersten made contact with Westerman Manufacturing Company, located in Castro Valley near Oakland. He had heard the company mentioned by Peter Mackin and had seen advertisements for its proprietary line of veterinary orthopedic surgical equipment and fiberglass animal cages in trade journals. Discussions began on a purchase agreement with the owner, Dan Westerman.

By the end of 1969 the expected sales of $100,000 had failed to materialize, and LRC was nearly out of money. A new prospectus was prepared. Oakland investment bankers were contacted for an offering to raise $300,-000 for working capital and purchase of another company. In March $298,000 was obtained by LRC through the sale of $325,000 worth of 7% convertible (at $2.50/share) debentures.

WESTERMAN MANUFACTURING COMPANY

After 6 months of discussions, LRC acquired Dan Westerman's company, excepting land and buildings, in June 1970 for $423,367. Of this amount, $100,000 was in cash at closing, with an additional $35,167 on January 1, 1971; and the balance in 120 equal monthly installments, including interest at 8%, beginning February 1, 1971.

Dan Westerman, whose father had sold veterinary equipment, became interested in

problems of animal bone fracture following World War II. He adapted techniques developed for human fractures during the war. The techniques involved using metal pins which allowed movement during healing and raised the probability of survival for animals. His technique was adopted by schools and the name "Westerman" became part of the veterinary lexicon. Westerman products included stainless steel and aluminum surgical tools and splints for smaller animals. Similar equipment for larger animals such as horses and cows had not yet been developed. Although by 1970 competitive products at lower prices had been developed, Westerman was described by two national distributors as still the leader.

In his frequent visits to veterinary clinics and laboratories, Mr. Westerman saw a need for cages easier to maintain and more attractive than those of wire mesh. As a result, he developed fiberglass cages in 1952 and by 1970 this product was offered through mail order only in a variety of sizes. Advertising was placed in journals and shows, and direct sales were made by Mr. Westerman. Price competition was described by management as intense, with a high turnover of competitors entering and leaving the field. Shipping charges were considered an appreciable handicap in sales to distant parts of the country.

In addition to the two major lines, Westerman offered a line of cages for environmental and germ-free studies, oxygen therapy units for use in treatment of cardiac, shock, and respiratory cases, and primate restraining chairs for behavioral and biomedical research. These and other miscellaneous items amounted to 10% of sales.

Mr. Westerman ran his company unassisted for over 20 years and became known as a leading authority on animal fracture equipment and its application. In 1968 a decline in sales prompted him to seek help, and he hired Edwin P. Laster who had previously worked in marketing with Canada Dry and General Mills. In mid-1969 Mr. Westerman became deaf and retired from active management, leaving Mr. Laster in charge. Lacking experience in orthopedics,

Mr. Laster concentrated on cage sales, and by 1970 these accounted for the major share of sales.

After LRC purchased the Westerman company Wallace Kelstan, former marketing manager of an Oakland bank who had been hired as marketing manager of LRC in January 1970, was put in charge of the new Westerman Division with Mr. Laster assigned to product development and sales. The shop superintendent of Westerman retired and was replaced by Sam Costello, formerly shop manager of In Motorcycles. By LRC decision, all Westerman advertising was discontinued. The plant was moved from the Valley to Oakland, and administrative offices, including records and accounting, were consolidated with those of LRC, which were a mile away.

Mr. Laster said that he felt the advertising could best be handled at LRC headquarters in order to realize discounts by placing it all through one source. He also thought that payroll and accounting should be done by LRC, as well as investment and major expenditure decisions. New product and pricing decisions, he thought, should involve LRC, but all decisions on plant personnel and the research and development of new products should be left at division level.

SETWORTH RESEARCH SUPPORT

In March 1970 Mr. Ersten learned from an employee that Setworth Research Support Corporation of Bloomington, Illinois might be for sale. In April at a convention Mr. Ott heard the same. The owner was TRW, a large Los Angeles company. When Mr. Ersten phoned TRW, a group executive there confirmed the proposed sale. Immediately following Ersten's call, the executive called him back to ask if, in addition to possibly buying Setworth, LRC might be interested in "going international." TRW owned a contract research laboratory (INBIFO) in Cologne, Germany, which was also for sale.

Ersten visited Setworth in June 1970, and after looking at the facilities told the representative, "I think you've sold your company." Two weeks later, TRW's group business manager flew to Oakland and set forth terms for purchase of both Setworth and INBIFO. The price was $420,463; with $20,463 down and additional payments of $50,000 on January 22, 1971; $100,000 on December 31, 1973; and $125,000 on December 31, 1976 and 1979. Of the total purchase price, it was understood that $29,237 was for INBIFO and the remainder for Setworth. The sale was completed July 16, 1970. To finance the initial payment, a $50,000 bank loan was secured by accounts receivable and inventory was obtained.

Setworth raised beagle dogs and guinea pigs for research purposes and sold them to such customers as Abbot Laboratories, University of Cincinnati, the U.S. Department of HEW, Procter & Gamble, du Pont, and Walter Reed Army Hospital. The largest portion of the company's $100,200 sales in 1969 came from continuing contracts, so that minimal effort was expended in selling.

The company employed a total of 75 people at its Bloomington headquarters and outlying facilities, each with its own resident manager reporting to the general manager, Dr. Kurtz. On 240 acres owned by the company in Champaign, Illinois the company raised beagle dogs in a modern facility built in 1967. There was room for approximately 500 females, which on the average had 2 litters of 6 pups per year. Contract boarding of other dogs was also provided.

At Callahan, Florida, near Jacksonville, the company owned 20 acres of land and buildings. This location had been operated as a beagle breeding and contract boarding facility, but was currently used primarily as a distribution center for beagles to the Midwest market. In Louisville, Kentucky the company produced guinea pigs on a 3½-acre leased facility. Formerly used for combination of mouse and guinea pig production, it now produced only guinea pigs because the market for them was considered better.

Increasing competition had led Setworth to discontinue raising mice, rats, and cats to concentrate on beagles and guinea pigs which sold easier. Charles River Laboratories was the main competitor in animals other than beagles. Competition in the beagle market was also increasing with new firms entering each year. Members of management expressed the view, however, that the modern facility at Champaign gave Setworth an advantage.

After the purchase of Setworth, Dr. Kurtz, the president and general manager, was replaced by Allan Watson, 34, a TRW employee who had formerly been business manager of Setworth. England recalled, "Although a capable veterinarian, Dr. Kurtz didn't have the business know-how we felt was necessary. Mr. Watson did and he also seemed to identify more readily with LRC."

The Callahan facility was closed by LRC; all beagle breeding was centered at Champaign. Headquarters of the company were moved to Louisville. For the first time in its history, the company earned a profit. But along with this favorable development, the market for dogs began to decline. Mr. Lancaster, the Setworth sales manager, commented:

> We got big in the dog market through a unique marketing technique developed several years ago when research institutions were taking almost anything they could get. We sold them the female dog and offered to breed her and raise the pups at a fixed rate per dog. Customers got a good dog, a guaranteed source of supply, and a very good price (about $72 per pup). But today other producers have entered the market with quality dogs and lower prices. At the same time, a reduction in research being done because of government funding cutbacks makes it less important to have a guaranteed source of animals.
>
> Guinea pigs are doing better. The competition is not as intense and demand is bigger than we can satisfy. We produce a good animal which holds up well under the stress of research studies. The researchers consider this important, and it has made our animals popular. Although we've gone through name changes in the last 10 years, I think we have a good reputation built up for SRS. Having the name of a major company like TRW associated with us was also a strength. Our customers seem to be taking a "wait-and-see" attitude toward LRC.

INBIFO

As part of the Setworth purchase agreement, INBIFO (Institut fur Industrielle und Biologische Forschung GMBH) was acquired in July 1970 for $29,237. Located in Cologne, Germany, the laboratory did contract research in pharmacology (preparation, qualities, and uses of drugs) and toxicology (poisons, their effects and antidotes, particularly in foods). Major customers were drug companies, but studies were also done for manufacturing, chemical, tobacco, and cosmetic industries. Most orders came to the laboratory through word-of-mouth from former clients. Most of these were German, but Swiss, Dutch, and Italian companies had also been served.

Occupying a 5,300-sq-ft building on a 10-year lease (ending in 1973), the laboratory employed 27 people, including part-time employees and consultants. The general manager, Dr. Halenstein, was an M.D. with postdoctoral studies in pharmacology and toxicology. His staff included one pathologist, one histologist, one toxicologist, and one pharmacologist. The remainder were apprentice researchers, animal caretakers, office staff, and maintenance personnel. Because of the crowded conditions of the laboratory, which was operating at full capacity, Dr. Halenstein claimed he was unable to recruit additional personnel even when additional orders were available.

Two smaller laboratories competed with INBIFO in Germany. According to a report prepared for TRW by an English consulting firm, both were considerably lower in quality. The main competitor was said to be the British firm of Huntington, which compared favorably to major U.S. laboratories and was, according to the report, the leading European firm.

> We bought this company because I thought having a lab in Europe sounded exciting. I also thought having a European division would catch the eye of investors, which it did. Secondly, we bought it because the price was book value, and it has a record of profits. Finally, it offered to open the door in Europe

for our other products. (Statement of Ralph Ersten.)

Several weeks after the purchase of INBIFO, Ersten toured the facility with Dr. Halenstein.

> I had been told by Dr. Halenstein on the phone that the lab facility was in bad shape and things were going downhill. But I came away optimistic and felt that things were not as bad as I had been led to believe. Dr. Halenstein seemed cautious with me. I explained LRC and what we were trying to do. Although he was interested, he was not willing to commit himself. He wanted me to know that what was essential to the lab was a new facility. (Statement of Ralph Ersten.)

After Ersten returned to the United States, he began receiving unsolicited offers to buy INBIFO. "After the first two, I didn't think much about selling. But after the third, I began to think about it more seriously. If we could get the right price, why not sell? The best offer so far had been $70,000, which was over twice what we had paid." Alternatively, it was estimated that with an investment of $500,000 a new lab could be built with twice the capacity.

BLATNER INCORPORATED

Discussions with the Blatners about the possibility of LRC's buying their company had begun in December 1969 and were concluded in June 1970, with the purchase to become effective September 1970 for $847,000. The initial payment at the time would be $250,000 in cash. On January 1, 1971 LRC would pay another $97,000 cash, plus $300,000 worth of LRC stock at $3.18 per share. Another $200,000 under an 8% note would be paid in equal installments on January 1, 1972, October 1, 1972, and October 1, 1973, with accrued interest paid quarterly. To finance the down payment a public offering of 100,000 shares of LRC stock at $2.50 per share was made in September, 1970.

Blatner manufactured over 200 products, such as animal cages and related equipment, including rat, mouse, cat, rabbit, dog,

and monkey cages, racks for holding cages, food hoppers, cage-cleaning equipment, and operating tables. According to the Constantin report, Blatner was an industry leader with a long-established reputation for quality. Although two other manufacturers of animal care equipment distributed such products on a national basis, most competition came from small metal fabricating shops which bid on contracts to utilize slack capacity. In a contract announced by Walter Reed Hospital in 1970, for instance, 75 firms submitted bids.

Principal customers for Blatner's products included universities, hospitals, pharmaceutical companies, independent research laboratories, and the U.S. Public Health Service. Sales were made through direct mail, trade shows, journal advertisements, and personal referrals. Manufacturers' representatives on a 10% commission basis were also used.

In addition to animal care products, the firm produced a variety of other metal-fabricated materials-handling equipment that accounted for about one-third of total sales. These included conveyor carriers, shop trucks, pouring spouts, commercial bakery racks and trays, and miscellaneous hospital and industrial equipment. This business came primarily by mail. Requests for bids were received from manufacturers (General Motors, Westinghouse, etc.) for special material-handling equipment. Demand fluctuated widely and the market was highly unpredictable in Blatner experience.

Blatner had operated as a family-owned company in Des Moines, Iowa since 1856. General manager and president, Stan Blatner, 64, was assisted by his brother, Erwin, 55, and a cousin, Walt Blatner, 62. The company employed 68 union and salaried people in a 44,000-sq-ft plant, which housed both offices and production. Ersten commented that there seemed to exist a healthy work atmosphere, resulting in high shop efficiency and workmanship.

Nat England considered Erwin Blatner particularly important to the success of the company because he was well-known and respected as a very knowledgeable person in the area of animal care. Stan Blatner managed administration and worked on development of material-handling equipment. Walt was plant superintendent. Stan's son-in-law, Jim Oneil, had been with Blatner 13 years and worked in both production and sales. Following the sale to LRC, Nat England told Stan Blatner of his confidence in existing management and his desire that LRC should learn from Blatner. "The last thing we wanted to do was upset the operation with new people," Nat recalled.

> But we were mistaken. Jim Oneil, who became plant superintendent when Walt retired, said he couldn't work with Stan as president. Erwin, who felt the same way, quit putting out. October became the worst month for production in company history. I sent Stew Ott to Des Moines to help, but he came into conflict with Oneil.
>
> In November we had a major convention in Chicago, to which we invited all our sales reps for an integrated LRC sales meeting. This was our first such meeting, and I considered it very important. But I found Jim Oneil, Erwin and Stan Blatner, and Stew Ott virtually not speaking to each other.
>
> After the meeting, I went to Des Moines to help reorganization. Jim Oneil became vice president and general manager reporting to Ott. Stan was appointed vice president and sales manager for material-handling equipment, and Erwin became vice president and sales manager of animal care equipment. Both Erwin and Stan Blatner became responsible to Wally Kelstan, LRC vice president for marketing.
>
> December plant performance was better than October, but it was still far below previous production. Stew Ott and Wally Kelstan moved from Oakland to Des Moines in early January 1971 and took with them the Automated Animal Housing System Division. [This division was the company originally bought from Pete Mackin. Mr. Mackin had left the company in August 1970 when his employment contract terminated.] (Statement of Nat England.)
>
> A Blatner sales representative expressed optimism for the future. "Our customers know what to expect when they buy our products. The company has always stood 100% behind

what it made and never competed just on price. When our customers hear about LRC, the first thing they want to know is whether they are still dealing with the same people. We tell them they are still dealing with Blatner and can depend on it."

CORPORATE HEADQUARTERS

As of March 1971, the company headquarters in downtown Oakland housed Ralph Ersten, Nat England, Bob Kappley, the controller, and two bookkeepers. Two salesmen of Westerman Division also shared the offices. In addition, there were two full-time secretaries. Much of the three LRC officers' time, when not on the road, was spent in each other's offices discussing problems and making decisions for the company jointly. Ersten and England traveled approximately 1 week per month, visiting divisions, meeting with prospective investors, or searching out possible acquisition candidates. Kappley had just spent 2 months in Des Moines and expected to travel still more in the future. An organization chart as Nat England saw it appears as Exhibit 3 on page 454.

> We've had disappointments in sales recently. I think that the general economic downturn of the country is largely to blame. I've gone out selling, particularly in the West where Blatner isn't represented. Since our dog sales were far below projections the last 2 months, I spent a week on the East Coast with our Setworth general manager selling dogs. Al Watson and Evan Lancaster said people just aren't buying dogs. When I asked about some customers in particular, they said they hadn't contacted them lately. I felt that both needed help in learning how we go about selling. They agreed over the phone, and Al and I spent a week together on calls. It appeared that people really weren't buying dogs. Apparently, many research studies were being delayed. We looked for other possible markets and visited medical centers where dogs were used for medical training. This looks like a new market LRC should enter. (Statement of Nat England.)

Ralph Ersten was spending his time almost entirely on possible acquisitions and sources of capital.

I recently completed work on a new brochure for distribution to potential investors. In addition, Nat and I have recently met with selected brokers and underwriters in Oakland to tell our story. I have lunch at least once a week with someone I think should know about us. (Statement of Ralph Ersten.)

Beyond what we are already working with, there are many other products and activities we could consider for the future. Some possibilities include contract laboratories in the United States, new products for veterinarians and humane societies, and complementary animal-care products such as automated watering devices, animal incinerators, cage-washing apparatus, and even animal food. We're now the largest single user of animal food outside the pet market.

Our most immediate worry is getting the cash budget back on schedule. Right now we're almost 6 months behind plan. But planning has been hard in a process of acquiring small family-run companies. Their records are all different, and some are incomplete. For instance, I can't tell you the costs or labor hours associated with manufacturing our products. These things are important to us as a manufacturer, and particularly now when we must be very careful of the dollars we spend. (Statement of Nat England.)

During Christmas vacation following the report, one of the students, Richard Piel, 28, a German national just graduating, visited INBIFO at the behest of LRC to meet with Dr. Halenstein about the problems of the lab and to clarify a legal matter concerning notarization of purchase of the company under German law. Upon his return, Piel reported that understaffing was a serious problem and that Dr. Halenstein did not even try to recruit people because he felt that the physical facility was so poor. The second major problem, he said, was a severe backlog of uncompleted work. Because Dr. Halenstein was trying to do everything himself, he was not doing a good job in any one area. Lower work output resulted. In one case, results of a research study completed 2 years prior had not been delivered to the customer. Because a few major customers accounted for most of INBIFO's work, he considered this serious. Piel's recommendation to Ersten was that if LRC could get a good price for INBIFO, it should sell. Shortly thereafter negotiations that had been underway for some time with an interested firm, produced an offer for INBIFO of $100,000.

By March 1971 LRC had 1,007,340 shares of stock outstanding held by 786 stockholders as follows: Synerco, 385,000; Pete Mackin, 110,500; three investment firms, 197,500; public, 217,000; Blatner family, 94,340; Jack Wilson, 3,000. The current trading price of the stock was 4½ bid, 5 asked.

In a letter to shareholders in early 1971, Nat England included the following comments:

> The combinations of several factors caused operations for the first 2 months of the quarter to be unprofitable. The losses were primarily the result of two plant moves . . . moving the Automated Systems Division from Concord, California to Des Moines, Iowa and moving the Westerman Scientific Division from Castro Valley, California to Oakland. . . . As a result of the lost production, it now appears that sales for the year will be under $3 million. The month of March was again profitable; however, it is likely that any profitability for the remainder of the fiscal year will not be sufficient to offset the earlier losses and the probability of inventory adjustment.

APPENDIX
The Industry

CAGES

There are approximately 2,500 institutions in the United States that use animals for biological, medical, and psychological research purposes. These include pharmaceutical firms, chemical companies, medical schools, hospitals, food companies, research institutes, cosmetic firms, psychologists, psychopharmacologists, universities, and testing laboratories.

Millions of animals are caged in metal or plastic boxes for this purpose. In order to feed, water, and clean the animals, a staff of maintenance personnel is required to attend to each cage containing an animal. The floor of a metal cage is usually either expanded metal or wire cloth to permit the animal's excreta to fall through into a pan covered with sawdust or paper. The pans must be changed several times a week. Water is provided by a small water bottle with a sipper tube hung on the outside of the cage, and food is hand-delivered at frequent intervals.

Because this work is so unpleasant, it is difficult to find employees, and as a result labor turnover is often high. Care of the animals is vital and is required 7 days a week, 24 hours a day. An experiment may last several months during studies. If the animal involved in the study dies because of improper care, thousands of dollars, as well as valuable research time, are lost.

Typical cage construction consists of stainless steel or galvanized metal, with some fiberglass construction found in veterinary clinics and animal pounds. Sources of supply for cages have been highly fragmented. Although three firms offer a product on a national basis, a great many cage products are manufactured on a local basis by metal fabrication shops, usually on a one-time basis. These local supply sources are many times able to offer a product at a significant cost savings over national brands because of their location advantage and because their pricing policies are designed to get the bid.

Automated caging is a very new concept in the housing and care of animals. It is an attempt to reduce the high cost of labor associated with maintaining conventional caging by providing caging that feeds, waters, and cleans the cages automatically. Various concepts have appeared on the market throughout the 1960s, but none has gained broad market acceptance. Resistance to automation has stemmed from poor performance of the early models, high costs of the product, and a general reluctance on the part of many researchers to switch to automated housing from conventional cages. Contamination and related health problems have been the paramount concerns of researchers.

By 1971 no more than 5% of existing facilities used an automated caging system, and this figure was not expected to exceed 20% in 5 years.

ANIMALS

A variety of animals are used for research purposes. The principal types and the approximate number used in 1969 are shown below:

Mice	35,625,000	Rabbits	577,000
Rats	12,322,000	Cats	162,000
Guinea pigs	888,000	Dogs	372,000
Hamsters	848,000	Primates	68,000

The order in which the animals are listed represents a hierarchy of usage by researchers. Generally as studies progress to advanced stages, a different and usually larger and more expensive animal is used. Some animals are particularly suited for certain types of research work. The guinea pig's skin resembles that of the human and therefore is used in dermatology studies. In addition, studies related to tumors, eye diseases, and cancer are common users of this animal. Dogs, particularly beagles, are considered the most suited for higher-level and more complex studies because of their temperament, cost of care, and durability.

Various sources of supply have been used by the institutions. In many cases, labs have taken what they could get. Beginning in 1965, more sophisticated suppliers emerged, supplying animals with carefully controlled breeding and environmental conditions. This allowed users to be more selective in their choice of animals and to choose those which would insure the best test results. In early 1971 the demand for guinea pigs outstripped the supply. Producers anticipated continued strong demand for the guinea pig following the temporary imbalance in the market supply. The entry by several producers into the beagle dog market in 1969 and 1970 created a ready supply of dogs of generally the same quality. The result was an oversupply of dogs and resulting price competition. It was anticipated that the beagle dog market would remain competitive and would force suppliers to find more economical means of production.

VETERINARY ORTHOPEDIC SURGICAL EQUIPMENT

In 1970 there were approximately 16,000 veterinary clinics in the United States. The equipment and supply needs for these clinics were met through hundreds of manufacturers and 2 national and 25 regional distributors that represented these many manufacturers.

One of the many products used by the veterinarian was equipment to set bone fractures. A technique similar to that used in human fracture repair was developed in the late 1940s by Dan Westerman, founder of Westerman Manufacturing, Castro Valley, California. This technique involved surgery on the animal and the use of pins, clamps, and splints to set the fracture. This technique was an innovation to veterinary medicine. To facilitate introduction of this technique, Westerman spent much of his time traveling to veterinary conventions and medical schools to demonstrate the technique. In addition, with the help of friends in veterinary practice, he wrote a procedures manual outlining the technique required and the tools necessary to set bones. This technique and equipment became widely accepted throughout the field of veterinary medicine.

Until the mid-1950s, Westerman was the only manufacturer of surgical equipment for use in setting animal fractures, although several major manufacturers of similar equipment for humans existed. Since then other manufacturers have developed similar techniques and related equipment to price competitively with the Westerman product. The effects of this competition were felt but were not significant enough to force Westerman to cut prices or force new product innovation. By 1970 the Westerman product remained the leader in supplying orthopedic surgical equipment to veterinarians.

ASSIGNMENT

Analyze this company and develop recommendations for management. Include as part of your analysis a concise definition of the strategy of this company both as it now exists and as you would propose it for the future.

Multivayer, Inc.

At 11:05 on a Friday morning in the spring of 1970, Bob Weaver, president of Multivayer, hung up his office phone, put both feet on the desk, and thoughtfully lit his pipe. A used manufacturing equipment broker had telephoned and, in discussing general business conditions, described the

Reprinted by permission. Copyright © Purdue Research Foundation, 1975.

situation of Aerospace Machining, Inc., a company in a small city 40 miles away. Aerospace Machining was in trouble and needed help. Since the executive group of Multivayer had recently discussed the desirability of applying excess corporate cash flow to acquisitions, Bob Weaver thought that this might be just what the group had been looking for.

By 11:50 the general manager, manufacturing manager, accountant, chief engineer, and the purchasing agent gathered in Mr. Weaver's office. Except to use telephones and for interviews, they were to remain there until 9:30 that night. Over the next few days the management group was to be almost fully involved in investigating Aerospace Machining and in deciding whether or not to offer to buy the business.

COMPANY BACKGROUND

Multivayer was founded in 1962 in Cincinnati by Bob Weaver, who at age 32 had had engineering and managerial experience with three companies. Most recently, he had been chief engineer and assistant to the vice president of administration for a small glass manufacturing firm that was acquired by a large company, Corrugated Boxes, Inc. His subsequent assignment was to develop plans for setting up a subsidiary that would develop manufacturing equipment for Corrugated Boxes' customers. After these plans were well-developed, the attorneys for the parent company advised that the venture might be interpreted as in violation of the antitrust laws.[1] Bob Weaver decided to quit. There was no ill will on the part of the parent company's management and he was told to feel free to pursue the venture if he wished to do so.

Weaver raised money for a new company by approaching seven businessmen and telling each, "I believe a good man, provided sufficient to live on for a year, can generate a profit. I intend to try. If you will agree to serve on our board of directors, we will sell

[1] Section Three of the Clayton Act provides, in its pertinent parts: ". . . it shall be unlawful for any person engaged in commerce . . . to lease or make a sale or contract for sale of goods . . . machinery, supplies, or other commodities . . . on the condition, agreement, or understanding that the . . . purchaser thereof shall not use or deal in the goods . . . machinery, supplies, or other commodities of a competitor or competitors of the lessor or seller . . . where the effect of such lease, sale . . . or agreement . . . may be to substantially lessen competition or tend to create a monopoly in any line of commerce." (15 U.S.C. Sec. 15, 38 Stat. 731.)

you a share." Six of the men contacted provided a total capital of $13,000 and received 51% equity. Mr. Weaver retained 49%.

The first 9 months were spent in the attic of the founder's garage with light and heat supplied by a single bulb, a broken popcorn popper, and a long extension cord. Through the process of elimination (there was no product to sell and there was insufficient capital for equipment or inventory) it became apparent that the company was in the consulting business. The founder's background was in machine design and industrial engineering; initially a variety of consulting jobs were pursued in the Cincinnati area.

About 18 months after founding, the firm began to concentrate on problems involving materials-handling for the corrugated box industry. Corrugated Boxes, Inc. contracted for about one-half of Bob Weaver's time. Initially, he concentrated on analyzing the use of forklift trucks with various attachments in the finishing department of one of their box plants. Since it appeared that conveyor systems might be superior to forklift trucks, this led to a series of assignments in designing conveyor systems for the finishing departments of Corrugated's plants. These were the first such conveyor systems in the industry.

Engineers were added and the company moved through a series of rented offices and, in the middle of the third year, into a leased building. Thereafter, the company moved once each year for the next 4 years into successively larger buildings. At each step, growth was financed from profit. Initially, debt was avoided because it could not be obtained. Later, when the company prospered and collateral became available, the company had learned to survive and grow without debt and this became a way of life.

By the fourth year the company had sales of $150,000 and 5 employees, including a secretary. At this time, the company made a major change in strategy by undertaking the manufacture of conveyor systems. Some parts of the conveyor systems that Multivayer designed were not commercially available. On three systems for Corrugated Boxes, Inc., Multivayer subcontracted the manufacturing of parts, but supervised the installation and "debugging" of the systems. Because of problems with the subcontractors Multivayer purchased a punch press and began manufacturing. Management found that a larger profit could be obtained by converting ideas into hardware and selling the finished product. Manufacturing also had the additional advantage of multiplication; an idea or machine design could be sold many times. The Company changed completely to manufacturing and no new consulting contracts were undertaken. This decision was made easier by the fact that other corrugated box companies were approaching them about buying conveyor systems.

To this point all personnel, with the exception of a bookkeeper/secretary, were engineers and for the next 9 months there continued to be no hourly paid employees. The staff taught themselves and each other the necessary production skills and subcontracted that small portion that could not be performed "in house." Production workers were added later, and by 1970 there were 40 production personnel, with average wage rates of $3 per hour. Manufacturing was described as a "blacksmith" operation, involving a relatively low level of manufacturing skill. Rollers, shafts, and cabinets were produced, but bearings, motors, belts, and electrical components were purchased.

During the early years talent was the only merchandisable commodity. For this reason, and out of pride, each new employee was outstanding in his area of specialization. To obtain talented personnel and maintain a high level of enthusiasm, employee compensation was normally 150% of what that person could obtain elsewhere. Corporate finances were completely open[2] and every employee was expected by all personnel to carry his full weight.[3] All personnel, including the president, were available for every job.[4]

Multivayer evolved a strategy of developing industrial products that required a high level of engineering innovation in an essential 10% of the system. To a prospective purchaser, the systems offered major cost savings over conventional methods of materials handling. In almost all instances the payback time for a system (costing from $20,000 to $30,000 for the earlier systems) was less than 1 year. Despite low manufacturing costs, it was possible to price systems on the basis of the cost savings provided, thus allowing high margins.

Capital requirements for manufacturing equipment were small, with the ratio of sales to fixed assets being in excess of 20 to 1. Increasing production, however, occasionally justified major equipment and in such instances it was often designed and built by the staff. The resulting high efficiency—special-purpose machinery, as contrasted to general-purpose equipment used by competition—usually developed additional economies.

Production and inventories were tightly controlled with absolutely no goods produced for inventory. Shipments went to customers directly from production and occasionally jobs would leave the plant with paint still wet and with metal warm to the touch from the heat of fabrication. Raw materials inventories were minimal with nothing being purchased unless required by a specific customer purchase order. Deliveries of raw materials were closely scheduled and the company became notorious among suppliers for specifying that a truck arrive at 2:32 p.m. of a given day.[5]

Competition consisted of 7 national manufacturers and approximately 90 regional companies. National competitors each produced sales volumes ranging from $40 mil-

---

2 *For many years financial statements were chalked on a blackboard and hung on the wall of the largest room. Revisions were performed much in the spirit of reporting ballgame scores.*

3 *It was never necessary to fire an employee. Group pressure compelled exceptional performance or the individual left usually within 30 days.*

4 *A standing joke, and actual occurrence, had a president in coveralls unplugging a restroom facility when a visiting salesman made a disparaging comment about the company. Ten minutes later, in the president's office, the company won record low prices on purchases.*

5 *They were often there.*

lion to more than $100 million per year. Regional competitors ranged from a few hundred thousand dollars to $20 million annually. Except for a few "back alley shops," the competitors supplied a complete line of products to a cross section of industry. Most competitors built substantial contingency allowances into their bids, because they lacked experience with specific problems of the corrugated box industry.

Multivayer specialized in the requirements of the corrugated box industry and declined business from all others. Management felt that its great familiarity with the industry permitted better estimation of system costs and had led to design features that gave the company advantages over competitors.

Multivayer's early sales involved design of conveyor systems for finishing departments of various box plants. (At that time there were about 1,500 corrugated box plants in the United States.) Many subsequent sales involved expanding the conveyor systems to other departments of the same box plants. In 1964 a box plant might have had from $20,000 to $30,000 of conveyor systems, but by 1970 the same plant might have more than $200,000 of such systems.

Early sales involved Mr. Weaver's calling personally upon the highest level manager he could contact in a box plant. Initially, he would try to convince the manager of the advantages of using conveyor systems; then he would emphasize the advantages of a Multivayer system. Potential customers might seek bids from as many as ten suppliers, many of whom had little experience with corrugated box plants. Multivayer was usually successful in winning the contract.

Although the savings promised by the conveyor systems might have permitted relatively high prices, management decided to price aggressively in order to remove a price umbrella under which less efficient manufacturers might hide. The thought was to drive them from the market before they gathered strength.

Traditionally, competitors sold through a network of distributors. The product was only one of many items offered by each distributor. Multivayer determined that it had developed a sufficiently focused market to sell through its own personnel and that the technical nature of the product required special knowledge in the customer's area of interest. Accordingly, nationally recognized experts were employed as salesmen. Typical of these was a man who had previously been chief engineer of a 21-plant company in the corrugated box industry. Another had been the plant manager of that industry's largest and most profitable plant. In 1970 there were 5 salesmen operating from offices in various parts of the country.

By early 1970 Multivayer felt secure in its field. Expansion was projected to continue at the current rate over the next several years. All anticipated capital expenditures had been made and a conveyor system for producers of cans had been successfully field tested. The company believed that this new line could, and should, be held until some slackening in demand for the existing product became apparent. At this time, as in all previous periods, approximately 62% of all employees had been with the company for less than a year. It was felt that internal expansion beyond 50% per year could not be sustained without damage to the corporate reputation for quality.

The company continued to avoid debt except accounts payable and very rare short-term bank borrowing for peak requirements. This was made possible by profits, sales terms, and demands on suppliers. Profits as a percent of sales were normally 100% to 150% greater than competitors. Sales terms were 30% upon receipt of purchase order, 60% upon shipment, and the remainder within 30 days. Better than 90% of their customers were listed in *Fortune* magazine's top 500 companies. Competitors' terms were "net 30 days after installation." Suppliers were required to carry Multivayer's accounts payable for 60 days.

Earnings on equity were routinely at or in excess of 100% per year, and because expansion was essentially self-financing, substantial cash surpluses were accumulating.

(See Exhibits 1 and 2.) At the direct and repeated suggestion of the Internal Revenue Service, dividends of $20,000 to $25,000 per year had been paid.[6] All original capital contributors were officers and majority stockholders of other companies and each was paying personal taxes at the 70% level. Dividends were strenuously objected to and no equity holder would set a price at which he would sell his stock.

Multivayer had made two small acquisitions in the past. One had been a company that manufactured equipment for the lock producing industry. The other produced overhead conveyors for various industrial markets; Multivayer had hoped to apply its product to the corrugated box market, but this had not worked out. Each company had about 10 employees and had been showing losses. Multivayer's outlay in each instance was about $20,000 plus the assumption of debts. By 1970 Multivayer was in the process of discontinuing each of the businesses and selling off the assets. It appeared that they would about break even on the two ventures.

Many of the Multivayer executives were ambitious, aggressive people who worked best when challenged. They grew restless if the business grew "uninteresting," and one reason for the past acquisitions had been to provide them with challenge. Bob Weaver believed that the current business was now becoming routine and that the management group was getting bored. In 1970 it would have been possible to transfer several of these people on a full-time basis to an acquired firm.

AEROSPACE MACHINING, INC.

Aerospace Machining had been founded in 1962 by James Channing and was located in

[6] *Section 531 of the Internal Revenue Code provided that a surtax might be assessed on undistributed earnings in excess of the reasonable needs of the business. Earnings are improperly retained when the purpose is to avoid personal income taxes on shareholder income. This penalty tax is 27½% on unreasonable additions to retained earnings up to $100,000 in any one year (after excluding $100,000 of retained earnings) and 38½% on annual improper accumulations in excess of $100,000.*

a small town about 30 miles from Cincinnati. The company specialized in high-precision machining of exotic metals, such as titanium. Virtually all sales were to the aerospace industry.

Marketing primarily involved developing bids for particular machining jobs that had been advertised by Aerospace prime contractors. The owner, an excellent salesman, handled all marketing and did not believe that it was necessary for the company to be located close to major customers. Aerospace Machining, like similar firms, was on a "qualified bidders list," having been inspected by prime contractors and the Defense Department.

In the past, Aerospace annual sales were believed to have been as high as $3 million, and the company had about 200 employees. By 1970 sales had declined precipitously, and there were about 30 employees. It was thought that the company was operating at about 20% of previous levels, primarily on two contracts. One was a subcontract for a wing flap assembly and the other was for an intricate component of a newly introduced and somewhat experimental military plane. Continued production of both units was contingent first upon government "follow on" orders of the aircraft and secondly upon Aerospace Machining's winning future competitive bids.

Industry sales of the aerospace industry had declined from $29.0 billion in 1968 to $24.9 billion in 1970 (see Exhibit 3). Many firms similar to Aerospace Machining were reputed to have closed within recent months. Opportunities to bid had decreased in recent months, and many machine shops were competing on each available job.

The Multivayer management group decided that Aerospace looked sufficiently attractive to warrant a full-scale investigation. The manufacturing manager talked to a new employee who had recently been laid off by Aerospace Machining. The purchasing agent began to contact suppliers and each of the others started to gather information from his area of specialization.

From the new employee, a former supervisor at Aerospace, the manufacturing man-

EXHIBIT 1 Multivayer, Inc., statement of financial condition.*

	December 31, 1968	December 31, 1969
ASSETS		
Current Assets		
Cash	$ 54,666	$ 24,348
Receivables:		
Trade accounts	$ 392,248	$1,019,023
Notes and amounts due from subsidiaries	66,002	71,263
Other accounts	3,879	4,827
	$ 465,732	$1,113,456
Less allowance for doubtful accounts	3,600	3,600
Net receivables	$ 462,132	$1,109,856
Inventories at lower of cost (first-in, first-out method) or market		
Work in progress	$ 80,956	$ 96,735
Raw material and supplies	142,621	276,292
Total inventories	$ 223,579	$ 373,028
Refundable federal and state income taxes, estimated	22,707	–0–
Principal payments due within 1 year on notes receivable from officers	$ 7,200	$ 16,200
Prepaid expenses	10,917	14,760
TOTAL CURRENT ASSETS	$ 781,203	$1,541,300
Other Assets		
Notes receivable from officers, less principal payments due within 1 year	$ 49,500	$ 33,300
Investment in Pemco, Inc., at cost, plus profits since acquisition	(33,057)	105,667
Investment in Un-O-Veyor Systems, Inc., at cost	–0–	51,377
Amounts due under consulting agreement	27,000	9,000
Real estate not used in operations, at cost less allowance for depreciation of $1,125	53,325	51,975
Miscellaneous investments, at cost	–0–	7,927
TOTAL OTHER ASSETS	$ 96,766	$ 260,575
Equipment and Leasehold Improvements, on the basis of cost		
Equipment	$ 119,604	$ 155,925
Vehicles	8,479	13,008
Furniture and fixtures	13,366	21,013
Leasehold improvements	20,770	22,681
	$ 168,224	$ 212,632
Less allowances for depreciation	50,013	78,390
TOTAL EQUIPMENT AND LEASEHOLD IMPROVEMENTS	$ 118,211	$ 134,242
Deferred Charges, at cost, less amortization		
Patents	$ 14,823	$ 15,114
Recapitalization costs	–0–	3,531
Research and development costs	10,683	12,744
TOTAL DEFERRED CHARGES	$ 25,506	$ 31,392
TOTAL ASSETS	$1,021,687	$1,944,736

EXHIBIT 1 *(Continued).*

	December 31, 1968	December 31, 1969
LIABILITIES AND STOCKHOLDERS' EQUITY		
Current Liabilities		
Note payable to bank	$ 27,000	$ –0–
Trade accounts payable	138,434	444,393
Notes and amounts owed to subsidiaries	111,445	133,565
Salaries, wages, and bonuses	22,100	58,546
Payroll taxes and amounts withheld from payrolls	10,983	26,551
State and local taxes	8,807	22,467
Deposits on projects in process	158,569	184,006
Accrued vacations	–0–	29,914
Accrued interest	2,835	–0–
Federal taxes on income, estimated	43	311,830
Principal payments due within 1 year on long-term debt	38,934	–0–
TOTAL CURRENT LIABILITIES	$ 519,159	$1,211,284
Long-Term Debt, less principal payments due within 1 year		
6% real estate mortgage note	$ 21,459	$ –0–
Installment note payable to bank	144,000	–0–
TOTAL LONG-TERM DEBT	$ 165,459	$ –0–
Stockholders' Equity		
Common stock, no par value	$ 205,488	$ 222,492
Retained earnings	167,704	580,924
	$ 373,192	$ 803,417
Less treasury stock, at cost	36,124	69,966
TOTAL STOCKHOLDERS' EQUITY	$ 337,068	$ 732,124
TOTAL LIABILITIES AND STOCKHOLDERS' EQUITY	$1,021,687	$1,944,736

* Any errors in totals result from rounding and deleting cents.

ager was able to supply firm data on hourly rates of pay, production rates, tooling, order backlog, and inventories.

Aerospace did not have a union and its wages were believed to be comparable to or lower than those of competitors. The company's machinists were highly skilled and able to do "superb" work. Average wage rates were about $4.50 per hour. The backlog on the two orders was $200,000.

It was learned that Aerospace leased its two buildings, and, under the guise of being a potential tenant, the general manager persuaded the building owner to conduct the general manager and Multivayer's chief engineer on a building inspection. From this they prepared a listing of equipment, a plant layout, a report on work process, an estimate of material inventories, and an appraisal of employee morale and general discipline.

Both buildings and equipment were judged to be in excellent condition. The little inventory that was on hand was owned by customers. Ingots of the valuable raw materials were registered, and records were kept on their status.

Plant discipline was described as "fantastic"; the owner appeared to be a tyrant. The machinists who remained with the firm were very skilled and it appeared that the company could do good work at relatively

EXHIBIT 2 Multivayer, Inc., statement of income and retained earnings, for the year ended December 31, 1969.

	Amount	Percent of net sales
Net sales	$5,265,379	100.00%
Cost of products sold	3,649,933	69.32
Gross profit on sales	$1,615,446	30.68%
Selling, administrative, and general expenses	1,013,817	19.25
Profit from operations	$ 601,626	11.43%
Other income:		
Cash discounts earned	$ 9,959	.19
Rent	6,660	.13
Interest	6,417	.12
Sundry	3,036	.05
	$ 26,073	.49%
	$ 627,701	11.92%
Other deductions:		
Interest	$ 8,857	.17%
Cash discounts allowed	8,203	.15
	$ 17,060	.32%
	$ 610,641	11.60%
Share of subsidiary net income*	133,499	2.53%
INCOME BEFORE FEDERAL TAXES THEREON	$ 744,139	14.13%
Federal taxes on income, estimated	311,830	5.92
NET INCOME	$ 432,309	8.21%
Retained earnings at January 1, 1969	167,704	
	$ 600,013	
Cash dividends paid	19,089	
RETAINED EARNINGS AT DECEMBER 31, 1969	$ 580,924	

* Subsidiary had been formed to invest in 3,000 steers in the Texas Panhandle.

low cost. During the recent decline in industry sales it appeared that Aerospace had at least "held its share" of industry business.

The purchasing agent, through telephone conversations and hastily arranged interviews with suppliers, determined that Aerospace was very slow on payments—as much as a year past due with most of them. The company was considered a poor risk by the majority of its suppliers and was on a cash basis with most of them. Working with selected suppliers, who in turn contacted others, the management of Multivayer prepared a list of the company's accounts payable. The list was estimated at 90% accuracy.

Multivayer's bank contacts, working privately and through personal channels, provided debt and other liability information. It was estimated that liabilities were about $300,000, including a bank loan of $80,000.

Aerospace was operating at an annual sales level of about $200,000. Although heavy losses had been shown earlier when the staff was larger, costs had recently been trimmed to the point where current operations were about the break-even level. (Few funds, however, were being generated to repay the large debts previously incurred.)

EXHIBIT 3 Aerospace Machining (billions of dollars). (Source: Standard & Poor's Industry Surveys, Aerospace Basic Analysis, October 31, 1974, p. A 11.)

1964	20.6
1965	20.7
1966	24.6
1967	27.3
1968	29.0
1969	26.1
1970	24.9

EXHIBIT 4 Aerospace Machining, equipment appraisal.

	A*	B†
Profile milling machines (10)	$154,000	$ 84,500
Vertical milling machines (10)	13,250	10,250
Planer (2)	7,000	4,000
Horizontal production mill (1)	7,000	4,500
Lathes (2)	3,000	1,800
Vertical boring mills (2)	15,500	10,500
Horizontal milling machines (3)	10,250	7,000
Planer (1)	27,500	20,000
Office furniture and equipment	3,600	3,000
Chevrolet van truck, new 1968	2,000	1,500
Grinders (2)	2,050	1,400
Miscellaneous equipment	19,700	13,775
	$264,850	$162,225

* Present market replacement value.
† Value expected if the equipment were sold in a quick forced sale.

The equipment broker who had originally brought the situation to Mr. Weaver's attention knew the machinery in the Aerospace plants. The special-purpose equipment was capable of producing to very tight tolerances. It had been beautifully maintained, and the capabilities of some pieces had been improved through changes made by Aerospace. It appeared that the equipment enabled Aerospace to produce precision parts of titanium at lower cost than many competitors. The resale value of this equipment under forced sale conditions was estimated at about $162,000 (see Exhibit 4). The machining capabilities of Aerospace were not needed for any present or contemplated products of Multivayer.

At this point, management decided to approach Mr. Channing formally about the possible sale of his business. Mr. Weaver found him very willing to discuss the sale of either the Aerospace common stock or the assets of the firm, but he was unwilling to disclose financial statements. He indicated that, if he sold the business, he would be willing to stay on as manager. Multivayer management judged that his technical knowledge would be critical to the operation of

EXHIBIT 5 Aerospace Machining, cash projections for the six months ended August 1970.

	March	April	May	June	July	August	Total
Collections, trade accounts	$ –0–	$18,350	$14,200	$11,900	$15,900	$21,350	$ 81,700
Disbursements:							
Direct labor and production supervision	9,000	8,800	9,300	9,000	12,300	12,300	60,700
Other production costs	4,000	4,000	4,000	4,400	4,400	4,400	25,200
Administrative salaries	3,450	3,150	3,150	3,450	3,150	3,150	19,500
Other sales, general, and administrative expense	400	400	400	400	400	400	2,400
Machinery modifications	–0–	–0–	1,000	–0–	–0–	–0–	1,000
Total disbursements	$16,850	$16,350	$17,850	$17,250	$20,250	$20,250	$108,800
Excess of disbursements over receipts	$16,850	$ (2,000)	$ 3,650	$ 5,350	$ 4,350	$ (1,100)	$ 27,100

Assumptions:
1. Trade accounts receivable will be collected in the month following shipment.
2. All payroll, suppliers, etc., are paid on a current basis.
3. The plant will be closed for a week in March 1970 and a week in April 1970 for vacation and payroll will be reduced by the fact that not all employees are eligible for vacation pay. Payroll will be reduced in May and June 1970 to correlate with the decrease in production.
4. Administrative salaries include payroll for two general managers for the remainder of 1970. Approximately $1,300 per month will be eliminated when the current general manager leaves.
5. $21,850 of the total $27,100 disbursements in excess of receipts is caused by the fact that there will be no cash received in 1970 for August 1970 sales and there will be two general managers until the fall of 1970.

EXHIBIT 6 Aerospace Machining, pro forma income statement for the six months ended August, 1970.

	March	April	May	June	July	August	Total
Sales, net	$18,350	$14,200	$11,900	$15,900	$21,350	$19,850	$101,550
Cost of sales	13,000	12,800	13,300	13,400	16,700	16,700	85,900
GROSS MARGIN	$ 5,350	$ 1,400	$ (1,400)	$ 2,500	$ 4,650	$ 3,150	$ 15,650
Sales, general, and administrative expense	3,850	3,550	3,550	3,850	3,550	3,550	21,900
Depreciation	1,350	1,350	1,350	1,350	1,350	1,350	8,100
NET LOSS (PROFIT)	$ (150)	$ 3,500	$ 6,300	$ 2,700	$ 250	$ 1,750	$ 14,350

Assumption:
The loss presented above does not take into consideration the effect of possible carrybacks of net operating losses, etc., should this corporation become a division of Multivayer, Inc.

the plant for the first year, which was estimated to be the time necessary for a Multivayer executive to learn the business. Mr. Channing appeared to be a good salesman, a harsh disciplinarian who "ran a tight ship," and a man with a fantastic ego, who might be difficult to direct.

Subsequent inquiries with creditors, primarily the bank and several key suppliers, indicated that they were pressuring Aerospace for payment. It appeared that they might be willing to accept about 50¢ on the dollar if Mr. Channing could obtain cash to settle on that basis. Multivayer learned that Aerospace had just been informed by one of its two major customers that its contract would be canceled if Aerospace did not get its financial house in order so that the customer's source of components was not jeopardized.

Multivayer management discussed the sales outlook with the current customers of Aerospace. They had a high opinion of Aerospace's machining capabilities and indicated a desire to have Aerospace keep these contracts, provided that the firm could be put on a sound financial and managerial basis. Additional future orders would depend on whether or not industry sales expanded. The SST program to develop a supersonic commercial airplane, if funded by the federal government, would result in a number of possible contracts.

Multivayer management encountered conflicting judgments about the outlook for the industry, but it also found a fair amount of optimism. Multivayer management had confidence in its own ability and believed that if anyone could increase sales of Aerospace Multivayer could.

Multivayer management then generated estimates of probable cash flows and monthly income statements if the facilities were operated by Multivayer management (see Exhibit 5). These assumed that the company's

two contracts would be continued and that no additional contracts would be obtained. Although based upon available information about current operations at Aerospace, management realized that there was substantial uncertainty, both in regard to expected revenues and expenses. Accordingly, there was substantial conservatism built into the forecast, and management believed that profitability might be improved substantially under Multivayer control. A loss of $14,000 for the next 6 months was forecast (see Exhibit 6).

Management was extremely hesitant to make an offer for the common stock of Aerospace. Under pressure, Mr. Channing would probably be willing to disclose financial statements, but the timeliness and quality of these statements might be open to question. In addition, even though Mr. Channing was thought to be honest, it was felt that extreme financial pressure might have led to undisclosed corporate liabilities. Therefore, management's inclination was to purchase the assets. It was believed that Mr. Channing would be reluctant to sell less than all of his assets.

Mr. Weaver arranged to meet with Mr. Channing again. It was believed that Mr. Channing had no other offers for his firm at this time. Management also believed that a decision should be made quickly. If the major customer of Aerospace were to cancel its contract and make arrangements with an alternative supplier, the consequences would be serious. The Multivayer management team met to consider making an offer and the possible terms to be proposed.

ASSIGNMENT

What should the management of Multivayer do?

12

Final Outcomes

A subject neglected by many operators of small companies concerns what will ultimately become of their firms. During start-up the owner is preoccupied with pulling pieces together to get the company going. As the company begins to develop, the owner often has to concentrate on survival to reach and pass the break-even point. Some companies never reach profitable operations, and of those that do many continue to be plagued with survival problems throughout their lives. If they break free of these problems and achieve high profits, their operators may shift their attention either to expanding and building growing concerns or else to enjoying the high profits by living more lavishly or by concentrating on community and other activities outside the firm. Ultimately, it must all end because nobody lives forever. It is easy to ignore this fact and operate without planning for the ultimate transfer of the firm to a new owner.

The result of this neglect can be a company that is ultimately cut adrift without direction, one whose employees are unprepared to cope either with continuation of operations or with seeking new jobs, and one whose value is much less than it might have been. Consequently, it makes sense to consider the possible ultimate outcomes of a small firm and lay plans for coping with them. Six possible outcomes are discussed in the following pages. It may happen that an entrepreneur cannot, because of unmanageable circumstances, choose among the possible outcomes freely, but he should at least be able to develop contingency plans. The six possible outcomes begin with the more attractive ones and then end with those that should be avoided.

GO PUBLIC

An attractive goal to many small companies is to sell stock publicly, because in that way the owners may be able to sell only part of the company, retain control, and obtain cash at the same time. If a market develops in which the stock is actively traded, they may be able to sell readily additional shares in the future. Upon the death of an owner, for example, part of the shares may be sold to cover estate taxes. The company may be able to raise additional money for expansion by issuing more shares and to attract desired personnel by offering stock or options to buy shares. These offers may be made even if the company is not publicly held, but if it is public, those who receive the options or shares will find them more attractive because they can see a market in which they can exchange them for money.

Counteracting these attractive features of making a company public are numerous laws, regulations, and other obstacles (see Chapter 5 on financial management). Generally, going public only makes sense for those who are not eager to put their money into stocks that do not offer promise of being salable at a profit, which requires both that the company be substantially and increasingly profitable and that it become large enough and have enough stock outstanding that it will enjoy an active market in which shares can be readily traded. This requirement rules out going public for most small companies, because most of them remain small.

MERGER

Merging is a common final outcome for small companies, particularly manufacturing companies. Typically, the acquiring company is seeking growth and either integration or diversification. Alternatively, a business is sometimes acquired for tax purposes, to take advantage of a tax loss in the small company or to use it as a vehicle for applying accumulated cash so that it will not have to be paid out and taxed as dividends.

An employment contract for the owner of the acquired company is often part of the consideration; sometimes that person will also have to sign an agreement not to enter competition in the same line of work for a stated time after the merger. One objective of the employment contract may be to reduce taxes by spreading out income over a longer period of time. Another objective may be to maintain access to the former owner's expertise in operating the acquired company. From the owner's point of view the employment contract can also be a way of selling off the business and yet maintaining some degree of contact with it.

In practice, however, there usually soon follows a parting of ways between the former owner and the new employer, whether there is an employment contract or not. Typically, the acquiring company introduces its own methods and various reform ideas into the acquired company. There will be new reporting requirements. Accounting and personnel practices of the acquiring company are imposed on the new acquisition. There may be changes in logo, products, and customer service policies. Changes in operating procedures and the introduction of managerial personnel from the new parent company may follow, together with the discharge ("housecleaning," "weeding out dead wood") of former employees of the acquired company. Most difficult of all to bear for the formerly independent owner will probably be the fact that major decisions will henceforth all have to be cleared with top management of the parent company ("who really don't understand the acquired business," its former owner might add). Thus, in actuality, the merger means that the small business is sold out, the same outcome as discussed in the section on sellout.

SUCCESSION RETIREMENT

If the owner is able to groom a manager to replace him, it may be possible for him to retire from the business and pass ownership to his heirs. Grooming a successor is sometimes difficult in a small company in which the owner has personally built the company, knows all about the company, and is inclined to keep a hand in everything. The owner tends not to attract employees who are inclined to leadership and he does not develop leadership qualities among his employees. If employees do not share in the ownership, they are less motivated to run the business well when the ownership changes and they are left running the business. (Of course, if one of the employees happens to be an heir, this problem is automatically solved.) The owner should consider providing ways for employees to acquire some share or all of the business.

Building toward succession requires that responsibilities for making managerial decisions be transferred to others. A typical way to begin is with relatively minor decisions and work toward major decisions. At first, the owner should put in shorter workweeks. Then he should take off from work and leave town for successively longer periods of time, leaving the business to "run itself." As time passes, he should receive fewer reports and he should receive them less frequently. The owner who is seeking to pass managerial functions along to others should not look daily at the bank balance and list of receivables. Monthly financial statements should be enough. It should also be possible to have others sign the checks. Ultimately, quarterly statements should be sufficient, as they are for stockholders in publicly held companies.

SELLOUT

A company that has profit-making potential can generally be sold for more than the liquidation value of its assets. Most businesses are sold this way. The owner who wants to get out of the business by selling it has several options for obtaining buyers. One way is to have employees take over the business and buy the owner out. A second way is to work through personal acquaintances, business connections, or advertisements to find an outside buyer. Some banks, for instance, circulate confidential internal newsletters among their branches telling about companies for sale. All metropolitan newspapers carry classified sections in which they list "business opportunities." *The Wall Street Journal* carries these advertisements regularly. Competitors and companies that wish to integrate or diversify through acquisition are also likely contacts.

A typical step in preparing to sell is to bring the company balance sheet up to date with detailed breakdowns of fixed assets and inventory, including original purchase prices and current market replacement costs and resale prices for the items included. Sometimes it is helpful to have a professional appraisal firm price the assets even though obviously buyers will tend to discount appraisals commissioned by the seller and will make their own more conservative estimates. Possible arrangements and terms between the buyer and seller are discussed in Chapter 9 on acquisition.

CLOSE DOWN

For the majority of new businesses formed the final outcome is to close down and go out of business. This approach makes sense if the company is losing money and can find no way to turn the business around. It also makes sense if the owner wants to get out of the business, either to retire or because some better opportunity has presented itself, and a buyer cannot be found to take over the business. Normally, if the business shows a profit, there will be people who will give a value to the going concern greater than the liquidation value of the assets, but sometimes it is not possible to find them. For instance, if the owner wants to get out fast, possibly for reasons of ill health or because he wishes to move into something else quickly, there may not be time enough to seek out or negotiate with a buyer. If the business is such that the owner himself is an asset, possibly because of his very specialized skill or know-how, or because of his special personal connections with key customers, the profits will stop and the going concern value will vanish if the owner is removed.

The procedure for closing down is usually simple. Utilities are shut off. Assets, such as plant, machinery, and inventory are sold either by advertisement or to dealers or by having an auctioneer come in and dispose of them. Even lists of customers can sometimes be sold to other firms that may be able to use them. Local, state, and federal agencies are notified that the company is ceasing business. Hopefully, this will be enough, but complications are possible. For example, one company was closed and its owners were preparing to write off the capital losses under internal revenue provisions applicable to section 1244 stock. The company was formally closed out to allow this. Suddenly a tax refund from the prior year arrived in the mail. The officers sent it back, saying that the corporation to which it was payable no longer existed. The tax officials said that they could not take it back. It had to be accepted. Ultimately, the owners and the tax officials worked out an agreement in which acceptance would not mean that the company was still in business.

BANKRUPTCY

The worst that can happen to a business is for it to go into bankruptcy. Generally, this happens because the business is losing money and can't pay its bills, but it sometimes happens when a business is making a profit but can't pay its bills because its inventory and accounts receivable have been allowed to grow too large. When creditors ask for payment and there is no cash to give them, the creditors can throw the company into bankruptcy. Bankruptcy can be either voluntary (the bankrupt person petitions for relief) or involuntray (creditors force the action).

There are two general types of bankruptcy, depending on the legal form of business: personal bankruptcy and corporate bankruptcy. In personal bankruptcy an individual can have his debts wiped out a maximum of once every 6 years. It is not necessary to have a lawyer. The person fills out the proper forms listing such things as how much money is owed to whom, what assets are owned, and how much they can be sold for. There may be a filing fee. After a few weeks the court notifies creditors to meet and the court appoints a "receiver" to preserve what is left of the property. After meeting, examining the lists, and questioning the bankrupt person, the creditors elect a trustee, usually a lawyer, to help divide the property among them. The property is then sold. The proceeds are divided as called for by the court appointed referee. State laws prevent everything from being taken away. In Washington, for instance, a voluntary bankrupt is allowed to retain up to $1,000 in household goods, $500 in clothes, jewels, tools or whatever trade is practiced, and $6,000 equity in a house.

Corporate bankruptcy may occur as often as an individual chooses to form corporations. Both state and federal laws apply, and generally it is advisable to engage a lawyer who specializes in such work. There are several different bankruptcy proceedings. These are normally referred to by the chapters of the 1938 federal bankruptcy act under which they are set forth. Most common is the Chapter 11 form under which the company continues to operate, often under the existing management, by arranging with the creditors to attempt to pay them some agreed upon fraction of what they are owed.

First to be paid from the assets of the company are the various fees for professionals, lawyers, accountants, appraisers, auctioneers, and so forth. Then come wages, taxes, rent, and other creditors. A supplier to other companies must remember that when a company goes bankrupt the supplier will be one of the last to be paid and most likely will not be paid at all. If new money is injected into the ailing company, that too will receive priority in repayment.

Other forms of bankruptcy include Chapters 10 and 12. Chapter 12 applies mainly to limited partnerships and mortgage holders but not to corporations. Chapter 10, sometimes called "straight bankruptcy," is harsher than Chapter 11, "arrangements with creditors," and is generally invoked if Chapter 11 cannot be worked out. Under Chapter 10, management loses full control to a receiver, who is charged with preserving the assets, and to a trustee who disposes of the assets. If the trustee decides to liquidate, the company is dissolved and its assets are sold, usually at auction, after which the proceeds are divided among the creditors. Bankruptcy lawyers prefer Chapter 11 over Chapter 10, because under Chapter 11 the larger fee goes to the lawyer for the company. Under Chapter 10, the court appoints the trustee and the trustee then selects a lawyer. The larger fee goes to the trustee. Under either chapter, it may be possible to save the company, but it more frequently happens under Chapter 11.

Out-of-court settlements are sometimes possible. The creditors meet in order to reach an agreement on payment. This can be tricky, however, because all the creditors must agree. If one of them decides to press legal action for full payment, the case is thrown into bankruptcy court.

It is best, of course, to take remedial action before the company reaches the point of insolvency. First, the company should perform financial management by keeping an eye on receivables, inventory, and payables so that they do not get out of line. Second, the company should be honest with creditors and should keep them fairly informed, so that the creditors will not become alarmed by possible rumors (an unscrupulous tactic sometimes used to torpedo a company). Third, the company should take action to cut back or even shut down before it goes broke. Even in a failing company it may be possible to salvage at least some value for shareholders, but if the company goes through bankruptcy, the residual will in all probability be totally consumed by fees of the bankruptcy professionals who carve up the carcass.

LONG-RANGE STRATEGY

Although most small businesses do very little formal planning, there may be good reasons for thinking ahead about what the final outcome of the company should be. For instance, if the company is to go public, under some types of offerings it will require 3 years' audited financial statements. This means that a starting audit will have to be performed at least 4 years before the offering. If the company is to be passed on to succeeding managers, then it will be necessary to select and train these managers. If the company is to provide a comfortable living as a stably small but prosperous enterprise, then some types of businesses are better to select (for example, manufacturing instead of barbering) than others.

There are many possible career options in small businesses. Two mentioned in Chapter 1 were to work as an employee or to become an owner. Another is to be a "staffer," not a "runner" of small companies. Some entrepreneurs' careers include starting many companies and then disposing of them (sometimes at a profit, sometimes at a loss) but always moving on. Other entrepreneurs become involved in several businesses at one time, shifting the time they spend at one firm versus another according to how exigencies and opportunities shift with time in each firm. Still others become "turnaround artists," acquiring control of a company in trouble, working it back to health, and then withdrawing to work on another company. Most banks know of people to call upon when they have to take over troubled companies or when the banks or trustees have to take control of companies that are parts of estates. Lawyers and courts have names of people who are considered qualified to manage companies as receivers should bankruptcy proceedings occur.

Examination of entrepreneurial careers in close detail shows that many of the choices made are largely influenced and often totally made possible by unforeseeable events. It can also be seen that the opportunities exploited successfully by some could also have been exploited successfully by others had the others been prepared to seize them and move aheaad. Having an idea about the desired outcome does not guarantee that it will come about, but it will in all probability greatly improve the odds.

13

Careers in
Small Firms

Most people are free to choose whether to seek out work in a small company or to join a large one. If a small company is chosen, there are still choices to be made among various types of firms and among different approaches to participating in ownership and management. This chapter will consider characteristics of careers in small firms, approaches to finding opportunities in established companies, and approaches to small business ownership, including starting a new business or buying an established one.

SMALL COMPANY EMPLOYMENT

"To be a bigger fish relative to the pond" is one reason some people deliberately seek employment in small companies. The employee knows all the people in the company, and all the people in the company, including the chief executive, know him. The employee in a small company will not be "just another number in the payroll computer," but will instead represent an appreciable percentage of the work force. It follows that he will be called upon to produce effectively, unlike some in large companies who are able to get by doing very little.

One small company president who had formerly worked for a large multinational corporation recalled that one day he had deliberately tried as an experiment to make it through the day without doing anything. "I wandered around the offices and took magazines into the men's room and read them like some of the other people did. A few times I was forced to do something because my phone rang and I felt obliged to answer it. Except for that, I was able to go through the whole day accomplishing absolutely nothing. I spent time talking with other people about this and that, but I did not work. Nobody even noticed. There I was, well-paid with all sorts of fringe benefits and a nice desk and title. I could do nothing and not be caught goofing off or even noticed for not getting anything done. In my present company, if any of our 30 people did that, I as president could not help but be aware of it personally."

At the same time, however, because a large organization is able to tolerate slack, it is also able to provide longer breaking-in periods for new employees. If training programs and job rotation are provided, a new person may be able to "shop around" in the large company to find a more suitable position. In contrast, managers of small companies often feel that new employees must contribute immediately, thereby lessening the opportunities for inexperienced young people.

Because each individual represents a larger fraction of the total manpower in a small company, it may be possible for a newcomer to see the impact of his efforts on overall company performance more readily. Usually, there is less "red tape" in the way of getting things done and less need to have decisions checked through committees for approval. Nevertheless, the company president may have to pass personally on major decisions. In a small company a person may be able to follow all the way through on a new project, but in a large company the project may pass from one specialist to another as it progresses. In a large company an individual may work on a small piece of a large project for weeks or even months, only to learn that a decision made elsewhere has made all of his efforts obsolete. In a small organization the person whose work is made obsolete is usually a participant in the decision.

Positions in large and small firms differ greatly in their degree of structure and breadth. Positions in large organizations are usually well-defined and are sometimes very narrow. For example, one may be a budget specialist for a particular department. Positions in a small company are often fluid and relatively broad, for example, it may not be uncommon to meet with a customer in the morning, discuss personnel policies at lunch, and to work on a production problem in the afternoon. Young people hired into small companies often fill new positions, and neither they nor management are sure how the job will evolve over the ensuing months.

Large firms have substantial experience in training and maturing young people who are just starting their professional careers. These firms know what to expect. People in small organizations often lack this experience and may expect too much or too little. Some may be apprehensive and a bit fearful that the university-trained person will "make them look bad" or move into positions that they had hoped to fill. Here, it is a challenge to the newcomer to be able to relate effectively to others in the organization, to earn their respect, and to contribute to the business. Since the management group of a small company is like a family, it is essential that the young person, no matter how brilliant or how well-trained, be able to "fit in."

It is also important for the prospective employee to evaluate the particular people in the small company management group. Can you learn from these people? Are your ethical standards similar? Can you work together well? In contrast, in the large organization the frequency of management moves and the opportunities for lateral transfers mean that the new employee can look forward to working with many managers.

Both large and small companies offer unique opportunities for learning. In a small company the new person will probably see more variety from any given position, because the entire company can be kept in view without necessarily being at the top. The large company may allow rotation in order to obtain variety, but the total organization will be difficult to view from any lower echelon position. The new employee may be able to land a staff job that allows perspective, but then the opportunity for line responsibility will be missing.

The largest companies in any industry will often be ones that have developed very effective ways of working. By joining one of these companies, one can learn their ways. General Motors and IBM, for instance, are known for having "alumni" who go on to high positions in other companies, applying those skills they learned with the industry leaders. The high degree of specialization possible in a large company allows certain functions to be developed to a high degree of perfection; this may not be possible in a small company where limited manpower must be spread among many functions. This has given rise to the view that "first you should join a large company to learn how they do things and then go on to a small company to apply that knowledge."

Although there may be some truth in this statement, there are also dangers. More than one small company has hired someone from a large company only to find that "the way he learned to do things there just won't work here. He wants to tie everything in forms, memos, and other red tape, and he isn't careful enough with money. The large company may deal in millions, but we have to watch every nickel around here."

The level and nature of compensation usually depends on the size of the firm. Large firms offer more fringe benefits, which, although they may not seem important to the young person, become important as families are formed and personal responsibilities increase. The typical large firm probably pays young people more than the typical small firm. Studies of alumni from several leading M.B.A. programs, however, have shown that those employed by small and medium-sized firms had, on the average, higher compensation than those employed by large companies. Compensation levels undoubtedly vary more in small firms. A critical determinant is whether or not a particular small firm has the earning power to support generous compensation and whether or not its management wishes to "share the rewards of success."

In a small firm there is a concentration of risk in a few products, a few markets, and a few people. Usually, there are fewer financial cushions. A prolonged downturn in a single important market, the death of a key officer, or a fire in the plant can place the company's survival in jeopardy. Sometimes a small company is sold out to a larger one, which in turn replaces the management of the small company with its own people. Or the small company may be handed over to other members of the owner's family who either obstruct or remove people who have been aspiring to succeed in management.

Capricious acts, however, can also take place in large companies. A change in top management may be brought about if the company's performance is flagging. The change may produce firings and transfers all down the line, even involving people who have been performing satisfactorily. An employee who has a comfortable job one day may be without a job the next day or may be forced by the company to move to a less desirable location.

Careers in large firms usually involve more geographic mobility. In contrast, the employees of a small business are usually committed, for better or worse, to a single location. Which is more desirable depends on the individual's values (and those of his spouse), his stage in the life cycle of raising a family, and the nature of the particular community.

A well-chosen small company can provide a good base for learning to be a company manager. It may be possible to work out terms for buying out the owner so that eventually the new employee ends up owning the business. There can be great freedom in self-expression. Income can be substantial. There will be no forced transfers, no need to clear through committees or play "company politics," no required retirement at age 65, . . . and nobody else to blame if things go wrong.

FINDING A SMALL COMPANY POSITION

Finding the right position with the right small firm is generally more difficult than finding a similar position in a large company. In large firms the process of adding new management people is institutionalized, with much of the effort focused on college campuses. Opportunities are advertised; personnel representatives recruit in various parts of the country; and the organization is geared toward screening, selecting, and training new people each year.

In small firms the process is less systematic; management people are added only occasionally, and there is much less emphasis on recruiting college graduates. Consequently, a student seeking a position who relies only on the college placement office is likely to generate only a limited number of opportunities.

Some other approaches to finding small company positions are as follows:

1. Term papers may sometimes be steered toward small company topics. These will enable the student to see inside one or more small companies and also provide contacts that might result in job offers.

2. After having chosen a preferred type of business and location, the student can identify all of the firms in that line of work through the Yellow Pages or the local Manufacturer's Directory. These businesses can then be contacted by letter, telephone, or personal visit.

3. After having chosen a location, the student can contact local businessmen, bankers, or lawyers to seek advice. The process can be continued through several replications, with each person contacted being asked to suggest others who could advise and provide assistance.

4. A joint effort can be organized with other students who want small company employment. Efforts can be pooled to generate "leads" and exchange information.

5. The conventional approach is to "ask around" and respond to want ads. Although this is a haphazard approach, it may generate possibilities.

6. The student may seek a position in a large company because the position will provide exposure to a large number of small firms. Positions in public accounting, management consulting, sales, and banking are examples. A career plan may involve a period of years with a large company, possibly followed by a move to a carefully selected small firm.

In seeking a job in a suitable small company, the student may have to contact a large number of companies. One large company may have many openings, but many small firms may have none or only a few.

SMALL BUSINESS OWNERSHIP

Presumably, the goal of most students in seeking employment in a small company is to work in the direction of substantial ownership positions. If the company is growing rapidly, then this ownership may be fractional and shared with others of the management group. If the company is stable and small, then the objective may be to become ultimately the sole owner of the business. Approaches to achieving immediate ownership include starting new ventures and acquiring businesses that are for sale.

New Venture. Life for the owner of a new company is usually tense and hectic. A satisfactory concept or strategy must be developed; the product must be produced or the service made available; and customers must be attracted and convinced to buy from an unproven firm. Meanwhile, funds must be raised and cash flow managed; legal requirements must be met; and people must be recruited and trained. Sometimes service enterprises break even within a few months or even weeks, but the failure rate is high. Manufacturing companies have a slightly lower failure rate, depending on the business, but it may take 1 or 2 years or more to break even. The pre-break-even period is almost always a time of severe strain for the company owner and for his family.

Buying a Company. Acquiring an established firm is another route to small business ownership. Many sons, daughters, and in-laws have taken over profitable family companies and have continued to enjoy comfortable earnings with relatively low risks. Others have bought companies from retiring owners. Many of these new owners were either employees who succeeded their former employers or outsiders who "bought in." It is true that the entrepreneur who buys a business may be acquiring problems, but he also acquires an ongoing organization, a reputation, and hopefully incoming orders and cash flow. It is unusual for an inexperienced person in a given field to start a new business and be successful. It is not uncommon for an inexperienced person to buy an existing business in that field and to succeed.

If the company that is taken over is not profitable, then the new owner must bring about a "turnaround." This too has often been done by new owners who were not experienced in the line of business. As might be expected, however, the rate of failure in companies that need turning around when they are acquired is much higher than in companies that are profitable at the time of acquisition. This is true whether the new owner is experienced in the line of work or not. It often happens that the reasons the company is unprofitable are beyond the control of the buyer.

CONCLUSION

Whether or not an individual should join an established firm or seek immediate ownership through starting a new venture or buying a company depends on many factors. These factors center primarily on the individual—his characteristics and available resources. Whatever path is taken to participate in the management of growing small firms, the individual can expect a challenging and often rewarding career.